Theories of Educational Leadership and Management

Fourth Edition

Tony Bush

SAGE

Los Angeles | London | New Delhi
Singapore | Washington DC

First edition published by Paul Chapman Publishing 1986
Second edition published by Paul Chapman Publishing 1995
Third edition published by SAGE Publications Ltd 2003
Reprinted 2003, 2005, 2006, 2008, 2009

SAGE Publications Ltd
1 Oliver's Yard
55 City Road
London EC1Y 1SP

SAGE Publications Inc.
2455 Teller Road
Thousand Oaks, California 91320

SAGE Publications India Pvt Ltd
B 1/I 1 Mohan Cooperative Industrial Area
Mathura Road
New Delhi 110 044

SAGE Publications Asia-Pacific Pte Ltd
33 Pekin Street #02–01
Far East Square
Singapore 048763

Library of Congress Control Number: 2010920844

British Library Cataloguing in Publication data
A catalogue record for this book is available from the British
Library

ISBN 978-1-84860-190-1
ISBN 978-1-84860-191-8 (pbk)

Typeset by Dorwyn, Wells, Somerset
Printed in Great Britain by the MPG Books Group, Bodmin, Cornwall
Printed on paper from sustainable resources

Mixed Sources
Product group from well-managed
forests and other controlled sources
www.fsc.org Cert no. SA-COC-1565
© 1996 Forest Stewardship Council
FSC

Contents

Preface

The significance of effective leadership and management for the successful operation of schools and colleges has been increasingly acknowledged in the twenty-first century. The trend towards self-management in the United Kingdom, and in many other parts of the world, has led to an enhanced appreciation of the importance of managerial competence for educational leaders. More recently, there has been a growing recognition of the differences between leadership and management and an understanding that school principals and senior staff need to be good leaders as well as effective managers. The leadership dimension embraces concepts of vision, values and transformational leadership. Managing capably is an important requirement but leadership is perceived to be even more significant in England, and in some other countries.

The first edition of this book was published in 1986, before the seismic changes to the English and Welsh educational system engendered by the Education Reform Act and subsequent legislation. The second edition, published in 1995, referred to the 'tentative steps' being taken to develop the managerial competence of senior staff, particularly headteachers. The School Management Task Force (SMTF, 1990) had set the agenda for management development in its 1990 report but, unlike many other countries, there was no national programme of management training for heads and very little provision of any kind for deputy heads and middle managers.

By the time the third edition was published in 2003, the English landscape had been transformed by the opening (in November 2000) and subsequent expansion of the National College for School Leadership (NCSL). As this fourth edition is being prepared, it has been renamed as the National College for Leadership of Schools and Children's Services (National College). The College manages the National Professional Qualification for Headship, which is now mandatory for new first time heads. It also offers provision for new heads, deputy heads, middle-level leaders, senior leadership teams, and directors of children's services. The College also commissions leadership research and external evaluations of its leadership programmes.

The decision to locate responsibility for leadership development in England in a single national agency contrasts sharply with arrangements in most other developed countries. In the United States and Canada, potential principals and assistant principals must complete a Masters degree in educational administration. Similarly, universities are centrally involved in the preparation of school leaders in Australia, Hong Kong, New Zealand, Singapore and South Africa (Bush, 2008). What these countries do have in common with England is an explicit recognition that preparation and development are essential if school leaders are to carry out their onerous responsibilities successfully. Just as teachers need training to be effective in the classroom, so leaders need specific preparation for their specialist roles.

There is now a substantial literature on management practice in educational organizations. Most of these books and journal articles have been written by academics and practitioners in the United States, the United Kingdom and Australia. However, there are still few sources addressing the theoretical foundations of good practice. The aim of this book is to provide conceptual frameworks to guide the practice of educational leaders and managers. The author seeks to present a complex body of theory in clear, straightforward terms and to illustrate the models by reference to examples of leadership and management in educational institutions. In making relevant theory more accessible to practitioners, the intention is to promote both greater understanding of the concepts underpinning effective leadership and management practice, and to develop the capability of senior and middle level leaders in schools and colleges.

In the third edition of the book, I integrated leadership concepts with the management models featured in the two previous editions to provide a comprehensive overview of educational leadership and management theory. For this fourth edition, I have made three major changes.

- To acknowledge the global significance of educational leadership and management by including much more material from a wide range of international settings.
- To update the literature by including many of the major sources published since 2003.
- To scrutinize the material in the previous edition, and to remove some of the less significant sources, while retaining those texts central to theory development in the twentieth century.

Chapter 1 defines educational management and stresses the centrality of aims or goals in guiding managerial practice. It also defines educational leadership and differentiates it from management. The historical development of educational management as a distinct subject is chronicled from its dependence on industrial models in the 1960s to its current status as an established discipline with an evolving specialist literature. The twin concepts of centralization and decentralization in education are discussed, and linked to the emergence of self-managing schools in many countries. The debate on whether education should be regarded as simply a different context for the application of general management principles, or a special case justifying a distinct approach, is also reflected in this chapter. Finally, there is a discussion of instructional leadership and the linked concept of learning-centred leadership.

Chapter 2 considers the relationship between theory and practice. The prospect of a theory/practice divide can be avoided by an appreciation of the relevance of theory. The nature and characteristics of educational management theory are discussed and the chapter also addresses issues of diversity in educational leadership. The six management models are introduced and, in a modified section, 10 leadership models are outlined.

The next six chapters are the heart of the book, each presenting one of the major models of educational management. The six perspectives are analysed in terms of the assumptions made about the goals of educational institutions, the nature of organizational structure, relations with the external environment and the most appropriate modes of leadership. The models are also linked to the 10 leadership theories.

Chapter 3 considers 'formal models', including structural, systems, bureaucratic, rational and hierarchical approaches. The concept of managerial leadership is linked to the formal models.

Chapter 4 outlines the collegial model and applies it to higher education, and to secondary and primary schools. The emphasis on the authority of expertise, the shared values and objectives of professional staff and decision-making based on consensus is noted and subjected to scrutiny. Collegiality is linked to three models of leadership – transformational and participative leadership, and, in a new section, distributed leadership.

Chapter 5 presents political models with their assumptions of conflict between interest groups and decision-making based on the resources of power deployed by the various factions. It also examines the relationship between micropolitics and transactional leadership.

Chapter 6 examines subjective models with their emphasis on individual interpretation of events and their rejection of the notions of organizational goals and structure. It assesses the relationship between subjectivity and qualitative research. It also discusses postmodern leadership, which is remarkably similar to subjective models of management, while there is a new section on emotional leadership.

Chapter 7 discusses ambiguity models which stress the unpredictability of organizations, the lack of clarity about goals and the fluid nature of participation in decision-making. These are linked to contingent leadership and its focus on adapting leadership styles to the specific context or event.

Chapter 8 considers the significance of culture for educational leadership and management. The chapter differentiates between societal and organizational culture. This model emphasizes the values and beliefs underpinning culture, and the symbols and rituals used to reinforce it. The chapter also discusses the concept of moral leadership.

Chapter 9 compares the six models and considers their validity for particular types of school or college. It also provides a comparative analysis of the 10 leadership models. The chapter considers several attempts to integrate some of the models and concludes by assessing how to use theory to improve practice.

I am grateful to the many people who have contributed to the development of this volume. Derek Glover and I have worked together for more than 20 years and he has again carried out a thorough review of the leadership and management literature, focusing on sources since 2003. Three generations of secretaries, Helen Knowles, Felicity Murray and Margaret King, provided excellent support for the first three editions, while Chabala Bush has supplied the indexes for this volume. Marianne Lagrange has been the commissioning editor for all four editions and has also been centrally involved in the production of many of my other books. I am grateful to all my academic colleagues, who have influenced my work in so many ways. Finally, I am thankful for the support of all those close to me, especially Graham and Cha.

References

Bush, T. (2008) *Leadership and Management Development in Education*, London: Sage.
School Management Task Force (SMTF) (1990) *Developing School Management: The Way Forward*, London: HMSO.

Tony Bush
University of Warwick
January 2010

CHAPTER 1

The importance of leadership and management for education

What is educational management?

Educational management is a field of study and practice concerned with the operation of educational organizations. There is no single generally accepted definition of the subject because its development has drawn heavily on several more firmly established disciplines, including sociology, political science, economics and general management. Interpretations drawn from different disciplines necessarily emphasize diverse aspects of educational management and these varying approaches are reflected in subsequent chapters of this book.

Bolam (1999: 194) defines educational management as 'an executive function for carrying out agreed policy'. He differentiates management from educational leadership which has 'at its core the responsibility for policy formulation and, where appropriate, organizational transformation' (ibid.: 194). Writing from an Indian perspective, Sapre (2002: 102) states that 'management is a set of activities directed towards efficient and effective utilization of organizational resources in order to achieve organizational goals'.

The present author has argued consistently (Bush, 1986; 1995; 1999; 2003) that educational management should be centrally concerned with the purpose or aims of education. These are the subject of continuing debate and disagreement, but the principle of linking management activities and tasks to the aims and objectives of schools or colleges remains vital. These purposes or goals provide the crucial sense of direction which should underpin the management of educational institutions. Management is directed at the achievement of certain educational objectives. Unless this link between purpose and management is clear and close, there is a danger of 'managerialism', 'a stress on procedures at the expense of educational purpose and values' (Bush, 1999: 240). Managerialism places the emphasis on managerial efficiency rather than the aims and purposes of education (Newman and Clarke, 1994; Gunter, 1997). 'Management possesses no super-ordinate goals or values of its own. The pursuit of efficiency may be the mission statement of management – but this is efficiency in the achievement of objectives which others define' (Newman and Clarke, 1994: 29).

While the emphasis on educational purpose is important, this does not mean that all aims or targets are appropriate, particularly if they are imposed from outside the school by government or other official bodies. Managing towards the achievement of educational aims is vital but these must be purposes agreed by the school and its community. If managers simply focus on implementing external initiatives, they risk becoming 'managerialist'. In England, the levers of central monitoring and target-setting have been tightened to allow government to manage schools more closely, for example through the National Literacy and Numeracy strategies (Whitty, 2008: 173). Successful internal management requires a clear link between values, aims, strategy and day-to-day activities.

The centrality of aims and purposes for the management of schools and colleges is common to most of the different theoretical approaches to the subject. There is disagreement, though, about three aspects of goal-setting in education:

1. the value of *formal* statements of purpose
2. whether the objectives are those of the organization or those of particular individuals
3. *how* the institution's goals are determined.

Formal aims

The formal aims of schools and colleges are sometimes set at a high level of generality. They usually command substantial support but, because they are often utopian, such objectives provide an inadequate basis for managerial action. A typical aim in a primary or secondary school might focus on the acquisition by each pupil of physical, social, intellectual and moral qualities and skills. This is worthy but it has considerable limitations as a guide to decision-making. More specific purposes often fail to reach the same level of agreement. A proposal to seek improved performance in one part of the curriculum, say literacy or numeracy, may be challenged by teachers concerned about the implications for other subjects.

The international trend towards self-management has led to a parallel call for managers, staff and other stakeholders to develop a distinctive vision for their schools with clearly articulated and specific aims. Beare, Caldwell and Millikan (1989: 99) say that 'outstanding leaders have a vision of their schools – a mental picture of a preferred future – which is shared with all in the school community'. Where educational organizations have such a vision, it is possible for effective managers to link functions with aims and to ensure that all management activity is purposeful. In practice, however, as we shall see later, many 'visions' are simply generalized educational objectives (Bolam et al., 1993) and may be derived from national government imperatives rather than being derived from a school-level assessment of needs.

Organizational or individual aims?

Some approaches to educational management are concerned predominantly with organizational objectives while other models strongly emphasize individual aims. There is a range of opinion between these two views, from those who argue that 'organizational' objectives may be imposed by leaders on the less powerful members of the school or college, to those who say that individual aims need to coalesce around specific themes for the organization to have meaning for its members and stakeholders. One problem is that individual and organizational objectives may be incompatible, or that organizational aims satisfy some, but not all, individual aspirations. It is reasonable to assume that most teachers want their school or college to pursue policies which are in harmony with their own interests and preferences. This issue will be explored later in this book, notably in Chapter 6.

The determination of aims

The process of deciding on the aims of the organization is at the heart of educational management. In some settings, aims are decided by the principal or headteacher, often working in association with senior colleagues and perhaps a small group of lay stakeholders. In many schools and colleges, however, goal-setting is a corporate activity undertaken by formal bodies or informal groups.

School and college aims are inevitably influenced by pressures emanating from the wider educational environment and lead to the questions about the viability of school 'visions', noted above. Many countries, including England and Wales, have a national curriculum, linked to national assessments and inspection systems, and such government prescriptions leave little scope for schools to decide their own educational aims. Institutions may be left with the residual task of interpreting external imperatives rather than determining aims on the basis of their own assessment of student need.

Wright's (2001) discussion of 'bastard leadership' develops this argument, suggesting that visioning is a 'sham' and that school leaders in England and Wales are reduced to implementing the values and policies of the government and its agencies:

> Leadership as the moral and value underpinning for the direction of schools is being removed from those who work there. It is now very substantially located at the political level where it is not available for contestation, modification or adjustment to local variations. (Wright, 2001: 280)

The key issue here is the extent to which school leaders are able to modify government policy and develop alternative approaches based on school-level values and vision. Do they have to follow the script, or can they ad lib? Gold et al.'s (2003) research with 10 'outstanding' English principals begins to address this central issue. They 'take for granted that school leaders are essentially "value carriers" ... school improvement is not a technocratic science, but rather a process of seeking ever better ways of embodying particular educational values in the working practices ... of particular schools' (2003: 128). These authors assert that their case study principals were developing just such value-led approaches to school leadership and management:

> The school leaders in our case study schools were clearly avoiding doing 'bastard leadership' by mediating government policy through their own values systems. We were constantly reminded by those to whom we spoke, of the schools' strong value systems and the extent to which vision and values were shared and articulated by all who were involved in them. (Ibid.: 131)

Wright's (2003) response to the Gold et al. research questions the extent to which even 'principled' leaders are able to challenge or modify government policies. In his view, these principals are still 'bastard leaders' because their values cannot challenge government imperatives:

> What is not provided [by Gold et al.] is clear evidence of how these values actually impinged at the interface between particular government initiatives and action in these schools ... 'bastard leadership' ... is actually about the lack of scope for school leaders to make decisions that legiti-

mately fly in the face of particular unrealistic and often inadequately researched government initiatives or requirements. (Wright, 2003: 140)

This debate is likely to continue but the central issue relates to the relative power of governments and school leaders to determine the aims and purpose of education in particular schools. Governments have the constitutional power to impose their will but successful innovations require the commitment of those who have to implement these changes. If teachers and leaders believe that an initiative is inappropriate for their children or students, they are unlikely to implement it with enthusiasm. Hence, governments would like schools to have visionary leadership as long as the visions do not depart in any significant way from government imperatives.

Furlong (2000) adds that the increased government control of education has significant implications for the status of teachers as professionals. He claims that, in England and Wales, professionalism is allowed to exist only by the grace of central government because of the dominance of a prescriptive national curriculum and the central monitoring of teacher performance.

The nature of the goal-setting process is a major variant in the different models of educational leadership and management to be discussed in subsequent chapters.

What is educational leadership?

Gunter (2004) shows that the labels used to define this field have changed from 'educational administration' to 'educational management', and, more recently, to 'educational leadership'. In England, this shift is exemplified most strongly by the opening of the National College for School Leadership in 2000, described as a 'paradigm shift' by Bolam (2004). We shall examine the differences between leadership and management later in this chapter. There are many different conceptualizations of leadership, leading Yukl (2002: 4–5) to argue that 'the definition of leadership is arbitrary and very subjective. Some definitions are more useful than others, but there is no "correct" definition.' Three dimensions of leadership may be identified as a basis for developing a working definition.

Leadership as influence

A central element in many definitions of leadership is that there is a process of influence.

Most definitions of leadership reflect the assumption that it involves a social influence process whereby intentional influence is exerted by one person [or group] over other people [or groups] to structure the activities and relationships in a group or organisation. (Yukl, 2002: 3)

Cuban's (1988: 193) definition shows that the influence process is purposeful in that it is intended to lead to specific outcomes: 'Leadership, then refers to people who bend the motivations and actions of others to achieving certain goals; it implies taking initiatives and risks'. Bush (2008a: 277) refers to three key aspects of these definitions:

- The central concept is *influence* rather than authority. Both are dimensions of power but the latter tends to reside in formal positions, such as the principal or headteacher, while the former could be exercised by anyone in the school or college. Leadership is independent of positional authority while management is linked directly to it.
- The process is *intentional*. The person seeking to exercise influence is doing so in order to achieve certain purposes.
- Influence may be exercised by *groups* as well as individuals. This notion provides support for the concept of distributed leadership and for constructs such as senior leadership teams. 'This aspect of leadership portrays it as a fluid process, potentially emanating from any part of the school, independent of formal management positions and capable of residing with any member of the organization, including associate staff and students' (ibid.: 277).

Leadership and values

The notion of 'influence' is neutral in that it does not explain or recommend what goals or actions should be pursued. However, leadership is increasingly linked with values. Leaders are expected to ground their actions in clear personal and professional values. Greenfield and Ribbins (1993) claim that leadership begins with the 'character' of leaders, expressed in terms of personal values, self-awareness and emotional and moral capability. Earlier, Greenfield (1991: 208) distinguished between values and rationality: 'Values lie beyond rationality. Rationality to be rationality must stand upon a value base. Values are asserted, chosen, imposed, or believed. They lie beyond quantification, beyond measurement'.

Day, Harris and Hadfield's (2001) research in 12 'effective' schools in England and Wales concludes that 'good leaders are informed by and communicate clear sets of personal and educational values which represent their moral purposes for the school' (ibid.: 53). This implies that values are 'chosen', but Bush (2008a: 277) argues that the dominant values are those of government and adds that these are 'imposed' on school leaders. Teachers and leaders are more likely to be enthusiastic about change when they 'own' it rather than having it imposed on them. Hargreaves (2004), drawing on research in Canadian schools, finds that teachers report largely positive emotional experiences of self-initiated change but predominantly negative ones concerning mandated change.

Leadership and vision

Vision has been regarded as an essential component of effective leadership for more than 20 years. Southworth (1993: 73–4) suggests that heads are motivated to work hard 'because their leadership is the pursuit of their individual visions' (ibid.: 74). Dempster and Logan's (1998) study of 12 Australian schools shows that almost all parents (97 per cent) and teachers (99 per cent) expect the principal to express his or her vision clearly, while 98 per cent of both groups expect the leader to plan strategically to achieve the vision.

These projects show the high level of support for the notion of visionary leadership but Foreman's (1998) review of the concept shows that it remains highly problematic. Fullan (1992a: 83) says that 'vision building is a highly sophisticated dynamic process which few organizations can sustain'. Elsewhere, Fullan (1992b) is even more critical, suggesting that visionary leaders may damage rather than improve their schools:

> The current emphasis on vision in leadership can be misleading. Vision can blind leaders in a number of ways ... The high-powered, charismatic principal who 'radically transforms the school' in four or five years can ... be blinding and misleading as a role model ... my hypothesis would be that most such schools decline after the leader leaves ... Principals are blinded by their own vision when they feel they must manipulate the teachers and the school culture to conform to it. (Ibid.: 19)

Bolam et al.'s (1993) research illustrates a number of problems about the development and articulation of 'vision' in English and Welsh schools. Their study of 12 self-selected 'effective' schools shows that most heads were able to describe 'some sort of vision' but 'they varied in their capacity to articulate the vision and the visions were more or less sophisticated' (ibid.: 33). Moreover, the visions were rarely specific to the school. They were 'neither surprising nor striking nor controversial. They are closely in line with what one might expect of the British system of education' (ibid.: 35).

It is evident that the articulation of a clear vision has the potential to develop schools but the empirical evidence of its effectiveness remains mixed. A wider concern relates to whether school leaders are able to develop a specific vision for their schools, given the centrality of government prescriptions of both curriculum aims and content. A few headteachers may be confident enough to challenge official policy in the way described by Bottery (1998: 24); 'from defy through subvert to ignore; on to ridicule then to wait and see to test; and in some (exceptional) cases finally to embrace'. However, most are more like Bottery's (2007: 164) 'Alison', who examines every issue in relation to their school's OFSTED report.

Hoyle and Wallace (2005: 11) are critical of the contemporary emphasis on vision. 'Visionary rhetoric is a form of managementspeak that has increased very noticeably in schools since the advent of educational reforms'. They contrast the 'visionary rhetoric' with 'the prosaic reality' experienced by staff, students and parents: 'If all the visionary rhetoric corresponded with reality, would a third of teachers be seeking to leave the profession?' (ibid.: 12). They add that visions have to conform to centralized expectations and to satisfy OFSTED inspectors; 'any vision you like, as long as it's central government's' (ibid.: 139).

Distinguishing educational leadership and management

As we noted earlier, the terminology used to describe the organization of educational bodies, and the activities of their principals and senior staff, has evolved from 'administration', which is still widely used in North America and Australia, for example, through 'management', to 'leadership'. Bush (2008a: 276) asks whether these are just semantic shifts or whether they represent a more fundamental change in the conceptualization of headship? Hoyle and Wallace (2005: viii) note that 'leadership' has only just overtaken 'management' as the main descriptor for what is entailed in running and improving public service organizations.

Cuban (1988) provides one of the clearest distinctions, linking leadership with change, and management with 'maintenance'. He also stresses the importance of both dimensions of organizational activity:

> By leadership, I mean influencing others' actions in achieving desirable ends. Leaders are people who shape the goals, motivations, and actions of others. Frequently they initiate change to reach existing and new goal ...

Leadership ... takes ... much ingenuity, energy and skill ...

Managing is maintaining efficiently and effectively current organizational arrangements. While managing well often exhibits leadership skills, the overall function is toward maintenance rather than change. I prize both managing and leading and attach no special value to either since different settings and times call for varied responses. (Ibid.: xx)

Day, Harris and Hadfield's (2001) study of 12 'effective' schools leads to the discussion of several dilemmas in school leadership. One of these relates to management, which is linked to systems and 'paper', and leadership, which is perceived to be about the development of people. 'Development and maintenance' are identified as another tension, linking to Cuban's (1988) distinction, identified above.

Bush (1998: 328) links leadership to values or purpose, while management relates to implementation or technical issues. Leadership and management need to be given equal prominence if schools and colleges are to operate effectively and achieve their objectives. While a clear vision may be essential to establish the nature and direction of change, it is equally important to ensure that innovations are implemented efficiently and that the school's residual functions are carried out effectively while certain elements are undergoing change:

Methods ... [are] as important as knowledge, understanding and value orientations ... Erecting this kind of dichotomy between something pure called 'leadership' and something 'dirty' called 'management', or between values and purposes on the one hand and methods and skills on the other, would be disastrous. (Glatter, 1997: 189)

Leading and managing are distinct, but both are important. Organizations which are over managed but under led eventually lose any sense of spirit or purpose. Poorly managed organizations with strong charismatic leaders may soar temporarily only to crash shortly thereafter. The challenge of modern organizations requires the objective perspective of the manager as well as the flashes of vision and commitment wise leadership provides. (Bolman and Deal, 1997: xiii–xiv)

These cautions are echoed by Leithwood (1994), who comments that the differences cannot easily be observed in the day-to-day practices of principals, and by Hallinger (2003), who argues that a leadership perspective on the role of the principal does not diminish the principal's managerial roles.

The dichotomy in Britain and elsewhere is that while leadership is normatively preferred, notably through the establishment and activities of the National College, governments are encouraging a technical–rational approach through their stress on performance and public accountability (Glatter, 1999; Levačić, et al., 1999; Gunter 2004). In practice, schools and colleges require visionary leadership, to the extent that this is possible with a centralized curriculum, *and* effective management.

The chronology of educational leadership and management

The origins and development of educational management as a distinct discipline have been chronicled by Hughes (1985), Hughes and Bush (1991), Bush (1999), Glatter (1999) and Bolam (2004). It began in the United States in the early part of this century. The work of Taylor (1947) was particularly influential and his 'scientific management movement' is still subject to vigorous debate, particularly by those who oppose a 'managerial' approach to education. Another important contributor to management theory was the French writer Fayol (1916) whose 'general principles of management' are still significant. Weber's (1947) work on 'bureaucracy' remains powerful and this will be given extended treatment in Chapter 3.

All these theories developed outside education and were subsequently applied to schools and colleges, with mixed results. The other models discussed in this book were developed in the educational context or have been applied to schools or colleges in their formative periods.

The development of educational management as a field of study in the United Kingdom came as late as the 1960s but there has been rapid expansion since then. In 1983 the Department of Education and Science (DES) sponsored a programme of management training for heads and established the National Development Centre for School Management Training at Bristol University. University courses on school and college management became increasingly popular (Hughes et al., 1981; Gunter, 1997).

The British government appointed a School Management Task Force in 1989 and its influential report (SMTF, 1990) set the agenda for school management development for the next few years. Probably its most important legacy was the establishment of mentoring schemes for new headteachers.

The next major development in England and Wales was the establishment of the Teacher Training Agency (TTA) which took an interest in leadership and management development as well as the pre-service training of teachers. The TTA set up the National Professional Qualification for Headship (NPQH), the first national qualification for aspiring heads, in 1997. The NPQH became mandatory for new heads in 2009.

The National College

The most important stage in this chronology was the setting up of the National College for School Leadership (NCSL) in November 2000. Significantly, the College's title excludes the term 'management', further emphasizing the current normative preference for 'leadership'. The College has taken over responsibility for leadership development programmes, including NPQH, and has introduced many new offerings, including provision for middle leaders, new heads, consultant heads, and leadership teams. Its scope was widened in 2009 to include leadership of children's services, with a modified title of National College for Leadership of Schools and Children's Services (National College). Its former Director of Research, Geoff Southworth, points out that the College was intended 'to provide a single national focus for school leadership development and research' (2004a: 340). He also refers to the 'widespread belief' that 'the quality of leadership makes a difference to organizational health, performance and growth' (ibid.: 341).

A full discussion of the achievements, and limitations, of the National College is beyond the scope of this book but five main strengths can be identified:

- a *national* focus
- programmes for different career stages
- an emphasis on practice
- programmes underpinned by research
- impressive reach and scale
  (Bush 2008b: 79–82).

Bush (2008b: 82–6) also identifies five main limitations of the College:

- Its intellectual demands are too modest.
- Its emphasis on practice is at the expense of theory and research.
- Its reliance on practitioners to lead programmes limits innovation.
- Its dominance of school leadership development is unhealthy.
- It is unduly influenced by the government.

It might be argued that its revised title and mission weakens the College 'brand' but this remains to be seen.

The National College also has a significant international role, although this appears to be declining (Bush, 2008c). One of its early decisions was to organize a series of study visits to international leadership centres. Each visit involved teams of two or three people, including school principals, College senior staff, and other professionals and academics directly connected with the College. Fifteen centres were visited in seven countries: Australia, Canada, Hong Kong, New Zealand, Singapore, Sweden and the United States.

The report of the visits (Bush and Jackson, 2002) showed that several other countries were well ahead of England and Wales in the development of national or state programmes for prospective principals. In Canada and most of the United States, for example, it is not possible to be appointed as a principal or vice-principal without an approved Masters degree in educational administration. Similarly, Singapore has had a national qualification for school principals since 1984.

The National College has also influenced the field of school leadership globally. In the United States, for example, Levine (2005: 54) says that the college 'proved to be the most promising model we saw, providing examples of good practice that educational administration programs might seek to emulate'. In South Africa, the Matthew Goniwe School of Leadership and Governance was modelled to some extent on the College, albeit on a much smaller scale and serving only a single province (Bush, 2008b: 79).

In summary, the climate for educational leadership and management has never been more buoyant. The recognition that high-quality leadership is central to educational outcomes has led to the view that training is desirable to develop people with the appropriate knowledge, skills and understanding to lead educational organizations in an increasingly global economy. This requirement is particularly important for self-managing schools and colleges.

Decentralization and self-management

Schools and colleges operate within a legislative framework set down by national, provincial or state parliaments. One of the key aspects of such a framework is the degree of decentralization in the educational system. Highly centralized systems tend to be bureaucratic and to allow little discretion to schools and local communities. Decentralized systems devolve significant powers to subordinate levels. Where such powers are devolved to the institutional level, we may speak of 'self-management'.

Lauglo (1997) links centralization to bureaucracy and defines it as follows:

> Bureaucratic centralism implies concentrating in a central ('top') authority decision-making on a wide range of matters, leaving only tightly programmed routine implementation to lower levels in the organization ... a ministry could make decisions in considerable detail as to aims and

objectives, curricula and teaching materials to be used, prescribed methods, appointments of staff and their job descriptions, admission of students, assessment and certification, finance and budgets, and inspection/evaluations to monitor performance. (Ibid.: 3–4)

Lauglo (1997: 5) says that 'bureaucratic centralism is pervasive in many developing countries' and links this to both the former colonial rule and the emphasis on central planning by many post-colonial governments. Tanzania is one example of a former colonial country seeking to reduce the degree of centralism (Babyegeya, 2000) while Seychelles illustrates the centralized nature of many former colonial countries (Purvis, 2007).

Centralized systems are not confined to former colonial countries. Derouet (2000: 61) claims that France 'was the most centralized system in the world' in the 1960s and 1970s while Fenech (1994: 131) states that Malta's educational system is 'highly centralized'. Bottery (1999: 119) notes that the United Kingdom education system 'has experienced a continued and intensified centralization for the last 30 years'. In Greece, the public education system is characterized by centralization and bureaucracy (Bush, 2001).

Decentralization involves a process of reducing the role of central government in planning and providing education. It can take many different forms:

Decentralization in education means a shift in the authority distribution away from the central 'top' agency in the hierarchy of authority ... Different forms of decentralization are diverse in their justifications and in what they imply for the distribution of authority. (Lauglo, 1997: 3)

The main forms of decentralization are:

- Federalism, for example in Australia, Germany, India and the United States.
- Devolution, for example in the United Kingdom.
- Deregulation, for example in the Czech Republic (Karstanje, 1999).
- Deconcentration, for example in Tanzania (Therkildsen, 2000).
- Participative democracy, involving strong participation by stakeholders at the institutional level, for example in Australia, Canada, England and Wales, and South Africa (Sayed, 1999).
- Market mechanism, for example in Britain and the United States.

Two or more of these modes may coexist within the same educational system. For example, the school-based management trend in many countries (England and Wales, Australia, New Zealand, Hong Kong) is underpinned by both participative democracy and the market mechanism. In England and Wales, schools and colleges are at the heart of 'the educational market place' with students and parents as customers, choosing from a range of providers. Caldwell and Spinks's (1992: 4) definition provides a clear link between self-management and decentralization: 'A self-managing school is a school in a system of education where there has been significant and consistent *decentralization* to the school level of authority to make decisions related to the allocation of resources'.

The research on self-management in England and Wales (Bush et al., 1993; Levačić, 1995; Thomas and Martin, 1996) largely suggests that the shift towards school autonomy has been beneficial. These UK perspectives are consistent with much of the international evidence on self-management (OECD, 1994). Caldwell (2008), one of the founders of the 'self-managing schools' movement, argues that the benefits of self-management are 'relatively straightforward':

> Self-managing schools have been one manifestation of a general trend to decentralization in public education ... Each school contains a unique mix of students' needs, interests, aptitudes and aspirations, and those at the school level are best placed to determine the particular mix of all the resources available to achieve optimal outcomes. (Ibid.: 249)

Autonomous schools and colleges may be regarded as potentially more efficient and effective but much depends on the nature and quality of internal leadership and management if these potential benefits are to be realized. Dellar's (1998) research in 30 secondary schools in Australia, for example, shows that 'site-based' management was most successful where there was a positive school climate and the involvement of staff and stakeholders in decision-making. Self-management also serves to expand the scope of leadership and management, providing the potential for principals and senior staff to have a greater impact on school outcomes than was possible in the era of state control.

The significance of the educational context

Educational management as a field of study and practice was derived from management principles first applied to industry and commerce, mainly in the United States. Theory development largely involved the application of industrial models to educational settings. As the subject became established as an academic discipline in its own right, its theorists and practitioners began to develop alternative models based on their observation of, and experience in, schools and colleges. By the twenty-first century the main theories, featured in this book, have either been developed in the educational context or have been adapted from industrial models to meet the specific requirements of schools and colleges.

Educational leadership and management has progressed from being a new field dependent upon ideas developed in other settings to become an established discipline with its own theories and significant empirical data testing their validity in education. This transition has been accompanied by lively argument about the extent to which education should be regarded as simply another field for the application of general principles of leadership and management, or should be seen as a separate discipline with its own body of knowledge.

One strand of opinion asserts that there are general principles of management which can be applied to all organizational settings. The case for a standard approach to the training and development of managers rests largely upon the functions thought to be common to different types of organization. These include financial management, human resource management, and relationships with the organization's clients and the wider community. The debate about the most appropriate relationship between general management and that specific to education was rekindled from 1995 with the TTA's emphasis on the need to take account of 'best practice outside education' in devising professional development programmes. For example, its National Standards document stated that 'the standards ... reflect the work undertaken on management standards by those outside the education profession' (TTA, 1998: 1) and 'the knowledge and understanding that headteachers need draw on sources both inside and outside education' (ibid.: 3).

Taking account of 'best practice outside education' appears uncontentious, but it assumes that definitions of 'best practice' are widely understood and accepted. In practice, there are several problematic issues:

- Who decides what good, let alone 'best', practice is?
- How is such good practice to be adapted for use in training school leaders and managers?
- Is good practice a universal trait or does it depend on the specific school setting?

In addressing this issue, Glatter (1997: 187) argues that 'it is not always clear what constitutes best practice in management outside education. As in education itself, there are different approaches and contending schools of thought'. Subsequently, Glatter and Kydd (2003: 240) add that 'it needs to be applied more rigorously and the criteria for assessing what practice is considered "best" should be clearly specified'.

There are several arguments to support the notion that education has specific needs that require a distinctive approach. These include:

- the difficulty of setting and measuring educational objectives
- the presence of children and young people as the 'outputs' or 'clients' of educational institutions
- the need for education professionals to have a high degree of autonomy in the classroom
- the fact that many senior and middle managers, particularly in primary schools, have little time for the managerial aspects of their work.

Even more important than these issues is the requirement for educational leaders and managers to focus on the specifically educational aspects of their work. The overriding purpose of schools and colleges is to promote effective teaching and learning. These core issues are unique to education and 'best practice outside education' is unlikely to be of any help in addressing these central professional issues. As 'learning-centred leadership' is increasingly advocated (e.g. by Southworth, 2004b), the main focus should be on learning from school leadership theory and practice. The business sector has little to offer in this domain, although other ideas have been borrowed for use in education, notably managing people (Bush and Middlewood, 2005) and marketing (Foskett, 2002). However, the special characteristics of schools and colleges imply caution in the application of management models or practices drawn from non-educational settings. As the leading American writer Baldridge suggested more than 30 years ago, careful evaluation and adaptation of such models is required before they can be applied with confidence to educational organizations.

> Traditional management theories cannot be applied to educational institutions without carefully considering whether they will work well in that unique academic setting ... We therefore must be extremely careful about attempts to manage or improve ... education with 'modern management' techniques borrowed from business, for example. Such borrowing may make sense, but it must be approached very carefully. (Baldridge et al., 1978: 9)

Instructional leadership

There are several models of educational leadership and these will be introduced in Chapter 2. Most of the models will be discussed in detail in subsequent chapters. However, instructional leadership does not fit the framework for this book, because it focuses on the direction of influence, rather than its nature and source, so it will be addressed here.

The increasing emphasis on managing teaching and learning as the core activities of educational institutions has led to 'instructional leadership', or 'learning-centred' leadership, being emphasized and endorsed, notably by the English National College. Leithwood, Jantzi and Steinbach (1999: 8) point to the lack of explicit descriptions of instructional leadership in the literature and suggest that there may be different meanings of this concept. 'Instructional leadership ... typically assumes that the critical focus for attention by leaders is the behaviour of teachers as they engage in activities directly affecting the growth of students'. Bush and Glover's definition stresses the direction of the influence process:

> Instructional leadership focuses on teaching and learning and on the behaviour of teachers in working with students. Leaders' influence is targeted at student learning via teachers. The emphasis is on the direction and impact of influence rather than the influence process itself. (2002: 10)

Blasé and Blasé's (1998) research with 800 principals in American elementary, middle and high schools suggests that effective instructional leadership behaviour comprises three aspects:

- talking with teachers (conferencing)
- promoting teachers' professional growth
- fostering teacher reflection.

The term 'instructional leadership' derives from North America and it has been superseded in England and elsewhere by the notion of 'learning-centred leadership'. Rhodes and Brundrett (2010) argue that the latter concept is broader and has greater potential to impact on school and student outcomes. They 'explore the transition from instructional leadership, concerned with ensuring teaching quality, to leadership for learning, which incorporates a wider spectrum of leadership action to support learning and learning outcomes' (ibid.). Southworth (2004b: 78–83) says that leaders influence learning through three main strategies:

- modelling
- monitoring
- dialogue.

Modelling is about the power of example. Learning-centred leaders are role models to others because they are interested in learning, teaching and classrooms, and want to know more about them. Monitoring involves visiting classrooms, observing teachers at work and providing them with feedback. Dialogue is about creating opportunities for teachers to talk with their colleagues and leaders about learning and teaching. While a strong emphasis on learning is important, leaders should also stay focused on other aspects of school life, such as socialization, student health, welfare and self-esteem, and such wider school-level issues as developing an appropriate culture and climate linked to the specific needs of the school and its community.

Conclusion

Effective leadership and management are essential if schools and colleges are to achieve the wide-ranging objectives set for them by their many stakeholders, notably the governments which provide most of the funding for public educational institutions. In an increasingly global economy, an educated workforce is vital to maintain and enhance competitiveness. Society expects schools, colleges and universities to prepare people for employment in a rapidly changing environment. Teachers, and their leaders and managers, are the people who are required to deliver higher educational standards.

The concept of management has been joined, or superseded, by the language of leadership but the activities undertaken by principals and senior staff resist such labels. Self-management is practised in many countries, expanding the scope and scale of leadership and providing greater potential for direct and indirect influences on school and pupil outcomes. Successful leaders are increasingly focused on learning, the central and unique focus of educational organizations. They also face unprecedented accountability pressures in what is clearly a 'results driven' business. As these environmental pressures intensify, leaders and managers require greater understanding, skill and resilience to sustain their institutions. Heads, principals and senior staff need an appreciation of the theory, as well as the practice, of educational management. Competence comprises an appreciation of concepts as well as a penchant for successful action. The next chapter examines the nature of theory in educational leadership and management, and its contribution to good practice.

References

Babyegeya, E. (2000) 'Education reforms in Tanzania: from nationalisation to decentralisation of schools', *International Studies in Educational Administration*, 28(1): 2–10.

Baldridge, J.V., Curtis, D.V., Ecker, G. and Riley, G.L. (1978) *Policy-Making and Effective Leadership*, San Francisco, CA: Jossey-Bass.

Beare, H., Caldwell, B. and Millikan, R. (1989) *Creating an Excellent School: Some New Management Techniques*, London: Routledge.

Blasé, J. and Blasé, J.R. (1998) *Handbook of Instructional Leadership: How Really Good Principals Promote Teaching and Learning*, London: Sage.

Bolam, R. (1999) 'Educational administration, leadership and management: towards a research agenda', in T. Bush, L. Bell, R. Bolam, R. Glatter and P. Ribbins (eds), *Educational Management: Redefining Theory, Policy and Practice*, London: Paul Chapman Publishing.

Bolam, R. (2004) 'Reflections on the NCSL from a historical perspective', *Educational Management, Administration and Leadership*, 32(3): 251–68.

Bolam, R., McMahon, A., Pocklington, K. and Weindling, D. (1993) *Effective Management in Schools*, London: HMSO.

Bolman, L.G. and Deal, T.E. (1997) *Reframing Organizations: Artistry, Choice and Leadership*, San Francisco, CA: Jossey-Bass.

Bottery, M. (1998) *Professionals and Policy*, London: Cassell.

Bottery, M. (1999) 'Education under the new modernisers: an agenda for centralisation, illiberalism and inequality?', *Cambridge Journal of Education*, 29 (1): 103–20.

Bottery, M. (2007) 'New Labour policy and school leadership in England: room for manouevre?', *Cambridge Journal of Education*, 37(2): 153–72.

Bush, T. (1986) *Theories of Educational Management*, London: Harper and Row.

Bush, T. (1995) *Theories of Educational Management*, 2nd edn, London: Paul Chapman Publishing.

Bush, T. (1998) 'The National Professional Qualification for Headship: the key to effective school leadership?', *School Leadership and Management*, 18(3): 321–34.

Bush, T. (1999) 'Crisis or crossroads? The discipline of educational management in the late 1990s', *Educational Management and Administration*, 27(3): 239–52.

Bush, T. (2001) 'School organisation and management: international perspectives', paper presented at the Federation of Private School Teachers of Greece Conference, Athens, May.

Bush, T. (2003) *Theories of Educational Management*, 3rd edn, London: Sage.

Bush, T. (2008a) 'From management to leadership: semantic or meaningful change?', *Educational Management, Administration and Leadership*, 36(2): 271–88.

Bush, T. (2008b) *Leadership and Management Development in Education*, London: Sage.

Bush, T. (2008c) *The NCSL's research role*, paper presented at the Standing Conference for Research on Educational Leadership and Management, Milton Keynes, October.

Bush, T. and Glover, D. (2002) *School Leadership: Concepts and Evidence*, Nottingham: National College for School Leadership.

Bush, T. and Jackson, D. (2002) 'Preparation for school leadership: international perspectives', *Educational Management and Administration*, 30(4): 417–29.

Bush, T. and Middlewood, D. (2005) *Leading and Managing People in Education*, London: Sage.

Bush, T., Coleman, M. and Glover, D. (1993) *Managing Autonomous Schools: The Grant-Maintained Experience*, London: Paul Chapman Publishing.

Caldwell, B. (2008) Reconceptualising the self-managing school, *Educational Management, Administration and Leadership*, 36(2): 235–52.

Caldwell, B. and Spinks, J. (1992) *Leading the Self-Managing School*, London: Falmer Press.

Cuban, L. (1988) *The Managerial Imperative and the Practice of Leadership in Schools*, Albany, NY: State University of New York Press.

Day, C., Harris, A. and Hadfield M. (2001) 'Challenging the orthodoxy of effective school leadership', *International Journal of Leadership in Education*, 4(1): 39–56.

Dellar, G. (1998) 'School climate, school improvement and site-based management', *Learning Environments Research*, 1(3): 353–67.

Dempster, N. and Logan, L. (1998) 'Expectations of school leaders', in J. MacBeath (ed.), *Effective School Leadership: Responding to Change*, London: Paul Chapman Publishing.

Derouet, J.L. (2000) 'School autonomy in a society with multi-faceted political references: the search for new ways of co-ordinating action', *Journal of Education Policy*, 15(1): 61–9.

Fayol, H. (1916) *General and Industrial Management*, London: Pitman.

Fenech, J. (1994) 'Managing schools in a centralised system: headteachers at work', *Educational Management and Administration*, 22(2): 131–40.

Foreman, K. (1998) 'Vision and mission', in D. Middlewood and J. Lumby (eds), *Strategic Management in Schools and Colleges*, London: Paul Chapman Publishing.

Foskett, N. (2002) 'Marketing', in T. Bush and L. Bell (eds), *The Principles and Practice of Educational Management*, London: Paul Chapman Publishing.

Fullan, M. (1992a) *Successful School Improvement*, Buckingham: Open University Press.

Fullan, M. (1992b) 'Visions that blind', *Educational Leadership*, 49(5): 19–20.

Furlong, J. (2000) 'Institutions and the crisis in teacher professionalism', in T. Atkinson and G. Claxton (eds), *The Intuitive Practitioner*, Buckingham: Open University Press.

Glatter, R. (1997) 'Context and capability in educational management', *Educational Management and Administration*, 25(2): 181–92.

Glatter, R. (1999) 'From struggling to juggling: towards a redefinition of the field of educational leadership and management', *Educational Management and Administration*, 27(3): 253–66.

Glatter, R. and Kydd, L. (2003) 'Best practice in educational leadership and management: can we identify it and learn from it?', *Educational Management and Administration*, 31(3): 231–44.

Gold, A., Evans, J., Earley, P., Halpin, D. and Collarbone, P. (2003) 'Principled principals? Values-driven leadership: evidence from ten case studies of "outstanding" school leaders', *Educational Management and Administration*, 31(2): 127–38.

Greenfield, T. (1991) 'Reforming and revaluing educational administration: whence and when cometh the phoenix', *Educational Management and Administration*, 19(4): 200–17.

Greenfield, T. and Ribbins, P. (eds) (1993) *Greenfield on Educational Administration: Towards a Humane Science*, London: Routledge.

Gunter, H. (1997) *Rethinking Education: The Consequences of Jurassic Management*, London: Cassell.

Gunter, H. (2004) 'Labels and labelling in the field of educational leadership', *Discourse – Studies in the Cultural Politics of Education*, 25(1): 21–41.

Hallinger, P. (2003) *Reshaping the Landscape of School Leadership: A Global Perspective*, Lisse: Swets and Zeitlinger.

Hargreaves, A. (2004) Inclusive and exclusive educational change: emotional responses of teachers and implications for leadership', *School Leadership and Management*, 24(3): 287–306.

Hoyle, E. and Wallace, M. (2005) *Educational Leadership: Ambiguity, Professionals and Managerialism*, London: Sage.

Hughes, M. (1985) 'Theory and practice in educational management', in M. Hughes, P. Ribbins and H. Thomas (eds), *Managing Education: The System and the Institution*, London: Holt, Rinehart and Winston.

Hughes, M. and Bush, T. (1991) 'Theory and research as catalysts for change', in W. Walker, R. Farquhar and M. Hughes (eds), *Advancing Education: School Leadership in Action*, London: Falmer Press.

Hughes, M., Carter, J. and Fidler, B. (1981) *Professional Development Provision for Senior Staff in Schools and Colleges*, Birmingham: University of Birmingham.

Karstanje, P. (1999) 'Decentralisation and deregulation in Europe: towards a conceptual framework', in T. Bush, L. Bell, R. Bolam, R. Glatter and P. Ribbins (eds), *Educational Management: Redefining Theory, Policy and Practice*, London: Paul Chapman Publishing.

Lauglo, J. (1997) 'Assessing the present importance of different forms of decentralisation in education', in K. Watson, C. Modgil and S. Modgil (eds), *Power and Responsibility in Education*, London: Cassell.

Leithwood, K. (1994) 'Leadership for school restructuring', *Educational Administration Quarterly*, 30(4): 498–518.

Leithwood, K., Jantzi, D. and Steinbach, R. (1999) *Changing Leadership for Changing Times*, Buckingham: Open University Press.

Levačić, R. (1995) *Local Management of Schools: Analysis and Practice*, Buckingham: Open University Press.

Levačić, R., Glover, D., Bennett, N. and Crawford, M. (1999) 'Modern headship for the rationally managed school: combining cerebral and insightful approaches', in T. Bush, L. Bell, R. Bolam, R. Glatter and P. Ribbins (eds), *Educational Management: Redefining Theory, Policy and Practice*, London: Paul Chapman Publishing.

Levine, A. (2005) *Educating School Leaders*, Washington, DC: Educating School Leaders Project.

Newman, J. and Clarke, J. (1994) 'Going about our business? The managerialism of public services', in J. Clarke, A. Cochrane and E. McLaughlin (eds), *Managing School Policy*, London: Sage.

Organisation for Economic Co-operation and Development (1994) *Effectiveness of Schooling and Educational Resource Management: Synthesis of Country Studies*, Paris: OECD.

Purvis, M.T. (2007) 'School Improvement in a Small Island Developing State: The Seychelles', unpublished PhD thesis, University of Warwick.

Rhodes, C. and Brundrett, M. (2010) 'Leadership for learning', in T. Bush, L. Bell, and D. Middlewood (eds), *The Principles of Educational Leadership and Management*. London: Sage.

Sapre, P. (2002) 'Realising the potential of educational management in India', *Educational Management and Administration*, 30(1): 101–8.

Sayed, Y. (1999) 'Discourses of the policy of educational decentralisation in South Africa since 1994: an examination of the South African Schools Act', *Compare*, 29(2): 141–52.

School Management Task Force (SMTF) (1990) *Developing School Management: The Way Forward*, London: HMSO.

Southworth, G. (1993) 'School leadership and school development: reflections from research', *School Organisation*, 12(2): 73–87.

Southworth, G. (2004a) 'A response from the National College for School Leadership', *Educational Management, Administration and Leadership*, 32(3): 339–54.

Southworth, G. (2004b) Learning-centred leadership, in Davies, B. (ed.), *The Essentials of School Leadership*, London: Paul Chapman Publishing.

Taylor, F.W. (1947) *Principles of Scientific Management*, New York: Harper and Row.

Teacher Training Agency (TTA) (1998) *National Standards for Headteachers; National Standards for Subject Leaders: National Standards for Qualified Teacher Status*, London: TTA.

Therkildsen, O. (2000) 'Contextual issues in decentralisation of primary education in Tanzania', *International Journal of Educational Development*, 20: 407–21.

Thomas, H. and Martin, J. (1996) *Managing Resources for School Improvement*, London: Routledge.

Weber, M. (1947) in T. Parsons (ed.), *The Theory of Social and Economic Organization*, Glencoe, IL: Free Press, and New York: Collier-Macmillan.

Whitty, G. (2008) 'Twenty years of progress? English education policy 1988 to the present', *Educational Management, Administration and Leadership*, 36(2): 165–84.

Wright, N. (2001) 'Leadership, "bastard leadership" and managerialism', *Educational Management and Administration*, 29(3): 275–90.

Wright, N. (2003) 'Principled "bastard leadership"?: A rejoinder to Gold, Evans, Earley, Halpin and Collarbone', *Educational Management and Administration*, 31(2): 139–44.

Yukl, G.A. (2002) *Leadership in Organizations*, 5th edn, Upper Saddle River, NJ: Prentice-Hall.

CHAPTER 2

Models of educational leadership and management

The theory/practice divide

Leadership and management are often regarded as essentially practical activities. The determination of vision, the articulation of aims, the allocation of resources, and the evaluation of effectiveness, all involve action. Practitioners tend to be dismissive of theories and concepts for their alleged remoteness from the 'real' school situation. The implementation of the Education Reform Act (1988), and subsequent legislation in England and Wales, and in other countries, have led to an emphasis on the *practice* of educational leadership and management. Heads and principals have been inundated with prescriptions from politicians, officials, officers of quangos, academics and consultants, about how to lead and manage their schools and colleges. Many of these prescriptions are atheoretical in the sense that they are not underpinned by explicit values or concepts (Bush, 1999: 246). Hoyle and Wallace (2005: 9) say that 'policies embodied in the educational reform movement of the past two decades have brooked little compromise, relying on the excessive resort to leadership and management that we will term "managerialism" to ensure implementation'.

There is some evidence that the explicit and systematic use of theory as a guide to practice is unusual. Some commentators regard management as atheoretical. Holmes and Wynne, for example, are sceptical about the value of theory in informing practice:

> There can be little genuine theory in educational administration. It is an applied field ultimately dependent on human will acting within a social context ... So, it is unproductive to look for a set of theories ... by which educational administrators may guide administrative behaviour. (1989: 1–2)

This comment suggests that theory and practice are regarded as separate aspects of educational leadership and management. Academics develop and refine theory while managers engage in practice. In short, there is a theory/practice divide, or 'gap':

> The theory–practice gap stands as the Gordian Knot of educational administration. Rather than be cut, it has become a permanent fixture of the landscape because it is embedded in the way we construct theories for use ... The theory–practice gap will be removed when we construct different and better theories that predict the effects of practice. (English, 2002: 1, 3)

Theory may be perceived as esoteric and remote from practice. Yet, in an applied discipline such as educational management, the acid test of theory is its relevance to practice. Theory is valuable and significant if it serves to explain practice and provide managers with a guide to action. The emphasis in this book is on the use of theory to inform practice and to guide managers:

> Theories are most useful for influencing practice when they suggest new ways in which events and situations can be perceived. Fresh insight may be provided by focusing attention on possible interrelationships that the practitioner has failed to notice, and which can be further explored and tested through empirical research. If the result is a better understanding of practice, the theory–practice gap is significantly reduced for those concerned. Theory cannot then be dismissed as irrelevant. (Hughes and Bush, 1991: 234)

Some writers argue that theories of educational leadership and management have failed to make adequate connections with practice. Fullan (1996), for example, says that more work needs to be done to develop a meaningful action-based theory of leadership. Harris (2003: 15) adds that 'the existing leadership literature is still dominated by theory that is premised upon a rational and technicist perspective'. These comments suggest that more work is required to provide meaningful explanations of practice that can build robust theories of educational leadership and management and help to guide school-level practice.

The relevance of theory to good practice

If practitioners shun theory then they must rely on experience as a guide to action. In deciding on their response to a problem they draw on a range of options suggested by previous experience with that type of issue. However, 'it is wishful thinking to assume that experience alone will teach leaders everything they need to know' (Copland et al., 2002: 75).

Teachers sometimes explain their decisions as just 'common sense'. However, such apparently pragmatic decisions are often based on implicit theories: 'Common-sense knowledge ... inevitably carries with it unspoken assumptions and unrecognized limitations. Theorizing is taking place without it being acknowledged as such' (Hughes, 1985: 31). When a teacher or a leader takes a decision it reflects in part that person's view of the organization. Such views or preconceptions are coloured by experience and by the attitudes engendered by that experience. These attitudes take on the character of frames of reference or theories which inevitably influence the decision-making process.

Day (2003: 45) stresses the value of 'critical reflection' for practitioners facing complex circumstances: 'Headteachers' responses to the increasing complexity and intensity of their lives caused by imposed reform had been to use their capacity for reflection in a variety of real and imagined circumstances'. The use of the term 'theory' need not imply something remote from the day-to-day experience of the teacher. Rather, theories and concepts can provide a framework for managerial decisions:

> Because organizations are complex, surprising, deceptive, and ambiguous, they are formidably difficult to understand and manage. We have to rely on the tools at hand, including whatever ideas and theories we have about what organizations are and how they work. Our theories, or frames, determine what we see and what we do ... Managers need better theories, as well as the ability to implement those theories with skill and grace. (Bolman and Deal, 1997: 38)

Theory serves to provide a rationale for decision-making. Managerial activity is enhanced by an explicit awareness of the theoretical framework underpinning practice in educational institutions. Day (2003: 46) cautions that 'many principals (and teachers) mistakenly rely mainly upon experience and intuition – with all the limitations to change which these contain – to guide them through their careers'.

There are three main arguments to support the view that managers have much to learn from an appreciation of theory, providing that it is grounded firmly (Glaser and Strauss, 1967) in the realities of practice:

1. Reliance on facts as the sole guide to action is unsatisfactory because all evidence requires *interpretation*. Life in schools and colleges is too complex to enable practitioners to make decisions simply on an event-by-event basis. Theory provides the framework for interpreting events. It provides 'mental models' (Leithwood et al., 1999: 75) to help in understanding the nature and effects of practice.

2. Dependence on personal *experience* in interpreting facts and making decisions is narrow because it discards the knowledge of others. Familiarity with the arguments and insights of theorists enables the practitioner to deploy a wide range of experience and understanding in resolving the problems of today. Grounded theory emerges by assessing a wide range of practice, and developing models which seem to help in explaining events and behaviour. An understanding of theory also helps by reducing the likelihood of mistakes occurring while experience is being acquired.

3. Experience may be particularly unhelpful as the sole guide to action when the practitioner begins to operate in a different *context*. Organizational variables may mean that practice in one school or college has little relevance in the new environment. A broader awareness of theory and practice may be valuable as the manager attempts to interpret behaviour in the fresh situation. As Leithwood et al (1999: 4) stress, 'outstanding leadership is exquisitely sensitive to the context in which it is exercised'. The significance of the leadership context has been emphasized even more strongly in the twenty-first century as the inadequacies of 'one-size-fits-all' models have been exposed. Southworth (2004: 77), for example, suggests that 'one of the most robust findings is that where you are affects what you do as a leader'.

Of course, theory is useful only so long as it has relevance to practice in education. Hoyle (1986) distinguishes between theory-for-understanding and theory-for-practice. While both are potentially valuable, the latter is more significant for practising leaders and managers in education. The relevance of theory should be judged by the extent to which it informs leadership action and contributes to the resolution of practical problems in schools and colleges.

The nature of theory

There is no single all-embracing theory of educational management. In part this reflects the astonishing diversity of educational institutions, ranging from small rural primary schools to very large universities and colleges. Given the centrality of context (see above), a universal theory to explain leadership behaviour in all types of school and college can be seen as too ambitious. This relates also to the varied nature of the problems encountered in schools and colleges, which require different approaches and solutions. Above all, this reflects the multifaceted nature of theory in education and the social sciences. 'The literature is full of competing theories and counter-claims that make any attempt at generating a single, over-arching theory impossible' (Harris, 2003: 15).

House (1981) argues that theories or 'perspectives' in education are not the same as scientific theories. The latter comprises a set of beliefs, values and techniques that are shared within a particular field of enquiry. The dominant theory eventually comes under challenge by the emergence of new facts which the theory cannot explain. Subsequently a new theory is postulated which does explain these new facts. However, the physical world itself remains constant.

Theories of education and the social sciences are very different from scientific theories. These perspectives relate to a changing situation and comprise different ways of seeing a problem rather than a scientific consensus as to what is true. House (1981) suggests that, in this sense, the perspective is a weaker claim to knowledge than a scientific theory. In education several perspectives may be valid simultaneously:

> Our understanding of knowledge utilization processes is conceived not so much as a set of facts, findings, or generalizations but rather as distinct perspectives which combine facts, values and presuppositions into a complex screen through which knowledge utilization is seen ... Through a particular screen one sees certain events, but one may see different scenes through a different screen. (Ibid.: 17)

The models discussed in this book should be regarded as alternative ways of portraying events, as House suggests. The existence of several different perspectives creates what Bolman and Deal (1997: 11) describe as 'conceptual pluralism: a jangling discord of multiple voices'. Each theory has something to offer in explaining behaviour and events in educational institutions. The perspectives favoured by managers, explicitly or implicitly, inevitably influence or determine decision-making.

Griffiths (1997) provides strong arguments to underpin his advocacy of 'theoretical pluralism'.

> The basic idea is that all problems cannot be studied fruitfully using a single theory. Some problems are large and complex and no single theory is capable of encompassing them, while others, although seemingly simple and straightforward, can be better understood through the use of multiple theories ... particular theories are appropriate to certain problems, but not others. (Griffiths, 1997: 372)

Morgan (1997) also emphasizes the diversity of theories of management and organization. He uses 'metaphors' to explain the complex and paradoxical character of organizational life and describes theory in similar terms to House (1981):

> All theories of organization and management are based on implicit images or metaphors that lead us to see, understand and manage organizations in distinctive yet partial ways ... the use of metaphor implies a *way of thinking* and a *way of seeing* that pervades how we understand our world ... We have to accept that any theory or perspective that we bring to the study of organization and management, while capable of creating valuable insights, is also incomplete, biased and potentially misleading. (Morgan, 1997: 4–5)

One of the confusing aspects of theory in educational leadership and management is the use of different terms to explain similar phenomena. While House (1981) prefers 'perspective', Bolman and Deal (1997) choose 'frame' and Morgan (1997) opts for 'metaphor'. Boyd (1992: 506) adds to the confusion by referring to 'paradigms', a term he admits to using 'loosely': 'By paradigm is meant a model or theory; with models or theories often guiding, consciously or subconsciously, our thinking about such things as organizations, leadership and policy'. These terms are broadly similar and reflect the preferences of the authors rather than any significant differences in meaning. They will be used interchangeably in this book.

The various theories of educational leadership and management reflect very different ways of understanding and interpreting events and behaviour in schools and colleges. They also represent what are often ideologically based, and certainly divergent, views about how educational institutions ought to be managed. Waite (2002: 66) refers to 'paradigm wars' in describing disagreements between academics holding different positions on theory and research in educational administration.

Theories of educational leadership and management are endowed with different terminology but they all emanate from organization theory or management theory. The former tends to be theory for understanding while management theory has more direct relevance for practice. Hoyle (1986) distinguishes between these two broad approaches:

> Organization theory is theory-for-understanding. We can thus make a broad distinction between organization theory and management theory, which is practical theory and hence has a narrower focus. However, the distinction cannot be pressed too hard since management theory is grounded in, and the research which it generates contributes to, organization theory ...

> [The] case for organization theory is that it enhances our understanding of the management component and ... that it provides a loose organizing framework for a variety of studies of schools. (Ibid.: 1, 20)

The models discussed in this book are broad compilations of the main theories of educational leadership and management and are largely based on organization theory. However, by applying theory to practice throughout the text, leadership and management theories are developed and tested for their applicability to schools and colleges.

The characteristics of theory

Most theories of educational leadership and management possess three major characteristics:

1. Theories tend to be *normative* in that they reflect beliefs about the nature of educational institutions and the behaviour of individuals within them. Theorists tend to express views about how schools and colleges should be managed as well as, or instead of, simply describing aspects of management or explaining the organizational structure of the school or college. When, for example, practitioners or academics claim that decisions in schools are reached following a participative process they may be expressing normative judgements rather than analysing actual practice.

   Simkins (1999) stresses the importance of distinguishing between descriptive and normative uses of theory:

   > This is a distinction which is often not clearly made. The former are those which attempt to describe the nature of organizations and how they work and, sometimes, to explain why they are as they are. The latter, in contrast, attempt to prescribe how organizations should or might be managed to achieve particular outcomes more effectively. (Ibid.: 270)

   The remaining chapters of this book will distinguish between the normative and descriptive aspects of theory.

2. Theories tend to be *selective* or partial in that they emphasize certain aspects of the institution at the expense of other elements. The espousal of one theoretical model leads to the neglect of other approaches. Schools and colleges are arguably too complex to be capable of analysis through a single dimension. An explanation of educational institutions using a political perspective, for example, may focus on the formation of interest groups and on the bargain-

ing between groups and individuals. This approach offers valuable insights, as we shall see in Chapter 5, but this emphasis necessarily means that other valid theories of school and college management may be underestimated. In the 1980s, a few writers (Enderud, 1980; Davies and Morgan, 1983; Ellstrom, 1983) attempted syntheses of different approaches, but with only limited success.

3. Theories of educational management are often based on, or supported by, *observation* of practice in educational institutions. English (2002: 1) says that observation may be used in two ways. First, observation may be followed by the development of concepts which then become theoretical frames. Such perspectives based on data from systematic observation are sometimes called 'grounded theory'. Because such approaches are derived from empirical inquiry in schools and colleges, they are more likely to be perceived as relevant by practitioners. As Glaser and Strauss (1967: 3) aptly claim, 'generating grounded theory is a way of arriving at theory suited to its supposed uses'.

   Secondly, researchers may use a specific theoretical frame to select concepts to be tested through observation. The research is then used to 'prove' or 'verify' the efficacy of the theory (English, 2002: 1).

   While many theories of educational management are based on observation, advocates of the subjective model are sceptical of this stance. As we shall see in Chapter 6, subjective theorists prefer to emphasize the perceptions and interpretations of individuals within organizations. In this view observation is suspect because it does not reveal the meanings placed on events by participants.

Theories of educational leadership and management thus tend to be normative and selective and may also be based on observation in educational settings. These qualities overlap, as Theodossin (1983: 89) demonstrates: 'Inevitably ... research involves selection; selection is determined by, and determines, perspective; perspective limits vision; vision generates questions; and questions in turn, help to shape and influence the answers'.

Diversity in educational leadership and management

Leadership in education in Western democracies has been dominated by what Lumby and Coleman (2007) describe as 'the white, male, middle class norm'. Women are greatly underrepresented in senior posts in education in the great majority of countries on every continent.

> It has become part of our taken-for-granted understanding that men dominate numerically in senior positions in all phases of education with the exception of nursery and infant schools. Analysts of education management acknowledge the disparity between women's numbers in the teaching profession and their representation at senior levels. (Hall, 1999: 159)

The normative view that management is a male pursuit inevitably impacts on women who seek, and those who access, leadership positions. Lumby and Coleman (2007: 46) report that half the English women principals surveyed in 2004 'were aware of resentment and/or surprise from peers, colleagues and others in finding a woman in the position of head teacher'. The position may be worse in many other countries. Davies (1990: 62) notes that 'formal decision-making is in the hands of men ... Educational administration is still seen as a masculine occupation in many countries'. Research by Coleman, Qiang and Li (1998) shows that there were no women principals in any of the 89 secondary schools in three counties of the Shaanxi province of China. Moorosi (2007) reports that women leaders in South Africa encounter a 'traditional stereotype', that associates school principalship with masculinity. The republic of Seychelles provides one rare exception, in that 90 per cent of school heads, and most senior Ministry of Education staff, are women (Purvis, 2007).

Among the reasons advanced for the low proportion of women in senior posts is the alleged 'male' image of management which may be unappealing to women. This model includes 'aggressive competitive behaviours, an emphasis on control rather than negotiation and collaboration, and the pursuit of competition rather than shared problem-solving' (Al-Khalifa, 1992: 100). The male domination, or 'androcentricity', of educational management is evident in the United States where school administration evolved into a largely male profession disconnected from the mainly female occupation of teaching. Boyd (1992) implies that this led to discrimination in the allocation of administrative posts:

> The abilities and values of women were passed over, as careers in school administration were more driven by male sponsorship than by merit and open competition ... school administration became far more concerned with hierarchy, control and efficiency than with issues of curriculum, pedagogy, and educational values. (Ibid.: 509)

Certain writers (e.g. Shakeshaft, 1987; Ozga, 1993) claim that theory has failed to acknowledge the different values of women and remains largely rooted in a male perspective. The difficulty is that there is little clarity about what constitutes a distinctive female theory of educational management. Hall (1993) concludes that:

> There is relatively little to date in research about women managers that can be used to challenge theories of educational management or lead to their reconceptualization to include both women and men ... Research is needed that challenges traditional stereotypes of what constitutes appropriate management behaviour and process. The association of management and masculinity has not been established as a fact yet it is treated as such, with negative consequences for women in education ... theory and prescriptions for action [would be] transformed by the inclusion of gender as a relevant concept for understanding educational management. (Ibid.: 43)

Wallace and Hall's (1994) research on senior management teams in secondary schools suggests that it is possible for management to incorporate both female and male styles:

> The decision to adopt a team approach seems to signify a shift in leadership style towards an 'androgynous' model which posits the possibility for leaders to exhibit the wide range of qualities which are present in both men and women. (Ibid.: 39)

Gray (1989) adopts a similar approach in distinguishing between 'feminine' and 'masculine' paradigms in school management. Feminine characteristics include 'caring', 'creative' and 'intuitive' dimensions, while the masculine paradigm features 'competitive', 'highly regulated' and 'disciplined' elements. Individual managers may possess qualities from both paradigms, regardless of their gender. This view is supported by the large-scale research on male and female secondary heads carried out by Coleman (2002). She shows that there is little difference in the ways that male and female heads respond to the Gray descriptors and concludes that 'the paradigms are not perceived as relevant in distinguishing women from men' (ibid.: 103).

A number of the six models presented in this book have been aligned with 'male' or 'female' qualities. The gender implications of the theories will be discussed at appropriate points in the text.

While there is now substantial research on gender aspects of leadership, in many countries, issues of race and ethnicity have been given much less attention. Lumby and Coleman (2007: 59) cite King's (2004: 73) notion of 'dysconscious racism' 'that tacitly accepts dominant White norms and privileges'. Bush and Moloi (2008) report that black and minority ethnic (BME) teachers are much less likely to be promoted to leadership positions than white teachers. Powney et al.'s (2003) research in England shows that 52 per cent of BME teachers remain in the classroom compared with 29 per cent of white women and 35 per cent of white men.

Several studies (e.g. Powney et al., 2003; Bush et al., 2006; 2007) identify barriers to BME progression at every stage in England, including lack of encouragement to apply for headship training, through racist attitudes during training, to uncomfortable experiences during the selection process, and continuing difficulties after appointment. Similarly, Bush and Moloi (2007) report on the discomfort experienced by black leaders in South Africa working in previously white schools, where racist attitudes persist 13 years after the election of the first democratic government. Bush and Moloi (2008) conclude that BME leaders need confidence building and targeted preparation, along with modified recruitment and selection practices, if the school leadership profile is going to match the diversity of schools and communities.

Leadership and management theory has paid little attention to issues of diversity but the discussion in the remaining chapters will show how theories could, or should, be adapted to make them suitable for the increasing diversity of school contexts.

Models of educational management: an introduction

Many different theories of educational management have been presented by various writers. These perspectives overlap in several respects. A further complication is that similar models are given different names or, in certain cases, the same term is used to denote different approaches. A degree of integration of these theories is required so that they can be presented in a clear and discrete manner. Cuthbert (1984) explains why there is a lack of clarity:

> The study of management in education is an eclectic pursuit. Models have been borrowed from a wide range of disciplines, and in a few cases developed specifically to explain unique features of educational institutions. To comprehend the variety of models available we need some labels and categories that allow us to consider different ideas in a sensible order. (Ibid.: 39)

The approach to theory adopted in this book has certain similarities with Cuthbert's (1984) presentation of models in five distinct groups. Cuthbert's categories are analytic-rational, pragmatic-rational, political, models that stress ambiguity, and phenomenological and interactionist models. The latter three groups are the same as three of the models discussed in this text although I prefer the term subjective rather than phenomenological or interactionist. Cuthbert compares his models in the following terms:

- the level of agreement among people in the organization about the objectives of their joint efforts

- different ideas about the way in which performance can and should be evaluated
- different ideas about the concept and the meaning of organization structure.

Two of the criteria used by Cuthbert are similar to two of the four main elements used in this text to distinguish between the models.

Several writers have chosen to present theories in distinct groups or bundles but they differ in the models chosen, the emphasis given to particular approaches and the terminology used to describe them. Two of the best known are those by Bolman and Deal (1997) and Morgan (1997).

- Bolman and Deal (1997); four 'perspectives or frames' – structural, human resource, political, symbolic.
- Morgan (1997); eight images or metaphors of organizations – as machines, organisms, brains, cultures, political systems, psychic prisons, flux and transformation, instruments of domination.

In this book the main theories are classified into six major models of educational management. While this division differs somewhat from the categorization of other writers, these models are given significant attention in the literature of educational management and have been subject to a degree of empirical verification in British education. The six theories are illustrated extensively by examples of practice drawn from primary schools, secondary schools and colleges in England and Wales, and in many other countries.

The six models are:

- formal
- collegial
- political
- subjective
- ambiguity
- cultural.

In the first edition of this book only five models were identified. A chapter on the cultural model was added to the second edition because of the increasing significance of this approach in the literature and because some empirical work had been undertaken in British schools and elsewhere in the English-speaking world.

Analysing the models

The analysis of these six models includes consideration of four main elements which are valuable in distinguishing the theories. These criteria are as follows:

1. The level of agreement about the *goals* or objectives of the institution. Cheng (2002: 51) shows that goal orientation is one of only two common factors within the numerous definitions of leadership.

   The theories differ in that some emphasize organizational aims, while others focus on individual purposes. Certain models feature agreement about objectives but others stress conflict over aims or point to difficulties in defining purpose within educational organizations.

2. The meaning and validity of organizational *structures* within educational institutions. Hoyle (1986) refers to the twin dimensions of people and structure. An emphasis on structure leads to the notion of individuals being defined by their roles, while a focus on people leads to the predominance of personality in determining behaviour.

   According to some theorists, structure is an objective fact while others believe that it is the subjective creation of individuals within the institution. Another group argues that structure is a matter for negotiation or dispute while others claim that the structure is one of the many ambiguous features of schools and colleges.

3. The relationship between the institution and its external *environment*. The shift to self-managing schools and colleges, discussed in Chapter 1, increases the significance of the relationships that staff and governors must have with a wide range of external groups and individuals. The nature of these external relationships is a key element in the differences between models. Some writers regard the head or principal as the sole or major contact with the outside world, while others suggest a wider range of contacts. Links may be regarded as essentially co-operative in nature or they may be thought of as political, with conflict between the institution and external agencies. Other approaches emphasize the ambiguity of such relationships.

4. The most appropriate *leadership* strategies for educational institutions. Analysts have different views about the nature of educational leadership according to the theories they espouse. Some assume that heads take the lead in establishing objectives and in decision-making while others regard the head as one figure within a participative system. Certain approaches stress conflict inside institutions and emphasize the head's role as negotiator, while others point to the limitations of

an active leadership role within essentially ambiguous institutions.

Given the heightened interest in the concept of educational leadership since the second edition of this volume, this subject will be given extended treatment in this edition. The main theories of leadership are introduced below and will also be addressed alongside the six management models, to demonstrate the links between these twin concepts.

These four criteria serve to emphasize the great differences in approach between the various models and reinforce the view that theories are normative and selective. In subsequent chapters of this book we examine these different interpretations of the nature of leadership and management in schools and colleges.

Models of educational leadership: an introduction

As with educational management, the vast literature on leadership has generated a number of alternative, and competing, models. Some writers have sought to cluster these various conceptions into a number of broad themes or 'types'. The best known of these typologies is that by Leithwood, Jantzi and Steinbach (1999), who identified six 'models' from their scrutiny of 121 articles in four international journals. Bush and Glover (2002) extended this typology to eight models. Table 2.1 elaborates these typologies to identify 10 leadership models and sets them against the six management models.

Table 2.1 Typology of management and leadership models

Management model	Leadership model
Formal	Managerial
Collegial	Participative
	Transformational
	Distributed
Political	Transactional
Subjective	Postmodern
	Emotional
Ambiguity	Contingency
Cultural	Moral
	Instructional

Source: adapted from Bush and Glover, 2002.

Instructional leadership, often described as learning-centred leadership, does not link to any of the management models because it focuses on the direction of influence, learning and teaching, rather than the nature of the influence process. This model was discussed in Chapter 1 while the other nine leadership models will be addressed alongside the appropriate management model in subsequent chapters of this book. The models in Table 2.1 are not exhaustive. In a single volume on leadership (Davies, 2004), seven other categories are identified:

- Strategic leadership
- Invitational leadership
- Ethical leadership
- Constructivist leadership
- Poetical and political leadership
- Entrepreneurial leadership
- Sustainable leadership.

These models add to the complexity of leadership theory and demonstrate the contested nature of the terrain. These constructs will be referred to as appropriate in the following chapters but the structure of the book will be based around the models shown in Table 2.1.

References

Al-Khalifa, E. (1992) 'Management by halves: women teachers and school management', in N. Bennett, M. Crawford and C. Riches (eds), *Managing Change in Education: Individual and Organizational Perspectives*, London: Paul Chapman Publishing.

Bolman, L.G. and Deal, T.E. (1997) *Reframing Organisations: Artistry, Choice and Leadership*, San Francisco, CA: Jossey-Bass.

Boyd, W. (1992) 'The power of paradigms: reconceptualizing educational policy and management', *Educational Administration Quarterly*, 28(4): 504–28.

Bush, T. (1999) 'Crisis or crossroads? The discipline of educational management in the late 1990s', *Educational Management and Administration*, 27(3): 239–52.

Bush, T. and Glover, D. (2002) *School Leadership: Concepts and Evidence*, Nottingham: NCSL.

Bush, T. and Moloi, K.C. (2007) 'Race, racism and discrimination in school leadership: evidence from England and South Africa', *International Studies in Educational Administration*, 35(1): 41–59.

Bush, T. and Moloi, K.C. (2008) 'Race and racism in leadership development', in J. Lumby, G. Crow and P. Pashiardis (eds), *International Handbook on the Preparation and Development of School Leaders*, New York: Routledge.

Bush, T., Glover, D. and Sood, K. (2006) 'Black and minority ethnic leaders in England: a portrait', *School Leadership and Management,* 26(3): 289–305.

Bush, T., Allen, T., Glover, D., Middlewood, D. and Sood, K. (2007) *Diversity and the*

National Professional Qualification for Headship, Nottingham: NCSL.

Cheng, Y.C. (2002) 'Leadership and strategy', in T. Bush and L. Bell (eds), *The Principles and Practice of Educational Management*, London: Paul Chapman Publishing.

Coleman, M. (2002) *Women as Headteachers: Striking the Balance*, Stoke-on-Trent: Trentham Books.

Coleman, M., Qiang, H. and Li, Y. (1998) 'Women in educational management in China: experience in Shaanxi province', *Compare*, 28(2): 141–54.

Copland, M., Darling-Hammond, L., Knapp, M., McLaugghlin, M. and Talbert, J. (2002) *Leadership for Teaching and Learning: A Framework for Research and Action*, April, New Orleans: American Educational Research Association.

Cuthbert, R. (1984) *The Management Process, E324 Management in Post-Compulsory Education, Block 3, Part 2*, Buckingham: Open University Press.

Davies, B. (2004) *The Essentials of School Leadership*, London: Paul Chapman.

Davies, J.L. and Morgan, A.W. (1983) 'Management of higher education in a period of contraction and uncertainty', in O. Boyd-Barrett, T. Bush, J. Goodey, I. McNay and M. Preedy (eds), *Approaches to Post-School Management*, London: Paul Chapman Publishing.

Davies, L. (1990) *Equity and Efficiency? School Management in an International Context*, London: Falmer Press.

Day, C. (2003) 'The changing learning needs of heads: building and sustaining effectiveness', in A. Harris, C. Day, D. Hopkins, M. Hadfield, A. Hargreaves and C. Chapman (eds), *Effective Leadership for School Improvement*, London: RoutledgeFalmer.

Ellstrom, P.E. (1983) 'Four faces of educational organisations', *Higher Education*, 12: 231–41.

Enderud, H. (1980) 'Administrative leadership in organised anarchies', *International Journal of Institutional Management in Higher Education*, 4(3): 235–53.

English, F. (2002) 'Cutting the Gordian Knot of educational administration: the theory–practice gap', *The Review*, 44(1): 1–3.

Fullan, M. (1996) 'Leadership for change', in K. Leithwood, J. Chapman, D. Corsan, P. Hallinger and A. Hart (eds), *International Handbook of Educational Leadership and Administration*, Vol. 2, Dordrecht and London: Kluwer.

Glaser, B.G. and Strauss, A.L. (1967) *The Discovery of Grounded Theory*, London: Weidenfeld and Nicolson.

Gray, H. (1989) 'Gender considerations in school management: masculine and feminine leadership styles', in C. Riches and C. Morgan (eds), *Human Resource Management in Education*, Buckingham: Open University Press.

Griffiths, D. (1997) 'The case for theoretical pluralism', *Educational Management and Administration*, 25(4): 371–80.

Hall, V. (1993) 'Women in educational management: a review of research in Britain', in J. Ouston (ed.), *Women in Educational Management*, Harlow: Longman.

Hall, V. (1999) 'Gender and education management: duel or dialogue?', in T. Bush, L. Bell, R. Bolam, R. Glatter and P. Ribbins (eds), *Educational Management: Redefining Theory, Policy and Practice*, London: Paul Chapman Publishing.

Harris, A. (2003) 'The changing context of leadership: research, theory and practice', in A. Harris, C. Day, D. Hopkins, M. Hadfield, A. Hargreaves and C. Chapman (eds), *Effective Leadership for School Improvement*, London: RoutledgeFalmer.

Holmes, M. and Wynne, E. (1989) *Making the School an Effective Community: Belief, Practice and Theory in School Administration*, Lewes: Falmer Press.

House, E.R. (1981) 'Three perspectives on innovation', in R. Lehming and M. Kane (eds), *Improving Schools: Using What We Know*, Beverly Hills, CA: Sage.

Hoyle, E. (1986) *The Politics of School Management*, Sevenoaks: Hodder and Stoughton.

Hoyle, E. and Wallace, M. (2005) *Educational Leadership: Ambiguity, Professionals and Managerialism*, London: Sage.

Hughes, M. (1985) 'Theory and practice in educational management', in M. Hughes, P. Ribbins and H. Thomas (eds), *Managing Education: The System and the Institution*, London: Holt, Rinehart and Winston.

Hughes, M. and Bush, T. (1991) 'Theory and research as catalysts for change', in W. Walker, R. Farquhar and M. Hughes (eds), *Advancing Education: School Leadership in Action*, London: Falmer Press.

King, J. (2004) 'Dysconscious racism: Ideology, identity, and the miseducation of teachers', in G. Ladson-Billings and D. Gillborn (eds), *The RoutledgeFalmer Reader in Multicultural Education*, Abingdon: RoutledgeFalmer.

Leithwood, K., Jantzi, D. and Steinbach, R. (1999) *Changing Leadership for Changing Times*, Buckingham: Open University Press.

Lumby, J. and Coleman, M. (2007) *Leadership and Diversity: Challenging Theory and Practice in Education*, London: Sage.

Moorosi, P. (2007) 'Creating linkages between private and public: Challenges facing women principals in South Africa', *South African Journal of Education*, 27(3): 507–21.

Morgan, G. (1997) *Images of Organization*, Newbury Park, CA: Sage.

Ozga, J. (1993) *Women in Educational Management*, Buckingham: Open University Press.

Powney, J., Wilson, V., Hall, S. et al. (2003) *Teachers' Careers: The Impact of Age, Disability, Ethnicity, Gender and Sexual Orientation*, London: DfES.

Purvis, M.T. (2007) 'School improvement in a small island developing state: The Seychelles', unpublished PhD thesis, University of Warwick.

Shakeshaft, C. (1987) *Women in Educational Administration*, Newbury Park, CA: Sage.

Simkins, T. (1999) 'Values, power and instrumentality: theory and research in education management', *Educational Management and Administration*, 27(3): 267–81.

Southworth, G. (2004) Learning-centred leadership, in B. Davies (ed.), *The Essentials of Schools Leadership*, London: Paul Chapman Publishing.

Theodossin, E. (1983) 'Theoretical perspectives on the management of planned educational change', *British Education Research Journal*, 9(1): 81–90.

Waite, D. (2002) 'The "paradigm wars" in educational administration: an attempt at transcendence', *International Studies in Educational Administration*, 30(1): 66–81.

Wallace, M. and Hall, V. (1994) *Inside the SMT: Teamwork in Secondary School Management*, London: Paul Chapman Publishing.

CHAPTER 3

Formal models

Central features of formal models

Formal model is an umbrella term used to embrace a number of similar but not identical approaches. The title 'formal' is used because these theories emphasize the official and structural elements of organizations. There is a focus on pursuing institutional objectives through rational approaches. The definition suggested below incorporates the main features of these perspectives.

> Formal models assume that organizations are hierarchical systems in which managers use rational means to pursue agreed goals. Heads and principals possess authority legitimized by their formal positions within the organization and are accountable to sponsoring bodies for the activities of their institutions.

The various formal models have several common features:

1. They tend to treat organizations as *systems*. A system comprises elements that have clear organizational links with each other. Within schools and colleges, for example, departments and other sub-units are systemically related to each other and to the institution itself.
2. Formal models give prominence to the *official structure* of the organization. Formal structures are often represented by organization charts

which show the authorized pattern of relationships between members of the institution. Structural models do not adequately reflect the many informal contacts within schools and colleges but they do help to represent the more stable and official aspects of organizations.

3. In formal models the official structures of the organization tend to be *hierarchical*. Organization charts emphasize vertical relationships between staff. In secondary schools and colleges staff are responsible to heads of department who, in turn, are answerable to heads and principals for the activities of their departments. The hierarchy thus represents a means of control for leaders over their staff.

4. All formal approaches typify schools and colleges as *goal-seeking* organizations. The institution is thought to have official purposes which are accepted and pursued by members of the organization. Cheng (2002: 52) claims that goal development and achievement is one of two main general elements in leadership: 'How to set goals, create meanings, direct actions, eliminate uncertainty or ambiguity and achieve goals is also a core part of leadership activities in education'. Increasingly, goals are set within a broader vision of a preferred future for the school (Beare et al., 1989).

5. Formal models assume that managerial decisions are made through a *rational* process. Typically, all the options are considered and evaluated in terms of the goals of the organization. The most suitable alternative is then selected to enable those objectives to be pursued. The essence of this approach is that decision-making is thought to be an objective, detached and intellectual process.

6. Formal approaches present the *authority* of leaders as essentially a product of their official positions within the organization. Heads and principals possess authority over other staff because of their formal roles within schools and colleges. Their power is regarded as positional and is held only while they hold these senior posts.

7. In formal models there is an emphasis on the *accountability* of the organization to its sponsoring body. Most English schools, for example, are responsible to the local authority (LA) and to their governing bodies. They are also answerable to the national inspection body, the Office for Standards in Education (OFSTED). In many centralized systems, school principals are accountable to national or provincial ministries of education. In decentralized systems, heads and principals are increasingly answerable to their governing boards which have enhanced responsibility for finance and staff management.

These seven basic features are present to a greater or lesser degree in each of the individual theories which together comprise the formal models. These are:

- structural models
- systems models
- bureaucratic models
- rational models
- hierarchical models.

These different theories overlap significantly and the main elements are often very similar despite their different titles. There are variations in emphasis but the central components appear in most of the individual theories.

Structural models

> Structure refers to the formal pattern of relationships between people in organizations. It expresses the ways in which individuals relate to each other in order to achieve organizational objectives. (Bush, 1997: 45)

Structural models stress the primacy of organizational structure but the key elements are compatible with the central features of any formal model. Bolman and Deal (1991: 48) argue that the structural perspective is based on six core assumptions:

1. Organizations exist primarily to accomplish established goals.
2. For any organization, a structural form can be designed and implemented to fit its particular set of circumstances.
3. Organizations work most effectively when environmental turbulence and the personal preferences are constrained by norms of rationality.
4. Specialization permits higher levels of individual expertise and performance.
5. Co-ordination and control are essential to effectiveness.
6. Organizational problems typically originate from inappropriate structures or inadequate systems and can be resolved through restructuring or developing new systems.

The structural assumptions identified by Bolman and Deal, including the goal orientation, the rationality, the exercise of authority and the reference to systems, are consistent with the central features of formal models discussed earlier.

Structural models are often expressed in terms of organizational levels. Five main levels can be identified:

1. The *central level*, including national, provincial or state governments, and official bodies appointed by them, which are collectively responsible for overall planning, resource allocation and the monitoring of standards.
2. The *local level*, including local and district authorities, which are responsible for interpreting government policies and, often, for administering the educational system.
3. The *institution* – schools, colleges, universities and other educational organizations.
4. *Sub-units,* such as departments or faculties in colleges and universities, and departments and pastoral units in schools.
5. The *individual level* – teachers, students or pupils and support staff (adapted from Becher and Kogan, 1992: 9).

In the twenty-first century, new forms of organization have become apparent that do not fit comfortably into the five-tier structure identified above. Increasingly, schools are becoming involved in networks or clusters in their local communities (Townsend, 2010). These networks are not part of the formal structure but arise organically, with or without an external stimulus, in order to meet the specified or emergent needs of the schools involved. In addition, schools in England, for example, are being linked through more formal structures such as federations where their individual character is becoming blurred by joint governance and leadership arrangements (Bush et al., 2009).

School and college structures are usually portrayed as vertical and hierarchical. Evetts (1992), for example, stresses the hierarchical nature of school structures and the authority of the headteacher. Similarly, the structures of English further education colleges have traditionally been hierarchical and Hall (1994) notes that the departmental, pyramid structure has dominated in colleges for 30 years. Lumby (2001) comments that, in the twenty-first century, many colleges are adopting different metaphors for structure, including the 'Christmas tree', 'a less stark image than a pyramid' (ibid.: 91–2), and a series of concentric circles. However, she concludes that 'some degree of bureaucratic hierarchy will always assert itself' (ibid.: 92).

Structures are not inevitably hierarchical. Those which are apparently hierarchical may be used to facilitate delegation and participation in decision-making. This may occur, for example, where budgets are delegated to departments.

The resilience of structure

It is easy to dismiss organizational structures as a rigid, over-formal presentation of relationships in educational institutions. Significantly, Porter (2006) notes that institutional structures have little or no impact on student engagement and development. All schools and colleges benefit from informal contacts not represented on organization charts, and the increasing interest in teacher leadership and distributed forms of leadership (Harris, 2004), suggests that more fluid and flexible arrangements are becoming apparent in many schools. While pyramidal structures can still be observed in many countries, they represent only part of the leadership activity in most schools. They may also conceal very different styles of management. Yet structures remain powerful influences on the nature and direction of development within institutions. Individuals are appointed to specific positions and this tends to influence, if not determine, the nature of their professional relationships. As Clark (1983: 114) makes clear, 'academic structures do not simply move aside or let go: what is in place heavily conditions what will be. The heavy hand of history is felt in the structures and beliefs that development has set in place'. Gaziel (2003) shows that structure is an important predictor of the management effectiveness of principals but has less influence on their leadership role.

Systems models

Systems theories emphasize the unity and integrity of the organization and focus on the interaction between its component parts, and with the external environment. These models stress the unity and *coherence* of the organization. Schools and colleges are thought to have integrity as prime institutions. Members of the organization, and those external to it, recognize the school or college as a meaningful entity. Staff and students may feel that they 'belong' to the place where they teach or learn. However, there are dangers in too great an emphasis on the organization rather than the people within it because of the risk of attributing human characteristics to schools and colleges. Greenfield (1973) has been the most trenchant critic of this tendency to reify organizations, as we shall see in Chapter 6.

Systems approaches share with other formal models the emphasis on agreed organizational *objectives*. It is assumed that the total system has objectives which have the support of its members. The institution is thought to develop policies in pursuit of these objectives and to assess the effectiveness of such policies. Systems theories play down or ignore the possibility that goals may be contested or that individuals may have purposes independent of the formal aims of the organization.

Systems models emphasize the concept of a system *boundary*. The boundary is an essential element in the definition of the system, distinguishing the organization and its members from the external environment:

> Environment is typically seen as everything outside the boundaries of an organisation, even though the boundaries are often nebulous and poorly drawn. It is the environment that provides raw materials to an organisation and receives the organisation's outputs ... Schools receive students from the community and later return graduates to the community. (Bolman and Deal, 1989: 24)

O'Shea (2007) argues that systems have become more complex because of the increasing diversity of the student body, a greater emphasis on collaboration, and the drive to replace simple 'delivery' models of teaching. He adds that these more complex systems are also more vulnerable to failure. Collaborative arrangements are consistent with open systems theory.

Closed or open systems

Systems theories are usually categorized as either *closed* or *open* in terms of the organization's relationships with its environment. Closed systems tend to minimize transactions with the environment and to take little account of external opinion in determining the purposes and activities of the organization. Bolman and Deal's (1991) structural assumptions, noted earlier, imply a 'closed systems' approach:

> These assumptions depict organizations as relatively closed systems pursuing fairly explicit goals. Such conditions make it possible for organizations to operate rationally, with high degrees of certainty, predictability and efficiency. Organizations highly dependent on the environment are continually vulnerable to external influences or interference. To reduce this vulnerability, a variety of structural mechanisms are created to protect central activities from fluctuation and uncertainty. (Bolman and Deal, 1991: 48–9)

The shift to self-management in many countries, and the associated requirement to collaborate with many groups and individuals, has made it more difficult to sustain a closed systems approach. Boyd (1999: 286), referring to the US, claims that the closed systems approach 'was inadequate for understanding or dealing with the most pressing problems of school administrators ... Failing the test of practical relevance, the closed systems model was abandoned and the search was on for more useful models'.

The alternative theory is that of 'open systems' which assumes permeable boundaries and an interactive two-way relationship between schools and colleges, and their environment. Hoy and Miskel (1987: 29) argue that 'school systems are now viewed as open systems, which must adapt to changing external conditions to be effective and, in the long term, survive'.

Open systems encourage interchanges with the environment, both responding to external influences and, in turn, seeking support for the objectives of the organization. In education, open systems theory shows the relationship between the institution and external groups such as parents, employers and the local education authority. In this model, schools and colleges have wide-ranging links across an increasingly permeable boundary but organizations are able to influence their environment and are not simply responding to external demands.

Educational institutions vary considerably in the extent to which they may be regarded as closed or open systems. English further education colleges have extensive and vital links with employers, who sponsor students on many part-time and some full-time courses, and with the Learning and Skills Councils, which largely determine their levels of funding. Most schools may also be regarded as open systems because of the constant interaction with various groups and individuals in their neighbourhoods. Selective schools and certain universities, which enjoy high reputations and which do not have to compete vigorously for students, may be sufficiently impervious to external influences to be categorized as closed systems.

The distinction between open and closed systems is more blurred in practice than it is in theory. It may be more useful to think of a continuum rather than a sharp distinction between polar opposites. All schools and colleges have a measure of interaction with their environments but the greater the dependence of the institution on external groups the more 'open' it is likely to be.

The educational reforms of the past 20 years, in Britain and elsewhere, have increased the salience of the open systems model. Schools have to compete for pupils and their income is tied closely to their levels of recruitment. To be attractive to potential parents, it is important to be responsive to their requirements. This can lead to permeable boundaries with parents and others influencing school policies and priorities. The clustering of some schools into informal networks provides one contemporary example of open systems, with teachers working together to address common issues.

Systems theorists believe that organizations can be categorized as systems with their parts interacting to achieve systemic objectives.
However, caution should be exercised in attributing these qualities to
schools and colleges, which are complex human organizations. Schools
do not operate smoothly like highly developed machines but some
integration of their activities is desirable and this lends some credence
to the systems model.

Bureaucratic models

The bureaucratic model is probably the most important of the formal
models. There is a substantial literature about its applicability to
schools and colleges. It is often used broadly to refer to characteristics
which are generic to formal organizations. The 'pure' version of the
bureaucratic model is associated strongly with the work of Weber who
argued that, in formal organizations, bureaucracy is the most efficient
form of management:

> The purely bureaucratic type of administrative organization ... is, from a
> technical point of view, capable of attaining the highest degree of effi-
> ciency and is in this sense formally the most rational means of carrying
> out imperative control over human beings. It is superior to any other
> form in precision, in stability, in the stringency of its discipline, and in its
> reliability. (Weber, 1989: 16)

Bureaucracy, then, describes a formal organization which seeks maximum efficiency through rational approaches to management. Its main
features are as follows:

1. It stresses the importance of the *hierarchical authority structure*, with
   formal chains of command between the different positions in the
   hierarchy. This pyramidal structure is based on the legal authority
   vested in the officers who hold places in the chain of command.
   Office holders are responsible to superordinates for the satisfactory
   conduct of their duties. In educational institutions teachers are
   accountable to the head or principal.
2. In common with other formal models, the bureaucratic approach
   emphasizes the *goal orientation* of the organization. Institutions are
   dedicated to goals which are clearly delineated by the officers at the
   apex of the pyramid. In colleges or schools goals are determined
   largely by the principal or head and endorsed without question by
   other staff.
3. The bureaucratic model suggests a *division of labour*, with staff spe-

cializing in particular tasks on the basis of expertise. The departmental structure in secondary schools and colleges is an obvious manifestation of division of labour, with subject specialists teaching a defined area of the curriculum. In this respect, English primary schools do not resemble bureaucracies because staff are typically class teachers who work with one group of children for much of their time.

4. In bureaucracies, decisions and behaviour are governed by *rules and regulations* rather than personal initiative. Schools typically have rules to regulate the behaviour of pupils and often guide the behaviour of teachers through bureaucratic devices such as the staff handbook. These rules may extend to the core issues of teaching and learning. In South Africa, 'the teachers … were subjected to tight bureaucratic regulation, especially in the matter of the curriculum' (Sebakwane, 1997: 397). In many centralized systems, including Greece, bureaucratic control extends to prescribing school textbooks (Bush, 2001). Sandholtz and Scribner (2006) note that increased regulation and bureaucratic controls at school and district levels undermine teachers' professional development.

5. Bureaucratic models emphasize *impersonal* relationships between staff, and with clients. This neutrality is designed to minimize the impact of individuality on decision-making. Good schools depend in part on the quality of personal relationships between teachers and pupils, and this aspect of bureaucracy has little influence in many schools. Yet where staff are required to make an appointment to see the head, this may be regarded as an example of bureaucracy in action.

6. In bureaucracies the recruitment and career progress of staff are determined on *merit*. Appointments are made on the basis of qualifications and experience, and promotion depends on expertise demonstrated in present and previous positions. Schools and colleges fulfil this criterion in that formal competitive procedures are laid down for the appointment of new staff and for some promoted posts. Internal promotions, however, depend on the recommendation of the head or principal and there may be no formal process.

Applying the bureaucratic model to education

All large organizations contain some bureaucratic elements and this is true of educational institutions:

> Schools and colleges have many bureaucratic features, including a hierar-

chical structure with the headteacher or principal at the apex. Teachers specialise on the basis of expertise in secondary schools and colleges and, increasingly, in primary schools also. There are many rules for pupils and staff, whose working lives are largely dictated by 'the tyranny of the timetable'. Heads and senior staff are accountable to the governing body and external stakeholders for the activities of the school or college. Partly for these reasons, bureaucratic theories pervade much of the literature on educational management. (Bush, 1994: 36)

The recognition that bureaucracy applies to many aspects of education is tempered by concern about its procedures becoming too dominant an influence on the operation of schools and colleges. There is a fear that the bureaucracy itself may become the *raison d'être* of the organization rather than being firmly subordinated to educational aims.

Bureaucracy is the preferred model for many education systems, including the Czech Republic (Svecova, 2000), China (Bush et al., 1998), Greece (Kavouri and Ellis, 1998), Israel (Gaziel, 2003), Poland (Klus-Stanska and Olek, 1998), Seychelles (Purvis, 2007), South Africa (Sebakwane, 1997), Slovenia (Becaj, 1994) and much of South America (Newland, 1995). Two of these authors point to some of the weaknesses of bureaucracy in education:

> The excessive centralization and bureaucratization, which continue to exist [in South America] in spite of the reforms undertaken, affect the efficiency of the system. (Newland, 1995: 113)

> The Greek state should start moving towards restructuring the organization of schools. Less complexity, formalization and centralization of the system, and more extended professionalism and autonomy of teachers and headteachers would be beneficial. (Kavouri and Ellis, 1998: 106)

These extracts suggest that bureaucracy is likely to be the preferred model in centralized education systems as the bureaucratic apparatus is the mechanism used to control subordinate levels in the hierarchy, including schools. Gamage's (2006) research in Victoria, Australia, suggests that the shift to site-based management has eased these controls and enhanced quality and innovation. 'When compared to what they experienced under centralized, bureaucratic models, the SBM [school-based management] has created more autonomous, flexible, better quality, effective schools' (ibid.: 27). However, where site-based management is accompanied by prescriptive policies and targets, as well as high levels of accountability (Taylor, 2007: 569), it may have the opposite effect of damaging the creativity and initiative of teachers, as Brehony and Deem (2005) argue in respect of England:

> Up to the mid 1980s, publicly funded educational organizations did dis-

play bureaucratic features, including rules, staff hierarchies and complex procedures. However, professionals employed in these organizations retained discretion and autonomy in their work. Since then, the introduction of an audit culture and a greater emphasis on management and regulation of the work of teachers and academics, has decreased discretion and autonomy. (Ibid.: 395).

The bureaucratic model has certain advantages for education but there are difficulties in applying it too enthusiastically to schools and colleges because of the professional role of teachers. If teachers do not 'own' innovations but are simply required to implement externally imposed changes, they are likely to do so without enthusiasm, leading to possible failure.

Rational models

Rational approaches differ from other formal models in that they emphasize managerial *processes* rather than organizational structure or goals. The focus is on the process of decision-making instead of the structural framework which constrains, but does not determine, managerial decisions. Although the distinctive quality of rational models is their emphasis on process, they share several characteristics with the other formal theories. These include agreed organizational objectives and a bureaucratic organizational structure. The decision-making process thus takes place within a recognized structure and in pursuit of accepted goals.

The process of rational decision-making is thought to have the following sequence:

1. Perception of a problem or a choice opportunity.
2. Analysis of the problem, including data collection.
3. Formulation of alternative solutions or choices.
4. Choice of the most appropriate solution to the problem to meet the objectives of the organization.
5. Implementation of the chosen alternative.
6. Monitoring and evaluation of the effectiveness of the chosen strategy.

Davies and Coates (2005: 109) add that 'rational planning … allows decision-makers to carefully weigh-up the consequences of alternatives and to choose a course of action that maximizes the achievement of objectives'. The process is essentially iterative in that the evaluation may lead to a redefinition of the problem or a search for an alternative solution (see Figure 3.1).

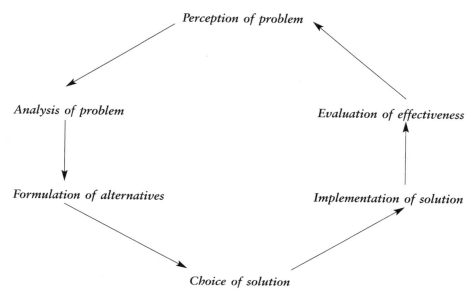

Figure 3.1 The rational process

Hoyle and Wallace (2005), however, note that, in practice, teachers and heads:

> make a multitude of decisions 'on the run' in contingent and evolving cir-cumstances. Despite the increasing scope for rational planning made possible by management systems, electronic means of communication, and sophisticated data storage and retrieval technology, there remain lim-its to scientific rationality. (Ibid.: 36–7)

In Chapter 2, we noted that theories tend to be *normative* in that they reflect views about how organizations and individuals ought to behave. The rational model is certainly normative in that it presents an ideal-ized view of the decision-making process. It has serious limitations as a portrayal of the decision-making process in education:

- There may be dispute over objectives, and the definition of the 'problem' is likely to be dependent on the particular standpoint of the individuals involved.
- Some of the data needed to make a decision may not be available.
- The assumption that the choice of solution can be detached and impartial is flawed. In practice, individuals and groups are likely to promote their own favoured solutions which in turn may reflect individual rather than organizational objectives.
- The perceived effectiveness of the chosen solution may also vary

according to the preferences of the people concerned.

Despite these practical limitations, Levačić (1995) shows that the rational model provides the preferred basis for the management of schools in England and Wales. She refers to the management consultancy report by Coopers and Lybrand (1988) which was influential in the introduction of local management in the early 1990s:

> The model of good management practice contained in the Coopers and Lybrand report is essentially a rational one. It advocates a system for allocating resources which is directed at the explicit achievement of institutional objectives. This requires clarity in the specification of objectives, gathering and analysing information on alternative ways of attaining the objectives, evaluating the alternatives and selecting those actions judged most likely to maximize achievement of the objectives. (Levačić, 1995: 62)

Watson and Crossley (2001: 114) show that similar principles underpin the management of further education in England and Wales: 'Many of the basic assumptions underpinning the [former] Further Education Funding Council's directives on strategy are rooted in a rational–scientific model that proposes the creation of a [strategic management process] that is sequential, linear and controllable'.

The application of rational principles to education can be illustrated through examining internal resource allocation in schools. There are five core principles (Bush, 2000: 105–6):

1. *Aims and priorities*. Resource allocation should be informed by clearly articulated aims and by determining priorities among these aims.
2. *Long-term planning*. Budgetary decisions should reflect an awareness of their long-term implications. This means going beyond the typical annual budget cycle to a consideration of the longer-term aims of the organization.
3. *Evaluating alternatives*. There should be a thorough consideration of alternative patterns of expenditure based on evaluation of past actions and assessment of the opportunity costs of different spending options.
4. *Zero-based budgeting*. This involves taking a fresh look at all areas of expenditure rather than simply making incremental changes to previous spending patterns.
5. *Selecting the most appropriate options*. Once the possible alternative spending patterns have been scrutinized, with an element of zero-basing, rational models require a choice of the most appropriate option linked to organizational objectives.

Levačić et al. (1999) conducted a large-scale review of inspection reports prepared by the Office for Standards in Education (OFSTED) in England and then carried out detailed case studies of 13 schools deemed by OFSTED to be offering good value for money. These authors cautiously conclude that applying the rational model is beneficial:

> Both OFSTED inspection report and case-study evidence showed that teachers are increasingly following the rational model in establishing aims for their schools and then endeavouring through planning processes to involve all staff ... we have found a tendency for schools which have sound planning approaches and developed monitoring and evaluation procedures to be more successful in relation to the quality of teaching and learning, student behaviour and attendance. (Levačić, 1999: 25–6)

Hierarchical models

Hierarchical approaches stress vertical relationships within organizations and the accountability of leaders to external sponsors. The organizational structure is emphasized with particular reference to the authority and responsibility of the managers at the apex of the structure. Packwood (1989) provides a precise definition of the hierarchical model and locates it firmly within the bureaucratic framework:

> One of the basic properties of bureaucratic organisation is the way in which occupational roles are graded in a vertical hierarchy. Authority to prescribe work passes from senior to junior roles, while accountability for the performance of work passes in the reverse direction from junior to senior. Authority and accountability are impersonal in that they are attached to roles, not to the personalities of the individuals who occupy the roles. The headteacher has authority to define the work of the deputy headteacher in a school because he or she occupies the role of headteacher not because of who he or she is as an individual. (Ibid.: 9–10)

This view subordinates individuals to the organizational hierarchy. Subjective theorists are very critical of this stance, as we shall see in Chapter 6.

Hierarchical models emphasize *vertical communication* patterns. Information is passed down the hierarchy to all appropriate levels, and subordinates are expected to implement the decisions made by the senior managers. Difficult issues may be referred upwards until they reach a level where they can be resolved. In schools and colleges, the head or principal is thought to inform heads of department or other staff about policies and is the final arbiter of problems incapable of resolution at lower levels in the hierarchy.

Horizontal communication also plays a part in the hierarchy but Packwood (1989) argues that such contacts are for co-ordination rather than management. The subject leader role in English primary schools is an example of a lateral relationship. These staff communicate with class teachers about aspects of their subject but they do not have managerial authority over them.

Central to hierarchical models is the concept of *accountability*. Leaders are responsible to external agencies for the performance of subordinates and the activities of the organization. In schools, the accountability of heads to the governing body, and to the local education authority, serves to underpin their internal authority.

Hierarchical models have certain limitations when applied to educational institutions. Teachers as professionals claim discretion in their classroom work and there is increasing participation in decision-making on wider school issues. As a result, the significance of the hierarchy may be modified by notions of collegiality (see Chapter 4) and teacher autonomy. Hatcher (2005: 253) also points to the contradictions between notions of distributed leadership and what he describes as 'the hierarchical power structure of schools'. Distributed leadership is independent of the hierarchy, based on personal qualities rather than designated positions. Despite this emerging model, and because of the clear legal authority of heads and principals, the hierarchy remains significant for schools and colleges.

In certain societies, the significance of the hierarchy is further reinforced by the tendency to accept unequal concentrations of power (Walker and Dimmock, 2002). Bush and Qiang (2000), for example, show that China is the archetypal high power-distance society and that teachers have considerable respect for the positional authority of principals.

Formal models: goals, structure, environment and leadership

Goals

Formal models characterize schools and colleges as *goal oriented*. There is an assumption that institutions pursue specific objectives. These goals are invariably determined by heads and senior staff and formal theories do not regard the support of other teachers as problematic. All members of the organization are thought to be working towards the achievement of these official aims. Begley (2008) stresses the close relationship between leadership and the purposes of education:

> Educational leaders should keep the fundamental purposes of education

in mind as they make decisions, manage people or resources, and generally provide leadership in their organizations. Otherwise they will be tossed about like a rudderless ship in a storm by the competing agendas and interest groups that make up any community. (Ibid.: 21)

Begley (ibid.: 21–3) argues that three 'broad and transcending' purposes characterize education:

1. Aesthetic purposes – the formation of character
2. Economic purposes – 'learning to earn'
3. Socialization functions – citizenship and social skills.

He adds (ibid.: 23) that 'a balanced attendance to all three fundamental purposes of education is critical to the educational leadership process'. Davies and Davies (2004: 11) claim that 'direction-setting' is a key element of strategic leadership while Cheng (2002: 61) stresses the role of leaders in goal development and achievement. He argues that leaders should be 'goal developers' and 'goal leaders' and should have two main strategies to promote quality:

- develop appropriate institutional missions and goals
- lead members to achieve goals, implement plans and programmes, and meet standards.

The portrayal of schools and colleges as organizations actively pursuing official goals set out in formal statements may be undermined by the recognition that they often have multiple objectives. The diverse goals of schools and colleges often emanate from different parts of the organization. For example, one can distinguish between individual, departmental and school goals. In a secondary school an official goal may refer to the fulfilment of the potential of all pupils. A departmental goal might relate to the attainment of particular standards of competence in certain subjects. Individual goals may well reflect personal career ambitions. These goals are not necessarily compatible.

Fishman (1999) makes a further distinction between external and internal goals in commenting on the differences between Russian and Western education. In centralized educational systems, there may be limited scope for institutional leaders to determine school aims because these are set by national or local government. However, even in highly directive systems, there has to be some scope for local interpretation, as Fishman demonstrates:

> Goal formulation cannot set one and the same result for all (that would be nothing but totalitarianism in education). Such goal setting should take into account the interests of the children, their abilities, the peculi-

arities of the social environment and the capabilities of the school itself ... the goal-setting process inside an educational system is not merely a banal transmission of the external goals. (Ibid.: 73)

Two examples of externally generated aims are the Millennium Development Goals applied to education: universal enrolment and completion of primary schooling; and gender equality in primary and secondary school access and achievement. Lewin (2005) argues that one consequence of these aims, which also strongly influence donor funding, is that many countries in sub-Saharan Africa have not developed coherent plans for the post-primary sub-sector. Elsewhere, I make a similar point and also raise concerns about quality:

> Focusing substantial resources on primary education often means that secondary, vocational or higher education can be neglected. There are also important questions about what is meant by 'quality education'. Increased enrolments often mean more children in the same space, leading to larger class sizes with inevitable consequences for quality. (Bush, 2008: 443)

Such broad externally developed goals are augmented by national and local policy, and by policy-making at the institutional level. The degree of centralization is likely to strongly influence, if not determine, the extent to which internal stakeholders can develop their own aims.

The organization's official goals may be a product of both external imperatives and internal requirements, but the assumption that they necessarily guide the behaviour and decisions of staff may be unrealistic or naive. As we shall see in subsequent chapters, formal goals may be contested or may provide only a limited guide to action. However, as a general rule, determining goals *within* schools, rather than *imposing them* on schools, is more likely to mean that they meet the needs of learners and the community. This should also enhance the prospect of staff 'owning' the goals and thus implementing them enthusiastically and effectively.

Organizational structure

Formal models present organizational *structure* as an objective fact. Schools and colleges are 'real' institutions which imbue teachers and pupils with a sense of belonging. Staff are thought to define their professional lives in terms of their position within the school or college. Structures may be typified in physical terms that imply permanence. Individuals are accorded a place in the structure such as teacher of year 2 or grade 3, or as head of the science department. The work of teachers and other staff is defined in terms of their roles within the formal structure. The structure is assumed to influence the behaviour of the individuals holding particular roles in the organization. Structure dominates and individuality is de-emphasized. The role of school leaders and managers is strongly influenced, or even determined, by the official requirements of the post and there is only limited scope for interpretation by the post-holder. In this model, the emphasis is on 'role taking', accepting the position as it is defined, rather than 'role-making', reinterpreting it in line with the post-holder's attributes and preferences (Hall, 1997). When office doors are marked 'principal', rather than having the incumbent's name identified, this symbolizes the dominance of the formal organizational structure.

As noted earlier, the organizational structure tends to be hierarchical and vertical, with staff being accountable to their superordinate in the hierarchy. In schools, teachers are accountable to the principal, often through a middle manager such as a head of department. The 'ethos of top-down management' (Johnson, 1995: 224) is evident in South African schools: 'It [is] important to bear in mind the nature of power relations within schools. In most cases, power resides with the principal who has legal authority and is legally accountable' (ibid.: 225).

Structure is not simply a matter of organization charts and formal relationships. It can also have a significant impact on the ways in which school goals are pursued and the extent of their achievement. Dupriez and Dumay (2006) for example, argue that the aim of equality of opportunity can be influenced specifically by the school's organization structure.

Organizational structure can be remarkably resilient, and resistant to change. Tripp (2003) reports on Singapore's shift from a highly centralized structure to a more diversified one, based around schools as autonomous learning organizations:

> Any paradigm shift is at best a slow and difficult process and, although the government is putting a lot of energy into it, the changes are very large scale and made all the more difficult by a history of strongly hierarchical thinking and bureaucratic processes. (Ibid.: 479)

The external environment

Formal approaches differ in the way they typify relationships between the organization and its environment. The more rigid models, such as 'closed systems', tend to limit environmental links to the minimum required to sustain accountability. These perspectives characterize relationships in terms of the official links between the head or principal and such formal groups as national and local governments, and the governing body. Interaction with other groups, such as parents, employers and other educational institutions, is de-emphasized. 'Closed systems' models assume that schools and colleges are impervious to such influences.

A significant aspect of bureaucracy, and particularly of closed systems, is that accountability to officials is regarded as more important than responsibility to clients such as students or parents. In South Africa, for example, despite an attempted shift towards self-managing schools in the post-Apartheid era, most principals still regard themselves as primarily accountable to the hierarchy, via district officials, rather than to the wider constituency of stakeholders such as parents, the community and learners themselves (Bush et al., 2008). This phenomenon is also evident in Slovenia:

> Heads know that parents and children are important but in fact they have been used to accepting the superior institutions and authorities as the real and powerful 'customers' on which they are really dependent. At the same time, parents and children have been used to seeing the school and its teachers as authorities who should be obeyed ... This kind of relationship between heads and parents also suits and supports bureaucratic organisation and head centred leadership very well. (Becaj, 1994: 11)

Other formal models, such as 'open systems', postulate wide-ranging links with the environment. Educational institutions are portrayed as interactive organizations, responding to a changing environment and displaying their achievements to the local community. Schools and colleges in self-managing systems are increasingly adopting a more 'open' stance, conscious of the need for a good reputation with present and prospective parents, employers and the local community. Few educational institutions justify the label 'closed' in the twenty-first century.

In many countries, formal accountability to the hierarchy is sharpened by a system of inspection or monitoring designed to ensure that schools are conforming to the national curriculum and achieving appropriate learning outcomes. 'To support and monitor the provision of education and attainment of expected standards ... , many countries put in place some form of external supervision often referred to as a schools' inspectorate' (McNab, 2004: 53). In England, the 'target-setting' culture means that many school leaders take decisions primarily on the basis of externally generated requirements, 'policed' by OFSTED, sometimes at the expense of their own professional judgement about what is best for their pupils. 'Any failure to meet centrally devised targets is guaranteed to bring an inspectorial body, like Ofsted, down upon their head' (Bottery, 2004: 53).

While recent research (Leithwood et al., 2006; Robinson et al., 2008) shows the importance of school leadership in improving student outcomes, other internal and external factors are also significant. Harris et al.'s (2006: 409) study of English schools in challenging contexts points to the centrality of external variables in school improvement: 'While schools can raise attainment and performance through their own efforts, the external environment remains an important influence upon a school's ability to improve'.

Leadership

Within formal models, leadership is ascribed to the person at the apex of the hierarchy. It is assumed that this individual sets the tone of the organization and establishes the major official objectives. Baldridge et al. discuss the nature of formal leadership:

> Under the bureaucratic model the leader is seen as the hero who stands at the top of a complex pyramid of power. The hero's job is to assess the problems, consider alternatives, and make rational choices. Much of the organisation's power is held by the hero, and great expectations are raised because people trust him [sic] to solve problems and fend off threats from the environment. (1978: 44)

The leader is expected to play a key part in policy-making, and adoption of innovations is assumed to follow. The possibility of opposition, or indifference, to change is not acknowledged. It is believed that implementation is unproblematic.

In education there are several features that support this characteristic of unidimensional leadership. Official bodies and individuals behave as if the head or principal is the fount of all knowledge and authority. The head is the focal point for most external communications, and parents and community leaders generally expect to contact the school via the head. Many other groups tend to regard the principal as the public face of the institution and behave accordingly. In primary schools, in particular, there is a perceived identity between the head and the school which reinforces the 'top down' perspective on leadership.

The assumption of an all-powerful leader at the apex of schools and colleges has several limitations. While formal authority resides with heads, they require the consent of colleagues if policy initiatives are to be carried through into departmental and classroom practice. It is now a truism that staff must 'own' decisions if they are to be implemented successfully.

Heads of self-managing schools and colleges have to share power with other staff in order to cope with the sheer volume of work arising from their enhanced responsibility for managing finance, staff and external relations. This pragmatic response to change serves to modify the notion of all-powerful heads, but in many cases the effect has been to increase the role of the senior leadership team and not to empower more junior staff. The hierarchy remains intact but the apex comprises a team rather than a single individual. Wallace (2004: 57) uses the concept of 'orchestration, narrowly distributed among senior formal leaders', in his study of district-wide change: 'Orchestration implies steering the change process by organizing and maintaining oversight of an intricate array of co-ordinated tasks. It is the over-arching "complex change management theme" of a hierarchically ordered typology'. Similarly, Bush et al. (2005) found that school leaders taking part in NCSL team development programmes often enhanced the effectiveness of their senior leadership teams but were sometimes perceived to be remote from the rest of the staff.

Managerial leadership

Various types of leadership have been identified in the literature, as we noted in Chapter 2. The type of leadership most closely associated with formal models is 'managerial':

> Managerial leadership assumes that the focus of leaders ought to be on functions, tasks and behaviours and that if these functions are carried out competently the work of others in the organisation will be facilitated. Most approaches to managerial leadership also assume that the behaviour of organizational members is largely rational. Authority and influence are allocated to formal positions in proportion to the status of those positions in the organizational hierarchy. (Leithwood et al., 1999: 14)

This definition shows that managerial leadership is strongly aligned with 'formal models', as the description of the latter on page 40 demonstrates. Leithwood et al. (ibid.: 15) say that 'there is evidence of considerable support in the literature and among practicing leaders for managerial approaches to leadership'. They add that 'positional power, in combination with formal policies and procedures, is the source of influence exercised by managerial leadership' (ibid.: 17).

Dressler's (2001: 175) review of leadership in Charter schools in the United States shows the significance of managerial leadership: 'Traditionally, the principal's role has been clearly focused on management responsibilities'.

Myers and Murphy (1995: 14) identify six specifically managerial functions for school principals. Four of these are described as 'hierarchical':

- supervision
- input controls (e.g. teacher transfers)
- behaviour controls (e.g. job descriptions)
- output controls (e.g. student testing).

It is significant to note that this type of leadership does not include the concept of vision which is central to most leadership models. Managerial leadership is focused on managing existing activities successfully rather than visioning a better future for the school. 'Management functions to support learning and teaching, the core of the educational enterprise' (Hoyle and Wallace, 2005: 68).

Managerialism

In Chapter 1 (p. 1), I introduced the notion of managerialism, a focus on management processes at the expense of educational purposes and values. In this section, I provide a longer discussion of this concept. The shift in the language of school organization to favour 'leadership' at the expense of 'management' is partly semantic (Bush, 2008) but also reflects anxiety about the dangers of value-free management, focusing on efficiency for its own sake, what Hoyle and Wallace (2005) describe as 'management to excess':

> Effective leadership and management 'take the strain' by creating structures and processes which allow teachers to engage as fully as possible in their key task. Managerialism, on the other hand, is leadership and management to excess. It transcends the support role of leadership and, in its extreme manifestation, becomes an end in itself. (Ibid.: 68)

Managerial leadership is the model which provides the greatest risk of a managerialist approach to school organization. By focusing on functions, tasks and behaviours, there is the possibility that the aims of education will be subordinated to the managerial aim of greater efficiency. Simkins (2005: 13–14) claims that managerialist values are being set against traditional professional values and points to four central elements of the 'managerialist agenda':

- The replacement of public sector values by those of the private sector and the market.

- The establishment of an impoverished concept of purpose within education that values measurable outcomes over those that are more elusive but more valuable.
- The imposition of models of leadership and management that emphasize individual accountability, rigid planning and target-setting as the prime means of organizational control.
- A redistribution of power, with the authority and autonomy of professionals being replaced by the power of managers to establish agendas and determine modes of work.

Evidence of a managerialist approach to education may be found in English and Scottish further education (Lumby, 2003; McTavish, 2003), in universities (Allen, 2003; Brehony and Deem, 2005) and in schools (Rutherford, 2006; Hoyle and Wallace, 2007). Goldspink (2007) aligns managerialism with 'New Public Management' and adds that 'tight linkage between teachers, schools and the centre is seen as both desirable and achievable' (ibid.: 29). Managerialism is often regarded with distaste, but Glatter (1997) warns that we should not regard 'leadership' as 'pure' and 'management' as 'dirty'. Rather, both are required to ensure that schools and colleges have a clear sense of moral purpose while also putting in place effective structures and processes to enable educational purposes to be achieved. Managerial leadership is an essential component of successful educational institutions but it should complement, not supplant, values-based approaches. Effective management is essential but value-free managerialism is inappropriate and damaging.

The limitations of formal models

The various formal models pervade much of the literature on educational management. They are normative approaches in that they present ideas about how people in organizations ought to behave. Schools and colleges are typified as goal-seeking organizations employing rational means to achieve the objectives established by official leaders. The educational reforms of the past 20 years, in England and many other countries, served to increase the significance of formal models. Because a 'top-down' model is operating in imposing change on schools and colleges, supported by a centralized inspection system, the assumption is that leaders should respond by managing their establishments in the same way, following a rational approach:

A major development in educational management in the last decade has been much greater emphasis on defining effective leadership by individuals in management posts in terms of the effectiveness of their organisation, which is increasingly judged in relation to measurable outcomes for students. In the UK both major political parties have pursued educational policies which seek to diminish the traditional ambiguity and lack of coupling between inputs, process and outcomes in educational organisations. This is argued to require a rational–technicist approach to the structuring of decision-making. (Levačić et al., 1999: 15)

The 'measurable outcomes' include, in England, league tables, target setting and benchmarking, leaving schools vulnerable to a range of bureaucratic pressures. MacBeath (1999) points to the resultant tension between meeting the requirements of a centrally determined agenda and the specific needs of the school as an educational community.

Formal models are selective as well as normative. In focusing on the bureaucratic and structural aspects of organizations they necessarily ignore or underestimate other salient features:

> A classical, rationalist model … fails to take into account the wider dimensions of organisational history, culture and context. There has been a failure of management … to understand that an apparently rational [process] may be a chimera in practice. (Watson and Crossley, 2001: 123)

There are five specific weaknesses associated with formal models:

1. It may be unrealistic to characterize schools and colleges as *goal-oriented* organizations. It is often difficult to ascertain the goals of educational institutions. Formal objectives may have little operational relevance because they are often vague and general, because there may be many different goals competing for resources, and because goals may emanate from individuals and groups as well as from the leaders of the organization. As we noted earlier (p. 56), goals may be imposed on schools by external agencies, such as local, state, provincial or national governments, or by global bodies such as the United Nations or the World Bank. These external aims jostle with internally-generated purposes, and with each other, to make goal-setting problematic.

   Even where the purposes of schools and colleges have been clarified, there are further problems in judging whether objectives have been achieved. Many of the goals associated with education are very difficult to measure. Policy-makers, practitioners and researchers often rely on examination performance to assess schools, but this is only one dimension of the educational process.

2. The portrayal of decision-making as a *rational* process is fraught with

difficulties. The belief that managerial action is preceded by a process of evaluation of alternatives and a considered choice of the most appropriate option is rarely substantiated. Decisions in schools and colleges are made by teachers, who draw on a whole range of experience as they respond to events. Much human behaviour is irrational and this inevitably influences the nature of decision-making in education. Hoyle and Wallace (2005: 37) add that there are 'cognitive' limits to rationality because leaders have limited awareness of what is happening inside and outside their schools. Moreover, rational pursuit of a particular goal may be derailed by the simultaneous prosecution of other, incompatible, purposes.

Educational institutions, in common with other organizations staffed by professionals, depend on decisions made by individuals and sub-units. Professional judgement is based as much on the expertise of the individual as on rational processes conditioned by the rule book. As Hoyle and Wallace (ibid.: 39) explain, teachers and other staff have 'the negative capacity to resist or undermine work towards achieving official goals'. That is why there is so much emphasis in twenty-first century literature on the need for teachers to 'own' change.

3. Formal models focus on the organization as an entity and ignore or underestimate the contribution of *individuals*. They assume that people occupy preordained positions in the structure and that their behaviour reflects their organizational positions rather than their individual qualities and experience. Critics argue that formal perspectives treat organizations as if they are independent of the people within them. Greenfield (1973) has been particularly critical of this view:

> Most theories of organisation grossly simplify the nature of the reality with which they deal. The drive to see the organisation as a single kind of entity with a life of its own apart from the perceptions and beliefs of those involved in it blinds us to its complexity and the variety of organisations people create around themselves. (Ibid.: 571)

Greenfield's alternative approach to organizations is discussed in Chapter 6 but the essence of his argument is that organizations are the creation of the people within them. He claims that formal models greatly underestimate individual variables and thus produce an inaccurate portrayal of schools and colleges. Samier (2002: 40) takes a similar view, expressing concern 'about the role technical rationality plays in crippling the personality of the bureaucrat, reducing him [sic] to a cog in a machine'.

4. A central assumption of formal models is that power resides at the apex of the pyramid. Heads and principals possess authority by virtue of their positions as the appointed leaders of their institutions. This focus on official authority leads to a view of institutional management which is essentially *top down*. Policy is laid down by senior managers and implemented by staff lower down the hierarchy. Their acceptance of managerial decisions is regarded as unproblematic.

The hierarchical aspect of the formal model is most relevant to organizations which depend on tight discipline for their effectiveness. The armed forces, for example, are expected to carry out their orders without any questioning or elaboration. The situation is assumed to require compliance with instructions from superordinates.

Organizations with large numbers of professional staff tend to exhibit signs of tension between the conflicting demands of professionalism and the hierarchy. Formal models assume that leaders, because they are appointed on merit, have the competence to issue appropriate instructions to subordinates. This is supported by the authority vested in them by virtue of their official position. Professional organizations have a rather different ethos, with expertise distributed widely within the institution:

> Traditional models of school organization favour peaked hierarchies that concentrate power and leadership responsibility on the office of the principal. As these models struggle to effectively meet the needs of education in the new millennium, leadership structures that distribute leadership influence and empower teachers to play a greater role in the leadership of the school, are slowly being implemented. (Rutherford, 2006: 59)

Where professionals specialize, as in secondary schools and colleges, the ability of leaders to direct the actions of subordinates may be questionable. A head who is a humanities graduate lacks the specific competence to supervise teaching in the faculty of technology. In professional organizations there is an authority of expertise which may come into conflict with positional authority.

Heads are responsible for the quality of teaching and learning in their schools, but their authority over teachers may be ambiguous. Professional staff claim zones of autonomy based on their specialist expertise. The classroom is still largely the domain of the teacher and pedagogic matters are primarily the responsibility of the practitioner as a qualified professional. These areas of discretion may lead to conflict between heads and other staff. Such difficulties can be avoided only if there is at least tacit acceptance of the head's overall responsibility for the activities of the school. This involves recognition by teachers of the head's right to take the initiative in many areas of school policy.

5. Formal approaches are based on the implicit assumption that organizations are relatively *stable*. Individuals may come and go but they slot into predetermined positions in a static structure. Bureaucratic and structural theories are most appropriate in stable conditions, as Bolman and Deal (1991: 77) suggest: 'Organisations operating in simpler and more stable environments are likely to employ less complex and more centralized structures, with authority, rules and policies as the primary vehicles for co-ordinating the work'.

It can be argued that assumptions of stability are unrealistic in many organizations and invalid in most schools and colleges. March and Olsen (1976: 21) are right to claim that 'individuals find themselves in a more complex, less stable and less understood world than that described by standard theories of organisational choice'. Rational perspectives require a measure of predictability to be useful as portrayals of organizational behaviour. The validity of formal models may be limited during phases of rapid and multiple change, such as that affecting most educational systems in the twenty-first century. The notion of a thorough analysis of a problem followed by identification of alternatives, choice of the preferred option and a process of implementation and evaluation, may be unrealistic during periods of turbulence.

Conclusion: are formal models still valid?

These criticisms of formal models suggest that they have serious limitations in respect of schools and colleges. The dominance of the hierarchy is compromised by the expertise possessed by professional staff. The supposed rationality of the decision-making process requires modification to allow for the pace and complexity of change. The concept of organizational goals is challenged by those who point to the existence of multiple objectives in education and the possible conflict between goals held at individual, departmental and institutional levels.

Despite these limitations, it would be inappropriate to dismiss formal approaches as irrelevant to schools and colleges. As Fitzgerald (2009: 63–4) indicates, bureaucracy is remarkably resilient and is being reinforced by new public management, for example in England and New Zealand: 'Despite almost two decades of change, the organization and hierarchy of school replicates industrial models of working that differentiates people and activities according to position'. The stress on standards and targets in the English system has led to what Ball (2003) and Strain (2009), describe as 'performativity', a mode of regulated control, with central requirements being imposed on schools and colleges. The hierarchy is the vehicle for external control of school activities.

The other models discussed in this book were all developed as a reaction to the perceived weaknesses of formal theories. However, these alternative perspectives have not succeeded in dislodging the formal models which remain valid as *partial* descriptions of organization and management in education. Formal models are inadequate but still have much to contribute to our understanding of schools and colleges as organizations. Owens and Shakeshaft (1992) refer to a reduction of confidence in bureaucratic models and a 'paradigm shift' to a more sophisticated analysis. In subsequent chapters we examine several alternative perspectives and assess the extent to which they have supplanted formal models as the best ways and means of understanding and leading schools and colleges.

References

Allen, D. (2003) 'Organisational climate and strategic change in higher education: organisational insecurity', Higher Education, 46(1): 61–79.

Baldridge, J.V., Curtis, D.V., Ecker, G. and Riley, G.L. (1978) *Policy-Making and Effective Leadership*, San Francisco, CA: Jossey-Bass.

Ball, S. (2003) 'The teacher's soul and the terrors of performativity', *Journal of Education Policy,* 18(2): 215–28.

Beare, H., Caldwell, B. and Millikan, R. (1989) *Creating an Excellent School*, London: Routledge.

Becaj, J. (1994) 'Changing bureaucracy to democracy', *Educational Change and Development*, 15(1): 7–14.

Becher, T. and Kogan, M. (1992) *Process and Structure in Higher Education*, London: Routledge.

Begley, P. (2008) 'The nature and specialized purposes of educational leadership', in J. Lumby, G. Crow and P. Pashiardis (eds), *International Handbook on the Preparation and Development of School Leaders*, New York: Routledge.

Bolman, L. and Deal, T. (1989) 'Organisations, technology and environment', in R. Glatter (ed.), *Educational Institutions and their Environments: Managing the Boundaries*, Buckingham: Open University Press.

Bolman, L. and Deal, T. (1991) *Reframing Organisations: Artistry, Choice and Leadership*, San Francisco, CA: Jossey-Bass.

Bottery, M. (2004) *The Challenges of Educational Leadership*, London: Paul Chapman.

Boyd, W. (1999) 'Environmental pressures, management imperatives and competing paradigms in educational administration', *Educational Management and Administration*, 27(3): 283–97.

Brehony, K. and Deem, R. (2005) 'Challenging the post-Fordist/flexible organization thesis: the case of reformed educational organizations', *British Journal of Sociology of Education*, 26(3): 395–417.

Bush, T. (1994) 'Theory and practice in educational management', in T. Bush and J. West-Burnham (eds), *The Principles of Educational Management*, Harlow: Longman.

Bush, T. (1997) 'Management structures', in T. Bush and D. Middlewood (eds), *Managing People in Education*, London: Paul Chapman Publishing.

Bush, T. (2000) 'Management styles: impact on finance and resources', in M. Coleman and L. Anderson (eds), *Managing Finance and Resources in Education*, London: Paul Chapman Publishing.

Bush, T. (2001) 'School organisation and management: international perspectives', paper presented at the Federation of Private School Teachers' Annual Conference, Athens, May.

Bush, T. (2008) 'Editorial: universal primary education – a legitimate goal?', *Educational Management, Administration and Leadership*, 36(4): 443–47.

Bush, T. and Qiang, H. (2000) 'Leadership and culture in Chinese education', *Asia Pacific Journal of Education*, 20(2): 58–67.

Bush, T., Coleman, M. and Si, X. (1998) 'Managing secondary schools in China', *Compare*, 28(2): 183–96.

Bush, T., Middlewood, D., Morrison, M. and Scott, D. (2005) *How Teams make a Difference? The Impact of Team Working*, Nottingham: NCSL.

Bush, T., Duku, N., Glover, D., Kiggundu, E., Kola, S., Msila, V. and Moorosi, P. (2008) *The Zenex ACE School Leadership Research: Second Interim Report*, Pretoria: Department of Education.

Bush, T., Allen, T., Glover, D., Middlewood, D., Parker, R. and Smith, R. (2009) *Succession Planning Programme Evaluation: Fourth Interim Report*, Nottingham: NCSL.

Cheng, Y.C. (2002) 'Leadership and strategy', in T. Bush and L. Bell (eds), *The Principles and Practice of Educational Management*, London: Paul Chapman Publishing.

Clark, B.R. (1983) 'The contradictions of change in academic systems', *Higher Education*, 12: 101–16.

Coopers and Lybrand (1988) *Local Management of Schools: A Report to the DES*, London: HMSO.

Davies, B. and Davies, B. (2004) 'Strategic leadership', in B. Davies (ed.), *The Essentials of School Leadership*, London: Paul Chapman Publishing.

Davies, P. and Coates, G. (2005) 'Competing conceptions and values in school strategy: rational planning and beyond', *Educational Management, Administration and Leadership*, 33(1): 109–24.

Dressler, B. (2001) 'Charter school leadership', *Education and Urban Society*, 33(2): 170–85.

Dupriez, V. and Dumay, X. (2006) 'Inequalities in school systems: effect of school structure or of society structure?', *Comparative Education*, 42(2): 243–60.

Evetts, J. (1992) 'The organisation of staff in secondary schools: headteachers' management structures', *School Organisation*, 12(1): 83–98.

Fishman, L. (1999) 'The cultural imperative and how we consider educational leadership', *International Journal of Leadership in Education*, 2(2): 69–79.

Fitzgerald, T. (2009) 'The tyranny of bureaucracy: continuing challenges of leading and managing from the middle', *Educational Management, Administration and Leadership*, 37(1): 51–65.

Gamage, D. (2006) 'School-based management: shared responsibility and quality in education', *Education and Society*, 24(1): 27–43.

Gaziel, H. (2003) 'Images of leadership and their effects upon school principals' performance', *International Review of Education*, 49(5): 475–86.

Glatter, R. (1997) 'Context and capability in educational management', *Educational Management and Administration*, 25(2): 181–92.

Goldspink, C. (2007) 'Rethinking educational reform: a loosely coupled and complex systems perspective', *Educational Management, Administration and Leadership*, 35(1): 27–50.

Greenfield, T.B. (1973) 'Organisations as social inventions: rethinking assumptions about change', *Journal of Applied Behavioural Science*, 9(5): 551–74.

Hall, V. (1994) *Further Education in the United Kingdom*, London: Collins Educational.

Hall, V. (1997) 'Management roles in education', in T. Bush and D. Middlewood (eds.), *Managing People in Education*, London: Paul Chapman Publishing.

Harris, A. (2004) 'Distributed leadership and school improvement: leading or misleading?', *Educational Management, Administration and Leadership*, 32(1): 11–24.

Harris, A., Chapman, C., Muijs, D., Russ, J. and Stoll, L. (2006) 'Improving schools in challenging circumstances: exploring the possible', *School Effectiveness and School Improvement*, 17(4): 409–24.

Hatcher, R. (2005) 'The distribution of leadership and power in schools', *British Journal of Sociology of Education*, 26(2): 253–67.

Hoy, W. and Miskel, C. (1987) *Educational Administration: Theory, Research and Practice*, New York: McGraw-Hill.

Hoyle, E. and Wallace, M. (2005) *Educational Leadership: Ambiguity, Professionals and Managerialism*, London: Sage.

Hoyle, E. and Wallace, M. (2007) 'Educational reform: an ironic perspective', *Educational Management, Administration and Leadership*, 35(1): 9–25.

Johnson, D. (1995) 'Developing an approach to educational management development in South Africa', *Comparative Education*, 31(2): 223–41.

Kavouri, P. and Ellis, D. (1998) 'Factors affecting school climate in Greek primary schools', *Welsh Journal of Education*, 7(1): 95–109.

Klus-Stanska, D. and Olek, H. (1998) 'Private education in Poland: breaking the mould', *International Review of Education*, 44(2–3): 235–49.

Leithwood, K., Jantzi, D. and Steinbach, R. (1999) *Changing Leadership for Changing Times*, Buckingham: Open University Press.

Leithwood, K., Day, C., Sammons, P., Harris, A. and Hopkins, D. (2006) *Seven Strong Claims about Successful School Leadership*, London: DfES.

Levačić, R. (1995) *Local Management of Schools: Analysis and Practice*, Buckingham: Open University Press.

Levačić, R., Glover, D., Bennett, N. and Crawford, M. (1999) 'Modern headship for the rationally managed school: combining cerebral and insightful approaches', in T. Bush and L. Bell (eds), *The Principles and Practice of Educational Management*, London: Paul Chapman Publishing.

Lewin, K. (2005) 'Planning post-primary education: taking targets to task', *International Journal of Educational Development*, 25(4): 408–22.

Lumby, J. (2001) *Managing Further Education: Learning Enterprise*, London: Paul Chapman Publishing.

Lumby, J. (2003) 'Culture change: the case of sixth form and general further education colleges', *Educational Management and Administration*, 31(2): 159–74.

MacBeath, J. (1999) *Schools Must Speak for Themselves: The Case for School Self-Evaluation*, London: Routledge.

McNab, D. (2004) 'Hearts, minds and external supervision of schools: direction and development', *Educational Review*, 56(1): 53–64.

McTavish, D. (2003) 'Aspects of public sector management: a case study of further education: ten years from the passage of the Further and Higher Education Act', *Educational Management and Administration*, 31(2): 175–88.

March, J.G. and Olsen, J.P. (1976) 'Organisational choice under ambiguity', in J.G. March and J.P. Olsen, *Ambiguity and Choice in Organisations*, Bergen: Universitetsforlaget.

Myers, E. and Murphy, J. (1995) 'Suburban secondary school principals' perceptions of administrative control in schools', *Journal of Educational Administration*, 33(3): 14–37.

Newland, C. (1995) 'Spanish American elementary education 1950–1992: bureaucracy, growth and decentralisation', *International Journal of Educational Development*, 15(2): 103–14.

O'Shea, P. (2007) 'A systems view of learning in education', *International Journal of Educational Development*, 27(6): 637–49.

Owens, R. and Shakeshaft, C. (1992) 'The new "revolution" in administrative theory', *Journal of Educational Management*, 30(9): 4–17.

Packwood, T. (1989) 'Return to the hierarchy', *Educational Management and Administration*, 17(1): 9–15.

Porter, S. (2006) 'Institutional structures and student engagement', *Research in Higher Education*, 47(5): 521–35.

Purvis, M.T. (2007) 'School Improvement in a Small Island Developing State: The Seychelles', unpublished PhD thesis, University of Warwick.

Robinson, V., Lloyd, C. and Rowe, K. (2008) 'The impact of leadership on student outcomes: an analysis of the differential effects of leadership types', *Educational Administration Quarterly*, XLIV(5): 635–74.

Rutherford, C. (2006) 'Teacher leadership and organizational structure', *Journal of Educational Change*, 7(1–2): 59–78.

Samier, E. (2002) 'Weber on education and its administration: prospects for leadership in a rationalised world', *Educational Management and Administration*, 30(1): 27–45.

Sandholtz, J. and Scribner, S. (2006) 'The paradox of administrative control in fostering teacher professional development', *Teaching and Teacher Education*, 22(8): 1104–12.

Sebakwane, S. (1997) 'The contradictions of scientific management as a mode of controlling teachers' work in black secondary schools: South Africa', *International Journal of Educational Development*, 17(4): 391–404.

Simkins, T. (2005) 'Leadership in education: "What works" or "what makes sense"?', *Educational Management, Administration and Leadership*, 33(1): 9–26.

Strain, M. (2009) 'Some cultural and ethical implications of the leadership "turn" in education', *Educational Management, Administration and Leadership*, 37(1): 67–84.

Svecova, J. (2000) 'Privatisation of education in the Czech Republic', *International Journal of Educational Development*, 20: 127–33.

Taylor, I. (2007) 'Discretion and control in education: the teacher as street-level bureaucrat', *Educational Management, Administration and Leadership*, 35(4): 555–72.

Townsend, A. (2010) 'Leadership and Educational Networks', in T. Bush, L. Bell and D. Middlewood (eds), *The Principles of Educational Leadership and Management*, London: Sage.

Tripp, D. (2003) 'Three resources for learning organizational change', *Educational Action Research*, 11(3): 479–98.

Walker, A. and Dimmock, C. (2002) 'Cross-cultural and comparative insights into educational administration and leadership', in A. Walker and C. Dimmock (eds), *School Leadership and Administration: Adopting a Cultural Perspective*, London: RoutledgeFalmer.

Wallace, M. (2004) 'Orchestrating complex educational change: local reorganisation of schools in England', *Journal of Educational Change*, 5(1): 57–78.

Watson, K. and Crossley, M. (2001) 'Beyond the rational: the strategic management process, cultural change and post-incorporation further education', *Educational Management and Administration*, 29(1): 113–25.

Weber, M. (1989) 'Legal authority in a bureaucracy', in T. Bush (ed.), *Managing Education: Theory and Practice*, Buckingham: Open University Press.

CHAPTER 4

Collegial models

Central features of collegial models

Collegial models include all those theories which emphasize that power and decision-making should be shared among some or all members of the organization. These approaches range from a 'restricted' collegiality where the leader shares power with a limited number of senior colleagues to a 'pure' collegiality where all members have an equal voice in determining policy. The definition suggested below captures the main features of these perspectives.

> Collegial models assume that organizations determine policy and make decisions through a process of discussion leading to consensus. Power is shared among some or all members of the organization who are thought to have a shared understanding about the aims of the institution.

The notion of collegiality became enshrined in the folklore of management as the most appropriate way to run schools and colleges in the 1980s and 1990s. It was then regarded as 'the official model of good practice' (Wallace, 1989: 182). Subsequently, in England, there was a re-emphasis on the power of the leader, who is expected to 'deliver' by meeting government targets as part of a centralized agenda. Latterly, however, there has been renewed interest in 'distributed leadership' (Lumby, 2003; Harris 2004; 2005; 2010; Leithwood et al., 2006; Gronn,

2010), which shares certain features with collegiality.

Brundrett (1998: 305) says that 'collegiality can broadly be defined as teachers conferring and collaborating with other teachers'. Little (1990) discusses the benefits of this approach:

> The reason to pursue the study and practice of collegiality is that, presumably, something is gained when teachers work together and something is lost when they do not; in effect, the perceived benefits must be great enough that the time teachers spend together can compete with time spent in other ways, on other priorities that are equally compelling or more immediate. (Ibid.: 166)

The time required to implement collegial approaches is a significant constraint as we shall see later in this chapter (p. 92). Collegial models have the following major features:

1. They are strongly *normative* in orientation. We noted in Chapter 2 that all theories tend to be normative but collegial approaches in particular reflect the prescriptive view that management ought to be based on agreement. Their advocates believe that decision-making should be based on democratic principles but do not necessarily claim that these principles actually determine the nature of management in action. It is an idealistic model rather than one that is founded firmly in practice: 'Credible evidence regarding the nature of participatory structures and processes in schools ... is thinner than one might expect' (Brown et al., 1999: 320).

   The normative dimension of collegiality is particularly evident in post-Apartheid South Africa. There is a powerful commitment to democratic institutions fuelled by an understandable reaction to the injustices and inequities of the past. This is particularly evident in the decision to establish governing bodies in all schools, and in the representation of both teachers and, in secondary schools, students, on these bodies. The South African government links governance to wider democratic objectives in its advice to school governors: 'Just like the country has a government, the school that your child and other children in the community attend needs a "government" to serve the school and the school community' (Department of Education, 1997: 2).

   The empowerment of school level governing bodies is largely a matter of faith (Bush and Heystek, 2003) and there is only limited evidence that this change is being matched by professional collegiality in schools.

2. Collegial models are seen as particularly appropriate for organiza-

tions such as schools and colleges that have significant numbers of professional staff. Teachers possess authority arising directly from their knowledge and skill. They have an *authority of expertise* that contrasts with the positional authority associated with formal models. Professional authority occurs where decisions are made on an individual basis rather than being standardized. Education necessarily demands a professional approach because pupils and students need personal attention. Teachers require a measure of autonomy in the classroom but also need to collaborate to ensure a coherent approach to teaching and learning. 'Professionalism has the effect of allowing teachers to come together with respect for one another's professional ability' (Brundrett, 1998: 307).

Collegial models assume that professionals also have a right to share in the wider decision-making process. Shared decisions are likely to be better informed and are also much more likely to be implemented effectively. Collegiality is also 'acclaimed as a way for teachers to benefit from the support and expertise of their colleagues' (Brown et al., 1999: 320). However, Hoyle and Wallace (2005: 126) caution that many teachers are ambivalent about participation rights. They welcome involvement in issues directly affecting the classroom but experience 'decision saturation' in administrative areas such as planning and staff appointments.

3. Collegial models assume a *common set of values* held by members of the organization. These may arise from the socialization which occurs during training and the early years of professional practice. These common values guide the managerial activities of the organization and, in particular, are thought to lead to shared educational objectives. The common values of professionals form part of the justification for the optimistic assumption that it is always possible to reach agreement about goals and policies. Brundrett (1998: 308) goes further in referring to the importance of 'shared vision' as a basis for collegial decision-making.

4. The *size* of decision-making groups is an important element in collegial management. They have to be sufficiently small to enable everyone to be heard. This may mean that collegiality works better in primary schools, or in sub-units, than at the institutional level in secondary schools and colleges. Meetings of the whole staff may operate collegially in small schools but may be suitable only for information exchange in larger institutions.

The collegial model deals with this problem of scale by building-in the assumption that staff have *formal representation* within the various decision-making bodies. Significant areas of policy are determined within the official committee system rather than being the prerogative of individual leaders. The democratic element of formal representation rests on the allegiance owed by participants to their constituencies. A teacher representing the English department on a committee is accountable to colleagues who may have the right to nominate or elect another person if they are not happy about the way they are being represented.

Informal consultations with staff do not constitute collegiality. Where heads seek the advice of colleagues before making a decision the process is one of consultation, whereas the essence of collegiality is participation in decision-making. Power is shared with staff in a democracy rather than remaining the preserve of the leader. Formal representation confers the right to participate in defined areas of policy while informal consultation is at the sole discretion of the leader, who is under no obligation to act on the advice received.

5. Collegial models assume that decisions are reached by *consensus* rather than division or conflict. The belief that there are common values and shared objectives lead to the view that it is both desirable and possible to resolve problems by agreement. There may be differences of opinion but they can be overcome by the force of argument. The decision-making process may be elongated by the search for compromise but this is regarded as an acceptable price to pay to maintain the aura of shared values and beliefs.

The case for consensual decision-making rests in part on the ethical dimension of collegiality. It is regarded as wholly appropriate to involve people in the decisions which affect their professional lives. Imposing decisions on staff is considered morally repugnant, and inconsistent with the notion of consent:

> The moral character of an exercise of authority is based on the presence of consent on the part of those subject to its jurisdiction ... the consent of the obligated is necessary for authority to assume moral status ... Where consent is not made a condition of authority, then we are not speaking of moral authority, but of the exercise of power, or of purely formal or legal authority. (Williams, 1989: 80)

These considerations also provide the rationale for the concept of 'moral leadership' which will be examined in Chapter 8.

These five central features of collegiality appear to a greater or lesser extent in each of the main sectors of education. We turn now to consider its application in higher education.

Collegial models in higher education

Collegial approaches in British education originated within the colleges of Oxford and Cambridge universities:

> Collegium designates a structure or structures in which members have equal authority to participate in decisions which are binding on each of them. It usually implies that individuals have discretion to perform their main operations in their own way, subject only to minimal collegial controls. (Becher and Kogan, 1992: 72)

The collegial model has been adopted by most universities. Authority of expertise is widespread within these institutions of scholarship and research. 'Any organisation which depends on high-level professional skills operates most efficiently if there is a substantial measure of collegiality in its management procedures' (Williams and Blackstone, 1983: 94).

The collegial model is most evident within the extensive committee system. Decisions on a whole range of academic issues take place within a labyrinth of committees rather than being the prerogative of the vice-chancellor. Issues are generally resolved by agreement or compromise rather than by voting or dissent: 'The members of a college take their own collective decisions, which have an authority legitimized by consensus, or at least compromise, amongst those to whom they apply' (Williams and Blackstone, 1983: 94).

Collegial approaches may have originated within higher education but in many universities democracy is compromised by a limited franchise. Certain institutions give full voting rights to all academic staff and some representation to students and, perhaps, also non-academic staff. Elsewhere membership of senate and the key committees is the preserve of senior staff. This restricted franchise serves to limit the extent to which universities can be regarded as collegial, and many might be regarded as elitist rather than democratic.

There is a dichotomy in universities and colleges between academic policy, which is generally the responsibility of the collegial senate or academic board, and resource management which is usually the preserve of the vice-chancellor and heads of faculty. The committee system fits the collegial model while the powers accorded directly to senior managers suggest one of the formal models.

The rapid growth of higher education in the 1990s and the early years of the twenty-first century may have made it more difficult for the collegial aspects of universities to maintain their previous significance in the decision-making process. Middlehurst and Elton (1992: 261) argue that universities have prospered by becoming more managerial. 'There ... has been a considerable loss in collegiality across the higher education system, with the resulting loss of a sense of ownership and shared professional responsibility for the operation of the institution'.

The threat to collegiality noted by Middlehurst and Elton (1992) has intensified during the 1990s and the early part of the twenty-first century. Deem's (2000: 48) large-scale research with academic managers suggested that 'the UK higher education system was now highly managerial and bureaucratic'. The shift to this 'corporate' model of management led Australian universities to seek a 'trusteeship' model as an alternative to both collegial and corporate styles (Harman and Treadgold, 2007).

The desire to maintain staff participation in decision-making is increasingly in conflict with external demands for accountability, notably in respect of funding, quality control and research assessment. This tension between participation and accountability is also evident in schools.

Collegial models in secondary schools

The introduction of collegial approaches in secondary schools has been slower, less complete and more piecemeal than in higher education. The tradition of all powerful heads, with authority over staff and accountability to external bodies, has stifled several attempts to develop participative modes of management. The formal position is that principals alone are responsible for the organization and management of schools. This consideration has acted as a brake on some heads who wish to share their power, and as a convenient justification for those reluctant to do so.

Brown, Boyle and Boyle (1999) carried out research on collegial models of management in 21 secondary schools in the north-west of England. The first phase involved interviews with middle managers in each school. Subsequently, the researchers interviewed the headteachers in 12 of these schools. Their analysis is thus based on paired responses from heads and middle managers in these schools.

The research was undertaken in the context of conflicting pressures on schools to be both collegial and managerial. The authors note that 'collegiality, or at least collaborative management, has become one of the biggest international trends in education' (Brown et al.: 320) but also point out that such developments may not be genuine:

> Headteachers may construct decision-making processes that seem on the surface to be participatory in order to gain greater acceptance of decisions and greater teacher satisfaction. However, they may be reluctant to extend genuine influence to teachers, assuming that they do not have the expertise

to make valuable contributions, or because they do not trust them to make decisions which are in the best interest of the school. (Ibid.: 319)

Brown, Boyle and Boyle (1999) found that only four of the 12 case-study schools could be categorized as 'operating fully' in a collegial way. These 'type A' schools had the following features:

- A commitment to regular formal opportunities for collaboration with other heads of department and colleagues from different subject areas.
- Departmental priorities correlated closely with the School Development Plan, with themes and issues identified and agreed collectively.
- Heads of department were actively involved and consulted in whole-school policy and decision-making.
- The headteacher saw the heads of department as having a wider wholeschool management role.

The participants explained why shared decision-making is desirable:

You need the collective support of your staff to implement any worth-while change, so involvement in the decision-making process is vital. (Headteacher) (Brown et al., 1999: 322)

Team work is the crucial ingredient for this school to be effective. There is no mystique and feeling of intimidation. It is almost a collaboration of equals. (Middle manager) (Ibid.: 323)

Type A schools overcame the problem of size by adopting flexible structures. One school changed its senior management team into a school management team and included representation from all areas of the teaching staff. Working parties or curriculum groups with cross-department and voluntary representation were also favoured ways of widening involvement.

Despite these strategies, the authors conclude that it is difficult to achieve collegiality in practice:

Collegial models of education management are becoming the dominant paradigm in the literature ... There are, however, pragmatic and ideological factors which raise the question of the attainability of collegiality. Collegiality offers many persuasive benefits but is, in reality, difficult to attain. (Ibid.: 329)

The concept of collegiality is similar to that of the 'jiaoyanzu' in Chinese schools. Paine and Ma (1993) refer to an 'assumption that teachers would work together in virtually every aspect of their work' and explain how the jiaoyanzu works:

> Many decisions about curriculum and instruction are made jointly through the jiaoyanzu ... teachers have a structured time to work together ... Teachers ... work together ... in an office that belongs to their jiaoyanzu. (Ibid.: 679)

Chinese teachers have substantial non-contact time to facilitate collaborative working. Research in secondary schools in the Shaanxi province of China (Bush et al., 1998) shows that departmental jiaoyanzu work collegially to discuss teaching materials, provide demonstration lessons, and observe and comment on each other's lessons. However, these discussions occur under the supervision of the teaching dean who, in turn, is appointed by the principal. This suggests a hierarchical dimension to the operation of jiaoyanzu.

Collegial models in primary schools

Collegiality became established during the 1980s and 1990s as the most appropriate way to manage primary schools. It remains the normative model of good practice in this phase of education in England, despite the contrary pressures arising from government imperatives. Little (1990: 177–80) describes how collegiality operates in practice:

- Teachers talk about teaching.
- There is shared planning and preparation.
- The presence of observers in classrooms is common.
- There is mutual training and development.

The model outlined by Little (1990) appears to depend on shared professional values leading to the development of trust and a willingness to give and receive criticism in order to enhance practice. It is a demanding approach which requires commitment from staff if it is to become an effective vehicle for beneficial change. It is also an elusive model to operate even where staff are committed to the concept.

Webb and Vulliamy (1996) examined the tension between collegiality and managerialism in their study of a national sample of 50 primary schools in England and Wales. They note the 'ideal type' of collegiality emerging in numerous reports in the 1980s and 1990s and state that 'aspirations for collaborative approaches to whole-school change still pervade much current advice to primary schools' (ibid.: 441–2). However, the pressures for external accountability mean that many schools are 'resorting to managerialism' (ibid.: 442). They express concern that 'tension between collegiality and managerialism is resulting in concepts like "whole school" being hijacked by a managerialist ethic'.

These authors report that all 50 heads in their sample 'spoke of the growth in openness, discussion and sharing among teachers since the introduction of the National Curriculum' (ibid.: 444). Subject leaders were viewed as playing a vital role in curriculum planning despite the lack of non-contact time for them to visit or work in colleagues' classrooms. Other difficulties reported by participants include:

- The time-consuming nature of meetings where 'the discussion phase seemed to go on and on' and 'I felt we weren't getting anywhere'
- Lack of agreement led to non-action
- The pace at which the external changes were introduced meant that teachers had insufficient time for critical reflection on existing practice (Webb and Vulliamy, 1996: 446).

They add that the policy climate 'encourages headteachers to be powerful and, if necessary, manipulative leaders' (ibid.: 448) and conclude that collegiality is being damaged by external demands and the pressures on headteachers to ensure compliance with national directives:

> We have documented a growing tension between collegial and top-down approaches to whole-school change ... strong ... forces appear to be combining to promote what we have termed managerialism and the directive management styles of headteachers associated with it, which undermine the feasibility and credibility of teachers working together collegially to formulate policies and promote continuity of practice ... The tensions generated by trying to create conditions for co-operative working in the context of increased managerialism were present to some extent in all schools. (Webb and Vulliamy, 1996: 455–6)

We shall return to these issues in examining the limitations of collegial models.

Collegial models: goals, structure, environment and leadership

Goals

Collegial models assume that members of an organization agree on its *goals*. There is a belief that staff have a shared view of the purposes of the institution. Agreement on aims is perhaps the central element in all participative approaches to school and college management. Goals have three main functions:

- They provide a general guide to activity, enabling teachers to link their work to school objectives.

■ Goals serve as a source of legitimacy, enabling activities to be justified if they contribute to achievement of the goals.

■ They are a means of measuring success; a school is effective if it achieves its objectives.

Agreement on goals provides a clear starting point for developing the structures and processes required to enhance learning. Southworth (2005: 84) stresses the need for 'a high measure of consistency in approach and action across the school. In fact, agreed systems and structures play a major part in developing and sustaining a sense of whole school'. He adds that 'the kind of culture we need in schools today is characterized by collaboration' (ibid.: 85).

In universities and colleges, and perhaps also in secondary schools, the various academic disciplines often have rather different ideas about the central purpose of their institutions. In these circumstances, as Baldridge et al. (1978) demonstrate, agreement on aims may be achieved only by obfuscation:

> Most organisations know what they are doing ... By contrast, colleges and universities have vague, ambiguous goals ... As long as goals are left ambiguous and abstract, people agree; as soon as they are concretely specified and put into operation, disagreement arises. (Ibid.: 20–1)

The acknowledgement of possible conflict over the goals of educational institutions threatens one of the central planks of collegial theory. The belief that staff can always reach agreement over institutional purposes and policies lies at the heart of all participative approaches. Recognition of goal conflict serves to limit the validity of collegial models.

Organizational structure

Collegial models share with formal approaches the view that organizational *structure* is an objective fact which has a clear meaning for all members of the institution. The major difference concerns the relationships between different elements of the structure. Formal models present structures as vertical or hierarchical, with decisions being made by leaders and then passed down the structure. Subordinates are accountable to superiors for the satisfactory performance of their duties. In contrast, collegial models assume structures to be lateral or horizontal, with participants having an equal right to determine policy and influence decisions.

In education, collegial approaches are often manifested through systems of committees, which may be elaborate in the larger and more complex institutions. The decision-making process inside committees is thought to be egalitarian with influence dependent more on specific expertise than an official position. The assumption is that decisions are reached by consensus or compromise rather than acquiescence to the views of the head or principal.

In schools, ad hoc working parties may be more effective than standing committees. Brown, Boyle and Boyle (1999: 323) report on the usefulness of such groups in their case study secondary schools, as one of their respondents illustrates: 'We have working parties who report back to faculties after consultation with the senior management team and collaborative policies are produced and implemented'.

The external environment

There are several difficulties in assessing the nature of relationships between the organization and its *external environment*. Collegial models characterize decision-making as a participative process with all members of the institution having an equal opportunity to influence policy and action. However, where decisions emerge from an often complex committee system, it is not an easy task to establish who is responsible for organizational policy.

The ambiguity of the decision-making process within collegial organizations creates a particular problem in terms of accountability to external bodies. The head or principal is invariably held responsible for the policies of the school or college. The assumptions of the formal models are in line with these expectations. Leaders are thought to determine or strongly influence decisions and are accountable to external bodies for these policies.

Collegial models do not fit comfortably with these formal accountability assumptions. Are principals expected to justify school policies determined within a participatory framework even where they do not enjoy their personal support? Or is the reality that collegial policy-making is limited by the head's responsibility to external agencies? Heads must agree with, or at minimum acquiesce in, collegial decisions, if they are not to be placed in a very difficult position.

Collegial models tend to overlook the possibility of conflict between internal participative processes and external accountability. The assumption that issues can be resolved by consensus leads to the normative conclusion that heads are always in agreement with decisions, and experience no difficulty in explaining them to external bodies. In practice, it may be that the head's accountability leads to a substantially modified version of collegiality in most schools and colleges. There is also the risk of tension for the principal who is caught between the conflicting demands of participation and accountability.

These pressures have intensified in many countries as governments pursue a 'standards' agenda through top-down policy implementation. As we noted earlier, these external demands have made it more difficult for schools to operate collegially. This is equally true for primary (Webb and Vulliamy, 1996) and secondary (Brown et al., 1999) schools.

Leadership

In collegial models the style of *leadership* both influences, and is influenced by, the nature of the decision-making process. Because policy is determined within a participative framework, the head or principal is expected to adopt strategies which acknowledge that issues may emerge from different parts of the organization and be resolved in a complex interactive process. Heroic models of leadership may be seen as inappropriate when influence and power are widely distributed within the institution. However, Gronn (2010: 70) also points to the historic significance of solo leadership and the need to adopt a hybrid model combining individual and shared leadership.

Collegial theorists ascribe the following qualities to leaders in schools and colleges:

1. They are responsive to the needs and wishes of their professional colleagues. Heads and principals acknowledge the expertise and skill of the teachers and seek to harness these assets for the benefit of the pupils and students. Invariably, they have been appointed to leadership posts after a long period as successful practitioners. Their experience makes them sensitive to the needs and rights of teacher professionals.

2. Collegial heads seek to create formal and informal opportunities for the testing and elaboration of policy initiatives. This is done to encourage innovation and to maximize the acceptability of school decisions. The headteacher of 'Uplands' school, for example, promotes and nurtures a culture of shared values and a modified form of collegiality:

> She believes in the importance of high quality human relationships and is very accessible. She teaches regularly, does bus duty every afternoon when she is in school, continually walks round the school talking to staff and pupils and partakes in social activities ... She consults and wants to involve staff in decision-making, although the ultimate deci-

sions clearly rest with the senior management team. (Glover, 1996: 146)

3. Collegial models emphasize the authority of expertise rather than official authority. It follows that authority in professional organizations such as schools or colleges resides as much with the staff as with the head. Instead of exerting authority over subordinates, the leader seeks to influence the decisions and actions of professional colleagues. The head also allows and encourages heads of department, subject leaders, teachers and other staff to become co-leaders.

> We need to move away from thinking of leadership in terms of one individual … and attend more to leadership as a collective endeavour … we need lots of leaders in schools. Peer leadership among teachers, learning assistants and support staff is essential if we are to make schools powerful learning organisations. (Southworth, 2005: 89)

In collegial models, then, the head or principal is typified as the facilitator of an essentially participative process. Their credibility with their colleagues depends on providing leadership to staff and external stakeholders while valuing the contributions of specialist teachers. However, Hoyle and Wallace (2005: 151) warn of several 'leadership ambiguities', including 'the pressure placed on teachers to share leadership while making it ever more risky to do so'.

We noted in Chapter 2 that the six management models are compared with leadership models throughout this book. Three of these leadership models appear to have links to collegiality. These are:

1. Transformational leadership
2. Participative leadership
3. Distributed leadership.

Transformational leadership

> This form of leadership assumes that the central focus of leadership ought to be the commitments and capacities of organisational members. Higher levels of personal commitment to organisational goals and greater capacities for accomplishing those goals are assumed to result in extra effort and greater productivity. (Leithwood et al., 1999: 9)

Leithwood (1994) conceptualizes transformational leadership along eight dimensions:

- building school vision
- establishing school goals
- providing intellectual stimulation
- offering individualized support
- modelling best practices and important organizational values
- demonstrating high performance expectations
- creating a productive school culture
- developing structures to foster participation in school decisions.

Caldwell and Spinks argue that transformational leadership is essential for autonomous schools:

> Transformational leaders succeed in gaining the commitment of followers to such a degree that ... higher levels of accomplishment become virtually a moral imperative. In our view a powerful capacity for transformational leadership is required for the successful transition to a system of self-managing schools. (1992: 49–50)

Leithwood's (1994) research suggests that there is some empirical support for the essentially normative transformational leadership model. He reports on seven quantitative studies and concludes that: 'Transformational leadership practices, considered as a composite construct, had significant direct and indirect effects on progress with school-restructuring initiatives and teacher-perceived student outcomes' (ibid.: 506).

More recently, Leithwood and Jantzi (2006) drew on data from a four-year evaluation of England's National Literacy and Numeracy strategies to show that transformational leadership produced significant effects on teachers' classroom practices, but not on student achievement.

The transformational model is comprehensive in that it provides a normative approach to school leadership which focuses primarily on the process by which leaders seek to influence school outcomes, rather than on the nature or direction of those outcomes. However, it may also be criticized as being a vehicle for control over teachers and more likely to be accepted by the leader than the led (Chirichello, 1999). Allix (2000) goes further and alleges that transformational leadership has the potential to become 'despotic' because of its strong, heroic and charismatic features. He believes that the leader's power ought to raise 'moral qualms' and serious doubts about its appropriateness for democratic organizations. His conception suggests a political (see Chapter 5) rather than a collegial stance.

The contemporary policy climate within which schools have to operate also raises questions about the validity of the transformational model, despite its popularity in the literature. Transformational language is used by governments to encourage, or require, practitioners to adopt and implement centrally-determined policies. In South Africa, for example, the language of transformation is used to underpin a non-racist post-Apartheid education system. The policy is rich in symbolism but weak in practice because many school principals lack the capacity and the authority to implement change effectively (Bush et al., 2009).

The English system increasingly requires school leaders to adhere to government prescriptions which affect aims, curriculum content and pedagogy as well as values. In this respect, transformation is a unilateral process of implementation not a context-specific assessment of the needs of individual schools and their communities. There is 'a more centralized, more directed, and more controlled educational system [that] has dramatically reduced the possibility of realising a genuinely transformational education and leadership' (Bottery, 2001: 215). Hartley (2004) makes the similar point that transformational leadership is mainly about the translation of government policy into practice.

Hoyle and Wallace (2005: 151) refer to the inconsistencies of the 'transformational rhetoric-transmissional reality' gap underlying English government prescriptions for practice, 'promoted through government-sponsored training and scrutinized in practice through OFSTED surveillance'. Bottery (2004: 17) adds that 'there is much to question' in assessing transformational leadership, arguing that it transforms and corrupts reality and may be more a heroic than a shared leadership model.

Transformational leadership is consistent with the collegial model in that it assumes that leaders and staff have shared values and common interests. When it works well, it has the potential to engage all stakeholders in the achievement of educational objectives. The aims of leaders and followers coalesce to such an extent that it may be realistic to assume a harmonious relationship and a genuine convergence leading to agreed decisions. When 'transformation' is a cloak for imposing the leader's values, or for implementing the prescriptions of the government, then the process is political rather than collegial, as we shall see in Chapter 5: 'The strongest advocacy of a transformational approach to reform has come from those whose policies ensure that the opportunity for transformation is in fact denied to people working in schools' (Hoyle and Wallace, 2005: 128).

Participative leadership

The second leadership model relevant to collegiality is 'participative leadership'. Hoyle and Wallace (2005: 124) say that participation refers to 'the opportunities that staff members have for engaging in the process of organizational decision-making'. Leithwood, Jantzi and Steinbach (1999: 12) add that 'participative leadership ... assumes that the decision-making processes of the group ought to be the central focus of the group'.

As with collegiality itself, this is a normative model which is based on three criteria:

- Participation will increase school effectiveness.
- Participation is justified by democratic principles.
- In the context of site-based management, leadership is potentially available to any legitimate stakeholder (ibid.: 12).

Sergiovanni (1984) points to the importance of a participative approach. This will succeed in 'bonding' staff together and in easing the pressures on school principals: 'The burdens of leadership will be less if leadership functions and roles are shared and if the concept of *leadership density* were to emerge as a viable replacement for principal leadership' (ibid.: 13).

Copland (2001) makes a similar point in claiming that participative leadership has the potential to ease the burden on principals and avoid the expectation that the formal leader will be a 'superhead':

> Leadership is embedded in various organisational contexts within school communities, not centrally vested in a person or an office ... exciting work is under way that explores specific ways in which schools might distribute leadership more broadly ... [There is] a need to identify and support aspects of leadership beyond the role of the principal. (Ibid.: 6)

Savery, Soutar and Dyson (1992) demonstrate that deputy principals in Western Australia wish to participate in school decision-making but their desire to do so varied across different types of decision. A majority of their 105 respondents wanted joint decision-making in school policy, student discipline, teaching load, general policy and time allocation, but fewer were interested in participating in what were described as 'economic variables', including budgets and staff selection, and in responding to parental complaints. The authors conclude that 'people are more likely to accept and implement decisions in which they have participated, particularly where these decisions relate directly to the individual's own job' (ibid.: 24).

Distributed leadership

Distributed leadership has become the normatively preferred leadership model in the twenty-first century, replacing collegiality as the favoured approach. Gronn (2010: 70) states that 'there has been an accelerating amount of scholarly and practitioner attention accorded [to] the phenomenon of distributed leadership'. Harris (2010: 55) adds that it 'represents one of the most influential ideas to emerge in the field of educational leadership in the past decade'. In this section, we examine this model and link it to notions of collegiality.

Defining distributed leadership

An important starting point for understanding this phenomenon is to uncouple it from posi   [arris (2004: 13) indicates,
'distributed leadership   ıging expertise wherever it
exists within the orga   seeking this only through
formal position or role   ; characterized as a form of
collective leadership'   that collegiality is 'at the
core of distributed lea   : adds that it involves both
vertical and lateral dir   ) practice, suggesting a link
to both formal and cc

Gronn (2010: 70)   e switch 'from heroics to
distribution', but al   a view that distributed
leadership necessaril   ion in the scope of the
principal's role. Indeed, Hartley (2010: 27) argues that 'its popularity may be pragmatic: to ease the burden of overworked headteachers'. Lumby (2009: 320) adds that distributed leadership 'does not imply that school staff are necessarily enacting leadership any differently' to the time 'when heroic, individual leadership was the focus of attention'. We shall consider later how to align solo and distributed leadership. Meanwhile, Lumby (2009: 320) also argues that distributed leadership should be extended to consideration of inter-school partnerships, rather than being confined to leadership within the organization.

Modes of distribution

A key issue in assessing the practice of distributed leadership is to consider how it is distributed. Does the principal cede some formal authority to others in a process analogous to delegation? Does s/he invite colleagues to adopt leadership roles or behaviours? Does s/he encourage others to initiate leadership actions? Do other staff take their own initiative in taking responsibility for leadership? Is distributed leadership a deliberate or an inadvertent process?

Bennett et al. (2003: 3) claim that distributed leadership is an emergent property of a group or network of individuals in which group members pool their expertise. Harris (2004: 19), referring to an English study of 10 English schools facing challenging circumstances (Harris and Chapman, 2002), says that there should be 'redistribution of power', not simply a process of 'delegated headship'. However, Hopkins and Jackson (2002) argue that formal leaders need to orchestrate and nurture the space for distributed leadership to occur, suggesting that it would be difficult to achieve without the active support of school principals. Given that leadership is widely regarded as an influence process, a central issue is 'who can exert influence over colleagues and in what domains?' (Harris, 2005: 165). Heads and principals retain much of the formal authority in schools, leading Hartley (2010: 282) to conclude that 'distributed leadership resides uneasily within the formal bureaucracy of schools'.

The role of the head in distributed leadership

Harris (2004: 16) argues that 'successful heads recognize the limitations of a singular leadership approach' and adopt a form of leadership 'distributed through collaborative and joint working' (ibid.). However, Arrowsmith's (in press) empirical study of distributed leadership in English secondary schools shows considerable caution in adopting this mode. Several heads regarded as 'non-negotiable' the 'delegation' or distribution of certain parts of their role, including strategic direction, and retained an acute sense of their personal accountability for school performance. This suggests that distribution may be subject to strict limits.

Gronn's (2010: 74) overview of four research projects leads him to conclude that principals retain considerable power: 'Certain individuals, while they by no means monopolized the totality of the leadership, nonetheless exercised disproportionate influence compared to their individual peers'. Bottery (2004: 21) asks how distribution is to be achieved 'if those in formal positions do not wish to have their power redistributed in this way?' Harris (2005: 167) argues that 'distributed and hierarchical forms of leadership are not incompatible', but it is evident that distribution can work successfully only if formal leaders allow it to take root.

The impact of distributed leadership

The interest in, and support for, distributed leadership is predicated on the assumption that it will bring about beneficial effects that would not occur with singular leadership. However, there has been little hard evidence on this issue, leading Harris (2005: 170) to comment that 'we do not know the impact of distributed leadership on schools, teachers and students'. Leithwood et al's (2006) important study of the impact of school leadership led to the articulation of 'seven strong claims' about successful school leadership. Two of these claims relate to distributed leadership:

1. School leadership has a greater influence on schools and students when it is widely distributed.
2. Some patterns of distribution are more effective than others.

Leithwood et al. show that multiple leadership is much more effective than solo leadership:

> Total leadership accounted for a quite significant 27 per cent variation in student achievement across schools. This is a much higher proportion of explained variation (two to three times higher) than is typically reported in studies of individual headteacher effects. (2006: 12)

Leithwood et al. (2006: 13) add that schools with the highest levels of student achievement attributed this to relatively high levels of influence from all sources of leadership. Hallinger and Heck (in press) also found that 'distributed leadership was significantly related to change in academic capacity' and, thus, to growth in student learning. These are important findings but more such research is required before a causal relationship can be established with confidence.

Barriers to distributed leadership

As suggested earlier, the existing authority structure in schools and colleges provides a potential barrier to the successful introduction and implementation of distributed leadership. 'There are inherent threats to status and the status quo in all that distributed leadership implies' (Harris, 2004: 20). Hartley (2010: 282) suggests that the origins of distributed leadership were essentially pragmatic, a response to the extra responsibilities imposed on schools as site-based management took root in many countries from the 1990s. 'It is little wonder there emerged a search for a structure whereby collective intelligence could be assembled'. However, he also notes that the requirements of the standards agenda mean that bureaucracy remains powerful and limits the scope for distributed leadership. Fitzgerald and Gunter (2008) also refer to the residual significance of authority and hierarchy and note the 'dark side' of distributed leadership – managerialism in a new guise. More neutrally, it can be argued that distributed leadership leads to the power relationship between followers and leaders becoming blurred (Law: 2010).

These reservations suggest that an appropriate climate is an essential pre-condition to meaningful distributed leadership. Harris (2005: 169) argues that 'the creation of collegial norms' are essential and adds that teachers need time to meet if collective leadership is to become a reality. She adds that cordial relationships are required with school managers, who may 'feel threatened' (ibid.) by teachers taking on leadership roles. Despite these reservations, however, the research does show that distributed leadership has the potential to expand the scope of leadership, leading to enhanced student outcomes while developing the formal leaders of the future. Gronn's (2010: 77) 'hybrid' model of leadership may offer the potential to harness the best of both individual and distributed approaches.

Limitations of collegial models

Collegial models have been popular in the literature on educational leadership and management, and in official pronouncements about school development, since the 1980s. Brundrett (1998: 307) argues that it has become 'one of the ubiquitous megatrends in education'. Advocates of collegiality believe that participative approaches represent the most appropriate means of conducting affairs in educational institutions. In the twenty-first century, leadership models linked to collegiality, transformational, participative and distributed approaches, have been encouraged. However, critics of collegial models point to a number of flaws which serve to limit their validity in schools and colleges. There are seven significant weaknesses of collegial perspectives.

1. Collegial models are so strongly *normative* that they tend to obscure rather than portray reality. Precepts about the most appropriate ways of managing educational institutions mingle with descriptions of behaviour. While collegiality is increasingly advocated, the evidence of its presence in schools and colleges tends to be sketchy and incomplete, leading Webb and Vulliamy (1996: 443) to state that 'the advocacy of collegiality is made more on the basis of prescrip-

tion than on research-based studies of school practice'.

2. Collegial approaches to decision-making tend to be *slow and cumbersome*. When policy proposals require the approval of a series of committees, the process is often tortuous and time-consuming. The participative ethic requires that a decision should be made by agreement where possible rather than by resorting to a voting process. The attempts to achieve consensus may lead to procedural delays such as a reference back to the sponsoring committee, or to consultation with other committees, individuals or external agencies. Participants may have to endure many lengthy meetings before issues are resolved. This requires patience and a considerable investment of time. Several primary school heads interviewed by Webb and Vulliamy (1996: 445–6) refer to 'the time-consuming nature of meetings' where 'the discussion phase seemed to go on and on' and 'I felt we weren't getting anywhere'. While planning time is essential, as noted earlier, spending valuable non-contact time in unproductive meetings is a recipe for frustration and apathy.

3. A fundamental assumption of democratic models is that decisions are reached by *consensus*. It is believed that the outcome of debate should be agreement based on the shared values of participants. In practice, though, professionals have their own views and there is no guarantee of unanimity on outcomes. In addition, participants often represent constituencies within the school or college. Individuals may be members of committees as representatives of the English department or the science faculty. Inevitably, these sectional interests have a significant influence on committees' processes. The participatory framework may become the focal point for disagreement between factions.

4. Collegial models have to be evaluated in relation to the special features of educational institutions. The participative aspects of decision-making exist alongside the structural and bureaucratic components of schools and colleges. Often there is tension between these rather different modes of management. The participative element rests on the authority of expertise possessed by professional staff, but this rarely trumps the positional authority of official leaders. Brundrett points to the inevitable contradiction between collegiality and bureaucracy in the English educational system:

> In an era of a national curriculum, centralised testing and increased bureaucratisation of education, it is interesting to note that collegiality is the preferred style of school-based management ... collegiality is inevitably the handmaiden of an ever increasingly centralised bureaucracy. (1998: 312–13)

5. Collegial approaches to school and college decision-making may be difficult to sustain in view of the requirement that heads and principals remain accountable to the governing body and to various external groups. Participation represents the internal dimension of democracy. *Accountability* may be thought of as the external aspect of democracy. Governors and external groups seek explanations of policy and invariably turn to the head or principal for answers to their questions. Heads may experience considerable difficulty in defending policies which have emerged from a collegial process but do not enjoy their personal support. Brundrett (1998: 310) is right to argue that 'heads need to be genuinely brave to lend power to a democratic forum which may make decisions with which the head-teacher may not themselves agree'.

6. The effectiveness of a collegial system depends in part on the attitudes of staff. If they actively support participation then it may succeed. If they display apathy or hostility, it seems certain to fail. Hellawell refers to the experience of one primary head who sought to introduce collegial approaches:

> I have worked very hard over the last few years, as the number of staff has grown, to build up a really collegial style of management with a lot of staff input into decisions that affect the school and they are saying that they don't like this. They would like an autocracy. They would like to be told what to do. (1991: 334)

Hoyle and Wallace (2005: 126) argue that teachers may not welcome increased participation, especially when this is 'institutionalized'. When formalized in this way, processes of collaboration 'cease to be satisfying to teachers; they increase workload and reduce opportunities for spontaneity'. A related consideration is the limited time available to work collegially. Teachers have only limited non-contact time, making it difficult for them 'to visit or work in colleagues' classrooms' (Webb and Vulliamy, 1996: 445).

7. Collegial processes in schools depend even more on the attitudes of heads than on the support of teachers. In colleges, the academic board provides a legitimate forum for the involvement of staff in decision-making and principals have to recognize and work with this alternative power source. In schools, participative machinery can be established only with the support of the head, who has the legal authority to manage the school. Wise heads take account of the views of their staff but this is a consultative process and not collegiality. 'Visions of distributed leadership need to take fully into

account the asymmetry of power between different actors' (Bottery, 2004: 21).

Contrived collegiality

Hargreaves (1994) makes a more fundamental criticism of collegiality, arguing that it is being espoused or 'contrived' by official groups in order to secure the implementation of national policy. He claims that genuine collegiality is spontaneous, voluntary, unpredictable, informal and geared to development. Contrived collegiality, in contrast, has the following contradictory features:

- administratively regulated rather than spontaneous
- compulsory rather than discretionary
- geared to the implementation of the mandates of government or the headteacher
- fixed in time and place
- designed to have predictable outcomes (Hargreaves, 1994: 195–6).

Within the post-Education Reform Act context in England and Wales, this analysis is persuasive. Brundrett (1998) and Webb and Vulliamy (1996) both argue that collegial frameworks may be used for essentially political activity, the focus of the next chapter:

> What is actually happening in many institutions where collaboration is espoused, is not a genuine collegial environment but rather an adept use of micro-political manipulation … In effect individuals and groups seek to realise their values and goals at the expense of others but seek to legitimate their power through assuming the cloak of the moral legitimacy lent to them by the apparent use of democratic procedures. (Brundrett, 1998: 311)

> The current climate … encourages headteachers to be powerful and, if necessary, manipulative leaders in order to ensure that policies and practices agreed upon are ones that they can wholeheartedly support and defend. (Webb and Vulliamy, 1996: 448)

These views are also consistent with the comments made by Allix (2000), noted earlier, about the potentially manipulative aspects of transformational leadership and of the 'dark side' of distributed leadership (Fitzgerald and Gunter, 2008). Hoyle and Wallace (2005: 127) also note the dangers of contrived collegiality leading to 'more time spent in formal meetings to the detriment of classroom work'.

Conclusion: is collegiality an unattainable ideal?

Collegial models are highly normative and idealistic. Their advocates believe that participative approaches represent the most appropriate means of managing educational institutions. Teachers exhibit that authority of expertise which justifies their involvement in the decision-making process. In addition, they are able to exercise sufficient discretion in the classroom to ensure that innovation depends on their co-operation. Collegial theorists argue that active support for change is more likely to be forthcoming where teachers have been able to contribute to the process of policy formulation and when they are able to participate in distributed leadership.

Collegial models contribute several important concepts to the theory of educational management. Participative approaches are a necessary antidote to the rigid hierarchical assumptions of the formal models. However, collegial perspectives provide an incomplete portrayal of management in education. They underestimate the official authority of the head and present bland assumptions of consensus which often cannot be substantiated. It may also be true that collegiality, and participative approaches to leadership, cannot easily co-exist with the bureaucratic and political realities of education systems. Little (1990: 187), following substantial research in the United States, concludes that collegiality 'turns out to be rare'.

A generation ago almost all schools and colleges could have been categorized as formal. Since the 1990s, many have developed collegial frameworks. There is a discernible trend towards collegiality, and participative or distributed leadership, despite the bureaucratic pressures imposed by central government. Despite Hargreaves's (1994) justifiable criticisms of 'contrived collegiality', the advantages of participation in professional organizations remain persuasive. Collegiality and distributed leadership are elusive concepts but a measure of participation is essential if schools are to be harmonious and creative organizations:

> While scholars have been increasingly persuaded of the shortcomings of leadership conceived as individually focused action, and have begun substituting a distributed or shared approach, they may have adopted a template which does not accurately accord with the realities of practice. Both a re-interpretation of data in accounts of distributed leadership and evidence from a handful of new studies points in the direction of leadership configurations that are mixed or hybrid in nature. (Gronn, 2010: 83)

References

Allix, N.M. (2000) 'Transformational leadership: democratic or despotic?', *Educational Management and Administration*, 28(1): 7–20.

Arrowsmith, T. (in press) 'How secondary headteachers address the challenges of distributing leadership across their schools', *Educational Management, Administration and Leadership*.

Baldridge, J.V., Curtis, D.V., Ecker, G. and Riley, G.L. (1978) *Policy Making and Effective Leadership*, San Francisco, CA: Jossey-Bass.

Becher, T. and Kogan, M. (1992) *Process and Structure in Higher Education*, 2nd edn, London: Routledge.

Bennett, N., Harvey, J., Wise, C. and Woods, P. (2003) 'Distributed leadership: a desk study', www.ncsl.org.uk/publications.

Bottery, M. (2001) 'Globalisation and the UK competition state: no room for transformational leadership in education?', *School Leadership and Management*, 21(2): 199–218.

Bottery, M. (2004) *The Challenges of Educational Leadership,* London: Paul Chapman Publishing.

Brown, M., Boyle, B. and Boyle, T. (1999) 'Commonalities between perception and practice in models of school decision-making in secondary schools', *School Leadership and Management*, 19(3): 319–30.

Brundrett, M. (1998) 'What lies behind collegiality, legitimation or control?', *Educational Management and Administration*, 26(3): 305–16.

Bush, T. and Heystek, J. (2003) 'School governance in the new South Africa', *Compare*, 33(2): 127–38.

Bush, T., Coleman, M. and Si, X. (1998) 'Managing secondary schools in China', *Compare*, 28(2): 183–96.

Bush, T., Duku, N., Glover, D., Kiggundu, E., Kola, S., Msila, V. and Moorosi, P. (2009) *The Zenex ACE School Leadership Research: Final Report*, Pretoria: Department of Education.

Caldwell, B. and Spinks, J. (1992) *Leading the Self-Managing School*, London: Falmer Press.

Chirichello, M. (1999) 'Building capacity for change: transformational leadership for school principals', paper presented at ICSEI Conference, 3–6 January, San Antonio.

Copland, M. (2001) 'The myth of the superprincipal', *Phi Delta Kappan*, 82: 528–32.

Deem, R. (2000) '"New Managerialism" and the management of UK universities', nd of award report of the findings of an Economic and Social Research Council ded project, Lancaster University.

f Education (1997) *Understanding the SA Schools Act*, Pretoria: Depart-

. (2008) 'Contesting the orthodoxy of teacher leader-
of Leadership in Education, 11(4): 331–41.

p, planning and resource management in four very
setting the scene', *School Organisation*, 16(2): 135–48.

Gronn, P. (2010) 'Where to next for educational leadership?', in Bush, T., Bell, L. and Middlewood, D. (eds), *The Principles of Educational Leadership and Management,* London: Sage.

Hallinger, P. and Heck, R. (in press) 'Leadership for learning: does distributed leadership make a difference in student learning', *Educational Management, Administration and Leadership.*

Hargreaves, A. (1994) *Changing Teachers, Changing Times: Teachers' Work and Culture in the Postmodern Age,* London: Cassell.

Harman, K. and Treadgold, E. (2007) 'Changing patterns of governance for Australian universities', *Higher Education Research and Development,* 26(1): 13–20.

Harris, A. (2004) 'Distributed leadership in schools: leading or misleading?', *Educational Management, Administration and Leadership,* 32(1): 11–24.

Harris, A. (2005), 'Distributed leadership', in B. Davies (ed.), *The Essentials of School Leadership,* London: Paul Chapman Publishing.

Harris, A. (2010) 'Distributed leadership: evidence and implications', in T. Bush, L. Bell and D. Middlewood, (eds), *The Principles of Educational Leadership and Management,* 2nd edn, London: Sage.

Harris, A. and Chapman, C. (2002) *Effective Leadership in Schools Facing Challenging Circumstances: Final Report,* Nottingham: NCSL.

Hartley, D. (2004) 'Management, leadership and the emotional order of the school', *Journal of Education Policy,* 19(5): 583–94.

Hartley, D. (2010) 'Paradigms: How far does research in distributed leadership "stretch"', *Educational Management, Administration and Leadership,* 38(3): 271–85.

Hellawell. D. (1991) 'The changing role of the head in the primary school in England', *School Organisation,* 11(3): 321–37.

Hopkins, D. and Jackson, D. (2002) 'Building the capacity for leading and learning', in A. Harris, C. Day, M. Hadfield, D. Hopkins, A. Hargreaves and C. Chapman (eds), *Effective Leadership for School Improvement.* London: Routledge.

Hoyle, E. and Wallace, M. (2005) *Educational Leadership: Ambiguity, Professionals and Managerialism,* London: Sage.

Law, E. (2010) 'Distributed curriculum leadership in action: a Hong Kong case study', *Educational Management, Administration and Leadership,* 38.3: 286–303.

Leithwood, K. (1994) 'Leadership for school restructuring', *Educational Administration Quarterly,* 30(4): 498–518.

Leithwood, K. and Jantzi, D. (2006) 'Transformational leadership for large-scale reform: effects on students, teachers and their classroom practices', *School Effectiveness and School Improvement,* 17(2): 201–27.

Leithwood, K., Jantzi, D. and Steinbach, R. (1999) *Changing Leadership for Changing Times,* Buckingham: Open University Press.

Leithwood, K., Day, C., Sammons, P., Harris, A. and Hopkins, D. (2006) *Seven Strong Claims about Successful School Leadership,* London: DfES.

Little, J. (1990) 'Teachers as colleagues', in A. Lieberman (ed.), *Schools as Collaborative Cultures: Creating the Future Now,* Basingstoke: Falmer Press.

Lumby, J. (2003) 'Distributed leadership in colleges: leading or misleading?', *Educational Management and Administration,* 31(3): 283–93.

Lumby, J. (2009) 'Collective leadership of local school systems: power, autonomy and ethics', *Educational Management, Administration and Leadership,* 373: 310–28.

Middlehurst, R. and Elton, L. (1992) 'Leadership and management in higher education', *Studies in Higher Education,* 17(3): 251–64.

Paine, L. and Ma, L. (1993) 'Teachers working together: a dialogue on organisational and cultural perspectives of Chinese teachers', *International Journal of Educational Research,* 19: 675–97.

Savery, L., Soutar, G. and Dyson, J. (1992) 'Ideal decision-making styles indicated by deputy principals', *Journal of Educational Administration*, 30(2): 18–25.

Sergiovanni, T. (1984) 'Leadership and excellence in schooling', *Educational Leadership*, 41(5): 4–13.

Southworth, G. (2005) 'Learning-centred leadership', in B. Davies (ed.), *The Essentials of School Leadership*, London: Paul Chapman Publishing.

Wallace, M. (1989) 'Towards a collegiate approach to curriculum management in primary and middle schools', in M. Preedy (ed.), *Approaches to Curriculum Management*, Buckingham: Open University Press.

Webb, R. and Vulliamy, G. (1996) 'A deluge of directives: conflict between collegiality and managerialism in the post-ERA primary school', *British Educational Research Journal*, 22(4): 441–58.

Williams, K. (1989) 'The case for democratic management in schools', *Irish Educational Studies*, 8(2): 73–86.

Williams, G. and Blackstone, T. (1983) *Response to Adversity*, Guildford: Society for Research into Higher Education.

CHAPTER 5

Political models

Central features of political models

Political models embrace those theories which characterize decision-making as a bargaining process. They assume that organizations are political arenas whose members engage in political activity in pursuit of their interests. Analysis focuses on the distribution of power and influence in organizations and on the bargaining and negotiation between interest groups. Conflict is regarded as endemic within organizations, and management is directed towards the regulation of political behaviour. The definition below incorporates the main elements of these approaches.

> Political models assume that in organizations, policy and decisions emerge through a process of negotiation and bargaining. Interest groups develop and form alliances in pursuit of particular policy objectives. Conflict is viewed as a natural phenomenon and power accrues to dominant coalitions rather than being the preserve of formal leaders.

Political models in schools and other educational institutions are often described as 'micropolitics' (Ball, 1987; Hoyle, 1999). Mawhinney defines micropolitics as:

> the interaction and political ideologies of social systems of teachers, administrators, teachers and pupils within school buildings. These may

be viewed as internal organizational subsystems. Micropolitical analysis is also concerned with external system issues such as those arising in the interaction between professional and lay subsystems. (1999: 161)

Micropolitics are important examples of political models but there are other political approaches that are not described as 'micropolitical'. Hence the wider concept of 'political models' is used in this volume. Deal (2005: 112) prefers the notion of 'frame'. 'The political frame relinquishes goals and needs in favour of the law of the jungle: scarce resources, competing interests and the role of power and conflict in determining both direction and outcomes … leadership is essentially political'.

Politics tend to be regarded as the concern of central and local government and to be associated strongly with the political parties who compete for our votes at national, provincial and local elections. It is useful to loosen this close identity between government and politics before seeking to apply political metaphors to educational institutions.

National and local politics strongly influence the context within which schools and colleges operate. In most societies, central government determines the broad character of the educational system and this is inevitably underpinned by the political views of the majority party. In England, for example, the 1988 Education Reform Act, and subsequent legislation, set the framework within which schools and colleges must operate. Similarly, the South African Schools Act (1996) provides the basis for the post-Apartheid education system.

Local politics have become less influential in England since the 1988 Act which allocated many former local authority (LA) responsibilities to central government or to the educational institutions. However, LAs retain the power to determine the financial position of most schools through their control over the funding formula. The elements of the formula, and their weighting, are the product of the political judgements of the majority party, within the limitations laid down in the legislation.

While national and local government determine the broad framework for education, political models apply to schools, colleges and other organizations just as much as they relate to political parties:

I take schools, in common with virtually all other social organizations, to be riven with actual or potential conflict between members; to be poorly coordinated; to be ideologically diverse. I take it to be essential that if we are to understand the nature of schools as organizations, we must achieve some understanding of these conflicts. (Ball, 1987: 19)

West (1999) points out that the international trend towards self-management in education expands the scope for political activity. As schools have greater responsibility for their own affairs, so the potential for conflict inevitably increases:

> The majority of decisions that concern teachers, and the responsibility for planning the individual school's future, now reside within the school ... schools in England and Wales have never offered more scope for micropolitical influence than they do now – within the self-managing school. We can speculate, therefore, that there has never been a time when an awareness of micropolitical processes and interactions was more useful to headteachers. (West, 1999: 190)

Hoyle (1999) makes a useful distinction between policy and management micropolitics:

> The concerns of policy micropolitics are essentially transboundary; how micropolitics constitute the means by which school staff respond to external pressures, e.g. resistance, retreatism, ritualism. Management micropolitics faces in the direction of the strategies whereby school leaders and teachers pursue their interests in the context of the management of the school ... although micropolitics is concerned with strategies deployed in the conflict of interests between teachers, perhaps the main focus is the conflict of interests between school leaders and teachers. (Ibid.: 214)

Baldridge's (1971) ground-breaking research in universities in the United States concluded that the political model, rather than the formal or collegial perspectives, best captured the realities of life in higher education:

> When we look at the complex and dynamic processes that explode on the modern campus today, we see neither the rigid, formal aspects of bureaucracy nor the calm consensus-directed elements of an academic collegium. On the contrary ... [interest groups] emerge ... These groups articulate their interests in many different ways, bringing pressure on the decision-making process from any number of angles ... Power and influence, once articulated, go through a complex process until policies are shaped, reshaped and forged out of the competing claims of multiple groups. (1971: 19–20)

Political models may be just as valid for schools and colleges as they are for universities.

Political models have the following major features:

1. They tend to focus on *group activity* rather than the institution as a whole. The emphasis is on sub-units such as departments or faculties, not the school or college level. Interaction between groups is at the heart of political approaches whereas formal and collegial models stress the institutional level: 'The basic unit of traditional political analysis is the sub group ... the basic unit of an apolitical

perspective is the total system' (Bacharach and Lawler, 1980).

Most schools and colleges are complex organizations and there are several different types of group. West (1999: 190) distinguishes between formal and informal groups. The former 'are created in order to fulfil specific goals and carry on specific tasks which are clearly linked to the school's overall mission'. Formal groups may be either permanent (the senior management, subject departments, etc.) or temporary (working parties or task forces). Informal groups exist to meet teachers' need for affiliation and can take many forms. Typically, they have their own leader and certain norms or rituals that underpin group behaviour (West, 1999).

Cranston (2008: 16) applies micropolitical theory to his analysis of senior management teams and argues that 'knowledge and understanding of micropolitics is useful in enhancing the operations and effectiveness of SMTs'.

Ball (1987) refers to 'baronial politics' and discusses the nature of conflict between the leaders of subgroups:

> In the middle ages the conflicts between English barons were essentially concerned with two matters: wealth and power. In the school the concerns and interests of academic and pastoral barons are fundamentally the same: allocations from the budget ... and influence over school policies. (Ibid.: 221)

Lindle (1999: 171) also stresses the significance of the competition for resources in fuelling political activity. 'The perennially scarce resources of schools ... provide the nutrients for school-based political activity'. Wallace and Hall's (1994) research on school management teams (SMTs) in England and Wales shows how issues of power and resources were strongly evident in the work of SMTs and in their relationships with other staff in the school.

2. Political models are concerned with *interests* and *interest groups*. Individuals are thought to have a variety of interests which they pursue within the organization. Morgan (1997: 161) explains their significance within the political model:

> In talking about 'interests', we are talking about pre-dispositions embracing goals, values, desires, expectations, and other orientations and inclinations that lead a person to act in one way rather than another. In everyday life, we tend to think of interests in a spatial way: as areas of concern that we wish to preserve or enlarge or as positions that we wish to protect or achieve ... the flow of politics is intimately connected with this way of positioning ourselves.

Hoyle (1986) distinguishes between personal and professional interests:

> Professional interests ... centre on commitments to a particular cur-
> riculum, syllabus, mode of pupil grouping, teaching method, etc ...
> professional interests become part of the micropolitical process accord-
> ing to the strategies used to further them. Personal interests focus on
> such issues as status, promotion and working conditions. (1986: 128)

Hoyle (1982) points to the development of interest groups as a principal means of seeking and achieving individual aims:

> Interests are pursued by individuals but frequently they are most effec-
> tively pursued in collaboration with others who share a common
> concern. Some of these may have the qualities of a group in that they
> are relatively enduring and have a degree of cohesion, but others ... will
> be looser associations of individuals who collaborate only infrequently
> when a common interest comes to the fore. (1982: 89)

The more permanent formal groups, such as departments, tend to be
cohesive because of shared values and beliefs. The individuals
within such groups often have common attitudes towards many of
the central issues in schools and colleges, although this was not the
case with the departments in Brown, Boyle and Boyle's (2000) 'Type
C' secondary schools where there was only limited co-operative
working between and among staff colleagues. However, there are
usually greater differences in goals and values *between* interest
groups, leading to fragmentation rather than organizational unity.
On particular issues, groups may form alliances to press for policies
which reflect their joint interests. These coalitions may well be temporary, disbanding when certain objectives have been achieved,
while the interest groups themselves often have enduring significance. Caffyn (2010: 336) notes the fragmentation that arises in
international schools because of cultural diversity and the transient
nature of the teaching force.

3. Political models stress the prevalence of *conflict* in organizations.
   Interest groups pursue their independent objectives which may contrast sharply with the aims of other sub-units within the institution
   and lead to conflict between them, or what Salo (2008: 502)
   describes as 'disputation'. 'Micropolitics is about conflict, and how
   people compete to get what they want in the face of scarce resources'
   (Mawhinney, 1999: 167–8).

   An important feature of political perspectives is the view that conflict
   is a normal feature of organizations (Deal, 2005: 112). Collegial models
   have a strong harmony bias and the possibility of disagreement is
   ignored or assumed away. In contrast, Morgan (1997) argues that conflict is the inevitable outcome of a clash of interests and interest groups:

Conflict arises whenever interests collide. The natural reaction to conflict in organisational contexts is usually to view it as a dysfunctional force that can be attributed to some regrettable set of circumstances or causes. 'It's a personality problem' ... Conflict is regarded as an unfortunate state that in more favourable circumstances would disappear ... [In practice] conflict will always be present in organisations ... its source rests in some perceived or real divergence of interests. (Ibid.: 167)

Caffyn (2010: 336) comments that, in international schools, transnational groups come into conflict with schools and educational systems. Milliken's (2001) study of a business school within a United Kingdom university also illustrates the prevalence of conflict. The school is divided into four specific divisions, each with its own goals. The interaction between these groups often generates conflict:

The interest groups cluster around the divergent values and this clustering is socially evident even to the organisation of their coffee breaks when members within a division often have their breaks together in the staff common room – a form of micro-political apartheid. (Ibid.: 78)

Vestiges of the Apartheid period remain in the experience of black teachers working in South Africa's former whites-only city schools. Many of them report that they are marginalized and often excluded from formal and social groups (Bush and Moloi, 2007).

4. Political models assume that the *goals* of organizations are unstable, ambiguous and contested. Individuals, interest groups and coalitions have their own purposes and act towards their achievement. Goals may be disputed and then become a significant element in the conflict between groups. Certain sub-units succeed in establishing their goals as the objectives of the institution while other interests seek to supplant the official purposes with their own objectives. Bolman and Deal (1991) explain the fluid nature of goals in political settings:

Traditional views of organisations ... assume that organisations have, or ought to have, clear and consistent goals. Generally, the goals are presumed to be established by those in authority ... The political frame, however, insists that organisational goals are set through negotiations among the members of coalitions. Different individuals and groups have different objectives and resources, and each attempts to bargain with other members or coalitions to influence goals and decision-making processes. (Ibid.: 190)

Interest groups are likely to promote their objectives in a variety of ways until they are supported by the policy-makers. This does not necessarily end the conflict because the endorsement of one set of purposes tends to be at the expense of other goals, whose proponents may continue to lobby for their own ideas. Disagreement over goals is a continuing feature of the policy process in organizations.

5. As noted above, decisions within political arenas emerge after a complex process of *bargaining and negotiation*. Formal models assume that decisions follow a rational process. Options are evaluated in terms of the objectives of the organization and the most appropriate alternative is selected. Policy-making in political settings is a more uncertain business. Interests are promoted in committees and at numerous unofficial encounters between participants. Policies cannot easily be judged in terms of the goals of the institution because these are subject to the same process of internal debate and subsequent change. The objectives are a moving target, as Bolman and Deal (1991: 186) suggest: organisational goals and decisions emerge from ongoing processes of bargaining, negotiation, and jockeying for position among members of different coalitions. Referring to Norwegian schools, Elstad (2008: 397) claims that bargaining is 'ubiquitous' and adds that teacher coalitions can strengthen interest groups' bargaining power.

The emphasis on the several stages of decision-making is significant because it multiplies the opportunities available to interest groups to exert influence on the policy process. Decisions on a subject at one forum do not necessarily resolve the issue because the unsuccessful groups are likely to pursue the matter whenever opportunities arise or can be engineered. Salo (2008: 497) notes that 'organisations are characterized by constant negotiations of pluralistic meanings' while Hoyle and Wallace (2005) comment that mediation is required to resolve disagreements.

6. The concept of *power* is central to all political theories. The outcomes of the complex decision-making process are likely to be determined according to the relative power of the individuals and interest groups involved in the debate. Salo (2008: 500) describes this process as 'a continuing struggle for control, power and influence'. Participants mobilize resources of power which are deployed in support of their interests and have a significant impact on policy outcomes. 'Power is the medium through which conflicts of interest are ultimately resolved. Power influences who gets what, when and how … the sources of power are rich and varied' (Morgan, 1997: 170–1). Deal (2005: 113) stresses the need for leaders to consolidate their 'power base'.

The nature and sources of power in education are examined on pages 108–112.

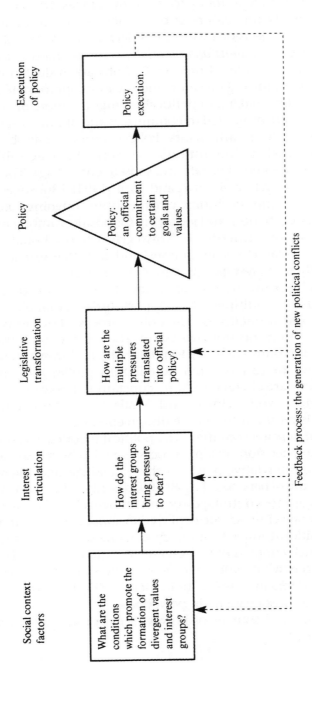

Figure 5.1 A political model (from Baldridge, 1971)

Baldridge's political model

Several of the ideas discussed in the previous section, notably the notion of stages of decision-making, are addressed in the classical political model developed by Baldridge (1971). The author considers the formation of interest groups and discusses the ways in which policies emerge from the kaleidoscope of conflicting pressures (see Figure 5.1). Baldridge postulates five stages in the policy process:

1. A *social structure* is a configuration of social groups with basically different lifestyles and political interests. These differences often lead to conflict, for what is in the interest of one group may damage another. The social structure, with its fragmented groups, divergent goal aspiration, and conflicting claims on the decision-makers, is the setting for political behaviour. Many conflicts have their roots in the complexity of the social structure and in the complex goals and values held by divergent groups.
2. *Interest articulation* is the process by which interests are advanced. Groups with conflicting values and goals must translate them into effective influence if they are to obtain favourable action by legislative bodies. How does a powerful group exert its pressure, what threats or promises can it make, and how does it translate its desires into political capital? There are many forms of interest articulation and it assumes a multitude of shapes.
3. The *legislative stage* is the process by which articulated interests are translated into policies. Legislative bodies respond to pressures, transforming the conflict into politically feasible policy. In the process many claims are played off against one another, negotiations are undertaken, compromises are forged, and rewards are divided. Committees meet, commissions report, negotiators bargain, and powerful people 'haggle' about the policy.
4. The *formulation of policy* is the end result of the legislative stage. The articulated interests have gone through conflict and compromise stages and the final legislative action is taken. The policy is the official climax to the conflict and represents an authoritative, binding decision to commit the organization to one set of possible alternative actions, to one set of goals and values.
5. Finally the *execution of policy* occurs. The conflict comes to a climax, the battle is at least officially over, and the resulting policy is turned over to the bureaucrats for routine execution. This may not be the end of the matter, however, for two things are likely to happen. First, the major losers in the conflict may take up their arms again for a new round of interest articulation. Second, the execution of policy

inevitably causes a feedback cycle, in which the policy generates new tensions, new vested interests, and a new cycle of political conflict. (Baldridge, 1971: 23–4)

Perhaps the most significant aspect of the Baldridge model is that it is essentially iterative. The policy-making process is rarely straightforward. Rather, it is capable of breakdown at any stage, as opposing interests coalesce to defeat proposals and seek to substitute their own plans. This leads to the feedback processes which inevitably follow the breakdown of particular proposals. Ultimately, the success or failure of interest groups in promoting their objectives depends on the resources of power which they are able to mobilize.

Sources of power in education

Power may be regarded as the ability to determine the behaviour of others or to decide the outcomes of conflict. Where there is disagreement, it is likely to be resolved according to the relative resources of power available to the participants.

There are many sources of power, but in broad terms a distinction can be made between authority and influence. *Authority* is legitimate power which is vested in leaders within formal organizations. Authority involves a legal right to make decisions which may be supported by sanctions. 'Authorities are defined essentially as the people who are entitled to make binding decisions' (Bolman and Deal, 1991: 193). School heads and principals typically have substantial authority by virtue of their formal leadership positions.

Influence represents an ability to affect outcomes and depends on personal characteristics and expertise. Bacharach and Lawler (1980: 44) identify seven distinctions between authority and influence:

1. Authority is the static, structural aspect of power in organizations; influence is the dynamic, tactical element.
2. Authority is the formal aspect of power; influence is the informal aspect.
3. Authority refers to the formally sanctioned right to make final decisions; influence is not sanctioned by the organization and is, therefore, not a matter of organizational rights.
4. Authority implies involuntary submission by subordinates; influence implies voluntary submission and does not necessarily entail a superior–subordinate relationship.

5. Authority flows downward, and it is unidirectional; influence is multidirectional and can flow upward, downward, or horizontally.
6. The source of authority is solely structural; the source of influence may be personal characteristics, expertise, or opportunity.
7. Authority is circumscribed, that is, the domain, scope, and legitimacy of the power are specifically and clearly delimited; influence is uncircumscribed, that is, its domain, scope, and legitimacy are typically ambiguous.

As we noted in Chapter 1, formal authority is often associated with management while influence is the key dimension of leadership. Heads and principals possess positional authority and have the formal power to impose their views. Leadership may arise in any part of the organization and relies on personal qualities and attributes.

Hoyle (1982) points to the ways in which these two aspects of power operate within educational institutions:

> Influence differs from authority in having a number of sources in the organization, in being embedded in the actual relationships between groups rather than located in an abstract legal source, and is not fixed but is variable and operates through bargaining, manipulation, exchange and so forth. The head teacher in Britain has a high degree of authority; but [the] exercise of that authority is increasingly modified as teachers' sources of influence ... increase and thus involves the head in a greater degree of exchange and bargaining behaviour. (Ibid.: 90)

There are six significant forms of power relevant to schools and colleges:

1. *Positional power.* A major source of power in any organization is that accruing to individuals who hold an *official position* in the institution. Formal positions confer authority on their holders, who have a recognized right to make decisions or to play a key role in the policy-making process. Handy (1993: 128) says that positional power is 'legal' or 'legitimate' power. In schools, the head is regarded as the legitimate leader and possesses legal authority which is inevitably a key determinant of school policy. Other staff who hold senior posts may also exercise positional power. These may include deputy or associate principals, heads of department and pastoral leaders. Chairs of governing bodies or school boards may also exert positional power within self-managing schools and colleges. Cameron (2010) also points to the power exercised by external partners, for example the Secondary National Strategy (SNS) consultant in London: 'The SNS consultant has reinforced the influence or power that secondary school hierarchies have over teachers and departments'

(ibid.: 356). In a hierarchy, the more highly placed individuals exert the greater authority:

> The first and most obvious source of power in an organization is formal authority, a form of legitimized power that is respected and acknowledged by those with whom one interacts ... legitimacy is a form of social approval that is essential for stabilizing power relations. It arises when people recognize that a person has a right to rule some area of human life and that it is their duty to obey. (Morgan, 1997: 172)

2. *Authority of expertise.* In professional organizations there is a significant reservoir of power available to those who possess appropriate *expertise*. Handy (1993: 130) says that 'expert power is the power that is vested in someone because of their acknowledged expertise ... In a meritocratic tradition people do not resent being influenced by those whom they regard as the experts'. Schools and colleges employ many staff who have specialist knowledge of aspects of the curriculum. The music specialist, for example, is regarded as the expert in their field, and principals may be cautious in substituting their own judgements for those of their heads of department in curricular matters. In certain circumstances, there may be conflict between formal leaders and experts but the outcome is by no means certain:

> Expert power relates to the use of knowledge and expertise as a means of legitimizing what one wishes to do. 'The expert' often carries an aura of authority and power that can add considerable weight to a decision that rests in the balance. (Morgan, 1997: 181)

3. *Personal power.* Individuals who are charismatic or possess verbal skills or certain other characteristics may be able to exercise *personal power*. Staff who are able to influence behaviour or decisions by virtue of personal abilities or qualities are often thought to possess the attributes of charismatic leadership. These personal skills are independent of the power accruing to individuals by virtue of their position in the organization. In school staff rooms, for example, there are often individuals who command the respect of colleagues because of their perceived wisdom or insight. These teachers may become alternative leaders whose views are sought on the key issues. 'Individuals with charisma, political skills, verbal facility, or the capacity to articulate vision are powerful by virtue of their personal characteristics, in addition to whatever other power they may have' (Bolman and Deal, 1991: 197).

4. *Control of rewards.* Power is likely to be possessed to a significant degree by individuals who have *control of rewards*. They are inevitably

perceived as powerful by those who value such returns. In education, rewards may include promotion, good references and allocation to favoured classes or groups. Individuals who control or influence the allocation of these benefits may be able to determine the behaviour of teachers who seek one or more of the rewards. Typically, the head or principal is the major arbiter of promotion and references, although advice may be sought from heads of department or others who possess relevant knowledge or information. Classes may be allocated by heads of department. This form of power represents a means of control over aspiring teachers but may have little influence on those staff who choose to spurn these rewards. Control of rewards may be regarded as authority rather than influence where it emanates from the leader acting in an official capacity.

5. *Coercive power*. The mirror image of the control of rewards may be *coercive power*. This implies the ability to enforce compliance with a request or requirement. Coercion is backed by the threat of sanctions. 'Coercive power rests on the ability to constrain, to block, to interfere, or to punish' (Bolman and Deal, 1991: 196).

Heads and principals may exercise coercive power by threatening not to supply a good reference for external applications or warning about the prospects for internal promotion. In certain circumstances, coercion may be used in conjunction with the control of rewards to manipulate the behaviour of others. This 'carrot and stick' combination may have a powerful double effect on staff and may be a latent factor in all schools and colleges. Wallace and Hall (1994: 33) question the legitimacy of such manipulative actions: 'We suggest that action ... is manipulative either where it is a conscious attempt, covertly, to influence events through means or ends which are not made explicit; or where it is illegitimate, whether overt or not.'

6. *Control of resources*. Control of the *distribution of resources* may be an important source of power in educational institutions, particularly in self-managing schools and colleges. Decisions about the allocation of resources are likely to be among the most significant aspects of the policy process in such organizations. Resources include revenue and capital finance, but also human and material resources such as staff and equipment. Control of these resources may give power over those people who wish to acquire them. There is often competition between interest groups for additional resources and success or failure in acquiring extra finance, staff and other resources is an indicator of the relative power of individuals and groups:

> Resource management is ... a micropolitical process, providing an arena within which participants compete for the resources which will enable them to develop programmes of activity which embody their values, further their interests and help to provide legitimation for the activities in which they are engaged. (Simkins, 1998: 110)

While these six forms of power might be regarded as the most significant, Bolman and Deal (1991), Handy (1993) and Morgan (1997) identify several other sources, including:

- physical power
- developing alliances and networks
- access to and control of agendas
- control of meanings and symbols
- control of boundaries
- gender and the management of gender relations.

Consideration of all these sources of power leads to the conclusion that heads and principals possess substantial resources of authority and influence. They have the capacity to determine many institutional decisions and to affect the behaviour of their colleagues. However, they do not have absolute power. Other leaders and staff also have power, arising principally from their personal qualities and expertise, although Young and Brooks (2004) show that part-time teachers, for example, are often marginalized. Lay governors may also be powerful, particularly if they chair the governing board or one of its important committees. These other sources of power may act as a counterbalance to the head's positional authority and control of rewards.

Political strategies in education

Educational leaders may adopt one or more political strategies in order to maintain or extend their control or to ensure a favoured outcome to a decision-making process. Using their significant resources of power, they are often able to ensure support for, or compliance with, their preferred position. Hoyle (1986: 140–6) outlines some of the more significant strategies:

1. *Dividing and ruling.* This may involve heads arranging separate 'deals' with individuals or departments, for example in respect of resource allocation.
2. *Co-optation.* This entails the involvement of those who support the leader or whose potential opposition has to be diverted. It may be used simply to involve a certain individual in the decision-making

process or may be an attempt to manipulate the outcome.

3. *Displacement*. This occurs where the apparent issue is used to cloak the real purpose of the participant. A good example is where personal interests, such as status, are presented as 'professional'. This might occur where heads of department argue for more time for their subject.

4. *Controlling information*. Information is an important source of power. Heads and principals are the main recipients of external information and may use this to influence decisions. Curriculum specialists may also receive information related to their specific expertise.

5. *Controlling meetings*. Leaders may be able to control the outcomes of meetings by using one or more of the following devices:
   (a) 'rigging' agendas
   (b) 'losing' recommendations
   (c) 'nobbling' members of the group
   (d) 'invoking' outside bodies
   (e) 'massaging' minutes.

Political models: goals, structure, environment and leadership

Goals

Political models differ from both the formal and collegial approaches in that they focus primarily on the *goals* of sub-units, or looser groups of individuals, rather than the objectives of the institution itself. Ball (1987: 11) claims that the focus on organizational goals in much of the literature is a 'major distortion' and he prefers to emphasize the goal diversity of organizations, as does Caffyn (2010).

These models assume that groups advance their interests in the form of goals that are pursued vigorously within the institution. The collegial assumption that there is agreement over the goals of the organization is challenged by political theorists who argue that there is no such consensus: 'An assumption of consensus ... has extremely limited validity in almost all types of organizations' (Ball, 1987: 11).

Schools and colleges have multiple goals reflecting their various interest groups. These groups endeavour to promote their own objectives as the official purposes of the institution. Inevitably, the goals of the various groups sometimes conflict with one another because a focus on one objective may be at the expense of another: 'Goals may be inherently in conflict and ... these conflicts will become manifest when the goals are given a specific form in terms of pedagogy or curriculum' (Hoyle, 1986: 58).

Brown, Boyle and Boyle (2000: 43–44) point to the risk of apparently collegial frameworks becoming political. Their research with secondary school departments in England suggests that they develop sub-cultures which lead to the formulation of common aims and enables 'jointly held beliefs and values to flourish', but is separate from that of other departments and from the values of the senior management team, leading to an essentially micropolitical structure.

As a result of this inter-group conflict, goals tend to be ambiguous, unstable and contested. Bolman and Deal (1991: 189) stress that 'organisational goals arise not from fiat at the top, but from an ongoing process of negotiation and interaction among the key players in any system'. The capacity to secure institutional backing for group objectives depends crucially on the power of the interest group and the ability of its members to mobilize support from other sub-units and institutional leaders. There is a continuing process of negotiation and alliance building to muster sufficient support for the group's policy objectives. Goals are unstable because alliances break down and new factors are introduced into the bargaining process. The extant objectives may be usurped by purposes advanced by new coalitions of interests.

Ultimately, goals become 'organizational' according to the resources of power that can be mobilized in their support. The purposes of the most powerful groups emerge as organizational goals.

Organizational structure

Political models assume that *organizational structure* emerges from the process of bargaining and negotiation and may be subject to change as the interest groups jockey for position. Formal and collegial approaches present structure as a stable aspect of the organization, while political theorists regard it as one of the uncertain and conflictual elements of the institution. The structure is developed not so much for organizational effectiveness, as formal theorists suggest, but rather to determine which interests are to be served by the organization: 'Organisational structures[s] … are often understood as products and reflections of a struggle for political control … organizational structure is frequently used as a political instrument' (Morgan, 1997: 175–6).

Schools and colleges provide many illustrations of structure being established or adapted following political activity. A management team drawn primarily from heads of department, for example, may be seen as a device to reinforce their baronial power. Deal (2005: 114) advises leaders to use structure as a political asset: 'Politically, it is a way for a leader to consolidate power, reward allies or punish opponents'.

Hoyle (1986) argues that schools are particularly prone to political activity because of their 'loosely-coupled' structure (see Chapter 7). The partial autonomy of teachers and their authority of expertise, together with the sectional interests of different sub-units, leads to this structural looseness and the prevalence of 'micropolitics':

> The loosely-coupled structure of the school invites micropolitical activity since, although the head has a high degree of authority and responsibility, the relative autonomy of teachers and the norms of the teaching profession serve to limit the pervasiveness and scope of this power ... Thus heads frequently have recourse to micropolitical strategies in order to have their way. But teachers, too, are not without their micropolitical resources. (Hoyle, 1986: 171)

Secondary schools in many countries experience political activity because of their highly differentiated structure. In the Netherlands, for example, there are two parallel structures representing subject departments and student guidance units. Imants, Sleegers and Witziers (2001: 290) argue that these are 'conflicting sub-structures', leading to tension, fragmentation and barriers between teachers of different subjects.

The external environment

Political models emphasize the significance of *external influences* on internal decision-making. The political process includes inputs from outside bodies and individuals which are often mediated by the internal participants. Sergiovanni (1984) explains the nature of the interaction between educational institutions and external groups:

> The political perspective is concerned with the dynamic interplay of the organisation with forces in its external environment. Schools and universities, for example, are viewed as open rather than closed systems, as integral parts of a larger environment not as bounded entities isolated from their environment. They receive inputs, process them, and return outputs to the environment. Inputs are presumed to be diverse and output demands often conflicting. As a result there is constant interplay between school and environment. (Ibid.: 6)

In this respect, political approaches are similar to the open systems theories considered in Chapter 3. The major difference concerns the ways in which external pressures are imported into school or college decision-making. In formal models, it is assumed that outside influences are transmitted through heads or principals whose knowledge of the external environment reinforces their official authority. The leaders' interpretation of these pressures may then be a significant element in the decision-making process.

In political models it is thought that external factors may be introduced by interest groups as well as by heads and principals. School or college staff whose courses are vulnerable because of low enrolments may cite evidence from employers who value the threatened courses. These environmental pressures mingle with the internal factors and add to the complexity and ambiguity of decision-making.

The various groups which have an interest in educational institutions tend to have rather different motivations for their involvement. Official bodies may be concerned about educational standards, or 'value for money', and may exert their authority through the head or principal. Unofficial groups usually pursue sectional interests. Employers may want the school to instil particular skills, while parents understandably focus on the progress of their own children. These pressures may be transmitted through the staff most involved with their interests, rather than via the leader. Lindle (1999), referring to the American context, points to the importance of managing the competing demands of diverse community groups:

> The school setting is more political due to the increasing and competing demands placed on schooling ... No one said that public schooling was easy, but its public mission and visibility in the community make it an easy political target. The intimate relationship between schools and communities creates micropolitics. While the context of school is indelibly situated in a larger community, all communities are inherently political. (Ibid.: 173)

In many countries, teacher unions have a significant impact on schools and may provide a counterpoint to the official authority of principals. The South African Democratic Teachers' Union (SADTU), for example, has a powerful influence on school leadership and management. Bush et al. (2009) report that SADTU secured the agreement of the Mpumalanga provincial Education Department for teachers to leave the school for several hours to attend a union meeting. Principals were advised to 'ensure' that this did not disrupt classes but this was impossible to achieve as so many educators were missing.

The management of the external environment is a significant issue for leaders and participants in political organizations. Control of the 'boundary' between schools and their environments is an important source of influence in the debate about policies and resources. Knowledge about the opinions and predilections of clients and interest groups confers power:

By monitoring and controlling boundary transactions, people are able to build up considerable power ... Most people in leadership positions at all levels of an organization can engage in this kind of boundary management in a way that contributes to their power. (Morgan, 1997: 181)

Hoyle (1999: 217) adds that 'the nature of micropolitics has changed with the increasing permeability of the school boundary' – an explicit recognition that the greater the decentralization of power to self-managing schools, the greater the requirement for effective boundary management within what is essentially a political framework. Governing boards have a political role in representing community interests and harmonizing them with the aims and culture of the school.

Leadership

There are two central facets of leadership within political arenas. First, the head or principal is a key participant in the process of bargaining and negotiation. Leaders have their own values, interests and policy objectives which they seek to advance as appropriate at meetings of committees and in informal settings. Heads have substantial reserves of power which they may deploy in support of their personal and institutional goals. Leaders also have a significant impact on the nature of the internal decision-making process and can exercise a controlling influence on the proceedings of committees and other decision-making groups. West (1999) criticizes the political behaviour of British heads, arguing that they often seem to promote division rather than emphasizing the school as a whole unit. Inappropriate actions include:

- setting group against group, for example in reviewing public examination results
- generating win–lose competition, for example in bidding for resources
- isolating groups from the rest of the school, for example in the work of task groups.

Even at this basic level of micropolitical understanding, all too often school leaders display a naivety that is likely to lead to frustration and discontent for many of their staff. Deliberately seeking to increase understandings of how the formal and the informal interact and, above all, reducing the 'area of struggle' between groups by creating a commitment to further the school's interests, rather than their own, are priorities for school leaders. (West, 1999: 195)

The second facet of leadership concerns heads' responsibility to sustain the viability of the organization and to develop the framework within which policies can be tested and, ultimately, receive the endorsement of the various interest groups. To achieve acceptable outcomes, leaders become mediators who attempt to build coalitions in support of policies. There is a recurring pattern of discussion with representatives of power blocks to secure a measure of agreement. Bennett (1999), drawing on her experience as a principal of two schools in Tasmania, argues that communication is a critical skill for political leaders:

> It is critical to spend the time providing updates to stake-holders through newsletters, promotional material, public relations and marketing so that the various interest groups within the community understand the background behind a decision or an action. Inside the school, developing and maintaining channels of communication ... assists the principal [in] working with interest groups ... It is the responsibility of the principal to create opportunities for educational dialogue inviting people to seek clarification and to question how or why an action has occurred or a decision has been made. (Ibid.: 199)

Portin (1998), referring to research in Belgium, New Zealand, the United Kingdom and the United States, points to the need for principals to develop 'political acumen' as part of their pre-service and in-service preparation:

> Political acumen need not be viewed pejoratively as either manipulative or dominating forms of positional power. Instead, the skills needed here are a deep understanding of the micropolitical dimension of organizational governance, the means by which constituency interests and values are expressed, and an ability to take 'soundings' of the environment in order to inform site decision making. (Ibid.: 386)

Bolman and Deal (1991) summarize several of the issues in this section, recommending four 'rules' for political leaders:

- Political leaders clarify what they want and what they can get. They are 'realists above all'.
- Political leaders assess the distribution of power and interests. They must 'map the political terrain'.
- Political leaders build linkages to other stakeholders. They 'build relationships and networks'.
- Political leaders persuade first, negotiate second, and use coercion only if necessary. Power needs to be used 'judiciously'.

Deal (2005: 110) argues that 'organisations long for leaders who are masterful politicians', to manage a 'culturally splintered' world, while

Cassidy et al. (2008) suggest that 'leaders need to harmonise a multiplicity of purposes'.

Transactional leadership

The leadership model most closely aligned with micropolitics is that of transactional leadership. This is often contrasted with the transformational leadership model examined in Chapter 4. Miller and Miller (2001) explain these twin phenomena:

> Transactional leadership is leadership in which relationships with teachers are based upon an exchange for some valued resource. To the teacher, interaction between administrators and teachers is usually episodic, short-lived and limited to the exchange transaction. Transformational leadership is more potent and complex and occurs when one or more teachers engage with others in such a way that administrators and teachers raise one another to higher levels of commitment and dedication, motivation and morality. Through the transforming process, the motives of the leader and follower merge. (Ibid.: 182)

Miller and Miller's (2001) definition refers to transactional leadership as an exchange process while Judge and Piccolo (2004: 755) add that transactional leaders 'focus on the proper exchange of resources'. Exchange is an established political strategy for members of organizations. Heads and principals possess authority arising from their positions as the formal leaders of their institutions. They also hold power in the form of key rewards such as promotion and references. However, the head requires the co-operation of staff to secure the effective management of the school. An exchange may secure benefits for both parties to the arrangement.

Judge and Piccolo (2004: 755) say that there are three dimensions of transactional leadership:

- *Contingent reward.* The degree to which the leader sets up constructive exchanges with followers
- *Management by exception – active.* Active leaders monitor follower behaviour, anticipate problems, and take corrective actions
- *Management by exception – passive.* Passive leaders wait until the behaviour has caused problems before taking action.

Bolivar and Moreno (2006) report on leadership in Spain, where principals are elected by teachers and the community. Despite the apparent democratic legitimacy of this process, the authors report that principals are in 'permanent transaction' with colleagues, and that such processes inhibit change.

The major limitation of transactional leadership is that it does not engage staff beyond the immediate gains arising from the transaction. As Miller and Miller's definition implies, it does not produce long-term commitment to the values and vision being promoted by school leaders. However, Bass (1998: 11) stresses that leaders often use both transformational and transactional approaches: 'Consistent honouring of transactional agreements builds trust, dependability, and perceptions of consistency with leaders by followers, which are each a basis for transformational leadership'. Judge and Piccolo (2004: 765) conclude that 'transformational and transactional leadership are so highly related that it makes it difficult to separate their unique effects'.

The limitations of political models

Political models are primarily descriptive and analytical whereas most other theories tend to be normative. The focus on interests, conflict between groups, and power, provides a valid and persuasive interpretation of the decision-making process in schools and colleges. Teachers and managers often recognize the applicability of political models in their own schools and colleges. However, these theories do have five major limitations:

1. Political models are immersed so strongly in the language of power, conflict and manipulation that they neglect other standard aspects of organizations. There is little attempt to discuss the various processes of management or any real acknowledgement that most organizations operate for much of the time according to routine bureaucratic procedures. The focus is heavily on policy formulation while the implementation of policy receives little attention. Political perspectives probably understate the significance of organizational structure as a constraint on the nature of political activity. The outcomes of bargaining and negotiation are endorsed, or may falter, within the formal authority structure of the school or college. Bolman and Deal (1991: 238) say that 'the political perspective is so thoroughly focused on politics that it underestimates the significance of both rational and collaborative processes'.

2. Political models stress the influence of interest groups on decision-making and give little attention to the institutional level. The assumption is that organizations are fragmented into groups which pursue their own independent goals. These sub-units compete to estab-

lish the supremacy of their policy objectives and to secure their endorsement within the institution. This aspect of political models may be inappropriate for most English primary schools, which do not have a departmental structure or any other apparatus which could become a focal point for political activity. The institutional level may be the centre of attention for staff in these schools, invalidating the political model's emphasis on interest group fragmentation.

3. In political models there is too much emphasis on conflict and a neglect of the possibility of professional collaboration leading to agreed outcomes. The assumption that staff are continually engaged in a calculated pursuit of their own interests underestimates the capacity of teachers to work in harmony with colleagues for the benefit of their pupils and students. The focus on power as the determinant of outcomes may not be wholly appropriate for a cerebral profession such as teaching. In many situations, staff may well be engaged in genuine debate about the best outcomes for the school rather than evaluating every issue in terms of personal and group advantage: 'The [political] frame is normatively cynical and pessimistic. It overstates the inevitability of conflict and understates the potential for effective collaboration' (Bolman and Deal, 1991: 238).

4. Political models are regarded primarily as descriptive or explanatory theories. Their advocates claim that these approaches are realistic portrayals of the decision-making process in schools and colleges. Unlike collegial models, these theories are not intended to be normative or idealistic. There is no suggestion that teachers *should* pursue their own self-interest, simply an assessment, based on observation, that their behaviour is consistent with a political perspective. Nevertheless, the less attractive aspects, or 'dark side' (Cranston, 2008: 16), of political models lead to a view that they are 'intrinsically wrong' (Caffyn, 2010: 324).

> The amorality that often characterises political perspectives raises questions of values. To what extent does the political perspective, even as it purports to be simply a description of reality, ratify and sanctify some of the least humane and most unsavoury aspects of human systems? (Bolman and Deal, 1984: 146)

Morgan (1997: 212) adds that the emphasis on the cynical and the selfish may lead to the notion that there must be winners and losers and that 'the effect is to reduce the scope for genuine openness and collaboration'. Deal (2005: 112) acknowledges that political approaches may be seen as 'manipulative, dishonest and destructive' but cautions that power and conflict are 'natural by-products of co-operative activity'.

5. Political models offer valid insights into the operation of schools and colleges but it is often difficult to discern what constitutes political behaviour and what may be typical bureaucratic or collegial activity. The interpretation of group processes as either 'collegial' or 'political' is particularly difficult. Campbell and Southworth's (1993: 77) research in primary schools illustrates this point: 'It would be simplistic to say the heads in the collaborative schools controlled what happened there but they certainly exerted a great deal of influence and they sometimes used their power directly ... the heads ... revealed a micropolitical dimension to collegiality'.

Conclusion: are political models valid?

Hoyle (1986; 1999) distinguishes between theory-for-understanding, a tool for academics and students, and theory-for-action, a source of guidance for management practice. Political models are important in helping to develop understanding of how educational institutions operate. They provide rich descriptions and persuasive analysis of events and behaviour in schools and colleges. The explicit recognition of interests as prime motivators for action is valid. The acceptance that competing interests may lead to conflict, and that differential power ultimately determines the outcome, is a persuasive element in the analysis of educational institutions: 'The model of interests, conflict, and power ... provides a practical and systematic means of understanding the relationship between politics and organization and emphasizes the key role of power in determining political outcomes' (Morgan, 1997: 209).

Bolman and Deal (1991) argue that political models capture several of the essential features of institutions:

> The political frame presents the only realistic portrayal of organizations ... The political frame says that power and politics are central to organizations and cannot be swept under the rug. This perspective represents an important antidote to the antiseptic rationality sometimes present in structural analysis. (Ibid.: 237)

For many teachers and school leaders, political models fit their experience of day-to-day reality in schools and provide a guide to 'theory-for-action'. Bennett (1999), a Tasmanian school principal, shows how politics have influenced practice in her schools:

> Micropolitics exist in schools. It is important to consider how they are manifested and we need to move beyond saying that it is just personality

clashes or differences which leads to divisions. We need to understand that staff have different views of the world, that we can see politics in the various groups of school and, if we can recognize actors and ascertain what they are struggling over, this will influence how principals as leaders communicate, collaborate and decide courses of action. (Ibid.: 200)

Lindle (1999: 176), a school administrator in the United States, makes a similar point about politics-in-action, arguing that it is a pervasive feature in schools:

> Education is a more overtly contested terrain for communities and governments, teachers, parents and administrators. Schools have become more overtly political arenas in this context. The study of micropolitics is absolutely a question of survival for school leaders and other educators ... Not only is the study of micropolitics inevitable, advisable and unavoidable, for most school leaders, it is an inherent occupational requirement.

In both respects, understanding and action, political models have much to offer in developing an appreciation of the nature of management in schools and colleges. Political theorists rightly draw attention to the significance of groups as a potent influence on policy formulation. The emphasis on conflict may be overdrawn but it is valuable as a counterbalance to the idealistic harmony bias of collegial models. The view that disagreement is likely to be resolved ultimately by the relative power of participants is also a persuasive contribution to understanding and practice in educational institutions. Political models provide valuable insights into the operation of schools and colleges but they need to be considered alongside the formal and collegial models.

References

Bacharach, S.B. and Lawler, E.J. (1980) *Power and Politics in Organisations*, San Francisco, CA: Jossey-Bass.

Baldridge, J.V. (1971) *Power and Conflict in the University*, New York: John Wiley.

Ball, S. (1987) *The Micropolitics of the School: Towards a Theory of School Organization*, London: Methuen.

Bass, B.M. (1998) *Transformational Leadership: Industry, Military and Educational Impact*, Mahwah, NJ: Erlbaum.

Bennett, J. (1999) 'Micropolitics in the Tasmanian context of school reform', *School Leadership and Management*, 19(2): 197–200.

Bolivar, A. and Moreno, J.M. (2006) 'Between transaction and transformation: the role of school principals as education leaders in Spain', *Journal of Educational Change*, 7(1): 19–31.

Bolman, L.G. and Deal, T.E. (1984) *Modern Approaches to Understanding and Managing Organizations*, San Francisco, CA: Jossey-Bass.

Bolman, L. and Deal, T. (1991) *Reframing Organisations: Artistry, Choice and Leadership*, San Francisco, CA: Jossey-Bass.

Brown, M., Boyle, B. and Boyle, T. (2000) 'The shared management role of the head of department in English secondary schools', *Research in Education*, 63: 33–47.

Bush, T. and Moloi, K.C. (2007) 'Race, racism and discrimination in school leadership: evidence from England and South Africa', *International Studies in Educational Administration*, 35(1): 41–59.

Bush, T., Duku, N., Glover, D., Kiggundu, E., Msila, V. and Moorosi, P. (2009) *The Zenex ACE School Leadership Programme: Final Report,* Pretoria: Department of Education.

Caffyn, R. (2010) '"We are in Transylvania and Transylvania is not in England": location as a significant factor in international school micropolitics', *Educational Management, Administration and Leadership*, 38(3): 321–40.

Cameron, D. (2010) 'Working with secondary school leaders in a large-scale reform in London: consultants' perspectives of their role as agents of school change and improvement', *Educational Management, Administration and Leadership*, 38(3): 341–59.

Campbell, P. and Southworth, G. (1993) 'Rethinking collegiality: teachers' views', in N. Bennett, M. Crawford and C. Riches (eds), *Managing Change in Education: Individual and Organizational Perspectives*, London: Paul Chapman Publishing.

Cassidy, C., Christie, D., Couuts, N., Dunn, J., Sinclair, C, Skinner, D. and Wilson, A. (2008) 'Building communities of educational enquiry', *Oxford Review of Education*, 34(2): 217–35.

Cranston, N. (2008) 'Leading Queensland schools: what some of the research can tell us?', *International Studies in Educational Administration*, 36(2): 7–21.

Deal, T.E. (2005) 'Poetical and political leadership', in B. Davies (ed.), *The Essentials of School Leadership,* London: Paul Chapman Publishing.

Elstad, E. (2008) 'Towards a theory of mutual dependency between school administrators and teachers: bargaining theory as research heuristic', *Educational Management, Administration and Leadership*, 36(3): 393–414.

Handy, C. (1993) *Understanding Organizations*, London: Penguin.

Hoyle, E. (1982) 'Micropolitics of educational organisations', *Educational Management and Administration*, 10(2): 87–98.

Hoyle, E. (1986) *The Politics of School Management*, Sevenoaks: Hodder and Stoughton.

Hoyle, E. (1999) 'The two faces of micropolitics', *School Leadership and Management*, 19(2): 213–22.

Hoyle, E. and Wallace, M. (2005) *Educational Leadership: Ambiguity, Professionals and Managerialism,* London: Sage.

Imants, J., Sleegers, P. and Witziers, B. (2001) 'The tension between organisational sub-structures in secondary schools and educational reform', *School Leadership and Management*, 21(3): 289–308.

Judge, T. and Piccolo, R. (2004) 'Transformational and transactional leadership: a meta-analytic test of their relative validity', *Journal of Applied Psychology*, 89(5): 755–68.

Lindle (1999) 'What can the study of micropolitics contribute to the practice of leadership in reforming schools', *School Leadership and Management*, 19(2): 171–8.

Mawhinney, H. (1999) 'Reappraisal: the problems and prospects of studying the micropolitics of leadership in reforming schools', *School Leadership and Management*, 19(2): 159–70.

Miller, T.W. and Miller, J.M. (2001) 'Educational leadership in the new millennium: a vision for 2020', *International Journal of Leadership in Education*, 4(2): 181–9.

Milliken, J. (2001) '"Surfacing" the micropolitics as a potential management change frame in higher education', *Journal of Higher Education Policy and Management*, 23(1): 75–84.

Morgan, G. (1997) *Images of Organization*, Thousand Oaks, CA: Sage.

Portin, B. (1998) 'From change and challenge to new directions for school leadership', *International Journal for Educational Research*, 29: 381–91.

Salo, P. (2008) 'Decision-making as a struggle and a play: on alternative rationalities in schools as organisations', *Educational Management, Administration and Leadership*, 36(4): 495–510.

Sergiovanni, T.J. (1984) 'Cultural and competing perspectives in administrative theory and practice', in T.J. Sergiovanni and J.E. Corbally (eds), *Leadership and Organizational Culture*, Chicago, IL: University of Illinois Press.

Simkins, T. (1998) 'Autonomy, constraint and the strategic management of resources', in D. Middlewood and J. Lumby (eds), *Strategic Management in Schools and Colleges*, London: Paul Chapman Publishing.

Wallace, M. and Hall, V. (1994) *Inside the SMT: Teamwork in Secondary School Management*, London: Paul Chapman Publishing.

West, M. (1999) 'Micropolitics, leadership and all that … the need to increase the micropolitical awareness and skills of school leaders', *School Leadership and Management*, 19(2): 189–96.

Young, B. and Brooks, M. (2004) 'Part-time politics: the micropolitical world of part-time teaching', *Educational Management, Administration and Leadership*, 32(2): 129–48.

CHAPTER 6

Subjective models

Central features of subjective models

Subjective models incorporate those approaches which focus on individuals within organizations rather than the total institution or its sub-units. The individual is placed at the centre of the organization. These perspectives suggest that each person has a subjective and selective perception of the organization. Events and situations have different meanings for the various participants in institutions. Organizations are portrayed as complex units which reflect the numerous meanings and perceptions of all the people within them. Organizations are social constructions in the sense that they emerge from the interaction of their participants. They are manifestations of the values and beliefs of individuals rather than the concrete realities presented in formal models. The definition below captures the main elements of these approaches.

> Subjective models assume that organizations are the creations of the people within them. Participants are thought to interpret situations in different ways and these individual perceptions are derived from their background and values. Organizations have different meanings for each of their members and exist only in the experience of those members.

Hermes (1999: 198) offers a similar definition in applying subjective models to higher education in Germany, using the term 'construction' to mean interpretation of events: 'Subjective theories presuppose that human beings are autonomous and reflective beings, actively constructing the world around them'.

Subjective models include phenomenological and interactive approaches. While these perspectives are not identical, they are sufficiently close to be treated together and, indeed, are used interchangeably in much of the literature (Innes-Brown, 1993). Hoyle (1986) defines phenomenology and explains its link with interactionism:

> [These] perspectives share certain characteristics which constitute a radically different way of conceiving social reality ... The phenomenological approach gives priority to people and their actions. The social world essentially consists of people interacting with each other, negotiating patterns of relationships and constructing a view of the world. (Ibid.: 10)

Subjective models became prominent in educational management as a result of the work of Thomas Greenfield in the 1970s and 1980s. Greenfield was concerned about several aspects of systems theory which he regarded as the dominant model of educational organizations. He argues that systems theory is 'bad theory' and criticizes its focus on the institution as a concrete reality:

> Most theories of organisation grossly simplify the nature of the reality with which they deal. The drive to see the organisation as a single kind of entity with a life of its own apart from the perceptions and beliefs of those involved in it blinds us to its complexity and the variety of organisations people create around themselves. (Greenfield, 1973: 571)

Greenfield's criticism of conventional (largely bureaucratic) theory is even more trenchant in his 1986 article on 'the decline and fall of science in educational administration':

> We have a science of administration which can deal only with facts and which does so by eliminating from its consideration all human passion, weakness, conviction, hope, will, pity, frailty, altruism, courage, vice and virtue ... in its own impotence [it] is inward-looking, self-deluding, self-defeating, and unnecessarily boring. (Greenfield, 1986: 61)

Greenfield's work has had a significant impact on theory development in educational management, as Hodgkinson (1993: x) suggests: 'It is not possible to properly comprehend the contemporary discipline of educational administration without some familiarity and aquaintanceship with the thoughts of Thomas Barr Greenfield'. Greenfield is closely associated with the application of subjective theories to schools and colleges and much of the theory development has come from him, or from others stimulated or provoked by his work. As Evers and

Lakomski (1991: 97) put it, 'no adequate understanding of organisations seems possible without some appeal to human subjectivity, to the interpretations people place on their own actions and those of others'.

Subjective models have the following major features:

1. They focus on the beliefs and perceptions of *individual* members of organizations rather than the institutional level or interest groups. While formal and collegial models stress the total institution, and political models emphasize sub-groups, the individual is at the heart of subjective or phenomenological theories. Subjective models 'focus on the individual and emphasize individual perspectives' (Hermes, 1999: 198).

   Within schools and colleges, subjective theorists point to the different values and aspirations of individual teachers, support staff and pupils. They all experience the institution from different standpoints and interpret events and situations according to their own background and motivations. Ribbins et al. (1981) argue that:

   > The school is not the same reality for all its teachers. Each teacher brings a perspective to the school, and to his place within it, which is to some extent unique. There are ... as many realities as there are teachers. (Ibid.: 170)

   The focus on individuals rather than the organization is a fundamental difference between subjective and formal models, and creates what Hodgkinson (1993) regards as an unbridgeable divide:

   > In the tension between individual and organization ... there is more than a mere dialectical conflict. There can also be a chasm, a Great Divide, an abyss. A fact can never entail a value, and an individual can never become a collective. (Ibid.: xii, original emphases).

   Strain (1996) takes a somewhat different view, pointing to the interdependence of individual and collective meanings:

   > The social world, of which education is an institutional part, spans the ... individual and the ... collectivity. The relationship between the two is reflexive ... The individual, by virtue of his imagining faculty, power to create meanings, cannot act meaningfully in isolation from the symbolically ordered collectivity ... but neither individual nor collectivity can be conceived of as subordinated to or originated by the other. (Ibid.: 51)

2. Subjective models are concerned with the *meanings* placed on events by people within organizations. The focus is on the individual interpretation of behaviour rather than the situations and actions

themselves. According to Greenfield (1975: 83), 'Organisations are to be understood in terms of people's beliefs about their behaviour within them', rather than on the basis of external observations of that behaviour. It is assumed that individuals may have different interpretations of the same event:

> What is most important about an event is not what happened but what it means. Events and meanings are loosely coupled: the same events can have very different meanings for different people because of differences in the schema that they use to interpret their experience. (Bolman and Deal, 1991: 244)

To explain any social phenomenon it is necessary to establish the subjective meanings which relevant actors attach to the phenomenon (Best et al., 1983: 58).

In schools there may be differences of interpretation between the head and other staff who often derive divergent meanings from the same event. Hoyle (1981: 45) draws attention to one familiar example of such discrepancies:

> When a head talks about his [sic] school on public occasions teachers often remark that they do not recognise the place, and, because this view of reality is different from that of the head's they may assume that he is deliberately misleading. But a phenomenological view would hold that we have here competing realities, the head and the teachers see the world differently with each perspective having its own legitimacy. (Ibid.: 45, original emphasis)

This case illustrates the point that the school or college may be conceptualized differently by the various individuals and groups in the organization. These participants construct a reality out of their interests and any commonality of perspective arises from the fortuitous fact that their interests are held in common (Hoyle, 1986).

In this respect, there are certain similarities between subjective theory and organizational culture. Culture is also an outcome of the meanings and values of the people who inhabit schools and colleges. 'Culture is a useful if intricate and elusive notion. In its broadest sense it is a way of constructing reality and different cultures are simply alternative constructions of reality' (Prosser, 1999: xii). The main difference between these two concepts is that subjective models focus on individual meanings while culture assumes that these coalesce to produce a distinctive whole-school or sub-unit culture. We shall examine culture in more detail in Chapter 8.

3. The different meanings placed on situations by the various participants are products of their *values, background* and *experience*. So the interpre-

tation of events depends on the beliefs held by each member of the organization. Holmes (1986) argues that it is 'bizarre' to develop a theory of educational administration outside a framework of values:

> The lack of consensus about the purpose of elementary and secondary schools makes it more important rather than less to have a clear framework of goals and values. The modern idea that schools can function in a value-free atmosphere brings the whole educational profession, and particularly administrators, into disrepute. (Ibid.: 80)

Allix (2000: 13) notes that the separation of objective facts and subjective values has 'had a profound impact on theorizing in educational administration'. Branson (2007: 226) adds that leaders' values closely guide their actions. Drawing on research with primary school principals in Queensland, he claims that 'authentic leaders' need to have self-knowledge of their values.

Strain (1996: 59) argues that 'choice ... is always a subjective affair' and identifies three sets of beliefs in examining the choice behaviour of individuals:
(a) beliefs about the world; how it works and should work
(b) beliefs about the chooser's own situation; what is feasible and desirable in relation to a set of actions which seem to be available
(c) beliefs about a range of desirable outcomes (ibid.: 54).
While leading on the basis of values is widely advocated, it is difficult for principals to substitute their values for those of their national education bodies. In England, for example, headteachers operate within a centralized policy framework (Bottery, 2001).

> The scope for leaders to act according to their own values is circumscribed by central power. To disagree is to risk censure by the Office for Standards in Education (Ofsted). Leaders are free to pursue their own values only if they are consistent with those of central government. (Bush, 2008: 278)

Greenfield (1979) asserts that formal theories make the mistake of treating the meanings of leaders as if they were the objective realities of the organization:

> Life in organisations is filled with contending ideologies ... Too frequently in the past, organisation and administrative theory has ... taken sides in the ideological battles of social process and presented as 'theory' the views of a dominating set of values, the views of rulers, elites, and their administrators. (Ibid.: 103)

One possible outcome of the different meanings placed on events may be conflict between participants. In this respect, subjective models may take on some of the characteristics of political theories. Where meanings coincide, individuals may come together in groups and engage in political behaviour in pursuit of objectives. Greenfield (1986: 72) relates conflict to differences in values: 'Conflict is endemic in organizations. It arises when different individuals or groups hold opposing values or when they must choose between accepted but incompatible values. Administrators represent values, but they also impose them'. In subjective models, then, conflict is regarded as the product of competing values. However, conflict is only one of several possible outcomes and should not be regarded as a norm. Rather the assumption is that meanings are highly personal, often subtle, and subject to the values and experience of participants.

4. Subjective models treat *structure* as a product of human interaction rather than something which is fixed or predetermined. The organization charts which are characteristic of formal models are regarded as fictions in that they cannot predict the behaviour of individuals. Subjective theorists reject the view that people have to conform to the structure of organizations. Rather, they argue that structure derives from what people do.

Subjective approaches move the emphasis away from structure towards a consideration of behaviour and process. Individual behaviour is thought to reflect the personal qualities and aspirations of the participants rather than the formal roles they occupy. Greenfield (1980) claims that the variable nature of human behaviour means that organizations are subject to change:

> There is no ultimate reality about organisations, only a state of constant flux. Organisations are at once both the products of action and its cause. We act out of past circumstances and drive towards those we intend for the future. Social realities are constantly created and reshaped. (Ibid.: 40)

Subjective theorists are particularly critical of those models which attribute 'human' characteristics to organizations or regard structure as something independent of its members. In this view, schools and colleges do not have an existence which is separate from the actions and behaviours of their staff, students and stakeholders. 'Organisations exist to serve human needs, rather than the reverse' (Bolman and Deal, 1991: 121).

This subjective perspective on the relative significance of structure and behaviour has implications for the management of organizations. It suggests that more attention should be given to the theory and practice of staff motivation, and to other aspects of human resource management, and that rather less significance should be attached to issues of organizational structure.

5. Subjective approaches emphasize the significance of individual purposes and deny the existence of organizational *goals*. Greenfield (1973: 553) asks, 'What is an organisation that it can have such a thing as a goal?' The view that organizations are simply the product of the interaction of their members leads naturally to the assumption that individuals, and not organizations, have objectives. The formal model's portrayal of organizations as powerful goal-seeking entities is treated with disdain. In this model, purposes and aims are individual, not organizational. However, Best et al.'s (1983) research on pastoral care in 'Rivendell' school shows that individual meanings clustered into five broad perspectives:

- child-centred
- pupil-centred
- discipline-centred
- administrator-centred
- subject-centred

This research demonstrates that a binary distinction between organizational and individual meanings may be too simplistic and fine-grained analysis needs to allow for clusters of interpretations to emerge.

Subjective models and qualitative research

The theoretical dialectic between formal and subjective models is reflected in the often lively debate about positivism and interpretivism in educational research. Positivist research, like the formal models, adheres to a scientific approach. People are the objects of research and 'scientific' knowledge is obtained through the collection of verified facts that are essentially 'value free' and can lead to generalizations (Morrison, 2007). 'Explanation proceeds by way of scientific description' (Cohen et al., 2000: 8). In contrast, subjective models relate to a mode of research which is predominantly interpretive or qualitative. This approach to enquiry is based on the subjective experience of individuals. The main aim is to seek understanding of the ways in which individuals create, modify and interpret the social world which they inhabit. It is concerned with meanings more than facts and this is one of the major differences between qualitative and quantitative research. The link between qualitative research and subjective models is evident in two definitions:

> [Qualitative research] stresses the importance of the subjective experience of individuals in the creation of the social world ... The principal concern is with an understanding of the way in which he or she finds himself or herself. The approach now takes on a qualitative ... aspect. (Cohen et al., 2000: 7)

> All human life is experienced and constructed from a subjective perspective. For an interpretivist, there cannot be an objective reality which exists irrespective of the meanings people bring to it ... Therefore, the data collected and analysed have qualitative rather than quantitative significance. (Morrison, 2007: 27)

The main features of interpretive, or qualitative, research echo those of the subjective models:

1. They focus on the perceptions of *individuals* rather than the whole organization. The subject's individual perspective is central to qualitative research (Morrison, 2007: 20). Interviews, for example, are respondent-centred and have few if any frameworks, so that the participants' meanings can predominate.
2. Interpretive research is concerned with the *meanings*, or interpretations, placed on events by participants. The focus is on individual interpretation rather than the situations or actions themselves. All human life is experienced from a subjective perspective. Cohen, Manion and Morrison (2000: 22) note that subjective consciousness has primacy in qualitative research and that 'the central endeavour ... is to understand the subjective world of human experience'.
3. Qualitative research pays much attention to detailed observation, leading to 'rich' and 'deep' description (Morrison, 2007: 27)
4. Research findings are interpreted using 'grounded' theory in contrast to positivist researchers who generally 'devise general theories of human behaviour and [seek] to validate them through the use of increasingly complex research methodologies' (Cohen et al., 2000: 23). The use of theory is very different for interpretive researchers: 'Theory is emergent and must arise from particular situations; it should be "grounded" on data generated by the research act. Theory should not precede research but follow it' (ibid.: 23).

Just as researchers seek the individual perceptions of participants, leaders and managers have to be aware of the individual needs of their colleagues and stakeholders. A recognition of the different values and motivations of the people who work in, or relate to, schools and colleges, is essential if they are to be led and managed effectively.

Subjective models: goals, structure, environment and leadership

Goals

Subjective models differ from other approaches in that they stress the goals of individuals rather than the objectives of the institution or its sub-units. Members of organizations are thought to have their own personal aims which they seek to achieve within the institution. The notion of organizational objectives, central to formal and collegial models, is rejected. Teachers and school leaders pursue their own goals, although principals, in particular, may present their personal aims as school purposes. Often, however, they are not concerned with wider institutional issues but reflect the personal wishes of the staff as individuals. Greenfield (1973: 568) argues that, 'Many people do not hold goals ... in the sense of *ends* that the organisation is to accomplish, but merely hold a set of beliefs about what it is *right* to do in an organisation' (original emphases).

The denial of the concept of organizational goals creates difficulties because teachers are usually aware of the purposes and aims of schools and colleges. Many staff acknowledge the existence of school-wide goals such as teaching all children to read or achieving a good record in public examinations. At a common-sense level, these are regarded as organizational objectives.

Greenfield (1973: 557) suggests that goals which appear to be those of the organization are really the objectives of powerful individuals within the institution: 'The goals of the organisation are the current preoccupations and intentions of the dominant organisational coalition'. In schools it is assumed that headteachers may possess sufficient power to promote their own purposes as the objectives of the institution. Organizational goals are a chimera; they are simply the personal aims of the most powerful individuals. In this respect, subjective models are similar to political theories.

Two of the nine English primary schools researched by Bennett et al. (2000) illustrate the view that school aims are really those of the head-teacher:

> The head [of Padingwick] was very much a visionary ... [T]he head had a clear view of what needed to be done to improve the school and how this created particular priorities at particular times. He spearheaded a series of improvement initiatives. (Ibid.: 341, 343)

The head [of Elms] was described as a strong leader, who led from the front but was sympathetic to others ... there was a clear sense of direction – to improve standards further and provide a lively and supportive learning environment for children. The head was a key figure in this: she was seen as 'knowing what she wants for the school'. (Ibid.: 342)

These examples support the subjective view that organizational goals are really the personal aims of influential people within schools and colleges. The subjective model's emphasis on individual goals is a valuable counter to the formal assumption about 'organizational' goals.

Hoyle and Wallace (2005) refer to the tendency to reify schools and add that school policies and 'visions' may simply reflect the wishes of the principal. Reification occurs where:

a collectivity such as a school is referred to as if it was a corporate entity capable of corporate action independent of the people who constitute it ... Reification is often allied with the visionary rhetoric now widely expected of school leaders. (Ibid.: 12–13)

They add that vision is usually expressed as the property of an entity (the school) rather than the individual (the headteacher).

Organizational structure

Subjective models regard *organizational structure* as an outcome of the interaction of participants rather than a fixed entity which is independent of the people within the institution. Structure is a product of the behaviour of individuals and serves to explain the relationships between members of organizations. Formal and collegial models tend to regard structure as a fixed and stable aspect of organizations while subjective theories emphasize the different meanings placed on structure by the individuals within the institution. For example, the senior leadership team might be portrayed as a participative forum by the headteacher but be regarded by other staff as a vehicle for the one-way dissemination of information.

Teachers interpret relationships in schools and colleges in different ways and, in doing so, they influence the structures within their institutions. However, there are variations in the amount of power which individuals can wield in seeking to modify structure. In education, heads and principals are often able to impose their interpretations of structure on the institutions they lead. They can introduce a faculty structure to promote inter-departmental co-operation, for example, but the effectiveness of such a change depends crucially on the attitudes of the staff concerned.

Lumby's (2001) research with English further education colleges demonstrates the complex relationship between organizational structure and the attitudes of managers and staff. She notes that, in the period following major reform in the early 1990s, most colleges had restructured but the motivation for change owed more to managers' desire for control than to any other factor:

> The restructuring process followed the appointment of a new principal or a merger, and did not seem to be in response to particular factors but, rather, the principal's vehicle for making a new start, placing people in new roles where they might have a vested interest in supporting the new order. Restructuring can therefore be seen as both a process for response to the external environment and an internal political process of reshaping power. (Lumby, 2001: 89)

Structural change alone may be ineffective if it lacks the support of the people within the organization, as Greenfield demonstrates:

> Shifting the external trappings of organisation, which we may call organisation structure if we wish, turns out to be easier than altering the deeper meanings and purposes which people express through organisation ... we are forced to see problems of organisational structure as inherent not in 'structure' itself but in the human meanings and purposes which support that structure. Thus it appears that we cannot solve organisational problems by either abolishing or improving structure alone; we must also look at their human foundations. (1973: 565)

While accepting the strictures of Greenfield about the limitations of structural change, there are obvious difficulties in understanding and responding to numerous personal interpretations of situations in organizations. The elusive and variable nature of human meanings suggests that organizational change may be a slow and uncertain process because it depends primarily on an understanding of individual wishes and beliefs.

Subjective theorists may be more interested in processes and relationships than in structure. While structure relates to the institutional level, subjective models focus on individuals and their interpretations of events and situations. The emphasis is on small-scale issues of concern to people rather than the macro-level of organizational structure: 'The phenomenologist is less concerned with structures than with processes involved at the microcosmic level as groups construct new realities within the framework of relatively enduring institutions' (Hoyle, 1986: 14).

The external environment

In subjective models little attention is paid to relationships between organizations and their *external environments*. This may be because organizations are not portrayed as viable entities. The focus is on the meanings placed on events by people within the organization rather than interaction between the institution and groups or individuals external to it. The notion of outside bodies exerting influence on the school or college makes little sense when subjective models claim that organizations have no existence independent of the individuals within them.

Where subjective models deal with the environment at all, the emphasis is on links between individuals within and outside the organization rather than external pressures on the total institution. The assumption that human behaviour stems from a personal interpretation of events raises the issue of the source of these meanings. Subjective theorists argue that they emanate from the external environment: 'The kinds of organisation we live in derive not from their structure but from attitudes and experiences we bring to organisations from the wider society in which we live' (Greenfield, 1973: 558).

In education, the interpretations of individuals may originate from several sources. For teachers a major influence is the socialization that results from their induction into the profession. The process of socialization may be reinforced through interaction with significant individuals who emanate from the same professional background. These may include other teachers and school leaders, education officers, inspectors and university lecturers. These professional contacts tend to produce shared meanings and values.

Teachers are also subject to personal influences, such as their family, friends and members of clubs and societies external to the school. These sources may lead to a diversity of meanings. Greenfield (1973) prefers to emphasize differences in interpretation rather than shared meanings:

> This notion of organisations as dependent upon meanings and purposes which individuals bring to organisations from the wider society does not require that all individuals share the same meanings and purposes. On the contrary, the views I am outlining here should make us seek to discover the varying meanings and objectives that individuals bring to the organisations of which they are a part. (Ibid.: 559)

Formal models stress the accountability of organizations, and senior staff within them, to certain groups and individuals in the external environment. Subjective theories give little attention to this issue but the focus is implicitly on the answerability of individual teachers rather than the accountability of the institution itself (Bush, 1994). Accountability may be primarily to the individual's own beliefs and values rather than to organizational leaders. While the focus on individual accountability is legitimate, because it is people who act, the subjective model fails to deal with the expectations of external groups and individuals who often require an explanation of institutional policies and practice.

Leadership

The concept of *leadership* fits rather uneasily within the framework of subjective models. Individuals place different meanings on events and this applies to all members, whatever their formal position in the organization. People who occupy leadership roles have their own values, beliefs and goals. All participants, including leaders, pursue their own interests. A significant difference, however, is that leaders of organizations may be in a position to impose their interpretations of events on other members of the institution. Leadership and management may be seen as forms of control, with heads and principals elevating their meanings to the status of school or college policy. These leaders may use their resources of power to require compliance with these interpretations even where other staff do not share those meanings.

Subjective theorists prefer to stress the personal qualities of individuals rather than their official positions in the organization. Situations require appropriate responses and these may arise from those best suited to address them, regardless of their formal position in the school. This emphasis on the personal attributes of staff suggests that formal roles are an inadequate guide to behaviour. Rather, individuals bring their own values and meanings to their work and interpret their roles in different ways according to their beliefs and experience.

The subjective view is that leadership is a product of personal qualities and skills and not simply an automatic outcome of official authority. However, positional power also remains significant. Perhaps the most effective leaders are those who have positional power *and* the personal qualities to command the respect of colleagues, a combination of the formal and subjective perspectives.

Postmodern leadership

The notion of postmodern leadership aligns closely with the principles of subjective models. This is a relatively recent model of leadership which has no generally agreed definition. For example, Starratt's (2001: 334) discussion of 'a postmodern theory of democratic leadership' does not define the concept beyond suggesting that postmodernism might legitimize the practice of democratic leadership in schools.

Keough and Tobin (2001: 2) say that 'current postmodern culture celebrates the multiplicity of subjective truths as defined by experience and revels in the loss of absolute authority'. They identify several key features of postmodernism:

- Language does not reflect reality.
- Reality does not exist; there are multiple realities.
- Any situation is open to multiple interpretations.
- Situations must be understood at local level with particular attention to diversity (ibid.: 11–13).

Similarly, Sackney and Mitchell (2001) refer to 'widely divergent meanings' (ibid.: 6) and to 'alternative truth claims' (ibid.: 9). They add that power is located throughout the organisation and 'enacted by all members' (ibid.: 11), leading to empowerment.

Grogan and Simmons (2007) stress that postmodern leadership developed as a reaction to theories presented as having universal application, such as several of the formal or scientific theories, and show its links to the subjective model:

> Central to most post-modern theories is an interest in language, subjectivity and meaning ... researchers taking a postmodern stance would shy away from utilising grand or formal theories in their work ... a postmodern stance on educational leadership questions the very notion of seeking truth and objectivity in research. (Ibid.: 39)

The postmodern model offers few clues to how leaders are expected to operate. This is also a weakness of the parallel Greenfield (1973) model. The most useful point to emerge from such analyses is that leaders should respect, and give attention to, the diverse and individual perspectives of stakeholders. They should also avoid reliance on the hierarchy because this concept has little meaning in such a fluid organization. Starratt (2001) aligns postmodernity with democracy and advocates a 'more consultative, participatory, inclusionary stance' (ibid.: 348), an approach which is consistent with collegiality (see Chapter 4).

Sackney and Mitchell (2001: 13–14) stress the centrality of individual interpretations of events while also criticizing transformational leadership as potentially manipulative: 'Leaders must pay attention to the cultural and symbolic structure of meaning construed by individuals and groups ... postmodern theories of leadership take the focus off vision and place it squarely on voice'. Instead of a compelling vision articulated by leaders, there are multiple visions and diverse cultural meanings.

Emotional leadership

Crawford (2009) demonstrates the links between the emerging notion of emotional leadership and the subjective model. She stresses that emotion is concerned with individual motivation and interpretation of events, rather than emphasizing the fixed and the predictable, and criticizes much of the current literature on leadership for underestimating this dimension:

> The educational leadership literature rarely considers headship from the perspective of the headteacher – in other words, 'what does it feel like to be in that role?'. This is probably because such subjectivity is viewed, in an accountability culture, as suspect. I would argue that understanding the emotions of leadership is a key to long-term sustainability and high functioning in headship. (Ibid.: 15)

Crawford (2009) adds that emotion is socially constructed and stresses the importance of individual interpretations of events and situations: 'perception is reality'.

Beatty (2005: 124) also notes the importance of emotional leadership and contrasts it with bureaucratic approaches: 'When I look at Weber's iron cage of bureaucracy … I see rungs of emotional silence. Emotional silence may be the most powerful self-replicating mechanism of bureaucratic hierarchy – in schools and elsewhere'. She adds that hierarchical stratifications and silos of specialization are anathema to the creation of dynamic learning communities. 'To overcome the anachronistic view of leadership as located exclusively at the top is itself an emotional challenge' (ibid.: 125). Crawford (2009: 164) concludes that 'educational leadership cannot, and does not, function without emotion'.

The limitations of subjective models

Subjective models are prescriptive approaches in that they reflect beliefs about the nature of organizations rather than presenting a clear framework for analysis. Their protagonists make several cogent points about educational institutions but this alternative perspective does not represent a comprehensive approach to the management of schools and colleges. Subjective models can be regarded as 'anti-theories' in that they emerged as a reaction to the perceived limitations of the formal models. Similarly, interpretivist approaches to research may be seen as anti-positivist (Morrison, 2007). Greenfield is zealous in his advocacy of subjective approaches and his rejection of many of the central assumptions of conventional organizational theory.

Although subjective models introduce several important concepts into the theory of educational management, they have four significant weaknesses which serve to limit their validity:

1. Subjective models are *strongly normative* in that they reflect the attitudes and beliefs of their supporters. Greenfield, in particular, has faced a barrage of criticism, much of it fuelled by emotion rather than reason, for his advocacy of these theories. As long ago as 1980, Willower claimed that subjective models are 'ideological':

   > [Phenomenological] perspectives feature major ideological components and their partisans tend to be true believers when promulgating their positions rather than offering them for critical examination and test ... The message is being preached by recent converts who ... now embrace it wholeheartedly and with the dedication of the convert. (Willower, 1980: 7)

   This comment serves to illustrate the intensity of feelings engendered by Greenfield's challenge to conventional theory. Nevertheless, there is substance in Willower's criticism. Subjective models comprise a series of principles, which have attracted the committed support of a few adherents, rather than a coherent body of theory: 'Greenfield sets out to destroy the central principles of conventional theory but consistently rejects the idea of proposing a precisely formulated alternative' (Hughes and Bush, 1991: 241).

2. Subjective models seem to assume the existence of an *organization* within which individual behaviour and interpretation occur but there is no clear indication of the nature of the organization. It is acknowledged that teachers work within a school or college, but these bodies are not recognized as viable organizations. Educational institutions are thought to have no structure beyond that created by their members. The notion of school and college objectives is dismissed because only people can have goals. So organizations are nothing more than a product of the meanings of their participants. In emphasizing the interpretations of individuals, subjective theorists neglect the institutions within which individuals behave, interact and derive meanings.

3. Subjective theorists imply that *meanings* are so individual that there may be as many interpretations as people. In practice, though, these meanings tend to cluster into patterns which do enable participants and observers to make valid generalizations about organizations. The notion of totally independent perceptions is suspect because individual meanings depend on participants' background and experience. Teachers, for example, emanate from a common professional background which often results in shared meanings and purposes. As noted earlier, perceptions of pastoral care at 'Rivendell' clustered into five broad perspectives (Best et al., 1983). Activities in schools cannot simply be reduced to a series of individual interpretations.

   Subjective models also fail to explain the many similarities between schools. If individual perceptions provide the only valid definitions of organizations, why do educational institutions have so many common features? A teacher from one school would find some unique qualities in other schools but would also come across many familiar characteristics. This suggests that there is an entity called a 'school' which may evoke similar impressions amongst participants and observers.

4. A major criticism of subjective models is that they provide few guidelines for managerial action. Leaders are left with little more than the need to acknowledge the individual meanings placed on events by members of organizations. Formal models stress the authority of heads to make decisions while pointing to the need to acknowledge the place of official groups such as management teams and governing bodies. Collegial models emphasize the desirability of reaching agreement with colleagues and providing opportunities for participation in decision-making. Political models accentuate the significance of building coalitions among interest groups in order to ensure support for policy proposals. Subjective models offer no such formula for the development of leadership strategies, but the focus on the individual may provide some guidance. The leader may seek to influence individual behaviour through the application of motivation theory in order to produce a better 'fit' between the participant's personal wishes and the leader's preferences. This stance may help leaders but it is much less secure than the precepts of the formal model. As Greenfield (1980: 27) acknowledges: 'This conception of organisations does not make them easy to control or to change'.

Conclusion: the importance of the individual

The subjective model has introduced some important considerations into the debate on the nature of schools and colleges. The emphasis on the primacy of individual meanings is a valuable aid to our understanding of educational institutions. A recognition of the different values and motivations of the people who work in organizations is an essential element if they are to be managed successfully. Certainly teachers are not simply automatons carrying out routine activities with mechanical precision. Rather, they deploy their individual skills and talents for the benefit of pupils and students.

The subjective model is also valuable in providing conceptual underpinning for interpretive research methodology. The focus on the individual perceptions of actors is at the heart of qualitative research. Similarly, subjective models have close links with the emerging, but still weakly defined, notion of postmodern leadership, as well as the developing sub-field of emotional leadership. Leaders need to attend to the multiple voices in their organizations and develop a 'power to' not a 'power over' model of leadership. However, as Sackney and Mitchell (2001: 19) note, 'we do not see how postmodern leadership … can be undertaken without the active engagement of the school principal'. In other words, the subjective approach works only if leaders wish it to work, a fragile basis for any approach to educational leadership.

Subjective models provide a significant new slant on organizations but the perspective is *partial*. The stress on individual interpretation of events is valid but ultimately it leads to a blind alley. If there are as many meanings as teachers, as Greenfield claims, our capacity to understand educational institutions is likely to be fully stretched. If individual meanings are themselves subject to variation according to the context, as Sackney and Mitchell (2001: 8) suggest, then the number of permutations is likely to be overwhelming. In practice, however, interpretations do cluster into patterns, if only because shared meanings emerge from the professional socialization undergone by teachers during training and induction. If there are common meanings, it is possible to derive some generalizations about behaviour.

The subjective perspective does offer some valuable insights which act as a corrective to the more rigid features of formal models. The focus on individual interpretations of events is a useful antidote to the uniformity of systems and structural theories. Similarly, the emphasis on individual aims, rather than organizational objectives, is an important contribution to our understanding of schools and colleges. Greenfield's work has broadened our understanding of educational institutions and exposed the weaknesses of the formal models. His admirers stress the significance of his contribution to organizational theory:

> Greenfield ... has almost single-handedly led a generation of educational administration theorists to a new perspective on their work. It seems indisputable that a decade from now ... Greenfield's work will be regarded as truly pioneering. (Crowther, 1990: 15)

> To understand Greenfield, whether one agrees with him or not, is to understand the nature of organizational reality better and to be better able to advance the state of the art. (Hodgkinson, 1993: xvi)

Despite these eulogies, it is evident that subjective models have supplemented, rather than supplanted, the formal theories Greenfield set out to attack. While his focus on individual meanings is widely applauded, the notion of schools and colleges as organizational entities has not been discarded. There is a wider appreciation of events and behaviour in education but many of the assumptions underpinning the formal model remain dominant in both theory and practice.

The search for a synthesis between formal models and Greenfield's analysis has scarcely begun. One way of understanding the relationship between formal and subjective models may be in terms of scale. Formal models are particularly helpful in understanding the total institution and its relationships with external bodies. In education, the interaction between schools and national or local government may be explained best by using bureaucratic and structural concepts. However, the subjective model may be especially valid in examining individual behaviour and relationships between individuals. Formal and subjective models thus provide complementary approaches to our understanding of organizations. The official structure of schools and colleges should be examined alongside consideration of the individual behaviour and perceptions of staff and students. While institutions cannot be understood fully without an assessment of the meanings of participants, these interpretations are of limited value unless the more formal and stable aspects of organizations are also examined.

References

Allix, N. (2000) 'Transformational leadership: democratic or despotic?', *Educational Management and Administration*, 28(1): 7–20.

Beatty, B. (2005) 'Emotional leadership', in B. Davies (ed.), *The Essentials of School Leadership*, London: Paul Chapman Publishing.

Bennett, N., Crawford, M., Levačić, R., Glover, D. and Earley, P. (2000) 'The reality of school development planning in the effective primary school: technicist or guiding plan?', *School Leadership and Management*, 20(3): 333–51.

Best, R., Ribbins, P., Jarvis, C. and Oddy, D. (1983) *Education and Care*, London: Heinemann.

Bolman, L. and Deal, T. (1991) *Reframing Organisations: Artistry, Choice and Leadership*, San Francisco, CA: Jossey-Bass.

Bottery, M. (2001), 'Globalisation and the UK competition state: no room for transformational leadership in education', *School Leadership and Management*, 21(2): 199–218.

Branson, C. (2007) 'Effects of structured self-reflection on the development of authentic leadership practices among Queensland primary school principals', *Educational Management, Administration and Leadership*, 35(2): 225–46.

Bush, T. (1994) 'Accountability in education', in T. Bush and J. West-Burnham (eds), *The Principles of Educational Management*, Harlow: Longman.

Bush, T. (2008) 'From management to leadership: semantic or meaningful change', *Educational Management, Administration and Leadership*, 36(2): 271–88.

Cohen, L., Manion, L. and Morrison, K. (2000) *Research Methods in Education*, 5th edn, London: RoutledgeFalmer.

Crawford, M. (2009) *Getting to the Heart of Leadership: Emotion and Educational leadership*, London: Sage.

Crowther, F. (1990) 'The pioneers in administration', *Practicing Administrator*, 12(3): 14–15.

Evers, C. and Lakomski, G. (1991) 'Educational administration as science: a post-positivist proposal', in P. Ribbins, R. Glatter, T. Simkins and L. Watson (eds), *Developing Educational Leaders*, Harlow: Longman.

Greenfield, T.B. (1973) 'Organisations as social inventions: rethinking assumptions about change', *Journal of Applied Behavioural Science*, 9(5): 551–74.

Greenfield, T.B. (1975) 'Theory about organisations: a new perspective and its implications for schools', in M. Hughes (ed.), *Administering Education: International Challenge*, London: Athlone Press.

Greenfield, T.B. (1979) 'Organisation theory is ideology', *Curriculum Enquiry*, 9(2): 97–112.

Greenfield, T.B. (1980) 'The man who comes back through the door in the wall: discovering truth, discovering self, discovering organisations', *Educational Administration Quarterly*, 16(3): 26–59.

Greenfield, T.B. (1986) 'The decline and fall of science in educational administration', *Interchange*, 17(2): 57–80.

Grogan, M. and Simmons, J. (2007) 'Taking a critical stance in research', A. Briggs and M. Coleman (eds), *Research Methods in Educational Leadership and Management*, 2nd edn, London: Sage.

Hermes, L. (1999) 'Learner assessment through subjective theories and action research', *Assessment and Evaluation in Higher Education*, 24(2): 197–204.

Hodgkinson, C. (1993) 'Foreword', in T.B. Greenfield and P. Ribbins (eds), *Greenfield on Educational Administration*, London: Routledge.

Holmes, M. (1986) 'Comment on "The decline and fall of science in educational administration"', *Interchange*, 17(2): 80–90.

Hoyle, E. (1981) *The Process of Management, E323 Management of the School, Block 3, Part 1*, Buckingham: Open University Press.

Hoyle, E. (1986) *The Politics of School Management*, Sevenoaks: Hodder and Stoughton.

Hoyle, E. and Wallace, M. (2005) *Educational Leadership: Ambiguity, Professionals and Managerialism*, London: Sage.

Hughes, M. and Bush, T. (1991) 'Theory and research as catalysts for change', in W. Walker, R. Farquhar and M. Hughes (eds), *Advancing Education: School Leadership in Action*, London: Falmer Press.

Innes-Brown, M. (1993) 'T. B. Greenfield and the interpretive alternative', *International Journal of Educational Management*, 7(2): 30–40.

Keough, T. and Tobin, B. (2001) 'Postmodern leadership and the policy lexicon: from theory, proxy to practice', paper for the Pan-Canadian Education Research Agenda Symposium, Quebec, May.

Lumby, J. (2001) *Managing Further Education: Learning Enterprise*, London: Paul Chapman Publishing.

Morrison, M. (2007) 'What do we mean by educational research?', in A. Briggs and M. Coleman (eds), *Research Methods in Educational Leadership and Management*, 2nd edn, London: Sage.

Prosser, J. (1999) 'Introduction', in J. Prosser (ed.), *School Culture*, London: Paul Chapman Publishing.

Ribbins, P.M., Jarvis, C.B., Best, R.E. and Oddy, D.M. (1981) 'Meanings and contexts: the problem of interpretation in the study of a school', *Research in Educational Management and Administration*, Birmingham: British Educational Management and Administration Society.

Sackney, L. and Mitchell, C. (2001) 'Postmodern expressions of educational leadership', in K. Leithwood and P. Hallinger (eds), *The Second International Handbook of Educational Leadership and Administration*, Dordrecht: Kluwer.

Starratt, R.J. (2001) 'Democratic leadership theory in late modernity: an oxymoron or ironic possibility?', *International Journal of Leadership in Education*, 4(4): 333–52.

Strain, M. (1996) 'Rationality, autonomy and the social context of education management', *Educational Management and Administration*, 24(1): 49–63.

Willower, D.J. (1980) 'Contemporary issues in theory in educational administration', *Educational Administration Quarterly*, 16(3): 1–25.

CHAPTER 7

Ambiguity models

Central features of ambiguity models

Ambiguity models include all those approaches that stress uncertainty and unpredictability in organizations. The emphasis is on the instability and complexity of institutional life. These theories assume that organizational objectives are problematic and that institutions experience difficulty in ordering their priorities. Sub-units are portrayed as relatively autonomous groups which are connected only loosely with one another and with the institution itself. Decision-making occurs within formal and informal settings where participation is fluid. Individuals are part-time members of policy-making groups who move in and out of the picture according to the nature of the topic and the interests of the potential participants. Ambiguity is a prevalent feature of complex organizations, such as schools and colleges, and is likely to be particularly acute during periods of rapid change. The definition below incorporates the main elements of these approaches.

> Ambiguity models assume that turbulence and unpredictability are dominant features of organizations. There is no clarity over the objectives of institutions and their processes are not properly understood. Participation in policy making is fluid as members opt in or out of decision opportunities.

Ambiguity models are associated with a group of theorists, mostly from the United States, who developed their ideas in the 1970s. They were dissatisfied with the formal models which they regarded as inadequate for many organizations, particularly during phases of instability. March (1982) points to the jumbled reality in certain kinds of organization:

> Theories of choice underestimate the confusion and complexity surrounding actual decision making. Many things are happening at once; technologies are changing and poorly understood; alliances, preferences, and perceptions are changing; problems, solutions, opportunities, ideas, people, and outcomes are mixed together in a way that makes their interpretation uncertain and their connections unclear. (Ibid.: 36)

Unlike certain other theories, the data supporting ambiguity models have been drawn largely from educational settings. Schools and colleges are characterized as having uncertain goals, unclear technology and fluid participation in decision-making. They are also subject to changing demands from their environments. These factors lead March and Olsen (1976: 12) to assert that 'ambiguity is a major feature of decision making in most public and educational organizations'.

Ambiguity models have the following major features:

1. There is a lack of clarity about the *goals* of the organization. Many institutions are thought to have inconsistent and opaque objectives. Formal models assume that organizations have clear purposes which guide the activities of their members. Ambiguity perspectives, by contrast, suggest that goals are so vague that they can be used to justify almost any behaviour. It may be argued that aims become clear only through the behaviour of members of the organization:

   > It is difficult to impute a set of goals to the organization that satisfies the standard consistency requirements of theories of choice. The organization appears to operate on a variety of inconsistent and ill-defined preferences. It can be described better as a loose collection of changing ideas than as a coherent structure. It discovers preferences through action more often than it acts on the basis of preferences. (Cohen and March, 1986: 3)

   Educational institutions are regarded as typical in having no clearly defined objectives. Hoyle and Wallace (2005: 33) say that school goals are 'diverse'. They add that it is a problematic concept because of the distinction between the 'official' goals of the school and the 'operational' goals of individuals or groups (ibid.: 34). The discretion available to teachers enables them to identify their own educational purposes and to act in accordance with those aims for some of their professional activities. Because teachers work independently for much of their time, they may experience little difficulty in pursuing their own interests. As a result schools and colleges are thought to have no coherent pattern of aims. As Bell (1989: 134) explains, schools face an ambiguity of purpose, the result of which is that the achievement of goals, which are educational in any sense, cease to be central to the functioning of the school.

2. Ambiguity models assume that organizations have a *problematic technology* in that their processes are not properly understood. Institutions are unclear about how outcomes emerge from their activities. This is particularly true of client-serving organizations where the technology is necessarily tailored to the needs of the individual client. In education it is not clear how pupils and students acquire knowledge and skills so the processes of teaching are clouded with doubt and uncertainty. Bell (1980) claims that ambiguity infuses the central functions of schools:

> The learning process is inadequately understood and therefore pupils may not always be learning effectively whilst the basic technology available in schools is often not understood because its purposes are only vaguely recognized ... Since the related technology is so unclear the processes of teaching and learning are clouded in ambiguity. (Ibid.: 188)

3. Ambiguity theorists argue that organizations are characterized by *fragmentation* and *loose coupling*. Institutions are divided into groups which have internal coherence based on common values and goals. Links between the groups are tenuous and unpredictable. Weick (1976) uses the term 'loose coupling' to describe relationships between sub-units:

> By loose coupling, the author intends to convey the image that coupled events are responsive, but that each event also preserves its own identity and some evidence of its physical or logical separateness ... their attachment may be circumscribed, infrequent, weak in its mutual effects, unimportant, and/or slow to respond ... Loose coupling also carries connotations of impermanence, dissolvability, and tacitness all of which are potentially crucial properties of the 'glue' that holds organizations together. (Ibid.: 3, original emphasis)

Weick subsequently elaborated his model by identifying eight particularly significant examples of loose coupling that occur between:
(a) individuals
(b) sub-units
(c) organizations
(d) hierarchical levels

(e) organizations and environments

(f) ideas

(g) activities

(h) intentions and actions

   (Orton and Weick, 1990: 208).

   The concept of loose coupling was developed for, and first applied to, educational institutions. It is particularly appropriate for organizations whose members have a substantial degree of discretion. Professional organizations, such as schools and colleges, fit this metaphor much better than, say, car assembly plants where operations are regimented and predictable. The degree of integration required in education is markedly less than in many other settings, allowing fragmentation to develop and persist. Hoyle and Wallace (2005: 170) refer to the loose-coupling arising from distinct teacher and headteacher 'zones' of influence but they add that, in England, this distinction has been eroded by enhanced accountability requirements.

4. Within ambiguity models *organizational structure* is regarded as problematic. There is uncertainty over the relative power of the different parts of the institution. Committees and other formal bodies have rights and responsibilities which overlap with each other and with the authority assigned to individual managers. The effective power of each element within the structure varies with the issue and according to the level of participation of committee members. The more complex the structure of the organization, the greater the potential for ambiguity. In this view, the formal structures discussed in Chapter 3 may conceal more than they reveal about the pattern of relationships in organizations.

   In education, the validity of the formal structure, as a representation of the distribution of power, depends on the size and complexity of the institution. Many primary schools have a simple authority structure centred on the head and there is little room for misunderstanding. In colleges and large secondary schools, there is often an elaborate pattern of interlocking committees and working parties. Noble and Pym's (1970) classic study of decision-making in an English college illustrates the ambiguity of structure in large organizations:

> The lower level officials or committees argue that they, of course, can only make recommendations. Departments must seek the approval of inter-departmental committees, these in turn can only submit reports and recommendations to the general management committee. It is there we are told that decisions must be made ... In the general management committee, however, though votes are taken and decisions formally reached, there was a widespread feeling, not infrequently

expressed even by some of its senior members, of powerlessness, a feeling that decisions were really taken elsewhere ... as a committee they could only assent to decisions which had been put up to them from one of the lower tier committees or a sub-committee ... The common attribution of effective decision making to a higher or lower committee has led the authors to describe the decision-making structure in this organisation as an involuted hierarchy. (Ibid.: 436)

These structural ambiguities lead to uncertainties about the authority and responsibility of individual leaders and managers. Referring to English further education colleges, Gleeson and Shain (1999: 469) point to 'the ambiguous territory which middle managers occupy between lecturers and senior managers', a position which also affects middle level leaders in schools (Bush, 2002). One middle manager interviewed by Gleeson and Shain (1999: 469) illustrates this point: 'The staff don't really know where we fit in and I don't think the senior management really knows either ... I don't know where we fit'. These uncertainties undoubtedly create tension for middle level leaders but also gives them a certain amount of scope to determine their own role. 'Ambiguity ... allows middle managers some room for manoeuvre' (Gleeson and Shain, 1999: 470).

5. Ambiguity models tend to be particularly appropriate for *professional client-serving* organizations. In education, the pupils and students often demand inputs into the process of decision-making, especially where it has a direct influence on their educational experience. Teachers are expected to be responsive to the perceived needs of their pupils rather than operating under the direct supervision of hierarchical superordinates. The requirement that professionals make individual judgements, rather than acting in accordance with managerial prescriptions, leads to the view that the larger schools and colleges operate in a climate of ambiguity. Hoyle and Wallace (2005: 167) argue that professional practice in education is 'endemically indeterminate' and that attempts to reduce ambiguity, and to enhance accountability, lead to a 'danger of impoverishing the quality of professional practice' (ibid.).

6. Ambiguity theorists emphasize that there is *fluid participation* in the management of organizations. Members move in and out of decision-making situations, as Cohen and March (1986) suggest:

> The participants in the organization vary among themselves in the amount of time and effort they devote to the organization; individual participants vary from one time to another. As a result standard theories of power and choice seem to be inadequate. (Ibid.: 3)

Bell (1989) elaborates this concept and applies it to education:

> By their very nature schools gain and lose large numbers of pupils each year and ... staff may move or change their roles ... Membership of the school also becomes fluid in the sense that the extent to which individuals are willing and able to participate in its activities may change over time and according to the nature of the activity itself. In this way schools are peopled by participants who wander in and out. The notion of membership is thus ambiguous, and therefore it becomes extremely difficult to attribute responsibility to a particular member of the school for some areas of the school's activities. (Ibid.: 139–40)

Changes in the powers of governing bodies in schools in England and Wales during the 1980s and 1990s add another dimension to the notion of fluid participation in decision-making. Lay governors now have an enhanced role in the governance of schools. Nominally, they have substantial responsibility for the management of staff, finance, external relations and the curriculum. In practice, however, they usually delegate most of their powers to the head-teacher and school staff. The nature of delegation, the extent of the participation of individual governors in committees and working parties, and the relationship between the headteacher and the chair of governors, may be unpredictable elements of the relationship.

7. A further source of ambiguity is provided by the signals emanating from the organization's *environment*. There is evidence that educational institutions are becoming more dependent on external groups. Self-managing schools and colleges are vulnerable to changing patterns of parental and student demand. Through the provision for school choice, parents and potential parents are able to exercise more power over schools. Funding levels, in turn, are often linked to recruitment, for example in the student-related element of school and college finance in England and Wales. The publication of examination and test results, and of OFSTED inspection reports, also serves to heighten dependence on elements in the external environment.

For all these reasons, institutions are becoming more open to external groups. In an era of rapid change, they may experience difficulties in interpreting the various messages being transmitted from the environment and in dealing with conflicting signals. The uncertainty arising from the external context adds to the ambiguity of the decision-making process within the institution. When there is exceptional environmental turbulence, as with schools and universities in post-Apartheid South Africa, the notion of ambiguity is particularly powerful (Bush, 2003).

8. Ambiguity theorists emphasize the prevalence of *unplanned decisions*. Formal models assume that problems arise, possible solutions are formulated and the most appropriate solution is chosen. The preferred option is then implemented and subject to evaluation in due course. Proponents of the ambiguity model claim that this logical sequence rarely occurs in practice. Rather the lack of agreed goals means that decisions have no clear focus. Problems, solutions and participants interact and choices somehow emerge from the confusion.

In England and Wales, ambiguity models can be illustrated by the resource allocation process in schools and colleges. Because there is little clarity about the goals of organizations, the notion of linking budgeting to aims is problematic. It is difficult to determine priorities among competing alternatives and the notion of an optimum choice is contentious (Bush, 2000: 113). Budgetary decisions are likely to be characterized by ambiguity rather than rationality, as Levačić's (1995) research suggests:

> The rational model is undermined by ambiguity, since it is so heavily dependent on the availability of information about relationships between inputs and outputs – between means and ends. If ambiguity prevails, then it is not possible for organizations to have clear aims and objectives. Reliable information about the relationships between different quantities and combinations of inputs and resulting outputs cannot be obtained. This state of affairs would explain why decision-making, particularly in the public sector, does not in fact follow the rational model, but is characterized by incrementalism. (Levačić, 1995: 82)

Bennett et al.'s (2000) study of development planning in English primary schools also casts doubt on the validity of rational models. They claim that primary schools are working in a highly turbulent environment and that this inevitably affects the planning process:

> It is impossible to predict the environment in which the school must operate, and management is so taken up with day-to-day responses to events as they occur that resources for strategic planning ... are unlikely to be available. (Ibid.: 349)

These examples serve to illustrate the problematic nature of the relationship between the decision-making process and the outcomes of that process. The rational assumption that implementation is a straightforward element in the decision-making process appears to be flawed. In practice, it is just as uncertain as the process of choice.

9. Ambiguity models stress the advantages of *decentralization*. Given the complexity and unpredictability of organizations, it is thought that

many decisions should be devolved to sub-units and individuals. Departments are relatively coherent and may be able to adapt rapidly to changing circumstances. Decentralized decision-making avoids the delays and uncertainties associated with the institutional level. Individual and departmental autonomy are seen as appropriate for professional staff, who are required to exercise their judgement in dealing with clients. Successful departments are able to expand and thrive, while weaker areas may contract or even close during difficult periods. Weick (1976: 7) argues that devolution enables organizations to survive while particular sub-units are threatened:

> If there is a breakdown in one portion of a loosely coupled system then this breakdown is sealed off and does not affect other portions of the organization ... when any element misfires or decays or deteriorates, the spread of this deterioration is checked in a loosely coupled system ... A loosely coupled system can isolate its trouble spots and prevent the trouble from spreading. (Ibid.: 7)

While decentralization does have certain merits, it may be difficult to sustain when leaders are increasingly answerable for all aspects of the institution. Underperforming departments or units can be identified through the inspection process, and the publication of performance indicators, and this limits the scope for 'sealing off' the weak sub-units. Rather, action must be taken to remedy the weakness if the institution is to thrive in a period of heightened market and public accountability. As Hoyle and Wallace (2005: 100) note, decentralization may be constrained by 'the iron cage of government policy'.

The garbage can model

The most celebrated of the ambiguity perspectives is the garbage can model developed by Cohen and March (1986). On the basis of empirical research, they conclude that ambiguity is one of the major characteristics of universities and colleges in the United States. They reject the sequential assumptions of the formal models in which decisions are thought to emanate from a rational process. Rather they regard decision-making as fundamentally ambiguous. They liken the process to that of a 'garbage can':

> A key to understanding the processes within organizations is to view a choice opportunity as a garbage can into which various problems and solutions are dumped by participants. The mix of garbage in a single can

depends partly on the labels attached to the alternative cans; but it also depends on what garbage is being produced at the moment, on the mix of cans available, and on the speed with which garbage is collected and removed from the scene. (Cohen and March, 1986: 81)

In their analysis of decision-making, the authors focus on four relatively independent streams within organizations. Decisions are outcomes of the interaction of the four streams as follows:

1. *Problems* are the concern of people inside and outside the organization. They arise over issues of: lifestyle; family; frustrations of work; careers; group relations within the organization; distribution of status, jobs and money; ideology; or current crises of mankind as interpreted by the mass media or the next-door neighbour. All require attention. Problems are, however, distinct from choices; and they may not be resolved when choices are made.
2. *Solutions.* A solution is somebody's product. A computer is not just a solution to a problem in payroll management, discovered when needed. It is an answer actively looking for a question. The creation of need is not a curiosity of the market in consumer products; it is a general phenomenon of processes of choice. Despite the dictum that you cannot find the answer until you have formulated the question, you often do not know what the question is in organizational problem-solving until you know the answer.
3. *Participants* come and go. Since every entrance is an exit somewhere else, the distribution of entrances depends on the attributes of the choice being left as much as it does on the attributes of the new choice. Substantial variation in participation stems from other demands on the participants' time (rather than from features of the decision under study).
4. *Choice opportunities.* These are occasions when an organization is expected to produce behaviour that can be called a decision. Opportunities arise regularly, and any organization has ways of declaring an occasion for choice. Contracts must be signed, people hired, promoted or fired, money spent and responsibilities allocated (Cohen and March, 1986: 82).

Cohen and March's analysis is persuasive. They argue that problems may well be independent of solutions, which may be 'waiting' for a problem to emerge. Participation in decision-making is fluid in many schools and colleges and the 'decision' emerging from choice opportunities may well depend more on who is present for that meeting than on the intrinsic merits of the potential solutions. Hoyle and Wallace

(2005) link the 'garbage can' model to complexity theory. They refer to Morrison's (2002: 9) four elements of complexity:

- 'Effects are not straightforward functions of causes.'
- 'Uncertainty and openness prevail.'
- 'The universe is irregular, diverse, uncontrollable and unpredictable.'
- 'Systems are indeterministic, non-linear and unstable.'

Morrison (2002: 189) adds that, within this scenario, 'the power of bosses is limited', but Hoyle and Wallace (2005: 41) assert that 'leaders and managers can at least give a steer to emergent events'.

Cohen and March regard their garbage can model as particularly appropriate for higher education but several of the concepts are also relevant for schools. The major characteristics of ambiguous goals, unclear technology and fluid participation often apply in the secondary sector, although they may be less evident in small primary schools.

The major contribution of the garbage can model is that it uncouples problems and choices. The notion of decision-making as a rational process for finding solutions to problems is supplanted by an uneasy mix of problems, solutions and participants, from which decisions may eventually emerge. The garbage can model has a clear application to educational institutions where there are many participants with ready-made solutions to apply to different problems. Levačić (1995: 82) contrasts this model with rational approaches: 'In the garbage can model, there is no clear distinction between means and ends, no articulation of organizational goals, no evaluation of alternatives in relation to organizational goals and no selection of the best means'.

Applying the ambiguity model: Oakfields School

The ambiguity model is an important contribution to the theory of educational management. It is a descriptive and analytical model which sets out its proponents' views of how organizations are managed rather than a normative approach extolling the 'right' way to manage institutions. However, there are few empirical studies which employ a conceptual framework drawn from the ambiguity perspective. One important example is Bell's (1989) research at Oakfields, then a newly amalgamated secondary school in the English East Midlands.

Oakfields was formed by the amalgamation of three schools as part of the LEA's strategy for dealing with falling pupil numbers. The new school opened with 1,500 pupils but numbers were expected to fall to about 900 within five years, with obvious implications for staffing levels. This uncertainty was aggravated by teachers' union action which meant that planning could not be undertaken at the end of the normal school day. The new school also operated on two sites. These factors created a turbulent environment with a high degree of ambiguity.

Bell refers to a lack of clarity about school aims, technology and school membership. The new head identified the goals but these were not shared by all staff. Attempts to resolve differences of view were inhibited by the teacher action, as the headteacher indicates:

> You may not agree with some of the policies and procedures, or even with the long term aims, but until we can discuss these I should like everyone to enforce them for all our sakes, but especially for the sake of the children. (Bell, 1989: 135)

Bell notes that the lack of clarity about aims emanated from different perceptions held by staff from each of the three constituent schools, particularly in respect of discipline and aspects of the curriculum. It was clear also that teachers' opinions about the nature of the former schools influenced their attitudes:

> Staff ... interpretation of the goals of the new school, and their stance towards operationalizing those goals, owed as much to their perception of the three constituent schools as it did to any statement of intent from the head of Oakfields. (Bell, 1989: 136)

Disagreement about the technology of the school centred around teaching styles and about the relative merits of separate or integrated subjects in science and humanities.

The notion of school membership was highly problematic because many staff retained a loyalty to their former school rather than to the newly amalgamated unit. This was particularly true of teachers at the former secondary school who returned to that school's site for certain lessons. The most potent example concerned the former head of the secondary school, who was based at the satellite campus as 'associate head', and also influenced the views of several colleagues:

> He could only be described as being a member of Oakfields school if the notion of membership is used to indicate the most tenuous of connections. Several of his erstwhile colleagues took up a similar position to the extent that they were in the new school but not of it. (Bell, 1989: 140)

The ambiguous aims, technology and membership were reflected in the decision-making process which was often unpredictable and irrational. Bell claims that Oakfields illustrates the limitations of formal theories and the salience of the ambiguity model:

> The traditional notion of the school as an hierarchical decision-making structure with a horizontal division into departments and a vertical division into authority levels needs to be abandoned. Such a conceptualization is unsuitable for the analysis of an organization attempting to cope with an unstable and unpredictable environment ... The fundamental importance of unclear technology, fluid membership and the problematic nature and position of educational goals has to be accorded due recognition in any analysis of the organization and management of a school such as Oakfields. (Bell, 1989: 146)

Ambiguity models: goals, structure, environment and leadership

Goals

Ambiguity models differ from all other approaches in stressing the problematic nature of *goals*. The other theories may emphasize the institution, or the sub-unit, or the individual, but they all assume that objectives are clear at the levels identified. The distinctive quality of the ambiguity perspective is that purposes are regarded not only as vague and unclear but also as an inadequate guide to behaviour:

> Events are not dominated by intention. The processes and the outcomes are likely to appear to have no close relation with the explicit intention of actors ... intention is lost in context dependent flow of problems, solutions, people, and choice opportunities. (Cohen et al., 1976: 37)

Ambiguity theorists argue that decision-making represents an opportunity for discovering goals rather than promoting policies based on existing objectives. The specific choice situation acts as a catalyst in helping individuals to clarify their preferences: 'Human choice behaviour is at least as much a process for discovering goals as for acting on them' (Cohen and March, 1986: 220).

Hoyle and Wallace (2007: 18–19) show how organizational goals often arise uneasily from external prescriptions and expectations. This leads 'headteachers and teachers to represent their work to the agencies of accountability in order to appear to be meeting the requirements of these agencies'. This requires a process of adaptation, which might be seen, broadly, as 'compliance', 'non-compliance' or 'mediation'. This may lead teachers to modify externally-generated goals so that they become more congruent with their professional values.

Organizational structure

Ambiguity models regard *organizational structure* as problematic. Institutions are portrayed as aggregations of loosely coupled sub-units with structures that may be both ambiguous and subject to change. In many educational organizations, and certainly in larger schools and colleges, policy is determined primarily by committees rather than by individuals. The various committees and working parties collectively comprise the structure of the organization.

Enderud (1980: 248) argues that organizational structure may be subject to a variety of interpretations because of the ambiguity and sub-unit autonomy that exists in many large and complex organizations: 'What really matters to the way in which the formal structure influences the processes is not what the structure formally "looks like", but the way it is actually used'. Enderud (1980) points to four factors which influence the interpretation of structure:

1. Institutions usually classify responsibilities into decision areas which are then allocated to different bodies or individuals. An obvious example is the distinction made between the academic and pastoral structures in many secondary schools. However, these decision areas may not be delineated clearly, or the topics treated within each area may overlap. A pupil's academic progress, for example, may be hampered by personal or domestic considerations. 'The result is that a given decision may quite reasonably be subject to different classifications of decision area. This again means that the circle of participants, who are to deal with the matter, is also open to interpretation' (Enderud, 1980: 249).
2. Decisions may also be classified in other ways. Issues may be major or minor, urgent or long term, administrative or political, and so on. These distinctions offer the same opportunities for different interpretations as exist with delineation by area.
3. Rules and regulations concerning the decision-making process within the formal structure may be unclear. The choice of rules for decision-making is often subject to ad hoc interpretation. The adoption of a voting process, or an attempt to reach consensus, or a proposal to defer a decision, may be unpredictable and have a significant influence on the final outcome.
4. Rules and regulations may be disregarded in certain circumstances. Most organizational structures have elements designed to deal with

emergencies or procedural conflicts. The formal structure may be circumvented to deal with particular occurrences where participants can agree on such practice (Enderud, 1980).

Ambiguity models portray structures as 'loosely coupled' (Weick, 2001). Goldspink (2007: 40) draws on this metaphor to discuss the 'rich multidimensional coupling' between the many agents involved in schools and colleges, who each make sense of their role in their own ways.

A further source of ambiguity concerns the extent of *participation* within the organizational structure. Certain individuals within the institution have the right to participate in decision-making through their membership of committees and working parties. Cohen, March and Olsen (1976: 27) stress that committee membership is only the starting point for participation in decision-making: 'Such rights are necessary, but not sufficient, for actual involvement in a decision. They can be viewed as invitations to participation. Invitations that may or may not be accepted'.

A basic assumption of ambiguity models is that participation in decision-making is fluid, as members underuse their decision rights. One consequence of such structural ambiguities is that decisions may be possible only where there are enough participants. Attempts to make decisions without sufficient participation may founder at subsequent stages of the process. Lumby's (2001: 99) research on English further education colleges suggests that staff roles are likely to be even more problematic than formal structures: 'Whether the official place within the structure of any role had changed or not, the way the role was seen by the role holder and by others continued to change, and was likely to be subject to ambiguity, conflict and overload'.

The external environment

The *external environment* is a source of ambiguity which contributes to the unpredictability of organizations. Schools and colleges have a continuing existence only as long as they are able to satisfy the needs of their external constituencies. People in educational institutions have to be sensitive and responsive to the messages transmitted by groups and individuals.

> Perhaps it needs to be recognized more explicitly that organizations, including schools, sometimes operate in a complex and unstable environment over which they exert only modest control and which is capable of producing effects which penetrate the strongest and most selective of boundaries ... many schools are now unable to disregard pressures emanating from their wider environment. (Bell, 1980: 186)

The development of a 'market economy' for education in many

countries means that schools and colleges have to be increasingly sensitive to the demands of clients and potential clients. Institutions which fail to meet the requirements of their environments may suffer the penalty of contraction or closure. The demise of certain schools as a result of falling rolls may be regarded as a failure to satisfy market needs. Closure is often preceded by a period of decline as parents opt to send their children to other schools which are thought to be more suitable. One way of assessing these events is to view the unpopularity of schools as a product of their inability to interpret the wishes of the environment.

Despite the environmental complexity engendered by decentralization, government policy remains the most potent influence on school actions and decision-making. In England, for example, the government exercises considerable power over schools through the national curriculum, patrolled by a tight inspection regime, through 'national strategies' for literacy and numeracy, and through a tightly defined target-setting culture. The paradoxically 'tight–loose' relationship between schools and government may be interpreted as representing a desire to leave school leaders with discretion about *how* to implement centrally-determined policies but not about *whether* to do so.

These external uncertainties interact with the other unpredictable aspects of organizations to produce a confused pattern, far removed from the clear, straightforward assumptions associated with the formal models. A turbulent environment combines with the internal ambiguities and may mean that management in education is often a hazardous and irrational activity, as Gunter's (1997) study of 'Jurassic' management suggests: 'The future is created by the sensitive response to fluctuations in the environment rather than proactive and systematic installations of new structures and tasks' (ibid.: 95).

Leadership

In a climate of ambiguity traditional notions of *leadership* require modification. The unpredictable features of anarchic organizations create difficulties for leaders and suggest a different approach to the management of schools and colleges. According to Cohen and March (1986: 195–203), leaders face four fundamental ambiguities:

1. There is an ambiguity of *purpose* because the goals of the organization are unclear. It is difficult to specify a set of clear, consistent goals which would receive the endorsement of members of the insti-

tution. Moreover, it may be impossible to infer a set of objectives from the activities of the organization. If there are no clear goals, leaders have an inadequate basis for assessing the actions and achievements of the institution.

2. There is an ambiguity of *power* because it is difficult to make a clear assessment of the power of leaders. Heads and principals do possess authority arising from their position as the formal leaders of their institutions. However, in an unpredictable setting, formal authority is an uncertain guide to the power of leaders. Decisions emerge from a complex process of interaction. Leaders are participants in the process but their 'solutions' may not emerge as the preferred outcomes of the organization.

3. There is an ambiguity of *experience* because, in conditions of uncertainty, leaders may not be able to learn from the consequences of their actions. In a straightforward situation, leaders choose from a range of alternatives and assess the outcome in terms of the goals of the institution. This assessment then provides a basis for action in similar situations. In conditions of ambiguity, however, outcomes depend on factors other than the behaviour of the leaders. External changes occur and distort the situation so that experience becomes an unreliable guide to future action.

4. There is an ambiguity of *success* because it is difficult to measure the achievements of leaders. Heads and principals are usually appointed to these posts after good careers as teachers and middle managers. They have become familiar with success. However, the ambiguities of purpose, power and experience make it difficult for leaders to distinguish between success and failure.

Cohen and March (1986) point to the problems for leaders faced with these uncertainties:

> These ambiguities are fundamental ... because they strike at the heart of the usual interpretations of leadership. When purpose is ambiguous, ordinary theories of decision-making and intelligence become problematic. When power is ambiguous, ordinary theories of social order and control become problematic. When experience is ambiguous, ordinary theories of learning and adaptation become problematic. When success is ambiguous, ordinary theories of motivation and personal pleasure become problematic. (Ibid.: 195)

These ambiguous features imply that leaders cannot control the institution in the manner suggested by the formal models. Rather they become facilitators of a complex decision-making process, creating opportunities for the discussion of problems, the participation of members and the exposition of solutions.

Two alternative leadership strategies are postulated for conditions of ambiguity. One stratagem involves a participative role for leaders to maximize their influence on policy. Cohen and March (1986) and March (1982) suggest the following approaches for the management of uncertainty:

1. Leaders should be ready to devote *time* to the process of decision-making. By taking the trouble to participate fully, leaders are likely to be present when issues are finally resolved and will have the opportunity to influence the decision.
2. Leaders should be prepared to *persist* with those proposals which do not gain the initial support of groups within the institution. Issues are likely to surface at several forums and a negative reception at one setting may be reversed on another occasion when there may be different participants.
3. Leaders should facilitate the *participation of opponents* of the leader's proposals. Occasional participants tend to have aspirations which are out of touch with reality. Direct involvement in decision-making increases members' awareness of the ramifications of various courses of action. The inclusion of opponents at appropriate fora may lead to the modification or withdrawal of alternative ideas and allow the leader's plans to prosper.
4. Leaders should *overload the system* with ideas to ensure the success of some of the initiatives. When the organization has to cope with a surfeit of issues, it is likely that some of the proposals will succeed, even if others fall by the wayside.

These tactical manoeuvres may appear rather cynical and they have certain similarities with the political models discussed in Chapter 5. The alternative stratagem is for leaders to forsake direct involvement in the policy-making process and to concentrate on structural and personnel matters. Attention to the formal structure enables leaders to influence the framework of decision-making. In deciding where issues should be discussed, there is an effect on the outcome of those discussions.

This second stratagem also requires leaders to pay careful attention to the selection and deployment of staff. If heads or principals recruit teachers who share their educational philosophies, then it is likely that their preferred solutions will become school or college policy. The structural and personnel aspects of management can overlap. Heads may encourage like-minded staff to join committees and working parties to improve the prospects of favourable outcomes.

Both these strategies suggest that leaders in ambiguous situations should proceed by stealth rather than through overt proclamation of particular policies. This approach may be appropriate for periods of high ambiguity but the tensions inherent in turbulent organizations may be very stressful for heads and principals who have to absorb these pressures, both to facilitate institutional development and to foster personal survival and growth.

The most appropriate leadership approach for turbulent conditions is the contingency model.

Contingent leadership

The models of leadership examined in the previous chapters are all partial. They provide valid and helpful insights into one particular aspect of leadership. Some focus on the process by which influence is exerted while others emphasize one or more dimensions of leadership. They are mostly normative and often have vigorous support from their advocates. None of these models provide a complete picture of school leadership. As Lambert (1995: 7) notes, there is 'no single best type'.

The contingent model provides an alternative approach, recognizing the diverse nature of school contexts and the advantages of adapting leadership styles to the particular situation, rather than adopting a 'one size fits all' stance:

> This approach assumes that what is important is how leaders respond to the unique organizational circumstances or problems ... [that] there are wide variations in the contexts for leadership and that, to be effective, these contexts require different leadership responses ... [I]ndividuals providing leadership, typically those in formal positions of authority, are capable of mastering a large repertoire of leadership practices. Their influence will depend, in large measure, on such mastery. (Leithwood et al., 1999: 15)

Yukl (2002: 234) adds that 'the managerial job is too complex and unpredictable to rely on a set of standardised responses to events. Effective leaders are continuously reading the situation and evaluating how to adapt their behaviour to it'. Hoyle and Wallace (2005: 189) extend this discussion by saying that the type of leader likely to be successful will depend on the specific set of circumstances facing the school. 'Some schools are in such a parlous state that only heroic leadership can "turn them round" ... But for many schools ... effective leadership is ... marked by the long haul towards improvement'. As Vanderhaar, Munoz and Rodosky (2007) suggest, leadership is contingent on the setting.

Bolman and Deal's (1991) 'conceptual pluralism' is similar to contingent leadership. An eclectic stance is required where leaders adapt their styles to the context in which they are operating. Leadership requires effective diagnosis of problems, followed by adopting the most appropriate response to the issue or situation (Morgan, 1997). This reflexive approach is particularly important in periods of turbulence when leaders need to be able to assess the situation carefully and react as appropriate rather than relying on a standard leadership model.

The limitations of ambiguity models

Ambiguity models add some important dimensions to the theory of educational management. The concepts of problematic goals, unclear technology and fluid participation are significant contributions to organizational analysis. Most schools and colleges possess these features to a greater or lesser extent, so ambiguity models should be regarded primarily as analytical or descriptive approaches rather than normative theories. They claim to mirror reality rather than suggesting that organizations *should* operate as anarchies.

The turbulence of educational policy in England, and in many other countries, in the twenty-first century, lends credence to ambiguity theories. The rapid pace of curriculum change, enhanced government expectations of schools and colleges, and the unpredictable nature of educational funding, lead to multiple uncertainty which can be explained adequately only within the ambiguity framework. Similarly, Sapre's (2002) analysis of educational reform in India points to the continual failure of top-down reforms, arising largely as a result of ambiguity: 'Repeated failure of reform initiatives is unsettling for practitioners and students. Reformers need a deeper understanding of the dynamics of change, what sustains a reform and what does not' (ibid.: 106).

The ambiguity model appears to be increasingly plausible but it does have four significant weaknesses:

1. It is difficult to reconcile ambiguity perspectives with the customary structures and processes of schools and colleges. Participants may move in and out of decision-making situations but the policy framework remains intact and has a continuing influence on the outcome of discussions. Specific goals may be unclear but teachers usually

understand and accept the broad aims of education.

2. Ambiguity models exaggerate the degree of uncertainty in educational institutions. Schools and colleges have a number of predictable features which serve to clarify the responsibilities of their members. Students, pupils and staff are expected to behave in accordance with standard rules and procedures. The timetable regulates the location and movement of all participants. There are usually clear plans to guide the classroom activities of teachers and pupils. Staff are aware of the accountability patterns, with teachers responsible ultimately to heads and principals who, in turn, are answerable to government and, in self-managing institutions, to governing bodies and funding agencies.

   The predictability of schools and colleges is reinforced by the professional socialization which occurs during teacher training, induction and mentoring. Teachers assimilate the expected patterns of behaviour and reproduce them in their professional lives. Socialization thus serves to reduce uncertainty and unpredictability in education. Educational institutions are rather more stable and predictable than the ambiguity perspective suggests.

3. Ambiguity models are less appropriate for stable organizations or for any institutions during periods of stability. The degree of predictability in schools depends on the nature of relationships with the external environment. Where institutions are able to maintain relatively impervious boundaries, they can exert strong control over their own processes. Oversubscribed schools, for example, may be able to rely on their popularity to insulate their activities from external pressures.

4. Ambiguity models offer little practical guidance to leaders in educational institutions. While formal models emphasize the head's leading role in policy-making, and collegial models stress the importance of team work, ambiguity models can offer nothing more tangible than contingent leadership.

Cohen and March (1986: 91) accept that their garbage can model has limitations while proclaiming its relevance to many organizations: 'We acknowledge immediately that no real system can be fully characterized in this way. Nonetheless, the simulated organizations exhibit behaviour that can be observed some of the time in almost all organizations and frequently in some'.

Conclusion: ambiguity or rationality?

Ambiguity models make a valuable contribution to the theory of educational leadership and management. The emphasis on the unpredictability of organizations is a significant counter to the view that problems can be solved through a rational process. The notion of leaders making a considered choice from a range of alternatives depends crucially on their ability to predict the consequences of a particular action. The edifice of the formal models is shaken by the recognition that conditions in schools and colleges may be too uncertain to allow an informed choice among alternatives.

In practice, however, educational institutions operate with a mix of rational and anarchic processes. The more unpredictable the internal and external environment, the more applicable is the ambiguity metaphor. As Hoyle and Wallace (2005: 60) suggest, there are limitations to the rationality of the implementation process, 'because of cognitive, logical, phenomenological and control ambiguities'.

Development planning, strongly advocated in England in the 1990s, provides a rational element of school and college management, although Bennett et al.'s (2000) work demonstrates its limitations in a climate of ambiguity and change. Wallace (1991: 182), for example, emphasizes that schools have to plan within a framework of uncertainty: 'The nature of many external innovations is liable to change unpredictably. It is in this rather frenetic context, which includes much ambiguity, that planning ... must take place'.

The ambiguity model has much to offer but it has to be assessed alongside the formal perspective and other theories of educational management. On its own, it is not sufficiently comprehensive to explain behaviour and events in education. Its relevance is overstated by its adherents but it does offer fascinating and valuable insights into the nature of school and college management.

References

Bell, L. (1980) 'The school as an organisation: a re-appraisal', *British Journal of Sociology of Education*, 1(2): 183–92.

Bell, L. (1989) 'Ambiguity models and secondary schools: a case study', in T. Bush (ed.), *Managing Education: Theory and Practice*, Buckingham: Open University Press.

Bennett, N., Crawford, M., Levačić, R., Glover, D. and Earley, P. (2000) 'The reality of school development planning in the effective primary school: technicist or guiding plan?', *School Leadership and Management*, 20(3): 333–51.

Bolman, L. and Deal, T. (1991) *Reframing Organizations: Artistry, Choice and Leadership*, San Francisco, CA: Jossey-Bass.

Bush, T. (2000) 'Management styles: impact on finance and resources', in M. Coleman and L. Anderson (eds), *Managing Finance and Resources in Education*, London: Paul Chapman Publishing.

Bush, T. (2002) *Middle Level Leaders' 'Think Piece'*, Nottingham: NCSL.

Bush, T. (2003) 'Theory and practice in educational management', in T. Bush, M. Coleman and M. Thurlow (eds), *Leadership and Strategic Management in South African Schools*, London: Commonwealth Secretariat.

Cohen, M.D. and March, J.G. (1986) *Leadership and Ambiguity: The American College President*, Boston, MA: Harvard Business School Press. (First published in 1974 by McGraw-Hill, New York.)

Cohen, M.D., March, J.G. and Olsen, J.P. (1976) 'People, problems, solutions and the ambiguity of relevance', in J.G. March and J.P. Olsen (eds), *Ambiguity and Choice in Organisations*, Bergen: Universitetsforlaget.

Enderud, H. (1980) 'Administrative leadership in organised anarchies', *International Journal of Institutional Management in Higher Education*, 4(3): 235–53.

Gleeson, D. and Shain, F. (1999) 'Managing ambiguity: between markets and managerialism – a case study of "middle" managers in further education', *Sociological Review*, 47(3): 461–91.

Goldspink, C. (2007) 'Rethinking educational reform: a loosely-coupled and complex systems perspective', *Educational Management, Administration and Leadership,* 35(1): 27–50.

Gunter, H. (1997) *Rethinking Education: The Consequences of Jurassic Management*, London: Cassell.

Hoyle, E. and Wallace, M. (2005) *Educational Leadership: Ambiguity, Professionals and Managerialism*, London: Sage.

Hoyle, E. and Wallace, M. (2007) 'Educational reform: an ironic perspective', *Educational Management, Administration and Leadership,* 35(1): 9–25.

Lambert, L. (1995) 'New directions in the preparation of educational leaders', *Thrust for Educational Leadership*, 24(5): 6–10.

Leithwood, K., Jantzi, D. and Steinbach, R. (1999) *Changing Leadership for Changing Times*, Buckingham: Open University Press.

Lumby, J. (2001) *Managing Further Education Colleges: Learning Enterprises*, London: Paul Chapman Publishing.

Levačič, R. (1995) *Local Management of Schools: Analysis and Practice*, Buckingham: Open University Press.

March, J.G. (1982) 'Theories of choice and making decisions', *Society*, 20(1). Copyright © by Transaction Inc. Published by permission of Transaction Inc.

March, J.G. and Olsen, J.P. (1976) 'Organisational choice under ambiguity', in J.G. March and J.P. Olsen (eds), *Ambiguity and Choice in Organisations*, Bergen: Universitetsforlaget.

Morgan, G. (1997) *Images of Organisation*, Newbury Park, CA: Sage.

Morrison, K. (2002) *School Leadership and Complexity Theory,* London: RoutledgeFalmer.

Noble, T. and Pym, B. (1970) 'Collegial authority and the receding locus of power', *British Journal of Sociology*, 21: 431–45.

Orton, J. and Weick, K. (1990) 'Loosely coupled systems: a reconceptualization', *Academy of Management Review*, 15(2): 203–23.

Sapre, P. (2002) 'Realizing the potential of educational management in India', *Educational Management and Administration*, 30(1): 101–8.

Vanderhaar, J, Munoz, M. and Rodosky, R. (2007) 'Leadership as accountability for learning: the effects of school poverty, teacher experience, previous achievement and principal preparation programs on student achievement', *Educational Assessment, Evaluation and Accountability*, 19(1): 17–32.

Wallace, M. (1991) 'Flexible planning: a key to the management of multiple innovations', *Educational Management and Administration*, 19(3): 180–92.

Weick, K.E. (1976) 'Educational organisations as loosely coupled systems', *Administrative Science Quarterly*, 21(1): 1–19.

Weick, K.E. (2001) *Making Sense of the Organisation,* Oxford: Blackwell.

Yukl, G.A. (2002) *Leadership in Organizations*, 5th edn, Upper Saddle River, NJ: Prentice-Hall.

CHAPTER 8

Cultural models

What do we mean by culture?

Cultural models emphasize the informal aspects of organizations, rather than their official elements. They focus on the values, beliefs and norms of individuals in the organization and how these individual perceptions coalesce into shared organizational meanings. Cultural models are manifested by symbols and rituals rather than through the formal structure of the organization. The definition below captures the main elements of these approaches.

> Cultural models assume that beliefs, values and ideology are at the heart of organizations. Individuals hold certain ideas and value-preferences which influence how they behave and how they view the behaviour of other members. These norms become shared traditions which are communicated within the group and are reinforced by symbols and ritual.

Cultural models have become increasingly significant in education since the first edition of this book was published in 1986. Walker (2010: 176), for example, comments that 'interest in building [learning] cultures has grown markedly over the past decade'. Harris (1992) claims that educational writers attach considerable value to culture:

Theorists argue that educational administration has a technical manage-

170

ment aspect but is mainly about the culture within an organization. This culture includes the rituals which occur (or should occur) within an organization ... Educational managers ... are taken to be those capable of shaping ritual in educational institutions. (Ibid.: 4)

This extract demonstrates that culture may be both operational and normative ('occur or should occur') and that leaders have a central role in influencing culture.

The increasing interest in culture as one element in school and college management may be understood as another example of dissatisfaction with the limitations of the formal models. Their emphasis on the technical aspects of institutions appears to be inadequate for schools and colleges aspiring to excellence. The stress on the intangible world of values and attitudes is a useful counter to these bureaucratic assumptions and helps to produce a more balanced portrait of educational institutions.

The developing importance of cultural models arises partly from a wish to understand, and operate more effectively within, this informal domain of the values and beliefs of teachers and other members of the organization. Morgan (1997) and O'Neill (1994) both stress the increasing significance of cultural factors in management. The latter charts the appearance of cultural 'labels' and explains why they became more prevalent in the 1990s:

The increased use of such cultural descriptors in the literature of educational management is significant because it reflects a need for educational organizations to be able to articulate deeply held and shared values in more tangible ways and therefore respond more effectively to new, uncertain and potentially threatening demands on their capabilities. Organizations, therefore, articulate values in order to provide form and meaning for the activities of organizational members in the absence of visible and certain organizational structures and relationships. In this sense the analysis and influence of organizational culture become essential management tools in the pursuit of increased organizational growth and effectiveness. (O'Neill, 1994: 116)

Beare, Caldwell and Millikan (1989) claim that culture serves to define the unique qualities of individual organizations:

An increasing number of ... writers ... have adopted the term 'culture' to define that social and phenomenological uniqueness of a particular organisational community ... We have finally acknowledged publicly that uniqueness is a virtue, that values are important and that they should be fostered. (Ibid.: 173)

The international trend towards decentralization and self-management reinforces the notion of schools and colleges as unique entities. Caldwell and Spinks (1992: 74) argue that there is 'a culture of self-management'. The essential components of this culture are the *empowerment* of leaders and their acceptance of *responsibility*.

Societal culture

Most of the literature on culture in education relates to organizational culture and that is also the main focus of this chapter. However, there is also an emerging literature on the broader theme of national or societal culture. Walker (2010: 178) notes that 'culture can be applied in big picture terms to nations, societies, religious or ethnic groups'.

Bottery (2004: 36) warns of 'cultural globalisation', where standardization arises from uncritical adoption of international, usually Western, norms rather than developing approaches based on a careful assessment of the specific needs of the society or of the individual school. Given the globalization of education, issues of societal culture are increasingly significant. Walker and Dimmock (2002: 1) refer to issues of context and stress the need to avoid 'decontextualized paradigms' in researching and analysing educational systems and institutions:

> The field of educational leadership and management has developed along ethnocentric lines, being heavily dominated by Anglo-American paradigms and theories ... Frequently, ... an implicit assumption is made that findings in one part of the world will necessarily apply in others. It is clear that a key factor missing from many debates on educational administration and leadership is context ... context is represented by societal culture and its mediating influence on theory, policy and practice. (Walker and Dimmock, 2002: 2)

Walker and Dimmock are by no means alone in advocating attention to issues of context. Crossley and Broadfoot (1992: 100) say that 'policies and practice cannot be translated intact from one culture to another since the mediation of different cultural contexts can quite transform the latter's salience', while Bush, Qiang and Fang (1998: 137) stress that 'all theories and interpretations of practice must be "grounded" in the specific context ... before they can be regarded as useful'. Southworth (2005: 77) stresses that school leadership is contextualized because 'where you are affects what you do as a leader'.

Dimmock and Walker (2002) have given sustained attention to these issues and provide a helpful distinction between societal and organizational culture:

> Societal cultures differ mostly at the level of basic values, while organizational cultures differ mostly at the level of more superficial practices, as

reflected in the recognition of particular symbols, heroes and rituals. This allows organizational cultures to be deliberately managed and changed, whereas societal or national cultures are more enduring and change only gradually over longer time periods. School leaders influence, and in turn are influenced by, the organizational culture. Societal culture, on the other hand, is a given, being outside the sphere of influence of an individual school leader. (Ibid.: 71)

Dimmock and Walker (2002) identify seven 'dimensions' of societal culture, each of which is expressed as a continuum:

1. *Power-distributed/power concentrated.* Power is either distributed more equally among the various levels of a culture or is more concentrated.
2. *Group-oriented/self-oriented.* People in self-oriented cultures perceive themselves to be more independent and self-reliant. In group-oriented cultures, ties between people are tight, relationships are firmly structured and individual needs are subservient to the collective needs.
3. *Consideration/aggression.* In aggression cultures, achievement is stressed, competition dominates and conflicts are resolved through the exercise of power and assertiveness. In contrast, consideration societies emphasize relationships, solidarity and resolution of conflicts by compromise and negotiation.
4. *Proactivism/fatalism.* This dimension reflects the proactive or 'we can change things around here' attitude in some cultures, and the willingness to accept things as they are in others – a fatalistic perspective.
5. *Generative/replicative.* Some cultures appear more predisposed towards innovation, or the generation of new ideas and methods, whereas other cultures appear more inclined to replicate or adopt ideas and approaches from elsewhere.
6. *Limited relationship/holistic relationship.* In limited relationship cultures, interactions and relationships tend to be determined by explicit rules which are applied to everyone. In holistic cultures, greater attention is given to relationship obligations, for example kinship, patronage and friendship, than to impartially applied rules.
7. *Male influence/female influence.* In some societies, the male domination of decision-making in political, economic and professional life is perpetuated. In others, women have come to play a significant role. (Adapted from Dimmock and Walker, 2002: 74–6.)

This model can be applied to educational systems in different countries. Bush and Qiang's (2000) study shows that most of these dimensions are relevant to Chinese education:

- *Power is concentrated* in the hands of a limited number of leaders. 'The principal has positional authority within an essentially bureaucratic system … China might be regarded as the archetypal high power-distance (power concentrated) society' (ibid.: 60).
- Chinese culture is *group-oriented*. 'Collective benefits [are] seen as more important than individual needs' (ibid.: 61).
- Chinese culture stresses *consideration* rather than aggression. 'The Confucian scholars advocate modesty and encourage friendly co-operation, giving priority to people's relationships. The purpose of education is to mould every individual into a harmonious member of society' (ibid.: 62).
- *Patriarchal leadership* dominates in education, business, government and the Communist Party itself. There are no women principals in the 89 secondary schools in three counties of the Shaanxi province. Coleman, Qiang and Li (1998: 144) attribute such inequalities to the continuing dominance of patriarchy.

Similar outcomes are evident in Hallinger and Kantamara's (2000) research in Thailand. They show that Thailand is a power-concentrated culture with collectivist values, replicative rather than generative approaches, and a focus on relationship-building in local communities.

Societal culture is one important aspect of the context within which school leaders must operate. They must also contend with organizational culture which provides a more immediate framework for leadership action. Principals and others can help to shape culture but they are also influenced by it. We turn now to examine the main features of organizational culture.

Central features of organizational culture

Organizational culture has the following major features:

1. It focuses on the *values and beliefs* of members of organizations. These values underpin the behaviour and attitudes of individuals within schools and colleges but they may not always be explicit. The assumption of 'shared' values is reflected in much of the literature on culture. Mitchell and Willower (1992: 6) say that culture is 'the way of life of a given collectivity (or organization), particularly as reflected in shared values, norms, symbols and traditions'.

   The sharing of values and beliefs is one way in which cultural models may be distinguished from the subjective perspective. While Greenfield (1991) and other subjective theorists stress the values of individuals, the cultural model focuses on the notion of a single or dominant culture in organizations. This does not necessarily mean that individual values are always in harmony with one another. Morgan (1997: 137) suggests that 'there may be different and competing value systems that create a mosaic of organizational realities rather than a uniform corporate culture'.

Large, multipurpose organizations, in particular, are likely to have more than one culture. 'Our experience with large organizations tells us that at a certain size, the variations among the sub-groups are substantial ... any social unit will produce subunits that will produce subcultures as a normal process of evolution' (Schein, 1997: 14).

Within education, sub-cultures are more likely in large organizations such as universities and colleges, but they may also exist in primary education. Fullan and Hargreaves (1992) argue that some schools develop a 'balkanized' culture made up of separate and sometimes competing groups:

> Teachers in balkanized cultures attach their loyalties and identities to particular groups of their colleagues. They are usually colleagues with whom they work most closely, spend most time, socialize most often in the staffroom. The existence of such groups in a school often reflects and reinforces very different group outlooks on learning, teaching styles, discipline and curriculum. (Ibid.: 71–2)

2. Organizational culture emphasizes the development of *shared norms and meanings*. The assumption is that interaction between members of the organization, or its subgroups, eventually leads to behavioural norms that gradually become cultural features of the school or college: 'The nature of a culture is found in its social norms and customs, and that if one adheres to these rules of behaviour one will be successful in constructing an appropriate social reality' (Morgan, 1997: 139). Walker (2010: 178) adds that these 'basic assumptions' comprise 'the "invisible" workings of schools, consisting of unconscious, taken for granted beliefs'.

   These group norms sometimes allow the development of a monoculture in a school with meanings shared throughout the staff – 'the way we do things around here'. We have already noted, however, that there may be several sub-cultures based on the professional and personal interests of different groups. These typically have internal coherence but experience difficulty in relationships with other groups whose behavioural norms are different. Wallace and Hall (1994) identify senior management teams (SMTs) as one example of group culture with clear internal norms but often weak connections to other groups and individuals:

> SMTs in our research developed a 'culture of teamwork' ... A norm com-
> mon to the SMTs was that decisions must be reached by achieving a
> working consensus, entailing the acknowledgement of any dissenting
> views ... there was a clear distinction between interaction inside the
> team and contact with those outside ... [who] were excluded from the
> inner world of the team. (Ibid.: 28, 127)

In this respect, cultural models are similar to collegiality where loyalty may be to a department or other sub-unit rather than to the
school or college as an entity.

3. Culture is typically expressed through *rituals and ceremonies* which
   are used to support and celebrate beliefs and norms. Schools, in particular, are rich in such symbols as assemblies, prize-givings and, in
   many voluntary schools, corporate worship. 'Symbols are a key
   component of the culture of all schools ... [they] have expressive
   tasks and symbols which are the only means whereby abstract values can be conveyed' (Hoyle, 1986: 150). Beare, Caldwell and
   Millikan (1989: 176) claim that culture is symbolized in three
   modes:
   (a) *Conceptually or verbally*, for example through use of language
       and the expression of organizational aims.
   (b) *Behaviourally*, through rituals, ceremonies, rules, support mecha-
       nisms, and patterns of social interaction.
   (c) *Visually or materially*, through facilities, equipment, memorabilia,
       mottoes, crests and uniforms.
   Schein (1997: 248) argues that 'rites and rituals [are] central to the
   deciphering as well as to the communicating of cultural assumptions'. Wallace and Hall (1994: 29) refer to rituals developed by
   SMTs, including seating arrangements for meetings and social occasions for team members.
4. Organizational culture assumes the existence of *heroes and heroines*
   who embody the values and beliefs of the organization. These honoured members typify the behaviours associated with the culture of
   the institution. Campbell-Evans (1993: 106) stresses that heroes or
   heroines are those whose achievements match the culture: 'Choice
   and recognition of heroes ... occurs within the cultural boundaries
   identified through the value filter ... The accomplishments of those
   individuals who come to be regarded as heroes are compatible with
   the cultural emphases'. Beare, Caldwell and Millikan (1989) stress
   the importance of heroes for educational organizations:

The heroes (and anti-heroes) around whom a saga is built personify the values, philosophy and ideology which the community wishes to sustain ... The hero figure invites emulation and helps to sustain group unity. Every school has its heroes and potential heroes; they can be found among principals and staff, both present and past; among students and scholars who have gone on to higher successes; and among parents and others associated with the school. Every school honour board contains hero material. (Ibid.: 191)

In practice, only those heroes whose achievements are consistent with the culture are likely to be celebrated. 'Whether religion or spirituality, pupils' learning, sporting achievements, or discipline are emphasized in assemblies provides a lens on one facet of school culture ... [schools] are making statements about what is considered important' (Stoll, 1999: 35). In South Africa, for example, the huge interest in school sport means that sporting heroes are frequently identified and celebrated. This was evident in a Durban school visited by the author, where former student Shaun Pollock, the South African cricketer, had numerous photographs on display and a room named after him.

Developing a learning culture

A dominant theme of this book is that leaders should focus strongly on the aims or purposes of their organizations. During the twenty-first century, there has been a growing recognition that the central purpose of schools and colleges should be learning (Southworth, 2005). Walker, (2010: 180) notes that this emphasis is reflected in the language of 'communities of practice' and 'professional learning communities'. He comments that educational reforms often fail to achieve their intended outcomes. 'One of the main reasons for this is that the cultural conditions are missing, misaligned or misunderstood' (ibid.). School staff may fail to reach a shared agreement about their aims or there is a lack of congruence between beliefs and actions (ibid.). In this scenario, people do not act in accordance with their values.

South Africa provides a powerful case study about the misalignment of values and practice. The predominant culture in South African schools reflects the wider social structure of the post-Apartheid era. Decades of institutionalized racism and injustice have been replaced by an overt commitment to democracy in all aspects of life, including education. The move from four separate and unequal education systems to integrated educational provision was underpinned by the rhetoric of democracy.

Badat (1995) traces the nature of educational transition since 1990 and links it to democratic values. He points out the difficulties involved in switching from racist and ethnic education to a system restructured 'along progressive and democratic lines' (ibid.: 141). Education was an important battleground in the struggle for national liberation, encapsulated in slogans such as 'Equal Education' and 'Education towards Democracy', and linked to the wider objective of political rights:

> The form and content of struggles around education have been shaped by a social structure characterized by severe economic and social inequalities of a race, class, gender and geographic nature, political authoritarianism and repression, and the ideology, politics, and organizational strengths and weaknesses of the social movements and organizations that have waged the struggle around apartheid education. (Badat, 1995: 145)

The years of struggle against apartheid inevitably affected schools, particularly those in the townships. One of the 'weapons' of the black majority was for youngsters to 'strike' and demonstrate against the policies of the white government. Similarly, teacher unions were an important aspect of the liberation movement and teachers would frequently be absent from school to engage in protest activity. It is perhaps inevitable that a culture of learning was difficult to establish in such a hostile climate. Badat (1995: 143) claims that 'the crisis in black education, including what has come to be referred to as the "breakdown" in the "culture of learning" ... continued unabated' while the National Education Policy Investigation links this problem to poor conditions in schools:

> South African teachers, especially those in black education, have had to contend with severe difficulties in rendering professional service to their clients, frequently because of the wretched physical conditions prevailing in their schools. Most teachers in black education have experienced a weakening of the social fabric in their communities, and the consequent disintegration of the culture of learning within their institutions. Most have experienced the trauma of having their bona fides questioned and their service rejected by their clients, as well as the humiliation of not being able to offer an adequate defence against these charges. (National Education Policy Investigation, 1992: 32)

This issue surfaced in the author's survey of school principals in the KwaZulu-Natal province. In response to a question about the aims of the school, principals stated that the school is striving:

- to instil in the minds of learners that 'education is their future'

- to show the importance of education within and outside the school
- to provide a conducive educational environment
- to develop a culture of learning.

The absence of a culture of learning in many South African schools illustrates the long-term and uncertain nature of cultural change. The long years of resistance to Apartheid education have to be replaced by a commitment to teaching and learning if South Africa is to thrive in an increasingly competitive world economy. However, educational values have to compete with the still prevalent discourse of struggle and it seems likely that the development of a genuine culture of learning will be slow and dependent on the quality of leadership in individual schools (Bush and Anderson, 2003).

Organizational culture: goals, structure, environment and leadership

Goals

The culture of a school or college may be expressed through its *goals*. The statement of purposes, and their espousal in action, serve to reinforce the values and beliefs of the organization. Where goals and values are consistent, the institution is likely to cohere:

> A clear description of the aims of a school, college or any section within it helps to provide a common vision and set of values. Well-stated aims will seize everybody's interest. Such aims will help in creating a strong culture. (Clark, 1992: 74)

Clark suggests that the process of goal-setting should be linked to organizational values. The core values help to determine the vision for the school or college. The vision is expressed in a mission statement which in turn leads to specific goals. This essentially rational process is similar to that set out in the formal models but within a more overt framework of values. In practice, however, the link between mission and goals is often tenuous:

> Consensus on the core mission does not automatically guarantee that the members of the group will have common goals. The mission is often understood but not well articulated. To achieve consensus on goals, the group needs a common language and shared assumptions about the basic logical operations by which one moves from something as abstract and general as a sense of mission to the concrete goals. (Schein, 1997: 56)

As Schein implies, official goals are often vague and tend to be inadequate as a basis for guiding decisions and action. Much then depends on the interpretation of aims by participants. This is likely to be driven by the values of the interpreter. Where there is a monoculture within the organization, a consistent policy is likely to emerge. If there are competing cultures, or 'balkanization' (Fullan and Hargreaves, 1992), the official aims may be subverted by members of sub-units who will interpret them in line with their own sectional values and goals.

Organizational structure

Structure may be regarded as the physical manifestation of the culture of the organization. 'There is a close link between culture and structure: indeed, they are interdependent' (Stoll, 1999: 40). The values and beliefs of the institution are expressed in the pattern of roles and role relationships established by the school or college. Schein (1997) cautions against a simplistic analysis of the relationship between structure and culture:

> The problem with inferring culture from an existing structure is that one cannot decipher what underlying assumptions initially led to that structure. The same structure could result from different sets of underlying assumptions ... The structure is a clear, visible artifact, but its meaning and significance cannot be deciphered without additional data. (Ibid.: 180–1)

Morgan (1997) argues that a focus on organizations as cultural phenomena should lead to a different conceptualization of structure based on shared meanings. He adopts a perspective similar to the subjective models in discussing the link between culture and structure:

> Culture ... must be understood as an active, living phenomenon through which people create and recreate the worlds in which they live ... we must root our understanding of organization in the processes that produce systems of shared meaning ... organizations are in essence socially constructed realities that are as much in the minds of their members as they are in concrete structures, rules and relations. (Ibid.: 141–2)

Structure is usually expressed in two distinct features of the organization. Individual roles are established and there is a prescribed, or recommended, pattern of relationships between role holders. There is also a structure of committees, working parties and other bodies which have regular or ad hoc meetings. These official encounters present opportunities for the enunciation and reinforcement of organizational culture. Hoyle (1986) stresses the importance of 'interpretation' at meetings:

> Ostensibly formal meetings are called to transact school business either in a full staff meeting or in various sub-committees and working parties. But meetings are rich in symbolic significance both as meetings and in the forms they take ... The teachers have the task of interpreting the purposes of the meeting and they may endow a meeting with functions which are significant to them. (Ibid.: 163–4, original emphasis)

The larger and more complex the organization, the greater the prospect of divergent meanings leading to the development of sub-cultures and the possibility of conflict between them:

> The relationship between organizational structure and culture is of crucial importance. A large and complex organizational structure increases the possibility of several cultures developing simultaneously within the one organization. A minimal organizational structure, such as that found in most primary schools, enhances the possibility of a solid culture guiding all areas of organizational activity. (O'Neill, 1994: 108)

The development of divergent cultures in complex organizations is not inevitable but the establishment of a unitary culture with wide and active endorsement within the institution requires skilled leadership to ensure transmission and reinforcement of the desired values and beliefs (see 'Leadership' section below).

The external environment

The external environment may be regarded as the source of many of the values and beliefs that coalesce to form the culture of the school or college. The professional background and experience of teachers yield the educational values that provide the potential for the development of a common culture. However, there is also the possibility of differences of interpretation, or multiple cultures, arising from the external interests, professional or personal, of teachers and other staff.

O'Neill (1994) charts the links between the external environment and the development of organizational culture. The environment is the source of the values, norms and behaviours that collectively represent culture:

> The well-being of schools and colleges depends increasingly on their ability to relate successfully to their external environments. As such they are

open rather than closed systems. It is therefore fundamentally important that the organization is able to offer visible and tangible manifestations of cultural 'match' to that environment. (Ibid.: 104)

O'Neill (1994) argues that the existence of complementary values should be publicized to external groups in order to sustain their sponsorship and support. This stance is particularly significant for autonomous colleges and schools whose success, or even survival, is dependent on their reputation with potential clients and the community. Caldwell and Spinks (1992) stress the need for self-managing schools to develop a concept of marketing that allows for the two-way transmission of values between the school and its community.

Leadership

Leaders have the main responsibility for generating and sustaining culture and communicating core values and beliefs, both within the organization and to external stakeholders (Bush, 1998). Heads and principals have their own values and beliefs arising from many years of successful professional practice. They are also expected to embody the culture of the school or college. Hoyle (1986) stresses the symbolic dimension of leadership and the central role of heads in defining school culture:

Few heads will avoid constructing an image of the school. They will differ in the degree to which this is a deliberate and charismatic task. Some heads ... will self-consciously seek to construct a great mission for the school. Others will convey their idea of the school less dramatically and construct a meaning from the basic materials of symbol-making: words, actions, artefacts and settings. (Ibid.: 155–6)

Schein (1997: 211) argues that cultures spring primarily from the beliefs, values and assumptions of founders of organizations. Nias, Southworth and Yeomans (1989: 103) suggest that heads are 'founders' of their school's culture. Deal (1985: 615–18) suggests several strategies for leaders who wish to generate culture:

- Document the school's history to be codified and passed on.
- Anoint and celebrate heroes and heroines.
- Review the school's rituals to convey cultural values and beliefs.
- Exploit and develop ceremony.
- Identify priests, priestesses and gossips and incorporate them into

mainstream activity. This provides access to the informal communications network.

However, it should be noted that cultural change is difficult and problematic. Hargreaves (1999: 59) claims that 'most people's beliefs, attitudes and values are far more resistant to change than leaders typically allow'. He identifies three circumstances when culture may be subject to rapid change:

- The school faces an obvious crisis, for example a highly critical inspection report or falling pupil numbers, leading to the prospect of staff redundancies or school closure.
- The leader is very charismatic, commanding instant trust, loyalty and followership. This may enable cultural change to be more radical and be achieved more quickly.
- The leader succeeds a very poor principal. Staff will be looking for change to instil a new sense of direction. (Adapted from Hargreaves, 1999: 59–60.)

Hargreaves (1999: 60) concludes that, 'if none of these special conditions applies, assume that cultural change will be rather slow'.

Leaders also have responsibility for sustaining culture, and cultural maintenance is often regarded as a central feature of effective leadership. Sergiovanni (1984a) claims that the cultural aspect is the most important dimension of leadership. Within his 'leadership forces hierarchy', the cultural element is more significant than the technical, human and educational aspects of leadership:

> The net effect of the cultural force of leadership is to bond together students, teachers, and others as believers in the work of the school ... As persons become members of this strong and binding culture, they are provided with opportunities for enjoying a special sense of personal importance and significance. (Ibid.: 9)

Walker (2010: 193) offers a five-part guide to designing and leading learning cultures:

- Develop a 'common schema'or framework to guide actions and relationships.
- Frame values and beliefs as 'simple rules' to guide behaviour.
- Encourage 'similarity at scale', meaning that the schema is embedded at all levels of the organization.

- Encourage 'emergent feedback' through a network of exchange among individuals and groups.
- Develop 'dispersed control', linked to distributed leadership, that enables self-organizing sub-systems to work collaboratively but in a way that is connected to other groups.

Walker (2010: 194) concludes that 'leaders play a key role in shaping a learning culture' but he also cautions that 'there is no recipe or guidebook for building learning cultures; it's not that simple'.

Moral leadership

The leadership model most closely linked to organizational culture is that of *moral leadership*. This model assumes that the critical focus of leadership ought to be on the values, beliefs and ethics of leaders themselves. Authority and influence are to be derived from defensible conceptions of what is right or good (Leithwood et al., 1999: 10). These authors add that this model includes normative, political/democratic and symbolic concepts of leadership. Several other terms have also been used to describe values-based leadership. These include ethical leadership (Starratt, 2005; Stefkovich and Begley, 2007), authentic leadership (Begley, 2007), spiritual leadership (Woods, 2007), and poetic leadership (Deal, 2005).

Sergiovanni (1984b: 10) says that 'excellent schools have central zones composed of values and beliefs that take on sacred or cultural characteristics'. Subsequently, he adds that 'administering' is a 'moral craft' (Sergiovanni, 1991: 322). The moral dimension of leadership is based on 'normative rationality; rationality based on what we believe and what we consider to be good' (ibid.: 326):

> The school must move beyond concern for goals and roles to the task of building purposes into its structure and embodying these purposes in everything that it does with the effect of transforming school members from neutral participants to committed followers. The embodiment of purpose and the development of followership are inescapably moral. (Ibid.: 323)

West-Burnham (1997: 239) discusses two approaches to leadership which may be categorized as 'moral'. The first he describes as 'spiritual' and relates to 'the recognition that many leaders possess what might be called "higher order" perspectives. These may well be ... represented by a particular religious affiliation'. Such leaders have a set of principles which provide the basis of self-awareness. Woods's (2007: 148) survey of headteachers in England found that 52 per cent 'were inspired or supported in their leadership by some kind of spiritual power'. Deal's (2005: 119) discussion of poetic leadership includes the claim that 'symbolic leaders first find their own spiritual core and then share their gifts with others'.

West-Burnham's (1997: 241) second category is 'moral confidence', the capacity to act in a way that is consistent with an ethical system and is consistent over time. The morally confident leader is someone who can:

- demonstrate causal consistency between principle and practice
- apply principles to new situations
- create shared understanding and a common vocabulary
- explain and justify decisions in moral terms
- sustain principles over time
- reinterpret and restate principles as necessary.

Gold et al.'s (2003: 127) research in English primary, secondary and special schools provides some evidence about the nature of the values held and articulated by heads regarded as 'outstanding' by OFSTED inspectors. These authors point to the inconsistency between 'the technicist and managerial view of school leadership operationalised by the Government's inspection regime' and the heads' focus on 'values, learning communities and shared leadership'. Gold et al. (2003: 136) conclude that their case study heads 'mediate the many externally generated directives to ensure, as far as possible, that their take-up was consistent with what the school was trying to achieve'.

Grace (2000: 241) adopts a temporal perspective in linking moral and managerial leadership in England and Wales. He asserts that, for more than 100 years, 'the position of the headteacher was associated with the articulation of spiritual and moral conceptions'. Subsequently, the requirements of the Education Reform Act led to the 'rising dominance' (ibid.: 234) of management, exemplified by the National Professional Qualification for Headship. Grace (2000: 244) argues, prescriptively, that 'the discourse and understanding of management must be matched by a discourse and understanding of ethics, morality and spirituality'.

Sergiovanni (1991) takes a different approach to the leadership/ management debate in arguing for both moral and managerial leadership. His conception points to the vital role of management but also shows that moral leadership is required to develop a learning community:

In the principalship, the challenge of leadership is to make peace with two competing imperatives, the managerial and the moral. The two imperatives are unavoidable and the neglect of either creates problems. Schools must be run effectively if they are to survive ... But for the school to transform itself into an institution, a learning community must emerge ... [This] is the moral imperative that principals face. (Ibid.: 329)

Greenfield (1991: 208) also stresses that managerial leadership must have a moral base: 'Values lie beyond rationality. Rationality to *be* rationality must stand upon a value base. Values are asserted, chosen, imposed or believed. They lie beyond quantification, beyond measurement' (original emphasis).

Moral leadership is consistent with organizational culture in that it is based on the values, beliefs and attitudes of principals and other educational leaders. It focuses on the moral purpose of education and on the behaviours to be expected of leaders operating within the moral domain. It also assumes that these values and beliefs coalesce into shared norms and meanings that either shape or reinforce culture. The rituals and symbols associated with moral leadership support these values and underpin school culture.

Limitations of organizational culture

Cultural models add several useful elements to the analysis of school and college leadership and management. The focus on the informal dimension is a valuable counter to the rigid and official components of the formal models. By stressing the values and beliefs of participants, cultural models reinforce the human aspects of management rather than their structural elements. The emphasis on the symbols of the organization is also a valuable contribution to management theory while the concept of moral leadership provides a useful way of understanding what constitutes a values-based approach to leadership. However, cultural models do have three significant weaknesses:

1. There may be ethical dilemmas in espousing the cultural model because it may be regarded as the imposition of a culture by leaders on other members of the organization. The search for a monoculture may mean subordinating the values and beliefs of some participants to those of leaders or of the dominant group. 'Shared' cultures may be simply the values of leaders imposed on less powerful participants. Morgan (1997) refers to 'a process of ideological control':

> Ideological manipulation and control is being advocated as an essential managerial strategy … such manipulation may well be accompanied by resistance, resentment and mistrust … where the culture controls rather than expresses human character, the metaphor may thus prove quite manipulative and totalitarian in its influence. (Ibid.: 150–1)

Prosser (1999: 4) refers to the 'dark underworld' of school culture and links it to the micropolitical ideas addressed in Chapter 5: 'The micropolitical perspective recognized that formal powers, rules, regulations, traditions and rituals were capable of being subverted by individuals, groups or affiliations in schools'. Hargreaves (1999: 60) uses the term 'resistance group' to refer to sub-units seeking to subvert leaders and their intended cultural change.

2. The cultural model may be unduly mechanistic, assuming that leaders can determine the culture of the organization (Morgan, 1997). While they have influence over the evolution of culture by espousing desired values, they cannot ensure the emergence of a monoculture. As we have seen, secondary schools and colleges may have several sub-cultures operating in departments and other sections. This is not necessarily dysfunctional, because successful sub-units are vital components of thriving institutions.

   In an era of self-managing schools and colleges in many countries, lay influences on policy are increasingly significant. Governing bodies often have the formal responsibility for major decisions and they share in the creation of institutional culture. This does not mean simple acquiescence to the values of the head or principal. Rather, there may be negotiation, leading to the possibility of conflict and the adoption of policies inconsistent with the leader's own values.

3. The cultural model's focus on symbols such as rituals and ceremonies may mean that other elements of organizations are underestimated. The symbols may misrepresent the reality of the school or college. Hoyle (1986) illustrates this point by reference to 'innovation without change'. He suggests that schools may go through the appearance of change but the reality continues as before:

> A symbol can represent something which is 'real' in the sense that it … acts as a surrogate for reality … there will be a mutual recognition by the parties concerned that the substance has not been evoked but they are nevertheless content to sustain the fiction that it has if there has been some symbolization of the substance … in reality the system carries on as formerly. (Ibid.: 166)

Schein (1997) also warns against placing too much reliance on ritual:

> When the only salient data we have are the rites and rituals that have
> survived over a period of time, we must, of course, use them as best we
> can ... however ... it is difficult to decipher just what assumptions lead-
> ers have held that have led to the creation of particular rites and rituals.
> (Ibid.: 249)

Conclusion: values and action

The cultural model is a valuable addition to our understanding of organizations. The emerging focus on societal culture provides the framework
within which school and college leaders must operate. It also serves to re-
emphasize the significance of context at a time when globalization
threatens to undermine it (Bottery 2004). Values and beliefs are not universal. A 'one size fits all' model does not work for nations any more than
it does for schools.

The recognition that school and college development needs to be preceded by attitudinal change is also salutary, and consistent with the
oft-stated maxim that teachers must feel 'ownership' of change if it is to be
implemented effectively. Externally imposed innovation often fails because
it is out of tune with the values of the teachers who have to implement it.
'Since organization ultimately resides in the heads of the people involved,
effective organizational change always implies cultural change' (Morgan,
1997: 150).

The emphasis on values and symbols may also help to balance the focus
on structure and process in many of the other models. The informal world
of norms and ritual behaviour may be just as significant as the formal elements of schools and colleges. Morgan (1997) stresses the symbolic
aspects of apparently rational phenomena such as meetings:

> Even the most concrete and rational aspects of organization – whether
> structures, hierarchies, rules, or organizational routines – embody
> social constructions and meanings that are crucial for understanding
> how organization functions day to day. For example meetings are
> more than just meetings. They carry important aspects of organiza-
> tional culture. (Ibid.: 146)

Cultural models also provide a focus for organizational action, a dimension
that is largely absent from the subjective perspective. Leaders often adopt
a moral approach and may focus on influencing values so that they
become closer to, if not identical with, their own beliefs. In this way, they
hope to achieve widespread support for, or 'ownership' of, new policies. By
working through this informal domain, rather than imposing change

through positional authority or political processes, heads and principals are more likely to gain support for innovation. An appreciation of the relevance of both societal and organizational culture, and of the values, beliefs and rituals that underpin them, is an important element in the leadership and management of schools and colleges.

References

Badat, S. (1995) 'Educational politics in the transition period', *Comparative Education*, 31(2): 141–59.

Beare, H., Caldwell, B. and Millikan, R. (1989) *Creating an Excellent School: Some New Management Techniques*, London: Routledge.

Begley, P. (2007) 'Editorial introduction: cross-cultural perspectives on authentic school leadership, *Educational Management, Administration and Leadership*, 35(2): 163–4.

Bottery, M. (2004) *The Challenges of Educational Leadership*, London: Paul Chapman Publishing.

Bush, T. (1998) 'Organisational culture and strategic management', in D. Middlewood and J. Lumby (eds), *Strategic Management in Schools and Colleges*, London: Paul Chapman Publishing.

Bush, T. and Anderson, L. (2003) 'Organizational culture', in T. Bush, M. Coleman and M. Thurlow (eds), *Leadership and Strategic Management in South African Schools*, London: Commonwealth Secretariat.

Bush, T. and Qiang, H. (2000) 'Leadership and culture in Chinese education', *Asia Pacific Journal of Education*, 20(2): 58–67.

Bush, T., Qiang, H. and Fang, J. (1998) 'Educational management in China: an overview', *Compare*, 28(2): 133–40.

Caldwell, B. and Spinks, J. (1992) *Leading the Self-Managing School*, London: Falmer Press.

Campbell-Evans, G. (1993) 'A values perspective on school-based management', in C. Dimmock (ed.), *School-Based Management and School Effectiveness*, London: Routledge.

Clark, J. (1992) *Management in Education*, Lancaster: Framework Press.

Coleman, M., Qiang, H. and Li, Y. (1998) 'Women in educational management in China: experience in Shaanxi province', *Compare*, 28(2): 141–54.

Crossley, M. and Broadfoot, P. (1992) 'Comparative and international research in education: scope, problems and potential', *British Educational Research Journal*, 18: 99–112.

Deal, T. (1985) 'The symbolism of effective schools', *Elementary School Journal*, 85(5): 605–20.

Deal, T. (2005) 'Poetical and political leadership', in B. Davies (ed.), *The Essentials of School Leadership*, London: Paul Chapman Publishing.

Dimmock, C. and Walker, A. (2002) 'School leadership in context – societal and organizational cultures', in T. Bush and L. Bell (eds), *The Principles and Practice of Educational Management*, London: Paul Chapman Publishing.

Fullan, M. and Hargreaves, A. (1992) *What's Worth Fighting for in Your School?* Buckingham: Open University Press.

Gold, A., Evans, J., Earley, P., Halpin, D. and Collarbone, P. (2003) 'Principled principals? Values-driven leadership: evidence from ten case studies of "outstanding" leaders', *Educational Management and Administration*, 31(2): 127–38.

Grace, G. (2000) 'Research and the challenges of contemporary school leadership: the contribution of critical scholarship', *British Journal of Educational Studies*, 48(3): 231–47.

Greenfield, T. (1973) 'Organisations as social inventions: rethinking assumptions about change', *Journal of Applied Behavioural Science*, 9(5): 551–74.

Greenfield, T. (1991) 'Re-forming and re-valuing educational administration: whence and when cometh the Phoenix?', *Educational Management and Administration*, 19(4): 200–17.

Hallinger, P. and Kantamara, P. (2000) 'Leading at the confluence of tradition and globalization: the challenge of change in Thai schools', *Asia Pacific Journal of Education*, 20(2): 46–57.

Hargreaves, D. (1999) 'Helping practitioners explore their school's culture', in J. Prosser (ed.), *School Culture*, London: Paul Chapman Publishing.

Harris, C. (1992) 'Ritual and educational management: a methodology', *International Journal of Educational Management*, 6(1): 4–9.

Hoyle, E. (1986) *The Politics of School Management*, Sevenoaks: Hodder and Stoughton.

Leithwood, K., Jantzi, D. and Steinbach, R. (1999) *Changing Leadership for Changing Times*, Buckingham: Open University Press.

Mitchell, J. and Willower, D. (1992), 'Organizational culture in a good high school', *Journal of Educational Administration*, 30(6): 6–16.

Morgan, G. (1997) *Images of Organization*, Newbury Park, CA: Sage.

National Education Policy Investigation (1992) *Teacher Education*, Cape Town: Oxford University Press.

Nias, J., Southworth, G. and Yeomans, R. (1989) *Staff Relationships in the Primary School*, London: Cassell.

O'Neill, J. (1994) 'Organizational structure and culture', in T. Bush and J. West-Burnham (eds), *The Principles of Educational Management*, Harlow: Longman.

Prosser, J. (ed.) (1999) *School Culture*, London: Paul Chapman Publishing.

Schein, E. (1997) *Organizational Culture and Leadership*, San Francisco, CA: Jossey-Bass.

Sergiovanni, T. (1984a) 'Cultural and competing perspectives in administrative theory and practice', in T. Sergiovanni and J. Corbally (eds), *Leadership and Organizational Culture*, Chicago, IL: University of Illinois Press.

Sergiovanni, T. (1984b) 'Leadership and excellence in schooling', *Educational Leadership*, 41(5): 4–13.

Sergiovanni, T.J. (1991) *The Principalship: A Reflective Practice Perspective*, Needham Heights, MA: Allyn and Bacon.

Southworth, G. (2005) 'Learning-centred leadership', in B. Davies (ed.), *The Essentials of School Leadership*, London: Paul Chapman Publishing.

Starratt, R. (2005) 'Ethical leadership', in B. Davies (ed.), *The Essentials of School Leadership*, London: Paul Chapman Publishing.

Stefkovich, J. and Begley, P. (2007) 'Ethical school leadership: defining the best interests of students', *Educational Management, Administration and Leadership*, 35(2): 205–24.

Stoll, L. (1999) 'School culture: black hole or fertile garden for school improvement?', in J. Prosser (ed.), *School Culture*, London: Paul Chapman Publishing.

Walker, A. (2010) 'Building and leading learning cultures', in T. Bush, L. Bell and D. Middlewood (eds), *The Principles of Educational Leadership and Management*, London: Sage.

Walker, A. and Dimmock, C. (2002) 'Introduction', in A. Walker and C. Dimmock (eds), *School Leadership and Administration: Adopting a Cultural Perspective*, London: RoutledgeFalmer.

Wallace, M. and Hall, V. (1994) *Inside the SMT: Teamwork in Secondary School Management*, London: Paul Chapman Publishing.

West-Burnham, J. (1997) 'Leadership for learning: reengineering "mind sets"', *School Leadership and Management*, 17(2): 231–43.

Woods, G. (2007) 'The "bigger feeling": the importance of spiritual experience in educational leadership', *Educational Management, Administration and Leadership*, 35(1): 135–55.

CHAPTER 9

Conclusion

Comparing the management models

The six management models discussed in this book represent different ways of looking at educational institutions. They are analogous to windows, offering a view of life in schools or colleges. Each screen offers valuable insights into the nature of management in education but none provides a complete picture. The six approaches are all valid analyses but their relevance varies according to the context. Each event, situation or problem may be understood by using one or more of these models but no organization can be explained by using only a single approach. In certain circumstances, a particular model may appear to be applicable, while another theory may seem more appropriate in a different setting. There is no single perspective capable of presenting a total framework for our understanding of educational institutions:

> [T]he search for an all-encompassing model is simplistic, for no one model can delineate the intricacies of decision processes in complex organizations such as universities and colleges ... there is a pleasant parsimony about having a single model that summarises a complicated world for us. This is not bad except when we allow our models to blind us to important features of the organization. (Baldridge et al., 1978: 28)

The formal models dominated the early stages of theory development in educational management. Formal structure, rational decision-making and 'top-down' leadership were regarded as the central concepts of effective management and attention was given to refining these processes to increase efficiency. Since the 1970s, however, there has been a gradual realization that formal models are 'at best partial and at worst grossly deficient' (Chapman, 1993: 215).

The other five models featured in this volume all developed in response to the perceived weaknesses of what was then regarded as 'conventional theory'. They have demonstrated the limitations of the formal models and put in place alternative conceptualizations that provide different portrayals of school and college management. While these more recent models are all valid, they are just as partial as the dominant perspective their advocates seek to replace. There is more theory and, by exploring different dimensions of management, its total explanatory power is greater than that provided by any single model:

> Traditional views ... still dominate understandings of theory, research and administrative practice but there are now systematic alternatives to this approach. As a result, educational administration is now theoretically much richer, more diverse and complex than at any other time in its short history. (Evers and Lakomski, 1991: 99)

The six models presented in this book are broad categories, encompassing a variety of different perspectives on management in education. Each has elements that provide a 'shock of recognition' and seem to be essential components of theory.

Collegial models are attractive because they advocate teacher participation in decision-making. The author's experience in postgraduate teaching and as a consultant, suggests that most heads aspire to collegiality, a claim which rarely survives rigorous scrutiny. The collegial framework all too often provides the setting for political activity or 'top-down' decision-making.

The cultural model's stress on values and beliefs, and the subjective theorists' emphasis on the significance of individual meanings, also appear to be both plausible and ethical. In practice, however, these may lead to manipulation as leaders seek to impose their own values on schools and colleges.

The increasing complexity of the educational context may appear to lend support to the ambiguity model with its emphasis on turbulence and anarchy. However, this approach provides few guidelines for managerial action and leads to the view that 'there has to be a better way'.

The six models differ along crucial dimensions but taken together they do provide a comprehensive picture of the nature of management in educational institutions. Throughout the book, four main aspects of management have been addressed:

- goals
- organizational structure
- the external environment
- leadership.

A review of these themes provides the focus for a comparative analysis of the six models.

Goals

There are significant differences in the assumptions made about the *goals* of educational organizations. In formal models, objectives are set at the institutional level. Goals are determined by senior staff and the support of other teachers is taken for granted. The activities of schools and colleges are evaluated in the light of these official purposes.

The advocates of collegial models claim that members of an organization agree on its goals. These approaches have a harmony bias in that they assume that it is always possible for staff to reach agreement based on common values. Unlike formal perspectives, the aims are not imposed from above but emerge from a participative process.

Political models differ from both the formal and collegial perspectives in stressing the goals of sub-units or departments rather than those of the institution. There is assumed to be conflict as groups seek to promote their own purposes. Goals are unstable as sub-units engage in negotiation and alliances form and break down.

Subjective models emphasize the goals of individuals rather than institutional or group purposes. The concept of organizational objectives is supplanted by the view that individuals have personal aims. Schools and colleges are regarded as the subjective creations of the people within them and the only reality is their individual perceptions of the organization. Goals attributed to organizations are thought to be the purposes of the most powerful individuals within them.

Ambiguity theorists claim that goals are problematic. While other perspectives assume that objectives are clear at institutional, group or individual levels, the ambiguity approach assumes that goals are opaque. Aims are also regarded as an unreliable guide to behaviour. In this view it is a mistake to regard policies or events as a corollary of the goals of the institution.

In cultural models, goals are an expression of the culture of the organization. The statement of purposes, and their espousal in action, serves to reinforce the beliefs of the institution. The core values help to determine a vision for the school or college. This vision is expressed in a mission statement which in turn leads to specific goals.

Organizational structure

The notion of *organizational structure* takes on different meanings within the various perspectives. Formal and collegial models regard structures as objective realities. Individuals hold defined positions in the organization and working relationships are assumed to be strongly influenced by these official positions. Formal models treat structures as hierarchical with decision-making as a 'top-down' process. Collegial models present structures as lateral with all members having the right to participate in the decision-making process.

Political models portray structure as one of the unstable and conflictual elements of the institution. The design of the structure is thought to reflect the interests of the dominant groups and individuals within the school or college. Committees and working parties may provide the framework for conflict between interest groups anxious to promote their policy objectives.

Subjective models regard organizational structure as a fluid concept that arises from relationships between individuals, rather than an established framework constraining the behaviour of its members. The emphasis is on the participants rather than the roles they occupy. The interaction of people within the organization is reflected in the structure, which is valid only as long as it represents those relationships accurately.

Ambiguity models assume that organizational structure is problematic because of the uncertain nature of the relationships between loosely coupled sub-units. It may not be clear which group has the power to determine outcomes. Committees and working parties are characterized by the fluid participation of their members. Attendance is variable and decisions may be compromised by the absence of certain individuals, who may challenge outcomes on other occasions.

In cultural models, structure may be regarded as the physical manifestation of the culture of the organization. The values and beliefs of the institution are thought to be expressed in the pattern of roles and role relationships established by the school or college. Committees and whole staff meetings provide opportunities for the enunciation and reinforcement of organizational culture.

The external environment

Relations with external groups are an increasingly important consideration for educational institutions if they are to survive and prosper. These links with the *environment* are portrayed in very different ways by the various models. Some of the formal approaches tend to regard schools and colleges as 'closed systems', relatively impervious to outside influences. Other formal theories typify educational organizations as 'open systems', responding to the needs of their communities and building a positive image to attract new clients.

Collegial models tend to be inadequate in explaining relationships with the environment. Policy is thought to be determined within a participatory framework which can make it difficult to locate responsibility for decisions. Heads may be held accountable for outcomes which do not enjoy their personal support, a position which is difficult to sustain for both the leader and the external group. Collegial approaches gloss over this difficulty by the unrealistic assumption that heads are always in agreement with decisions. In practice, heads and principals have to navigate skilfully between the expectations of their professional colleagues and the requirements of schools' external constituencies.

Political models tend to portray relationships with the environment as unstable. External bodies are regarded as interest groups, which may participate in the complex bargaining process that characterizes decision-making. Internal and external groups may form alliances to press for the adoption of certain policies. Interaction with the environment is seen as a central aspect of an essentially political decision-making process.

In subjective models, the environment is treated as a prime source of the meanings placed on events by people within the organization. Individuals are thought to interpret situations in different ways and these variations in meaning are attributed in part to the different external influences upon participants.

Ambiguity models regard the environment as a source of the uncertainty which contributes to the unpredictability of organizations. The signals from outside groups are often unclear and contradictory, leading to confusion inside schools and colleges. Interpretation of messages from a turbulent environment may be difficult, adding to the ambiguity of the decision-making process.

In cultural models, the external environment may be regarded as the source of many of the values and beliefs that coalesce to form the culture of the school or college. The professional background and experience of teachers yield the educational values that provide the potential for the development of a common culture. However, there is also the possibility of multiple cultures arising from the divergent external interests, professional or personal, of teachers and other staff.

Leadership

The perceived styles of *leadership* inevitably reflect the particular features of the diverse models of management. Within formal perspectives, the official leader is thought to have the major role in goal-setting, decision-making and policy formulation. Heads and principals are located at the apex of a hierarchy and they are acknowledged as the leaders, both inside and outside the institution. The positional leader is assumed to be the most powerful person in the organization.

In collegial models, policies are thought to emerge from a complex process of discussion at committees and in other formal and informal settings. Influence is distributed widely within the institution and the leader is one participant in a collegial style of decision-making. Principals are assumed to have the prime responsibility for the promotion of consensus among their fellow professionals. A hierarchical approach is thought to be inappropriate for participative organizations and the leader is portrayed as *primus inter pares*.

Political models assume that leaders are active participants in the process of bargaining and negotiation, which characterizes decision-making in organizations. Heads and principals have significant resources of power which they are able to deploy in support of their interests and objectives. Leaders may also mediate between groups in order to develop acceptable policy outcomes.

Subjective models de-emphasize the concept of leadership, preferring to stress the personal attributes of individuals rather than their official positions in the organization. All participants, including leaders, are assumed to have their own values and objectives which necessarily influence their interpretation of events. Heads and principals may be able to exert control over colleagues by enunciating institutional policies in line with their own personal interests and requiring the compliance of staff with these interpretations.

Ambiguity models stress the uncertainty facing leaders and the difficulties associated with the management of unpredictability. There are two schools of thought about the most appropriate leadership strategies for conditions of ambiguity. One mode involves active participation, with the leader engaging in various tactical machinations, an approach similar to that assumed in the political models. The alternative stance is to adopt an unobtrusive style with an emphasis on personnel and structural issues. Here the leader sets the framework for decision-making but avoids direct involvement in the policy-making process.

In cultural models, the leader of the organization has the main responsibility for developing and sustaining its culture. Heads and principals have their own values and beliefs arising from many years of successful professional practice and these may become the fulcrum of institutional culture. Leaders are expected to communicate the organization's core values and beliefs, both internally and to external stakeholders. Promotion and maintenance of the culture are regarded as central features of effective leadership.

The six perspectives differ significantly in the ways in which they treat the various components of institutional management, including goals, structure, environment and leadership. The major features of the six models are compared, and linked to the leadership models, in Figure 9.1.

Comparing the leadership models

Leadership can be understood as a process of influence based on clear values and beliefs and leading to a 'vision' for the school. The vision is articulated by leaders who seek to gain the commitment of staff and stakeholders to the ideal of a better future for the school, its students and stakeholders.

Each of the leadership models discussed in this book is partial. In this respect, they are similar to the management models. They provide distinctive but unidimensional perspectives on school leadership. Sergiovanni (1984: 6) adds that much 'leadership theory and practice provides a limited view, dwelling excessively on some aspects of leadership to the virtual exclusion of others'.

The 10 models, adapted from Leithwood, Jantzi and Steinbach (1999), and Bush and Glover (2002), collectively suggest that concepts of school leadership are complex and diverse. They provide clear normative frameworks by which leadership can be understood but relatively weak empirical support for these constructs. They are also artificial distinctions, or 'ideal types', in that most successful leaders are likely to embody most or all of these approaches in their work. Since the previous edition of this book, 'distributed leadership' has been added to the analysis (see Chapter 4). This model has gained ground, partly as a reaction to the perceived inadequacies of singular, or 'heroic', leadership. It also serves to illustrate the fluidity of leadership concepts as theorists seek new ways to explain the phenomenon or to make normative judgements about how schools *should* be led.

Hallinger (1992) provides a helpful, although dated, perspective on three of the most important models: managerial, instructional and transformational. He argues that there has been a shift in expectations

Elements of management	Type of model					
	Formal	Collegial	Political	Subjective	Ambiguity	Cultural
Level at which goals are determined	Institutional	Institutional	Subunit	Individual	Unclear	Institutional or subunit
Process by which goals are determined	Set by leaders	Agreement	Conflict	Problematic May be imposed by leaders	Unpredictable	Based on collective values
Relationship between goals and decisions	Decisions based on goals	Decisions based on agreed goals	Decisions based on goals of dominant coalitions	Individual behaviour based on personal objectives	Decisions unrelated to goals	Decisions based on goals of the organisation or its subunits
Nature of decision process	Rational	Collegial	Political	Personal	Garbage can	Rational within a framework of values
Nature of structure	Objective reality Hierarchical	Objective reality Lateral	Setting for subunit	Constructed through human interaction	Problematic	Physical manifestation of culture
Links with environment	May be 'closed' or 'open' Head accountable	Accountability blurred by shared decision making	Unstable external bodies portrayed as interest groups	Source of individual meanings	Source of uncertainty	Source of values and beliefs
Style of leadership	Head establishes goals and initiates policy	Head seeks to promote consensus	Head is both participant and mediator	Problematic May be perceived as a form of control	May be tactical or unobtrusive	Symbolic
Related leadership model	Managerial	Transformational Participative Distributed	Transactional	Postmodern Emotional	Contingent	Moral

Figure 9.1 Comparing the management models

Note: Figure 9.1 has certain similarities with Cuthbert's (1984) tabular representation of five models using the criteria noted on page 33.

of American principals which can be explained as changing conceptions of school leadership. These three phases were:

1. M*anagerial*. During the 1960s and 1970s, principals came to be viewed as change agents for government initiatives:

   > These categorical programmes and curriculum reforms represented innovations conceived and introduced by policymakers outside the local school ... the principal's role, though apparently crucial, was limited to managing the implementation of an externally devised solution to a social or educational problem. (Hallinger, 1992: 36, original emphasis)

2. *Instructional*. By the mid-1980s, the emphasis had shifted to the 'new orthodoxy' of instructional leadership. 'The instructional leader was viewed as the primary source of knowledge for development of the school's educational programme' (ibid.: 37).

   As noted earlier, this model is primarily about the direction rather than the process of influence. This view is reflected in two contemporary criticisms of instructional leadership:

   (a) an inability 'to document the processes by which leaders helped their schools to become instructionally effective' (ibid.: 37–8)

   (b) principals did not have 'the instructional leadership capacities needed for meaningful school improvement' (ibid.: 38).

3. *Transformational*. During the 1990s, a new conception of leadership emerged based on the assumption that schools were becoming the 'unit responsible for the initiation of change, not just the implementation of change conceived by others' (ibid.: 40). This led to the notion of transformational leadership, as principals sought to enlist support from teachers and other stakeholders to participate in a process of identifying and addressing school priorities.

Hallinger (1992) claims that instructional leadership should not be the predominant role of principals: 'The legitimate instructional leaders ... ought to be teachers. And principals ought to be leaders of leaders: people who develop the instructional leadership in their teachers' (ibid.: 41). In this view, transformational leadership is the vehicle for promoting and developing the instructional leadership capabilities of classroom teachers and those leaders with direct responsibility for promoting learning.

The Hallinger (1992) distinction provides a starting point for an assessment of school leadership in the twenty-first century, beginning with an overview of the 10 leadership models.

Managerial leadership

Managerial leadership is analogous to the formal models of management. It has been discredited and dismissed as limited and technicist, but it is an essential component of successful leadership, ensuring the implementation of the school's vision and strategy. When vision and mission have been defined, and goals agreed, they have to be converted into strategic and operational management. The implementation phase of the decision-making process is just as crucial as the development of the school's vision. Management without vision is rightly criticized as 'managerialist' but vision without effective implementation is bound to lead to frustration. Managerial leadership is a vital part of the armoury of any successful principal.

Instructional leadership

Instructional leadership is different to the other models in focusing on the direction rather than the process of leadership. As suggested in Chapter 1, there is a firm emphasis on the purpose of education and the instructional leadership model stresses the need to focus on teaching and learning as the prime purpose of educational institutions. This model has been endorsed by the English National College, which included it as one of its 10 leadership propositions (NCSL, 2001), but it has two major weaknesses:

- It underestimates the other important purposes of education, including pupil welfare, socialization and the process of developing young people into responsible adults. It also de-emphasizes the less academic aspects of education, including sport, drama and music.
- It says little about the process by which instructional leadership is to be developed. It focuses on the 'what' rather than the 'how' of educational leadership. In this respect, it is a limited and partial model.

Transformational leadership

Transformational leadership is currently in vogue as it accords closely with the present emphasis on vision as the central dimension of leadership. Successful leaders are expected to engage with staff and other stakeholders to produce higher levels of commitment to achieving the goals of the organization which, in turn, are linked to the vision. As Miller and Miller (2001: 182) suggest, 'through the transforming process, the motives of the leader and follower merge'.

There is evidence to suggest that transformational leadership is effective in improving student outcomes (Leithwood, 1994) but this model also has two major limitations:

- It may be used as a vehicle for the manipulation or control of teachers who are required to support the 'vision' and aims of the leader.
- In England, the government uses the language of transformation but this is about the implementation of centrally determined policies, not the identification of, and commitment to, school-level vision and goals.

Participative leadership

Participative leadership is an attractive model because it appears to provide for teachers and other stakeholders to become involved in the decision-making process. It was the normatively preferred approach in the late twentieth and early twenty-first centuries and may be described as shared, collaborative or collegial, as well as participative. The model may be manifested in collective decision-making and/or in the allocation of responsibility for decision-making to specific individuals and groups.

This model is likely to be effective in increasing the commitment of participants, and in the development of team work, but the price may be an increase in the time taken to reach agreement, and there may be difficulties for the formal leader, who remains accountable for decisions reached through the collective process.

Distributed leadership

Distributed leadership has become the normatively preferred leadership model in the twenty-first century, replacing collegiality as the favoured approach. One of its major advocates (Harris, 2010) argues that it is one of the most influential ideas to emerge in the field of educational leadership. It can be differentiated from several other models by its focus on collective, rather than singular, leadership. Gronn (2010) refers to a normative switch 'from heroics to distribution' but also cautions against a view that distributed leadership necessarily means any reduction in the scope of the principal's role. Leithwood et al.'s (2006) important study of the impact of school leadership led to an evidence-based claim that leadership has a greater influence on schools and students when it is widely distributed. Gronn's (2010) 'hybrid' model of leadership may offer the potential to harness the best of both individual and distributed approaches.

Transactional leadership

In transactional leadership, relationships with teachers and other stake-holders are based on a process of exchange. Leaders offer rewards or inducements to followers rather than seeking to improve their commitment or motivation, as in the transformational model. At its most basic, this model is demonstrated in contracts of employment where the employee's terms and conditions of work are articulated and the rewards structure and processes are clarified. In day-to-day management, principals may offer inducements, such as promotion or discretionary salary increments, to persuade others to support their plans, or to undertake certain tasks.

The main limitation of the transactional model is that the exchange is often short-term and limited to the specific issue under discussion. It does not have a wider impact on the behaviour of the teacher or on school outcomes. Transactional leadership does not produce long-term commitment to the values and vision being promoted by school leaders.

Postmodern leadership

Postmodern leadership is very similar to the subjective model of management in focusing on multiple individual perceptions rather than 'objective' reality. There can be as many meanings as there are people in the organization, with power being distributed throughout the school rather than being the preserve of the formal leader. Each participant has a unique view of the institution. There is no absolute truth, only a set of individual insights. There are multiple visions and diverse cultural meanings instead of a single vision enunciated by leaders.

The main limitation of this model, as with the parallel subjective perspective, is that it offers few guidelines for leadership action. Its main contribution to leadership theory is its focus on individual perceptions and its emphasis on the need to deal with people as individuals rather than as an undifferentiated group.

Emotional leadership

Emotional leadership relates to the subjective model in that it concerns individual motivation and interpretation of events. Crawford (2009) shows that emotion is socially constructed and stresses the importance of individual interpretations of events and situations: 'perception is reality'. As she also notes, 'educational leadership cannot, and does not, function without emotion' (ibid.: 164). The distinctive feature of emotional leadership is that it is concerned with feelings rather than facts, recognizing that rational approaches, inherent to the formal models, do not fully explain how principals, for example, enact their leadership role.

Contingent leadership

Contingent leadership acknowledges the diverse nature of school contexts and the advantages of adapting leadership styles to the particular situation, rather than adopting a 'one size fits all' stance. As Leithwood, Jantzi and Steinbach (1999: 15) suggest, 'what is important is how leaders respond to the unique organizational circumstances or problems'. The educational context is too complex and unpredictable for a single leadership approach to be adopted for all events and issues. Given the turbulent environment, leaders need to be able to read the situation and adopt the most appropriate response.

Contingent leadership, then, is not a single model but represents a mode of responsiveness which requires effective diagnosis followed by careful selection of the most appropriate leadership style. It is analogous to selecting the right club for each golf shot or the appropriate clothes for each occasion. It is pragmatic, rather than principled, and can be criticized for having no overt sense of the 'big picture'.

Moral leadership

Moral leadership is based on the values, beliefs and ethics of leaders themselves. Leaders are expected to operate on the basis of what is 'right' or 'good'. It has similar characteristics to transformational leadership, in its emphasis on developing the commitment of followers, but its distinctive element is the focus on values and moral purpose. Leaders are expected to behave with integrity and to develop and support goals underpinned by explicit values. Such leadership may be found in religious schools, where the values are essentially spiritual, or may be a product of the leader's own background and experience. The main difficulty arises when staff or stakeholders do not support the values of leaders. This is likely to be uncomfortable for the people concerned and may lead to dissonance within the school.

Applying the models to schools and colleges

The six management models represent conceptually distinct

approaches to the management of educational institutions. Similarly, the 10 leadership models illustrate different approaches to educational leadership. However, as we have seen, it is rare for a single theory to capture the reality of leadership or management in any particular school or college. Rather, aspects of several perspectives are present in different proportions within each institution. The applicability of each approach may vary with the event, the situation and the participants. The validity of the various models also depends on five overlapping considerations:

1. size of the institution
2. organizational structure
3. time available for management
4. the availability of resources
5. the external environment.

We first examine the impact of institutional size.

1. The *size of the institution* is an important influence on the nature of management structure and process. A small two-teacher primary school necessarily operates very differently from a large multipurpose college. The two primary teachers are likely to determine policy by informal agreement while the head is acknowledged as the official leader by external groups and individuals. It may be appropriate to regard the management of such schools as comprising elements of both the collegial and formal models.

   In large and complex institutions, such as colleges and most secondary schools, there are numerous decision points leading to the development of alternative power centres. Staff may owe their first loyalty to their discipline and their department. These sub-units compete for the resources they require to advance their objectives in a process encapsulated by the political model. In certain circumstances, the situation may be so fluid that the ambiguity perspective appears to be appropriate.

   Size may also be a factor influencing leadership styles. It is easier to adopt a participative approach, and to distribute leadership, in small organizations, while managerial leadership is likely to be an essential dimension in larger schools and colleges. It is straightforward to be sensitive to individual meanings in smaller schools, making the postmodern model, and the emotional dimension, more salient in such settings. Transactional approaches are likely to be most useful in large institutions where leaders may have to bargain with staff as individuals or in groups. Transformational and moral leadership models may be applicable in both large and small organizations although it may be easier to secure the adherence of followers in smaller units.

2. The nature of the *organizational structure* is likely to have a significant impact on school and college management. Heads who establish participative machinery may be motivated by a desire to involve professional colleagues in decision-making. The intention, then, is to create a collegial framework for policy formulation and to lead in a participative style. However, the introduction of committees and working parties also provides several focal points for political behaviour and transactional leadership. Interest groups seek representation on these bodies, engage in bargaining and attempt to build coalitions in order to secure favourable outcomes.

   Leadership styles may also be influenced by organizational structure, although leaders do have the power to modify structure to achieve their own policy objectives. For example, committees and working parties could be restructured to ensure a stronger focus on teaching and learning, a strategy consistent with the instructional leadership model. Distributed leadership may be regarded as independent of the formal structure, as it relates to participants' expertise rather them their official position.

3. The nature of the leadership and management process depends on the *time available for management*. Participants differ in the amount of time they are able and willing to devote to the wider organizational and managerial aspects of their work. Limited time is a major problem for English primary and secondary school teachers despite the provision for 10 per cent PPA (planning, preparation and assessment) time. This is also an issue for heads of department in English secondary schools (Wise and Bush, 1999). The limited time available for management may serve to reinforce the 'top-down' leadership style associated with the formal model and managerial leadership. It also exacerbates the fluid participation in decision-making, which is one of the central characteristics of the ambiguity model.

4. The *availability of resources* is likely to play a part in determining the relevance of the various models. In periods of expansion, it may be possible to adopt a rational approach to the distribution of resources, or to rely on a collegial stance. When funding is limited, departments may face the possibility of reductions in real resources such as staff, books or equipment. In these circumstances, units are likely to seek to defend their interests. Committees and working parties may begin to resemble political arenas as sub-units seek to retain existing resource levels. Simkins (1998) shows how political models

and transactional leadership are likely to thrive when resource allocation is being decided:

> Resource management is … a micropolitical process, providing an arena within which participants compete for the resources which will enable them to develop programmes of activity which embody their values, further their interests and help to provide legitimation for the activities in which they are engaged. (Ibid.: 71)

5. *The external environment* inevitably influences the process of management inside schools and colleges. The shift to self-management in many countries means that schools and colleges have to be responsive to signals from their environment if they are to thrive. Hoy and Miskel (1987: 103) stress the links between the environment and school management: 'The emergence of open-systems theory during the past two decades has highlighted the importance [of the] external environment on internal school structures and processes'.

In periods of relative stability, organizations may be able to adopt formal or collegial approaches. This may be true of institutions with good reputations; they may have an assured clientele and be insulated from environmental turbulence. Fluctuating levels of recruitment in many schools and colleges, however, lead to unpredictable funding with clear implications for staffing and other real resources. The ambiguity model is particularly salient in such an unstable climate and leaders may need to adopt a contingent approach.

While these issues are important influences on management structure and process, it is rarely appropriate to label any school or college as typifying a single model. Rather, elements of many or all of the models may be found in almost all organizations. In any one institution, certain models may be more prevalent than the others but it is a question of relative not absolute significance.

This caution is important but it is possible to conclude that small schools are likely to possess most of the characteristics of formal or collegial organizations, particularly in periods of stability, and be able to operate with a mix of transformational, participative, distributed and managerial leadership. Large, multipurpose colleges undergoing rapid change may display many of the features of the political and ambiguity theories, and leaders may adopt transactional and contingent models. Many secondary schools have elements of all these models, whose significance varies from time to time according to the nature of the activity and the nature and level of participation. Adherents of the subjective and cultural models, and the postmodern and moral leadership approaches, would add that much depends on the values, perceptions and interpretations of individuals and groups in the organization.

Attempts at synthesis

Each of the models discussed in this volume offers valid insights into the nature of leadership and management in schools and colleges. Yet all the perspectives are limited in that they do not give a complete picture of educational institutions. Rather, they turn the spotlight on particular aspects of the organization and consequently leave other features in the shade. As we have seen, most educational institutions display features from most or all of the models:

> Organizations are many things at once! They are complex and multifaceted. They are paradoxical. That's why the challenges facing management are so difficult. In any given situation, there may be many different tendencies and dimensions, all of which have an impact on effective management. (Morgan, 1997: 347)

The inadequacies of each theory, taken singly, have led to a search for a comprehensive model that integrates concepts to provide a coherent analytical framework. The attempt to develop coherence is not just a matter of esoteric interest for educational theorists. Chapman (1993: 212) stresses the need for leaders to develop this broader perspective in order to enhance organizational effectiveness: 'Visionary and creative leadership and effective management in education require a deliberate and conscious attempt at integration, enmeshment and coherence.'

Enderud (1980) developed an integrative model, incorporating ambiguity, political, collegial and formal perspectives. His synthesis is based on the assumption that policy formation proceeds through four distinct phases, which all require adequate time if the decision is to be successful. Attempts by leaders to omit certain stages or to proceed too fast with initiatives may lead to a breakdown of the decision-making process or create the necessity for a 'loopback' to earlier phases.

Enderud assumes an initial period of high ambiguity, as problems, solutions and participants interact at appropriate choice opportunities. This anarchic phase serves to identify the issues and acts as a preliminary sifting mechanism. If conducted properly it should lead to an initial coupling of problems with potential solutions.

The output of the ambiguous period is regarded as the input to the political phase. This stage is characterized by bargaining and negotiations, and usually involves relatively few participants in small, closed committees. The outcome is likely to be a broad measure of agreement on possible solutions.

In the third collegial phase, the participants committed to the proposed solution attempt to persuade less active members to accept the compromise reached during the political stage. The solutions are tested against criteria of acceptability and feasibility, and may result in minor changes. Eventually this process should lead to agreed policy outcomes and a degree of commitment to the decision.

The final phase is the formal or bureaucratic stage during which agreed policy may be subject to modification in the light of administrative considerations. The outcome of this period is a policy which is both legitimate and operationally satisfactory.

Enderud (1980: 241) emphasizes that the significance of each phase varies according to the different perceptions of participants as well as the nature of the issue: 'Different participants often can interpret the same decision as largely anarchic, political, collegial or bureaucratic, according to the phase which is most visible to them, because of their own participation or for other reasons'. Although Enderud acknowledges that the individual interpretations of participants may influence the visibility of the models, the subjective perspective is not featured explicitly in his synthesis. However, Theodossin (1983: 88) does link the subjective approach to the formal or systems model using an analytical continuum. He argues that a systems perspective is the most appropriate way of explaining national developments, while individual and sub-unit activities may be understood best by utilizing the individual meanings of participants.

Theodossin's analysis is interesting and plausible. It helps to delineate the contribution of the formal and subjective models to educational management theory. In focusing on these two perspectives, however, the contribution of other approaches, including the cultural model which has not been incorporated into any of the syntheses applied to education, is necessarily ignored.

The Enderud (1980) model is valuable in suggesting a plausible sequential link between four of the major theories. However, it is certainly possible to postulate different sets of relationships between the models. For example, a collegial approach may become political as participants engage in conflict instead of seeking to achieve consensus. It is perhaps significant that there have been few attempts to integrate the management models since the 1980s. There are probably too many potential combinations for an integration of the 10 leadership models to be a profitable activity.

Gronn (2010) advocates a more limited synthesis, in bringing together singular and distributed leadership into what he describes as a 'hybrid' model. He argues that 'scholars have been increasingly persuaded of the shortcomings of leadership conceived as individually focused action, and have begun substituting a distributed or shared approach', but adds that 'a handful of new studies points in the direction of leadership configurations that are mixed or hybrid in texture'. He concludes that this is likely to lead to 'a grounded understanding of the dynamism of leadership configurations', while providing 'a viable, learning-informed and non-heroic alternative way of thinking about and practicing educational leadership'.

Using theory to improve practice

The 16 models (six management and 10 leadership) present different approaches to the management of education and the syntheses indicate a few of the possible relationships between them. However, the ultimate test of theory is whether it improves practice. Theory which is arid and remote from practice will not improve leadership and management, or help to enhance teaching and learning, which should be at the heart of the educational process.

There should be little doubt about the *potential* for theory to inform practice. School and college managers generally engage in a process of implicit theorizing in deciding how to formulate policy or respond to events. Theory provides the analytical basis for determining the response to events, and helps in the interpretation of management information. Facts cannot simply be left to speak for themselves. They require the explanatory framework of theory in order to ascertain their real meaning.

The multiplicity of competing models means that no single theory is sufficient to guide practice. Rather, managers need to develop 'conceptual pluralism' (Bolman and Deal, 1984) in order to be able to select the most appropriate approach to particular issues and avoid a uni-dimensional stance:

> Understanding organizations is nearly impossible when the manager is unconsciously wed to a single, narrow perspective ... Managers in all organizations ... can increase their effectiveness and their freedom

through the use of multiple vantage points. To be locked into a single path is likely to produce error and self-imprisonment. (Bolman and Deal, 1984: 4)

Conceptual pluralism is similar to the notion of contingent leadership. Both recognize the diverse nature of educational contexts, and the advantages of adapting leadership styles to the particular situation, rather than adopting a 'one size fits all' stance. Leaders should choose the theory most appropriate for the organization and for the particular situation under consideration. Appreciation of the various models is the starting point for effective action. It provides a 'conceptual tool-kit' for the manager to deploy as appropriate in addressing problems and developing strategy.

This eclectic approach may be illustrated by reference to the task of chairing a meeting. The chair may begin by adopting the normatively preferable collegial model and a participative leadership style. If consensus cannot be achieved, s/he may need to adopt the political strategy of mediation to achieve a compromise. If the emerging outcome appears to contradict governing body policy, it may be necessary to stress accountability, a central concept in both the formal model and managerial leadership. During the meeting, there may be different interpretations of the same phenomena and sensitivity may be required to this essentially subjective or postmodern position. There may also be elements of the ambiguity model, particularly if there is fluid participation in the discussion. Throughout the process, the chair may seek to ensure that the tone of the debate, and any policy proposals, are consistent with the values and cultural norms of the organization.

Morgan (1997: 359) argues that organizational analysis based on these multiple perspectives comprises two elements:

- a diagnostic reading of the situation being investigated, using different metaphors to identify or highlight key aspects of the situation
- a critical evaluation of the significance of the different interpretations resulting from the diagnosis.

These skills are consistent with the concept of the 'reflective practitioner', whose managerial approach incorporates both good experience and a distillation of theoretical models, based on wide reading and discussion with both academics and fellow practitioners. This combination of theory and practice enables the leader to acquire the overview required for strategic management. Middlewood (1998: 8) claims that this 'helicopter' quality is a central element of strategic thinking.

While it is widely recognized that appreciation of theory is likely to enhance practice, there remain relatively few published accounts of how the various models have been tested in school or college-based research. More empirical work is needed to enable judgements on the validity of the models to be made with confidence. While observation is important, it may not be sufficient to judge the validity of the models: 'Empirical adequacy is not a sufficient criterion for deciding the merits of competing theories: the same empirical foundation may adequately confirm any number of different theories' (Evers and Lakomski, 1991: 101). Adherents of the subjective model, and of postmodern leadership, would argue that observation is inadequate because it overlooks the perceptions of participants, whose interpretations of events are central to any real understanding of educational institutions. Research is required which combines observation and participants' perceptions to provide a comprehensive analysis of school and college management. The objectives of such a research programme would be to test the validity of the models presented in this volume and to develop an overarching conceptual framework. It is a tough task, but if awareness of theory helps to improve practice, as we have sought to demonstrate, then more rigorous theory should produce more effective practitioners and better schools and colleges.

References

Baldridge, J.V., Curtis, D.V., Ecker, G. and Riley, G.L. (1978) *Policy Making and Effective Leadership*, San Francisco, CA: Jossey-Bass.

Bolman, L. and Deal, T. (1984) *Modern Approaches to Understanding and Managing Organizations*, San Francisco, CA: Jossey-Bass.

Bush, T. and Glover, D. (2002) *School Leadership: Concepts and Evidence*, Nottingham: National College for School Leadership.

Chapman, J. (1993) 'Leadership, school-based decision-making and school effectiveness', in C. Dimmock (ed.), *School-based Management and School Effectiveness*, London: Routledge.

Crawford, M. (2009) *Getting to the Heart of Leadership: Emotion and Educational Leadership*, London: Sage.

Enderud, H. (1980) 'Administrative leadership in organised anarchies', *International Journal of Institutional Management in Higher Education*, 4(3): 235–53.

Evers, C. and Lakomski, G. (1991) 'Educational administration as science: a post-positivist proposal', in P. Ribbins, R. Glatter, T. Simkins and L. Watson (eds), *Developing Educational Leaders*, Harlow: Longman.

Gronn, P. (2010) 'Where to next for educational leadership?', in T. Bush, L. Bell and D. Middlewood (eds), *The Principles of Educational Leadership and Management*, London: Sage.

Hallinger, P. (1992) 'The evolving role of American principals: from managerial to instructional to transformational leaders', *Journal of Educational Administration*, 30(3): 35–48.

Harris, A. (2010) 'Distributed leadership: Current evidence and future directions', in T. Bush, L. Bell and D. Middlewood (eds), *The Principles of Educational Leadership and Management,* London: Sage.

Hoy, W. and Miskel, C. (1987) *Educational Administration: Theory, Research and Practice*, New York: Random House.

Leithwood, K. (1994) 'Leadership for school restructuring', *Educational Administration Quarterly*, 30(4): 498–518.

Leithwood, K., Jantzi, D. and Steinbach, R. (1999) *Changing Leadership for Changing Times*, Buckingham: Open University Press.

Leithwood, K., Day, C., Sammons, P., Harris, A. and Hopkins, D. (2006) *Seven Strong Claims about Successful School Leadership*, London: DfES.

Middlewood, D. (1998) 'Strategic management in education: an overview', in D. Middlewood and J. Lumby (eds), *Strategic Management in Schools and Colleges*, London: Paul Chapman Publishing.

Miller, T.W. and Miller, J.M. (2001) 'Educational leadership in the new millennium: a vision for 2020', *International Journal of Leadership in Education*, 4(2): 181–9.

Morgan, G. (1997) *Images of Organization*, Newbury Park, CA: Sage.

National College for School Leadership (NCSL) (2001) *Leadership Development Framework*, Nottingham: NCSL.

Sergiovanni, T. (1984) 'Leadership and excellence in schooling', *Educational Leadership*, 41(5): 4–13.

Simkins, T. (1998) 'Autonomy, constraint and the strategic management of resources', in D. Middlewood and J. Lumby (eds), *Strategic Management in Schools and Colleges*, London: Paul Chapman Publishing.

Theodossin, E. (1983) 'Theoretical perspectives on the management of planned organizational change', *British Educational Research Journal*, 9(1): 81–90.

Wise, C. and Bush, T. (1999) 'From teacher to manager: the role of the academic middle manager in secondary schools', *Educational Research*, 41(2): 183–96.

Author index

Subject index

THE NINE TAILORS

Stranded in the Fenlands on New Year's Eve, Lord Peter Wimsey is offered hospitality by a local Rector and his wife, and offers to take the place of an incapacitated bell-ringer for that night's nine-hour peal in the village church. With New Year's Day comes a death — Lady Thorpe, whose family's lives have for years been overshadowed by the theft of an emerald necklace. By Easter, Sir Henry Thorpe has joined his wife in eternal sleep. But when her grave is opened to inter her husband alongside her, another body is discovered in there — one mutilated beyond recognition . . .

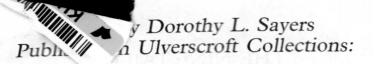

y Dorothy L. Sayers
Publ.... n Ulverscroft Collections:

CLOUDS OF WITNESS
WHOSE BODY?
UNNATURAL DEATH
THE UNPLEASANTNESS AT
THE BELLONA CLUB
FIVE RED HERRINGS
STRONG POISON
STRIDING FOLLY

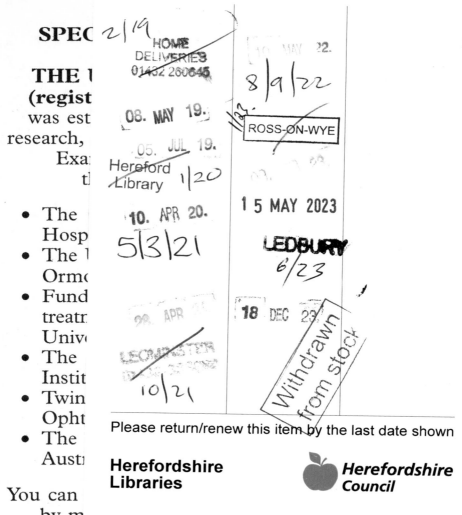

DOROTHY L. SAYERS

◆

THE NINE TAILORS

A Lord Peter Wimsey Mystery

Complete and Unabridged

ULVERSCROFT
Leicester

First published in Great Britain in 1934 by
Victor Gollancz
London

This Ulverscroft Edition
published 2019
by arrangement with
Hodder & Stoughton
An Hachette UK Company
London

A catalogue record for this book is available
from the British Library.

ISBN 978–1–4448–3989–0

Published by
F. A. Thorpe (Publishing)
Anstey, Leicestershire

Set by Words & Graphics Ltd.
Anstey, Leicestershire
Printed and bound in Great Britain by
T. J. International Ltd., Padstow, Cornwall

This book is printed on acid-free paper

Foreword

From time to time complaints are made about the ringing of church bells. It seems strange that a generation which tolerates the uproar of the internal combustion engine and the wailing of the jazz band should be so sensitive to the one loud noise that is made to the glory of God. England, alone in the world, has perfected the art of change-ringing and the true ringing of bells by rope and wheel, and will not lightly surrender her unique heritage.

I have to ask the indulgence of all change-ringers for any errors I may have made in dealing with their ancient craft. The surnames used in this book are all such as I have myself encountered among the people of East Anglia, but every place and person described is wholly fictitious, as are also the sins and negligences of those entirely imaginary bodies, the Wale Conservancy Board, the Fen Drainage Board and the East Level Waterways Commission.

My grateful thanks are due to Mr W.J. Redhead, who so kindly designed for me the noble Parish Church of Fenchurch St Paul and set it about with cherubims.

DOROTHY L. SAYERS

I

A SHORT TOUCH OF KENT TREBLE BOB MAJOR

(Two Courses)

704

By the Course Ends

64352

23456

8th the Observation
Call her in the middle with a double, before,
wrong and home.
Repeated once.   (TROYTE)

the first course

THE BELLS ARE RUNG UP

The coil of rope which it is necessary to hold in the hand, before, and whilst raising a bell, always puzzles a learner; it gets into his face, and perhaps round his neck (in which case he may be hanged!).

TROYTE *On Change-Ringing*

'That's torn it!' said Lord Peter Wimsey.

The car lay, helpless and ridiculous, her nose deep in the ditch, her back wheels cocked absurdly up on the bank, as though she were doing her best to bolt to earth and were scraping herself a burrow beneath the drifted snow. Peering through a flurry of driving flakes, Wimsey saw how the accident had come about. The narrow, hump-backed bridge, blind as an eye-less beggar, spanned the dark drain at right-angles, dropping plumb down upon the narrow road that crested the dyke. Coming a trifle too fast across the bridge, blinded by the bitter easterly snowstorm, he had overshot the road and plunged down the side of the dyke into the deep ditch beyond, where the black spikes of a thorn hedge stood bleak and unwelcoming in the glare of the headlights.

Right and left, before and behind, the fen lay

3

shrouded. It was past four o'clock and New Year's Eve; the snow that had fallen all day gave back a glimmering greyness to a sky like lead.

'I'm sorry,' said Wimsey. 'Whereabouts do you suppose we've got to, Bunter?'

The manservant consulted a map in the ray of an electric torch.

'I think, my lord, we must have run off the proper road at Leamholt. Unless I am much mistaken, we must be near Fenchurch St Paul.'

As he spoke, the sound of a church clock, muffled by the snow, came borne upon the wind; it chimed the first quarter.

'Thank God!' said Wimsey. 'Where there is a church, there is civilisation. We'll have to walk it. Never mind the suitcases; we can send somebody for them. Br'rh! it's cold. I bet that when Kingsley welcomed the wild northeaster he was sitting indoors by a good fire, eating muffins. I could do with a muffin myself. Next time I accept hospitality in the Fen-country, I'll take care that it's at midsummer, or else I'll go by train. The church lies to windward of us, I fancy. It would.'

They wrapped their coats about them and turned their faces to the wind and snow. To left of them, the drain ran straight as a rule could make it, black and sullen, with a steep bank shelving down to its slow, unforgiving waters. To their right was the broken line of the sunk hedge, with, here and there, a group of poplars or willows. They tramped on in silence, the snow beating on their eyelids. At the end of a solitary mile the gaunt shape of a windmill loomed up

4

upon the farther bank of the drain, but no bridge led to it, and no light showed.

Another half-mile, and they came to a signpost and a secondary road that turned off to the right. Bunter turned his torch upon the signpost and read upon the single arm:

'Fenchurch St Paul.'

There was no other direction; ahead, road and dyke marched on side by side into an eternity of winter.

'Fenchurch St Paul for us,' said Wimsey. He led the way into the side-road, and as he did so, they heard the clock again — nearer — chiming the third quarter.

A few hundred yards of solitude, and they came upon the first sign of life in this frozen desolation: on their left, the roofs of a farm, standing some way back from the road, and, on the right, a small, square building like a box of bricks, whose sign, creaking in the blast, proclaimed it to be the Wheat-sheaf public-house. In front of it stood a small, shabby car, and from windows on the ground and first floors light shone behind red blinds.

Wimsey went up to it and tried the door. It was shut, but not locked. He called out, 'Anybody about?'

A middle-aged woman emerged from an inner room.

'We're not open yet,' she began, abruptly.

'I beg your pardon,' said Wimsey. 'Our car has come to grief. Can you direct us — ?'

'Oh, I'm sorry, sir. I thought you were some of the men. Your car broke down? That's bad. Come in. I'm afraid we're all in a muddle — '

5

'What's the trouble, Mrs Tebbutt?' The voice was gentle and scholarly, and, as Wimsey followed the woman into a small parlour, he saw that the speaker was an elderly parson.

'The gentlemen have had an accident with their car.'

'Oh, dear,' said the clergyman. 'Such a terrible day, too! Can I be of any assistance?'

Wimsey explained that the car was in the ditch, and would certainly need ropes and haulage to get it back to the road again.

'Dear, dear,' said the clergyman again. 'That would be coming over Frog's Bridge, I expect. A most dangerous place, especially in the dark. We must see what can be done about it. Let me give you a lift into the village.'

'It's very good of you, sir.'

'Not at all, not at all. I am just getting back to my tea. I am sure you must be wanting something to warm you up. I trust you are not in a hurry to reach your destination. We should be delighted to put you up for the night.'

Wimsey thanked him very much, but said he did not want to trespass upon his hospitality.

'It will be a great pleasure,' said the clergyman, courteously. 'We see so little company here that I assure you you will be doing my wife and myself a great favour.'

'In that case — ' said Wimsey.

'Excellent, excellent.'

'I'm really most grateful. Even if we could get the car out tonight, I'm afraid the axle may be bent, and that means a blacksmith's job. But couldn't we get rooms at an inn or something?

6

I'm really ashamed — '

'My dear sir, pray don't think twice about it. Not but what I am sure Mrs Tebbutt here would be delighted to take you in and would make you very comfortable — very comfortable indeed; but her husband is laid up with this dreadful influenza — we are suffering from quite an epidemic of it, I am sorry to say — and I fear it would not be altogether convenient, would it, Mrs Tebbutt?'

'Well, sir, I don't know as how we could manage very well, under the circumstances, and the Red Cow has only one room — '

'Oh, no,' said the clergyman, quickly, 'not the Red Cow; Mrs Donnington has visitors already. Indeed, I will take no denial. You must positively come along to the Rectory. We have ample accommodation — too much, indeed, too much. My name, by the way, is Venables — I should have mentioned it earlier. I am, as you will have gathered, rector of the parish.'

'It's extremely good of you, Mr Venables. If we're really not putting you out, we will accept your invitation with pleasure. My name is Wimsey — here is my card — and this is my man, Bunter.'

The Rector fumbled for his glasses, which, after disentangling the cord, he perched very much askew on his long nose, in order to peer at Wimsey's card.

'Lord Peter Wimsey — just so. Dear me! The name seems familiar. Have I not heard of it in connection with — ah! I have it! *Notes on the Collection of Incunabula*, of course. A very

7

scholarly little monograph, if I may say so. Yes. Dear me. It will be charming to exchange impressions with another book-collector. My library is, I fear, limited, but I have an edition of the *Gospel of Nicodemus* that may interest you. Dear me! Yes. Delightful to have met you like this. Bless my heart, there's five o'clock striking. We must be off, or I shall get a scolding from my wife. Good afternoon, Mrs Tebbutt. I hope your good man will be much improved by tomorrow; I really think he is looking better already.'

'Thank you, sir; Tom's always so pleased to see you. I'm sure you do him a lot of good.'

'Tell him to keep his spirits up. Such a nasty, depressing complaint. But he's over the worst now. I will send a little bottle of port wine as soon as he is able to take it. Tuke Holdsworth '08,' added the Rector, in an aside to Wimsey; 'couldn't harm a fly you know. Yes. Dear me! Well! We really must be going. I'm afraid my car is not much to boast of, but there's more room in it than one would think. Many's the christening party we've managed to squeeze into it, eh, Mrs Tebbutt? Will you sit beside me, Lord Peter? Your man and your — dear me! have you any luggage . . . Ah! down at Frog's Bridge? I will send my gardener to fetch it. It will be quite safe where it is; we're all honest people about here, aren't we, Mrs Tebbutt? That's right. You must have this rug about your legs — yes, I insist. No, no, thank you. I can start her up quite well. I am so well accustomed to do it. There, you see! A few good pulls and she comes up as brisk as a bell. All right behind, my man? Good.

Excellent. *Good* afternoon, Mrs Tebbutt!'

The ancient car, shuddering to her marrow-bones, lurched away down the straight and narrow road. They passed a cottage, and then, quite suddenly, on their right, there loomed out of the whirling snow a grey, gigantic bulk.

'Great Heavens!' exclaimed Wimsey, 'is that your church?'

'Yes, indeed,' said the Rector, with pride. 'You find it impressive?'

'Impressive!' said Wimsey. 'Why, it's like a young cathedral. I'd no idea. How big is your parish, then?'

'You'll be surprised when I tell you,' said the Rector, with a chuckle. 'Three hundred and forty souls — no more. Astonishing, is it not? But you find the same thing all over the fens. East Anglia is famous for the size and splendour of its parish churches. Still, we flatter ourselves we are almost unique, even in this part of the world. It was an abbey foundation, and in the old days Fenchurch St Paul must have been quite an important place. How high should you say our tower was?'

Wimsey gazed up at the great pile.

'It's difficult to tell in this darkness. Not less than a hundred and thirty feet, surely.'

'Not a bad guess. A hundred and twenty-eight, to be exact, to the top of the pinnacles, but it looks more, because of the comparative lowness of the clerestory roof. There aren't many to beat us. St Peter Mancroft, of course — but that's a town church. And St Michael's, Coventry, is one hundred and thirty feet without the spire. But I would venture to back Fenchurch St Paul against

9

them all for beauty of proportion. You will see that better when we turn the corner. Here we are. I always blow my horn here; the wall and the trees make it so very dangerous. I sometimes think we ought to have the churchyard wall set back a little, in the public interest. Ah! now you get a little idea. Very fine, is it not, the piling of the aisle and clerestory? You will be able to judge better in daylight. Here is the Rectory — just opposite the church. I always blow my horn at the gate for fear anybody should be about. The bushes make it so very dark. Ah! safely negotiated. I'm sure you will be glad to get into the warm and have a cup of tea — or possibly something stronger. I always blow my horn at the door, so as to tell my wife I am back. She gets nervous when I am out after lighting-up time; the dykes and drains make these roads so very awkward, and I am not as young as I was. I fear I am already a little late. Ah! here is my wife. Agnes, my dear, I am sorry to be a little behind time, but I have brought a guest back with me. He has had an accident with his car and will stay the night with us. The rug! Allow me! I fear that seat is something of a *res angusta*. Pray be careful of your head. Ah! all is well. My dear — Lord Peter Wimsey.'

Mrs Venables, a plump and placid figure in the lamplight from the open door, received the invasion with competent tranquillity.

'How fortunate that my husband should have met you. An accident? I do hope you are not hurt. I always say these roads are perfect death-traps.'

'Thank you,' said Wimsey. 'There is no harm done. We stupidly ran off the road — at Frog's Bridge, I understand.'

'A very nasty place — quite a mercy you didn't go into the Thirty-foot Drain. Do come in and sit down and get yourselves warm. Your man? Yes, of course. Emily! Take this gentleman's manservant into the kitchen and make him comfortable.'

'And tell Hinkins to take the car and go down to Frog's Bridge for the luggage,' added the Rector. 'He will find Lord Peter's car there. He had better go at once, before the weather gets worse. And, Emily! tell him to send over to Wilderspin and arrange to get the car out of the dyke.'

'Tomorrow morning will do for that,' said Wimsey.

'To be sure. First thing tomorrow morning. Wilderspin is the blacksmith — an excellent fellow. He will see to the matter most competently. Dear me, yes! And now, come in, come in! We want our tea. Agnes, my dear, have you explained to Emily that Lord Peter will be staying the night?'

'That will be all right,' said Mrs Venables, soothingly. 'I do hope, Theodore, you have not caught cold.'

'No, no, my dear. I have been well wrapped up. Dear me, yes! Ha! What do I see? Muffins?'

'I was just wishing for muffins,' said Wimsey.

'Sit down, sit down and make a good meal. I'm sure you must be famished. I have seldom known such bitter weather. Would you prefer a whisky-and-soda, perhaps?'

'Tea for me,' said Wimsey. 'How jolly all this looks! Really, Mrs Venables, it's tremendously good of you to take pity upon us.'

'I'm only so glad to be able to help,' said Mrs Venables, smiling cheerfully. 'Really, I don't think there's anything to equal the dreariness of these fen roads in winter. It's most fortunate your accident landed you comparatively close to the village.'

'It is indeed.' Wimsey gratefully took in the cosy sitting-room, with its little tables crowded with ornaments, its fire roaring behind a chaste canopy of velvet overmantel, and the silver tea-vessel winking upon the polished tray. 'I feel like Ulysses, come to port after much storm and peril.'

He bit gratefully into a large and buttery muffin.

'Tom Tebbutt seems a good deal better today,' observed the Rector. 'Very unfortunate that he should be laid up just now, but we must be thankful that it is no worse. I only hope there are no further casualties. Young Pratt will manage very well, I think; he went through two long touches this morning without a single mistake, and he is extremely keen. By the way, we ought, perhaps to warn our visitor — '

'I'm sure we ought,' said Mrs Venables. 'My husband has asked you to stay the night, Lord Peter, but he ought to have mentioned that you will probably get very little sleep, being so close to the church. But perhaps you do not mind the sound of bells.'

'Not at all,' said Wimsey.

'My husband is a very keen change-ringer,' pursued Mrs Venables, 'and, as this is New Year's Eve — '

The Rector, who seldom allowed anybody else to finish a sentence, broke in eagerly.

'We hope to accomplish a real feat tonight,' he said, 'or rather, I should say, tomorrow morning. We intend to ring the New Year in with — you are not, perhaps, aware that we possess here one of the finest rings in the country?'

'Indeed?' said Wimsey. 'Yes, I believe I have heard of the Fenchurch bells.'

'There are, perhaps, a few heavier rings,' said the Rector, 'but I hardly know where you would rival us for fullness and sweetness of tone. Number seven, in particular, is a most noble old bell, and so is the tenor, and the John and Jericho bells are also remarkably fine — in fact, the whole ring is most 'tuneable and sound', as the old motto has it.'

'It is a full ring of eight?'

'Oh, yes. If you are interested. I should like to show you a very charming little book written by my predecessor, giving the whole history of the bells. The tenor, Tailor Paul, was actually cast in a field next the church-yard in the year 1614. You can still see the depression in the earth where the mould was made and the field itself is called the Bell-Field to this day.'

'And have you a good set of ringers?' inquired Wimsey, politely.

'Very good indeed. Excellent fellows and most enthusiastic. That reminds me, I was about to say that we have arranged to ring the New Year

13

in tonight with no less,' said the Rector, emphatically, 'no less than fifteen thousand, eight hundred and forty Kent Treble Bob Majors. What do you think of that? Not bad, eh?'

'Bless my heart!' said Wimsey. 'Fifteen thousand — '

'Eight hundred and forty,' said the Rector.

Wimsey made a rapid calculation.

'A good many hours' work there.'

'Nine hours,' said the Rector, with relish.

'Well done, sir,' said Wimsey. 'Why, that's equal to the great performance of the College Youths in eighteen hundred and something.'

'In 1868,' agreed the Rector. 'That is what we aim to emulate. And, what's more, but for the little help I can give, we shall be obliged to do as well as they did, and ring the whole peal with eight ringers only. We had hoped to have twelve, but unhappily, four of our best men have been laid low by this terrible influenza, and we can get no help from Fenchurch St Stephen (which has a ring of bells, though not equal to ours) because there they have no Treble Bob ringers and confine themselves to Grandsire Triples.'

Wimsey shook his head, and helped himself to his fourth muffin.

'Grandsire Triples are most venerable,' he said solemnly, 'but you can never get the same music — '

'That's what I say,' crowed the Rector. 'You never can get the same music when the tenor is rung behind — not even with Stedman's, though we are very fond here of Stedman's and ring them, I venture to say, very well. But for interest and variety and for sweetness in the peal, give me Kent Treble Bob every time.'

'Quite right, sir,' said Wimsey.

'You will never beat it,' said Mr Venables, soaring away happily to the heights of the belfry, and waving his muffin in the air, so that the butter ran down his cuff. 'Take even Grandsire Major — I cannot help feeling it as a defect that the blows come behind so monotonously at the bobs and singles — particularly at the singles, and the fact that the treble and second are confined to a plain hunting course — '

The rest of the Rector's observations on the Grandsire method of change-ringing were unhappily lost, for at that moment Emily made her appearance at the door, with the ominous words:

'If you please, sir, could James Thoday speak to you for a moment?'

'*James* Thoday?' said the Rector, 'Why, certainly, of course. Put him in the study, Emily, and I will come in a moment.'

The Rector was not long gone, and when he returned his face was as long as a fiddle. He let himself drop into his chair in an attitude off utter discouragement.

'This,' he ejaculated, dramatically, 'is an irreparable disaster!'

'Good gracious, Theodore! What in the world is the matter?'

'William Thoday! Of all nights in the year! Poor fellow, I ought not to think of myself, but it is a bitter disappointment — a bitter disappointment.'

15

'Why, what has happened to Thoday?'

'Struck down,' said the Rector, 'struck down by this wretched scourge of influenza. Quite helpless. Delirious. They have sent for Dr Baines.'

'T'chk, t'chk,' said Mrs Venables.

'It appears,' went on the Rector, 'that he felt unwell this morning, but insisted — most unwisely, poor man — on driving in to Walbeach on some business or other. Foolish fellow! I thought he looked seedy when he came in to see me last night. Most fortunately, George Ashton met him in the town and saw how bad he was and insisted on coming back with him. Poor Thoday must have taken a violent chill in all this bitter cold. He was quite collapsed when they got him home and they had to put him to bed instantly, and now he is in a high fever and worrying all the time because he cannot get to the church tonight. I told his brother to make every effort to calm his mind, but I fear it will be difficult. He is so enthusiastic, and the thought that he has been incapacitated at this crisis seems to be preying on his mind.'

'Dear, dear,' said Mrs Venables, 'but I expect Dr Baines will give him something to quiet him down.'

'I hope so, sincerely. It is a disaster, of course, but it is distressing that he should take it so to heart. Well, well. What can't be cured must be endured. This is our last hope gone. We shall be reduced to ringing minors.'

'Is this man one of your ringers, then, padre?'

'Unfortunately, he is, and there is no one now

16

to take his place. Our grand scheme will have to be abandoned. Even if I were to take a bell myself, I could not possibly ring for nine hours. I am not getting younger, and besides, I have an Early Service at eight o'clock, in addition to the New Year service which will not release me till after midnight. Ah. well! Man proposes and God disposes — unless' — the Rector turned suddenly and looked at his guest — 'you were speaking just now with a good deal of feeling about Treble Bob — you are not, yourself, by any chance, a ringer?'

'Well,' said Wimsey, 'I used at one time to pull quite a pretty rope. But whether, at this time of day — '

'Treble Bob?' inquired the Rector, eagerly.

'Treble Bob, certainly. But it's some time since — '

'It will come back to you,' cried the Rector, feverishly. 'It will come back. Half an hour with the handbells — '

'My dear!' said Mrs Venables.

'Isn't it wonderful?' cried the Rector. 'Is it not really providential? That just at this moment we should be sent a guest who is actually a ringer and accustomed to ringing Kent Treble Bob?' He rang for the maid. 'Hinkins must go round at once and call the lads together for a practice ring on the handbells. My dear, I am afraid we shall have to monopolise the dining-room, if you don't mind. Emily, tell Hinkins that I have here a gentleman who can ring the peal with us and I want him to go round immediately — '

'One moment, Emily. Theodore, is it quite fair

17

to ask Lord Peter Wimsey, after a motor accident, and at the end of a tiring day, to stay up ringing bells from midnight to nine o'clock? A short peal, perhaps, if he really does not mind, but even so, are we not demanding rather a lot of his good nature?'

The Rector's mouth dropped like the mouth of a hurt child, and Wimsey hastened to his support.

'Not in the least, Mrs Venables. Nothing would please me more than to ring bells all day and all night. I am not tired at all. I really don't need rest. I would far rather ring bells. The only thing that worries me is whether I shall be able to get through the peal without making stupid mistakes.'

'Of course you will, of course you will,' said the Rector, hurriedly. 'But as my wife says — really, I am afraid I am being very thoughtless. Nine hours is too much. We ought to confine ourselves to five thousand changes or so — '

'Not a bit of it,' said Wimsey. 'Nine hours or nothing. I insist upon it. Probably, once you have heard my efforts, it will be nothing.'

'Pooh! nonsense!' cried the Rector. 'Emily, tell Hinkins to get the ringers together here by — shall we say half-past six? I think they can all be here by then, except possibly Pratt, who lives up at Tupper's End, but I can make the eighth myself. How delightful this is! Positively, I cannot get over the amazing coincidence of your arrival. It shows the wonderful way in which Heaven provides even for our pleasures, if they be innocent. I hope, Lord Peter, you will not mind if I make a little reference to it in my sermon tonight? At least, it will hardly be a sermon — only a few thoughts appropriate to the New Year and its opportunities. May I ask where you usually ring?'

'Nowhere, nowadays; but when I was a boy I used to ring at Duke's Denver, and when I go home at Christmas and so on, I occasionally lay hand to a rope even now.'

'Duke's Denver? Of course — St John ad-Portam-Latinam — a beautiful little church; I know it quite well. But I think you will admit that our bells are finer. Well, now, if you will excuse me, I will just run and put the dining-room in readiness for our practice.'

He bustled away.

'It is very good of you to indulge my husband's hobby,' said Mrs Venables; 'this occasion has meant so much to him, and he has had so many disappointments about it. But it seems dreadful to offer you hospitality and then keep you hard at work all night.'

Wimsey again assured her that the pleasure was entirely his.

'I shall insist on your getting a few hours' rest at least,' was all Mrs Venables could say. 'Will you come up now and see your room? You will like a wash and brush-up at any rate. We will have supper at 7.30, if we can get my husband to release you by then, and after that, you really must go and lie down for a nap. I have put you in here — I see your man has everything ready for you.'

'Well, Bunter,' said Wimsey, when Mrs Venables had departed, leaving him to make himself presentable by the inadequate light of a small oil-lamp and a candle, 'that looks a nice bed — but I am not fated to sleep in it.'

'So I understand from the young woman, my lord.'

'It's a pity you can't relieve me at the rope, Bunter.'

'I assure your lordship that for the first time in my existence I regret that I have made no practical study of campanology.'

'I am always so delighted to find that there are things you cannot do. Did you ever try?'

'Once only, my lord, and on that occasion an accident was only narrowly averted. Owing to my unfortunate lack of manual dexterity I was very nearly hanged in the rope, my lord.'

'That's enough about hanging,' said Wimsey, peevishly. 'We're not detecting now, and I don't want to talk shop.'

'Certainly not, my lord. Does your lordship desire to be shaved?'

'Yes — let's start the New Year with a clean face.'

'Very good, my lord.'

★ ★ ★

Descending, clean and shaven, to the dining-room, Wimsey found the table moved aside and eight chairs set in a circle. On seven of the chairs sat seven men, varying in age from a gnarled old gnome with a long beard to an embarrassed

20

youth with his hair plastered into a cowlick; in the centre, the Rector stood twittering like an amiable magician. 'Ah! there you are! Splendid! excellent! Now, lads, this is Lord Peter Wimsey, who has been providentially sent to assist us out of our difficulty. He tells me he is a little out of practice, so I am sure you will not mind putting in a little time to enable him to get his hand in again. Now I must introduce you all. Lord Peter, this is Hezekiah Lavender, who has pulled the tenor for sixty years and means to pull it for twenty years longer, don't you, Hezekiah?'

The little gnarled man grinned toothlessly and extended a knobbly hand.

'Proud to meet you, my lord. Yes, I've pulled old Tailor Paul a mort o' times now. Her and me's well acquainted, and I means to go on a-pulling of her till she rings the nine tailors for me, that I do.'

'I hope you will long be spared to do it, Mr Lavender.'

'Ezra Wilderspin,' went on the Rector. 'He's our biggest man, and he pulls the smallest bell. That's often the way of things, isn't it? He is our blacksmith, by the way, and has promised to get your car put right for you in the morning.'

The blacksmith laughed sheepishly, engulfed Wimsey's fingers in an enormous hand and retired to his chair in some confusion.

'Jack Godfrey,' continued the Rector. 'Number Seven. How's Batty Thomas going now, Jack?'

'Going fine, thank you, sir, since we had them new gudgeons put in.'

'Jack has the honour of ringing the oldest bell

21

we have,' added the Rector. 'Batty Thomas was cast in 1338 by Thomas Belleyetere of Lynn; but she gets her name from Abbot Thomas who recast her in 1380 — doesn't she, Jack?'

'So she do, sir,' agreed Mr Godfrey. Bells, it may be noted, like ships and kittens, have a way of being female, whatever names they are given.

'Mr Donnington, the landlord of the Red Cow, our churchwarden,' went on the Rector, bringing forward a long, thin man with a squint. 'I ought to have mentioned him first of all, by right of his office, but then you see, though he himself is very distinguished, his bell is not so ancient as Tailor Paul or Batty Thomas. He takes charge of Number Six — Dimity, we call her — a comparative newcomer in her present shape, though her metal is old.'

'And a sweeter bell we haven't got in the ring,' averred Mr Donnington, stoutly. 'Pleased to meet you, my lord.'

'Joe Hinkins, my gardener. You have already met. I think. He pulls Number Five. Harry Gotobed, Number Four; our sexton, and what better name could a sexton have? And Walter Pratt — our youngest recruit, who is going to ring Number Three and do it very well indeed. So glad you were able to get here in time, Walter. That's all of us. You, Lord Peter, will take poor William Thoday's bell, Number Two. She and Number Five were recast in the same year as Dimity — the year of the old Queen's Jubilee; her name is Sabaoth. Now, let's get to work. Here is your handbell; come and sit next to Walter Pratt. Our good old friend Hezekiah will be the conductor, and you'll find he can sing out his calls as loud and clear as the bells, for all he's seventy-five years past. Can't you, Granddad?'

'Ay, that I can,' cried the old man, cheerfully. 'Now, boys, if you be ready, we'll ring a little touch of 96, just to put this gentleman in the way of it, like. You'll remember, my lord, that you starts by making the first snapping lead with the treble and after that you goes into the slow hunt till she comes down to snap with you again.'

'Right you are,' said Wimsey. 'And after that I make the thirds and fourths.'

'That's so, my lord. And then it's three steps forward and one back till you lay the blows behind.'

'Carry on, sergeant-major.'

The old man nodded, adding: 'And you, Wally Pratt, mind what you're about, and don't go a-follerin' your course bell beyond third place. I've telled yew about that time and again. Now, are you ready, lads — go!'

★　★　★

The art of change ringing is peculiar to the English, and, like most English peculiarities, unintelligible to the rest of the world. To the musical Belgian, for example, it appears that the proper thing to do with a carefully tuned ring of bells is to play a tune upon it. By the English campanologist, the playing of tunes is considered to be a childish game, only fit for foreigners; the proper use of bells is to work out mathematical permutations and combinations. When he speaks

23

of the music of his bells, he does not mean
musician's music — still less what the ordinary
man calls music. To the ordinary man, in fact,
the pealing of bells is a monotonous jangle and
a nuisance, tolerable only when mitigated by
remote distance and sentimental association. The
change-ringer does, indeed, distinguish musical
differences between one method of producing
his permutations and another; he avers, for
instance, that where the hinder bells run 7, 5, 6,
or 5, 6, 7, or 5, 7, 6, the music is always prettier,
and can detect and approve, where they occur,
the consecutive fifths of Tittums and the
cascading thirds of the Queen's change. But
what he really means is, that by the English
method of ringing with rope and wheel, each
several bell gives forth her fullest and her noblest
note. His passion — and it is a passion — finds
its satisfaction in mathematical completeness
and mechanical perfection, and as his bell
weaves her way rhythmically up from lead to
hinder place and down again, he is filled with the
solemn intoxication that comes of intricate ritual
faultlessly performed. To any disinterested
spectator, peeping in upon the rehearsal, there
might have been something a little absurd about
the eight absorbed faces; the eight tense bodies
poised in a spellbound circle on the edges of
eight dining-room chairs; the eight upraised right
hands, decorously wagging the handbells upward
and downward; but to the performers, everything
was serious and important as an afternoon with
the Australians at Lords.

Mr Hezekiah Lavender having called three

successive bobs, the bells came back into rounds without mishap.

'Excellent,' said the Rector. 'You made no mistake about that.'

'All right, so far,' said Wimsey.

'The gentleman will do well enough,' agreed Mr Lavender. 'Now, boys, once again. What 'ull we make it this time, sir?'

'Make it a 704,' said the Rector, consulting his watch. 'Call her in the middle with a double, before, wrong and home, and repeat.'

'Right you are, sir. And you, Wally Pratt, keep your ears open for the treble and your eyes on your course bell, and don't go gapin' about or you'll have us all imbrangled.'

The unfortunate Pratt wiped his forehead, curled his boots tightly round the legs of his chair, and took a firm hold of his bell. Whether out of nervousness or for some other cause, he found himself in trouble at the beginning of the seventh lead, 'imbrangled' himself and his neighbours very successfully and broke into a severe perspiration.

'Stand!' growled Mr Lavender, in a disgusted tone. 'If that's the way you mean to set about it, Wally Pratt, we may just so well give up the ringing of this here peal. Surely you know by this time what to do at a bob?'

'Come, come,' said the Rector. 'You mustn't be disheartened, Wally. Try again. You forgot to make the double dodge in 7, 8, didn't you?'

'Yes, sir.'

'Forgot!' exclaimed Mr Lavender, waggling his beard. 'Now, just yew take example by his

25

lordship here. *He* didn't go forgettin' things, none the more for bein' out o' practice.'

'Come, come, Hezekiah,' cried the Rector again. 'You mustn't be hard on Wally. We haven't all had sixty years' experience.'

Mr Lavender grunted, and started the whole touch again from the beginning. This time Mr Pratt kept his head and his place and the ringing went on successfully through to its conclusion.

'Well rung, all,' cried the Rector. 'Our new recruit will do us credit, I think, Hezekiah?'

'I almost fell down in the second lead, though,' said Wimsey, laughing. 'I as nearly as possible forgot to lay the four blows in fourths place at the bob. However, nearly isn't quite.'

'You'll keep your place all right, my lord,' said Mr Lavender. 'As for you, Wally Pratt — '

'I think,' said the Rector hastily, 'we'd better run across to the church now and let Lord Peter get the feel of his bell. You may as well all come over and ring the bells up for service. And, Jack, see to it that Lord Peter's rope is made comfortable for him. Jack Godfrey takes charge of the bells and ropes,' he added in explanation, 'and keeps them in apple-pie order for us.'

Mr Godfrey smiled.

'We'll need to let the tuckings down a goodish bit for his lordship,' he observed, measuring Wimsey with his eye; 'he's none so tall as Will Thoday, not by a long chalk.'

'Never you mind,' said Wimsey. 'In the words of the old bell-motto: I'd have it to be understood that though I'm little, yet I'm good.'

'Of course,' said the Rector, 'Jack didn't mean

anything else. But Will Thoday is a very tall man indeed. Now where did I put my hat? Agnes, my dear! Agnes! I can't find my hat. Oh, here, to be sure. And my muffler — I'm so much obliged to you. Now, let me just get the key of the belfry and we — dear me, now! When did I have that key last?'

'It's all right, sir,' said Mr Godfrey. 'I have all the keys here, sir.'

'The church-key as well?'

'Yes, sir, and the key of the bell-chamber.'

'Oh, good, good — excellent. Lord Peter will like to go up into the bell-chamber. To my mind, Lord Peter, the sight of a ring of good bells — I beg your pardon, my dear?'

'I said. Do remember dinner-time, and don't keep poor Lord Peter too long.'

'No, no, my dear, certainly not. But he will like to look at the bells. And the church itself is worth seeing. Lord Peter. We have a very interesting twelfth-century font, and the roof is considered to be one of the finest specimens — yes, yes, my dear, we're just going.'

The hall-door was opened upon a glimmering world. The snow was still falling fast; even the footprints made less than an hour earlier by the ringers were almost obliterated. They straggled down the drive and crossed the road. Ahead of them, the great bulk of the church loomed dark and gigantic. Mr Godfrey led the way with an old-fashioned lantern through the lych-gate and along a path bordered with tombstones to the south door of the church, which he opened, with a groaning of the heavy lock. A powerful ecclesiastical odour, compounded of ancient wood, varnish, dry rot, hassocks, hymn-books, paraffin lamps, flowers and candles, all gently baking in the warmth of slow-combustion stoves, billowed out from the interior. The tiny ray of the lantern picked out here the poppy-head on a pew, here the angle of a stone pillar, here the gleam of brass from a mural tablet. Their footsteps echoed queerly in the great height of the clerestory.

'All Transitional here,' whispered the Rector, 'except the Late Perpendicular window at the end of the north aisle, which of course you can't see. Nothing is left of the original Norman foundation but a couple of drums at the base of the chancel arch, but you can trace the remains of the Norman apse, if you look for it, underneath the Early English sanctuary. When we have more light, you will notice — Oh, yes, Jack, yes, by all means. Jack Godfrey is quite right, Lord Peter — we must not waste time. I am apt to be led away by my enthusiasm.'

He conducted his guest westwards under the tower arch, and thence, in the wake of Godfrey's lantern up a steep and winding belfry stair, its stone treads worn shallow with the feet of countless long-dead ringers. After a turn or so, the procession halted: there was a jingling of keys and the lantern moved away to the right through a narrow door. Wimsey, following, found himself in the ringing-chamber of the belfry.

It was in no way remarkable, except in being perhaps a little loftier than the average, on account of the exceptional height of the tower.

By daylight, it was well lit, having a fine window of three lights on each of its three exterior sides, while low down in the eastern wall, a couple of unglazed openings, defended by iron bars against accident, gave upon the interior of the church, a little above the level of the clerestory windows. As Jack Godfrey set the lantern on the floor, and proceeded to light a paraffin lamp which hung against the wall, Wimsey could see the eight bellropes, their woollen sallies looped neatly to the walls and their upper ends vanishing mysteriously into the shadows of the chamber roof. Then the light streamed out and the walls took shape and colour. They were plainly plastered, with a painted motto in Gothic lettering running round below the windows: 'They Have Neither Speech nor Language but their Voices are Heard Among Them, their Sound is Gone Forth into All Lands.' Above this, various tablets of wood, brass and even stone, commemorated the ringing of remarkable peals in the past.

'We shall hope to put up a new tablet after tonight,' said the Rector's voice in Wimsey's ear.

'I only hope I may do nothing to prevent it,' said Wimsey. 'I see you have the old regulations for your ringers. Ah! 'Keep stroak of time and goe not out. Or elles you forfeit out of doubt. For every fault a Jugg of beer.' It doesn't say how big a jug, but there is something about the double g that suggests size and potency. 'If a bell you over throw 'Twill cost you sixpence ere you goe.' That's cheap, considering the damage it does. On the other hand, sixpence for every swear or curse is rather on the dear side, I think, don't you, padre? Where's this bell of mine?'

'Here, my Lord.' Jack Godfrey had unhitched the rope of the second bell, and let down to its full length the portion of rope below the sallie.

'When you've got her raised,' he said, 'we'll fix them tuckings proper. Unless you'd like me to raise her for you?'

'Not on your life,' said Wimsey. 'It's a poor ringer that can't raise his own bell.' He grasped the rope and pulled it gently downwards, gathering the slack in his left hand. Softly, tremulously, high overhead in the tower, Sabaoth began to speak, and her sisters after her as the ringers stood to their ropes. 'Tin-tin-tin,' cried Gaude in her silvery treble; 'tan-tan,' answered Sabaoth; 'din-din-din,' 'dan-dan-dan,' said John and Jericho, climbing to their places; 'bim, bam, bim, bam,' Jubilee and Dimity followed; 'bom,' said Batty Thomas; and Tailor Paul, majestically lifting up her great bronze mouth, bellowed 'bo, bo, bo,' as the ropes hauled upon the wheels.

Wimsey brought his bell competently up and set her at backstroke while the tuckings were finally adjusted, after which, at the Rector's suggestion, a few rounds were rung to let him 'get the feel of her.'

'You can leave your bells up, boys,' said Mr Hezekiah Lavender, graciously, when this last rehearsal was concluded, 'but don't you go a-taking that for what they calls preceedent, Wally Pratt. And listen here, all on you; don't make no mistake. You comes here, sharp at the quarter to eleven, see — and you rings same as usual for service, and after Rector has finished

30

his sermon, you comes up here again quiet and decent and takes your places. Then, while they're a-singin' their 'ymn, I rings the nine tailors and the 'alf-minute passing-strokes for Old Year, see. Then you takes your ropes in hand and waits for the clock to strike. When she's finished striking, I says 'Go!' and mind as you're ready to go. And when Rector's done down below, he's promised to come up and give a 'and from time to time to any man as needs a rest, and I'm sure it's very kind of him. And I take leave to suppose, Alf Donnington, as you won't forget the usual.'

'Not me,' said Mr Donnington. 'Well, so long, boys.'

The lantern led the way from the ringing-chamber, and a great shuffling of feet followed it.

'And now,' said the Rector, 'and now, Lord Peter, you will like to come and see — Dear me!' he ejaculated, as they groped upon the dark spiral stair, 'where in the world is Jack Godfrey? Jack! He has gone on down with the others. Ah, well, poor fellow, no doubt he wants to get home to his supper. We must not be selfish. Unfortunately he has the key of the bell-chamber, and without it we cannot conduct our researches. However, you will see much better tomorrow. Yes, Jack, yes — we are coming. Do be careful of these stairs — they are very much worn, especially on the inside. Here we are, safe and sound. Excellent! Now, before we go, Lord Peter, I should so much like to show you — '

The clock in the tower chimed the three-quarters.

'Bless my heart!' cried the Rector, conscience-striken, 'and dinner was to be at half-past! My

31

wife — we must wait till tonight. You will get a general idea of the majesty and beauty of our church if you attend the service, though there are many most interesting details that a visitor is almost bound to miss if they are not pointed out to him. The font, for instance — Jack! bring the lantern here a moment — there is one point about our font which is most uncommon, and I should like to show it to you. Jack!'

But Jack, unaccountably deaf, was jingling the church keys in the porch, and the Rector, sighing a little, accepted defeat.

'I fear it is true,' he said as he trotted down the path, 'that I am inclined to lose count of time.'

'Perhaps,' replied Wimsey politely, 'the being continually in and about this church brings eternity too close.'

'Very true,' said the Rector, 'very true — though there are mementoes enough to mark the passage of time. Remind me tomorrow to show you the tomb of Nathaniel Perkins — one of our local worthies and a great sportsman. He refereed once for the great Tom Sayers, and was a notable figure at all the 'mills' for miles around, and when he died — Here we are at home. I will tell you later about Nathaniel Perkins. Well, my dear, we're back at last! Not so very late after all. Come along, come along. You must make a good dinner, Lord Peter, to fit you for your exertions. What have we here? Stewed oxtail? Excellent! Most sustaining! I trust, Lord Peter, you can eat stewed oxtail. For what we are about to receive . . . '

the second course

THE BELLS IN THEIR COURSES

When mirth and pleasure is on the wing we
  ring;
At the departure of a soul we toll.
    Ringers' Rules at Southhill, Bedfordshire

After dinner, Mrs Venables resolutely asserted
her authority. She sent Lord Peter up to his
room, regardless of the Rector, who was
helplessly hunting through a set of untidy
bookshelves in search of the Rev. Christopher
Woollcott's *History of the Bells of Fenchurch St
Paul*.

'I can't imagine what has become of it,' said
the Rector. 'I fear I'm sadly unmethodical. But
perhaps you would like to look at this — a
trifling contribution of my own to campanologi-
cal lore. I know, my dear, I know — I must not
detain Lord Peter — it is thoughtless of me.'

'You must get some rest yourself, Theodore.'

'Yes, yes, my dear. In a moment. I was
only — '

Wimsey saw that the one way to quiet the
Rector was to desert him without compunction.
He retired, accordingly, and was captured at the
head of the stairs by Bunter, who tucked him
firmly beneath the eiderdown with a hot-water

bottle and shut the door upon him.

A roaring fire burned in the grate. Wimsey drew the lamp closer to him, opened the little brochure presented to him by the Rector, and studied the title-page:

An Inquiry into
the Mathematical Theory
of the
IN AND OUT OF COURSE
together with
Directions for
Calling Bells into Rounds
from any position
in all the recognised Methods
upon a
New and Scientific Principle
by
Theodore Venables, M.A.
Rector of Fenchurch St Paul
sometime Scholar of Caius Coll: Camb:
author of
'Change-ringing for Country Churches,'
'Fifty Short Touches of Grandsire Triples,' etc.
'God is gone up with a merry noise.'
MCMII

The letterpress was of a soporofic tendency; so was the stewed oxtail; the room was warm; the day had been a tiring one: the lines swam before Lord Peter's eyes. He nodded; a coal tinkled from the grate; he roused himself with a jerk and read: ' . . . if the 5th is in course after the 7th (says Shipway), and 7th after the 6th, they are

34

right, when the small bells, 2, 3, 4, are brought as directed in the preceding peals; but if 6, 7, are together without the 5th, call the 5th into the hunt . . . '

Lord Peter nodded away into dreams.

★ ★ ★

He was roused by the pealing of bells.

For a moment, memory eluded him — then he flung the eiderdown aside and sat up, ruffled and reproachful, to encounter the calm gaze of Bunter.

'Good God! I've been asleep! Why didn't you call me? They've begun without me.'

'Mrs Venables gave orders, my lord, that you were not to be disturbed until half-past eleven, and the reverend gentleman instructed me to say, my lord, that they would content themselves with ringing six bells as a preliminary to the service.'

'What time is it now?'

'Nearly five minutes to eleven, my lord.'

As he spoke, the pealing ceased, and Jubilee began to ring the five-minute bell.

'Dash it all!' said Wimsey. 'This will never do. Must go and hear the old boy's sermon. Give me a hairbrush. Is it still snowing?'

'Harder than ever, my lord.'

Wimsey made a hasty toilet and ran downstairs, Bunter following him decorously. They let themselves out by the front door, and, guided by Bunter's electric torch, made their way through the shrubbery and across the road

35

to the church, entering just as the organ boomed out its final notes. Choir and parson were in their places and Wimsey, blinking in the yellow lamplight, at length discovered his seven fellow-ringers seated on a row of chairs beneath the tower. He picked his way cautiously over the coco-nut matting towards them, while Bunter, who had apparently acquired all the necessary information beforehand, made his unperturbed way to a pew in the north aisle and sat down beside Emily from the Rectory. Old Hezekiah Lavender greeted Wimsey with a welcoming chuckle and thrust a prayer-book under his nose as he knelt down to pray.

'Dearly beloved brethren — '

Wimsey scrambled to his feet and looked round.

At the first glance he felt himself sobered and awe-stricken by the noble proportion of the church, in whose vast spaces the congregation — though a good one for so small a parish in the dead of a winter's night — seemed almost lost. The wide nave and shadowy aisles, the lofty span of the chancel arch — crossed, though not obscured, by the delicate fan-tracery and crenellated moulding of the screen — the intimate and cloistered loveliness of the chancel, with its pointed arcading, graceful ribbed vault and five narrow east lancets, led his attention on and focused it first upon the remote glow of the sanctuary. Then his gaze, returning to the nave, followed the strong yet slender shafting that sprang fountain-like from floor to foliated column-head, spraying into the light, wide arches that carried the clerestory, And there, mounting to the steep pitch of the roof, his eyes were held entranced with wonder and delight. Incredibly aloof, flinging back the light in a dusky shimmer of bright hair and gilded out-spread wings, soared the ranked angels, cherubim and seraphim, choir over choir, from corbel and hammer-beam floating face to face uplifted.

'My God!' muttered Wimsey, not without reverence. And he softly repeated to himself: 'He rode upon the cherubims and did fly; He came flying upon wings of the wind.'

Mr Hezekiah Lavender poked his new colleague sharply in the ribs, and Wimsey became aware that the congregation had settled down to the General Confession, leaving him alone and agape upon his feet. Hurriedly he turned the leaves of his prayer-book and applied himself to making the proper responses. Mr Lavender, who had obviously decided that he was either a half-wit or a heathen, assisted him by finding the psalms for him and by bawling every verse loudly in his ear.

' . . . Praise Him in the cymbals and dances: praise Him upon the strings and pipe.'

The shrill voices of the surpliced choir mounted to the roof, and seemed to find their echo in the golden mouths of the angels.

'Praise Him upon the well-tuned cymbals; praise Him upon the loud cymbals.

'Let everything that hath breath praise the Lord.'

★   ★   ★

37

The time wore on towards midnight. The Rector, advancing to the chancel steps, delivered, in his mild and scholarly voice, a simple and moving little address, in which he spoke of praising God, not only upon the strings and pipe, but upon the beautiful bells of their beloved church, and alluded, in his gently pious way, to the presence of the passing stranger — 'please do not turn round to stare at him; that would be neither courteous nor reverent' — who had been sent 'by what men call chance' to assist in this work of devotion. Lord Peter blushed, the Rector pronounced the Benediction, the organ played the opening bars of a hymn and Hezekiah Lavender exclaimed sonorously: 'Now, lads!' The ringers, with much subdued shuffling, extricated themselves from their chairs and wound their way up the belfry stair. Coats were pulled off and hung on nails in the ringing-chamber, and Wimsey, observing on a bench near the door an enormous brown jug and nine pewter tankards, understood, with pleasure, that the landlord of the Red Cow had, indeed, provided 'the usual' for the refreshment of the ringers.

The eight men advanced to their stations, and Hezekiah consulted his watch.

'Time!' he said.

He spat upon his hands, grasped the sallie of Tailor Paul, and gently swung the great bell over the balance.

Toll-toll-toll; and a pause; toll-toll-toll; and a pause; toll-toll-toll; the nine tailors, or teller-strokes, that mark the passing of a man. The year is dead; toll him out with twelve strokes more, one for every passing month. Then silence. Then, from the faint, sweet tubular chimes of the clock overhead, the four quarters and the twelve strokes of midnight. The ringers grasped their ropes.

'Go!'

The bells gave tongue: Gaude, Sabaoth, John, Jericho, Jubilee, Dimity, Batty Thomas and Tailor Paul, rioting and exulting high up in the dark tower, wide mouths rising and falling, brazen tongues clamouring, huge wheels turning to the dance of the leaping ropes. Tin tan din dan bim bam bom bo — tan tin din dan bam bim bo bom — tin tan dan din bim bam bom bo — tan tin dan din bam bim bo bom — tan dan tin bam din bo bim bom — every bell in her place striking tuneably, hunting up, hunting down, dodging, snapping, laying her blows behind, making her thirds and fourths, working down to lead the dance again. Out over the flat, white Wastes of fen, over the spear-straight, steel-dark dykes and the wind-bent, groaning poplar trees, bursting from the snow-choked louvres of the belfry, whirled away southward and westward in gusty blasts of clamour to the sleeping counties went the music of the bells — little Gaude, silver Sabaoth, strong John and Jericho, glad Jubilee, sweet Dimity and old Batty Thomas, with great Tailor Paul bawling and striding like a giant in the midst of them. Up and down went the shadows of the ringers upon the walls, up and down went the scarlet sallies flickering roofwards and floorwards, and up and down, hunting in their courses, went the bells of Fenchurch St Paul.

39

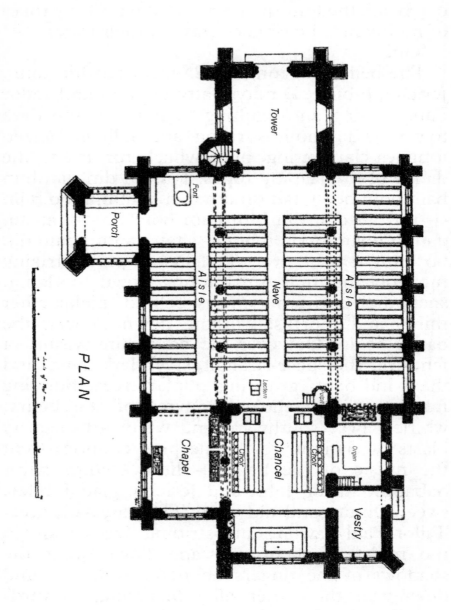

Wimsey, his eye upon the ropes and his ear pricked for the treble's shrill tongue speaking at lead, had little attention to give to anything but his task. He was dimly conscious of old Hezekiah, moving with the smooth rhythm of a machine, bowing his ancient back very slightly at each pull to bring Tailor Paul's great weight over, and of Wally Pratt, his face anxiously contorted and his lips moving in the effort to keep his intricate course in mind. Wally's bell was moving down now towards his own, dodging Number Six and passing her, dodging Number Seven and passing her, passing Number Five, striking her two blows at lead, working up again, while the treble came down to take her place and make her last snapping lead with Sabaoth. One blow in seconds place and one at lead, and Sabaoth, released from the monotony of the slow hunt, ran out merrily into her treble bob hunting course. High in the air above them the cock upon the weather-vane stared out over the snow and watched the pinnacles of the tower swing to and fro with a slowly widening sweep as the tall stalk of stone gathered momentum and rocked like a windblown tree beneath his golden feet.

The congregation streamed out from the porch, their lanterns and torches flitting away into the whirling storm like sparks tossed from a bonfire. The Rector, pulling off his surplice and stole, climbed in his cassock to the ringing-chamber and sat down upon the bench, ready to give help and counsel. The clock's chimes came faintly through the voices of the bells. At the end of the first hour the Rector took the rope from

41

the hand of the agitated Wally and released him for an interval of rest and refreshment. A soft glugging sound proclaimed that Mr Donnington's 'usual' was going where it would do most good.

Wimsey, relieved at the end of the third hour, found Mrs Venables seated among the pewter pots, with Bunter in respectful attendance beside her.

'I do hope,' said Mrs Venables, 'that you are not feeling exhausted.'

'Far from it; only rather dry.' Wimsey remedied this condition without further apology, and asked how the peal sounded.

'Beautiful!' said Mrs Venables, loyally. She did not really care for bell-music, and felt sleepy; but the Rector would have felt hurt if she had withdrawn her sympathetic presence.

'It's surprising, isn't it?' she added, 'how soft and mellow it sounds in here. But of course there's another floor between us and the bell-chamber.' She yawned desperately. The bells rang on. Wimsey, knowing that the Rector was well set for the next quarter of an hour, was seized with a fancy to listen to the peal from outside. He slipped down the winding stair and groped his way through the south porch. As he emerged into the night, the clamour of the bells smote on his ears like a blow. The snow was falling less heavily now. He turned to his right, knowing that it is unlucky to walk about a church widdershins, and followed the path close beneath the wall till he found himself standing by the west door. Sheltered by the towering bulk of the masonry, he lit a sacrilegious cigarette, and, thus fortified, turned right again. Beyond the foot of the tower, the pathway ended, and he stumbled among the grass and tombstones for the whole length of the aisle, which, on this side, was prolonged to the extreme east end of the church. Midway between the last two buttresses on the north side he came upon a path leading to a small door; this he tried, but found it locked, and so passed on, encountering the full violence of the wind as he rounded the east end. Pausing a moment to get his breath, he looked out over the Fen. All was darkness, except for a dim stationary light which might have been shining from some cottage window. Wimsey reckoned that the cottage must lie somewhere along the solitary road by which they had reached the Rectory, and wondered why anybody should be awake at three o'clock on New Year's morning. But the night was bitter and he was wanted back at his job. He completed his circuit, re-entered by the south porch and returned to the belfry. The Rector resigned the rope to him, warning him that he had now to make his two blows behind and not to forget to dodge back into eighth's place before hunting down.

At six o'clock, the ringers were all in pretty good case. Wally Pratt's cow-lick had fallen into his eyes, and he was sweating freely, but was still moving well within himself. The blacksmith was fresh and cheerful, and looked ready to go on till next Christmas. The publican was grim but determined. Most unperturbed of all was the aged Hezekiah, working grandly as though he were part and parcel of his rope, and calling his bobs without a tremor in his clear old voice.

At a quarter to eight the Rector left them to prepare for his early service. The beer in the jug had sunk to low tide and Wally Pratt, with an hour and a half to go, was beginning to look a little strained. Through the southern window a faint reflection of the morning light came, glimmering frail and blue.

At ten minutes past nine the Rector was back in the belfry, standing watch in hand with a beaming smile on his face.

At thirteen minutes past nine the treble came shrilling triumphantly into her last lead.

Tin tan din dan bim bam bom bo.

Their long courses ended, the belts came faultlessly back into rounds, and the ringers stood.

'Magnificent, lads, magnificent!' cried Mr Venables. 'You've done it, and it couldn't have been better done.'

'Eh!' admitted Mr Lavender, 'it was none so bad.' A slow toothless grin overspread his countenance. 'Yes, we done it. How did it sound from down below, sir?'

'Fine,' said the Rector. 'As firm and true as any ringing I have ever heard. Now you must all be wanting your breakfasts. It's all ready for you at the Rectory. Well now, Wally, you can call yourself a real ringer now, can't you? You came through it with very great credit — didn't he Hezekiah?'

'Fair to middlin',' said Mr Lavender grudgingly. 'But you takes too much out o' yourself,

Wally. You've no call to be gettin' all of a muck o' sweat that way. Still, you ain't made no mistakes an' that's something, but I see you a mumblin' and countin' to yourself all the time. If I've telled yew once I've telled yew a hundred times to keep your eye on the ropes and then you don't need — '

'There, there!' said the Rector. 'Never mind, Wally, you did very well indeed. Where's Lord Peter — oh! there you are. I'm sure we owe you a great deal. Not too fatigued, I hope?'

'No, no,' said Wimsey, extricating himself from the congratulatory handshakes of his companions. He felt, in fact, exhausted to dropping-point. He had not rung a long peal for years, and the effort of keeping alert for so many hours had produced an almost intolerable desire to tumble down in a corner and go to sleep. 'I — ah — oh — I'm perfectly all right.'

He swayed as he walked and would have pitched headlong down the steep stair, but for the blacksmith's sustaining arm.

'Breakfast,' said the Rector, much concerned, 'breakfast is what we all want. Hot coffee. A very comforting thing. Dear me, yes, I for one am looking forward to it very much. Ha! the snow has ceased falling. Very beautiful, this white world — if only there were not a thaw to follow. This will mean a lot of water down the Thirty-foot, I expect. Are you sure you're all right? Come along, then, come along! Why, here is my wife — come to chide my tardiness, I expect. We're just coming, my dear — Why, Johnson, what is it?'

45

He addressed a young man in chauffeur's livery, who was standing at Mrs Venables's side. Mrs Venables broke in before he could reply.

'My dear Theodore — I have been saying, you can't go just yet. You must have something to eat — '

Mr Venables put the interruption aside with an unexpected, quiet authority.

'Agnes, my dear, permit me. Am I wanted Johnson?'

'Sir Henry sent me to say, sir, that the mistress was very bad this morning and they're afraid she's sinking, sir, and she is very anxious to receive the Sacrament if you could see your way — '

'Good Heavens!' exclaimed the Rector. 'So ill as that? Sinking? I am terribly grieved to hear it. Of course, I will come immediately. I had no idea — '

'No more hadn't any of us, sir. It's this wicked influenza. I'm sure nobody ever thought yesterday — '

'Oh, dear, oh, dear! I hope it's not as bad as you fear! But I mustn't delay. You shall tell me about it as you go. I will be with you in one moment. Agnes, my dear, see that the men get their breakfasts and explain to them why I cannot join them. Lord Peter, you must excuse me. I shall be with you later. Bless my heart! Lady Thorpe — what a scourge this influenza is!'

He trotted hurriedly back into the church. Mrs Venables looked ready to cry, between anxiety and distress.

'Poor Theodore! After being up all night — of

course he has to go, and we ought not to think about ourselves. Poor Sir Henry! An invalid himself! Such a bitter morning, and no breakfast! Johnson, please say to Miss Hilary how sorry I am and ask if there is anything I can do to help Mrs Gates. The housekeeper, you know, Lord Peter — such a nice woman, and the cook away on holiday, it does seem so hard. Troubles never come singly. Dear me, you must be famished. Do come along and be looked after. You'll be sure to send round, Johnson, if you want any help. Can Sir Henry's nurse manage, I wonder? This is such an isolated place for getting any help. Theodore! are you sure you are well wrapped up?'

The Rector, who now rejoined them, carrying the Communion vessels in a wooden case, assured her that he was well protected. He was bundled into the waiting car by Johnson, and whirled away westwards towards the village.

This untoward incident cast a certain gloom over the breakfast table, though Wimsey, who felt his sides clapping together like an empty portmanteau, was only too thankful to devour his eggs and bacon and coffee in peace. Eight pairs of jaws chumped steadily, while Mrs Venables dispensed the provisions in a somewhat distracted way, interspersing her hospitable urgings with ejaculations of sympathy for the Thorpe family and anxiety for her husband's well-being.

'Such a lot of trouble as the Thorpes have had, too, one way and another,' she remarked. 'All that dreadful business about old Sir Charles, and

47

the loss of the necklace, and that unfortunate girl and everything, though it was a merciful thing the man died, after killing a warder and all that, though it upset the whole family very much at the time. Hezekiah, how are you getting on? A bit more bacon, Mr Donnington? Hinkins, pass Mr Godfrey the cold ham. And of course, Sir Henry never has been strong since the War, poor man. Are you getting enough to eat down there, Wally? I do hope the Rector won't be kept too long without his breakfast. Lord Peter, a little more coffee?'

Wimsey thanked her, and asked what, exactly, was the trouble about old Sir Charles and the necklace.

'Oh, of course, you don't know. So silly of me! Living in this solitary place, one imagines that one's little local excitements are of world-wide importance. It's rather a long story, and I shouldn't have mentioned it at all' — here the good lady lowered her voice — 'if Will Thoday had been here. I'll tell you after breakfast. Or ask Hinkins. He knows all about it. How is William Thoday this morning, I wonder? Has anybody heard?'

'He's mortal bad, ma'am, I'm afraid,' replied Mr Donnington, taking the question to himself. 'I saw my missus after service, and she told me she'd heard from Joe Mullins as he was dreadful delirious all night, and they couldn't hardly keep him in his bed, on account of him wanting to get up and ring.'

'Dear, dear! It's a good thing for Mary that they've got James at home.'

48

'So it is,' agreed Mr Donnington. 'A sailor's wonderful handy about the house. Not but what his leave's up in a day or two, but it's to be hoped as they'll be over the worst by then.'

Mrs Venables clucked gently.

'Ah!' said Hezekiah. ' 'Tis a mortal bad thing, this influenza. And it do take the young and strong cruel often, and leave the old uns be. Seems like old fellers like me is too tough fer it.'

'I hope so, Hezekiah, I'm sure,' said Mrs Venables. 'There! Ten o'clock striking, and the Rector not back. Well, I suppose one couldn't expect — why, there's the car coming up the drive! Wally, would you please ring that bell? I want some fresh eggs and bacon for the Rector, Emily, and you'd better take the coffee out and hot it up for him.'

Emily took out the jug, but returned almost immediately.

'Oh, if you please, ma'am, the Rector says, will you all excuse him, please, and he'll take his breakfast in the study. And oh! if you please, ma'am, poor Lady Thorpe's gone, ma'am, and if Mr Lavender's finished, he's please to go over to the church at once and ring the passing bell.'

'Gone!' cried Mrs Venables. 'Why, what a terrible thing!'

'Yes, ma'am. Mr Johnson says it was dreadful sudden. The Rector hadn't hardly left her room, ma'am, when it was all over, and they don't know how they're to tell Sir Henry.'

Mr Lavender pushed back his chair and quavered to his ancient feet.

'In the midst of life,' he said solemnly, 'we are

in death. Terrible true that is, to be sure. If so be as you'll kindly excuse me, ma'am, I'll be leaving you now, and thank you kindly. Good mornin' to you all. That were a fine peal we rung, none the more for that, and now I'll be gettin' to work on old Tailor Paul again.'

He shuffled sturdily out, and within five minutes they heard the deep and melancholy voice of the bell ringing, first the six tailors for a woman and then the quick strokes which announce the age of the dead. Wimsey counted them up to thirty-seven. Then they ceased, and were followed by the slow tolling of single strokes at half-minute intervals. In the dining-room, the silence was only broken by the shy sound of hearty feeders trying to finish their meal inconspicuously.

The party broke up quietly. Mr Wilderspin drew Wimsey to one side and explained that he had sent around to Mr Ashton for a couple of farm-horses and a stout rope, and hoped to get the car out of the ditch in a very short time, and would then see what was needed in the way of repairs. If his lordship cared to step along to the smithy in an hour or so, they could go into consultation about the matter. His (Mr Wilderspin's) son George was a great hand with motors, having had considerable experience with farm engines, not to mention his own motorbike. Mrs Venables retired into the study to see that her husband had everything he wanted and to administer such consolation as she might for the calamity that had befallen the parish. Wimsey, knowing that his presence at Frog's Bridge would not help and would probably only hinder the breakdown team, begged his hostess not to trouble about him, and wandered out into the garden. At the back of the house, he discovered Joe Hinkins polishing the Rector's aged car. Joe accepted a cigarette, passed a few remarks about the ringing of the peal, and thence slid into conversation about the Thorpe family.

'They live in the big red-brick house t'other side the village. A rich family they were once. They do say as they got their land through putting money into draining of the Fen long ago under the Earl of Bedford. You'd know all about that, my lord, I dare say. Anyhow, they reckon to be an old family hereabouts. Sir Charles, he was a fine, generous gentleman; did a lot of good in his time, though he wasn't what you'd call a rich man, not by no means. They do say his father lost a lot of money up in London, but I don't know how. But he farmed his land well, and it was a rare trouble to the village when he died along of the burglary.'

'What burglary was that?'

'Why, that was the necklace the mistress was talking about. It was when young Mr Henry — that's the present Sir Henry — was married. The year of the War, it was, in the spring — April 1914 — I remember it very well. I was a youngster at the time, and their wedding-bells was the first long peal I ever rang. We gave them 5,040 Grandsire Triples, Holt's Ten-part Peal — you'll find the record of it in the church yonder, and there was a big supper at the Red House afterwards, and a lot of fine visitors came

51

down for the wedding. The young lady was an orphan, you see, and some sort of connection with the family, and Mr Henry being the heir they was married down here. Well, there was a lady come to stay in the house, and she had a wonderful fine emerald necklace — worth thousands and thousands of pounds it was — and the very night after the wedding, when Mr Henry and his lady was just gone off for their honeymoon, the necklace was stole.'

'Good lord!' said Wimsey. He sat down on the running-board of the car and looked as encouraging as he could.

'You may say so,' said Mr Hinkins, much gratified. 'A big sensation it made at the time in the parish. And the worst part of it was, you see, that one of Sir Charles's own men was concerned in it. Poor gentleman, he never held up his head again. When they took this fellow Deacon and it came out what he'd done — '

'Deacon was — ?'

'Deacon, he was the butler. Been with them six years, he had, and married the housemaid, Mary Russell, that's married to Will Thoday, him as rings Number Two and has got the influenzy so bad.'

'Oh!' said Wimsey. 'Then Deacon is dead now, I take it.'

'That's right, my lord. That's what I was a-telling you. You see, it 'appened this way. Mrs Wilbraham woke up in the night and saw a man standing by her bedroom window. So she yelled out, and the fellow jumped out into the garden and dodged into the shrubbery, like. So she screamed again, very loud, and rang her bell and made a to-do, and everybody came running out to see what was the matter. There was Sir Charles and some gentlemen that was staying in the house, and one of them had a shotgun. And when they got downstairs, there was Deacon in his coat and trousers just running out at the back door, and the footman in pyjamas; and the chauffeur as slept over the garage, he came running out too, because the first thing as Sir Charles did, you see, was to pull the house-bell what they had for calling the gardener. The gardener, he came too, of course, and so did I, because, you see, I was the gardener's boy at the time, and wouldn't never have left Sir Charles, only for him having to cut down his establishment, what with the War and paying Mrs Wilbraham for the necklace.'

'Paying for the necklace?'

'Yes, my lord. That's just where it was, you see. It wasn't insured, and though of course nobody could have held Sir Charles responsible he had it on his conscience as he ought to pay Mrs Wilbraham the value of it, though how anybody calling herself a lady could take the money off him I don't understand. But as I was a-saying, we all came out and then one of the gentlemen see the man a-tearing across the lawn, and Mr Stanley loosed off the shot-gun at him and hit him, as we found out afterwards, but he got away over the wall, and there was a chap waiting for him on the other side with a motor-car, and he got clear away. And in the middle of it all, out comes Mrs Wilbraham and her maid, a-hollering that the emerald necklace has been took.'

'And didn't they catch the man?'

'Not for a bit, they didn't, my lord. The chauffeur, he gets the car out and goes off after them, but by the time he'd got started up, they were well away. They went up the road past the church, but nobody knew whether they'd gone through Fenchurch St Peter or up on to the Bank, and even then they might have gone either by Dykesey and Walea or Walbeach way, or over the Thirty-foot to Leamholt or Holport. So the chauffeur went after the police. You see, barring the village constable at Fenchurch St Peter there's no police nearer than Leamholt, and in those days they didn't have a car at the police-station even there, so Sir Charles said to send the car for them would be quicker than telephoning and waiting till they came.'

'Ah!' said Mrs Venables, suddenly popping her head in at the garage door. 'So you've got Joe on to the Thorpe robbery. He knows a lot more about it than I do. Are you sure you aren't frozen to death in this place?'

Wimsey said he was quite warm enough, thanks, and he hoped the Rector was none the worse for his exertions.

'He doesn't seem to be,' said Mrs Venables, 'but he's rather upset, naturally. You'll stay to lunch of course. No trouble at all. Can you eat shepherd's pie. You're sure? The butcher doesn't call today, but there's always cold ham.'

She bustled away. Joe Hinkins passed a chamois leather thoughtfully over a headlight. 'Carry on,' said Wimsey.

'Well, my lord, the police did come and of course they hunted round a good bit, and didn't we bless them, the way they morrised over the flower-beds, a-looking for footprints and breaking down the tulips. Anyhow, there 'twas, and they traced the car and got the fellow that had been shot in the leg. A well-known jewel thief he was, from London. But you see, they said it must have been an inside job, because it turned out as the fellow as jumped out o' the window wasn't the same as the London man, and the long and the short of it was, they found out as the inside man was this here Deacon. Seems the Londoner had been keeping his eye on that necklace, like, and had got hold of Deacon and got him to go and steal the stuff and drop it out of the window to him. They was pretty sure of their ground — I think they found finger-prints and such like — and they arrested Deacon. I remember it very well, because they took him one Sunday morning, just a-coming out of church, and a terrible job it was to take him; he near killed a constable. The robbery was on the Thursday night, see? and it had took them that time to get on to it.'

'Yes, I see. How did Deacon know where to find the jewels?'

'Well, that was just it, my lord. It came out as Mrs Wilbraham's maid had let out something, stupid-like, to Mary Russell — that is, her as had married Deacon, and she, not thinking no harm, had told her husband. Of course, they had them two women up too. All the village was in a dreadful way about it, because Mary was a very

55

decent, respectable girl, and her father was one of our sidesmen. There's not an honester, better family in the Fenchurches than what the Russells are. This Deacon, he didn't come from these parts, he was a Kentish man by birth. Sir Charles brought him down from London. But there wasn't no way of getting him out of it, because the London thief — Cranton, he called himself, but he had other names — he blew the gaff and gave Deacon away.'

'Dirty dog!'

'Ah! but you see, he said as Deacon had done him down and so, if Cranton was telling the truth, he had. Cranton said as Deacon dropped out nothing but the empty jewel-case and kept the necklace for himself. He went for Deacon 'ammer-and-tongs in the dock and tried for to throttle him. But, of course, Deacon swore as it was all a pack of lies. His tale was, that he heard a noise and went to see what was the matter, and that when Mrs Wilbraham saw him in her room, he was just going to give chase to Cranton. He couldn't deny he'd been in the room, you see, because of the finger-prints and that. But it went against him that he'd told a different story at the beginning, saying as how he'd gone out by the back door, hearing somebody in the garden. Mary supported that, and it's a fact that the back door was unbolted when the footman got to it. But the lawyer on the other side said that Deacon had unbolted the door himself before-hand, just in case he had to get out by the window, so as to leave himself a way back into the house. But as for the necklace, they never

56

could settle that part of it, for it wasn't never found. Whether Cranton had it, and was afraid to get rid of it, like or whether Deacon had it and hid it, I don't know and no more does anybody. It ain't never turned up to this day, nor yet the money Cranton said he'd given Deacon, though they turned the place upside-down looking for both on 'em. And the upshot was, they acquitted the two women, thinking as how they'd only been chattering silly-like, the way women do, and they sent Cranton and Deacon to prison for a good long stretch. Old Russell, he couldn't face the place after that, and he sold up and went off, taking Mary with him. But when Deacon died — '

'How was that?'

'Why, he broke prison and got away after killing a warder. A bad lot, was Deacon. That was in 1918. But he didn't get much good by it, because he fell into a quarry or some such place over Maidstone way, and they found his body two years later, still in his prison clothes. And as soon as he heard about it, young William Thoday, that had always been sweet on Mary went after her and married her and brought her back. You see, nobody here ever believed as there was anything against Mary. That was ten year ago, and they've got two fine kids and get along first-class. This fellow Cranton got into trouble again after his time was up and was sent back to prison, but he's out again now, so I'm told, and Jack Priest — that's the bobby at Fenchurch St Peter — he says he wouldn't wonder if we heard something about that necklace again, but I don't know. Cranton may know where it is, and again he may not, you see.'

'I see. So Sir Charles compensated Mrs Wilbraham for the loss of it.'

'Not Sir Charles, my lord. That was Sir Henry. He came back at once, poor gentleman, from his honeymoon, and found Sir Charles terrible ill. He'd had a stroke from the shock, when they took Deacon, feeling responsible-like, and being over seventy at the time. After the verdict, Mr Henry as he was then, told his father he'd see that the thing was put right, and Sir Charles seemed to understand him; and then the War came and Sir Charles never got over it. He had another stroke and passed away, but Mr Henry didn't forget, and when the police had to confess as they'd almost give up hope of the necklace, then he paid the money, but it came very hard on the family. Sir Henry got badly wounded in the Salient and was invalided home, but he's never been the same man since, and they say he's in a pretty bad way now. Lady Thorpe dying so sudden won't do him no good, neither. She was a very nice lady and very much liked.'

'Is there any family?'

'Yes, my lord; there's one daughter, Miss Hilary. She'll be fifteen this month. She's just home from school for the holidays. It's been a sad holiday for her, and no mistake.'

'You're right,' said Lord Peter. 'Well, that's an interesting tale of yours, Hinkins. I shall look out for news of the Wilbraham emeralds. Ah! here's my friend Mr Wilderspin. I expect he's come to say that the car's on deck again.'

This proved to be the case. The big Daimler stood outside the Rectory gate, forlornly hitched to the back of a farm waggon. The two stout horses who drew it seemed, judging by their sleek complacency, to have no great opinion of it. Messrs. Wilderspin senior and junior, however, took a hopeful view of the matter. A little work on the front axle, at the point where it had come into collision with a hidden milestone would, they thought, do wonders with it, and, if not, a message could be sent to Mr Brownlow at Fenchurch St Peter, who ran a garage, to come and tow it away with his lorry. Mr Brownlow was a great expert. Of course, he might be at home or he might not. There was a wedding on at Fenchurch St Stephen, and Mr Brownlow might be wanted there to take the wedding-party to church, they living a good way out along Digg's Drove, but if necessary the postmistress could be asked to telephone and find out. She would be the right party to do it, since leaving out the post-office, there was no other telephone in the village, except at the Red House, which wouldn't be convenient at a time like the present.

Wimsey, looking dubiously at his front axle, thought it might perhaps be advisable to procure the skilled assistance of Mr Brownlow and said he would approach the postmistress for that purpose, if Mr Wilderspin would give him a lift into the village. He scrambled up, therefore, behind Mr Ashton's greys, and the procession took its way past the church for the better part of a quarter of a mile, till it reached the centre of the village.

The parish church of Fenchurch St Paul, like a good many others in that part of the country, stands completely isolated from the village itself, with only the Rectory to neighbour it. The village itself is grouped about a crossroads, one arm of which runs southward to Fenchurch St Stephen and northwards to join the Fenchurch St Peter road a little south of the Thirty-foot; while the other, branching off from the same road by the church, degenerates at the western end of the village into a muddy drove by which, if you are not particular about your footing, you may, if you like, emerge once more on to the road by the Thirty-foot at Frog's Bridge. The three Fenchurches thus form a triangle, with St Paul to the north, St Peter to the south, and St Stephen to the west. The L.N.E.R. line connects St Peter with St Stephen, passing north to cross the Thirty-foot at Dykesey Viaduct on its way to Leamholt.

Of the three, Fenchurch St Peter is the largest and most important, possessing, in addition to a railway station, a river with two bridges. It has, however, but a bare and uninteresting church built in the latest and worst period of Perpendicular, with a slate spire and no bells to speak of. Fenchurch St Stephen has a railway station — though only, as it were, by accident, through lying more or less upon the direct line between Leamholt and St Peter. Still, there the station is; moreover, there is a church with a respectable fourteenth-century tower, a rather remarkable rood-screen, a Norman apse and a ring of eight bells. Fenchurch St Paul is the smallest village, and has neither river nor railway; it is, however, the oldest;

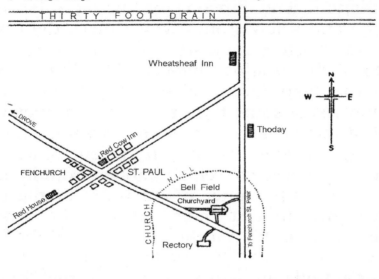

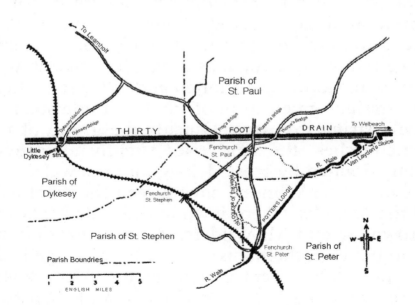

its church is by far the largest and the noblest, and its bells beyond question the finest. This is due to the fact that St Paul is the original abbey foundation. The remains of the first Norman church and a few stones which mark the site of the old cloisters may still be seen to east and south of the existing chancel. The church itself, with the surrounding glebe, stands on a little mound rising some ten or twelve feet above the level of the village — an elevation which, for the Fens, is considerable and, in ancient times, was sufficient to save church and abbey from inundation during the winter months. As for the river Wale, Fenchurch St Peter had no right to boast about that, for did not the old course of the Wale run close by St Paul's church, until the cutting of Potter's Lode in King James I's time drained away its waters by providing them with a shorter and more direct channel? Standing on the roof of the tower at Fenchurch St Paul, you can still trace the old river bed, as it wanders circuitously across meadow and ploughland, and see where the straight green dyke of Potter's Lode spans it like a string to a bow. Outside the group of the Fenchurches, the land rises slightly all round, being drained by cross-dyking into the Wale.

Lord Peter Wimsey, having seen the front axle of the Daimler taken down and decided that Mr Brownlow and Mr Wilderspin could possibly fix it up between them, dispatched his message from the post office, sent a wire to the friends who were expecting him at Walbeach, and then cast about him for some occupation. The village presented nothing of interest, so he determined to go and have a look at the church. The tolling of the bell had ceased and Hezekiah had gone home; the south door was, however, open, and entering, he discovered Mrs Venables putting fresh water in the altar vases. Catching sight of him as he stood gazing at the exquisite oak tracery of the screen, she came forward to greet him.

'It *is* beautiful, isn't it? Theodore is so proud of his church. And he's done a lot, since we've been here, to keep it looking nice. Fortunately the man before us was conscientious and did his repairs properly, but he was *very* Low and allowed all manner of things that quite shocked us. This beautiful chapel, for instance, would you *believe* that he allowed it to be used for furnace-coke? Of course, we had all that cleared out. Theodore would like a lady-altar here, but we're afraid the parishioners would think it popish. Yes — it's a magnificent window, isn't it? Later than the rest, of course, but so fortunate that it's kept its old glass. We were so afraid when the Zeppelins came over. You know, they dropped a bomb at Walbeach, only twenty miles off, and it might just as easily have been here. Isn't the parclose lovely? Like lace, I always think. The tombs belong to the Gaudy family. They lived here up to Queen Elizabeth's time, but they've all died out now. You'll find the name on the Treble bell: GAUDE, GAUDY, DOMINI IN LAUDE. There used to be a chantry on the north side, corresponding to this: Abbot Thomas's chantry, it was, and that's his tomb. Batty Thomas is named after him — a corruption of

'Abbot', of course. Some vandal in the nineteenth century tore down the screen behind the choir stalls to put the organ in. It's a hideous thing, isn't it? We put in a new set of pipes a few years ago, and now the bellows want enlarging. Poor Potty has his work cut out to keep the wind-chest filled when Miss Snoot is using the full organ. They all call him Potty Peake, but he's not really potty, only a little lacking, you know. Of course, the angel roof is our great showpiece — I think myself it's even lovelier than the ones at March or Needham Market, because it has all the original colouring. At least, we had it touched up here and there about twelve years back, but we didn't add anything. It took ten years to persuade the churchwardens that we could put a little fresh gold-leaf on the angels without going straight over to Rome, but they're proud of it now. We hope to do the chancel roof too, one day. All these ribs ought to be painted, you can still see traces of colour, and the bosses ought to be gilt. The east window is Theodore's *béte noire*. That dreadful crude glass — about 1840, I think it is. Quite the worst period, Theodore says. The glass in the nave has all gone, of course — Cromwell's men. Thank goodness they left part of the clerestory. I suppose it was rather a job to get up there. The pews are modern; Theodore got them done ten years ago. He'd have preferred chairs, but the congregation wouldn't have liked it, being used to pews, and he had them copied from a nice old design that wasn't too offensive. The old ones were terrible — like bathrooms — and there was a frightful gallery along both sides, blocking the aisle windows completely and ruining the look of the pillars. We had that taken down at the same time. It wasn't needed, and the school-children *would* drop hymn-books and things on people's heads. Now, the choir-stalls are different. *They* are the original monks' stalls, with misereres. Isn't the carving fine? There's a piscina in the sanctuary, but not a very exciting one.'

Wimsey admitted that he was unable to feel great excitement about piscinas.

'And the altar-rails are very poor, of course — Victorian horrors. We want very much to put up something better in their place when we can find the money. I'm sorry I haven't the key to the tower. You'd like to go up. It's a wonderful view, though it's all ladders above the ringing-chamber. It makes my head swim, especially going over the bells. I think bells are rather frightening, somehow. Oh, the font! You must look at the font. That carving is supposed to be quite remarkable. I forget exactly what it is that's so special about it — stupid of me. Theodore must show you, but he's been sent for in a hurry to take a sick woman off to hospital, right away on the other side of the Thirty-foot, across Thorpe's Bridge. He rushed off almost before he'd finished his breakfast.'

('And they say,' thought Wimsey, 'that Church of England parsons do nothing for their money.')

'Would you like to stay on and look round? Do you mind locking the door and bringing the key back? It's Mr Godfrey's key — I can't *think* where Theodore has put his bunch. It does seem

65

wrong to keep the church locked, but it's such a solitary place. We can't keep an eye on it from the Rectory because of the shrubbery and there are sometimes very unpleasant-looking tramps about. I saw a most horrible man go past only the other day, and not so long ago someone broke open the alms-box. That wouldn't have mattered so much, because there was very little in it, but they did a lot of wanton damage in the sanctuary — out of disappointment, I suppose, and one can't really allow that, can one?'

Wimsey said, No, one couldn't, and Yes, he would like to look round the church a little longer and would remember about the key. He spent the first few minutes after the good lady had left him putting a suitable donation into the alms-box and in examining the font, whose carvings were certainly curious and, to his mind, suggestive of a symbolism neither altogether Christian nor altogether innocent. He noted a heavy old cope-chest beneath the tower, which, on being opened, proved to contain nothing more venerable than a quantity of worn bell-ropes, and passed on into the north aisle, noticing that the corbels supporting the principals of the angel-roof were very appropriately sculptured with cherubs' heads. He brooded for a little time over the tomb of Abbot Thomas, with its robed and mitred effigy. A stern old boy, he thought, this fourteenth-century cleric, with his strong, harsh face, a ruler rather than a shepherd of his people. Carved panels decorated the sides of the tomb, and showed various scenes in the life of the abbey; one of them depicted the casting of a bell, no doubt of 'Batty Thomas', and it was evident that the Abbot had taken particular pride in his bell, for it appeared again, supporting his feet, in place of the usual cushion. Its decorations and mottoes were realistically rendered: on the shoulder: + NOLI + ESSE + INCREDVLVS + SED + FIDELIS +; on the sound-bow: + *Abbat Thomas sett mee heare + and bad mee ringe both lovd and cleer +* 1380 +; and on the waist: O SANCTE THOMA, which inscription, being embellished with an abbot's mitre, left the spectator in a pleasing uncertainty whether the sanctity was to be attributed to the Apostle or the ecclesiastic. It was as well that Abbot Thomas had died long before the spoliation of his house by King Henry. Thomas would have made a fight for it, and his church might have suffered in the process. His successor, douce man, had meekly acquiesced in the usurpation, leaving his abbey to moulder to decay, and his church to be purified peaceably by the reformers. So, at least, the Rector informed Wimsey over the shepherd's pie at lunch.

It was only very reluctantly that the Venables consented to let their guest go; but Mr Brownlow and Mr Wilderspin between them had made such good progress on the car that it was ready for use by two o'clock, and Wimsey was anxious to press on to Walbeach before dusk set in. He started off, therefore, speeded by many handshakes and much earnest solicitation to come again soon and help to ring another peal. The Rector, at parting, thrust into his hands a copy of *Venables on the In and Out of Course,* while Mrs Venables insisted on his drinking an amazingly powerful hot whisky-and-water, to keep the cold out. As the car turned right along the Thirty-foot Bank Wimsey noticed that the wind had changed. It was hauling round to the south, and, though the snow still lay white and even over the Fen, there was a softness in the air.

'Thaw's coming, Bunter.'

'Yes, my lord.'

'Ever seen this part of the country when the floods are out?'

'No, my lord.'

'It looks pretty desolate; especially round about the Welney and Mepal Washes, when they let the waters out between the Old and New Bedford Rivers, and across the fen between Over and Earith Bridge. Acres of water, with just a bank running across it here and there or a broken line of willows. Hereabouts I think it's rather more effectively drained. Ah! look — over to the right — that must be Van Leyden's Sluice that turns the tide up the Thirty-foot Drain — Denver Sluice again on a smaller scale. Let's look at the map. Yes, that's it. See, here's where the Drain joins the Wale, but it meets it at a higher level; if it wasn't for the Sluice, all the Drain water would turn back up the Wale and flood the whole place. Bad engineering — but the seventeenth-century engineers had to work piecemeal and take things as they found 'em. That's the Wale coming down through Potter's Lode from Fenchurch St Peter. I shouldn't care for the sluice-keeper's job — dashed lonely, I should think.'

They gazed at the ugly little brick house, which stood up quaintly on their right, like a pricked ear, between the two sides of the Sluice. On the one side a weir, with a small lock, spanned the Thirty-foot, where it ran into the Wale six feet above the course of the river. On the other, the upper course of the Wale itself was spanned by a sluice of five gates, which held the Upper Level waters from turning back up the river.

'Not another house within sight — oh, yes — one cottage about two miles further up the bank. Boo! Enough to make one drown one's self in one's own lock. Hullo! what happens to the road here? Oh, I see; over the Drain by the bridge and turn sharp right — then follow the river. I do wish everything wasn't so rectangular in this part of the world. Hoops-a-daisy, over she goes! There's the sluice-keeper running out to have a look at us. I expect we're his great event of the day. Let's wave our hats to him — Hullo-ullo! Cheerio! — I'm all for scattering sunshine as we pass. As Stevenson says, we shall pass this way but once — and I devoutly hope he's right. Now then, what's this fellow want?'

Along the bleak white road a solitary figure, plodding towards them, had stopped and extended both arms in appeal. Wimsey slowed the Daimler to a halt.

'Excuse me stopping you, sir,' said the man, civilly enough. 'Would you be good enough to tell me if I'm going right for Fenchurch St Paul?'

'Quite right. Cross the bridge when you come to it and follow the Drain along in the direction you are going till you come to the signpost. You can't miss it.'

'Thank you, sir. About how far would it be?'

'About five and a half miles to the signpost and then half a mile to the village.'

'Thank you very much, sir.'

'You've got a cold walk, I'm afraid.'

'Yes, sir — not a nice part of the country. However, I'll be there before dark, that's a comfort.'

He spoke rather low, and his voice had a faint London twang; his drab overcoat, though very shabby, was not ill-cut. He wore a short, dark, pointed beard and seemed to be about fifty years old, but kept his face down when talking as if evading close scrutiny.

'Like a fag?'

'Thank you very much, sir.'

Wimsey shook a few cigarettes out of his case and handed them over. The palm that opened to receive them was calloused, as though by heavy manual labour, but there was nothing of the countryman about the stranger's manner or appearance.

'You don't belong about these parts?'

'No, Sir.'

'Looking for work?'

'Yes, sir'

'Labourer?'

'No, sir. Motor mechanic.'

'Oh, I see. Well, good luck to you.'

'Thank you, sir. Good afternoon, sir.'

'Good afternoon.'

Wimsey drove on in silence for about half a mile. Then he said:

70

'Motor mechanic possibly, but not recently, I think. Stone-quarrying's more about the size of it. You can always tell an old lag by his eyes, Bunter. Excellent idea to live down the past, and all that, but I hope our friend doesn't put anything across the good Rector.'

II

A FULL PEAL OF GRANDSIRE TRIPLES

(Holt's Ten-Part Peal)

5,040
By the Part Ends

First Half	Second Half
246375	257364
267453	276543
275634	264735
253746	243657
235476	234567

2nd the Observation.

Call her: 1st Half) Out of the hunt, middle, in and out at 5, right, middle, wrong, right, middle and into the hunt (4 times repeated).

2nd Half) Out of the hunt, wrong, right, middle, wrong, right, in and out at 5, wrong and into the hunt (4 times repeated).

The last call in each half is a single; Holt's Single must be used in ringing this peal.

the first part

MR GOTOBED IS CALLED WITH A DOUBLE

> Thou shalt pronounce this hideous thing
> With cross, and candle, and bell-knelling.
> > JOHN MYRC: *Instructions for*
> > *Parish Priests (15th Century)*

Spring and Easter came late together that year to Fenchurch St Paul. In its own limited, austere and almost grudging fashion the Fen acknowledged the return of the sun. The floods withdrew from the pastures; the wheat lifted its pale green spears more sturdily from the black soil; the stiff thorns bordering dyke and grass verge budded to a softer outline; on the willows, the yellow catkins danced like little bell-rope sallies, and the silvery pussies plumped themselves for the children to carry to church on Palm Sunday; wherever the grim banks were hedge-sheltered, the shivering dog-violets huddled from the wind.

In the Rectory garden, the daffodils were (in every sense of the word) in full blow, for in the everlasting sweep and torment of wind that sweeps across East Anglia, they tossed desperately and madly. 'My poor daffodils!' Mrs Venables would exclaim, as the long leaf-tufts streamed over like blown water, and the golden trumpets kissed the ground, 'this dreadful old

75

wind! I don't know how they stand it!' She felt both pride and remorse as she cut them — sound stock varieties, Emperor, Empress, Golden Spur — and took them away to fill the altar-vases and the two long, narrow, green-painted tin troughs that on Easter Sunday stood one on either side of the chancel screen. 'The yellow looks so bright,' thought Mrs Venables, as she tried to persuade the blossoms to stand upright among the glossy green of periwinkle and St John's Wort, 'though it really seems a shame to sacrifice them.'

She knelt before the screen on a long red cushion, borrowed from a pew-seat to protect her 'bones' from the chill of the stone floor. The four brass altar-vases stood close beside her, in company with a trug full of flowers and a watering-can. Had she tried to fill them at the Rectory and carry them over, the sou' wester would have blown them into ruin before she had so much as crossed the road. 'Tiresome things!' muttered Mrs Venables, as the daffodils flopped sideways, or slid helplessly out of sight into the bottom of the trough. She sat up on her heels and reviewed her work, and then turned, hearing a step behind her.

A red-haired girl of fifteen, dressed in black, had come in, bearing a large sheaf of pheasant-eye narcissi. She was tall and thin and rather gawky, though with promise of becoming some day a striking-looking woman.

'Are these any use to you, Mrs Venables? Johnson's trying to get the arums along, but the wind's so terrific, he's afraid they'll be broken all to bits in the barrow. I think he'll have to pack them into the car, and drive them down in state.'

'My dear Hilary, how kind of you! Yes, indeed — I can do with all the white flowers I can get. These are beautiful, and *what* a delicious scent! Dear things! I thought of having some of our plants stood along there in front of Abbot Thomas, with some tall vases among them. And the same on the other side under old Gaudy. But I am *not*' — here she became very much determined — 'I am *not* going to tie bunches of greenery on to the font and the pulpit this year. They can have that at Christmas and Harvest Festival, if they like, but at Easter it's unsuitable and absurd, and now that old Miss Mallow's gone, poor dear, there's no need to go on with it.'

'I hate Harvest Festivals. It's a shame to hide up all this lovely carving with spiky bits of corn and vegetable marrows and things.'

'So it is, but the village people like it, you know. Harvest Festival is *their* festival, Theodore always says. I suppose it's wrong that it should mean so much more to them than the Church seasons, but it's natural. It was much worse when we came here — before you were born or thought of, you know. They actually used to drive spikes into the pillars to hold up wreaths of evergreens. Quite wicked. Just thoughtlessness, of course. And at Christmas they had horrible texts all across the screens and along the abominable old gallery — done in cottonwool on red flannel. Disgusting, dirty old things. We found a great bundle of them in the vestry when we came here, full of moths and mice. The Rector put his foot down about *that*.'

'And I suppose half the people went over to the Chapel.'

'No, dear — only two families, and one of them has come back since — the Wallaces, you know, because they had some sort of dispute with the Minister about their Good Friday beanfeast. Something to do with the tea urns, but I forget what. Mrs Wallace is a funny woman; she takes offence rather easily, but so far — touch wood' — (Mrs Venables performed this ancient pagan rite placidly on the oak of the screen) — 'so far, I've managed to work in quite smoothly with her over the Women's Institute. I wonder if you'd just step back a little way and tell me if these two sides match.'

'You want a few more daffs on the decani side, Mrs Venables.'

'Here? Thank you, dear. Is that better? Well, I think it will have to do. Oo-oh! my poor old bones! Yes, it'll pass in a crowd with a push, as they say. Oh, here's Hinkins with the aspidistras. People may say what they like about aspidistras, but they do go on all the year round and make a background. That's right, Hinkins. Six in front of this tomb and six on the other side — and have you brought those big pickle-jars? They'll do splendidly for the narcissi, and the aspidistras will hide the jars and we can put some ivy in front of the pots. Hinkins, you might fill up my watering-can. How is your father today, Hilary? Better, I hope.'

'I'm afraid he isn't any better, Mrs Venables.

Doctor Baines is very much afraid he won't get over it. Poor old Dad!'

'Oh, my dear! I'm terribly sorry. This has been a dreadful time for you. I'm afraid the shock of your dear mother's death coming so suddenly was too much for him.'

The girl nodded.

'We'll hope and pray it isn't as bad as the doctor thinks. Dr Baines always takes a pessimistic view of everything. I expect that's why he's only a country practitioner, because I think he's really very clever; but patients do like a doctor to be cheerful. Why don't you get a second opinion?'

'We're going to. There's a man called Hordell coming down on Tuesday. Dr Baines tried to get him today, but he's away for Easter.'

'Doctors oughtn't to go away,' said Mrs Venables, rather uncharitably. The Rector never took holidays at the greater festivals, and scarcely ever at any other time, and she could not quite see that there was any necessity for the rest of the world to do so.

Hilary Thorpe laughed rather ruefully.

'I feel a little like that myself. But he's supposed to be the very best man there is, and we're hoping that a couple of days won't make all that difference.'

'Good gracious, no, I hope not,' said the Rector's wife. 'Is that Johnson with the arums? Oh, no, it's Jack Godfrey. I expect he's going up to grease the bells.'

'Is he? I'd like to watch him. May I go up to the belfry, Mrs Venables?'

'I'm sure you may, my dear. But do be careful. I never think those great high ladders are really safe.'

'Oh, I'm not afraid of them. I love looking at the bells.'

Hilary hastened down the church and caught Jack Godfrey up just as he emerged from the winding stair into the ringing chamber.

'I've come to watch you do the bells, Mr Godfrey. Shall I be in your way?'

'Why, no, Miss Hilary, I'd be very pleased for you to come. You better go first up them ladders, so as I can help you if you was to slip.'

'I shan't slip,' said Hilary, scornfully. She climbed briskly up the thick and ancient rungs, to emerge into the chamber which formed the second story of the tower. It was empty, except for the case which housed the chiming mechanism of the church clock, and the eight bell-ropes rising through the sallie-holes in the floor to vanish through the ceiling in the same way. Jack Godfrey followed her up soberly, carrying his grease and cleaning-rags.

'Be a bit careful of the floor, Miss Hilary,' he urged, 'it's none too good in places.'

Hilary nodded. She loved this bare, sun-drenched room, in whose four tall walls were four tall windows. It was like a palace of glass lifted high into the air. The shadows of the splendid tracery of the south window lay scrawled on the floor like a pattern of wrought iron on a gate of brass. Looking down through the dusty panes, she could see the green fen spread out mile upon mile.

'I'd like to go up to the top of the tower, Mr Godfrey.'

'All right, Miss Hilary; I'll take you up, if so be as there's time when I've done with the bells.'

The trap-door that led to the bell-chamber was shut; a chain ran down from it, vanishing into a sort of wooden case upon the wall. Godfrey produced a key from his bunch and unlocked this case, disclosing the counterpoise. He pulled it down and the trap swung open.

'Why is that kept locked, Mr Godfrey?'

'Well, Miss Hilary, now and again it has happened as the ringers has left the belfry door open, and Rector says it ain't safe. You see, that Potty Peake might come atraipsing round, or some of they mischeevious lads might come up here and get larking about with the bells. Or they might go up the tower and fall off and hurt theirselves. So Rector said to fix a lock the way they couldn't get the trap-door open.'

'I see.' Hilary grinned a little. 'Hurt theirselves' was a moderate way of expressing the probable result of a hundred-and-twenty-foot fall. She led the way up the second ladder.

By contrast with the brilliance below, the bell-chamber was sombre and almost menacing. The main lights of its eight great windows were darkened throughout their height; only through the slender panelled tracery above the slanting louvres the sunlight dripped rare and chill, striping the heavy beams of the bell-cage with bars and splashes of pallid gold, and making a curious fantastic patterning on the spokes and rims of the wheels. The bells, with mute black

81

mouths gaping downwards, brooded in their ancient places.

Mr Godfrey, eyeing them with the cheerful familiarity born of long use, fetched a light ladder that stood against the wall, set it up carefully against one of the crossbeams, and prepared to mount.

'Let me go up first, or I shan't see what you're doing.'

Mr Godfrey paused and scratched his head. The proposal did not seem quite safe to him. He voiced an objection.

'I shall be quite all right; I can sit on the beam. I don't mind heights one bit. I'm very good at gym.'

Sir Henry's daughter was accustomed to have her own way, and got it — with the stipulation that she should hold on very tightly by the timber of the cage and not let go or 'morris about'. The promise being given, she was assisted to her lofty perch. Mr Godfrey, whistling a lively air between his teeth, arranged his materials methodically about him and proceeded with his task, greasing the gudgeons and trunnions, administering a spot of oil to the pulley-axle, testing the movement of the slider between the blocks and examining the rope for signs of friction where it passed over wheel and pulley.

'I've never seen Tailor Paul as close as this before. She's a big bell, isn't she?'

'Pretty fair,' said Jack Godfrey, approvingly, giving the bell a friendly pat on her bronze shoulder. A shaft of sunshine touched the soundbow, lighting up a few letters of the inscription, which ran, as Hilary very well knew:

NINE+TAYLERS+MAKE+A+MANNE+IN+CHRIST+
IS+DETH+ATT+END+IN +ADAM+YET+BEGANNE+
1614

'She've done her bit in her time, have old
Tailor Paul — many a good ring have we had out
of her, not to say a sight of funerals and
passing-bells. And we rung her with Gaude for
them there Zeppelin raids, to give the alarm like.
Rector was saying the other day as she did soon
ought ter be quarter-turned, but I don't know.
Reckon she'll go a bit longer yet. She rings out
true enough to my thinking.'

'You have to ring the passing-bell for everyone
that dies in the parish, don't you, whoever they
are?'

'Yes, dissenter and church alike. That was laid
down by old Sir Martin Thorpe, your great-great-
grandfather, when he left the money for the
bell-fund. 'Every Christian soul' was the words in
his will. Why, we even had to ring for that woman
as lived up the Long Drove, as was a Roman
Catholic. Old Hezekiah was rare put out.' Mr
Godfrey chuckled reminiscently. ' "What, ring old
Tailor Paul for a Roman?' he says. 'You wouldn't
call the like o' them Christians, would you, Rector?'
he says. 'Why, Hezekiah,' says Rector, 'we was all
Romans in this country once; this church was
built by Romans,' he says. But Hezekiah, he
wouldn't see it. He never had much education,
you see. Well, now, Miss Hilary, that'll do for
Tailor Paul, I'm thinking, so if you'll give me
your hand I'll be helping you down.'

Gaude, Sabaoth, John, Jericho, Jubilee, and

Dimity each in her turn was visited and anointed. When, however, it came to the turn of Batty Thomas, Mr Godfrey displayed a sudden and unexpected obstinacy.

'I'm not taking you up to Batty Thomas, Miss Hilary. She's an unlucky bell. What I mean, she's a bell that has her fancies and I wouldn't like for to risk it.'

'What *do* you mean?'

Mr Godfrey found it difficult to express himself more plainly.

'She's my own bell,' he said; 'I've rung her close on fifteen years now and I've looked after her for ten, ever since Hezekiah got too old for these here ladders. Her and me knows one another and she've no quarrel with me nor I with her. But she's queer-tempered. They do say as how old Batty down below, what had her put up here, was a queer sort of man and his bell's took after him. When they turned out the monks and that — a great many years ago, that'd be — they do say as Batty Thomas tolled a whole night through on her own like, without a hand laid to the rope. And when Cromwell sent his men to break up the images an' that, there was a soldier come up here into the belfry, I don't know for what, maybe to damage the bells, but anyhow, up he come; and some of the others, not knowing he was here, began to haul on the ropes, and it seems as how the bells' must have been left mouth up. Careless ringers they must have been in those days, but anyhow, that's how 'twas. And just as this soldier was leaning over to look at the bells, Batty Thomas came swinging down and killed him dead. That's history, that is, and Rector says as how Batty Thomas saved the church, because the soldiers took fright and ran away thinking it was a judgement, though to my thinking, it was just carelessness, leaving the bell that fashion. Still, there it was. And then, there was a poor lad in old Rector's time learning to ring, and he tried to raise Batty Thomas and got hisself hanged in the rope. A terrible thing that was, and there again, I say it was carelessness and the lad didn't ought to have been let practise all alone, and it's a thing Mr Venables never will allow. But you see, Miss Hilary, Batty Thomas has killed two men, and while it's quite understandable as there was carelessness both times or it wouldn't have happened — well! I wouldn't like to take any risks, like I said.'

And with this as his last word on the subject, Mr Godfrey mounted aloft to grease the gudgeons of Batty Thomas unassisted. Hilary Thorpe, dissatisfied but recognising an immovable obstacle when she met one, wandered vaguely about the belfry, scuffing up the dust of ages with her square-toed, regulation-pattern school shoes and peering at the names which bygone rustics had scrawled upon the plastered walls. Suddenly in a remote corner, something gleamed white in a bar of sunlight. Idly she picked it up. It was a sheet of paper, flimsy and poor in quality and ruled in small, faint squares. It reminded her of the letters she occasionally received from a departed French governess and, when she examined it, she saw that it was covered with writing in the very same purple ink that she associated with 'Mad'm'selle,' but the hand was English — very neat, and yet somehow not the hand of a well-educated person. It had been folded in four and its under side was smeared with fine dust from the floor on which it had lain, but it was otherwise fairly clean.

'Mr Godfrey!'

Hilary's voice was so sharp and excited that Jack Godfrey was quite startled. He very nearly fell off the ladder, adding thereby one more to Batty Thomas's tale of victims.

'Yes, Miss Hilary?'

'I've found such a funny thing here. Do come and look at it.'

'In one moment, Miss Hilary.'

He finished his task and descended. Hilary was standing in a splash of sunshine that touched the brazen mouth of Tailor Paul and fell all about her like Danaë's shower. She was holding the paper where the light could catch it.

'I found this on the floor. Do listen to it. It's absolutely loony. Do you think Potty Peake could have written it?'

Mr Godfrey shook his head.

'I couldn't say, I'm sure Miss Hilary. He's queer, is Potty, and he did use to come up here one time, before Rector locked up the trap-door chain. But that don't look to me like his writing.'

'Well, I don't think anybody but a lunatic could have written it. Do read it. It's so funny.' Hilary giggled, being of an age to be embarrassed by lunacy.

Mr Godfrey set down his belongings with deliberation, scratched his head and perused the document aloud, following the lines with a somewhat grimy forefinger.

'I thought to see the fairies in the fields, but I saw only the evil elephants with their black backs. Woe! how that sight awed me! The elves danced all around and about while I heard voices calling clearly. Ah! how I tried to see — throw off the ugly cloud — but no blind eye of a mortal was permitted to spy them. So then came minstrels, having gold trumpets, harps and drums. These played very loudly beside me, breaking that spell. So the dream vanished, whereat I thanked Heaven. I shed many tears before the thin moon rose up, frail and faint as a sickle of straw. Now though the Enchanter gnash his teeth vainly, yet shall he return as the Spring returns. Oh, wretched man! Hell gapes, Erebus now lies open. The mouths of Death wait on thy end.'

'There, now,' said Mr Godfrey, astonished. 'That's a funny one, that is. Potty it is, but, if you follow me, it ain't Potty neither. Potty ain't no scholar. This here, now, about Ereebus — what do you take that to mean?'

'It's a kind of an old name for hell,' said Hilary.

'Oh, that's what it is, is it? Chap that wrote this seems to have got that there place on his mind, like. Fairies, too, and elephants. Well, I don't know. Looks like a bit of a joke, don't it now? Perhaps' — (his eye brightened with an idea) — 'perhaps somebody's been copying out something out of a book. Yes, I wouldn't wonder if that's what this is. One of them old-fashioned books. But it's a funny thing how it got up here. I'd show it to Rector, Miss Hilary, that's what I'd do. He knows a lot of books and maybe he'd know where it come from.'

'That's a good idea. I will. But it's awfully mysterious, isn't it? Quite creepy. Can we go up the tower now, Mr Godfrey?'

Mr Godfrey was quite willing, and together they climbed the last long ladder, stretching high over the hells and leading them out by way of a little shelter like a dog-kennel on to the leaded roof of the tower. Leaning against the wind was like leaning against a wall. Hilary pulled off her hat and let her thick bobbed hair blow out behind her, so that she looked like one of the floating singing angels in the church below. Mr Godfrey had no eyes for this resemblance; he thought Miss Hilary's angular face and straight hair rather unattractive, if the truth were known. He contented himself with advising her to hold tight by the iron stays of the weathercock. Hilary paid no attention to him, but advanced to the parapet, leaning over between the pierced battlements to stare out southward over the Fen. Far away beneath her lay the churchyard, and, while she looked, a little figure, quaintly foreshortened, crawled beetle-like from the porch and went jogging down the path. Mrs Venables, going home to lunch. Hilary watched her struggle with the wind at the gate across the road and enter the Rectory garden. Then she turned and moved to the east side of the tower, and looked out along the ridged roofs of the nave and chancel. A brown spot in the green churchyard caught her eye and her heart seemed to turn over in her body. Here, at the north-east angle of the church, her mother lay buried, her grave not yet turfed over; and now it looked as though, before long, the earth would have to be opened up again to let the husband join his wife. 'Oh, God!' said Hilary, desperately, 'don't let Dad die — You can't — You simply can't.' Beyond the churchyard wall lay a green field, and in the middle of the field there was a slight hollow. She knew that hollow well. It had been there now for over three hundred years. Time had made it shallower, and in three hundred years more it might disappear altogether, but there it still was — the mark left by the great pit dug for the founding of Tailor Paul.

Jack Godfrey spoke close beside her.

'Time I was getting along now, Miss Hilary.'

'Oh, yes. I'm sorry. I wasn't thinking. Are you ringing a peal tomorrow?'

'Yes, Miss Hilary. We're going to have a try at Stedman's. They're difficult to ring, are Stedman's, but very fine music when you get them going proper. Mind your head, Miss Hilary. A full peal of 5,040 we're going to give them — that's three hours. It's a fortnit thing as Will Thoday's all right again, because neither Tom Tebbutt nor young George Wilderspin is what you might call reliable in Stedman's, and of course, Wally Pratt's no good at all. Excuse me one minute, Miss Hilary, while I gather up my traps. But to my mind, there's more interest, as you might say, in Stedman's than in any other method, though it takes a bit of thinking about to keep it all clear in one's head. Old Hezekiah don't so much care about it, of course, because he likes the tenor rung in. Triples ain't much fun for him, he says, and it ain't to be wondered at. Still, he's an old man now, and you couldn't hardly expect him to learn Stedman's at his age, and what's more, if he could, you'd never get him to leave Tailor Paul. Just a moment, Miss Hilary, while I lock up this here counterpoise. But give me a nice peal of Stedman's and I ask no better. We never had no Stedman's till Rector come, and it took him a powerful long time to learn us to ring them. Well I mind the trouble we had with them. Old John Thoday — that's Will's father, he's dead and gone now — he used to say, 'Boys,' he said, 'it's my belief the Devil himself couldn't get no sense out of this dratted method.' And Rector fined him sixpence for swearing, like it says in they old rules. Mind you don't slip on the stair, Miss Hilary, it's terrible worn. But we learned Stedman to rights, none the more for that, and to my mind it's a very pretty method of ringing. Well, good morning to you, Miss Hilary.'

★   ★   ★

The peal of 5,040 Stedman's Triples was duly rung on Easter Sunday morning. Hilary Thorpe heard it from the Red House, sitting beside the great old four-poster bed, as she had sat on New Year's morning to hear the peal of Treble Bob Major. Then the noise of the bells had come full

90

and clear; today, it reached her only in distant bursts, when the wind, rollicking away with it eastward, bated for a moment or veered round a little to the south.

'Hilary!'

'Yes, Dad.'

'I'm afraid — if I go west this time — I'll be leaving you rottenly badly off, old girl.'

'I don't care a dash about that, old thing. Not that you are going west. But if you did, I should be quite all right.'

'There'll be enough to send you to Oxford, I dare say. Girls don't seem to cost much there — your uncle will see to it.'

'Yes — and I'm going to get a scholarship, anyway. And I don't want money. I'd rather make my own living. Miss Bowler says she doesn't think anything of a woman who can't be independent.' (Miss Bowler was the English mistress and the idol of the moment.) 'I'm going to be a writer, Dad. Miss Bowler says she wouldn't wonder if I'd got it in me.'

'Oh? What are you going to write? Poetry?'

'Well, perhaps. But I don't suppose that pays very well. I'll write novels. Best sellers. The sort that everybody goes potty over. Not just bosh ones, but like *The Constant Nymph*.'

'You'll want a bit of experience before you can write novels, old girl.'

'Rot, Daddy. You don't want experience for writing novels. People write them at Oxford and they sell like billy-ho. All about how awful everything was at school.'

'I see. And when you leave Oxford, you write

one about how awful everything was at college.'

'That's the idea. I can do that on my head.'

'Well, dear, I hope it'll work. But, all the same, I feel a damned failure, leaving you so little. If only that rotten necklace had turned up! I was a fool to pay that Wilbraham money for it, but she as good as accused the old Governor of being an accessory, and I — '

'Oh, Dad, please — *please* don't go on about that silly necklace. Of course you couldn't do anything else about it. And I don't want the beastly money. And, anyhow, you're not going to peg out yet.'

But the specialist, arriving on Tuesday, looked grave and, taking Dr Baines aside, said to him kindly:

'You have done all you could. Even if you had called me in earlier, it would have made no possible difference.'

And to Hilary, still kindly:

'We must never give up hope, you know, Miss Thorpe. I can't disguise from you that your father's condition is serious, but Nature has marvellous powers of recuperation . . . '

Which is the medical man's way of saying that, short of miraculous intervention, you may as well order the coffin.

* * *

On the following Monday afternoon, Mr Venables was just leaving the cottage of a cantankerous and venomous-tongued old lady on the extreme outskirts of the parish, when a deep, booming sound smote his ear from afar. He stood still with his hand upon the gate.

'That's Tailor Paul,' said the Rector to himself.

Three solemn notes and a pause.

'Man or woman?'

Three notes, and then three more.

'Man,' said the Rector. He stilt stood listening. 'I wonder if poor old Merryweather has gone at last? I hope it isn't that boy of Hensman's.' He counted twelve strokes, and waited But the bell tolled on, and the Rector breathed a sigh of relief. Hensman's boy, at least, was safe. He hastily reckoned up the weaklings of his flock. Twenty strokes, thirty strokes — a man of full age. 'Heaven send,' thought the Rector, 'it isn't Sir Henry. He seemed better when I saw him yesterday.' Forty strokes, forty-one, forty-two. Surely it must be old Merryweather — a happy release for him, poor old man. Forty-three forty-four, forty-five, forty-six. Now it must go on — it could not stop at that fatal number. Old Merryweather was eighty-four. The Rector strained his ears. He must have missed the next stroke — the wind was pretty strong, and his hearing was perhaps not as good as it had been.

But he waited full thirty seconds before Tailor Paul spoke again; and after that there was silence for another thirty seconds.

The cantankerous old lady, astonished to see the Rector stand so long bare-headed at her gate, came hobbling down the garden path to know what it was all about.

'It's the passing-bell,' said Mr Venables, 'they have rung the nine tailors and forty-six strokes, and I'm afraid it must be for Sir Henry.'

'Oh, dear,' said the cantankerous old woman. 'That's bad. Terrible bad, that is.' A peevish kind of pity came into her eyes. 'What's to become of Miss Hilary now, with her mother and father gone so quick, and her only fifteen, and nobody to keep her in check? I don't hold with girls being left to look after themselves. They're troublesome at the best and they didn't ought to have their parents took away from them'

'We mustn't question the ways of Providence,' said the Rector.

'Providence?' said the old woman. 'Don't yew talk to me about Providence. I've had enough o' Providence. First he took my husband, and then he took my 'taters, but there's One above as'll teach him to mend his manners, if he don't look out.'

The Rector was too much distressed to challenge this remarkable piece of theology.

'We can but trust in God, Mrs Giddings,' he said, and pulled up the starting-handle with a jerk.

★　★　★

Sir Henry's funeral was fixed for the Friday afternoon. This was an occasion of mournful importance to at least four persons in Fenchurch St Paul. There was Mr Russell, the undertaker, who was a cousin of that same Mary Russell who had married William Thoday. He was determined to excel himself in the matter of polished oak and brass plates, and his hammer and plane had been keeping up a dismal little harmony of their own during the early part of the week. His, also, was the delicate task of selecting the six bearers so that they might be well-matched in height and step. Mr Hezekiah Lavender and Mr Jack Godfrey went into conference about the proper ringing of a muffled peal — Mr Godfrey's business being to provide and adjust the leather buffets about the clappers of the bells, and Mr Lavender's to arrange and conduct the ringing. And Mr Gotobed, the sexton, was concerned with the grave — so much concerned that he had declined to take part in the peal, preferring to give his whole mind to the graveside ceremonies, although his son, Dick, who assisted him with the spadework, considered himself quite capable of carrying on on his own. There was not, indeed, very much to do in the way of digging. Rather to Mr Gotobed's disappointment. Sir Henry had expressed a wish to be buried in the same grave with his wife, so that there was little opportunity for any fine work in the way of shaping, measuring and smoothing the sides of the grave. They had only to cast out the earth — scarcely yet firm after three rainy months — make all neat and tidy and line the grave with fresh greenery. Nevertheless, liking to be well beforehand with his work Mr Gotobed took measures to carry this out on the Thursday afternoon.

The Rector had just come in from a round of visits, and was about to sit down to his tea, when Emily appeared at the sitting-room door.

'If you please, sir, could Harry Gotobed speak

to you for a moment?'

'Yes, certainly. Where is he?'

'At the back door, sir. He wouldn't come in on account of his boots being dirty.'

Mr Venables made his way to the back door; Mr Gotobed stood awkwardly on the step, twirling his cap in his hands.

'Well, Harry, what's the trouble?'

'Well, sir, it's about this here grave. I thought I better come and see you, being as it's a church matter. You see, when Dick and me come to open it up, we found a corpus a-lying inside of it, and Dick says to me — '

'A corpse? Well, of course there's a corpse. Lady Thorpe is buried there. You buried her yourself.'

'Yes, sir, but this here corpus ain't Lady Thorpe's corpus. It's a man's corpus, that's what it is, and it du seem as though it didn't have no right to be there. So I says to Dick — '

'A man's corpse! What do you mean? Is it in a coffin?'

'No, sir, no coffin. Just an ordinary suit o' clothes, and he du look as though he's a-been a-laying there a goodish while. So Dick says, 'Dad,' he says, 'this looks like a police matter to me. Shall I send for Jack Priest?' he says. And I says, 'No,' I says, 'this here is church property, this is, and Rector did ought to be told about it. That's only right and respectful,' I says. 'Throw a bit o' summat over it,' I says, 'while I goes and fetches Rector, and don't let any o' they boys come into the churchyard.' So I puts on my coat and comes over, because we don't rightly know what to do about it.'

'But what an extraordinary thing, Harry!' exclaimed the Rector, helplessly. 'I really — I never — who is this man? Do you know him?'

'It's my belief, sir, his own mother wouldn't know him. Perhaps you'd like to step across and take a look at him?'

'Why, yes, of course, I'd better do that. Dear me, dear me! how very perplexing. Emily! Emily! have you seen my hat anywhere? Ah, thank you. Now, Harry. Oh, Emily, please tell Mrs Venables that I am unexpectedly detained, and not to wait tea for me. Yes, Harry, I'm quite ready now.'

Dick Gotobed had spread a tarpaulin over the half-open grave, but he lifted this as the Rector approached. The good gentleman gave one look and averted his eyes hastily. Dick replaced the tarpaulin.

'This is a very terrible thing,' said Mr Venables. He had removed his clerical felt in reverence for the horrid thing under the tarpaulin, and stood bewildered, his thin grey hair ruffled by the wind. 'We must certainly send for the constable — and — and' — here his face brightened a little — 'and for Dr Baines, of course. Yes, yes — Dr Baines will be the man. And, Harry, I think I have read that it is better in these cases to disturb things as little as possible. Er — I wonder who this poor fellow can possibly be. It's nobody belonging to the village, that's certain, because if anybody was missing we should have heard about it. I cannot imagine how he can have come here.'

'No more can't we, sir. Looks like he was a

proper stranger. Excuse me, sir, but didn't we ought to inform the coroner of this here?'

'The coroner? Oh, dear! yes, naturally; I suppose there will have to be an inquest. What a dreadful business this is! Why, we haven't had an inquest in the village since Mrs Venables and I came to the Rectory, and that's close on twenty years. This will be a very shocking blow for Miss Thorpe, poor child. Her parent's grave — such a fearful desecration. Still, it can't be hushed up, of course. The inquest — well, well, we must try to keep our wits about us. I think, Dick, you had better run up to the post office and get a call put through to Dr Baines and ask him to come over at once and you had better ring through to St Peter and get someone to send a message to Jack Priest. And you, Harry, had better stay here and keep an eye on — on the grave. And I will go up to the Red House myself and break the shocking news to Miss Thorpe, for fear she should hear it in an abrupt and painful way from somebody else. Yes, I think that is what I had better do. Or perhaps it would be more suitable if Mrs Venables were to go round. I must consult her. Yes, yes, I must consult Mrs Venables. Now, Dick, off you go, and be sure you don't say a word about this to anybody till the constable comes.'

There is no doubt that Dick Gotobed did his best in the matter, but, since the post office telephone lived in the postmistress's sitting-room, it was not altogether easy to keep any message confidential. At any rate, by the time that P.C. Priest arrived, rather blown, upon his push-cycle, a small knot of men and women had gathered in and about the churchyard, including Hezekiah Lavender, who had run as fast as his ancient legs could carry him from his cottage-garden and was very indignant with Harry Gotobed for not letting him lift the tarpaulin.

''Ere!' said the constable, running his machine adroitly into the midst of a bunch of children clustered round the lychgate and tipping himself bodily sideways. ''Ere! what's all this? You run along home to yer mothers, see? And don't let me catch you here again. 'Afternoon, Mr Venables, sir. What's the trouble here?'

'There's been a body found in the churchyard,' said Mr Venables.

'Body, eh?' said the constable. 'Well, it's come to the right place, ain't it? What have you done with it? Oh, you've left it where you found it. Quite right, sir. And where might that be? Oh, 'ere. *I* see. All right; let's have a look at him. Oh! ah! that's it, is it? Why, Harry, whatever have you been a-doing of? Tryin' to bury him?'

The Rector began to explain, but the constable stopped him with an upraised hand.

'One moment, sir. We'll take this here matter in the proper and correct order. Just a moment while I gets out my notebook, Now, then. Date. Call received 5.15 pee hem. Proceeded to the churchyard, arriving 5.30 pee hem. Now, who found this here body?'

'Dick and me.'

'Name?' said the constable.

'Go on, Jack. You know me well enough.'

'That don't matter. I've got to do it in the

proper way. Name?'

'Harry Gotobed.'

'Hoccupation?' 'Sexton.'

'Righto, Harry. Go ahead.'

'Well, Jack, we was a-openin' this here grave, which is Lady Thorpe's grave what died last New Year's Day, for to be ready for her 'usband's body, see, what's to be buried tomorrow. We begins to shovel away the earth, one at each end, like, and we hadn't got much more than a foot or so below ground level, as you might say, when Dick drives his spade down a good spit, and he says to me, 'Dad,' he says, 'there's something in here.' And I says to him, 'What's that?' I says, 'what do you mean? Something in here?' and then I strikes my spade down hard and I feels something sort of between hard and soft, like, and I says, 'Dick,' I says, 'that's a funny thing, there *is* something here.' So I says, 'Go careful, my boy,' I says, 'because it feels funny like to me,' I says. So we starts at one end and shovels away gentle, and arter a bit we sees something sticking up like it might be the toe of a boot. So I says, 'Dick,' I says, 'that's a boot, that is.' And he says, 'You're right, Dad, so 'tis.' So I says, 'Looks to me like we begun at the wrong end of this here, so to say.' So he says, 'Well, Dad, now we've gone so far we may as well have a look at him.' So we gets ashovellin' again, still going very careful, and arter a bit more we sees something lookin' like 'air. So I says, 'You put that there shovel away and use your 'ands, because we don't want to spile it.' And he says, 'I don't like it.' And I says, 'Don't you be a fool, my boy. You can wash your

100

'ands, can't you, when you've done?' So we clears away very careful, and at last we sees him plain. And I says, 'Dick, I don't know who he is or nor yet how he got here, but he didn't ought to be here.' And Dick says, 'shall I go for Jack Priest?' And I says, 'No. 'Tis Church ground and we better tell Rector.' So that's what we done.'

'And I said,' put in the Rector, 'that we had better send at once for you and for Dr Baines — and here he is, I see.'

Dr Baines, a peremptory-looking little man, with a shrewd Scotch face, came briskly up to them.

'Good afternoon, Rector. What's happened here? I was out when your message came, so I — Good Lord!'

A few words put him in possession of the facts, and he knelt down by the graveside.

'He's terribly mutilated — looks as though somebody had regularly beaten his face in. How long has he been here?'

'That's what we'd like you to tell us, Doctor.'

'Half a minute, half a minute, sir,' interrupted the policeman. 'What day was it you said you buried Lady Thorpe, Harry?'

'January 4th, it were.' said Mr Gotobed, after a short interval for reflection.

'And was this here body in the grave when you filled it up?'

'Now don't you be a fool, Jack Priest,' retorted Mr Gotobed. ''Owever can you suppose as we'd fill up a grave with this here corpus in it? It ain't a thing as a man might drop in careless like, without noticing. If it was a pocket-knife or a

101

penny-piece, that'd be another thing, but when it comes to the corpus of a full-grown man, that there question ain't reasonable.'

'Now, Harry, that ain't a proper answer to my question. I knows my duty.'

'Oh, all right. Well, then, there weren't no body in that there grave when I filled it up on January 4th — leavin' out, of course, Lady Thorpe's body. That was there, I don't say it wasn't, and for all I know it's there still. Unless him as put this here corpus where it is took the other away with him, coffin and all.'

'Well,' said the doctor, 'it can't have been here longer than three months, and so far as I can tell, it hasn't been there much less. But I'll tell you that better when you get it out.'

'Three months, eh?' Mr Hezekiah Lavender had pushed his way to the front. 'That 'ud be about the time that stranger chap disappeared — him as was stayin' at Ezra Wilderspin's and wanted a job to mend up moty-cars and sich. He had a beard, too, by my recollection.'

'Why, so he had,' cried Mr Gotobed. 'What a head you have on you, Hezekiah! That's who it is, sure-lie. To think o' that, now! I always thought that chap was after no good. But who could have gone for to do a thing like this here?'

'Well,' said the doctor. 'If Jack Priest has finished with his interrogation, you may as well get the body dug out. Where are you going to put it? It won't be a very nice thing to keep hanging about.'

'Mr Ashton have a nice airy shed, sir. If we was to ask him, I dessay he could make shift to move his ploughs out for the time being. And it's got a decent-sized window and a door with a lock to it.'

'That'll do well. Dick, run round and ask Mr Ashton and get him to lend us a cart and a hurdle. How about getting hold of the coroner, Rector? It's Mr Compline, you know, over at Leamholt. Shall I ring him up when I get back?'

'Oh, thank you, thank you. I should be very grateful.'

All right. Can they carry on now, Jack?'

The constable signified his assent, and the digging was resumed. By this time the entire village seemed to have assembled in the churchyard and it was with the greatest difficulty that the children were prevented from crowding round the grave, since the grown-ups who should have restrained them were themselves struggling for positions of vantage. The Rector was just turning upon them with the severest rebuke he knew to utter, when Mr Lavender approached him.

'Excuse me, sir, but did I ought to ring Tailor Paul for that there?'

'Ring Tailor Paul? Well, really, Hezekiah, I hardly know.'

'We got to ring her for every Christian soul dyin' in the parish,' protested Mr Lavender. 'That's set down for us. And seemin'ly he must a-died in the parish, else why should anybody go for to bury him here?'

'True, true, Hezekiah.'

'But as for bein' a Christian soul, who's to say?'

'That, I fear, is beyond me, Hezekiah.'

'As to bein' a bit behindhand with him,' went on the old man, 'that ain't no fault of ours. We only knowed today as he'd died, so it stands to reason we couldn't ring for him earlier. But Christian — well, there! that's a bit of a puzzle, that is.'

'We'd better give him the benefit of the doubt, Hezekiah. Ring the bell by all means.'

The old man looked dubious, and at length approached the doctor.

'How old?' said the latter, looking round in some surprise. 'Why, I don't know. It's hard to say. But I should think he was between forty and fifty. Why do you want to know? The bell? Oh, I see. Well, put it at fifty.'

So Tailor Paul tolled the mysterious stranger out with nine strokes and fifty and a hundred more, while Alf Donnington at the Red Cow and Tom Tebbutt at the Wheatsheaf did a roaring trade and the Rector wrote a letter.

the second part

LORD PETER IS CALLED INTO THE HUNT

Hunting is the first part of change ringing which it is necessary to understand.
TROYTE *On Change-Ringing*

'My dear Lord Peter (wrote the Rector), —

'Since your delightful visit to us in January, I have frequently wondered, with a sense of confusion, what you must have thought of us for not realising how distinguished an exponent of the methods of Sherlock Holmes we were entertaining beneath our roof. Living so very much out of the world, and reading only *The Times* and the *Spectator*, we are apt, I fear, to become somewhat narrow in our interests. It was only when my wife wrote to her cousin Mrs Smith (whom you may know, perhaps, as she lives in Kensington) and mentioned your stay with us, that we were informed, by Mrs Smith's reply, what manner of man our guest was.

'In the hope that you will pardon our lamentable ignorance, I venture to write and ask you to give us some advice out of your great experience. This afternoon we have been jerked rudely out of 'the noiseless tenor of our way,' by a most mysterious and shocking occurrence. On opening the grave of the late Lady Thorpe to receive the body of her husband — whose sad death you no doubt saw in the Obituary columns of the daily Press — our sexton was horrified to discover the dead body of a completely strange man, who appears to have come by his end in some violent and criminal manner. His face has been terribly mutilated, and — what seems even more shocking — the poor fellow's hands have been cut right off at the wrists! Our local police have, of course, the matter in hand, but the sad affair is of peculiar and painful interest to me (being in some sort connected with our parish church), and I am somewhat at a loss to know how I personally should proceed. My wife, with her usual great practical ability, suggested that we should seek your aid and advice, and Superintendent Blundell of Leamholt, with whom I have just had an interview, most obligingly says that he will give you every facility for investigation should you care to look into the matter personally. I hardly like to suggest to so busy a man that you should actually come and conduct your investigations on the spot, but, in case you thought of doing so, I need not say how heartily welcome you would be at the Rectory.

'Forgive me if this letter is somewhat meandering and confused; I am writing in some perturbation of mind. I may add that our Ringers retain a most pleasant and grateful recollection of the help you gave us with our famous peal, and would, I am sure, wish me to remember them to you.

'With kindest regards from my wife and myself,

'Most sincerely yours,
       'THEODORE VENABLES.'

'P.S. — My wife reminds me to tell you that the inquest is at 2 o'clock on Saturday.'

This letter, dispatched on the Friday morning, reached Lord Peter by the first post on Saturday. He wired that he would start for Fenchurch St Paul at once, joyfully cancelled a number of social engagements, and at two o'clock was seated in the Parish Room, in company with a larger proportion of the local population than had probably ever gathered beneath one roof since the spoliation of the Abbey.

The coroner, a florid-faced country lawyer, who seemed to be personally acquainted with everybody present, got to work with the air of an immensely busy person, every moment of whose time was of value.

'Come now, gentlemen . . . No talking over there *if* you please . . . all the jury this way . . . Sparkes, give out these Testaments to the jury . . . choose a foreman, please . . . Oh! you have chosen Mr Donnington . . . very good . . . Come along, Alf . . . take the Book in your right hand . . . diligently inquire . . . Sovereign Lord the King . . . man unknown . . . body . . . view . . . skill and knowledge . . . help you God . . . kiss the Book . . . sit down . . . table over there . . . now the rest of you . . . take the Book in your right hand . . . your *right* hand, Mr Pratt . . . don't you know your left from your right, Wally? . . . No laughing, please, we've no time to waste . . . same oath that your foreman

. . . you and each of you severally to keep . . .
help you God . . . kiss the Book . . . on that
bench by Alf Donnington . . . Now then, you
know what we're here for . . . inquire how this
man came by his death . . . witnesses to identity
. . . understand no witnesses to identity . . . Yes,
Superintendent? . . . Oh, I see . . . why didn't
you say so? Very well . . . this way, please . . . I
beg your pardon, sir? . . . Lord Peter . . . do you
mind saying that again . . . Whimsy? . . . Oh, no
H . . . just so . . . Wimsey with an E . . . quite
. . . occupation? . . . what? . . . Well, we'd better
say, Gentleman . . . now then, my lord, you say
you can offer evidence as to identity?'

'Not exactly, but I rather think . . . '

'One moment, please . . . take the Book in
your right hand . . . evidence . . . inquiry
. . . truth, whole truth and nothing but the
truth . . . kiss the Book . . . yes . . . name,
address, occupation we've got all that . . . If you
can't keep that baby quiet, Mrs Leach, you'll
have to take it out . . . Yes?'

'I have been taken to see the body, and from
my observation I think it possible that I saw this
man on January 1st last. I do not know who he
was, but if it is the same man he stopped my car
about half a mile beyond the bridge by the sluice
and asked the way to Fenchurch St Paul. I never
saw him again, and had never seen him before to
my knowledge.'

'What makes you think it may be the same
man?'

'The fact that he is dark and bearded and that
the man I saw also appeared to be wearing a

dark suit similar to that worn by deceased. I say 'appeared', because he was wearing an overcoat, and I only saw the legs of his trousers. He seemed to be about fifty years of age, spoke in a low voice with a London accent and was of fairly good address. He told me that he was a motor mechanic and was looking for work. In my opinion, however . . . '

'One moment. You say you recognise the beard and the suit. Can you swear . . . ?'

'I cannot swear that I definitely recognise them. I say that the man I saw resembled the deceased in these respects.'

'You cannot identify his features?'

'No: they are too much mutilated.'

'Very well. Thank you. Are there any more witnesses to identity?'

The blacksmith rose up rather sheepishly.

'Come right up to the table, please. Take the Book . . . truth . . . truth . . . truth . . . Name Ezra Wilderspin. Well, now, Ezra, what have you got to say?'

'Well, sir, if I was to say I recognised the deceased, I should be telling a lie. But it's a fact that he ain't unlike a chap that come along same as his lordship here says, last New Year's Day a-looking for a job along of me. Said he was a motor mechanic out o' work. Well, I told him I might do with a man as knowed somethin' about motors, so I takes him on and gives him a trial. He did his work pretty well near as I could judge, for three days, livin' in our place, and then, all of a sudden, off he goes in the middle of the night and we never seen no more of him.'

'What night was that?'

'Same day as they buried her ladyship it was . . .'

Here a chorus of voices broke in:

'January 4th, Ezra! that's when it were.'

'That's right. Saturday, January 4th, so 'twere.'

'What was the name of this man?'

'Stephen Driver, he called hisself. Didn't say much; only that he'd been trampin' about a goodish time, lookin' for work. Said he'd been in the Army, and in and out of work ever since.'

'Did he give you any references?'

'Why, yes, sir, he did, come to think on it. He give me the name of a garridge in London where he'd been, but he said it had gone bankrupt and shut up. But he said if I was to write to the boss, he'd put in a word for him.'

'Have you got the name and address he gave you?'

'Yes, sir. Leastways, I think the missus put it away in the teapot.'

'Did you take up the reference?'

'No, sir. I did think of it but being no great hand at writing I says to myself I'd wait till the Sunday, when I'd have more time, like. Well, you see, before that he was off, so I didn't think no more about it. He didn't leave nothing behind him, bar an old toothbrush. We 'ad to lend him a shirt when he came.'

'You had better see if you can find that address.'

'That's right, sir. Liz!' (in a stentorian bellow). 'You cut off home and see if you can lay your 'and on that bit o' paper what Driver give me.'

Voice from the back of the room: 'I got it here, Ezra,' followed by a general upheaval, as the blacksmith's stout wife forced her way to the front.

'Thanks, Liz,' said the coroner. 'Mr Tasker, 103 Little James St, London, W.C. Here, Superintendent, you'd better take charge of that. Now Ezra, is there anything more you can tell us about this man Driver?'

Mr Wilderspin explored his stubble with a thick forefinger.

'I dunno as there is, sir.'

'Ezra! Ezra! don't yew remember all them funny questions he asked?'

'There now,' said the blacksmith, 'the missus is quite right. That was a funny thing about them questions, that was. He said he 'adn't never been in this here village before, but he knowed a friend as had and the friend had told him to ask after Mr Thomas. 'Mr Thomas!' I says. 'There ain't no Mr Thomas in this here village, nor never has been to my knowledge.' 'That's queer,' he says, 'but maybe he's got another name as well. Far as I can make out,' he says, 'this Thomas ain't quite right in his 'ead. My friend said as he was potty, like.' 'Why,' I says, 'you can't mean Potty Peake? Because Orris is his Chrissen name.' 'No,' he says, 'Thomas was the name. Batty Thomas, that's right. And another name my friend gi'n me,' he says, 'was a fellow called Paul — a tailor or some'in o' that, living next door to him, like.' 'Why,' I says to him, 'your friend's been havin' a game with you. Them ain't men's names, them's the names of bells,' I says.

111

'Bells?' he says. 'Yes,' I says, 'church bells, that's what they is. Batty Thomas and Tailor Paul, they call 'em.' And then he went on and asked a sight o' questions about they bells. 'Well,' I says, 'if you want to know about Batty Thomas and Tailor Paul, you better ask Rector,' I says. 'He knows all about they old bells.' I dunno if he ever went to Rector, but he come back one day — that was the Friday — and says he been in the church and see a bell carved on old Batty Thomas's tomb, like, and what did the writing on it mean. And I says to ask Rector, and he says: 'Did all bells have writing on 'em,' and I says, 'Mostly'; and arter that he didn't say no more about it.'

Nobody being able to make very much sense out of Mr Wilderspin's revelations, the Rector was called, who said that he remembered having seen the man called Stephen Driver on one occasion when he was distributing the parish magazine at the smithy, but that Driver had said nothing then, or at any other time, about bells. The Rector then added his own evidence about finding the body and sending for the police, and was dismissed in favour of the sexton.

Mr Gotobed was very voluble, repeating, with increased circumlocutory detail and reference to what he had said to Dick and Dick to him, the account he had originally given to the police. He then explained that Lady Thorpe's grave had been dug on the 3rd of January and filled in on the 4th, immediately after the funeral.

'Where do you keep your tools, Harry?'

'In the coke-house, sir.'

'Where's that?'

'Well, sir, it's down underneath the church — where Rector says the old cryp used to be. Makes a sight o' work, that it du, a-carryin' coke up and down they stairs and through the chancel and sweepin' up arter it. You can't 'elp it a-dribbling out o' the scuttle, do as you like.'

'Is the door kept locked?'

'Oh, yes, sir, always kept locked. It's the little door under the organ, sir. You can't get to it without you have the key and the key of the west door as well. That is to say, either the key of the west door or one of the church keys, sir, if you take my meaning. I has the west door key, bein' 'andiest for me where I live, but either of the others would do as well.'

'Where do you keep these keys?'

'Hanging up in my kitchen, sir.'

'Has anybody else got a key to the coke-house door?'

'Yes, sir; Rector has all the keys.'

'Nobody else?'

'Not as I knows, sir. Mr Godfrey hasn't them all, only the key of the cryp.'

'I see. When these keys are in your kitchen, I suppose any of your family has access to them?'

'Well, sir, in a manner of speakin', yes, but I 'opes as how you ain't tryin' to put anything on me and my missus, nor yet Dick, let alone the children. I been sexton in this here village twenty year follerin' on Hezekiah, and none of us ain't never yet been suspected of 'ittin' strangers over the 'ead and buryin' of them. Come to think of it, this chap Driver came round to my place one

113

morning on a message and 'ow do I know what he did? Not but what, if he'd a-took the keys I'd be bound to miss them; still, none the more for that . . . '

'Come, come, Harry! Don't talk nonsense. You don't suppose this unfortunate man dug his own grave and buried himself? Don't waste time.'

(Laughter, and cries of 'That's a good 'un, Harry!')

'Silence, *if* you please. Nobody's accusing you of anything. Have you in fact ever missed the keys at any time?'

'No, sir,' (sulkily).

'Or even noticed that your tools had been disturbed?'

'No, sir.'

'Did you clean them after digging Lady Thorpe's grave?'

'Course I cleaned 'em. I always leaves me tools clean.'

'When did you use them next after that?'

This puzzled Mr Gotobed for a moment. The voice of Dick supplied helpfully: 'Massey's baby.'

('Don't prompt the witness, please.')

'That's right,' agreed Mr Gotobed. 'Massey's baby it were, as you can see by the Register. And that 'ud be about a week later — ah! just about.'

'You found the tools clean and in their right place when you dug the grave for Mrs Massey's baby?'

'I ain't noticed nothing different.'

'Not at any time since?'

'No, sir.'

'Very well. That will do. Constable Priest.'

The constable, taking the oath briskly, informed the court of his having been called to the scene of action, having communicated with Superintendent Blundell, having assisted at the removal of the body and of having helped to search the clothes of the deceased. He then made way for the Superintendent, who corroborated his evidence and produced a brief list of the dead man's belongings. These were: a suit of navy-blue serge of poor quality, much deteriorated by its burial in the earth, but apparently purchased fairly recently from a well-known firm of cheap outfitters; much-worn vest and pants, bearing (unexpectedly enough) the name of a French manufacturer; a khaki shirt (British army type): a pair of working-man's boots, nearly new; a cheap spotted tie. In his pockets they had found a white cotton handkerchief; a packet of Woodbines; twenty-five shillings and eight-pence in cash; a pocket-comb; a ten-centime piece; and a short length of stiff wire, bent at one end into a hook. The body had worn no overcoat.

The French money and underclothing and the piece of wire were the only objects which seemed to suggest any kind of clue. Ezra Wilderspin was recalled, but could not bring to mind that Driver had ever said anything about France, beyond mentioning that he had served in the war; and the Superintendent, asked whether he thought the wire could be anything in the nature of a pick-lock, shook his head, and said it didn't look like anything of that sort to *him*.

The next witness was Dr Baines, and his evidence produced the only real sensation of the day. He said:

'I have examined the body of deceased and made an autopsy. I should judge the subject to be a man aged between 45 and 50. He appears to have been well nourished and healthy. Taking into account the nature of the soil, which tends to retard putrefaction, the position of the body when found, that is, about two feet beneath the level of the churchyard and from three to four feet beneath the actual surface of the mound, I should judge the extent of decomposition found to indicate that deceased had been lying in the grave between three and four months. Decay does not proceed so rapidly in a buried body as in one exposed to the air, or in a clothed body as in a naked body. In this case, the internal organs and the soft tissues generally were all quite distinguishable and fairly well preserved. I made a careful examination and could discover no signs of external injury on any part of the body except upon the head, arms, wrist and ankles. The face had apparently been violently battered in with some blunt instrument which had practically reduced all the anterior — that is, the front — part of the skull to splinters. I was not able to form any exact estimate of the number of blows inflicted, but they must have been numerous and heavy. On opening the abdomen — '

'One moment, Doctor. I take it we may assume that the deceased died in consequence of one or some of these blows upon the skull?'

'No; I do not think that the blows were the cause of death.'

At this point an excited murmur ran around

116

the little hall, and Lord Peter Wimsey was distinctly observed to rub his finger-tips lightly together with a gratified smile.

'Why do you say that, Dr Baines?'

'Because, to the best of my judgement and belief, all the blows were inflicted after death. The hands also were removed after death, apparently with a short, heavy knife, such as a jack-knife.'

Further sensation; and Lord Peter Wimsey audibly observed: 'Splendid!'

Dr Baines added a number of technical reasons for his opinion, chiefly connected with the absence of any extravasation of blood and the general appearance of the skin; adding, with proper modesty, that he was, of course, not an expert and could only proffer his opinion for what it was worth.

'But why should anybody inflict such savage injuries on a dead body?'

'That,' said the doctor dryly, 'is outside my province. I am not a specialist in lunacy or neurosis.'

'That is true. Very well, then. In your opinion, what was the cause of death?'

'I do not know. On opening the abdomen, I found the stomach, intestine, liver and spleen considerably decomposed, the kidneys, pancreas and oesophagus in a fairly good state of preservation.' (Here the doctor wandered off into medical detail.) 'I could not see,' he resumed, 'any superficial signs of disease or injury by poison. I, however, removed certain organs' (he enumerated them) 'and placed them in sealed jars' (further technical details) 'and propose dispatching them today for expert examination by Sir James Lubbock. I should expect to receive his report in about a fortnight's time — possibly earlier.'

The coroner expressed himself satisfied with this suggestion, and then went on:

'You mentioned injuries to the arms and ankles, Doctor; what was the nature of those?'

'The skin of the ankles seemed to have been very much broken and abraded — as though the ankles had been tightly bound with cord or rope which had cut through the socks. The arms also showed the pressure marks of a rope above the elbows. These injuries were undoubtedly inflicted before death.'

'You suggest that somebody tied the deceased up with ropes, and then, by some means or other, brought about his death?'

'I think that the deceased was undoubtedly tied up — either by another person or by himself. You may remember that there was a case in which a young man at one of the universities died in circumstances which suggested that he had himself bound his own wrists and arms.'

'In that case, the cause of death was suffocation, I believe?'

'I believe it was. I do not think that was the case here. I found nothing to indicate it.'

'You do not, I suppose, suggest that the deceased went so far as to bury himself?'

'No; I do not suggest that.'

'I am glad to hear it,' said the coroner, sarcastically. 'Can you suggest any reason why, if a man had accidentally or intentionally killed himself by tying himself up — ?'

118

'After tying himself up; the tying of the arms and ankles would not in themselves be likely to cause death.'

'After tying himself up — why somebody else should then come along, smash his face in and then bury him secretly?'

'I could suggest a variety of reasons; but I do not think that is my province.'

'You are very correct, Doctor.'

Dr Baines bowed.

'He might, I suppose, have perished of starvation, if he had tied himself up and been unable to free himself.'

'No doubt. Sir James Lubbock's report will tell us that.'

'Have *you* anything further to tell us?'

'Only that, as a possible aid to identification, I have made as careful a note as I can — in view of the extensive mutilation of the jaws — of the number and condition of deceased's teeth, and of the dental work done upon them at various times. I have handed his note over to Superintendent Blundell in order that he may issue an inquiry.'

'Thank you, Doctor; that will no doubt be very helpful.'

The coroner paused, glanced through his notes and then turned to the Superintendent.

'In the circumstances, Superintendent, it seems to be advisable to adjourn the inquest until you have completed your investigations. Shall we say, till today fortnight? Then, if you should see your way to making any charge against anybody in connection with this crime, or accident, or, whatever it is, we may if you like adjourn the inquiry *sine die.*'

'I think that would be the best way, Mr Compline.'

'Very well. Gentlemen, we will adjourn until today fortnight.'

The jury, a little puzzled and disappointed at not being asked for any opinion, filed slowly out from behind the long trestle table at which they had been seated — a table dedicated, under happier circumstances, chiefly to parish teas.

'A beautiful case,' said Lord Peter, enthusiastically, to Mr Venables. 'Quite charming. I am uncommonly grateful to you for drawing my attention to it. I wouldn't have missed it for the world. I like your doctor.'

'We consider him a very able man.'

'You must introduce me to him; I feel that we should get on well together. The coroner doesn't like him. Some trifling personal antagonism, no doubt. Why, here is my old friend Hezekiah! How do you do, Mr Lavender? How's Tailor Paul?'

There was general greeting. The Rector caught the arm of a tall, thin man hurrying past their little group.

'Just a moment, Will, I want to introduce you to Lord Peter Wimsey. Lord Peter, this is Will Thoday, whose bell you rang on your last visit.'

Hands were shaken.

'Very sorry I was to miss that peal,' said Thoday. 'But I was pretty bad, wasn't I, Rector?'

'You were indeed. You don't look to have quite got over it yet.'

'I'm all right, sir, except for being troubled by

a bit of a cough. But that'll pass away with the spring weather coming.'

'Well, you must take care of yourself, How's Mary?'

'Fine, sir, thank you. She was for coming to this here inquest, but I said as it wasn't no place for a woman. I'm thankful I got her to stop at home.'

'Yes; the doctor's evidence was very disagreeable. Children all right? That's splendid. Tell your wife Mrs Venables will be coming round to see her in a day or two. Yes, she's very well, thank you — distressed, naturally, by all this sad business. Ah! There's Dr Baines. Doctor! Lord Peter Wimsey wants very much to make your acquaintance. You'd better come and have a cup of tea at the Rectory. Good day, Will, good day! . . . I don't like the looks of that fellow,' added the Rector, as they turned towards the Rectory. 'What do you think of him, Doctor?'

'He's looking a bit white and strained today. Last week I thought he was a lot better, but he had a bad bout of it and he's rather a nervous subject. You don't expect farm-labourers to have nerves, do you, Lord Peter? But they're human, like the rest of us.'

'And Thoday is a very superior man,' said the Rector, as though superiority conveyed a licence to keep a nervous system. 'He used to farm his own land till these bad times set in. Now he works for Sir Henry — that is to say, he did. I'm sure I don't know what will happen now, with only the poor child left at the Red House. I suppose the trustee will let the place, or put in a steward to run it for her. It doesn't bring in very much these days, I fear.'

At this point a car overtook them and stopped a little way ahead. It proved to contain Superintendent Blundell and his assistants, and the Rector, apologising fussily for his remissness, made him and Wimsey acquainted with one another.

'Pleased to meet you, my lord. I've heard of you through my old friend Inspector Snugg. He's retired now — did you know? — and got a nice little place the other side of Leamholt. He often talks about you. Says you used to pull his leg something cruel. This is a bad job, this is. Between you and me, my lord, what was it you were going to say when the coroner interrupted you — about this chap Driver's not being a motor mechanic?'

'I was going to say that he gave me the impression of having done most of his manual labour lately at Princetown or somewhere like that.'

'Ah!' said the Superintendent, thoughtfully. 'Struck you that way, did he? How was that?'

'Eyes, voice, attitude — all characteristic, what?'

'Ah!' said the Superintendent again. 'Ever heard of the Wilbraham emeralds, my lord?'

'Yes.'

'You know that Nobby Cranton's out again? And it seems he ain't reported himself lately, neither. Last heard of six months ago in London. They've been looking for him. Maybe we've found him. In any case, I wouldn't be surprised if we was to hear of those emeralds again before very long.'

'Loud cheers!' said Wimsey. 'I'm all for a treasure-hunt. This is all confidential, of course?'

'If you please, my lord. You see, if somebody thought it worth while to kill Cranton and smash him up and bury him, *and* cut off his hands where he keeps his fingerprints, there's somebody in this village that knows something. And the less they think we guess, the more free they'll act and speak. And that's why, my lord, I was rather glad when the reverend gentleman suggested you coming down here. They'll talk freer to you than to me — see?'

'Perfectly. I'm a terrific success at pottering round asking sloppy questions. And I can put away quite a lot of beer in a good cause.'

The Superintendent grinned, begged Wimsey to come and see him at any time, clambered into his car and drove off.

★ ★ ★

The great difficulty about any detective inquiry is knowing where to start. After some thought Lord Peter made out the following list of queries:

A. *Identity of the Corpse*
  1. Was it Cranton? — Wait for report on teeth and police report.
  2. Consider the question of the ten-centime piece and the French underclothing. Has Cranton been in France? When? If not Cranton, is anyone known in the village also known to have been in France at any period since the war?
  3. The destruction of the hands and features after death suggests that the murderer had

123

an interest in making recognition impossible. If the body is Cranton, who knew Cranton (a) by sight? (b) personally?

4. (Note: Deacon knew him; but Deacon is dead. Did Mary Thoday know him?) Many people must have seen him at the trial.

B. *The Wilbraham Emeralds*

1. Resulting from the above: Was Mary Thoday (formerly Mary Deacon, née Russell) really after all concerned in the theft?

2. Who really had the emeralds — Deacon or Cranton?

3. Where are the emeralds now? Did Cranton (if it was Cranton) come to Fenchurch St Paul to look for them?

4. If the answer to 3 is 'Yes,' why did Cranton wait till now to make his search? Because some fresh information had lately reached him? Or merely because he was continuously in prison till just lately? (Ask the Superintendent.)

5. What is the meaning of 'Driver's' interest in Batty Thomas and Tailor Paul? Is anything to be gained from a study of the bells and/or their mottoes?

C. *The Crime*

1. What did deceased die of? (Wait for experts' report.)

2. Who buried (and presumably also killed) him?

3. Can any clue to the time of the burial be gained by looking up the weather reports? (Snow? Rain? Footprints?)
4. Whereabouts did the murder take place? The churchyard? the church? somewhere in the village?
5. If the sexton's tools were used, who had access to them? ('Driver,' apparently, but who else?)

Quite a lot of questions, thought his lordship, and some of them unanswerable till outside reports came in. The matter of the bell-mottoes could, of course, be looked into at once. He sought the Rector and asked whether he could without too much trouble, lay his hand on Woollcott's *History of the Bells of Fenchurch St Paul*, which he had once spoken about. The Rector thought he could, and after he had hunted through all his study shelves and enlisted the aid of Mrs Venables and Emily, the book was in fact discovered in a small room devoted to the activities of the Clothing Club ('and how it could have got there I cannot imagine!'). From this work Wimsey distilled the following facts interesting to archaeologists, but not immediately suggestive of anything in the way of corpses or emeralds:

Batty Thomas (No. 7. Weight 30½ cwt. Note: D). The oldest bell in the ring in her present form, and oldest still in her original metal. First cast by Thomas Belleyetere of Lynn in 1338. Recast, with additional metal, by Abbot Thomas of Fenchurch (fl: 1356–1392) in

1380. (This abbot also built the tower and the greater part of the existing nave, though the aisle windows were enlarged in Perpendicular style by Abbot Martin, *circ.* 1423.)

Inscriptions:

Shoulder — NOLI + ESSE + INCREDV-
LVS + SED + FIDELIS +

Waist — O SANCTE THOMA.

Soundbow — ABBAT . THOMAS . SETT .
MEE . HEARE . AND . BAD
. MEE . RINGE . BOTH . LOVD
. AND . CLEER . 1380 .

No record of any other bells at this time, though there was probably at least one other. We know, however, that in the reign of Elizabeth there was a ring of five bells in D of which

John (No. 3. Weight 8 cwt. Note: A) was the original treble. She bears the name of her founder, John Cole, an itinerant founder of the period.

Inscriptions:

Soundbow — JHON . COLE. MAD .
MEE. JHON . PRESBYTER .
PAYD . MEE . JHON EVAGE-
LIST . AID . MEE . MDLVII.

Jericho (No. 4. Weight 8½ cwt. Note: G) was the No. 2 of the old peal and her maker seems to have thought aggressively well of her.

Inscriptions:

Shoulder — FROM . IERICHO . TO
IOHN . AGROAT . YR . IS .
NOE . BELLE . CAN .
BETTER . MY . NOTE. 1559.

Of the original No. 4, nothing is known. The original No. 3 (F#) was a poor bell, flat in pitch and weak in quality. In James I's reign, this bell was further flattened by the grinding away of its inner surface so as to produce some sort of approximation to F#, and the great tenor bell was added to make a ring of six in C.

Tailor Paul (No. 8. Weight 41 cwt. Note: C). A very noble bell of superb truth and tone. She was cast in the Bellfield by the church. (See parish records.)

Inscriptions:

Shoulder — PAVLE + IS + MY + NAME
+ HONOVR + THAT + SAME +
Soundbow — NINE + TAYLERS + MAKE
+ A + MANNE + IN + CHRIST
+ IS + DETH + ATT + END +
IN + ADAM + YAT + BEGANNE
+ 1614

The bells survived the tumults of the Great Rebellion, and in the later part of the century, when the fashion for change-ringing set in, a new treble and second were added to bring the number up to eight.

Gaude (Treble. Weight 7 cwt. Note: C). The gift of the Gaudy family, she bears a 'canting' motto.

Inscriptions:
    Soundbow — GAVDE. GAUDY . DNI. IN. LAVDE . MDCLXVI.

The No. 2 of that period was known as *Carolus*, having been given in honour of the King's Restoration. This bell, however, was cracked in the 18th century, as a result of the abominable practice of 'clappering' the two smallest bells for occasional services, so that the ring was again reduced to six, of which No. 5 (F#) had always been unsatisfactory. In the first half of the 19th century (that period of ecclesiastical apathy) the worm was allowed to get into the timbers of the bell-cage, as a result of which No. 6 (the Elizabethan No. 4) fell and was broken. Nothing was done until the eighties, when an energetic High Church rector called public attention to the bad state of the bells. Subscriptions were raised, the framework of the bell-cage was repaired and put in order, and three bells were recast:

Sabaoth (No. 2. Weight 7¼ cwt. Note: B) was the gift of the Rector.

Inscriptions:
    Shoulder — SANCTUS . SANCTUS . SANCTUS . DOMINUS. DEUS. SABAOTH

Soundbow — RECAST BY JOHN TAYLOR
OF LOUGHBOROUGH 1887.

Dimity (No. 6. Weight 14 cwt. Note: E) was given in memory of Sir Richard Thorpe, who died in 1883.

Inscriptions:
Shoulder — RECAST BY JOHN TAYLOR OF LOUGHBOR-OUGH 1887.
Soundbow — IN . PIAM . MEMORIAM . RICARDI . THORPE . ARMIGERI . NUNC DIMIT-TIS . DOMINE . SERVUM . TUUM . IN . PACE .

Jubilee (No. 5. Weight 9½ cwt. Note: F#). The funds for this bell were raised by public subscription in commemoration of the Queen's Jubilee.

Inscriptions:
Shoulder — JUBILATE . DEO . OMNIS . TERRA .
Waist — RECAST . IN . THE . YEAR . OF . THE . QUEEN'S . JUBI-LEE . BY . JOHN . TAYLOR . AND . CO . E . HINKINS . AND . B . DONNINGTON . CHURCH-WARDENS.

Wimsey puzzled his head for some time over this information, but without very much result.

The dates, the weights and the mottoes — was there anything here that could serve as a guide to buried treasure? Batty Thomas and Tailor Paul had been particularly mentioned, but try as he would, for him they had neither speech nor language. After a time he gave up his calculations. Possibly there was something about the bells themselves that did not appear in Mr Woollcott's work. Something written or carved on the timbers, possibly. He must go up and look some time.

It was Sunday morning. As he lifted his head from his calculations, he heard the bells begin to ring for matins. He hastened out in the hall, where he found his host winding the grandfather clock.

'I always wind it when the bells begin on a Sunday morning,' explained Mr Venables, 'otherwise I might forget. I fear I am none too methodical. I hope you will not feel obliged to come to church merely because you are our guest. I always make a point of telling our visitors that they are quite free to do as they wish. What time do *you* make it? Ten thirty-seven — we will put the hands at 10.45. He always loses about a quarter of an hour during the week, you see, and by putting him a little forward each time he is wound, we strike a happy mean. If you will just remember that he is always *fast* on Sundays, Mondays and Tuesday, *right* on Wednesdays, and *slow* on Thursdays, Fridays and Saturdays, you will find him a very reliable guide.'

Wimsey said he was sure of it, and turned to find Bunter at his elbow, offering him with one hand his hat and with the other two leather-bound volumes on a small salver.

'You see, padre, we have every intention of going to church; we have, in fact, come prepared. Hymns A. & M. — I suppose that is the right work?'

'I took the liberty of ascertaining as much beforehand, my lord.'

'Of course you did, Bunter. You always ascertain everything. Why, padre, what's the trouble? Have you lost anything?'

'I — er — it's very odd — I could have declared that I laid them down just here. Agnes! Agnes, my dear! Have you seen those banns anywhere?'

'What is it, Theodore?'

'The banns, my dear. Young Flavel's banns. I know I had them with me. I always write them out on a slip of paper, you see, Lord Peter; it is so very inconvenient to carry the register to the lectern. Now what in the world — ?'

'Are they on the top of the clock, Theodore?'

'My dear, what a — ! Bless me, though, you are quite right. How did that come about, I wonder! I must have put them up there unconsciously when I was picking up the key. Very strange indeed, but the little mishap is now remedied, thanks to my wife. She always knows where I have put things. I believe she knows the workings of my mind better than I do myself. Well, I must go across to the church now. I go early, because of the choirboys. My wife will show you the Rectory pew.'

The pew was conveniently situated for observation, towards the rear of the nave on the north side. From it, Mrs Venables was able to survey the south porch, by which the congregation entered, and also to keep an admonitory eye on the school-children who occupied the north aisle, and to frown at those who turned round to stare or make faces. Lord Peter, presenting a placid front to the inquisitive glances of his fellow-worshippers, also watched the south porch. There was a face he was particularly anxious to see. Presently he saw it. William Thoday came in, and with him a thin, quietly dressed woman accompanied by two little girls. He guessed her to be about forty, though, as is frequently the case with country women, she had lost most of her front teeth and looked older. But he could still see in her the shadow of the smart and pretty parlour-maid that she must have been sixteen years before. It was, he thought, an honest face, but its expression was anxious and almost apprehensive — the face of a woman who had been through trouble and awaited, with nervous anticipation, the next shock which fate might hold in store for her. Probably, thought Wimsey, she was worried about her husband. He did not look well; he, too, had the air of being braced in self-defence. His uneasy eyes wandered about the church and then returned, with a curious mingling of wariness and protective affection, to his wife. They took their seats almost immediately opposite the Rectory pew, so that Wimsey from his corner seat was able to watch them without any appearance of particularity. He gained the impression, however, that Thoday felt his scrutiny and resented it. He turned his eyes away, therefore, and fixed them on the splendours of the angel roof, lovelier than ever in the soft spring sunshine that streamed through the rich reds and blues of the clerestory windows.

The pew which belonged to the Thorpe family was empty, except for an upright, middle-aged gentleman who was pointed out in a whisper by Mrs Venables as being Hilary Thorpe's uncle from London. The housekeeper, Mrs Gates, and the Red House servants sat in the south aisle. In the pew immediately in front of Wimsey was a stout little man in a neat black suit, who, Mrs Venables further informed him, was Mr Russell, the village undertaker, and a cousin of Mary Thoday. Mrs West, the postmistress, arrived with her daughter, and greeted Wimsey, whom she remembered from his last visit, with a smile and something between a nod and a bob. Presently, the bells ceased, with the exception of the five-minute bell, and the ringers came clattering up to their places. Miss Snoot, the schoolmistress, struck into a voluntary, the choir came in from the vestry with much noise of hobnailed boots, the Rector entered his stall.

The service was devoid of incident, except that Mr Venables again mislaid the banns, which had to be fetched from the vestry by the tenor on the cantoris side, and that, in his sermon, he made a solemn little allusion to the unfortunate stranger whose funeral was to take place on the morrow, whereat Mr Russell nodded, with an air of importance and approbation. The Rector's progress to the pulpit was marked by a loud and gritty crunching, which caused Mrs Venables to mutter in an exasperated tone, 'That's the coke again — Gotobed *will* be so careless with it.' At

133

the conclusion, Wimsey found himself stranded with Mrs Venables in the porch, while handshakings and inquiries passed.

Mr Russell and Mr Gotobed came out together, busily talking, and the former was introduced to Lord Peter.

'Where are they a-putting of him, Harry?' asked Mr Russell, eagerly turning from ceremony to business.

'Over on the north side, next to old Susan Edwards,' replied the sexton. 'We got him dug last night, all very fit and proper. Maybe his lordship would like to come and see.'

Wimsey expressed suitable interest, and they made their way round to the other side of the church.

'We're giving him a nice bit of elm,' said Mr Russell, with some satisfaction, when the handsome proportions of the grave had been duly admired. 'He did ought by rights to have come on the parish, and that means deal, as you know, but the Rector says to me, 'Poor fellow,' he says, 'let's put him away nice and seemly, and I'll pay for it,' he says. And I've trued up the boards good and tight, so there won't be no unpleasantness. Of course, lead would be the right thing for him, but it ain't a thing as I'm often asked for, and I didn't think as I could get it in time, and the fact is, the sooner he's underground again, the better. Besides, lead is cruel 'ard work on the bearers. Six of them we're giving him — wouldn't want to be thought lacking in respect for the dead, however come by, so I says to Rector, 'No, sir,' I says, 'not that old

134

handcart,' I says, 'but six bearers just the same as if he was one of ourselves.' And Rector, he quite agreed with me. Ah! I daresay there'll be a sight of folk come in from round about, and I wouldn't like them to see the thing done mean or careless like.'

'That's right,' said Mr Gotobed. 'I've heerd as there's a reglar party comin' from St Stephen in John Brownlow's sharrer. It'll he a rare frolic for 'em.'

'Rector's giving a wreath, too,' pursued Mr Russell, 'and Miss Thorpe's sending another. And there'll be a nice bunch o' flowers from the school-children and a wreath from the Women's Institute. My missus was round collecting the pennies just as soon as we knowed we'd have the buryin' of him.'

'Ah! she's a quick worker and no mistake,' said the sexton, admiringly.

'Ah! and Mrs Venables, she made the money up to a guinea, so it'll be a real good one. I like to see a nice lot of flowers at a funeral. Gives it tone, like.'

'Is it to be choral?'

'Well, not what you might call fully choral, but just a 'ymn at the graveside. Rector says, 'Not too much about parted friends,' he says. ''Twouldn't be suitable, seeing we don't know who his friends was.' So I says, 'What about *God moves in a myster'ous way?* I says. 'That's a good solemn-like, mournful 'ymn, as we all knows the tune on, and if anything can be said to be myster'ous, it's this here death,' I says. So that's what was settled.'

'Ah!' said the voice of Mr Lavender, 'you're right there, Bob Russell. When I was a lad, there wasn't none of this myster'ousness about. Everything was straightforward an' proper. But ever since eddication come in, it's been nothing but puzzlement, and fillin' up forms and 'ospital papers and sustificates and such, before you can get even as much as your Lord George pension.'

'That may be, Hezekiah,' replied the sexton, 'but to my mind it all started with that business of Jeff Deacon at the Red House, bringin' strangers into the place. First thing as 'appened arter that was the war, and since then we been all topsy-turvy like.'

'As to the war,' said Mr Russell, 'I daresay we'd a had that anyhow, Jeff Deacon or no Jeff Deacon. But in a general way you're quite right. He was a bad 'un, was Jeff, though even now, poor Mary won't hear a word again him.'

'That's the way with women,' said Mr Lavender, sourly. 'The wusser a man is, the more they dotes on him. Too soft-spoken he were, to my liking, were that Deacon. I don't trust these London folk, if you'll excuse me, sir.'

'Don't mention it,' said Wimsey.

'Why, Hezekiah; remonstrated Mr Russell, 'you thought a sight o' Jeff Deacon yourself at one time. Said he was the quickest chap at learning Kent Treble Bob as you ever had to do with.'

'That's a different thing,' retorted the old gentleman. 'Quick he was, there ain't no denyin', and he pulled a very good rope. But quickness in the 'ed don't mean a good 'eart. There's many evil men is as quick as monkeys. Didn't the good Lord say as much? The children o' this world is wiser in their generation than the children o' light. He commended the unjust steward, no doubt, but he give the fellow the sack just the same, none the more for that.'

'Ah, well,' said the sexton, 'Jeff Deacon 'ull be put in his proper place where he've gone, and the same with this poor chap, whoever he be. We ain't got nothing to meddle wi' that, only to do our dooties in the station whereto we are called. That's Scripture, that is, and so I says, Give him a proper funeral for we don't know when it may be our turn next.'

'That's very true, Harry; very true, that is. It may be you or me to be 'it on the 'ed one o' these days — though who can be going about to do such things beats me. Now then, Potty, what do you want here?'

'Nothing, nothing, Bob. Only to see where you was a-putting of the dead 'un. Ah! he was reglar smashed up, he were, weren't he? Beat all to a pulp, eh? Whack! whack! I a-liked to a-seen that, I would.'

'Clear off,' said the undertaker. 'I'm disgusted wi' you, Potty. Fair disgusted. Don't you get talkin' that a-way, or I'll tell Rector on you, and he won't let you blow the organ no more. See! What do you mean by it?'

'Nothing, Bob, nothing.'

'That's a good thing.'

Mr Russell watched the imbecile uneasily as he shuffled away, his big head rolling and his hands swinging loosely at his sides.

137

'He's getting very queer, is Potty,' said he. 'I 'ope as he's safe. I reckon he did ought to be shut up.'

'No, no,' said the sexton. 'Potty's safe enough. I don't 'old with these 'ere asylums.'

At this point Mrs Venables joined them to take possession of her guest.

'Poor little Hilary Thorpe wasn't in church,' she observed. 'Such a nice child. I should have liked you to see her. But she's quite prostrated, poor child, so Mrs Gates tells me. And you know, the village people do stare so at anybody who's in trouble and they will want to talk and condole. They mean well, but it's a terrible ordeal. I'll take you along to the Red House one day. Come along now — I'm sure you want your dinner.'

the third part

LORD PETER IS TAKEN FROM LEAD AND MAKES THIRD PLACE

The bell that the treble takes from lead makes thirds place and returns to lead again; while the bells in 4, 5 and 6, 7 dodge when the place is made.

Rules for Ringing Grandsire Triples

Lord Peter watched the coffin borne up the road.

'Here comes my problem,' said he to himself, 'going to earth on the shoulders of six stout fellows. Finally, this time, I suppose, and I don't seem to have got very much out of it. What a gathering of the local worthies — and how we are all enjoying it! Except dear old Venables — he's honestly distressed . . . This everlasting tolling makes your bones move in your body . . . Tailor Paul . . . For Mr Paul . . . two mortal tons of bawling bronze . . . 'I am the Resurrection and the Life . . . ' that's all rather sobering. This chap's first resurrection was ghastly enough — let's hope there won't be another this side of Doomsday . . . Silence that dreadful bell! . . . Tailor Paul . . . though even that might happen, if Lubbock finds anything funny . . . 'Though after my skin worms destroy this body . . . ' How queer that fellow Thoday looks . . . something wrong there, I shouldn't wonder . . . Tailor Paul . . . 'We brought nothing into this world and it is certain we can carry nothing out . . . ' except our secrets, old Patriarch; we take those with us all right.' The deep shadows of the porch swallowed up priest, corpse and bearers, and Wimsey, following with Mrs Venables, felt how strange it was that he and she should follow that strange corpse as sole and unexpected mourners.

'And people may say what they like,' thought Wimsey again, 'about the services of the Church of England, but there was genius in the choosing of these psalms. 'That I may be certified how long I have to live' — what a terrifying prayer; Lord, let me never be certified of anything of the kind. 'A stranger with Thee and a sojourner' — that's a fact, God knows . . . 'Thou hast set our misdeeds before Thee' . . . very likely, and why should I, Peter Wimsey, busy myself with digging them up? I haven't got so very much to boast about myself, if it comes to that . . . Oh, well . . . 'world without end, Amen.' Now the lesson, I suppose we sit down for this — I'm not very well up in the book of words . . . This is the place where the friends and relations usually begin to cry — but there's nobody here to do it — not a friend, nor a — How do I know that? I don't know it. Where's the man or woman who would have recognised that face, if the murderer hadn't taken all those pains to disfigure it? . . . That red-haired kid must be Hilary Thorpe . . . decent of her to come . . . interesting type . . . I can see her making a bit of a splash in five years' time . . . 'I have fought with beasts at Ephesus' . . . what on earth has that got to do with it? . . . 'raised a spiritual body' — what does old Donne say? 'God knows in what part of the world every grain of every man's dust lies . . . He whispers, he hisses, he beckons for the bodies of his saints' . . . do all these people believe that? Do I? Does anybody? We all take it pretty placidly, don't we? 'In a flash, at a trumpet crash, this Jack, joke, poor potsherd, patch, matchwood, immortal diamond is — immortal diamond.' Did the old boys who made that amazing roof believe? Or did they just make those wide wings and adoring hands for fun, because they liked the pattern? At any rate, they made them *look* as though they believed something, and that's where they have us beat. What next? Oh, yes, out again to the grave, of course. Hymn 373 . . . there must be some touch of imagination in the good Mr Russell to have suggested this, though he looks as if he thought of nothing but having tinned salmon to his tea . . . 'Man that is born of woman . . . ' not very much further to go now; we're coming into the straight . . . 'Thou knowest, Lord, the secrets of our hearts . . . ' I knew it, I knew it! Will Thoday's going to faint . . . No, he's got hold of himself again. I shall have to have a word with that gentleman before long . . . 'for any pains of death, to fall from Thee.' Damn it! that goes home. Why? Mere splendour of rhythm, I expect — there were plenty of worse pains . . . 'Our dear brother departed' . . . *brother* . . . we're all dear when we're dead, even if beforehand

141

somebody hated us enough to tie us up and . . . Great Scott, yes! What about that rope?'

The problem of the rope — absurdly overlooked and now absurdly insistent — took such possession of Wimsey that he forgot to join in the Lord's Prayer; nor had he even wits to spare for a sardonic commentary on the means used by Providence to deliver this our brother out of the miseries of this sinful world. He was amazed that he had not earlier seized upon the rope as a clue to the labyrinth. For the tying-up of the dead man implied so much.

Where had the rope come from? How had it happened to be handy for the tying-up, and where had that tying taken place? You might kill a man in hot blood, but you did not first tie him. The death of a bound man meant premeditation — a calf roped for the shambles. The rope had been removed before burial; there was a horrid thrift about that . . . At this point Wimsey shook himself. There was no need to fancy things; there were plenty of other reasons for the removal of the rope. It had been removed before death. It had been removed and replaced where it came from, lest its absence should arouse suspicion. It had been removed for the same reason that the face had been mutilated — lest anyone finding the body should recognise it. Finally, it had been removed because it had tied the body *to* something — and that, perhaps, was the likeliest reason. For the body must have been brought from somewhere — how? Car, lorry, cart, waggon, wheelbarrow, truck . . . ? It reminded one of 'Tinker tailor . . . '

'Everything *very* nicely done, Mr Russell,' said Mrs Venables.

'Yes'm,' said Mr Russell. 'Very glad you think so, 'm. We done what we could to the best of our ability.'

'I'm sure,' said Mrs Venables, 'that if his own people had been here, they couldn't have wished for anything *nicer*.'

'No'm,' agreed Mr Russell, much gratified, 'and it's a pity they couldn't a-been present, for there's no doubt a handsome funeral is a great comfort to them as is left. Of course, it ain' so grand as a London funeral would be — ' He glanced wistfully at Wimsey.

'But much nicer,' said Wimsey, in a ridiculous echo of Mrs Venables. 'You see, it has so much more of the personal touch.'

'That's very true,' said the undertaker, much encouraged. 'Why, I dessay these London men get as much as three or four funerals every week, and it stands to reason as they can't put the same 'eart into it — let alone not knowing the parties. Well, I'll be getting along now. There's someone wants to speak to you, my lord.'

'No,' said Wimsey, firmly, to a gentleman in well-worn tweeds, who approached briskly. 'I have no story for the *Morning Star*. Nor for the other paper. Hop it. I have other things to do.'

'Yes,' added Mrs Venables, addressing the reporter as though he were an importunate child at a school treat, 'run along now, the gentleman's busy. How tiresome these newspapers are! You must get sick to death of them. Come along, I want to introduce you to Hilary Thorpe. Hilary, my dear, how are you? Very sweet of you to come — so trying for you. How is your uncle? This is Lord Peter Wimsey.'

'I'm ever so glad to meet you, Lord Peter. Dad used to read all about your cases — he'd have loved to have a talk with you. You know, I think he'd have been frightfully amused to think of being mixed up in one himself — if only it hadn't been Mother's grave. I'm glad he didn't know about that. But it is a mystery, isn't it? And he was — well, quite a kid about mysteries and things.'

'Was he? I should have thought he'd had about enough of them.'

'You mean about the necklace? That was pretty awful for him, poor dear. Of course, it all happened before I was born, but he often used to talk about it. He always used to say he believed Deacon was the worse of the two men, and that Granddad ought never to have had him in the house. It was funny, but I believe he rather took a liking to the other man — the London thief. He only saw him at the trial, of course, but he said he was an amusing beggar and he believed he was telling the truth.'

'That's dashed interesting.' Lord Peter turned suddenly and savagely on the young man from the *Morning Star*, who still hovered at a little distance. 'See here, my lad, if you don't make a noise like a hoop and roll away, I shall have something to say to your editor. I will not have this young lady followed about and bothered by you. Go right away, and if you're good I'll see you later and tell you any lies you like. See? Now vanish! . . . Curse the Press!'

'That lad's a sticker,' said Miss Thorpe. 'He badgered poor Uncle nearly out of his senses this morning. That's Uncle, talking to the Rector. He's a Civil Servant, and he disapproves of the Press altogether. He disapproves of mysteries, too. It's rotten for Uncle.'

'I expect he'll disapprove of me.'

'Yes, he does. He thinks your hobby unsuited to your position in life. That's why he's rather carefully avoiding an introduction. Uncle's a comic old bird, but he isn't a snob and he's rather decent, really. Only he's not a bit like Dad. You and Dad would have got on splendidly. Oh, by the way — you know where Dad and Mother are buried, don't you? I expect that was the first place you looked at.'

'Well, it was; but I'd rather like to look at it again. You see, I'm wondering just exactly how the — the — '

'How they got the body there? Yes, I thought you'd be wondering that. I've been wondering, too. Uncle doesn't think it's nice of me to wonder anything of the sort. But it really makes things easier to do a little wondering, I mean, if you're once interested in a thing it makes it seem less real. That's not the right word, though.'

'Less personal?'

'Yes; that's what I mean. You begin to imagine how it all happened, and gradually it gets to feel more like something you've made up.'

'H'm!' said Wimsey. 'If that's the way your mind works, you'll be a writer one day.'

'Do you think so? How funny! That's what I

want to be. But why?'

'Because you have creative imagination, which works outwards, till finally you will be able to stand outside your own experience and see it as something you have made, existing independently of yourself. You're lucky.'

'Do you really think so?' Hilary looked excited.

'Yes — but your luck will come more at the end of life than at the beginning, because the other sort of people won't understand the way your mind works. They will start by thinking you dreamy and romantic, and then they'll be surprised to discover that you are really hard and heartless. They'll be quite wrong both times — but they won't ever know it, and *you* won't know it at first, and it'll worry you.'

'But that's just what the girls say at school. How did you know? . . . Though they're all idiots — mostly, that is.'

'Most people are,' said Wimsey, gravely, 'but it isn't kind to tell them so. I expect you do tell them so. Have a heart; they can't help it . . . Yes, this is the place. Well, you know, it isn't very much overlooked, is it? That cottage is the nearest — whose is that?'

'Will Thoday's.'

'Oh, is it? . . . And after that, there's only the Wheatsheaf and a farm. Whose is the farm?'

'That's Mr Ashton's place. He's quite a well-to-do kind of man, one of the churchwardens. I liked him very much when I was a kid; he used to let me ride on the farmhorses.'

'I've heard of him; he pulled my car out of the

ditch one day — which reminds me. I ought to call and thank him personally.'

'That means you want to ask him questions.'

'If you *do* see through people as clearly as that, you oughtn't to make it so brutally plain to them.'

'That's what Uncle calls my unfeminine lack of tact. He says it comes of going to school and playing hockey.'

'He may be right. But why worry?'

'I'm not worrying — only, you see, Uncle Edward will have to look after me now, and he thinks it's all wrong for me to be going to Oxford . . . What are you looking at? The distance from the South gateway?'

'Uncomfortably discerning woman — yes, I was. You could bring the body in a car and carry it round without too much difficulty. What's that, there, close by the north wall of the churchyard? A well?'

'Yes; that's the well where Gotobed gets the water for washing out the porch and scrubbing the chancel and all that. I think it's rather deep. There used to be a pump there at one time, but the village people used to come and use it for drinking water, when the village well ran dry, and Mr Venables had to stop it because he said it wasn't sanitary, drinking water out of a graveyard; so he took the pump away, and paid for having the village well dug deeper and put in order. He's a frightfully good old sort. When Gotobed wants water he has to haul it up as best he can in a bucket. He grumbles a lot about it. The well's a great nuisance, anyway, because it makes the graves on that side very damp, and sometimes in the winter you can't dig them properly. It was worse before Mr Venables had the churchyard drained.'

'Mr Venables seems to do a lot for the parish.'

'He does. Dad used to subscribe to things, of course, but Mr Venables generally starts things, when it's anything to do with the Church. At least, when it's things like drains, it's probably Mrs Venables. Why did you want to know about the well?'

'I wanted to know whether it was used or disused. As it's used, of course nobody would think of hiding anything large in it.'

'Oh, you mean the body? No, that wouldn't have done.'

'All the same,' said Wimsey . . . 'Look here! forgive my asking, but, supposing your father hadn't died when he did, what sort of tombstone would he have been likely to put up to your mother? Any idea?'

'None at all. He hated tombstones and wouldn't discuss them, poor darling. It's horrid to think that he's got to have one.'

'Quite. So that for all anybody knew, he might have had a flat stone put down, or one of those things with a marble kerb round and chips in the middle.'

'A thing like a fender? Oh, no he'd never have done *that*. And certainly not chips. They always reminded him of that fearfully genteel kind of coffee-sugar you get at the sort of places where everything's served on mats and all the wine-glasses are coloured.'

'Ah! but did the murderer know your father's feelings about coffee-sugar and wine-glasses?'

'Sorry — I don't know what you're driving at.'

'My fault; I'm always so incoherent. I mean — when there are such lots of good places for putting bodies — dykes and drains and so on, why cart one at great risk and trouble to a churchyard to plant it where it might quite easily be dug up by a stonemason smoothing away the earth for a fenderful of marble chips? I know the body was a good two feet below ground-level, but I suppose they have to dig down a bit when they set up gravestones. It all seems so odd and so rash. And yet, of course, I can see the fascination of the idea. You'd think a grave was about the last place where anyone would look for a stray body. It was sheer bad luck that it should have had to be opened up again so soon. All the same — when you think of the job of getting it here, and digging away at night in secret — ! But it looks as though it must have been done that way, because of the rope-marks, which show that the man was tied up somewhere first. It must, I mean, all have been deliberate and thought-out beforehand.'

'Then the murderer couldn't have thought about it earlier than New Year's Day when Mother died. I mean, he couldn't have counted on having a grave handy.'

'Of course he couldn't; but it may have happened at any time since.'

'Surely not at *any* time. Only within a week or so after Mother died.'

'Why?' asked Wimsey, quickly.

'Why, because old Gotobed would be certain to notice if anybody had been digging his grave about after the earth had been firmed up properly. Don't you think it must have happened quite soon — probably while the wreaths were still on the grave? They stayed there for a week, and then they looked dead and beastly, and I told Gotobed to chuck them away.'

'That's an idea,' said Wimsey. 'I never thought about that — not having had very much to do with the digging of graves. I must ask Gotobed about it. Can you remember how long the snow lay after your mother died?'

'Let me see. It stopped snowing on New Year's Day, and they swept the path up to the south door. But it didn't start to thaw till — wait! I know! It was during the night of the second though it had been getting sort of warmer for two days, and the snow was kind of damp. I remember quite well now. They dug the grave on the third, and everything was all sloshy. And on the day of the funeral it rained like billy-oh! It was dreadful. I don't think I shall ever forget it.'

'And that took all the snow away, of course.'

'Oh, yes.'

'So it would have been easy enough for anybody to get to the grave without leaving footprints. Yes, I suppose you never noticed yourself that the wreaths had been moved, or anything?'

'Oh, no! As a matter of fact, I didn't come here much. Dad was so ill, I had to be with him — and anyway, I didn't think of Mother as being *here*, you know. Lord Peter, I think all this business about graves is hateful, don't you? But I'll tell you who would have noticed anything, and that's Mrs Gates — our housekeeper, you know. She came down every day. She's a perfect ghoul. She kept on trying to talk to me about it, and I wouldn't listen to her. She's quite nice, really, but she ought to live in a Victorian novel, where people wear crêpe and weep into the teacups . . . Oh, dear! there's Uncle Edward looking for me. He looks quite dyspeptic with disapproval. I'm going to introduce you to him, just to embarrass the poor dear . . . Uncle Edward! This is Lord Peter Wimsey. He's been so kind. He says I have a creative imagination, and ought to be a writer.'

'Ah! how do you do?' Mr Edward Thorpe, forty-four, very correct and formal, presented a bland Civil Service front to the impact of Wimsey's personality. 'I believe I have met your brother, the Duke of Denver. I hope he is quite well . . . Quite . . . quite so . . . It is very good of you to take an interest in my niece's young ambitions. All these young women mean to do great things, don't they? But I tell her, authorship is a good stick, but a bad crutch. Very distressing business, this. I am so sorry she should be dragged into it, but of course, in her position, the village people expect her to — ah! — enter into their — ah! — their — um — '

'Amusements?' suggested Wimsey. It came upon him with a shock that Uncle Edward could not be many years older than himself. He felt for him the apprehensive reverence which one feels for a quaint and brittle piece of antiquity.

151

'For anything which touches them nearly,' said Mr Thorpe. Gallant fellow! Deeply disapproving, he yet sought to defend his niece against criticism. 'But I am taking her away for a little peace and quietness,' he added. 'Her aunt, unhappily, was unable to come to Fenchurch — she suffers sadly from rheumatoid arthritis — but she is looking forward to seeing Hilary at home.'

Wimsey, glanced at Hilary's sullen face, saw rebellion rising; he knew exactly the kind of woman who would have married Uncle Edward.

'In fact,' said Mr Thorpe, 'we are leaving tomorrow, I am so sorry we cannot ask you to dine, but under the circumstances — '

'Not at all,' said Wimsey.

'So I fear it must be a case of Hail and Farewell,' continued Mr Thorpe, firmly. 'Delighted to have met you. I could wish that it were under happier circumstances. Ah — good afternoon. Please remember me to your brother when you see him.'

★ ★ ★

'Warned off!' said Wimsey, when he had shaken hands with Uncle Edward and bestowed on Hilary Thorpe a grin of understanding sympathy. 'Why? Corrupting the morals of youth? Or showing too much zeal about digging up the family mystery? Is Uncle Edward a dark horse or a plain ass, I wonder? Did he go to his brother's wedding? I must ask Blundell. Where is Blundell? I wonder if he is free tonight?'

He hastened to catch the Superintendent, who

152

had dutifully attended the funeral, and arranged to run over to Leamholt after dinner. Gradually the congregation melted away. Mr Gotobed and his son Dick removed their official 'blacks' and fetched the spades that leaned against the wall near the covered well.

As the earth thudded heavily upon the coffin lid, Wimsey joined the small group that had gathered to discuss the ceremony and read the cards upon the wreaths. He stooped idly to examine an exceptionally handsome and exotic floral tribute of pink and purple hothouse exhibits, wondering who could have gone to so much expense for the unknown victim. With a slight shock he read, on a visiting card: 'With reverent sympathy. Lord Peter Wimsey. St Luke xii. 6.'

'Very appropriate,' said his lordship, identifying the text after a little thought (for he had been carefully brought up). 'Bunter, you are a great man.'

★　★　★

'What I really want to know,' said Lord Peter, as he stretched comfortable legs upon the Superintendent's hearth, 'is the relation between Deacon and Cranton. How did they get into touch? Because a lot seems to turn on that.'

'So it does,' agreed Mr Blundell; 'but the trouble is, we have only got their words to go on, and which was the biggest liar, the Lord God only knows, though Mr Justice Bramhill made a guess. There's no doubt of one thing, and that is that they knew each other in London. Cranton was one of those smooth-spoken, gentlemanly sort of crooks that you meet hanging about the lounge in cheapsmart restaurants — you know the type. He'd been in trouble before, but he gave out he was a reformed character, and made quite a spot of money writing a book. At least, I suppose somebody wrote it for him, but he had his name put on the cover, and all that. There've been several of that sort since the War, but this chap was a smart lad — a bit ahead of his time, really. He was thirty-five in 1914; not educated anything to speak of, but with a kind of natural wit, sharpened by having had to look out for himself, if you take my meaning.'

'Just so. A graduate in the University of the World.'

'That's very well put,' said Mr Blundell, welcoming the cliché as an inspiration. 'Very cleverly put indeed. Yes — that's just what he was. Deacon, now, he was different. A very superior man indeed, he was, and a great reader. In fact, the chaplain down at Maidstone said he was quite a remarkable scholar in his way, with a poetic imagination, whatever that may be exactly. Sir Charles Thorpe took quite a fancy to the fellow, treated him friendly and all that, and gave him the run of the library. Well, these two met in some dance place or other, some time in 1912, when Sir Charles was staying in London. Cranton's story is that some girl that Deacon had picked up — Deacon was always after a skirt — pointed him out to Deacon as the author of this book I was telling you about, and that

Deacon made out to be tremendously interested in the book and pumped him a lot about crooks and their doings and the way they worked their little games and all that. He said Deacon made a dead set at him and wouldn't leave him alone, and was always kind of hinting that he was bound to go back to the old life in the end. Deacon said different. He said that what interested him was the literary side of the business, as he called it. Says he thought, if a crook could write a book and make money, why not a butler? According to him, it was Cranton made a dead set at *him*, and started pumping him about what sort of place he'd got, and suggesting if there was anything to be pinched, they should pinch it together and go shares. Deacon working the inside part of the job and Cranton seeing to the rest — finding a fence and settling the terms and so on. I daresay it was six of one and half-a-dozen of the other, if you ask me. A pretty pair they were, and no mistake.'

The Superintendent paused to take a long draught of beer from a pewter mug and then resumed.

'You understand,' he said, 'this was the story they told after we'd got hold of 'em both for the robbery. At first, naturally, they both lied like Ananias and swore they'd never seen each other before in their lives, but when they found what the prosecution had up against them, they changed their tune. But there was this about it. As soon as Cranton realised that the game was up, he adopted this story and stuck to it. In fact, he pleaded guilty at the trial and his one idea

155

seemed to be to get Deacon into trouble and have him gaoled good and hard. He said Deacon had double-crossed him and he was out to get his own back — though whether there was any truth in that, or whether he thought he would get off easy by making himself out to be the poor unfortunate victim of temptation, or whether it was all pure malice, I don't know. The jury had their own idea about it, and so had the judge.

'Well, now. In April 1914 this wedding of Mr Henry Thorpe's came along, and it was pretty well known that Mrs Wilbraham was going to be there with her emerald necklace. There wasn't a thief in London that didn't know all about Mrs Wilbraham. She's a sort of cousin of the Thorpes, a lot of times removed, and long way back, and she's got a stack of money and the meanness of fifty thousand Scotch Jews rolled into one. She'll be about eighty-six or seven now and getting childish, so I'm told; but in those days she was just eccentric. Funny old lady, stiff as a ramrod, and always dressed in black silks and satins — very old-fashioned — with jewels and bangles and brooches and God knows what stuck all over her. That was one of her crazes, you understand. And another was, that she didn't believe in insurance and she didn't believe a lot in safes, neither. She had a safe in her town house, naturally and kept her stuff locked up in it, but I don't suppose she'd have done that if the safe hadn't been put in by her husband when he was alive. She was too mean to buy as much as a strong-box for herself, and when she went away on a visit, she preferred to trust to her own wits.

Mad as a March hare, she must have been,' said the Superintendent, thoughtfully, 'but there! you'd be surprised what a lot of these funny old ladies there are going about loose in the world. And, of course, nobody ever liked to say anything to her, because she was disgustingly rich and had the full disposal of her own property. The Thorpes were about the only relations she had in the world, so they invited her to Mr Henry's wedding, though it's my belief they all hated the sight of her. If they hadn't have asked her, she'd have taken offence, and — well, there! You can't offend your rich relations, can you?'

Lord Peter thoughtfully refilled his own beer-mug and said, 'Not on any account.'

'Well, then,' pursued the Superintendent, 'here's where Cranton and Deacon tell different tales again. According to Deacon, he got a letter from Cranton as soon as the wedding-day was announced, asking him to come and meet him at Leamholt and discuss some plan for getting hold of the emeralds. According to Cranton, it was Deacon wrote to him. Neither of 'em could produce a scrap of evidence about it, one way or the other, so, there again, you paid your money and you took your choice. But it was proved that they did meet in Leamholt and that Cranton came along the same day to have a look at the house.

'Very good. Now Mrs Wilbraham had a lady's maid, and if it hadn't been for her and Mary Thoday, the whole thing might have come to nothing. You'll remember that Mary Thoday was

Mary Deacon then. She was housemaid at the Red House, and she'd got married to Deacon at the end of 1913. Sir Charles was very kind to the young couple. He gave them a nice bedroom to themselves away from the other servants, just off a little back stair that runs up by the butler's pantry, so that it was quite like a little private home for them. The plate was all kept in the pantry, of course, and it was supposed to be Deacon's job to look after it.

'Now, this maid of Mrs Wilbraham's — Elsie Bryant was her name — was a quick, smart sort of girl, full of fun and high spirits, and it so happened that she'd found out what Mrs Wilbraham did with her jewels when she was staying away from home. It seems the old girl wanted to be too clever by half. I think she must have been reading too many detective stories, if you ask me, but anyway; she got it into her head that the best place to keep valuables wasn't a jewel-case or a strong-box or anything of that kind, that would be the first thing a burglar would go for, but some fancy place where nobody would think of looking, and, to cut a long story short, the spot she pitched upon was — if you'll excuse me mentioning it — was underneath one of the bedroom utensils. You may well laugh — so did everybody in court, except the judge, and he happened to get a fit of coughing at the time and his handkerchief was over his face, so nobody could see how he took it. Well, this Elsie, she was a bit inquisitive, as girls are, and one day — not very long before the wedding — she managed to take a peep through

158

a keyhole or something of that kind, and caught the old lady just in the act of putting the stuff away. Naturally, she couldn't keep a thing like that to herself, and when she and her mistress got to Fenchurch — which they did a couple of days before the wedding — the first thing she had to do was to strike up a bosom friendship with Mary Deacon (as she was then) for the express purpose, as it seems to me, of telling her all about it in confidence. And, of course, Mary, being a devoted wife and all that, had to share the joke with her husband. I dare say it's natural. Anyhow, counsel for the defence made a big point of it, and there's no doubt it was that utensil kept Elsie and Mary out of quod. 'Gentlemen,' he said to the jury, in his speech, 'I see you smiling over Mrs Wilbraham's novel idea of a safe-deposit, and I've no doubt you're looking forward to passing the whole story on to your wives when you get home. And, that being so, you can very well enter into the feelings of my client Mary Deacon and her friend, and see how — in the most innocent manner in the world — the secret was disclosed to the one man who might have been expected to keep it quiet.' He was a clever lawyer, he was, and had the jury eating out of his hand by the time he'd done with them.

'Now we've got to guess again. There was a telegram sent off to Cranton from Leamholt — no doubt about that, for we traced it. He said it came from Deacon, but Deacon said that if anybody sent it, it must have been Elsie Bryant. She and Deacon were both in Leamholt that afternoon, but we couldn't get the girl at the post office to recognise either of them, and the telegram was written in block letters. To my mind, that points to Deacon, because I doubt if the girl would have thought of such a thing, but needless to say, when the two of them were told to show a specimen of their printing, it wasn't a mite like the writing on the form. Whichever of them it was, either they were pretty clever, or they got somebody else to do it for them.

'You say you've heard already about what happened that night. What you want to know is the stories Cranton and Deacon told about it. Here's where Cranton, to my mind, shows up better than Deacon, unless he was very deep indeed. He told a perfectly consistent tale from start to finish. It was Deacon's plan first and last. Cranton was to come down in a car and be under Mrs Wilbraham's window at the time mentioned in the telegram. Deacon would then throw out the emerald necklace, and Cranton would go straight off with it to London and get it broken up and sold, dividing the loot fifty-fifty with Deacon, less £50 he'd given him on account. Only he said that what came out of the window was only the jewel-case and not the emeralds, and he accused Deacon of taking the stuff himself and rousing the house on purpose to put the blame on him — on Cranton, that is. And, of course, if that was Deacon's plan, it was a very good one. He would get the stuff and the kudos as well.

'The trouble was, of course, that none of this came out till some time after Cranton had been arrested, so that when Deacon was taken and made his first statement to the police, he didn't know what story he'd got to meet. The first account he gave was very straightforward and simple, and the only trouble about it was that it obviously wasn't true. He said he woke up in the night and heard somebody moving about in the garden, and at once he said to his wife: 'I believe there's somebody after the plate.' Then, he said, he went downstairs, opened the back door and looked out, in time to see somebody on the terrace under Mrs Wilbraham's window. Then (according to him) he rushed back indoors and upstairs, just quick enough to catch a fellow making off through Mrs Wilbraham's window.'

'Hadn't Mrs Wilbraham locked her door?'

'No. She never did, on principle — afraid of fire, or something. He said he shouted loudly to alarm the house, and then the old lady woke up and saw him at the window. In the meantime the thief had climbed down by the ivy and got away. So he rushed off downstairs and found the footman just coming out of the back door. There was a bit of confusion about the back door part of the story, because Deacon didn't explain, first go-off, how he happened to be in Mrs Wilbraham's bedroom at all. His very first tale, to Sir Charles, had been that he went straight out when he heard the noise in the garden, but by the time the police got him, he'd managed to fit the two accounts together, and said that he'd either been too upset at the time to explain himself clearly or else that everybody else had been too upset to understand what he said. Well, that was all right, until they started to unearth all

161

the history of his having met Cranton before, and the telegram and so on. Then Cranton, seeing that the game was up, told his tale in full, and of course, that made it pretty awkward for Deacon. He couldn't deny it altogether, so he now admitted knowing Cranton, but said it was Cranton who had tried to tempt him into stealing the emeralds, while he had been perfectly sea-green incorruptible. As for the telegram, he denied that altogether, and put it on Elsie. And he denied the £50 altogether, and it's a fact that they never traced it to him.

'Of course, they cross-examined him pretty fiercely. They wanted to know, first, why he hadn't warned Sir Charles about Cranton, and secondly, why he'd told a different tale at first. He declared that he thought Cranton had given up all idea of the theft, and he didn't want to frighten anybody; but that when he heard noises in the garden, he guessed what was happening. He also said that afterwards he was afraid to own up to knowing Cranton for fear he should be accused of complicity. But it sounded a pretty thin story, and neither the judge nor the jury believed a word of it. Lord Bramhill spoke very severely to him after the verdict, and said that if it hadn't been his first offence, he'd have given him the heaviest sentence it was in his power to bestow. He called it aggravated larceny of the very worst type, being committed by a servant in a position of trust, in a dwelling-house and his master's dwelling-house at that, and accompanied by the opening of a window, which made it into burglary, and then he had violently resisted arrest, and so forth and so on; and in the end he gave Deacon eight years' penal servitude and told him he was lucky to get off with that. Cranton was an old offender and might have got a lot more, but the judge said he was unwilling to punish him much more heavily than Deacon, and gave him ten years. So that was that. Cranton went to Dartmoor, and served his full time as a perfectly good old lag, without giving much trouble to anybody. Deacon, being a first offender, went to Maidstone, where he set up to be one of those model prisoners — which is a kind you always want to look out for, because they are always up to some mischief or other. After nearly four years — early in 1918, it was — this nice, refined, well-conducted convict made a brutal attack on a warder and broke prison. The warder died, and of course the whole place was scoured for Deacon, without any success. I daresay, what with the War and one thing and another, they hadn't as many men to carry on the job as they ought to have had. Anyhow, they didn't find him, and for two years he enjoyed the reputation of being about the only man who had ever broken prison successfully. Then his bones turned up in one of those holes — dene-holes, I think they call them, in a wood in North Kent, so they found it was one up to the prison system after all. He was still in his convict clothes and his skull was smashed in, so he must have tumbled over during the night — probably within a day or two of his escape. And that was the end of *him*.'

'I suppose there's no doubt he was guilty.'

'Not the slightest. He was a liar from beginning to end, and a clumsy liar at that. For one thing, the ivy on the Red House showed clearly enough that nobody had climbed down by it that night — and, in any case, his final story was as full of holes as a sieve. He was a bad lot, and a murderer as well, and the country was well rid of him. As for Cranton, he behaved pretty well for a bit after he came out. Then he got into trouble again for receiving stolen goods, or goods got by false pretences or something, and back he went into quod. He came out again last June, and they kept tabs on him till the beginning of September. Then he disappeared, and they're still looking for him. Last seen in London — but I shouldn't be surprised if we'd seen the last of him today. It's my belief, and always was, that Deacon had the necklace, but what he did with it, I'm damned if I know. Have another spot of beer, my lord. It won't do you any harm.'

'Where do you think Cranton was, then, between September and January?'

'Goodness knows. But if he's the corpse, I should say France, at a guess. He knew all the crooks in London, and if anybody could wangle a forged passport, he could.'

'Have you got a photograph of Cranton?'

'Yes, my lord, I have. It's just come. Like to have a look at it?'

'Rather!'

The Superintendent brought out an official photograph from a bureau which stood, stacked neatly with documents, in a corner of the room. Wimsey studied it carefully.

'When was this taken?'

'About four years ago, my lord, when he went up for his last sentence. That's the last we have.'

'He had no beard then. Had he one in September?'

'No, my lord. But he'd have plenty of time to grow one in four months.'

'Perhaps that's what he went to France for.'

'Very likely indeed, my lord.'

'Yes — well — I can't be dead positive, but I think this is the man I saw on New Year's Day.'

'That's very interesting,' said the Superintendent.

'Have you shown the photograph to any of the people in the village?'

Mr Blundell grinned ruefully.

'I tried it on the Wilderspins this afternoon, but there! Missus said it was him, Ezra said 'twas nothing like him — and a bunch of neighbours agreed heartily with both of them. The only thing is to get a beard faked on to it and try 'em again. There's not one person in a hundred can swear to a likeness between a bearded face and one that's clean-shaven.'

'H'm, too true. Defeat thy favour with an usurped beard . . . And, of course, you couldn't take the body's finger-prints, since he had no hands.'

'No, my lord, and that's a sort of an argument, in a way, for it's being Cranton.'

'If it *is* Cranton, I suppose he came here to look for the necklace, and grew a beard so that he shouldn't be recognised by the people that had seen him in court.'

'That's about it, my lord.'

'And he didn't come earlier simply because he had to let his beard grow. So much for my bright notion that he might have received some message within the last few months. What I can't understand is that stuff about Batty Thomas and Tailor Paul. I've been trying to make out something from the inscriptions on the bells, but I might as well have left it alone. Hear the tolling of the bells, iron bells — though I'd like to know when church bells were ever made of iron — what a world of solemn thought their monody compels! Was Mr Edward Thorpe at his brother's wedding, do you know?'

'Oh, yes, my lord. He was there, and a terrible row he made with Mrs Wilbraham after the theft. It upset poor old Sir Charles very much, Mr Edward as good as told the old lady that it was all her own fault, and he wouldn't hear a word against Deacon. He was certain Elsie Bryant and Cranton had fixed it all up between them. I don't believe myself that Mrs Wilbraham would ever have cut up so rough if it weren't for the things Mr Edward said to her, but she was — is — a damned obstinate old girl, and the more he swore it was Elsie, the more *she* swore it was Deacon. You see, Mr Edward had recommended Deacon to his father — '

'Oh, had he?'

'Why, yes. Mr Edward was working in London at the time — quite a lad, he was, only twenty-three — and hearing that Sir Charles was wanting a butler, he sent Deacon down to see him.'

'What did he know about Deacon?'

'Well, only that he did his work well and

looked smart. Deacon was a waiter in some club that Mr Edward belonged to, and it seems he mentioned that he wanted to try private service, and that's how Mr Edward came to think of him. And, naturally, having recommended the fellow he had to stick up for him. I don't know if you've met Mr Edward Thorpe, but if you have, my lord, you'll know that anything that belongs to him is always perfect. He's never been known to make a mistake, Mr Edward hasn't — and so, you see, he couldn't possibly have made a mistake about Deacon.'

'Oh, yes?' said Wimsey. 'Yes, I've met him. Frightful blithering ass. Handy thing to be, sometimes. Easily cultivated. Five minutes' practice before the glass every day, and you will soon acquire that vacant look so desirable for all rogues, detectives and Government officials. However, we will not dwell on Uncle Edward. Let us return to our corpse. Because, Blundell, after all, even if it is Cranton, come to look for emeralds — who killed him, and why?'

'Why,' returned the policeman, 'supposing he found the emeralds all right and somebody lammed him on the head and took them off him. What's wrong with that?'

'Only that he doesn't seem to have been lammed on the head.'

'That's what Dr Baines says; but we don't know that he's right.'

'No — but anyway, the man was killed somehow. Why kill him, when you'd already got him tied up and could take the emeralds without any killing at all?'

167

'To prevent him squealing. Stop! I know what you're going to say — Cranton wasn't in a position to squeal. But he was, don't you see. He'd already been punished for the theft — they couldn't do anything more to him for that, and he'd only to come and tell us where the stuff was to do himself quite a lot of good. You see his game. He could have done the sweet injured innocence stuff. He'd say: 'I always told you Deacon had the stuff, so the minute I could manage it, I went down to Fenchurch to find it, and I did find it — and of course I was going to take it straight along to the police-station like a good boy, when Tom, Dick or Harry came along and took it off me. So I've come and told you all about it, and when you lay your hands on Tom, Dick or Harry and get the goods you'll remember it was me gave you the office.' Oh, yes — that's what he could have done, and the only thing we'd have been able to put on him would be failing to report himself, and if he'd put us on to getting the emeralds, he'd be let off light enough, you bet. No! anybody as wanted those emeralds would have to put Cranton where he couldn't tell any tales. That's clear enough. But as to who it was, that's a different thing.'

'But how was this person to know that Cranton knew where the necklace was? And how did he know, if it comes to that? Unless it really was he who had them after all, and he hid them somewhere in Fenchurch instead of taking them to London. It looks to me as though this line of argument was going to make Cranton the black sheep after all.'

'That's true. How'd he come to know? He can't have got the tip from anybody down here, or they'd have got the stuff for themselves, and not waited for him. They've had long enough to do it, goodness knows. But why should Cranton have left the stuff behind him?'

'Hue and cry. Didn't want to be caught with it on him. He may have parked it somewhere when he drove off, meaning to come back and fetch it later. You never know. But the longer I look at these photographs, the more positive I feel that the man I met was Cranton. The official description agrees, too — colour of eyes and all that. And if the corpse isn't Cranton, what's become of him?'

'There you are,' said Mr Blundell. 'I don't see as we can do much more till we get the reports from London. Except, of course, as regards the burying. We ought to be able to get a line on that. And what you say about Miss Thorpe's notion — I mean, as to the wreaths and that — may have something in it. Will you have a chat with this Mrs Gates, or shall I? I think you'd better tackle Mr Ashton. You've got a good excuse for seeing him, and if I went there officially, it might put somebody on his guard. It's a nuisance, the churchyard being so far from the village. Even the Rectory doesn't overlook it properly, on account of the shrubbery.'

'No doubt that circumstance was in the mind of the murderer. You mustn't quarrel with your bread and butter, Superintendent. No difficulty, no fun.'

'Fun?' said the Superintendent. 'Well, my lord,

it's nice to be you. How about Gates?'

'You'd better do Gates. If Miss Thorpe's leaving tomorrow, I can't very well call without looking a nosey parker. And Mr Thorpe doesn't approve of me. I daresay he's issued an order: No information. But *you* can invoke all the terrors of the law.'

'Not much, I can't. Judges' Rules and be damned. But I'll have a try. And then there's — '

'Yes, there's Will Thoday.'

'Ah! . . . but if Miss Thorpe's right, he's out of it. He was laid up in bed from New Year's Eve till the 14th January. I know that for certain. But somebody in his house may have noticed something. It'll be a bit of a job getting anything out of them, though. They've had a taste of the dock once, and they'll get frightened, ten to one, the minute they see me.'

'You needn't worry about that. You can't very well frighten them worse than they're frightened already. Go and read the Burial Service to them and watch their reactions.'

'Oh!' said the Superintendent. 'Religion's a bit out of my line, except on Sundays. All right — I'll take on that part of it. Maybe, if I don't mention that dratted necklace . . . but there, my mind's that full of it, it'll be a mercy if it don't slip out.'

Which shows that policemen, like other people, are at the mercy of their subconscious preoccupations.

the fourth part

LORD PETER DODGES WITH
MR BLUNDELL AND PASSES HIM

'Dodging' is taking a retrograde movement, or moving a place backwards out of the ordinary hunting course . . . She will be seen to dodge with a bell, and pass a bell alternately throughout her whole work.

TROYTE

'Well now, ma'am,' said Superintendent Blundell.

'Well, officer?' retorted Mrs Gates.

It is said, I do not know with how much reason, that the plain bobby considers 'officer' a more complimentary form of address than 'my man', or even 'constable'; while some people, of the Disraelian school of thought, affirm that an unmerited 'sergeant' is not taken amiss. But when a highly refined lady with a grey glacé gown and a grey glacé eye addresses a full-blown Superintendent in plain clothes as 'officer', the effect is not soothing, and is not meant to be so. At this rate, thought Mr Blundell, he might just as well have sent a uniformed inspector, and had done with it.

'We should be greatly obliged, ma'am,' pursued Mr Blundell, 'for your kind assistance in this little matter.'

'A little matter?' said Mrs Gates. 'Since when have murder and sacrilege been considered little matters in Leamholt? Considering that you have had nothing to do for the last twenty years but run in a few drunken labourers on market day, you seem to take your new responsibilities very coolly. In my opinion, you ought to call in the assistance of Scotland Yard. But I suppose, since being patronised by the aristocracy, you consider yourself quite competent to deal with any description of crime.'

'It does not lie with me, ma'am, to refer anything to Scotland Yard. That is a matter for the Chief Constable.'

'Indeed?' said Mrs Gates, not in the least disconcerted. 'Then why does the Chief Constable not attend to the business himself? I should prefer to deal directly with him.'

The Superintendent explained patiently that the interrogation of witnesses was not, properly speaking, the duty of the Chief Constable.

'And why should I be supposed to be a witness? I know nothing about these disgraceful proceedings.'

'Certainly not, ma'am. But we require a little information about the late Lady Thorpe's grave, and we thought that a lady with your powers of observation would be in a position to assist us.'

'In what way?'

'From information received, ma'am, it appears probable that the outrage may have been committed within a very short period after Lady Thorpe's funeral. I understand that you were a frequent visitor at the graveside after the melancholy event — '

'Indeed? And who told you that?'

'We have received information to that effect, ma'am.'

'Quite so. But from whom?'

'That is the formula we usually employ, ma'am,' said Mr Blundell, with a dim instinct that the mention of Hilary would only make bad worse. 'I take it, that is a fact, is it not?'

'Why should it not be a fact? Even in these days, some respect may be paid to the dead, I trust.'

'Very proper indeed, ma'am. Now can you tell me whether, on any occasion when you visited the grave, the wreaths presented the appearance of having been disturbed, or the earth shifted about, or anything of that kind?'

'Not,' said Mrs Gates, 'unless you refer to the extremely rude and vulgar behaviour of that Mrs Coppins. Considering that she is a Noncomformist, you would think she would have more delicacy than to come into the churchyard at all. And the wreath itself was in the worst possible taste. I suppose she was entitled to send one if she liked, considering the great and many favours she had always received from Sir Charles's family. But there was no necessity whatever for anything so large and ostentatious. Pink hot-house lilies in January were entirely out of place. For a person in her position, a simple bunch of chrysanthemums would have been ample to show respect, without going out of her way to draw attention to herself.'

'Just so, ma'am,' said the Superintendent.

'Merely because,' pursued Mrs Gates, 'I am here in a dependent position, that does not mean that I could not have afforded a floral tribute quite as large and expensive as Mrs Coppins'. But although Sir Charles and his lady, and Sir Henry and the late Lady Thorpe after them, were always good enough to treat me rather as a friend than a servant, I know what is due to my position, and should never have dreamed of allowing my modest offering to compete in any way with those of the Family.'

'Certainly not, ma'am,' agreed the Superintendent, heartily.

'I don't know what you mean by 'Certainly not',' retorted Mrs Gates. 'The Family themselves would have raised no objection, for I may say that they have always looked on me as one of themselves, and seeing that I have been housekeeper here thirty years, it is scarcely surprising that they should.'

'Very natural indeed, ma'am. I only meant that a lady like yourself would, of course, take the lead in setting an example of good taste and propriety, and so forth. My wife,' added Mr Blundell, lying with great determination and an appearance of the utmost good faith, 'my wife is always accustomed to say to our girls, that for an example of ladylike behaviour, they cannot do better than look up to Mrs Gates of the Red House at Fenchurch. Not' — (for Mrs Gates looked a little offended) — 'that Mrs Blundell would presume to think our Betty and Ann in any way equal to *you*, ma'am, being only one of them in the post office and the other a clerk in

174

Mr Compline's office, but it does young people no harm to look well above themselves, ma'am, and my wife always says that if they will model themselves upon Queen Mary, or — since they cannot have very much opportunity of studying her Gracious Majesty's behaviour — upon Mrs Gates of the Red House, they can't fail to grow up a credit to their parents, ma'am.'

Here Mr Blundell — a convinced Disraelian — coughed. He thought he had done that rather well on the spur of the moment, though, now he came to think of it, 'deportment' would have been a better word than 'behaviour'.

Mrs Gates unbent slightly, and the Superintendent perceived that he would have no further trouble with her. He looked forward to telling his wife and family about this interview. Lord Peter would enjoy it, too. A decent sort of bloke, his lordship, who would enjoy a bit of a joke.

'About the wreath, ma'am,' he ventured to prompt.

'I am telling you about it. I was disgusted — really *disgusted*, officer, when I found that Mrs Coppins had had the *impertinence* to remove my wreath and put her own in its place. There were, of course, a great many wreaths at Lady Thorpe's funeral, some of them extremely handsome, and I should have been quite content if my little tribute had been placed on the roof of the hearse, with those of the village people. But Miss Thorpe would not hear of it. Miss Thorpe is always very thoughtful.'

'A very nice young lady,' said Mr Blundell.

'Miss Thorpe is one of the Family,' said Mrs

Gates, 'and the Family are always considerate of other people's feelings. True gentlefolk always are. Upstarts are not.'

'That's very true indeed, ma'am,' said the Superintendent, with so much earnestness that a critical listener might almost have supposed the remark to have a personal application.

'My wreath was placed upon the coffin itself,' went on Mrs Gates, 'with the wreaths of the Family. There was Miss Thorpe's wreath, and Sir Henry's, of course, and Mr Edward Thorpe's and Mrs Wilbraham's and mine. There was quite a difficulty to get them all upon the coffin, and I was quite willing that mine should be placed elsewhere, but Miss Thorpe insisted. So Mrs Wilbraham's was set up against the head of the coffin, and Sir Henry's and Miss Thorpe's and Mr Edward's *on* the coffin, and mine was given a position at the foot — which was practically the same thing as being on the coffin itself. And the wreaths from the Servants' Hall and the Women's Institute were on one side and the Rector's wreath and Lord Kenilworth's wreath were on the other side. And the rest of the flowers were placed, naturally, on top of the hearse.'

'Very proper, I'm sure, ma'am.'

'And consequently,' said Mrs Gates, 'after the funeral, when the grave was filled in, Harry Gotobed took particular notice that the Family's wreaths (among which I include mine) were placed in suitable positions on the grave itself. I directed Johnson the chauffeur to attend to this — for it was a very rainy day, and it would not have been considerate to ask one of the maids to

176

go — and he assured me that this was done. I have always found Johnson sober and conscientious in his work and I believe him to be a perfectly truthful man, as such people go. He described to me exactly where he placed the wreaths, and I have no doubt that he carried out his duty properly. And in any case, I interrogated Gotobed the next day, and he told me the same thing.'

'I daresay he did,' thought Mr Blundell, 'and in his place I'd have done the same. I wouldn't get a fellow into trouble with this old cat, not if I knew it.' But he merely bowed and said nothing.

'You may judge of my surprise,' went on the lady, 'when, on going down the next day after Early Service. to see that everything was in order, I found Mrs Coppins's wreath — not at the side, where it should have been — but *on* the grave, as if she were somebody of importance, and *mine* pushed away into an obscure place and actually covered up, so that nobody could see the card at all. I was extremely angry, as you may suppose. Not that I minded in the least where my poor little remembrance was placed, for that can make no difference to anybody, and it is the thought that counts. But I was so much incensed by the woman's insolence — merely because I had felt it necessary to speak to her one day about the way in which her children behaved in the post office. Needless to say, I got nothing from her but impertinence.'

'That was on the 5th of January, then?'

'It was the morning after the funeral. That, as you say, would be Sunday the fifth. I did not accuse the woman without proof. I had spoken to Johnson again, and made careful inquiries of Gotobed, and they were both positive of the position in which the wreaths had been left the night before.'

'Mightn't it have been some of the school-children larking about, ma'am?'

'I could well believe anything of *them*,' said Mrs Gates, 'they are always ill-behaved, and I have frequently had to complain to Miss Snoot about them, but in this case the insult was too pointed. It was quite obviously and definitely aimed at myself, by that vulgar woman. Why a small farmer's wife should give herself such airs, I do not know. When I was a girl, village people knew their place, and kept it.'

'Certainly,' replied Mr Blundell, 'and I'm sure we were all much happier in those days. And so, ma'am you never noticed any disturbance except on that one occasion?'

'And I should think that was quite enough,' replied Mrs Gates. 'I kept a very good look-out after that, and if anything of a similar kind had occurred again, I should have complained to the police.'

'Ah, well,' said the Superintendent, as he rose to go, 'you see, it's come round to us in the end, and I'll have a word with Mrs Coppins, ma'am, and you may be assured it won't happen again. Whew! What an old catamaran!' (this to himself, as he padded down the rather neglected avenue beneath the budding horse-chestnuts). 'I suppose I had better see Mrs Coppins.'

Mrs Coppins was easily found. She was a

small, shrewish woman with light hair and eyes which boded temper.

'Oh, well,' she said, 'Mrs Gates did have the cheek to say it was me. As if I'd have touched her mean little wreath with a hayfork. Thinks she's a lady. No real lady would think twice about where her wreath was or where it wasn't. Talking that way to me, as if I was dirt! Why shouldn't we give Lady Thorpe as good a wreath as we could get? Ah! she was a sweet lady — a *real* lady, she was — and her and Sir Henry were that kind to us when we were a bit put about, like, the year we took this farm. Not that we were in any real difficulty — Mr Coppins has always been a careful man. But being a question of capital at the right moment, you see, we couldn't just have laid our hands on it at the moment, if it hadn't been for Sir Henry. Naturally, it was all paid back — with the proper interest. Sir Henry said he didn't want interest, but that isn't Mr Coppins's way. Yes — January 5th, it would be — and I'm quite sure none of the children had anything to do with it, for I asked them. Not that my children would go and do such a thing, but you know what children are. And it's quite true that her wreath was where she said it was, last thing on the evening of the funeral, for I saw Harry Gotobed and the chauffeur put it there with my own eyes, and they'll tell you the same.'

They did tell the Superintendent so, at some considerable length; after which, the only remaining possibility seemed to be the school-children. Here, Mr Blundell enlisted the aid of Miss Snoot. Fortunately, Miss Snoot was not only able to reassure him that none of her scholars was in fault ('for I asked them all very carefully at the time, Superintendent, and they assured me they had not, and the only one I might be doubtful of is Tommy West and he had a broken arm at the time, through falling off a gate'); she was also able to give valuable and unexpected help as regards the time at which the misdemeanour was committed.

'We had a choir-practice that night, and when it was over — that would be about half-past seven — the rain had cleared up a little, and I thought I would just go and give another little look at dear Lady Thorpe's resting-place; so I went round with my torch, and I quite well remember seeing Mrs Coppins's wreath standing up against the side of the grave next to the church, and thinking what a beautiful one it was and what a pity the rain should spoil it.'

The Superintendent felt pleased. He found it difficult to believe that Mrs Coppins or anybody else had gone out to the churchyard on a dark, wet Saturday night to remove Mrs Gates's wreath. It was surely much more reasonable to suppose that the burying of the corpse had been the disturbing factor, and that brought the time of the crime down to some hour between 7.30 p.m. on the Saturday and, say, 8.30 on the Sunday morning. He thanked Miss Snoot very much and, looking at his watch, decided that he had just about time to go along to Will Thoday's. He was pretty sure to find Mary at home, and, with luck, might catch Will himself when he came home to dinner. His way led him past the churchyard. He drove slowly, and, glancing over the churchyard wall as he went, observed Lord Peter Wimsey, seated in a reflective manner and apparently meditating among the tombs.

''Morning!' cried the Superintendent cheerfully. 'Morning, my lord!'

'Oy,' responded his lordship. 'Come along here a minute. You're just the man I wanted to see.'

Mr Blundell stopped his car at the lych-gate, clambered out, grunting (for he was growing rather stout), and made his way up the path.

Wimsey was sitting on a large, flat tombstone, and in his hands was about the last thing the Superintendent might have expected to see, namely, a large reel of line, to which, in the curious, clumsy-looking but neat and methodical manner of the fisherman, his lordship was affixing a strong cast adorned with three salmon-hooks.

'Hullo!' said Mr Blundell. 'Bit of an optimist, aren't you? Nothing but coarse fishing about here.'

'Very coarse,' said Wimsey. 'Hush! While you were interviewing Mrs Gates, where do you think I was? In the garage, inciting our friend Johnson to theft. From Sir Henry's study. Hist! not a word!'

'A good many years since he went fishing, poor soul,' said Mr Blundell, sympathetically.

'Well, he kept his tackle in good order all the same,' said Wimsey, making a complicated knot and pulling it tight with his teeth. 'Are you busy, or have you got time to look at something?'

'I was going along to Thoday's, but there's no great hurry. And, by the way, I've got a bit of news.'

181

Wimsey listened to the story of the wreath.

'Sounds all right,' he said. He searched in his pocket, and produced a handful of lead sinkers, some of which he proceeded to affix to his cast.

'What in the world are you thinking of catching with that?' demanded Mr Blundell. 'A whale?'

'Eels,' replied his lordship. He weighed the line in his hand and gravely added another piece of lead.

Mr Blundell, suspecting some kind of mystification, watched him in discreet silence.

'That will do,' said Wimsey, 'unless eels swim deeper than ever plummet sounded. Now come along. I've borrowed the keys of the church from the Rector. He had mislaid them, of course, but they turned up eventually among the Clothing Club accounts.'

He led the way to the cope-chest beneath the tower, and threw it open.

'I have been chattin' with our friend Mr Jack Godfrey. Very pleasant fellow. He tells me that a complete set of new ropes was put in last December. One or two were a little dicky, and they didn't want to take any chances over the New Year peal, so they renewed the lot while they were about it. These are the old ones, kept handy in case of sudden catastrophe. Very neatly coiled and stowed. This whopper belongs to Tailor Paul. Lift 'em out carefully — eighty feet or so of rope is apt to be a bit entanglin' if let loose on the world. Batty Thomas. Dimity. Jubilee. John, Jericho. Sabaoth. But where is little Gaude? Where and oh where is she? With her

182

sallie cut short and her rope cut long, where and oh where can she be? No — there's nothing else in the chest but the leather buffets and a few rags and oilcans. No rope for Gaude. *Gaudeamus igitur, juvenes dum sumus.* The mystery of the missing bell-rope. *Et responsum est ab omnibus: Non est inventus* — -a or -um.'

The Superintendent scratched his head and gazed vaguely about the church.

'Not in the stove,' said Wimsey. 'My first thought, of course. If the burying was done on Saturday, the stoves would be alight, but they'd be banked down for the night, and it would have been awkward if our Mr Gotobed had raked out anything unusual on Sunday morning with his little scraper. As a matter of fact, he tells me that one of the first things he does on Sunday morning is to open the top thingumajig on the stove and take a look inside to see that the flue-pipe is clear. Then he stirs it up a-top, rakes it out at the bottom door and sets it drawing for the day. I don't *think* that was where the rope went. I hope not, anyway. I think the murderer used the rope to carry the body by, and didn't remove it till he got to the graveside. Hence these salmon-hooks.'

'The well?' said Mr Blundell, enlightened.

'The well,' replied Wimsey. 'What shall we do, go fishing?'

'I'm on; we can but try.'

'There's a ladder in the vestry,' said Wimsey. 'Bear a hand. Along this way — out through the vestry-door — and here we are. Away, my jolly boys, we're all bound away. Sorry! forgot this was consecrated ground. Now then — up with the cover. Half a jiff. We'll sacrifice half a brick to the water-gods. Splosh! — it's not so very deep. If we lay the ladder over the mouth of the well, we shall get a straight pull.'

He extended himself on his stomach, took the reel in his left hand and began to play the line cautiously out over the edge of the ladder, while the Superintendent illuminated the proceedings with a torch.

The air came up cold and dank from the surface of the water. Far below a circle of light reflected the pale sky and the beam of the torch showed hooks and line working steadily down-wards. Then a tiny break in the reflection marked the moment when the hook touched the water.

A pause. Then the whirr of the reel as Wimsey rewound the line.

'More water than I thought. Where are those leads? Now then, we'll try again.'

Another pause. Then:

'A bite, Super, a bite! What's the betting it's an old boot? It's not heavy enough to be the rope. Never mind. Up she comes. Ahoy! up she rises! Sorry, I forgot again. Hullo, 'ullo, 'ullo! What's this? Not a boot, but the next thing to it. A hat! Now then, Super! Did you measure the head of the corpse? You did? Good! then we shan't need to dig him up again to see if his hat fits. Stand by with the gaff. Got him! Soft felt, rather the worse for wear and water. Mass production. London maker. Exhibit One. Put it aside to dry. Down she goes again . . . *And* up she comes. Another tiddler. Golly! what's this? Looks like a German sausage. No, it isn't. No, it isn't. It's a sallie. Sallie in our alley. She is the darling of my heart. Little Gaude's sallie. Take her up tenderly, lift her with care. Where the sallie is, the rest will be . . . Hoops-a-daisy! . . . I've got it . . . It's caught somewhere . . . No, don't pull too hard, or the hook may come adrift. Ease her. Hold her . . . Damn! . . . Sorry, undamn! I mean, how very provoking, it's got away . . . *Now* I've got it . . . Was that the ladder cracking or my breastbone, I wonder? Surprisin'ly sharp edge a ladder has . . . There now, there now! there's your eel — all of a tangle. Catch hold. Hurray!'

'It's not all here,' said the Superintendent, as the slimy mass of rope was hauled over the edge of the well.

'Probably not,' said Wimsey, 'but this is one of the bits that were used to do the tying. He's cut it loose and left the knots in.'

'Yes. Better not touch the knots, my lord. They might tell us something about who tied 'em.'

'Take care of the knots and the noose will take care of itself. Right you are. Here we go again.'

In process of time, the whole length of the rope — as far as they could judge — lay before them in five sections, including the sallie.

'Arms and ankles tied separately. Then body tied up to something or other and the slack cut off. And he removed the sallie because it got in the way of his knots. H'm!' said Mr Blundell. 'Not very expert work, but effective, I dare say. Well, my lord, this is a very interesting discovery of yours. But — it's a bit of a facer, isn't it? Puts rather a different complexion on the crime, eh?'

185

'You're right, Super. Well, one must face up to things, as the lady said when she went to have hers lifted. Hullo! what the — '

A face, perched in a bodiless sort of way on the churchyard wall, bobbed suddenly out of sight as he turned, and then bobbed up again.

'What the devil do you want, Potty?' demanded the Superintendent.

'Oh, nothing,' replied Potty. 'I don't want nothing. Who're you goin' to hang with that there, mister? That's a rope, that is. They've got eight on 'em hanging up the tower there,' he added, confidentially. 'Rector don't let me go up there no more, because they don't want nobody to know. But Potty Peake knows. One, two, three, four, five, six, seven, eight — all hung up by the neck. Old Paul, he's the biggest — Tailor Paul — but there did ought to be nine tailors by rights. I can count, you see; Potty can count. I've counted 'em over time and again on my fingers. Eight. And one is nine. And one is ten — but I ain't telling you *his* name. Oh, no. He's waiting for the nine tailors — one, two, three, four — '

'Here, you hop it!' cried the Superintendent, exasperated. 'And don't let me catch you hanging round here again.'

'Who's a-hanging? Listen — you tell me, and I'll tell you. There is Number Nine a-coming, and that's a rope to hang him, ain't it, Mister? Nine of 'em, and eight's there already. Potty knows. Potty can say. But he won't. Oh, no! Somebody might be listening.' His face changed to its usual vacant look and he touched his cap.

'Good-day, sir. Good-day, mister. I got to feed

186

the pigs, that's Potty's work. Yes, that's right. They pigs did ought to be fed. 'Morning, sir; 'morning, mister.'

He slouched away across the fields towards a group of outhouses some distance away.

'There!' said Mr Blundell, much vexed. 'He'll go telling everybody about this rope. He's got hanging on the brain, ever since he found his mother hanging in the cowhouse when he was a kid. Over at Little Dykesey, that was, a matter of thirty year back. Well, it can't be helped. I'll get these things taken along to the station, and come back later on for Will Thoday. It'll be past his lunch-time now.'

'It's past mine, too,' said Wimsey, as the clock chimed the quarter past one. 'I shall have to apologise to Mrs Venables.'

★ ★ ★

'So you see, Mrs Thoday,' said Superintendent Blundell, pleasantly, 'if anybody can help us over this awkward business it's you.'

Mary Thoday shook her head.

'I'm sure I would if I could, Mr Blundell, but there! how can I? It's right enough to say I was up all night with Will. I hardly had my clothes off for a week, but he was that bad, and the night after they laid poor Lady Thorpe to rest, he was just as bad as he could be. It turned to pneumonia, you know, and we didn't think as we should ever pull him through. I'm not likely to forget that night, nor the day neither. Sitting here, listening to old Tailor Paul and wondering

187

if he was going to ring for Will before the night was out.'

'There, there!' said her husband, embarrassed, and sprinkling a great quantity of vinegar on his tinned salmon, 'it's all over now, and there's no call to get talking that way.'

'Of course not,' said the Superintendent. 'Not but what you had a pretty stiff time of it, didn't you, Will? Delirious and all that kind of thing, I'll lay. I know what pneumonia is, for it carried off my old mother-in-law in 1922. It's a very trying thing to nurse, is pneumonia.'

'So 'tis,' agreed Mrs Thoday. 'Very bad he was that night. Kept on trying to get out of his bed and go to church. He thought they was ringing the peal without him, though I kept on telling him that was all rung and finished with New Year's Day. A terrible job I had with him, and nobody to help me, Jim having left us that very morning. Jim was a great help while he was here, but he had to go back to his ship. He stayed as long as he could, but of course he's not his own master.'

'No,' said Mr Blundell. 'Mate on a merchant-man, isn't he? How's he getting along? Have you heard from him lately?'

'We had a postcard last week from Hong Kong,' said Mary, 'but he didn't say much. Only that he was well and love to the children. He hasn't sent nothing but postcards this voyage, and he must be terrible busy, for he's such a man for writing letters as a rule.'

'They'll be a bit shorthanded, maybe,' said Will. 'And it's an anxious time for men in his line of business, freights being very scarce and hard to come by. It'll be all this depression, I suppose.'

'Yes, of course. When do you expect him back?'

'Not for I don't know when,' replied Will. The Superintendent looked sharply at him, for he seemed to detect a note almost of satisfaction in his tone. 'Not if trade's decent, that is. You see, his ship don't make regular trips. She follows cargo, as they call it, tramping round from port to port wherever there's anything to be picked up.'

'Ah, yes, of course. What's the name of the ship, again?'

'The *Hannah Brown*. She belongs to Lampson & Blake of Hull. Jim is doing very well, I'm told, and they set great store by him. If anything happened to Captain Woods, they'd give the ship to Jim. Wouldn't they, Will?'

'So he says,' replied Thoday uneasily. 'But it don't do to count on anything these days.'

The contrast between the wife's enthusiasm and the husband's lack of it was so marked, that Mr Blundell drew his own conclusions.

'So Jim's been making trouble between 'em, has he?' was his unspoken comment. 'That explains a lot. But it doesn't help me much. Better change the subject.'

'Then you didn't happen to see anything going on at the church that night?' he said. 'No lights moving about? Nothing of that kind?'

'I didn't move from Will's bedside all night,' replied Mrs Thoday, with a hesitating glance at her husband. 'You see, he was so ill, and if I left him a minute, he'd be throwing the clothes off and trying to get up. When it wasn't the peal that was in his mind, it was the old trouble — you know.'

'The old Wilbraham affair?'

'Yes. He was all muddled up in his head, thinking the — the — that dreadful trial was on and he had to stand by me.'

'That'll *do*!' cried Thoday, suddenly, pushing his plate away so violently that the knife and fork clattered from the plate upon the table. 'I won't have you fretting yourself about that old business no more. All that's dead and buried. If it come up in my mind when I wasn't rightly in my senses, I can't help that. God knows, I'd be the last to put you in mind of it if I'd been able to help myself. You did ought to know that.'

'I'm not blaming you, Will.'

'And I won't have nothing more said about it in my house. What do you want to come worrying her this way, Mr Blundell? She's told you as she don't know a thing about this chap that was buried, and that's all there is to it. What I may have said and done, when I was ill, don't matter a hill of beans.'

'Not a scrap,' admitted the Superintendent, 'and I'm very sorry such an allusion should have come up, I'm sure. Well, I won't keep you any longer. You can't assist me and that's all there is to it. I'm not saying it isn't a disappointment, but a policeman's job's all disappointments, and one must take the rough with the smooth. Now I'll be off and let the youngsters come back to their tea. By the way, what's wrong with the parrot?'

'We've put him in the other room,' said Will, with a scowl. 'He's taken to shrieking fit to split your head.'

'That's the worst of parrots,' said Mr Blundell. 'He's a good talker, though. I've never heard a better.'

He bade them a cheerful good evening and went out. The two Thoday children — who had been banished to the woodshed during the discussion of murders and buryings, unsuited to their sex and tender years — ran down to open the gate for him.

' 'Evening, Rosie,' said Mr Blundell, who never forgot anybody's name, ' 'evening, Evvie. Are you being good girls at school?'

But, the voice of Mrs Thoday calling them at that moment to their tea, the Superintendent received but a brief answer to his question.

⋆ ⋆ ⋆

Mr Ashton was a farmer of the old school. He might have been fifty years old, or sixty or seventy, or any age. He spoke in a series of gruff barks, and held himself so rigidly that if he had swallowed a poker it could only have produced unseemly curves and flexions in his figure. Wimsey, casting a thoughtful eye upon his hands, with their gnarled and chalky joints, concluded, however, that his unbending aspect was due less to austerity than to chronic arthritis. His wife was considerably younger than himself; plump where he was spare, bounce-about where he was stately, merry where he was

191

grave, and talkative where he was monosyllabic. They made his lordship extremely welcome and offered him a glass of home-made cowslip wine.

'It's not many that makes it now,' said Mrs Ashton. 'But it was my mother's recipe, and I say, as long as there's peggles to be got, I'll make my peggle wine. I don't hold by all this nasty stuff you get at the shops. It's good for nothing but to blow out the stomach and give you gas.'

'Ugh!' said Mr Ashton, approvingly.

'I quite agree with you, Mrs Ashton,' said his lordship. 'This is excellent.' And so it was. 'It is another kindness I have to thank you for.' And he expressed his gratitude for the first-aid given to his car the previous January.

'Ugh!' said Mr Ashton. 'Pleased, I'm sure.'

'But I always hear of Mr Ashton engaged in some good work or other,' went on his lordship. 'I believe he was the Good Samaritan who brought poor William Thoday back from Walbeach the day he was taken ill.'

'Ugh!' repeated Mr Ashton. 'Very fortunate we happened to see him. Ugh! Very bad weather for a sick man. Ugh! Dangerous thing, influenza.'

'Dreadful,' said his wife. 'Poor man — he was quite reeling with it as he came out of the Bank. I said to Mr Ashton, 'How terrible bad poor Will do look, to be sure! I'm sure he's not fit to go home.' And sure enough, we hadn't got but a mile or so out of the town when we saw his car drawn up by the side of the road, and him quite helpless. It was God's mercy he didn't drive into the Drain and kill himself. And with all that money on him, too! Dear, dear! What a terrible loss it would have been. Quite helpless and out of his head he was, counting them notes over and dropping of them all over the place. Now, Will, I said, you just put them notes back in your pocket and keep quiet and we'll drive you home. And you've no call to worry about the car, I said, for we'll stop at Turner's on the way and get him to bring it over next time he comes to Fenchurch. He'll do it gladly, and he can go back on the bus. So he listened to me and we got him into our car and brought him home. And a hard time he had, dear, dear! He was prayed for in church two weeks running.'

'Ugh!' said Mr Ashton.

'What he ever wanted to come out for in such weather I can't think,' went on Mrs Ashton, 'for it wasn't market day, and we wouldn't have been there ourselves, only for Mr Ashton having to see his lawyer about Giddings's lease, and I'm sure if Will had wanted any business done, we'd have been ready to do it for him. Even if it was the Bank, he could have trusted us with it, I should think. It's not as though Mr Ashton couldn't have taken care of two hundred pounds, or two thousand, for that matter. But Will Thoday was always very close about his business.'

'My dear!' said Mr Ashton, 'ugh! It may have been Sir Henry's business. You wouldn't have him anything but close about what's not, rightly speaking, his affair.'

'And since when, Mr Ashton,' demanded his lady, 'has Sir Henry's family banked at the London and East Anglia? Let alone that Sir

193

Henry was always a deal too considerate to send a sick man out to do business for him in a snow-storm? I've told you before that I don't believe that two hundred pounds had anything to do with Sir Henry, and you'll find out one of these days I'm right, as I always am. Aren't I, now?'

'Ugh!' said Mr Ashton. 'You make a lot of talk, Maria, and some of it's bound to be right. Funny if it wasn't, now and again. Ugh! But you've no call to be interfering with Will's money. You leave that to him.'

'That's true enough,' admitted Mrs Ashton, amiably. 'I do let my tongue run on a bit, I'll allow. His lordship must excuse me.'

'Not at all,' said Wimsey. 'In a quiet place like this, if one doesn't talk about one's neighbours, what is there to talk about? And the Thodays are really your only near neighbours, aren't they? They're very lucky. I'll be bound, when Will was laid up, you did a good bit of the nursing, Mrs Ashton.'

'Not as much as I'd have liked,' said Mrs Ashton. 'My daughter was took ill at the same time — half the village was down with it, if it comes to that. I managed to run in now and again, of course — 'twouldn't be friendly else — and our girl helped Mary with the cooking. But what with being up half the night —

This gave Wimsey his opportunity. In a series of tactful inquiries he led the conversation to the matter of lights in the churchyard.

'There, now!' exclaimed Mrs Ashton. 'I always thought as there might be something in that tale as little Rosie Thoday told our Polly. But children

194

do have so many fancies, you never know.'

'Why, what tale was that?' asked Wimsey.

'Ugh! foolish nonsense, foolish nonsense,' said Mr Ashton. 'Ghosts and what not.'

'Oh, *that's* foolish enough, I dare say,' retorted his lady, 'but you know well enough, Luke Ashton, that the child might be telling the truth, ghost or no ghost. You see, your lordship, it's this way. My girl Polly — she's sixteen now and going out to service next autumn, for whatever people may say and whatever airs they may give themselves, I will maintain there's nothing like good service to train a girl up to be a good wife, and so I told Mrs Wallace only last week. It's not standing behind a counter all day selling ribbons and bathing-dresses (if they call them dresses, with no legs and no backs and next to no fronts neither) will teach you how to cook a floury potato, let alone the tendency to fallen arches and varicose veins. Which,' added Mrs Ashton triumphantly, 'she couldn't hardly deny, suffering badly from her legs as she do.'

Lord Peter expressed his warm appreciation of Mrs Ashton's point of view and hinted that she had been about to say that Polly —

'Yes, of course. My tongue do run on and no mistake, but Polly's a good girl, though I say it, and Rosie Thoday's always been a pet of Polly's like, ever since she was quite a baby and Polly only seven. Well then, it was a good time ago, now — when would it be, Luke? End of January, maybe, near enough — it was pretty near dark at six o'clock, so it couldn't be much later — well, call it end of January — Polly comes on Rosie

195

and Evvie sitting together under the hedge just outside their place, both of them crying. Why, Rosie, says Polly, what's the matter? And Rosie says, Nothing, now that Polly's come and can they walk with her to the Rectory, because their Dad has a message for Rector. Of course, Polly was willin' enough, but she couldn't understand what they was cryin' about, and then, after a bit — for you know how difficult it is to get children to tell you what they're frightened on — it comes out that they're afraid to go past the churchyard in the dark. Well, Polly being a good girl, tells 'em there's no call to be frighted, the dead being in the arms of our Saviour and not having the power to come out o' their graves not to do no harm to nobody. But that don't comfort Rosie, none the more for that, and in the end Polly makes out that Rosie's seen what she took to be the spirit of Lady Thorpe a-flittin' about her grave. And it seems the night she see her was the night of the funeral.'

'Dear me,' said Wimsey. 'What exactly did she see?'

'No more than a light, by what Polly could make out. That was one of the nights Will Thoday was very bad, and it seems Rosie was up and about helping her mother — for she's a good, handy, child is Rosie — and she looks out o' the window and sees the light just a-rising out of where the grave would be.'

'Did she tell her mother and father?'

'Not then, she didn't. She didn't like to, and I remember well, as a child I was just the same, only with me it was a funny sort of thing that used to groan in the washhouse, which I took to be bears — but as to telling anybody, I'd ha' died first. And so would Rosie, only that night her father wanted her to go a message to the Rectory and she tried everything to get off doing it, and at last he got angry and threatened to take a slipper to her. Not that he meant it, I don't suppose,' said Mrs Ashton, 'for he's a kind man as a rule, but he hadn't hardly got over his illness and he was fratchety, like, as sick people will be. So then Rosie made up her mind to tell him what she seen. Only that made him angrier still, and he said she was to go and no more nonsense, and never to speak about ghosts and such like to him again. If Mary had been there, she'd a-gone, but she was out getting his medicine from Dr Baines, and the bus don't come back till half-past seven and Will wanted the message sent particular, though I forget now what it were. So Polly told Rosie it couldn't have been Lady Thorpe's spirit, for that was at rest, and if it had been, Lady Thorpe wouldn't do harm to a living soul; and she said Rosie must a-seen Harry Gotobed's lantern. But it couldn't well a-been that, for by what the child said it was one o'clock in the morning past that Rosie see the light. Dear me an' all! I'm sure if I'd a-known then what I know now, I'd a-paid more attention to it.'

Superintendent Blundell was not pleased when this conversation was repeated to him.

'Thoday and his wife had better be careful,' he observed.

'They told you the exact truth, you know,' said Wimsey.

197

'Ah!' said Mr Blundell. 'I don't like witnesses to be so damned particular about exact truth. They get away with it as often as not, and then where are you? Not but what I did think of speaking to Rosie, but her mother called her away double quick — and no wonder! Besides, I don't care, somehow, for pumping kids about their parents. I can't help thinking of my own Betty and Ann.'

If that was not quite the exact truth, there was a good deal of truth in it; for Mr Blundell was a kindly man.

the fifth part

TAILOR PAUL IS CALLED
BEFORE WITH A SINGLE

The canal has been dangerously ignored.
Each year of the Republic, our family have
reported to the Capital that there were silted
channels and weakened dykes in our neigh-
bourhood. My husband and Maida's father
have just interviewed the present President.
They were received politely, but their conclusion is that nothing will be done.

NORA WALN: *The House of Exile*

Lord Peter Wimsey sat in the schoolroom at the
Rectory, brooding over a set of underclothing.
The schoolroom was, in fact, no longer the
schoolroom, and had not been so for nearly
twenty years. It had retained its name from the
time when the Rector's daughters departed to a
real boarding-school. It was now devoted to
Parish Business, but a fragrance of long-vanished
governesses still hung about it — governesses
with straight-fronted corsets and high-necked
frocks with bell sleeves, who wore their hair *à la*
Pompadour. There was a shelf of battered
lesson-books, ranging from *Little Arthur's
England* to Hall & Knight's *Algebra*, and a
bleached-looking Map of Europe still adorned

one wall. Of this room, Lord Peter had been made free, 'except,' as Mrs Venables explained, 'on Clothing Club nights, when I am afraid we shall have to turn you out.'

The vest and pants were spread upon the table, as though the Clothing Club, in retiring, had left some forlorn flotsam and jetsam behind. They had been washed, but there were still faint discolorations upon them, like the shadow of corruption, and here and there the fabric had rotted away, as the garments of mortality will, when the grave has had its way with them. Wafted in through the open window came the funeral scent of jonquils.

Wimsey whistled gently as he examined the underclothes, which had been mended with scrupulous and economical care. It puzzled him that Cranton, last seen in London in September, should possess a French vest and pants so much worn and so carefully repaired. His shirt and outer garments — now also clean and folded — lay on a chair close at hand. They, too, were well worn, but they were English. Why should Cranton be wearing secondhand French underclothes?

Wimsey knew that it would be hopeless to try tracing the garments through the makers. Underwear of this mark and quality was sold by the hundred thousand in Paris and throughout the provinces. It lay stacked up outside the great linen-drapers' shops, marked 'Occasions,' and thrifty housewives bought it there for cash. There was no laundry-mark; the washing had doubtless been done at home by the housewife herself or the *bonne à tout faire*. Holes here and there had been carefully darned; under the armpits, patches of a different material had been neatly let in; the wrists of the vest, frayed with use, had been oversewn; buttons had been renewed upon the pants. Why not? One must make economies. But they were not garments that anyone would have gone out of his way to purchase, even at a second-hand dealer's. And it would be hard for even the most active man to reduce his clothes to such a state of senility in four months' wear.

Lord Peter thrust his fingers into his hair till the sleek yellow locks stood upright. 'Bless his heart!' thought Mrs Venables, looking in upon him through the window. She had conceived a warm maternal affection for her guest. 'Would you like a glass of milk, or a whisky-and-soda, or a cup of beef-tea?' she suggested, hospitably. Wimsey laughed and thanked her, but declined.

'I hope you won't catch anything from those dreadful old clothes,' said Mrs Venables. 'I'm sure they can't be healthy.'

'Oh, I don't expect to get anything worse than brain-fever,' said Wimsey. 'I mean' — seeing Mrs Venables look concerned — 'I can't quite make out these underthings. Perhaps you can suggest something.' Mrs Venables came in, and he laid his problem before her.

'I'm sure I don't know,' said Mrs Venables, gingerly examining the objects before her. 'I'm afraid I'm not a Sherlock Holmes. I should think the man must have had a very good, hard-working wife, but I can't say more.'

'Yes, but that doesn't explain why he should get his things in France. Especially as everything else is British. Except, of course, the ten-centime piece, and they're common enough in this country.'

Mrs Venables, who had been gardening and was rather hot, sat down to consider the question.

'The only thing I can think of,' she said, 'is that he got his English clothes as a disguise — you said he came here in disguise, didn't you? But, of course, as nobody would see his underneaths, he didn't bother to change them.'

'But that would mean that he came from France.'

'Perhaps he did. Perhaps he was a Frenchman. They often wear beards, don't they?'

'Yes; but the man I met wasn't a Frenchman.'

'But you don't know he was the man you met. He may be somebody quite different.'

'Well, he *may*,' said Wimsey, dubiously.

'He didn't bring any other clothes with him, I suppose?'

'No; not a thing. He was just a tramping out-of-work. Or he said he was. All he brought was an old British trenchcoat, which he took with him, and a toothbrush. He left that behind him. Can we wangle a bit of evidence out of that? Can we say that he must have been murdered because, if he had merely wandered away, he would have taken his toothbrush with him? And if he was the corpse, where is his coat? For the corpse had no coat.'

'I can't imagine,' replied Mrs Venables, 'and that reminds me, do be careful when you go down the bottom of the garden. The rooks are building and they *are* so messy. I should wear a hat if I were you. Or there's always an old umbrella in the summer-house. Did he leave his hat behind too?'

'In a sense he did,' said Wimsey. 'We've found that, in rather a queer place. But it doesn't help us much.'

'Oh!' said Mrs Venables, 'how tiresome it all is. I'm sure you'll wear your brains right out with all these problems. You mustn't overdo yourself. And the butcher says he has some nice calf's liver today, only I don't know if you can eat it. Theodore is very fond of liver-and-bacon, though I always think it's rather rich. And I've been meaning to say, it's very good of that nice manservant of yours to clean the silver and brass so beautifully, but he really shouldn't have troubled. I'm quite used to giving Emily a hand with it. I hope it isn't very dull for him here. I understand he's a great acquisition in the kitchen and extraordinarily good at music-hall imitations. Twice as good as the talkies, Cook says.'

'Is he indeed?' said Wimsey. 'I had no idea of it. But what I don't know about Bunter would fill a book.'

Mrs Venables bustled away, but her remarks remained in Wimsey's mind. He put aside the vest and pants, filled a pipe and wandered down the garden, pursued by Mrs Venables with an ancient and rook-proof linen hat, belonging to the Rector. The hat was considerably too small for him, and the fact that he immediately put it on, with expressions of gratitude, may attest the kind heart which, despite the poet, is frequently found in close alliance with coronets; though the shock to Bunter's system was severe when his master suddenly appeared before him, wearing this grotesque headgear, and told him to get the car out and accompany him on a short journey.

'Very good, my lord,' said Bunter. 'Ahem! there is a fresh breeze, my lord.'

'All the better.'

'Certainly, my lord. If I may venture to say so, the tweed cap or the grey felt would possibly be better suited to the climatic conditions.'

'Eh? Oh! Possibly you are right, Bunter. Pray restore this excellent hat to its proper place, and if you should see Mrs Venables, give her my compliments and say that I found its protection invaluable. And, Bunter, I rely on you to keep a check upon your Don Juan fascination and not strew the threshold of friendship with the wreckage of broken hearts.'

'Very good, my lord.'

On returning with the grey felt, Bunter found the car already out and his lordship in the driving-seat.

'We are going to try a long shot, Bunter, and we will begin with Leamholt.'

'By all means, my lord.'

They sped away up the Fenchurch Road, turned left along the Drain, switchbacked over Frog's Bridge without mishap and ran the twelve or thirteen miles to the little town of Leamholt. It was market day, and the Daimler had to push her way decorously through droves of sheep and pigs and through groups of farmers, who stood carelessly in the middle of the street, disdaining to move till the mudguards brushed their thighs.

In the centre of one side of the market-place stood the post office.

'Go in here, Bunter, and ask if there is any letter here for Mr Stephen Driver, to be left till called for.'

Lord Peter waited for some time, as one always waits when transacting business in rural post offices, while pigs lurched against his bumpers and bullocks blew down his neck. Presently, Bunter returned, having drawn a blank despite a careful search conducted by three young ladies and the postmaster in person.

'Well, never mind,' said Wimsey. 'Leamholt is the post town, so I thought we ought to give it the first chance. The other possibilities are Holport and Walbeach, on this side of the Drain. Holport is a long way off and rather unlikely. I think we'll try Walbeach. There's a direct road from here — at least, as direct as any fen road ever is . . . I suppose God could have made a sillier animal than a sheep, but it is very certain that He never did . . . Unless it's cows. Hoop, there, hup! hup! get along with you, Jemima!'

Mile after mile the flat road reeled away behind them. Here a windmill, there a solitary farmhouse, there a row of poplars strung along the edge of a reed-grown dyke. Wheat, potatoes, beet, mustard and wheat again, grassland, potatoes, lucerne, wheat, beet and mustard. A long village street with a grey and ancient church tower, a red-brick chapel, and the vicarage set in a little oasis of elm and horse-chestnut, and then once more dyke and windmill, wheat, mustard and grassland. And as they went, the land flattened more and more, if a flatter flatness were possible, and the windmills became more numerous, and on the right hand the silver streak of the Wale River came back into view, broader now, swollen with the water of the Thirty-foot and of Harper's Cut and St Simon's Eau, and winding and spreading here and there, with a remembrance of its ancient leisure. Then, ahead of the great circle of the horizon, a little bunch of spires and roofs and a tall tree or so, and beyond them the thin masts of shipping. And so, by bridge and bridge the travellers came to Walbeach, once a great port, but stranded now far inland with the silting of the marshes and the choking of the Wale outfall; yet with her maritime tradition written unerringly upon her grey stones and timber warehouses, and the long lines of her half-deserted quays.

Here, at the post office in the little square, Lord Peter waited in the pleasant hush that falls on country towns where all days but market days are endless Sabbaths. Bunter was absent for some time, and, when he emerged, did so with a trifle less than his usual sedateness, while his usually colourless face was very slightly flushed about the cheekbones.

'What luck?' inquired Wimsey, genially.

To his surprise, Bunter replied by a hasty gesture enjoining silence and caution. Wimsey waited till he had taken his place in the car and altered his question to:

'What's up?'

'Better move on quickly, my lord,' said Bunter, 'because, while the manoeuvre has been attended with a measure of success, it is possible that I have robbed His Majesty's mails by obtaining a postal packet under false pretences.'

Long before this handsome period had thundered to its close, the Daimler was running down a quiet street behind the church.

'What *have* you been doing, Bunter?'

'Well, my lord, I inquired, as instructed, for a letter addressed to Mr Stephen Driver, poste restante, which might have been lying here some time. When the young person inquired how long a time, I replied, according to our previous arrangement, that I had intended to visit Walbeach a few weeks ago, but had been prevented from doing so, and that I understand that an important letter had been forwarded to me at this address under a misapprehension.'

'Very good,' said Wimsey. 'All according to Cocker.'

'The young person, my lord, then opened a species of safe or locker, and searched in it, and after the expiration of a considerable period, turned round with a letter in her hand and inquired what name I had said.'

'Yes? These girls are very bird-witted. It would have been more surprising if she hadn't asked you to repeat the name.'

'Quite so, my lord. I said, as before, that the name was Stephen or Steve Driver, but at the same time I observed from where I was standing that the letter in her hand bore a blue stamp. There was only the counter between us, and, as you are aware, my lord, I am favoured with excellent sight.'

207

'Let us always be thankful for blessings.'

'I hope I may say that I always am, my lord. On seeing the blue stamp, I added quickly (calling to mind the circumstances of the case) that the letter had been posted in France.'

'Very good, indeed,' said Wimsey, nodding approval.

'The young person, my lord, appeared to be puzzled by this remark. She said, in a doubtful tone, that there was a letter from France, which had been lying in the post office for three weeks, but that it was addressed to another person.'

'Oh, hell!' said Wimsey.

'Yes, my lord; that thought passed through my own mind. I said, Are you quite sure, miss, that you have not mistaken the handwriting? I am happy to say, my lord, that the young person — being young, and, no doubt, inexperienced — succumbed to this somewhat elementary strategy. She answered immediately, Oh, no — it's as plain as print: M. Paul Taylor. At that point — '

'Paul Taylor!' cried Wimsey, in sudden excitement. 'Why, that was the name — '

'Precisely, my lord. As I was about to say, at that point it was necessary to act promptly. I said at once: Paul Taylor? Why, that is the name of my chauffeur. You will excuse me, my lord, if the remark should appear to carry any disrespectful implication, seeing that you were at that moment in the car and might conceivably be supposed to be the person alluded to, but in the momentary agitation of my spirits, my lord, I was not in a position to think as quickly or as clearly as I should have wished.'

'Bunter,' said his lordship, 'I warn you that I am growing dangerous. Will you say at once, yes or no, did you get that letter?'

'Yes, my lord, I did. I said, of course, that since the letter for my chauffeur was there, I would take it to him, adding some facetious observations to the effect that he must have made a conquest while we were travelling abroad and that he was a great man for the ladies. We were quite merry on the subject, my lord.'

'Oh, were you?'

'Yes, my lord. At the same time, I said it was exceedingly vexatious that my own letter should have gone astray, and I requested the young person to institute another search. She did so, with some reluctance, and in the end I went away, after remarking that the postal system in this country was very undependable and that I should certainly write to *The Times* about it.'

'Excellent. Well, it's all very illegal, either way, but we'll get Blundell to put it right for us — I'd have suggested his doing it himself, but it was such a shot at a venture that I didn't think he'd cotton to it, and I hadn't a devil of a lot of faith in it myself. And anyway' — here Wimsey was seized with an uprush of candour to the lips — 'anyway, it was *my* jolly old idea and I wanted us to have the fun of it ourselves. Now, don't start apologising any more. You were perfectly brilliant in two places and I'm as bucked as hell. What's that? It mayn't be the right letter? Rot! It *is* the right letter. It's damn well got to be the right letter, and we're going to go straight along to the Cat and Fiddle, where the port is remarkable and the claret not to be despised, to celebrate our deed of darkness and derring do.'

Accordingly, within a very short time, Wimsey and his follower found themselves established in a dark old upper room, facing away from the square looking out upon the squat, square church tower, with the rooks wheeling over it and the seagulls swooping and dipping among the gravestones. Wimsey ordered roast lamb and a bottle of the far from despicable claret and was soon in conversation with the waiter, who agreed with him that things were very quiet.

'But not so quiet as they used to be, sir. The men working on the Wash Cut make a difference to the town. Oh, yes, sir — the Cut's nearly finished now, and they say it will be opened in June. It will be a good thing, so they say, and improve the draining very much. It's hoped as it will scour the river out ten feet or more and take the tide up again to the head of the Thirty-foot Drain, like it was in the old days, by what they tell us. Of course, I don't know about that, sir, for it seems that was in Oliver Cromwell's time, and I've only been here twenty year, but that's what the Chief Engineer says. They've brought the Cut to within a mile of the town now, sir, and there's to be a great opening in June, with a gala and a cricket match and sports for the young people, sir. And they say as they're asking the Duke of Denver to come down and open the Cut, but we haven't heard yet if he'll come.'

'He'll come all right,' said Wimsey. 'Dash it, he shall come. He does no work and it will do him good.'

'Indeed, sir?' said the waiter, a little dubiously, not knowing the cause of this certainty, but unwilling to offend. 'Yes, sir, it would be much appreciated in the town if he were to come. Will you take another potato, sir?'

'Yes, please,' said Wimsey. 'I'll make a point of jogging old Denver up to do his duty. We'll all come. Great fun. Denver shall present gold cups to all the winners and I will present silver rabbits to all the losers, and with luck somebody will fall into the river.'

'That,' said the waiter, seriously, 'will be very gratifying.'

Not till the port (Tuke Holdsworth '08) was set upon the table did Wimsey draw the letter from his pocket and gloat upon it. It was addressed in a foreign hand to 'M. Paul Taylor, Poste Restante, Walbeach, Lincolnshire, Angleterre.'

'My family,' observed Lord Peter, 'have frequently accused me of being unrestrained and wanting in self-control. They little know me. Instead of opening this letter at once, I reserve it for Superintendent Blundell. Instead of rushing off at once to Superintendent Blundell, I remain quietly at Walbeach and eat roast mutton. It is true that the good Blundell is not at Leamholt today, so that nothing would be gained if I did rush back, but still — it just shows you. The envelope bears a postmark which is only half-decipherable, but which I make out to be something ending in y in the department of either Marne or Seine-et-Marne — a district endeared to many by the recollection of mud, blood, shell-holes and trench-feet. The envelope is of slightly worse quality than even the majority of French envelopes, and the writing suggests that it was carried out with what may be called a post office pen and ink to match, by a hand unaccustomed to the exercise. The ink and pen mean little, for I have never yet encountered in any part of France a pen and ink with which any normal person could write comfortably. But the handwriting is suggestive, because, owing to the system of State education in that country, though all the French write vilely, it is rare to find one who writes very much more vilely than the rest. The date is obscure, but, since we know the time of arrival, we may guess the time of dispatch. Can we deduce anything further from this envelope?'

'If I may be allowed to say so, my lord, it is possibly a little remarkable that the name and address of the sender does not appear on the back.'

'That is well observed. Yes, Bunter, you may have full marks for that. The French, as you have no doubt often noticed, seldom head their letters with an address as we do in England, though they occasionally write at the foot some such useless indication as Paris or Lyon, without adding the number of the house and the name of the street. They do, however, frequently place these necessary indications on the flap of the envelope, in the hope that they may be thrown into the fire and irrecoverably lost before the letter is answered or even read.'

'It has sometimes occurred to me, my lord, to be surprised at that habit.'

'Not at all, Bunter. It is quite logical. To begin

with, it is a fixed idea with the French that the majority of letters tend to be lost in the post. They put no faith in Government departments, and I think they are perfectly right. They hope, however, that if the post office fails to deliver the letter to the addressee, it may, in time, return it to the sender. It seems a forlorn hope, but they are again perfectly right. One must explore every stone and leave no avenue unturned. The Englishman, in his bluff, hearty way, is content that under such circumstances the post office should violate his seals, peruse his correspondence, extract his signature and address from the surrounding verbiage, supply a fresh envelope and return the whole to him under the blushing pseudonym of Hubbykins or Dogsbody for the entertainment of his local postman. But the Frenchman, being decorous, not to say secretive, by nature, thinks it better to preserve his privacy by providing, on the exterior of the missive, all the necessary details for the proper functioning of this transaction. I do not say he is wrong, though I do think it would be better if he wrote the address in both places. But the fact that this particular letter provides no address for the return does perhaps suggest that the sender was not precisely out for publicity. And the devil of it is, Bunter, that ten to one there will be no address on the inside, either. No matter. This is very excellent port. Be good enough to finish the bottle, Bunter, because it would be a pity to waste it and if I have any more I shall be too sleepy to drive.'

They took the direct road back from Walbeach to Fenchurch following the bank of the river.

'If this country had been drained intelligently and all of a piece,' remarked Wimsey, 'by running all the canals into the rivers instead of the rivers into the canals, so as to get a good scour of water, Walbeach might still be a port and the landscape would look rather less like a crazy quilt. But what with seven hundred years of greed and graft and laziness, and perpetual quarrelling between one parish and the next, and the mistaken impression that what suits Holland must suit the Fens, the thing's a mess. It answers the purpose, but it might have been a lot better. Here's the place where we met Cranton — if it was Cranton. By the way, I wonder if that fellow at the sluice saw anything of him. Let's stop and find out. I love dawdling round locks.'

He twisted the car across the bridge and brought it to a standstill close beside the sluice-keeper's cottage. The man came out to see what was wanted and was lured, without difficulty, into a desultory conversation, beginning with the weather and the crops and going on to the Wash Cut, the tides and the river. Before very long, Wimsey was standing on the narrow wooden footbridge that ran across the sluice, gazing down thoughtfully into the green water. The tide was on the ebb and the gates partly open, so that a slow trickle ran through them as the Wale water discharged itself sluggishly towards the sea.

'Very picturesque and pretty,' said Wimsey. 'Do you ever get artists and people along here to paint it?'

The sluice-keeper didn't know as he did.

'Some of those piers would be none the worse

for a bit of stone and mortar,' went on Wimsey; 'and the gates look pretty ancient.'

'Ah!' said the sluice-keeper. 'I believe you.' He spat into the river. 'This here sluice has been needing repairs — oh! a matter of twenty year, now. And more.'

'Then why don't they do it?'

'Ah!' said the sluice-keeper.

He remained lost in melancholy thought for some minutes, and Wimsey did not interrupt him. Then he spoke, weightily, and with long years of endurance in his voice.

'Nobody knows whose job this here sluice is, seemin'ly. The Fen Drainage Board, now — they say as it did oughter be done by the Wale Conservancy Board. And *they* say the Fen Drainage Board did oughter see to it. And now they've agreed to refer it, like, to the East Level Waterways Commission. But they ain't made their report yet.' He spat again and was silent.

'But,' said Wimsey, 'suppose you got a lot of water up this way, would the gates stand it?'

'Well, they might and they mightn't,' replied the sluice-keeper. 'But we don't get much water up here these days. I have heard tell as it was different in Oliver Cromwell's time, but we don't get a great lot now.'

Wimsey was well used to the continual intrusion of the Lord Protector upon the affairs of the Fen, but he felt it to be a little unjustified in the present case.

'It was the Dutchmen built this sluice, wasn't it?' he said.

'Ah!' agreed the sluice-keeper. 'Yes, that's who

built this sluice. To keep the water out. In Oliver Cromwell's time this country was all drowned every winter, so they say. So they built this sluice. But we don't get much water up nowadays.'

'You will, though, when they've finished the New Wash Cut.'

'Ah! So they say. But I don't know. Some says it won't be no different. And some says as it'll drown the land round about Walbeach. All I know, they've spent a sight of money, and where's it coming from? To my mind, things was all very well as they was.'

'Who's responsible for the Wash Cut? The Fen Drainage Board?'

'No, that's the Wale Conservancy, that is.'

'But it must have occurred to them that it might make a difference to this sluice. Why couldn't they do it all at the same time?'

The fenman gazed at Wimsey with a slow pity for his bird-witted feebleness of mind.

'Ain't I telling yew? They don't rightly know if it did oughter be paid for by the Fen Drainage or the Wale Conservancy. Why,' and a note of pride crept into his tone, 'they've had five law actions about this here sluice. Ah! they took one on 'em up to Parliament, they did. Cost a heap of money, so they say.'

'Well, it seems ridiculous,' said Wimsey. 'And with all this unemployment about, too. Do you get many of the unemployed tramping round this way?'

'Times we do, times we don't.'

'I remember meeting a chap along the Bank last time I was down here — on New Year's Day.

216

I thought he looked a bit of a tough nut.'

'Oh, him? Yes. He got took on at Ezra Wilderspin's place, but he soon had enough o' that. Didn't want to do no work. Half on 'em don't. He came along askin' for a cup o' tea, but I told him to get out. It wasn't tea he was lookin' for. Not him. I know his sort.'

'I suppose he'd come from Walbeach.'

'I suppose he had. He said so, anyhow. Said he'd been trying to get work on the Wash Cut.'

'Oh? He told me he was a motor mechanic.'

'Ah!' The sluice-keeper spat once more into the tumbling water. 'They'd say anything.'

'He looked to me as though he'd worked a good bit with his hands. Why shouldn't there be work for men on the Cut? That's what I was saying.'

'Yes, sir, it's easy to say them things. But with plenty o' skilled men out of a job, they don't need to go taking on the like of him. That's where it is, you see.'

'Well,' said Wimsey, 'I still think that the Drainage Board and the Conservancy Board and the Commission between them ought to be able to absorb some of these men and give you a fresh set of gates. However, it's not my business, and I'll have to be pushing along.'

'Ah!' said the sluice-keeper. 'New gates? Ah!'

He remained hanging on the rail and spitting thoughtfully into the water till Wimsey and Bunter had regained the car. Then he came hobbling after them.

'What I says is,' he observed, leaning so earnestly over the door of the Daimler that

217

Wimsey hurriedly drew back his feet, thinking that the usual expectoration was about to follow, 'what I says is, Why don't they refer it to Geneva? Why don't they refer it to Geneva? Then we might get it, same time as they gets disarmament, see?'

'Ha, ha!' said Wimsey, rightly supposing this to be irony. 'Very good! I must tell my friends about that. Good work, what? Why don't they refer it to Geneva? Ha, ha!'

'That's right,' said the sluice-keeper, anxious that the point of the jest should not be lost. 'Why don't they refer it to Geneva? see?'

'Splendid!' said Wimsey. 'I won't forget that. Ha, ha, ha!'

He gently released the clutch. As they moved away, he glanced back and saw the sluice-keeper convulsed by the remembrance of his own wit.

★　★　★

Lord Peter's misgivings about the letter were duly confirmed. He honourably submitted it, unopened, to Superintendent Blundell, as soon as the latter returned from attendance at the Quarter Sessions where he had been engaged all day. The Superintendent was alarmed by Wimsey's unorthodox raid on the post office, but pleased by his subsequent discretion, and readily allowed him full credit for zeal and intelligence. Together they opened the envelope. The letter, which bore no address, was written on thin paper of the same poor quality as the envelope, and began:

218

'*Mon cher mari* — '

'Hey!' said Mr Blundell. 'What's that mean? I'm not much of a French scholar, but doesn't *mari* mean *husband?*'

'Yes. My dear husband, it begins.'

'I never knew that Cranton — dash it!' exclaimed Mr Blundell. 'Where does Cranton come into this? I never heard of his having any wife at all, let alone a French one.'

'We don't know that Cranton comes into it at all. He came to St Paul and asked for a Mr Paul Taylor. This, presumably, is addressed to the Paul Taylor he asked for.'

'But they said Paul Taylor was a bell.'

'Tailor Paul is a bell, but Paul Taylor may be a person.'

'Who is he, then?'

'God knows. Somebody with a wife in France.'

'And, the other chap, Batty Something — is he a person?'

'No, he's a bell. But he may be a person, too.'

'They can't both be persons,' said Mr Blundell, 'it's not reasonable. And where is this Paul Taylor, anyhow?'

'Perhaps he was the corpse.'

'Then where's Cranton? They can't,' added the Superintendent, 'both be the corpse. That's not reasonable, either.'

'Possibly Cranton gave one name to Wilderspin and another to his correspondent.'

'Then what did he mean by asking for Paul Taylor at Fenchurch St Paul?'

'Perhaps that was the bell, after all.'

'See here,' said Mr Blundell, 'it doesn't seem

reasonable to me. This Paul Taylor or Tailor Paul can't be both a bell and a person. At least, not both at once. It sounds kind of, well, batty to me.'

'Why bring Batty into it? Batty is a bell. Tailor Paul is a bell. Paul Taylor is a person, because he gets a letter. You can't send letters to a bell. If you did you'd be batty. Oh, bother!'

'Well, I don't understand it,' said Mr Blundell. 'Stephen Driver, he's a person, too. You don't say he's a bell, do you? What I want to know is, which of 'em all is Cranton. If he's been and fixed himself up with a wife in France between this and last September — I mean, between this and January — no, I mean between September and January — I mean — here, dash it all, my lord, let's read the blooming letter. You might read it out in English, would you? My French is a bit off, these days.'

'My dear husband' (Wimsey translated), ' — You told me not to write to you, without great urgency, but three months are past and I have no news of you. I am very anxious, asking myself if you have not been taken by the military authorities. You have assured me that they could not now have you shot, the War being over so long ago, but it is known that the English are very strict. Write, I beseech you, a little word to say that you are safe. It begins to be very difficult to do the work of the farm alone, and we have had great trouble with the Spring sowing. Also the red cow is dead. I am obliged to carry the fowls to

220

market myself, because Jean is too exigent, and prices are very low. Little Pierre helps me as much as he can, but he is only nine. Little Marie has had the whooping-cough and the Baby also. I beg your pardon if I am indiscreet to write to you, but I am very much troubled. Pierre and Marie send kisses to their papa.

'Your loving wife,
'SUZANNE.'

Superintendent Blundell listened aghast; then snatched the paper from Wimsey, as though he mistrusted his translation and thought to tear out some better meaning from the words by mere force of staring at them.

'Little Pierre — nine years old — kisses to their papa — and the red cow's dead — t'cha!' He did a little arithmetic on his fingers. 'Nine years ago, Cranton was in gaol.'

'Stepfather, perhaps?' suggested Wimsey.

Mr Blundell paid no heed. 'Spring sowing — since when has Cranton turned farmer? And what's all that about military authorities? And the War. Cranton never was in the War. There's something here I can't make head or tail of. See here, my lord — this can't be Cranton. It's silly, that's what it is. It can't be Cranton.'

'It begins to look as if it wasn't,' said Wimsey. 'But I still think it was Cranton I met on New Year's Day.'

'I'd better get on the telephone to London,' said Mr Blundell. 'And then I'll have to be seeing the Chief Constable about this. Whatever it is, it's got to be followed up. Driver's disappeared and we've found a body that looks like his and we've got to do something about it. But France — well, there! How we're to find this Suzanne I don't know, and it'll cost a mint of money.'

the sixth part

MONSIEUR ROZIER HUNTS
THE TREBLE DOWN

The remaining bell . . . does nothing but
plain hunting, and is therefore said to be 'in
the hunt with the Treble.'
             TROYTE *On Change-Ringing*

There are harder jobs in detective work than
searching a couple of French departments for a
village ending in 'y' containing a farmer's wife
whose first name is Suzanne whose children are
Pierre, aged nine, Marie and a baby of unknown
age and sex, and whose husband is an
Englishman. All the villages in the Marne district
end, indeed, in 'y', and Suzanne, Pierre and
Marie are all common names enough, but a
foreign husband is rarer. A husband named Paul
Taylor would, of course, be easily traced, but
both Superintendent Blundell and Lord Peter
were pretty sure that 'Paul Taylor' would prove to
be an alias.

It was about the middle of May when a report
came in from the French police which looked
more hopeful than anything previously received.
It came through the Sûreté, and originated with
M. le commissaire Rozier of Chateau-Thierry in
the Department of Marne.

It was so exceedingly promising that even the Chief Constable, who was a worried gentleman with an itch for economy, agreed that it ought to be investigated on the spot.

'But I don't know whom to send,' he grumbled. 'Dashed expensive business, anyhow. And then there's the language. Do you speak French, Blundell?'

The Superintendent grinned sheepishly. 'Well, sir, not to say speak it. I could ask for a spot of grub in an *estaminet*, and maybe swear at the garsong a bit. But examining witnesses — that's a different question.'

'I can't go myself,' said the Chief Constable, sharply and hastily, as though anticipating a suggestion that nobody had had the courage to make. 'Out of the question.' He tapped his fingers on his study table and stared vaguely over the Superintendent's head at the rooks wheeling high over the elms at the end of the garden. 'You've done your best, Blundell, but I think we had better hand the thing over, lock, stock and barrel, to Scotland Yard. Perhaps we ought to have done so earlier.'

Mr Blundell looked chagrined. Lord Peter Wimsey, who had come with him, ostensibly in case help should be needed to translate the commissaire's letter, but actually because he was determined not to be left out of anything, coughed gently.

'If you would entrust the inquiry to me, sir,' he murmured, 'I could pop over in two ticks — at my own expense, of course,' he added, insinuatingly.

'I'm afraid it would be rather irregular,' said the Chief Constable, with the air of one who only needs to be persuaded.

'I'm more reliable than I look, really I am,' said his lordship. 'And my French is my one strong point. Couldn't you swear me in as a special constable or something? with a natty little armlet and a truncheon? Or isn't interrogation part of a special constable's duties?'

'It is not,' said the Chief Constable. 'Still,' he went on, 'still — I suppose I might stretch a point. And I suppose' — he looked hard at Wimsey — 'I suppose you'll go in any case.'

'Nothing to prevent me from making a private tour of the battlefields,' said Wimsey, 'and, of course, if I met one of my old Scotland Yard pals knocking round there, I might join up with him. But I really think that, in these hard times, we ought to consider the public purse, don't you, sir?'

The Chief Constable was thoughtful. He had no real wish to call in Scotland Yard. He had an idea that a Yard man might make himself an officious nuisance. He gave way. Within two days, Wimsey was being cordially received by M. le commissaire Rozier. A gentleman who has '*des relations intimes*' with the Paris Sûreté, and who speaks perfect French, is likely to be well received by country *commissaires de police*. M. Rozier produced a bottle of very excellent wine, entreated his visitor to make himself at home, and embarked upon his story.

'It does not in any way astonish me, milord, to receive an inquiry concerning the husband of

Suzanne Legros. It is evident that there is there a formidable mystery. For ten years I have said to myself, 'Aristide Rozier, the day will come when your premonitions concerning the so-called Jean Legros will be justified.' I perceive that the day is at hand, and I congratulate myself upon my foresight.'

'Evidently,' said Wimsey, 'M. le commissaire possesses a penetrating intelligence.'

'To lay the matter clearly before you, I am obliged to go back to the summer of 1918. Milord served in the British Army? Ah! then milord will remember the retreat over the Marne in July. *Quelle histoire sanglante!* On that occasion the retreating armies were swept back across the Marne pell-mell and passed in disorder through the little village of C — y, situated upon the left bank of the river. The village itself, you understand, milord, escaped any violent bombardment, for it was behind the frontline trenches. In that village lived the aged Pierre Legros and his granddaughter Suzanne. The old man was eighty years of age and refused to leave his home. His grandchild, then aged twenty-seven, was a vigorous and industrious girl who, single-handed, kept the farm in a sort of order throughout the years of conflict. Her father, her brother, her affianced husband had all been killed.

'About ten days after the retreat, it was reported that Suzanne Legros and her grandfather had a visitor at the farm. The neighbours had begun to talk, you understand, and the curé, the reverend Abbé Latouche, now in paradise, thought it his duty to inform the authorities here. I myself, you comprehend, was not here at that time; I was in the Army; but my predecessor, M. Dubois, took steps to investigate the matter. He found that there was a sick and wounded man being kept at the farm. He had suffered a severe blow upon the head and various other injuries. Suzanne Legros, and her grand-father, being interrogated, told a singular story.

'She said that, on the second night after the retreat had passed through the village, she went to a distant out-house and there found this man lying sick and burning with fever, stripped to his underclothing, with his head roughly bandaged. He was dirty and bloodstained and his clothes were bedaubed with mud and weeds as though he had been in the river. She contrived to carry him home with the old man's help, washed his wounds and nursed him as best she might. The farm is a couple of kilometres distant from the village itself, and she had no one whom she could send for assistance. At first, she said, the man had raved in French about the incidents of the battle, but afterwards he had fallen into a heavy stupor, from which she could not rouse him. When seen by the curé and by the commissaire he lay inert, breathing heavily and unconscious.

'She showed the clothing in which she had found him — a vest, underpants, socks, and shirt of regulation army pattern, very much stained and torn. No uniform; no boots, no identity disc; no papers. It seemed evident that he had been in the retreat and had been obliged to swim across the river in making his way back from the front line — this would account for the abandoning of his boots, uniform and kit. He seemed to be a man of some thirty-five or forty years of age, and when first seen by the authorities, he had a dark beard of about a week's growth.'

'Then he had been clean-shaven?'

'It would seem so, milord. A doctor from the town was found to go out and see him, but he could only say that it appeared to be a severe case of injury to the brain from the wound in the head. He advised ameliorative measures. He was only a young student of small experience, incapacitated from the Army by reason of frail health. He has since died.

'It was at first supposed that they had only to wait till the man came to himself to learn who he was. But when, after three more weeks of coma, he slowly regained consciousness, it was found that his memory, and, for some time, his speech also, was gone. Gradually, the speech was regained, though for some time he could express himself only in a thick mumbling manner, with many hesitations. It seemed that there were injuries to the locutory centres in the brain. When he was well enough to understand and make himself understood he was, naturally, interrogated. His replies were simply that his mind was a blank. He remembered nothing of his past — but nothing. He did not know his name, or his place of origin; he had no recollection of the war. For him, his life began in the farmhouse at C — y.'

M. Rozier paused impressively, while Wimsey

registered amazement.

'Well, milord, you will understand that it was necessary to report the case at once to the Army authorities. He was seen by a number of officers, none of whom could recognise him, and his portrait and measurements were circulated without result. It was thought at first that he might be an Englishman — or even a Boche — and that, you understand, was not agreeable. It was stated, however, that when Suzanne first found him, he had deliriously muttered in French, and the clothes found upon him were undoubtedly French also. Nevertheless, his description was issued to the British Army, again without result, and, when the Armistice was signed, inquiries were extended to Germany. But they knew nothing of him there. Naturally, these inquiries took some time, for the Germans had a revolution, as you know, and everything was much disordered. In the meanwhile, the man had to live somewhere. He was taken to hospital — to several hospitals — and examined by psychologists, but they could make nothing of him. They tried — you understand, milord — to set traps for him. They suddenly shouted words of command at him in English, French and German, thinking that he might display an automatic reaction. But it was to no purpose. He seemed to have forgotten the war.'

'Lucky devil!' said Wimsey, with feeling.

'*Je suis de votre avis.* Nevertheless, a reaction of some kind would have been satisfying. Time passed, and he became no better. They sent him back to us. Now you know, milord, that it is impossible to repatriate a man who has no nationality. No country will receive him. Nobody wanted this unfortunate man except Suzanne Legros and her *bon-papa*. They needed a man to work on the farm and this fellow, though he had lost his memory, had recovered his physical strength and was well suited for manual labour. Moreover, the girl had taken a fancy to him. You know how it is with women. When they have nursed a man, he is to them in a manner their child. Old Pierre Legros asked leave to adopt this man as his son. There were difficulties — *que voulez-vous?* But, *enfin*, since something had to be done with the man, and he was quiet and well behaved and gave no trouble, the consent was obtained. He was adopted under the name of Jean Legros and papers of identity were made out for him. The neighbours began to be accustomed to him. There was a man — a fellow who had thought of marrying Suzanne — who was his enemy and called him *sale Boche* — but Jean knocked him down one evening in the *estaminet* and after that there was no more heard of the word Boche. Then, after a few years it became known that Suzanne had the wish to marry him. The old curé opposed the match — he said it was not known but that the man was married already. But the old curé died. The new one knew little of the circumstances. Besides, Suzanne had already thrown her bonnet over the windmill. Human nature, milord, is human nature. The civil authorities washed their hands of the matter; it was better to regularise the position. So Suzanne Legros wedded this

230

Jean, and their eldest son is now nine years of age. Since that time there has been no trouble — only Jean still remembers nothing of his origin.'

'You said in your letter,' said Wimsey, 'that Jean had now disappeared.'

'Since five months, milord. It is said he is in Belgium, buying pigs, cattle, or I know not what. But he has not written, and his wife is concerned about him. You think you have some information about him?'

'Well,' said Wimsey, 'we have a corpse. And we have a name. But if this Jean Legros has conducted himself in the manner you describe, then the name is not his, though the corpse may be. For the man whose name we have was in prison in 1918 and for some years afterwards.'

'Ah! then you have no further interest in Jean Legros?'

'On the contrary. An interest of the most profound. We still have the corpse.'

'A la bonne heure,' said M. Rozier cheerfully. 'A corpse is always something. Have you any photograph? any measurements? any marks of identification?'

'The photograph will assuredly be of little use, since the corpse when found was four months old and the face had been much battered. Moreover, his hands had been removed at the wrists. But we have measurements and two medical reports. From the latest of these, recently received from a London expert, it appears that the scalp bears the mark of an old scar, in addition to those recently inflicted.'

'Aha! that is perhaps some confirmation. He

was, then, killed by being beaten on the head, your unknown?'

'No,' said Wimsey. 'All the head injuries were inflicted after death. The expert opinion confirms that of the police-surgeon on this point.'

'He died, then, of what?'

'There is the mystery. There is no sign of fatal wound, or of poison, or of strangling, nor yet of disease. The heart was sound; the intestines show that he had not died of starvation — indeed, he was well nourished, and had eaten a few hours before his death.'

'*Tiens!* an apoplexy, then?'

'It is possible. The brain, you understand, was in a somewhat putrefied condition. It is difficult to say with certainty, though there are certain signs that there had been an effusion of blood into the cortex. But you comprehend that, if a thundering apoplexy killed this man, it was not so obliging as to bury him also.'

'Perfectly. You are quite right. Forward, then, to the farm of Jean Legros.'

The farm was a small one, and did not seem to be in too flourishing a state. Broken fences, dilapidated out-houses and ill-weeded fields spoke of straitened means and a lack of the necessary labour. The mistress of the house received them. She was a sturdy, well-muscled woman of some forty years of age, and carried in her arms a nine-months-old child. At the sight of the commissaire and his attendant gendarme a look of alarm came unmistakably into her eyes. Another moment, and it had given place to that expression of mulish obstinacy which no one can better assume at will than the French peasant.

'M. le commissaire Rozier?'

'Himself, madame. This gentleman is milord Vainsé, who has voyaged from England to make certain inquiries. It is permitted to enter?'

It was permitted, but at the word 'England' the look of alarm had come again; and it was not lost on either of the men.

'Your husband, Mme Legros,' said the commissaire, coming brusquely to the point, 'he is absent from home. Since how long?'

'Since December, M. le commissaire.'

'Where is he?'

'In Belgium.'

'Where, in Belgium?'

'Monsieur, in Dixmude, as I suppose.'

'You suppose? You do not know? You have had no letter from him?'

'No, monsieur.'

'That is strange. What took him to Dixmude?'

'Monsieur, he had taken the notion that his family lived perhaps at Dixmude. You know, without doubt, that he had lost his memory. *Eh, bien!* In December, one day, he said to me, 'Suzanne, put a record on the gramophone.' I put on the record of a great *diseuse*, reciting *Le Carillon*, a poem of Verhaeren, to music. *C'est un morceau très impressionnant.* At that moment, filled with emotion where the carillons are named turn and turn, my husband cried out: 'Dixmude! There is then a town of Dixmude in Belgium?' 'But certainly,' I replied. He said, 'But that name says something to me! I am convinced, Suzanne, that I have a beloved mother residing in Dixmude. I shall not rest till I have gone to Belgium to make inquiries about this dear mother.' M. le commissaire, he would listen to nothing. He went away, taking with him our small savings, and since that time I have heard nothing from him.'

'*Histoire très touchante*,' said the commissaire, drily. 'You have my sympathy, madame. But I cannot understand that your husband should be a Belgian. There were no Belgian troops engaged at the third battle of the Marne.'

'Nevertheless, monsieur, his father may have married a Belgian. He may have Belgian relations.'

'*C'est vrai.* He left you no address?'

'None, monsieur. He said he would write on his arrival.'

'Ah! And he departed how? By the train?'

'Oh, yes, monsieur.'

'And you have made no inquiries? From the mayor of Dixmude, for example?'

'Monsieur, you understand that I was sufficiently embarrassed. I did not know where to begin with such an inquiry.'

'Nor of us, the police, who exist for that? You did not address yourself to us?'

'M. le commissaire, I did not know — I could not imagine — I told myself every day, 'Tomorrow he will write,' and I waited, *et enfin* — '

'*Et enfin* — it did not occur to you to inform yourself. *C'est bien remarquable.* What gave you the idea that your husband was in England?'

'In England, monsieur?'

'In England, madame. You wrote to him under the name of Paul Taylor, did you not? At the

town of Valbesch in the county of Laincollone?'
The commissaire excelled himself in the render-
ing of these barbarian place-names. 'At Valbesch
in Laincollone you address yourself to him in the
name of Paul Taylor — *voyons, madame, voyons,*
and you tell me now that you suppose him to be
all the time in Belgium. You will not deny your
own handwriting, I suppose? Or the names of your
two children? Or the death of the red cow? You
do not imagine that you can resurrect the cow?'

'Monsieur — '

'Come, madame. During all these years you
have been lying to the police, have you not? You
knew very well that your husband was not a
Belgian but an Englishman? That his name was
actually Paul Taylor? That he had not lost his
memory at all? Ah! you think that you can trifle
with the police in that way? I assure you,
madame, that you will find it a serious matter.
You have falsified papers, that is a crime!'

'Monsieur, monsieur — '

'That is your letter?'

'Monsieur, since you have found it, I cannot
deny it. But — '

'Good, you admit the letter. Now, what is this
about falling into the hands of the military
authorities?'

'I do not know, monsieur. My husband
— monsieur, I implore you to tell me, where is
my husband?'

The commissaire Rozier paused, and glanced
at Wimsey, who said:

'Madame, we are greatly afraid that your
husband is dead.'

235

'*Ah, mon dieu! je le savais bien*. If he had been alive he would have written to me.'

'If you will help us by telling the truth about your husband, we may be able to identify him.'

The woman stood looking from one to the other. At last she turned to Wimsey:

'You, milord, you are not laying a trap for me? You are sure that my husband is dead?'

'Come, come,' said the commissaire, 'that makes no difference. You must tell the truth, or it will be the worse for you.'

Wimsey took out of the attache case which he had brought with him the underclothing which had been found upon the corpse.

'Madame,' he said, 'we do not know whether the man who wore these is your husband, but on my honour, the man who wore these is dead and they were taken from his body.'

Suzanne Legros turned the garments over, her work-hardened fingers slowly tracing each patch and darn. Then, as though the sight of them had broken down something in her, she dropped into a chair and laid her head on the mended vest and burst out into loud weeping.

'You recognise the garments?' asked the commissaire presently, in a milder tone.

'Yes, they are his, I mended these garments myself. I understand that he is dead?'

'In that case,' said Wimsey, 'you can do him no harm by speaking.'

When Suzanne Legros had recovered herself a little, she made her statement, the commissaire calling in his attendant gendarme to take a shorthand note of it.

'It is true that my husband was not a Frenchman or a Belgian. He was an Englishman. But it is true also that he was wounded in the retreat of 1918. He came to the farm one night. He had lost much blood and was exhausted. Also his nerves were shattered, but it is not true that he had lost his memory. He implored me to help him and to hide him, because he did not want to fight any more. I nursed him till he was well and then we arranged what we should say.'

'It was shameful, madame, to harbour a deserter.'

'I acknowledge it, monsieur, but consider my position. My father was dead, my two brothers killed, and I had no one to help me with the farm. Jean-Marie Picard, that was to have married me, was dead also. There were so few men left in France, and the war had gone on so long. And also, monsieur, I grew to love Jean. And his nerves were greatly deranged. He could not face any more fighting.'

'He should have reported to his unit and applied for sick leave,' said Wimsey.

'But then,' said Suzanne, simply, 'they would have sent him back to England and separated us. And besides, the English are very strict. They might have thought him a coward and shot him.'

'It appears at least, that he made you think so,' said Monsieur Rozier.

'Yes, monsieur. I thought so and he thought so too. So we arranged that he should pretend to have lost his memory, and since his French accent was not good, we decided to make out that his speech was affected by his injury. And I burnt his uniform and papers in the copper.'

'Who invented the story — you or he?'

'He did, monsieur. He was very clever. He thought of everything.'

'And the name also?'

'The name also.'

'And what was his real name?'

She hesitated. 'His papers were burnt, and he never told me anything about himself.'

'You do not know his name. Was it then not Taylor?'

'No, monsieur. He adopted that name when he went back to England.'

'Ah! and what did he go to England for?'

'Monsieur, we were very poor, and Jean said that he had property in England which could be disposed of for a good sum, if only he could get hold of it without making himself known. For, you see, if he were to reveal himself he would be shot as a deserter.'

'But there was a general amnesty for deserters after the war.'

'Not in England, monsieur.'

'He told you that?' said Wimsey.

'Yes, milord. So it was important that nobody should know him when he went to fetch the property. Also there were difficulties which he did not explain to me, about selling the goods — I do not know what they were — and for that he had to have the help of a friend. So he wrote to this friend and presently he received a reply.'

'Have you that letter?'

'No, monsieur. He burnt it without showing it to me. This friend asked him for something — I

238

did not quite understand that, but it was some sort of guarantee, I think. Jean shut himself up in his room for several hours the next day to compose his answer to the letter, but he did not show that to me, either. Then the friend wrote back and said he could help him, but it would not do for Jean's name to appear — neither his own name nor the name of Legros, you understand. So he chose the name of Paul Taylor, and he laughed very much when the idea came to him to call himself so. Then the friend sent him papers made out in the name of Paul Taylor, British subject. I saw those. There was a passport with photograph; it was not very much like my husband, but he said they would not pay great attention to it. The beard was like his.'

'Had your husband a beard when you last knew him?'

'No, he was clean-shaven, like all the English. But of course, he grew his beard when he was ill. It altered him very much, because he had a small chin, and with the beard it looked bigger. Jean took with him no luggage: he said he would buy clothes in England, because then he would again look like an Englishman.'

'And you know nothing of the nature of this property in England?'

'Nothing whatever, monsieur.'

'Was it land, securities, valuables?'

'I know nothing about it, monsieur. I asked Jean often, but he would never tell me.'

'And you expect us to believe you do not know your husband's real name?'

Again the hesitation. Then: 'No, monsieur, I

do not know. It is true that I saw it upon his papers, but I burnt those and I do not now remember it. But I think it began with a C, and I should know it if I saw it again.'

'Was it Cranton?' asked Wimsey.

'No, I do not think it was that, but I cannot say what it was. As soon as he was able to speak at all, he told me to give him his papers, and I asked him then what his name was, because I could not pronounce it — it was English and difficult — and he said that he would not tell me his name then, but I could call him what I liked. So I called him Jean, which was the name of my *fiancé*, who was killed.'

'I see,' said Wimsey. He hunted through his pocket-book and laid the official photograph of Cranton before her. 'Is that your husband as you first knew him?'

'No, milord. That is not my husband. It is not in the least like him.' Her face darkened. 'You have deceived me. He is not dead and I have betrayed him.'

'He is dead,' said Wimsey. 'It is this man who is alive.'

★ ★ ★

'And now,' said Wimsey, 'we are no nearer than before to a solution.'

'*Attendez*, milord. She has not yet told all she knows. She does not trust us, and she is concealing the name. Only wait, and we shall find the means to make her speak. She still thinks that her husband may be alive. But we shall convince her.

We shall have this man traced. It is some months old, the trail, but it will not be too difficult. That he started from here by train to go to Belgium I already know, by my inquiries. When he sailed for England, it was doubtless from Ostend, unless — *voyons*, milord, what resources could this man command?'

'How can I tell? But we believe that this mysterious property had to do with an emerald necklace of many thousands of pounds value.'

'*Ah, voilà!* It would be worth while to spend money, then. But this man, you say he is not the man you thought. If that other man was the thief how does this one come into it?'

'There is the difficulty. But look! There were two men concerned in the theft; one, a London *cambrioleur*, the other, a domestic servant. We do not know which of them had the jewels; it is a long story. But you heard that this Jean Legros wrote to a friend in England, and that friend may have been Cranton, the burglar. Now Legros cannot have been the servant who stole the jewels in the first place, for that man is dead. But before dying, the thief may have communicated to Legros the secret of where the emeralds are hidden, and also the name of Cranton. Legros then writes to Cranton and proposes a partnership to find the jewels. Cranton does not believe, and asks for proof that Legros really knows something. Legros sends a letter which satisfies Cranton, and Cranton in turn procures the necessary papers for Legros. Then Legros goes to England and meets Cranton. Together they go and discover the jewels. Then Cranton kills his confederate, so as to have all for himself. How is that, monsieur? For Cranton also has disappeared.'

'It is very possible, milord. In that case, both the jewels and the murderer are in England — or wherever this Cranton may be. You think, then, that the other dead man, the servant, communicated the hiding-place of the necklace — to whom?'

'Perhaps to some fellow-prisoner who was only in gaol for a short term.'

'And why should he do that?'

'In order that this fellow-prisoner should provide him with a means of escape. And the proof is that the servant did break prison and escape, and afterwards his dead body was found in a pit many miles from the prison.'

'Aha! the affair begins to outline itself. And the servant — how did he come to be found dead? Eh?'

'He is supposed to have fallen over the edge of the pit in the dark. But I begin to think that he was killed by Legros.'

'Milord, our thoughts chime together. Because, voyez-vous, this story of desertion and military authorities will not hold water. There is more than a desertion behind this change of name and this fear of the British police. But if the man was an old gaol-bird, and had committed a murder into the bargain, the thing understands itself. Twice he changes his name, so that he shall not be traced even to France, because he, Legros, under his English name, had enlisted after his release from prison and the records of your Army

242

might reveal him. Only, if he was in the Army, it is strange that he should have found the leisure to plan a prison-breaking for his comrade and commit murder. No, there are still difficulties, but the outline of the plot is clear and will develop itself more clearly still as we proceed. In the meanwhile, I will undertake inquiries here and in Belgium. I think, milord, we must confine ourselves to the ordinary passenger-routes, or even to the ports. A motor-boat might well make the journey to the coast of Laincollone. Your police, also, will make inquiries on their part. And when we have shown the progress of Legros from the front door of his house to his grave in England, then, I think, Mme Suzanne will speak a little more. And now, milord, I beg you will honour us by sharing our dinner tonight. My wife is an excellent cook, if you will condescend to a *cuisine bourgeoise* garnished with a tolerable *vin de Bourgogne*. Monsieur Delavigne of the Sûreté informs me that you have the reputation of a *gourmet*, and it is only with a certain diffidence that I make the suggestion, but it would give Mme Rozier unheard-of delight if you would give her the pleasure of making your acquaintance.'

'Monsieur,' said Lord Peter, 'I am infinitely obliged to you both.'

the seventh part

PLAIN HUNTING

First, Lucas Mortis; then Terra Tenebrosa; next, Tartarus, after that, Terra Oblivionis; then Herebus; then Barathrum; then Gehenna; and then Stagnum Ignis.

SHERIDAN LEFANU: *Wylder's Hand*

'Well,' said Superintendent Blundell, 'if that's how it is, we've got to find Cranton. But it's a funny thing to me. From what they tell me, I wouldn't have thought Cranton was the man for that sort of job. He's never been suspected of killing anyone, and he never looked to me like a killer. And you know, my lord, that it's very rare for one of them sort of smart burglars to go all off the rails and take to violence. What I mean, it isn't in them, as a rule, if you get my meaning. It's true he went for Deacon in the dock but that was more of a scrimmage, as you might say, and I don't think he meant much harm. Supposing as it was the other chap that killed Cranton? He might have changed clothes with him to prevent identification.'

'So he might. But what becomes of that old scar on the head? That seems to fit in with the body being this fellow they call Jean Legros. Unless Cranton had a scar too.'

'He'd no scar up to last September,' said the Superintendent, thoughtfully. 'No, I reckon you're right, and that won't work. Some of the measurements seem a bit different, too — though, of course, it's not easy to be as accurate as all that when you're comparing a live man with a four-months-old corpse. And there were so many teeth gone and busted from the corpse that we've not got much out of that, either. No, we've got to find Cranton. If he's alive, he's lying uncommon low. Looks as though he'd done something pretty bad — I give you that.'

The conversation took place in the church-yard, where Mr Blundell had been undertaking an exhaustive search for unspecified clues. The Superintendent thoughtfully decapitated a nettle, and resumed:

'Then there's that chap Will Thoday. I can't make him out at all. I'll swear he knows something — but what *can* he know? It's as certain as anything can be that he was sick in bed when it all happened. He sticks to that, and says he knows nothing. What can you do with a man who says he knows nothing? Why, nothing. And as for his wife, *she* couldn't have tied a man up and buried him. She's not a powerful sort of woman by any means. And I've got hold of the children. It went against me to do it, but I did it all the same. And they say their Mother and Dad were both in the house all night. There's one other person might know something, and that's James Thoday. Look here, my lord, here's a queer thing. James Thoday left Fenchurch St Paul on January 4th, early in the morning, to

245

join his ship. He was seen to go, all right — the station-master saw him. But he never got to Hull that day. I've been on to Lampson & Blake, and they say they had a wire from him to say he couldn't get back in time, but would arrive on the Sunday night — which he did. Had some story of being taken suddenly ill — and they say he looked ill enough when he did arrive. I've told them to get in touch with him as quick as they can.'

'Where was the wire sent from?'

'London. From a post office near Liverpool Street. About the time when the train Jim Thoday took at Dykesey would get up there. Looks as though he'd been taken queer on the way up.'

'He might have picked up influenza from his brother.'

'So he might. Still, he was fit to sail the next day, and it looks funny, don't you think? He'd have had plenty of time to go up to London and come down here again. He wouldn't come to Dykesey, of course, but he might have come part of the way by train and done the rest by car or motor-bike or what-not.'

Wimsey whistled. 'You think he was in with Will over the thing. Yes, I see. Will is in a conspiracy with Legros to get the emeralds — is that it? And he gets flu and can't do the job himself, so he arranges with Brother Jim to do it for him. Then Jim meets Legros and kills him and buries him and vamooses with the emeralds to Hong Kong. Well, that would explain one thing, and that is, why those infernal stones haven't been put on the European market. He could easily get rid of them over in the East. But look here, Super — how did Will Thoday get into touch with Legros in the first place? It was easy when we put it all on Cranton, because he could have got the papers and things made out for Legros by one of his pals in Town. But you can't imagine that Thoday produced forged papers and provided Legros with his passage facilities and all that. How would a fellow like that know how to set about it?'

Mr Blundell shook his head.

'But there's that two hundred pounds,' he said.

'So there is, but that was after Legros had started.'

'And when Legros was killed, the money was returned to the bank.'

'Was it?'

'Oh, yes. I had a word with Thoday. He made no difficulties. He said he had an idea of purchasing a bit of land and starting to farm again on his own, but that, after his illness, he gave up the idea, thinking that for some time he wouldn't be strong enough. He gave me permission to go over his bank account. It was all in order — no suspicious withdrawals of money up to that £200 on December 31st, and that was paid in again in January, as soon as he was able to get about. And it's true about the land, too. He did think of buying it. All the same, £200 all in one-pound notes — '

The Superintendent broke off, and made a sudden dive behind a tall tombstone. There was a squeak and a scuffle. Mr Blundell emerged, rather flustered. His large hand held Potty Peake's coat-collar in a firm grip.

'Now, you clear off,' said the Superintendent, giving his captive a rough, but not unkindly, shake. 'You'll get yourself in trouble, my lad, hanging round the churchyard and listening to private conversations. See?'

'Ar!' said Potty, 'you needn't choke a fellow. You needn't choke poor Potty. If you knew what Potty knows — '

'What do you know?'

Potty's eyes gleamed cunningly.

'I seen him — Number Nine — I seen him a-talking to Will in the church. But the tailors was too much for him. Him with the rope — he got him, and he'll get you too. Potty knows. Potty ain't lived all these years, in and out of the church, for nothing.'

'Who was talking to Will in the church?'

'Why, him!' Potty jerked his head towards the Thorpe grave. 'Him they found over there. The black-bearded man. There's eight in the belfry and one in the grave. That makes nine. You think Potty can't count, but he can. But him as calls the peal — you won't get him, oh, no!'

'See here,' said Wimsey, 'you're a clever fellow, Potty. When did you see Will Thoday talking to the black-bearded man? See if you can count that far.'

Potty Peake grinned at him. 'Potty can count all right,' he said, with great satisfaction. 'Oh, yes.' He began an elaborate calculation on his fingers. 'Ah! it was Monday night, that's when it was. There was cold pork and beans for dinner — that's good, cold pork and beans. Ah! Parson he preached about thankfulness. Be thankful for Christmas, he says. There was roast fowl, Christmas day, and boiled pork and greens Sunday and be thankful, that's what Parson says. So Potty slips out at night, for to be thankful again. You got to go to church to be thankful proper, ain't you, sir? And there was the church door standing open. So Potty creeps in, careful-like, see? And there's a light in the vestry. Potty was frightened. There's things hanging in the vestry. Ah! So Potty hides behind ole Batty Thomas, and then Will Thoday comes in, and Potty hears them talking in the vestry. 'Money', Will says. 'Tis a great wickedness, is money. And then Will Thoday he cries out — he fetches a rope from the chest and — ah! Potty's afraid. He thinks about hanging. Potty don't want to see no one hanged. Potty runs away. He looks in at the vestry window,' and there's the black-bearded man a-laying on the floor, and Will a-standing over him with the rope. Ah, dear! oh, dear! Potty don't like ropes. Potty's allus a-dreamin' of ropes. One, two, three, four, five, six, seven, eight — and this one's nine. Potty seen him a-hangin' there. Ooh!'

'I think you was a-dreaming all the time,' said the Superintendent. 'There's nobody been hanged that I know of.'

'I see him a-hanging,' persisted Potty. 'Terrible it were. But don't you pay no attention. 'Tis only one o' poor Potty's dreams.' His face changed. 'You lemme go, mister, I gotter feed my pigs.'

'Bless my heart,' said Superintendent Blundell. 'And what do you suppose we're to make of
that?'

Wimsey shook his head.

'I think he saw something — or how did he
know that the rope was gone from the cope-
chest? But as for hanging, no! He's crazed about
hanging. Got a hanging complex, or whatever
they call it. The man wasn't hanged. Which Monday
night do you suppose Potty meant?'

'Can't be January 6th, can it?' said the
Superintendent. 'The body was buried on the
4th, as far as we can make out. And it can't very
well be December 30th, because Legros only got
here on January 1st — if that was Legros you
saw. And besides, I can't make out whether he
means Sunday or Monday, with his boiled pork!'

'I can,' said Wimsey. 'He had boiled pork and
greens on Sunday, and Parson told him to be
thankful and so he was. And on Monday, he had
the pork cold with beans — probably the tinned
variety if I know the modern countrywoman
— and he felt thankful again. So he went down
to the church to be thankful in the proper place.
It would be some time in the evening, as there
was a light in the vestry.'

'That's right. Potty lives with an aunt of his
— a decent old soul, but not very sharp. He's
always slipping out at night. They're cunning as
the devil, these naturals. But which evening was
it?'

'The day after Parson had preached on thankfulness,' said Wimsey. 'Thankfulness for Christmas.
That looks like December 30th. Why not? You

don't know that Legros didn't get here before January 1st. That's when Cranton got here.'

'But I thought we'd washed Cranton out of it,' objected Mr Blundell, 'and put Will Thoday in his place.'

'Then who was it I met on the road over the bridge?'

'That must have been Legros.'

'Well, it may be — though I still think it was Cranton, or his twin brother. But if I met Legros on January 1st, he can't have been hanged by Will Thoday on December 30th. And in any case, he wasn't hanged. And,' said Wimsey, triumphantly, 'we still don't know how he did die!'

The Superintendent groaned.

'What I say is, we've got to find Cranton, somehow. And as for December 30th, how are you going to be sure of that, anyway?'

'I shall ask the Rector which day he preached about thankfulness. Or Mrs Venables. She's more likely to know.'

'And I'd better see Thoday again. Not that I believe a single word Potty says. And how about Jim Thoday? How does he come into it now?'

'I don't know. But one thing I'm sure of, Super. It was no sailor put those knots into Gaude's rope. I'll take my oath on that.'

'Oh, well!' said the Superintendent.

★ ★ ★

Wimsey went back to the house and found the Rector in his study, busily writing out a touch of Treble Bob Major.

'One moment, my dear boy,' he said, pushing the tobacco-jar towards his guest, 'one moment. I am just pricking this little touch to show Wally Pratt how to do it. He has got himself 'imbrangled' as they call it — fine old English word, that. Now what has the foolish lad done here? The ninth lead should bring Queen's, change — let me see, let me see — 51732468, 15734286 — that's the first thirds and fourths all right — 51372468, 15374286 — and that's the first fourths and thirds — 13547826 — ah! here is the trouble! The eighth should be at home. What has happened? — To be sure! What a beetle-headed cuckoo I am! He has forgotten to make the bob. She can't come home till she's called.' He ran a red-ink line down the page and started to write figures furiously. 'There! 51372468, 15374286 — and *now* she comes home like a bird! — 13572468. That's better. Now it should come round at the second repeat. I will just check it. Second to fifth, third to second — yes, yes — that brings 15263748, with Tittums at the end of the second course, and repeated once again brings it round. I will just jot down the lead-ends for him to check it by. Second to third, third to, fifth, fourth to second, fifth to seventh, sixth to fourth, seventh to eighth, eighth to sixth for the plain lead, Then the bob. Plain, bob, bob, three plain and a bob. I cannot understand why red ink should distribute itself so lavishly over one's person. There! I have a large smear on my cuff! Call her in the middle, in and out and home. Repeat twice. A lovely little touch.' He pushed aside several sheets of paper covered with figures, and transferred a quantity of red ink from his fingers to his trouser-leg. 'And now, how are you getting along? Is there anything I can do to help you?'

'Yes, padre. You can tell me on which Sunday this winter you preached about thankfulness.'

'Thankfulness? Well, now, that's rather a favourite subject of mine. Do you know, I find people very much disposed to grumble — I do indeed — and when you come to think of it, they might all be very much worse off. Even the farmers. As I said to them last Harvest Festival — oh! you were asking about my Thankfulness sermon — well, I nearly always preach about it at Harvest Festival . . . Not so long ago as that? . . . Let me think. My memory is getting very unreliable, I fear . . . ' He made a dive for the door. 'Agnes, my dear! Agnes! Can you spare us a moment? . . . My wife is sure to remember . . . My dear, I am so sorry to interrupt you, but can you recollect when I last preached about Thankfulness? I touched on the subject in my Tithe sermon, I remember — would you be thinking of that? Not that we have had any trouble about tithe in this parish. Our farmers are very sensible. A man from St Peter came to talk to me about it, but I pointed out to him that the 1918 adjustment was made in the farmers' interests and that if they thought they had reason to complain of the 1925 Act, then they should see about getting a fresh adjustment made. But the law, I said, is the law. Oh, on the matter of tithe I assure you I am adamant. Adamant.'

'Yes, Theodore,' said Mrs Venables, with rather

a wry smile, 'but if you didn't so often advance people money to pay the tithe with, they mightn't be as reasonable as they are.'

'That's different,' said the Rector, hurriedly, 'quite different. It's a matter of principle, and any small personal loan has nothing to do with it. Even the best of women don't always grasp the importance of a legal principle, do they, Lord Peter? My sermon dealt with the principle. The text was: 'Render unto Caesar'. Though whether Queen Anne's Bounty is to be regarded as Caesar or as God — and sometimes, I admit, I feel that it is a little unfortunate that the Church should appear to be on Caesar's side, and that disestablishment and disendowment — '

'A Caesarian operation is indicated, so to speak?' suggested Wimsey.

'A — ? Oh, yes! Very good,' said the Rector. 'My dear, that is very good, don't you think? I must tell the Bishop — no, perhaps not. He is just a leetle bit strait-laced. But it is true — if only one could separate the two things, the temporal and the spiritual — but the question I ask myself is always, the churches themselves — the buildings — our own beautiful church — what would become of it in such a case?'

'My dear,' said Mrs Venables, 'Lord Peter was asking about your sermons on Thankfulness. Didn't you preach one on the Sunday after Christmas? About Thankfulness for the Christmas message? Surely you remember. The text was taken from the Epistle for the day; 'Thou art no more a servant, but a son.' It was about how happy we ought to be as God's children and about making a habit of saying 'Thank-you, Father' for all the pleasant things of life, and being as pleasant-tempered as we should wish our own children to be. I remember it so well, because Jackie and Fred Holliday got quarrelling in church over those prayer-books we gave them and had to be sent out.'

'Quite right, my dear. You always remember everything. That was it, Lord Peter. The Sunday after Christmas. It comes back to me very clearly now. Old Mrs Giddings stopped me in the porch afterwards to complain that there weren't enough plums in her Christmas pudding.'

'Mrs Giddings is an ungrateful old wretch,' said his wife.

'Then the next day *was* the 30th December,' said Wimsey. 'Thanks, padre, that's very helpful. Do you recollect Will Thoday coming round to see you on the Monday evening, by any chance?'

The Rector looked helplessly at his wife, who replied readily enough:

'Of course he did, Theodore. He came to ask you something about the New Year's peal. Don't you remember saying how queer and ill he looked? Of course, he must have been working up for that attack of flu, poor man. He came late — about 9 o'clock — and you said you couldn't understand why he shouldn't have waited till the morning.'

'True, true,' said the Rector. 'Yes, Thoday came round to me on the Monday night. I hope you are not — well! I mustn't ask indiscreet questions, must I?'

'Not when I don't know the answers,' said

Wimsey, with a smile and a shake of the head. 'About Potty Peake, now. Just how potty is he? Can one place any sort of reliance on his account of anything?'

'Well,' said Mrs Venables, 'sometimes one can and sometimes one can't. He gets mixed up, you know. He's quite truthful, as far as his understanding goes, but he gets fancies and then tells them as if they were facts. You can't trust anything he says about ropes or hanging — that's his little peculiarity. Otherwise — if it was a question of pigs, for instance, or the church organ — he's quite good and reliable.'

'I see,' said Wimsey. 'Well, he has been talking a good bit about ropes and hanging.'

'Then don't believe a word of it,' replied Mrs Venables, robustly. 'Dear me! here's that Superintendent coming up the drive. I suppose he wants you.'

Wimsey caught Mr Blundell in the garden and headed him away from the house.

'I've seen Thoday,' said the Superintendent. 'Of course he denies the whole story. Says Potty was dreaming.'

'But how about the rope?'

'There you are! But that Potty was hiding behind the churchyard wall when you and I found the rope in the well, and how much he may have heard, I don't know. Anyway, Thoday denies it, and short of charging him with the murder, I've got to take his word for it. You know these dratted regulations. No bullying of witnesses. That's what they say. And whatever Thoday did or didn't do, he couldn't have buried the body, so where are you? Do you think any jury is going to convict on the word of a village idiot like Potty Peake? No. Our job's clear. We've got to find Cranton.'

★　★　★

That afternoon, Lord Peter received a letter.

'DEAR LORD PETER, — I have just thought of something funny you ought to know about, though I don't see how it can have anything to do with the murder. But in detective stories the detective always wants to know about anything funny, so I am sending you the paper. Uncle Edward wouldn't like me writing to you, because he says you encourage me about wanting to be a writer and mixing myself up in police work — he *is* a silly old stick-in-the-mud! So I don't suppose Miss Garstairs — that's our H.M. — would let me send you a letter, but I'm putting this into one to Penelope Dwight and I do hope she sends it on all right.

'I found the paper lying in the belfry on the Saturday before Easter Day and I meant to show it to Mrs Venables because it was so funny, but Dad dying made me forget all about it. I thought it must be some rubbish of Potty Peake's, but Jack Godfrey says it isn't Potty's writing, but it's quite mad enough to be him, isn't it? Anyway, I thought you might like to have it. I don't see how Potty could have got hold of that foreign paper, do you?

'I hope you are still getting on well with the investigations. Are you still at Fenchurch St Paul? I am writing a poem about the founding of Tailor Paul. Miss Bowler says it is quite good and I expect they will put it in the School Magazine. That will be one in the eye for Uncle Edward, anyhow. He can't stop me being printed in the School Mag. Please write if you have time and tell me if you find out anything about the paper.

'Yours sincerely,

'HILARY THORPE.'

'A colleague, as Sherlock Holmes would say, after my own heart,' said Wimsey, as he unfolded the thin enclosure. 'Oh, lord! 'I thought too see the fairies in the fields' — a lost work by Sir James Barrie, no doubt! Literary sensation of the year. 'But I saw only the evil elephants with their black backs.' This is neither rhyme nor reason. Hum! there is a certain dismal flavour about it suggestive of Potty, but no reference to hanging, so I conclude that it is not his — he surely couldn't keep King Charles's Head out of it so long. Foreign paper — wait a minute! I seem to know the look of that paper. By God, yes! Suzanne Legros's letter! If the paper isn't the dead spit of this I'm a Dutchman. Let me think. Suppose this was the paper Jean Legros sent to Cranton, or Will Thoday, or whoever it was? Blundell had better have a look at it. Bunter, get the car out. And what do you make of this?'

'Of this, my lord? I should say that it was

written by a person of no inconsiderable literary ability, who had studied the works of Sheridan Lefanu and was, if I may be permitted the expression, bats in the belfry, my lord.'

'It strikes you that way? It does not look to you like a cipher message, or anything of that kind?'

'It had not occurred to me to regard it in that light, my lord. The style is cramped, certainly, but it is cramped in what I should call a consistent manner, suggestive of — ah! — literary rather than mechanical effort.'

'True, Bunter, true. It certainly isn't anything simple and bucolic of the every-third-word type. And it doesn't look as if it was meant to be read with a grid, because, with the possible exception of 'gold', there isn't a single word in it that's significant — or could be significant of anything but moonshine. That bit about the moon is rather good, of its kind. Mannered, but imaginative. 'Frail and faint as a sickle of straw.' Alliteration's artful aid, what? 'So then came minstrels, having gold trumpets, harps and drums. These played very loudly beside me, breaking that spell.' Whoever wrote that had an ear for a cadence. Lefanu, did you say? That's not a bad shot, Bunter. It reminds me a little of that amazing passage in *Wylder's Hand* about Uncle Lorne's dream.'

'That was the passage I had in mind, my lord.'

'Yes. Well — in that case the victim was due to 'be sent up again, at last, a thousand, a hundred, ten and one, black marble steps, and then it will be the other one's turn.' He *was* sent up again, Bunter, wasn't he?'

'From the grave, my lord? I believe that was so. Like the present unknown individual.'

'As you say — very like him. 'Hell gapes, Erebus now lies open,' as our correspondent has it. 'The mouths of Death wait on thy end.' Does he mean anything by that, Bunter?'

'I could not say, my lord.'

'The word 'Erebus' occurs in the Lefanu passage too, but there, if I remember rightly, it is spelt with an H. If the man who wrote this got his inspiration there, he knew enough, at any rate, about Erebus to be familiar with both spellings. All very curious, Bunter mind. We'll go along to Leamholt and get the two sheets of paper put side by side.'

★　★　★

There was a great wind blowing over the fen, and immense white clouds sailing fast in the wide blue dome of sky. As they drew up before the police-station at Leamholt, they met the Superintendent just about to step into his own car.

'Coming to see me, my lord?'

'I was. Were you coming to see me?'

'Yes.'

Wimsey laughed.

'Things are moving. What have you got?'

'We've got Cranton.'

'No!'

'Yes, my lord. They've run him to earth in a place in London. I heard from them this morning. Seems he's been ill, or something.

Anyway, they've found him. I'm going up to interrogate him. Would you like to come?'

'Rather! Shall I run you up there? Save the Force a bit of money, you know, on train fares. And be quicker and more comfortable.'

'Thank you very much, my lord.'

'Bunter, wire to the Rector that we have gone to Town. Hop in, Super. You will see how safe and swift modern methods of transport are when there is no speed limit. Oh, wait a moment. While Bunter is wiring, have a look at this. It reached me this morning.'

He handed over Hilary Thorpe's letter and the enclosure.

'Evil elephants?' said Mr Blundell. 'What in the name of goodness is all this about?'

'I don't know. I'm hoping your friend Cranton can tell us.'

'But it's potty.'

'I don't think Potty could rise to such heights. No, I know what you mean — don't trouble to explain. But the paper, Superintendent, the paper!'

'What about it? Oh, I get you. You think this came from the same place as Suzanne Legros's letter. I shouldn't wonder if you're right. Step in and we'll have a look. By Jove, my lord, and you *are* right. Might have come out of the same packet. Well, I'll be — Found in the belfry, you say. What do you think it all means, then?'

'I think this is the paper that Legros sent to his friend in England — the 'guarantee' that he composed, shut up in his room for so many hours. And I think it's the clue to where the

261

emeralds were hidden. A cipher, or something of that sort.'

'Cipher, eh? It's a queer one, then. Can you read it?'

'No, but I jolly well will. Or find somebody who can. I'm hoping that Cranton will read it for us. I bet he won't though,' added his lordship, thoughtfully. 'And even if we do read it, it isn't going to do us much good, I'm afraid.'

'Why not?'

'Why, because you can bet your sweet life that the emeralds were taken away by whoever it was killed Legros — whether it was Cranton or Thoday or somebody else we don't know about yet.'

'I suppose that's a fact. Anyhow, my lord, if we read the cipher and find the hiding-place, and the stuff's gone, that'll be pretty good proof that we're working along the right lines.'

'So it will. But,' added Wimsey, as the Superintendent and Bunter piled into the car and were whisked away out of Leamholt at a speed which made the policeman gasp, 'if the emeralds are gone, and Cranton says he didn't take them, and we can't prove he did, and we can't find out who Legros really was, or who killed him, why then — where are we?'

'Just where we were before,' said Mr Blundell.

'Yes,' said Wimsey. 'It's like Looking-Glass Country. Takes all the running we can do to stay in the same place.'

The Superintendent glanced about him. Flat as a chess-board, and squared like a chess-board with intersecting dyke and hedge, the fen went flashing past them.

'Very like Looking-Glass Country,' he agreed, 'same as the picture in the book. But as for staying in the same place — all I can say is, it don't look like it, my lord — not where you're concerned.'

the eighth part

LORD PETER FOLLOWS
HIS COURSE BELL TO LEAD

I will again urge on the young conductor the
great advantage that it will be to him to write
out touches or even whole peals . . . whereby
he will gain a great insight into the working
of the bells.

TROYTE *On Change-Ringing*

'Well, of course,' admitted Mr Cranton, grinning
up ruefully from his pillow into Lord Peter's face,
'if your lordship recognises me, that's done it. I'll
have to come clean, as the sheet said to the patent
washer. It's a fact I was in Fenchurch St Paul on
New Year's Day, and a lovely place it is to start a
happy New Year in, I don't think. And it's true I
failed to report myself as from last September.
And if you ask me, I think it's damned slack of
you flatties not to have dug me out earlier. What
we pay rates and taxes for I don't know.'

He stopped and shifted restlessly.

'Don't waste your breathe in giving us lip,'
said Chief Inspector Parker of the C.I.D., kindly
enough. 'When did you start growing that
face-fungus? In September? I thought so. What
was the idea? You didn't think it was becoming,
did you?'

'I didn't,' said Mr Cranton. 'Went to my heart, I may say, to disfigure myself. But I thought, 'They'll never know Nobby Cranton with his handsome features all hidden in black hair,' so I made the sacrifice. It's not so bad now, and I've got used to it, but it looked horrible while it was growing. Made me think of those happy times when I lived on His Majesty's bounty. Ah! and look at my hands. They've never got over it. I ask you, how can a gentleman carry on with his profession after all those years of unrefined manual labour? Taking the bread out of a man's mouth, I call it.'

'So you had some game on, which started last September,' said Parker, patiently. 'What was it, now? Anything to do with the Wilbraham emeralds, eh?'

'Well, to be frank, it was,' replied Nobby Cranton. 'See here, I'll tell you the truth about that. I didn't mind — I never *have* minded — being put inside for what I did do. But it's offensive to a gentleman's feelings when his word isn't believed. And when I said I never had those emeralds, I meant what I said. I never did have them, and you know it. If I had had them, I wouldn't be living in a hole like this, you can bet your regulation boots. I'd have been living like a gentleman on the fat of the land. Lord!' added Mr Cranton, 'I'd have had 'em cut up and salted away before you could have said 'knife'. Talk about tracing them — you'd never have traced them the way I'd have worked it.'

'So you went to Fenchurch St Paul to try and find them, I suppose?' suggested Wimsey.

'That's right, I did. And why? Because I knew they must be there. That swine — you know who I mean — '

'Deacon?'

'Yes, Deacon.' Something that might have been fear and might have been mere anger twisted the sick man's face. 'He never left the place. He couldn't have got them away before you pinched him. You watched his correspondence, didn't you? If he'd have packed them up and posted them, you'd have known it, eh? No. He had them there — somewhere — I don't know — but he had them. And I meant to get them, see? I meant to get them, and I meant to bring them along and show 'em to you and make you take back what you said about my having had them. Pretty silly, you'd have looked, wouldn't you, when you had to own up that I was right?'

'Indeed?' said Parker. 'That was the idea, was it? You were going to find the stuff and bring it along like a good little boy?'

'That's right.'

'No idea of making anything out of them, of course?'

'Oh, dear, no,' replied Cranton.

'You didn't come to us in September and suggest that we should help you to find them?'

'Well, I didn't,' agreed Mr Cranton. 'I didn't want to be bothered with a lot of clumsy cops. It was my own little game, see? All my own work, as the pavement-artists say.'

'Delightful,' said Parker. 'And what made you think you knew where to look for them?'

'Ah!' said Mr Cranton, cautiously. 'Something

266

Deacon once said gave me an idea. But he was a liar about that, too. I never met such a liar as that fellow was. He was so crooked, you could have used his spine for a safety-pin. It serves me right for having to do with menials. A mean, sneaking spirit, that's what you find in that sort. No sense of honour at all.'

'Very likely,' said the Chief Inspector. 'Who is Paul Taylor?'

'There you are!' said Mr Cranton, triumphantly. 'Deacon said to me — '

'When?'

'In the — oh, well! — in the dock, if you will excuse my mentioning such a vulgar place. 'Want to know where those shiners are?' he said. 'Ask Paul Taylor or Batty Thomas' — and grinned all over his face. 'Who're they?' said I. 'You'll find 'em in Fenchurch,' he said, grinning still more. 'But you aren't likely to see Fenchurch again in a hurry,' he said. So then I biffed him one — excuse the expression — and the blinking warder interfered.'

'Really?' said Parker, incredulously.

'Cross my heart and wish to die,' said Mr Cranton. 'But when I got down to Fenchurch, you see, I found there were no such people — only some rubbish about bells. So I dismissed the matter from my mind.'

'And sneaked off on the Saturday night. Why?'

'Well, to be frank with you,' replied Mr Cranton, 'there was an individual in that place I didn't like the looks of, I got the idea that my face struck a chord in her mind, in spite of the exterior decorations. So, not wishing for argument — which is always ungentlemanly — I went quietly away.'

'And who was the penetrating individual?'

'Why, that woman — Deacon's wife. We had stood shoulder to shoulder, as you might say, under unfortunate circumstances, and I had no wish to renew the acquaintance. I never expected to see *her* in that village, and candidly, I thought she showed a lack of taste.'

'She came back when she married a man named Thoday,' said Wimsey.

'Married again, did she?' Cranton's eyes narrowed. 'Oh, I see. I didn't know that. Well, I'm damned!'

'Why the surprise?'

'Why? — Oh, well — somebody wasn't too particular, that's all.'

'See here,' said Parker, 'you may as well tell the truth now. Did that woman have anything to do with the theft of the emeralds?'

'How should I know? But to be frank, I don't believe she did. I think she was just a plain fool. Deacon's cat's-paw. I'm sure the fellow put her on to find out about the stuff, but I don't think she was wise to what she was doing. Honestly, I don't think so, because I can't see that man Deacon giving his game away. But hell! What do I know about it?'

'You don't think she knows where the stuff is?'

Cranton thought for a moment. Then he laughed. 'I'd pretty well take my oath she doesn't.'

'Why?'

He hesitated.

'If she knew and was straight, she'd have told

268

the police, wouldn't she? If she knew and was crooked, she'd have told me or my pals. No. You won't get it out of her.'

'H'm! You say you think she recognised you?'

'I got a sort of idea that she was beginning to find my face familiar. Mind you, it was only a kind of hunch I got. I might have been wrong. But I anticipated argument, and I have always considered argument ill-bred. So I went away. In the night. I was working for the blacksmith — an excellent fellow, but crude. I didn't want any argument with him, either. I just went quietly home to think things out, and then I got laid up with rheumatic fever, and it's left my heart dickey, as you see.'

'Quite so. How did you get rheumatic fever?'

'Well, wouldn't anybody get rheumatic fever, if he'd fallen into one of those cursed dykes? I never saw such a country, never. Country life never did suit me — particularly in the blasted middle of winter, with a thaw going on. I was damn nearly found dead in a ditch, which is no end for a gentleman.'

'You didn't investigate the matter of Batty Thomas and Tailor Paul any further, then?' said Parker, placidly putting aside the eloquence which Mr Cranton seemed ready to lavish on any side-issue. 'I am referring to the bells. You did not, for instance, visit the belfry, to see if the emeralds were hidden up there?'

'No, of course I didn't. Besides,' went on Mr Cranton, much too hastily, 'the confounded place was always locked.'

'You tried it, then?'

269

'Well, to be frank, I may just have laid my hand on the door, so to speak.'

'You never went up into the bell-chamber?'

'Not me.'

'Then how do you account for that?' demanded Parker, suddenly producing the mysterious cipher and thrusting it under the sick man's eyes.

Mr Cranton turned extremely white.

'That?' he gasped. 'That? — I never — ' He fought for breath. 'My heart — here, give me some of the stuff in that glass — '

'Give it him,' said Wimsey, 'he's really bad.'

Parker gave him the medicine with a grim face. After a time the blue pallor gave place to a healthier colour, and the breathing became more natural.

'That's better,' said. Cranton. 'You startled me. What did you say? That? I never saw that before.'

'You're lying,' said the Chief Inspector, curtly. 'You have seen it. Jean Legros sent it to you, didn't he?'

'Who's he? Never heard of him'

'That's another lie. How much money did you send him to get him to England?'

'I tell you I never heard of him,' repeated Cranton, sullenly. 'For God's sake, can't you leave me alone? I tell you I'm ill.'

He looked ill enough. Parker swore under his breath.

'Look here, Nobby, why not come across with the truth? It'll save us bothering you. I know you're ill. Cough it up and get it over.'

'I know nothing about it. I've told you — I went down to Fenchurch and I came away again. I never saw that paper and I never heard of Jean

What's-his-name. Does that satisfy you?'

'No, it doesn't.'

'Are you charging me with anything?'

Parker hesitated. 'Not as yet,' he said.

'Then you've got to take my answer,' said Mr Cranton, faintly, but as one who is sure of his position.

'I know that,' said Parker, 'but, hang it, man! do you *want* to be charged? If you'd rather come down with us to the Yard — '

'What's the idea? What have you got to charge me with? You can't try me for stealing those bloody emeralds all over again. I haven't got them. Never seen them — '

'No; but we might charge you with the murder of Jean Legros.'

'No — no — no!' cried Cranton. 'It's a lie! I never killed him. I never killed anybody. I never — '

'He's fainted,' said Wimsey.

'He's dead,' said Superintendent Blundell, speaking for the first time.

'I hope to goodness not,' said Parker. 'No — it's all right, but he looks pretty queer. Better get hold of that girl. Here, Polly!'

A woman came in. She gave one resentful glance at the three men and hurried across to Cranton.

'If you've killed him,' she muttered, 'it's murder. Coming and threatening one that's as sick as him. You get out, you great bullies. He's done nobody any harm.'

'I'll send the doctor along,' said Parker. 'And I'll be coming to see him again. And when I do come, see that I find him here all right. Understand? We shall want him elsewhere, you know, as soon as he's fit to be moved. He hasn't reported himself since last September.'

The girl shrugged a disdainful shoulder, and they left her bending over the sick man.

'Well, Superintendent,' said Parker. 'I'm afraid that's the best we can do for you at the moment. The man's not shamming — he's really ill. But he's holding something out on us. All the same, I don't think it's murder, somehow. That wouldn't be like Cranton. He knew that paper all right.'

'Yes,' said Wimsey. 'Produced quite a reaction, didn't it? He's frightened about something, Charles. What is it?'

'He's frightened about the murder.'

'Well,' said Blundell, 'it looks to me as though he did it. He admits he was there, and that he ran away on the night the body was buried. If he didn't do it, who did? He could have got the key of the crypt from the sexton all right, we know that.'

'So he could,' said Wimsey, 'but he was a stranger to the place. How did he know where the sexton kept his tools? Or where to find the bell-rope? He might have noticed the well, of course, in the daytime, but it's funny that he should have had the whole scheme so pat. And where does Legros come into it? If Deacon told Cranton in the dock where to find the emeralds, where was the sense of bringing Legros to England? He didn't want him. And, if he did for some reason need Legros, and killed him to get the emeralds, where are the emeralds? If he sold them, you ought to have found it out by now. If he's still got

272

them, you'd better have a hunt for them.'

'We'll search the house,' said Parker, dubiously, 'but I don't somehow think he's got them. He wasn't alarmed about the emeralds. It's a puzzle. But we'll turn the place upside-down, and if they're here, we'll get them.'

'And if you do,' said Blundell, 'then you can arrest that chap for the murder. Whoever's got the emeralds did the murder. I'm sure of that.'

'Where thy treasure is, there shall thy heart be also,' said Wimsey. 'The heart of this crime is down at St Paul. That's my prophecy, Charles. Will you have a bet on it?'

'No, I won't,' said the Chief Inspector. 'You're right too often, Peter, and I've no money to waste.'

★ ★ ★

Wimsey went back to Fenchurch St Paul and shut himself up with the cipher. He had untwisted cryptograms before, and he felt certain that this would prove to be a simple one. Whether the inventor was Cranton or Jean Legros or Will Thoday or any other person connected with the affair of the Wilbraham emeralds, he was hardly likely to be an expert in the art of secret writing. Yet the thing had the signs of a cunning hand about it. He had never seen a secret message that looked so innocent. Sherlock Holmes's Little Dancing Men were, by comparison, obviously secretive.

He tried various simple methods, such as taking every second, third or fourth letter, or skipping letters in accordance with a set combination of figures, but without result. He tried assigning a number to each letter and adding the results, word by word and sentence by sentence. This certainly produced enough mathematical problems to satisfy a Senior Wrangler, but none of them seemed to make sense. He took all the bell-inscriptions and added them up also, with and without the dates, but could find nothing significant. He wondered whether the book contained the whole of what was on the bells. Leaving his papers strewn over the table, he went to the Rector to borrow the keys to the belfry. After a slight delay, caused by the keys having been taken downstairs by mistake for the keys of the wine-cellar, he secured them and made his way to the church.

He was still puzzled about the finding of the cryptogram. The keys jingled together in his hand — the two great keys of the west and south doors, all by themselves on a steel chain, and then, in a bunch on a ring together, the keys of the crypt and vestry, the key of the belfry, the key of the ringing-chamber and the key that unlocked the counterpoise of the, belfry. How had Cranton known where to find them? He could, of course, have taken them from the sexton's house — if he had known already. But if 'Stephen Driver' had been asking questions about the church keys, somebody would have taken notice of it. The sexton had the key of the west door and of the crypt. Had he the other keys as well? Wimsey suddenly turned back and shot the question through the study window at the Rector, who was struggling with the finances of the Parish Magazine.

Mr Venables rubbed his forehead.

'No,' he said at last. 'Gotobed has the west-door key and, the key of the crypt, as you say, and he also has the key of the belfry stair and of the ringing-chamber, because he rings the single bell for Early Service and sometimes deputises for Hezekiah when he's ill. And Hezekiah has the keys of the south porch and the belfry stair and the ringing-chamber, too. You see, Hezekiah was sexton before Gotobed, and he likes to keep his privilege of ringing the passing-bell, though he's too old for the other work, and he has the necessary keys. But neither of them has the key to the counterpoise. They don't need it. The only people who have that are Jack Godfrey and myself. I have a complete set of everything, of course, so that if one of the others is lost or mislaid, I can supply it.'

'Jack Godfrey — has he the key of the crypt as well?'

'Oh, no — he doesn't need that.'

Curiouser and curiouser, thought Wimsey. If the man who left the paper in the bell-chamber was the same man who buried the body, then either he took *all* the Rector's keys, or he had access to *two* sets, and those two sets had to be Jack Godfrey's (for the key of the counterpoise) and Gotobed's (for the key of the crypt). And if the man had been Cranton, then how did he *know*? Of course, the criminal might have brought his own spade (though that added to the complication). If so he must have had either the Rector's keys or Jack Godfrey's. Wimsey went round to the back and got hold of Emily and Hinkins. They were both quite sure that they had never seen the man who called himself Stephen Driver inside the Rectory gates, much less inside the Rector's study, which was the proper place for the keys when they were in their proper place.

'But they weren't there at all, my lord,' said Emily, 'because, if you remember, they keys was missing on New Year's night, and it wasn't till near a week after we found them in the vestry — bar the key of the church porch and that was in the lock where Rector left it after choir-practice.'

'After choir-practice? On the Saturday?'

'That's right,' said Hinkins. 'Only, don't you remember, Emily, Rector said it couldn't have been him as left it, because it was gone a-missing, and he didn't have it, on Saturday and had to wait for Harry Gotobed?'

'Well, I don't know,' said Emily, 'but that's where it was. Harry Gotobed said he found it there when he went to ring for Early Service.'

More confused than ever, Wimsey trotted back to the study window. Mr Venables, arrested with a carrying-figure at the tip of his pen, was at first not very clear in his recollection, but said presently that he believed Emily was right.

'I must have left the keys in the vestry the week before,' he suggested, 'and whoever left the church last after choir-practice must have found the church key and used it — but who that would be, I don't know, unless it was Gotobed. Yes, it would be Gotobed, because he would wait behind to make up the stoves. But it was funny that he should leave the key in the lock. Dear me! You don't think it could have been the murderer, do you?'

'I do, indeed,' said Wimsey.

'There now!' exclaimed the Rector. 'But if I left the keys in the vestry, how did he get in to find them? He couldn't get in without the church key. Unless he came to choir-practice. Surely, nobody belonging to the choir — '

The Rector looked horribly distressed. Wimsey hastened to comfort him.

'The door would be unlocked during choir-practice. He might have slipped in then.'

'Oh, yes — of course! How stupid I am! No doubt that is what occurred. You have relieved my mind very much.'

Wimsey had not, however, relieved his own mind. As he resumed his way to the church, he turned the matter over. If the keys had been taken on New Year's Eve, then Cranton had not taken them. Cranton had not arrived till New Year's Day. Will Thoday had come, unnecessarily, to the Rectory on December 30th, and might have taken the keys then, but he had certainly not been in the church on the night of January 4th to restore them. It remained possible that Will Thoday had taken the keys and the mysterious James Thoday had returned them — but in that case, what was Cranton doing in the business? And Wimsey felt sure that Cranton knew something about the paper found in the bell-chamber.

Meditating, thus, Wimsey let himself into the church, and, unlocking the door in the tower, made his way up the spiral stair. As he passed through the ringing-chamber, he noticed with a smile that a new board had made its appearance on the wall, announcing that: 'On New Year's morning, 19 — , a peal of 15,840 Kent Treble Bob Major was Rung in 9 Hours and 15 Minutes, the Ringers being: Treble, Ezra Wilderspin; 2, Peter D. B. Wimsey; 3, Walter Pratt; 4, Henry Gotobed; 5, Joseph Hinkins; 6, Alfred Donnington; 7, John P. Godfrey; Tenor, Hezekiah Lavender; Theodore Venables, Rector, assisting. Our Mouths shall shew forth Thy Praise.' He passed up through the great, bare clock-chamber, released the counterpoise and climbed again till he came out beneath the bells. There he stood for a moment, gazing up into their black mouths while his eyes grew accustomed to the semi-darkness. Presently their hooded silence oppressed him. A vague vertigo seized him. He felt as though they were slowly collapsing together and coming down upon him. Spellbound, he spoke their names: Gaude, Sabaoth, John, Jericho, Jubilee, Dimity, Batty Thomas and Tailor Paul. A soft and whispering echo seemed to start from the walls and die stealthily among the beams. Suddenly he shouted in a great voice: 'Tailor Paul!' and he must somehow have hit upon a harmonic of the scale, for a faint brazen note answered him, remote and menacing, from overhead.

'Come!' said Wimsey, pulling himself together, 'this won't do. I'm getting as bad as Potty Peake, coming here and talking to the bells. Let's find the ladder and get to work.'

He switched on his torch and turned it on the dim corners of the belfry. It showed him the ladder, and it showed him something else also. In the gloomiest and dustiest corner of the floor, there was a patch that was not so dusty. He stepped forward eagerly, the menace of the bells forgotten. Yes, there was no mistake. A portion of the floor had at some fairly recent time been scrubbed, for the dust which in other places lay centuries thick was here only a thin film.

He knelt to examine it, and new thoughts went swooping and turning through his brain like bats. Why should anybody trouble to swab the floor of a belfry, unless to remove some very sinister stain. He saw Cranton and Legros climbing to the belfry, with the cipher in their hands for guidance. He saw the green glint of the jewels, dragged from their old hiding-place in the light of the lantern. He saw the sudden leap, the brutal blow, and the blood gushing to the floor, the cipher fluttering, unheeded, into a corner. And then the murderer, trembling and glancing over his shoulder, as he snatched the emeralds from dead fingers, took up the body and stumbled panting down the creaking ladders. The sexton's spade from the crypt, the bucket and scrubbing-brush from the vestry, or wherever they were kept, the water from the well —

There he stopped. The well? The well meant the rope, and what had the rope to do with this? Had it been used merely as a convenient means to carry the corpse? But the experts had been so sure that the victim had been bound before he was dead. And besides, there were the blow and the blood. It was all very well making horrible pictures for one's self, but there had been no blow till the man had been dead too long to leave any pool of blood. And if there was no blood, why scrub the floor?

He sat back on his heels and looked up again to the bells. If their tongues could speak, they could tell him what they had seen, but they had neither speech nor language. Disappointed, he again took up the torch and searched further. Then he broke out into a harsh and disgusted laughter. The whole cause of the mystery revealed itself absurdly. An empty quart beer-bottle lay there, rolled into an obscure place behind a quantity of worm-eaten beams that were stacked against the wall. Here was a pretty ending to his dreams! Some unlicensed trespasser on consecrated ground — or possibly some workman legitimately engaged in repairs to the bell-cage — had spilt his beer and had tidily removed the stains, while the bottle, rolling out of sight, had been forgotten. No doubt that was all. Yet a lingering suspicion caused Wimsey to take up the bottle very carefully, by means of a finger inserted into the neck. It was not very dusty. It could not, he thought, have lain there long. It would bear somebody's finger-prints — perhaps.

He examined the rest of the floor, very carefully, but could find only a few jumbled footprints in the dust — large, male prints, he thought. They might be Jack Godfrey's or Hezekiah Lavender's, or anybody's. Then he took the ladder and made an exhaustive search of the bells and timbers. He found nothing. No secret mark. No hiding-place. And nothing whatever suggestive of fairies or elephants, enchanters or Erebus. After several dirty and fatiguing hours, he descended again, carrying the bottle as his sole reward.

★ ★ ★

Curiously enough, it was the Rector who solved the cipher. He came into the schoolroom that night as the hall-clock struck eleven, thoughtfully bearing a glass of hot toddy in one hand and an old-fashioned foot-muff in the other.

'I do hope you are not working yourself to death,' he said, apologetically. 'I have ventured to bring a little comfort for the inner man. These nights of early summer are so chilly. And my wife thinks you might like to put your feet in this. There is always a draught under that door. Allow me — it is slightly moth-eaten, I fear, but still affords protection. Now, you must not let me disturb you. Dear me! What is that? Are you pricking out a peal? Oh, no — I see they are letters, not figures. My eyesight is not as good as it was. But I am rudely prying into your affairs.'

'Not a bit, padre. It does look rather like a peal. It's still this wretched cipher. Finding that the number of letters formed a multiple of eight, I had written it out in eight columns, hoping forlornly that something might come of it. Now you mention it, I suppose one might make a simple sort of cipher out of a set of changes.'

'How could you do that?'

'Well, by taking the movements of one bell and writing the letters of your message in the appropriate places and then filling up the places of the other bells with arbitraries. For instance. Take a

281

Plain Course of Grandsire Doubles,[1] and suppose you want to convey the simple and pious message 'Come and worship'. You would select one bell to carry the significants — let us say, No. 5. Then you would write out the beginning of your plain course, and wherever No. 5 came you would put one letter of your message. Look.'

1 2 3 4 5 6	
2 1 3 5 4 6	. . . C . .
2 3 1 4 5 6	. . . . O .
3 2 4 1 5 6	. . . . M .
3 4 2 5 1 6	. . . E . .
4 3 5 2 1 6	. . A . . .
4 5 3 1 2 6	. N . . . .
5 4 1 3 2 6	D . . . . .
5 1 4 2 3 6	W . . . . .
1 5 2 4 3 6	. O . . . .
1 2 5 3 4 6	. . R . . .
2 1 5 4 3 6	. . S . . .
2 5 1 3 4 6	. H . . . .
5 2 3 1 4 6	I . . . . .
5 3 2 4 1 6	P . . . . .
etc.	

He rapidly scribbled down the two columns:

'Then you could fill up the other places with any sort of nonsense letters — say XLOCMP, JQIWON, NAEMMB, TSHEZP, and so on. Then you would write the whole thing out in one paragraph, dividing it so as to look like words.'

'Why?' inquired the Rector.

'Oh, just to make it more difficult. You could

---

[1] 'Doubles' is the name given to a set of changes rung on 5 bells, the tenor (No. 6) being rung last or 'behind' in each change.

write, for example, 'XLOC MPJQI. WON NAE M MBTS! HEZP?' and so on to the end. It wouldn't matter what you did. The man who received the message and had the key would simply divide the letters into six columns again, run his pencil along the course of No. 5 and read the message.'

'Dear me!' said Mr Venables, 'so he would! How very ingenious. And I suppose that with a little further ingenuity, the cipher might be made to convey some superficial and misleading information. I see, for instance, that you already have the word WON and the Scotch expression NAE. Could not the idea be extended further, so that the entire message might appear completely innocuous?'

'Of course it could. It might look like this.' Wimsey flicked Jean Legros's communication with his finger.

'Have you — ? But pardon me. I am unwarrantably interfering. Still — have you tried this method on the cryptogram?'

'Well, I haven't,' admitted Wimsey. 'I've only just thought of it. Besides, what would be the good of sending a message like that to Cranton, who probably knows nothing about bell-ringing? And it would take a bell-ringer to write it, and we have no reason to suppose that Jean Legros was a ringer. It is true,' he added thoughtfully, 'that we have no reason to suppose he was not.'

'Well, then,' said the Rector. 'Why not try? You told me, I think, that this paper was picked up in the belfry. Might not the person to whom it was sent, though not himself a ringer and not knowing how to interpret it, have connected it in his mind with the bells and supposed that the key was to be found in the belfry? No doubt I am very foolish, but it appears to me to be possible.'

Wimsey struck his hand on the table.

'Padre, that's an idea! When Cranton came to Fenchurch St Paul, he asked for Paul Taylor, because Deacon had told him that Tailor Paul or Batty Thomas knew where the emeralds were. Come on. Have at it. We'll ask Tailor Paul ourselves.'

He picked up the paper on which he had already written the cryptogram in eight columns.

'We don't know what method the fellow used, or which bell to follow. But we'll take it that the bell is either Batty Thomas or Tailor Paul. If the method is Grandsire Triples, it can't be Tailor Paul, for the Tenor would be rung behind the whole way and we should find the message running down the last column. And it's not likely to be Grandsire Major, because you never ring that method here. Let us try Batty Thomas. What does the 7th bell give us? GHILSTETHCWA. That's not very encouraging. For form's sake we'll try the other bells. No. No. No. Could the man possibly have started off with a bob or single?'

'Surely not.'

'Well, you never know. He's not pricking a peal, he's only making a cipher and he might do something unusual on purpose.'

His pencil traced the letter again.

'No. I can't make anything of it. Wash out

Grandsires. And I think we can probably wash out Stedman's, too — that would keep the significants too close together. Try Kent Treble Bob, and we'll take Tailor Paul first, since the Tenor is the usual observation bell for that method. She starts in the 7th place, H. Then 8th place, E. Back to 7th, S; to 6th, I; to 5th, T. 'HESIT.' Well, it's pronounceable, at any rate. Dodge up into 6ths place, T again. Down to 5th, E; to 4th, T; to 3rds, H. 'HESITTETH.' Hullo, padre! we've got two words, anyhow. 'He sitteth.' Perhaps 'He' is the necklace. We'll carry on with this.'

The Rector, his glasses sliding down his long nose with excitement, pored over the paper as the pencil made its rapid way down the letters.

' 'He sitteth between' — it's part of a verse from Psalm xcix — there, what did I tell you? 'He sitteth between the cherubims.' Now, what can that mean? Oh, dear! there is some mistake — the next letter should be a B — 'be the earth never so unquiet.' '

'Well, it isn't a B; it's another T. There isn't a B anywhere. Wait a moment. THE is coming — no, THEI — no, as you were. It's THE ISLES. I can't help it, padre. It couldn't come like that by accident. Just a second, and we'll have it all sorted out and then you can say what you like . . . Oy! what's happened here at the end? Oh, dash it! I was forgetting. This must be the end of the lead. Yes' — he calculated rapidly — 'it is, and we've got to make the 3rds and 4ths. There you are. Message complete; and what it means is more than I can tell you.'

The Rector polished his glasses and stared.

'It's verses from three psalms,' he said. 'Most singular. 'He sitteth between the cherubims'; that's Ps. xcix. 1. Then 'The isles may be glad thereof'; that's Ps. xcvii. 1. Both those psalms begin alike: 'Dominus regnavit', 'The Lord is King'. And then we get, 'as the rivers in the south'. That's Ps. cxxvi. 5, 'In convertendo', 'When the Lord turned the captivity of Sion'. This is a case of *obscurum per obscuriora* — the interpretation is even more perplexing than the cipher.'

'Yes,' said Wimsey. 'Perhaps the figures have something to do with it. We have 99.1. 97.1.126. 5. Are they to be taken as one figure 9919711265? or to be left as they are? or re-divided? The permutations are almost endless. Or perhaps they ought to be added. Or converted into letters on some system we haven't discovered yet. It can't be a simple a=1 substitution. I refuse to believe in a message that runs IIAIGIABFE. I shall have to wrestle with this quite a lot more. But you have been simply marvellous, padre. You ought to take to deciphering codes as a profession.'

'It was pure accident,' said Mr Venables, simply, 'and due entirely to my failing vision. That is a curious thing. It has given me the idea for a sermon about evil being overruled for good. But I should never have thought of the possibility that one might make a cipher out of change-ringing. Most ingenious.'

```
I THOUGHT       L Y C L O U D B       N Y T E A R S B
T O S E E T H E  U T N O B L I N      E F O R E T H E
F A I R I E S I  D E Y E O F A M      T H I N M O O N
N T H E F I E L  O R T A L W A S      R O S E U P F R
D S B U T I S A  P E R M I T T E      A I L A N D F A
W O N L Y T H E  D T O S P Y T H      I N T A S A S I
E V I L E L E P  E M S O T H E N      C K L E O P S T
H A N T S W I T  C A M E M I N S      R A W N O W T H
H T H E I R B L  T R E L S H A V      O U G H T H E E
A C K B A C K S  I N G G O L D T      N C H A N T E R
W O E H O W T H  R U M P E T S H      G N A S H H I S
A T S I G H T A  A R P S A N D D      T E E T H V A I
W E D M E T H E  R U M S T H E S      N L Y Y E T S H
E L V E S D A N  E P L A Y E D V      A L L H E R E T
C E D A L L A R  E R Y L O U D L      U R N A S T H E
O U N D A N D A  Y B E S I D E M      S P R I N G R E
B O U T W H I L  E B R E A K I N      T U R N S O H W
E I H E A R D V  G T H A T S P E      R E T C H E D M
O I C E S C A L  L L S O T H E D      A N H E L L G A
L I N G C L E A  R E A M V A N I      P E S E R E B U
R L Y X H H O W  S H E D W H E R      S N O W L I E S
I T R I E D T O  E A T I T H A N      O P E N T H E M
S E E T H R O W  K E D H E A V E      O U T H S O F D
O F F T H E U G  N I S H E D M A      E A T H W A I T
                                      O N T H Y E N D
```

'It could have been done still more ingeniously,' said Wimsey, 'I can think of lots of ways to improve it. Suppose — but I won't waste time with supposing. The point is, what the dickens is one to do with 99. 1.97.1. 126. 5?'

He clutched his head between his hands, and the Rector, after watching him for a few minutes, tiptoed away to bed.

the ninth part

EMILY TURNS BUNTER FROM BEHIND

Let the bell that the Treble turns from behind make thirds place, and return behind again.
Rules for Change-Making on Four Bells

'I should like,' panted Emily between her sobs, 'to give my week's warning.'

'Good gracious, Emily,' cried Mrs Venables, pausing as she passed through the kitchen with a pail of chicken-feed, 'what on earth is the matter with you?'

'I'm sure,' said Emily, 'I ain't got no fault to find with you and Rector as has always been that kind, but if I'm to be spoken to so by Mr Bunter, which I'm not his servant and never want to be and ain't no part of my duties, and anyway how was I to know? I'm sure I'd have cut my right hand off rather than disoblige his lordship, but I did ought to have been told and it ain't my fault and so I told Mr Bunter.'

Mrs Venables turned a little pale. Lord Peter presented no difficulties, but Bunter she found rather alarming. But she was of the bulldog breed, and had been brought up in the knowledge that a servant was a servant, and that to be afraid of a servant (one's own or anybody else's) was the first step to an Avernus of domestic inefficiency.

She turned to Bunter, standing white and awful in the background.

'Well now, Bunter,' she said firmly. 'What is all this trouble about?'

'I beg your pardon, madam,' said Bunter in a stifled manner. 'I fear that I forgot myself. But I have been in his lordship's service now for going on fifteen years (counting my service under him in the war), and such a thing has never yet befallen me. In the sudden shock and the bitter mortification of my mind, I spoke with considerable heat. I beg, madam, that you will overlook it. I should have controlled myself better. I assure you that it will not occur again.'

Mrs Venables put down the chicken-pail.

'But what was it all about?'

Emily gulped, and Bunter pointed a tragic finger at a beer-bottle which stood on the kitchen table.

'That bottle, madam, was entrusted to me yesterday by his lordship. I placed it in a cupboard in my bedroom, with the intention of photographing it this morning, before despatching it to Scotland Yard. Yesterday evening, it seems that this young woman entered the room during my absence, investigated the cupboard and removed the bottle. Not content with removing it, she dusted it.'

'If you please, 'm,' said Emily, 'how was I to know it was wanted? A nasty, dirty old thing. I was only adusting the room, 'm, and I see this old bottle on the cupboard shelf, and I says to myself, 'Look at that dusty old bottle, why however did that get there? It must have got left accidental.' So I takes it down and when Cook sees it she says, 'Why, whatever have you got there, Emily? That'll just do,' she says, 'to put the methylated.' So I gives it a dust — '

'And now the finger-prints have all gone,' concluded Bunter in a hollow tone, 'and what to say to his lordship I do not know.'

'Oh, dear! oh dear!' said Mrs Venables, helplessly. Then she seized on the one point of domestic economy which seemed to call for inquiry. 'How did you come to leave your dusting so late?'

'If you please, 'm, I don't know how it was. I got all behind yesterday, somehow, and I said to myself, 'Better late than never,' and I'm sure if I'd only have known — '

She wept loudly, and Bunter was touched.

'I am sorry I expressed myself with so much acerbity,' he said, 'and I take blame to myself for not removing the key from the cupboard door. But you will understand my feelings, madam, when I think of his lordship innocently waking to a new day, if I may say so, and not knowing of the blow which is in store for him. It goes to my heart, if you will pardon my mentioning the organ in such a connection. There, madam, is his morning tea, only waiting for my hand to put the boiling water to it, and I feel, madam, as though it were the hand of a murderer which no perfumes of Arabia — supposing such to be suitable to my situation — could sweeten. He has rung twice,' added Bunter, in desperate tones, 'and he will know by the delay that something of a calamitous nature has occurred — '

'Bunter!'

'My lord!' cried Bunter, in a voice like prayer.

'What the devil has happened to my tea? What the — ? Oh, I beg your pardon, Mrs Venables. Excuse my language and my bath-robe, won't you? I didn't know you were here.'

'Oh, Lord Peter!' exclaimed Mrs Venables, 'such a dreadful thing's happened. Your man is so terribly upset, and this silly girl — she meant well, of course, and it's all a mistake — but we've dusted all the finger-prints off your bottle!'

'Wah-ha-ha!' sobbed Emily. 'O-oh! Wah-ha-ha! I did it. I dusted it. I didn't know — ho-ho.'

'Bunter,' said his lordship, 'what is the verse about the struck eagle stretched upon the plain, Never through something clouds to soar again? It expresses my feelings exactly. Take up my tea and throw the bottle in the dustbin. What's done cannot be undone. In any case the finger-prints were probably of no importance. William Morris once wrote a poem called *The Man Who Never Laughed Again*. If the shout of them that triumph, the song of them that feast, should never again be heard upon my lips, you will know why. My friends will probably be devoutly thankful. Let it be a warning to you never to seek for happiness out of a bottle. Emily, if you cry any more, your young man won't know you from Sunday. Don't worry about the bottle Mrs Venables — it was a beastly bottle, anyhow, and I always loathed the sight of it. It is a beautiful morning for early rising. Allow me to carry the chicken-pail. I beg you will not give another thought to the bottle, or Emily either. She's a particularly nice girl, isn't she? What's her surname, by the way?'

'Holliday,' said Mrs Venables. 'She's a niece of Russell's, the undertaker, you know, and some sort of relation to Mary Thoday, though of course, everybody is, in this village, related to somebody or the other, I mean. It comes of being such a small place, though now that they all have motor-bicycles and the buses running twice a week it isn't so bad, and there won't be so many unfortunate creatures like Potty Peake. All the Russells are very nice, superior people.'

'Just so,' said Lord Peter Wimsey. He did a certain amount of thinking as he spooned out mash into the chicken-trough.

★   ★   ★

He spent the early part of the morning in fresh unavailing study of the cryptogram, and as soon as he thought the pubs would be open, went round to the Red Cow for a pint of beer.

'Bitter, my lord?' inquired Mr Donnington with his hand upon the tap.

Wimsey said No, not today. He would have a bottle of Bass for a change.

Mr Donnington produced the Bass, observing that his lordship would find it in very nice condition.

'Condition is nine-tenths of the bottle,' said Wimsey, 'and a lot of it depends upon the bottling. Who are your bottlers?'

'Griggs of Walbeach,' said Mr Donnington. 'Very sound people they are, too; I've got no complaints to make. Just you try for yourself

293

— though you can tell by the look of it, if you see what I mean. Clear as a bell — though, of course, you have to be able to trust your cellarman. I had a chap once that never could be taught not to pack his Bass 'ead down in the basket, same as if it was stout. Now stout will stand being stood on its 'ead, though it's not a thing I ever would do myself and I don't recommend it, but Bass *must* be stood right ways up and not shook about, if you're to do justice to the beer.'

'Very true indeed,' said Wimsey. 'There's certainly nothing wrong with this. Your health. Won't you take something yourself?'

'Thank you, my lord, I don't mind if I do. Here's luck. Now, that,' said Mr Donnington, raising the glass to the light, 'is as nice a glass of Bass as you could wish to see.'

Wimsey asked whether he did much with quart bottles.

'Quarts?' said Mr Donnington. 'No. Not with quarts, I don't. But I believe Tom Tebbutt down at the Wheatsheaf does a bit. Griggs bottles for him, too.'

'Ah!' said Wimsey.

'Yes. There's one or two prefers quarts. Though, mind you, most of the business about here is draught. But there's a farmer here and there as likes the quarts delivered at their homes. Ah! in the old days they all did their own brewing — there's plenty farms now with the big brewing coppers still standing, and there's a few as still cures their own sides of bacon — Mr Ashton's one on 'em, he won't have nothing new-fangled. But what with these chain stores and their grocery vans, and the girls all wanting to be off to the pictures in their silk stockings and so many things coming in tins, it's not many places where you can see a bit of real home-cured. And look at the price of pig-feed. What I say is, the farmers did ought to have some protection. I was brought up a Free Trader myself, but times has changed. I don't know if you've ever thought of these things, my lord. They may not come your way. Or — there — I'm forgetting. Maybe you sit in the 'Ouse of Lords, now. Harry Gotobed will have it that that's so, but I said he was mistook — but there! you'll know better than me about that.'

Wimsey explained that he was not qualified to sit in the House of Lords. Mr Donnington observed with pleasure that in that case the sexton owed him half-a-crown, and while he made a note of the fact on the back of an envelope, Wimsey escaped and made his way to the Wheatsheaf.

Here, by exercising a certain amount of tact, he obtained a list of those households to which Bass was regularly supplied in quarts. Most of those names were those farmers in outlying places, but as an afterthought, Mrs Tebbutt mentioned one which made Wimsey prick up his ears.

'Will Thoday, he had a few while Jim was at home — a dozen or so, it might be. He's a nice chap, is Jim Thoday — makes you laugh by the hour telling his tales of foreign parts. He brought back that there parrot for Mary, though as I says

295

to her, that bird ain't no proper example for the children. How it do go on, to be sure. I'm sure, if you'd heard what it said to Rector the other day! I didn't know where to look. But it's my belief, Rector didn't understand half of it. He's a real gentleman, is Mr Venables, not like old parson. He was a kind man, too, but different from Rector, and they say he used to swear something surprising in a clergyman. But there, poor man! He had a bit of a weakness, as they say. 'Do as I say, don't do as I do' — that's what he used to say in his sermons. Terrible red in the face he were, and died sudden, of a stroke.'

Wimsey tried in vain to steer the conversation back to Jim Thoday. Mrs Tebbutt was fairly launched into reminiscences of Old Rector, and it was half an hour before he was able to make his way out of the Wheatsheaf. Turning back towards the Rectory, he found himself at Will Thoday's gate. Glancing up the path, he saw Mary, engaged in hanging out washing. He suddenly determined on a frontal attack.

'I hope you'll forgive me, Mrs Thoday,' he said, when he had announced himself and been invited to enter, 'if I take your mind back to a rather painful episode. I mean to say, bygones are bygones and all that and one hates digging anything up, what? But when it comes to dead bodies in other people's graves and so on, well, sometimes one gets pondering about them and all that sort of thing, don't you know.'

'Yes, indeed, my lord. I'm sure if there's anything I can do to help, I will. But as I told Mr Blundell, I never knew a thing about it, and I can't imagine how it came there. That was the Saturday night he was asking me about, and I'm sure I've thought and thought, but I couldn't call to mind as I'd seen anything.'

'Do you remember a man who called himself Stephen Driver?'

'Yes, my lord. Him that was at Ezra Wilderspin's. I remember seeing him once or twice. They said at the inquest that the body might have been him.'

'But it wasn't,' said Wimsey.

'Wasn't it, my lord?'

'No. Because we've found this chap Driver and he's still alive and kicking. Had you ever seen Driver before he came here?'

'I don't think so, my lord; no, I can't say as I ever did.'

'He didn't remind you of anybody?'

'No, my lord.'

She appeared to be answering quite frankly, and he could not see any signs of alarm in voice or expression.

'That's odd,' said Wimsey, 'because he says that he ran away from St Paul because he thought you had recognised him.'

'Did he? Well, that's a strange thing, my lord.'

'Did you ever hear him speak?'

'I don't think I ever did, my lord.'

'Suppose he hadn't been wearing a beard, now — would he remind you of anybody?'

Mary shook her head. Like most people, she found the effort of imagination beyond her.

'Well, do you recognise this?'

He took out a photograph of Cranton, taken

at the time of the Wilbraham emeralds affair.

'That?' Mrs Thoday turned pale. 'Oh, yes, my lord. I remember him. That was Cranton, that took the necklace and was sent to prison same time as — as my first husband, my lord. I expect you know all about that. That's his wicked face. Oh, dear! it's given me quite a turn, seeing that again.'

She sat down on a bench and stared at the photograph.

'This isn't — it couldn't be Driver?'

'That's Driver,' said Wimsey. 'You had no idea of it?'

'That I never had, my lord. If I'd ever had such a thought, I'd have spoken to him, don't you fear! I'd have got out of him where he put those emeralds too. You see, my lord, that was what went so hard against my poor husband, this man saying as my husband had kept the necklace himself. Poor Jeff, there's no doubt he was tempted — all through my fault, my lord, talking so free — and he did take the jewels, I'm sorry to say. But he didn't have them afterwards. It was this Cranton had them all the time. Don't you think it hasn't been a bitter hard cross to me, my lord, all these years, knowing as I was suspected? The jury believed what I said, and so did the judge, but you'll find some as thinks now that I had a hand in it and knew where the necklace was. But I never did, my lord, never. If I'd been able to find it, I'd have crawled to London on my hands and knees to give it back to Mrs Wilbraham. I know what poor Sir Henry suffered with the loss of it. The police searched our place, and I searched it myself, over and over — '

'Couldn't you take Deacon's word for it?' asked Wimsey, softly.

She hesitated, and her eyes clouded with pain.

'My lord, I did believe him. And yet, all the same — well! it was such a terrible shock to me that he could have done such a thing as to rob a lady in the master's house, I didn't know but what he mightn't perhaps have done the other too. I didn't rightly know what to believe, if you understand me, my lord. But *now* I feel quite sure that my husband was telling the truth. He was led away by this wicked Cranton, there's no doubt of that, but that he was deceiving us all, afterwards, I don't believe. Indeed, my lord, I don't think he was — I'm quite sure of it in my own mind.'

'And what do you suppose Cranton came down here for?'

'Doesn't that show, my lord, that it was him as hid them after all? He must have got frightened and hid them away in some place that night, before he got away.'

'He says himself that Deacon told him in the dock that the emeralds were here, and he was to ask Tailor Paul and Batty Thomas to find them for him.'

Mary shook her head. 'I don't understand that, my lord. But if my husband had said such a thing to him then, Cranton wouldn't have kept quiet about it. He'd have told the jury, he was that mad with Jeff.'

'Would he? I'm not so sure. Suppose Deacon

299

told Cranton where to find the emeralds, don't you think Cranton would have waited in the hope of getting hold of them when he came out of prison? And mightn't he have come down here last January to look for them? And then, thinking you'd spotted him, mightn't he have run away in a fright?'

'Well, my lord, I suppose he might. But then, who would that poor dead man be?'

'The police think he may have been an accomplice of Cranton's, who helped him to find the emeralds and was killed for his pains. Do you know whether Deacon made any friends among the other convicts or the warders at Maidstone?'

'I couldn't say, I'm sure, my lord. He was allowed to write now and again, of course, but naturally he wouldn't tell anybody a thing like that, because his letters would be read.'

'Naturally. I wondered whether perhaps you'd had a message from him at some time — through a released prisoner, or anything like that?'

'No, my lord, never.'

'Have you ever seen this writing?'

He handed her the cryptogram.

'That writing? Why, of course — '

'Shut up, you fool! Shut up, you bloody fool! Come on, Joey! Show a leg there!'

'Good lord!' exclaimed Wimsey, startled. Peering round the door into the inner room, he encountered the bright eye of a grey African parrot fixed knowingly upon him. At sight of a stranger, the bird stopped talking, cocked its head aslant, and began to sidle along its perch.

'Damn your eyes!' said his lordship, pleasantly. 'You made me jump.'

'Aw!' said the bird, with a long, self-satisfied chuckle.

'Is that the bird your brother-in-law gave you? I've heard about him from Mrs Tebbutt.'

'Yes, my lord, that's him. He's a wonderful talker, but he does swear and that's the truth.'

'I've no use for a parrot that doesn't,' said Wimsey. 'Seems unnatural. Let me see — what were we — ? Oh, yes, that bit of writing. You were just saying — '

'I said, of course I'd never seen it before, my lord.'

Wimsey could have sworn that she had been going to say just the opposite. She was looking at — no, not at, but through and past him, with the face of someone who sees an incredible catastrophe approaching.

'It's queer-looking stuff, isn't it?' she went on, in a flat voice, 'don't seem to mean anything. What made you think I should know anything about the like of that?'

'We had an idea that it might have been written by some man your late husband knew at Maidstone. Did you ever hear of anyone called Jean Legros?'

'No, my lord. That's a French name, isn't it? I've never seen a Frenchman, except a few of those Beljums that came over here in the war.'

'And you never knew anyone called Paul Taylor?'

'No, never.'

The parrot laughed heartily.

301

'Shut up, Joey!'

'Shut up, you fool! Joey, Joey, Joey! Scratch a poll, then. Aw!'

'Oh, well,' said Wimsey. 'I just wondered.'

'Where did that come from?'

'What? Oh, this? It was picked up in the church, and we had an idea it might be Cranton's. But he says it isn't, you know.'

'In the *church*?'

As though the words were a cue, the parrot picked it up, and began muttering excitedly:

'Must go to church. Must go to church. The bells. Don't tell Mary. Must go to church. Aw! Joey! Joey! Come on, Joey! Must go to church.'

Mrs Thoday stepped hurriedly into the other room and flung a cloth over the cage, while Joey squawked protestingly.

'He goes on like that,' she said. 'Gets on my nerves. He picked it up the night Will was so bad. They were ringing the peal, and it worried him, like, that he couldn't be there. Will gets that angry with Joey when he starts mocking him. Shut up, now, Joey, do.'

Wimsey held out his hand for the cryptogram, which Mary surrendered — reluctantly, he thought, and as though her thoughts were elsewhere.

'Well, I mustn't bother you any more, Mrs Thoday. I just wanted to clear up that little point about Cranton. I expect you are right after all, and he just came down here to snoop about on his own. Well, you aren't likely to be bothered with him again. He's ill, and in any case, he'll have to go back to prison to work out his time.

Forgive my bargin' along and botherin' you about what's best forgotten.'

But all the way back to the Rectory, he was haunted by Mary Thoday's eyes and by the hoarse muttering voice of the parrot: 'The bells! the bells! Must go to the church! Don't tell Mary!'

Superintendent Blundell clicked his tongue a good deal over all this.

'It's a pity about the bottle,' he said. 'Don't suppose it would have told us anything, but you never know. Emily Holliday, eh? Of course, she's a cousin of Mary Thoday's. I'd forgotten that. That woman beats me — Mary, I mean. Damned if I know what to make of her, or her husband either. We're in touch with those people at Hull, and they're arranging to get James Thoday shipped back to England as soon as possible. We told them he might be wanted as a witness. Best way to work it — he can't skip his orders; or if he does, we'll know there's something wrong and go after him. It's a queer business altogether. As regards that cipher, what do you say to sending it along to the Governor of Maidstone? If this fellow Legros or Taylor or whatever he is was ever in there, they may be able to spot the handwriting.'

'So they may,' said Wimsey, thoughtfully. 'Yes, we'll do that. And I'm hoping we'll hear from M. Rozier again soon. The French haven't any of our inhibitions about dealing with witnesses.'

'Lucky them, my lord,' replied Mr Blundell, with fervour.

the tenth part

LORD PETER IS CALLED WRONG

And he set the cherubims within the inner house: and they stretched forth the wings of the cherubims.

1 Kings vi. 27

And above were costly stones.

1 Kings vii. 11

'I hope,' said the Rector on the following Sunday morning, 'there is nothing wrong with the Thodays. Neither Will nor Mary was at Early Service. I've never known them both miss before, except when he was ill.'

'No more they were,' said Mrs Venables. 'Perhaps Will has taken a chill again. These winds are very treacherous. Lord Peter, do have another sausage. How are you getting along with your cipher?'

'Don't rub it in, I'm hopelessly stuck.'

'I shouldn't worry,' said Mr Venables. 'Even if you have to lie still a whole pull now and again, you'll soon find yourself back in the hunt.'

'I wouldn't mind that,' said Wimsey. 'It's lying behind the whole way that gets on my nerves.'

'There's always something that lies behind a mystery,' said the Rector, mildly enjoying his little witticism. 'A solution of some kind.'

'What I say is,' observed Mrs Venables darkly, 'there are always wheels within wheels.'

'And where there's a wheel there's usually a rope,' added his lordship.

'Unhappily,' said the Rector, and there was a melancholy pause.

★   ★   ★

Anxiety about the Thodays was somewhat allayed by their appearance together at Matins, but Wimsey thought he had never seen two people look so ill and unhappy. In wondering about them, he lost all consciousness of what was going on about him, sat down for the Venite, lost the Psalms for the day, embarked on a loud and solitary 'For thine is the Kingdom' at the end of the second 'Our Father,' and only pulled himself together when Mr Venables came down to preach his sermon. As usual, Mr Gotobed had failed to sweep the chancel properly, and a hideous crunching of coke proclaimed the Rector's passage to the pulpit. The Invocation was pronounced, and Wimsey sank back with a sigh of relief into the corner of the pew, folded his arms and fixed his gaze firmly on the roof.

'Who hast exalted thine only son with great triumph into the Heavens. Those words are from the collect for the day. What do they mean to us? What picture do we make of the glory and triumph of Heaven? Last Thursday we prayed that we also might in heart and mind thither ascend and continually dwell, and we hope that after death we shall be admitted — not only in heart and mind but in soul and body — to that blessed state where cherubim and seraphim continually sing their songs of praise. It is a beautiful description that the Bible gives us — the crystal sea and the Lord sitting between the cherubims, and the angels with their harps and crowns of gold, as the old craftsmen imagined them when they built this beautiful roof that we are so proud of — but do we, do you and I really believe — ?'

It was hopeless. Wimsey's thoughts were far away again. 'He rode upon the cherubim and did fly. He sitteth between the cherubims.' He was suddenly reminded of the little architect who had come down to advise about the church roof at Duke's Denver. 'You see, your Grace, the rot has got into the timbers; there are holes behind those cherrybims you could put your hand in.' *He sitteth between the cherubims.* Why, of course! Fool that he was — climbing up among the bells to look for cherubims when they were here over his head, gazing down at him, their blank golden eyes blind with excess of light. The cherubim? Nave and aisle were thick with cherubim, as autumn leaves in Vallombrosa. Nave and aisle — 'the *isles* may be glad thereof' — and then the third text — 'as the rivers in the *south.*' Between the cherubims in the south aisle — what could be clearer than that? In his excitement he nearly shot out of his seat. It only remained to discover which particular pair of cherubims was concerned, and that ought not to be very difficult. The emeralds themselves would be gone, of course, but if one could find even the

306

empty hiding place, that would prove that the cryptogram was connected with the necklace and that all the queer tragedy brooding over Fenchurch St Paul was in some way connected with the emeralds too. Then, if the handwriting of the cryptogram could be traced back to Maidstone Gaol and to Jean Legros they would know who Legros was, and with luck they would also link him up with Cranton. After that, if Cranton could escape from the murder charge, he would be a lucky man.

Over the Sunday beef and Yorkshire pudding, Wimsey tackled the Rector.

'How long ago was it, sir, that you took away the galleries from the aisles?'

'Let me see,' said Mr Venables, 'about ten years ago, I think. Yes, that is right. Ten years. Hideous, cumbersome things they were. They ran right across the aisle windows, obscuring all the upper tracery and blocking the light, and were attached to the arcading. As a matter of fact, what with those horrible great pews, like bathing machines, sprouting up from the floor, and the heavy galleries, you could scarcely see the shafts of the pillars at all.'

'Or anything else,' said his wife. 'I always used to say it was regular blind man's holiday underneath those galleries.'

'If you want to see what it was like,' added the Rector, 'go and look at Upwell Church near Wisbech. You'll find the same sort of gallery in the north aisle there (though ours was larger and uglier), and they have an angel roof, too, though not as fine as ours, because their angels are only attached to the roof itself, instead of being on the hammer-beams. In fact, you can't see the angels in their north aisle, at all, unless you climb up into the gallery.'

'I suppose there was the usual amount of opposition when you took the galleries down?'

'A certain amount, of course. There are always some people who oppose any change. But it did seem absurd, when the church was far too large for the parish in any case, to have all that unnecessary seating. There was plenty of room for the school-children in the aisle.'

'Did anybody sit in the gallery besides the schoolchildren?'

'Oh, yes. The Red House servants and a few of the oldest inhabitants, who had been there from time immemorial. Indeed, we really had to wait for one poor old soul to die before we embarked on the improvements. Poor old Mrs Wilderspin, Ezra's grandmother. She was ninety-seven and came regularly to church every Sunday, and it would have broken her heart to have turned her out.'

'Which side did the Red House servants sit?'

'At the west end of the south aisle. I never liked that, because one couldn't see what they were doing, and sometimes their behaviour wasn't as reverent as it might have been. I do not think the House of God is a proper place for flirtation, and there was so much nudging and giggling that it really was very unseemly.'

'If that woman Gates had done her duty and sat with the servants it would have been all right,' said Mrs Venables, 'but she was far too much of a lady. She always had to have her own seat, just inside the south door, for fear she should feel faint and have to go out.'

'Mrs Gates is not a robust woman, my dear.'

'Rubbish!' said Mrs Venables. 'She eats too much and gets indigestion, that's all.'

'Perhaps you are right, my dear.'

'I can't stand the woman,' said Mrs Venables. 'The Thorpes ought to sell that place, but apparently they can't under Sir Henry's will. I don't see how it can be kept up, and the money would be more use to Hilary Thorpe than the great tumbledown house. Poor little Hilary! If it hadn't been for that horrible old Wilbraham creature and her necklace — I suppose there's no hope of recovering the necklace, Lord Peter, after all this time?'

'I'm afraid we're a day after the fair. Though I'm pretty sure it was in this parish up to last January.'

'In the parish? Where?'

'I think it was in the church,' said Wimsey. 'That was a very powerful sermon of yours this morning, padre. Very inspiring. It inspired me to guess the riddle of the cryptogram.'

'No!' exclaimed the Rector. 'How did it do that, I wonder?' Wimsey explained.

'Good gracious! How very remarkable! We must investigate the place at once.'

'Not at once, Theodore.'

'Well, no, my dear, I didn't mean today. I'm afraid it wouldn't do to take ladders into the church on Sunday. We are still rather touchy here about the Fourth Commandment. Besides, I have the Children's Service this afternoon and three baptisms, and Mrs Edwards is coming to be churched. But, Lord Peter, how do you suppose the emeralds got up in the roof?'

'Why, I was just thinking about that. Isn't it true that this fellow Deacon was arrested after church on Sunday morning? I expect he got some idea of what was going to happen to him, and concealed his loot somehow during the service.'

'Of course, he was sitting up there that morning. Now I understand why you asked so many questions about the gallery. What a sad villain the man must have been! He really did — what is that word they use when one malefactor deceives another?'

'Double-cross?' suggested Wimsey.

'Ah! that is the very expression I was looking for. He did double-cross his accomplice. Poor man! I mean the accomplice. Ten years in prison for a theft of which he never enjoyed the fruits. One cannot help feeling some sympathy for him. But in that case, Lord Peter, who constructed the cryptogram?'

'I think it must have been Deacon, because of the bell-ringing.'

'Ah, yes. And then he gave it to this other man, Legros. Why did he do that?'

'Probably as an inducement to Legros to help him to escape from Maidstone.'

'And Legros waited all these years before making use of it?'

'Legros obviously had very good reasons for keeping out of England. Eventually he must have passed the cryptogram on to somebody here — Cranton, perhaps. Possibly he couldn't decipher it himself, and in any case he wanted Cranton's help to get back from France.'

'I see. Then they found the emeralds and Cranton killed Legros. How sad it makes me to think of all this violence for the sake of a few stones!'

'It makes me still sadder to think of poor Hilary Thorpe and her father,' said Mrs Venables. 'You mean to say that while they needed that money so badly, the emeralds were hidden in the church all the time within a few feet of them?'

'I'm afraid so.'

'And where are they now? Has this man Cranton got them? Why hasn't somebody found them by now? I can't think what the police are doing.'

★ ★ ★

Sunday seemed an unusually long day. On the Monday morning, a great many things happened at once.

The first thing was the arrival of Superintendent Blundell, in great excitement.

'We've got that letter from Maidstone,' he announced, 'and whose do you suppose the writing is?'

'I've been thinking it over,' said Wimsey. 'I think it must have been Deacon's.'

'There!' said Mr Blundell, disappointed. 'Well, you're quite right, my lord; it is.'

311

'It must be the original cipher,' said Wimsey. 'When we found out that it had to do with bell-ringing, I realised that Deacon must be the author. To have two bell-ringing convicts in Maidstone Gaol at once seemed rather too much of a coincidence. And then, when I showed the paper to Mrs Thoday, I felt sure that she recognised the writing. It might have meant that Legros had written to her, but it was still more likely that she knew it to be her husband's.'

'Well, then, how did it come to be written on that foreign paper?'

'Foreign paper is much of a muchness,' said Wimsey. 'Did Lady Thorpe ever have a foreign maid? Old Lady Thorpe, I mean.'

'Sir Charles had a French cook,' said the Superintendent.

'At the time of the theft?'

'Yes. She left them when the war broke out, I remember. She wanted to get back to her family, and they scraped her across on one of the last boats.'

'Then that's clear enough. Deacon invented his cryptogram before he actually hid the emeralds. He couldn't have taken it into prison with him. He must have handed it to somebody — '

'Mary,' said the Superintendent, with a grim smile.

'Perhaps. And she must have sent it to Legros. It's all rather obscure.'

'Not so obscure as that, my lord.' Mr Blundell's face grew still grimmer. 'I thought it was a bit reckless, if you'll excuse me, showing that paper to Mary Thoday. She's skipped.'

312

'Skipped?'

'First train to town this morning. And Will Thoday with her. A precious pair.'

'Good God!'

'You may say so, my lord. Oh, we'll have them, don't you fear. Gone off, that's what they've done, and the emeralds with them.'

'I admit,' said Wimsey, 'I didn't expect that.'

'Didn't you?' said Mr Blundell. 'Well, I didn't either, or I'd have kept a sharper eye on them. And by the way, we know now who that Legros fellow was.'

'You're a perfect budget of news today, Super.'

'Ah! well — we've had a letter from your friend M. Rozier. He had that woman's house searched, and what do you think they found? Legros's identification disc — no less. Any more guesses coming, my lord?'

'I might make a guess, but I won't. I'll buy it. What was the name?

'Name of Arthur Cobbleigh.'

'And who's Arthur Cobbleigh when he's at home?'

'You hadn't guessed that, then?'

'No — my guess was quite different. Go on, Super. Spill the beans.'

'Well, now. Arthur Cobbleigh — seems he was just a bloke. But can you guess where he came from?'

'I've given up guessing.'

'He came from a little place near Dartford — only about half a mile from the wood where Deacon's body was found.'

'Oho! now we're coming to it.'

'I got on the phone straight away as soon as this letter came. Cobbleigh was a chap aged somewhere about twenty-five in 1914. Not a good record. Labourer. Been in trouble once or twice with the police for petty thieving and assault. Joined up in the first year of the war and considered rather a good riddance. Last seen on the last day of his leave in 1918, and that day was just two days after Deacon's escape from prison. Left his home to rejoin his unit. Never seen again. Last news of him, 'Missing believed killed' in the retreat over the Marne. Officially, that is. Last actual news of him — over there!'

The Superintendent jerked his thumb in the general direction of the churchyard.

Wimsey groaned.

'It makes no sense, Super, it makes no sense! If this man Cobbleigh joins up in the first year of the war, how on earth could he have been elaborately in league with Deacon, who went to Maidstone in 1914? There was no time. Damn it! You don't get a man out of quod in a few spare hours spent on leave. If Cobbleigh had been a warder — if he'd been a fellow-convict — if he'd been anything to do with the prison, I could understand it. Had he a relation in the gaol or anything of that sort. There must have been something more to it than that.'

'Must there? Look here, my lord, how's this? I've been working this thing out coming over, and this is what I make out of it. Deacon bust away from a working-party, didn't he? He was found still wearing his prison dress, wasn't he? Doesn't that show his escape wasn't planned out

314

elaborately beforehand? They'd have found him fast enough, if he hadn't gone and pitched down that denehole, wouldn't they? Now, you listen to this and see if it don't hold water. I can see it plain as a pikestaff. Here's this Cobbleigh — a hard nut, by all accounts. He's walking through the wood on the way from his mother's cottage, to take the train to Dartford for wherever he might be going to join up with the troops going back to France. Somewhere on that moor he finds a chap lurking about. He collars him, and finds he's pinched the escaped convict that everybody's looking for. The convict says, 'Let me go, and I'll make you a rich man,' see? Cobbleigh's got no objection to that. He says, 'Lead me to it. What is it?' The convict says, 'The Wilbraham emeralds, that's what it is.' Cobbleigh says, 'Coo! tell us some more about that. How'm I to know you ain't kidding me? You tell us where they are and we'll see about it.' Deacon says, 'No fear — catch me telling you, without you helps me first.' Cobbleigh says, 'You can't help yourself,' he says, 'I only got to give you up and then where'll you be?' Deacon says, 'You won't get much out o' that. You stick by me and I'll put hundreds of thousands of pounds in your hands.' They go on talking, and Deacon, like a fool, let's out that he's made a note of the hiding-place and has it on him. 'Oh, have you?' says Cobbleigh, 'then you damn well take that.' And lams him over the head. Then he goes over him and finds the paper, which he's upset to find he can't make head or tail of. Then he has another look at Deacon and sees he's done him good and proper. 'Oh, hell!' he says, 'that's torn it. I better shove him out of the way and clear off.' So he pops him down the hole and makes tracks for France. How's that, so far?'

'Fine, full-blooded stuff,' said Wimsey. 'But why should Deacon be carrying a note of the hiding-place about with him? And how did it come to be written on foreign paper?'

'I don't know. Well, say it was like you said before. Say he'd given the paper to his wife. He spills his wife's address like a fool, and then it all happens the way I said. Cobbleigh goes back to France, deserts, and gets taken care of, by Suzanne. He keeps quiet about who he is, because he don't know whether Deacon's body's been found or not and he's afraid of being had up for murder if he goes home. Meanwhile, he's stuck to the paper — no, that's wrong. He writes to Mrs Deacon and gets the paper out of her.'

'Why should she give it up?'

'That's a puzzler. Oh, I know! I've got it this time. He tells her he's got the key to it. That's right. Deacon told him, 'My wife's got the cipher, but she's a babbling fool and I ain't trusted her with the key. I'll give you the key and that'll show you I know what I'm talking about.' Then Cobbleigh kills him, and when he thinks it's safe he writes to Mary and she sends him the paper.'

'The original paper?'

'Why, yes.'

'You'd think she'd keep that and send him a copy.'

'No. She sends the original, so that he can see

it's in Deacon's writing.'

'But he wouldn't necessarily know Deacon's writing.'

'How's she to know that? Cobbleigh works out the cipher and they help him to get across.'

'But we've been into all that and decided the Thodays couldn't do it.'

'All right, then. The Thodays bring Cranton into it. Cobbleigh comes over, anyhow, under the name of Paul Taylor, and he comes along to Fenchurch and they get the emeralds. Then Thoday kills him, and *he* takes the emeralds. Meanwhile, along comes Cranton to see what's happening and finds they've been ahead of him. He clears off and the Thodays go about looking innocent till they see we're getting a bit close on their trail. Then *they* clear.'

'Who did the killing, then?'

'Any one of them, I should say.'

'And who did the burying?'

'Not Will, anyhow.'

'And how was it done? And why did they want to tie Cobbleigh up? Why not kill him straight off with a bang on the head? Why did Thoday take £200 out of the bank and put it back again? When did it all happen? Who was the man Potty Peake saw in the church on the night of the 30th? And, above all, why was the cipher found in the belfry of all places?'

'I can't answer everything at once, can I? That's the way it was done between 'em, you can take it from me. And now I'm going to have Cranton charged, and get hold of those precious Thodays, and if I don't put my hand on the emeralds among them, I'll eat my hat.'

'Oh!' said Wimsey, 'that reminds me. Before you came, we were just going to look at the place where Deacon hid those jolly old emeralds. The Rector solved the cipher — '

'Him?'

'He. So, just for fun, and by way of shutting the stable door after the steed was stolen, we're going to climb up aloft and have a hunt among the cherubims. In fact, the Rector is down at the church, champing his bit at this very moment. Shall we go?'

'Sure — though I haven't a lot of time to waste.'

'I don't suppose it will take long.'

The Rector had procured the sexton's ladder and was already up in the south aisle roof, covering himself with cobwebs as he poked about vaguely among the ancient oak.

'The servants sat just about here,' he said, as Wimsey came in with the Superintendent. 'But now I come to think of it, we had the painters up here last year, and they ought to have found anything there was to be found.'

'Perhaps they did,' said Wimsey; and Mr Blundell uttered a low moan.

'Oh, I hope not. I really think not. They are most honest men.' Mr Venables came down from the ladder. 'Perhaps you had better try, I am not clever about these things.'

'Beautiful old work this is,' said his lordship. 'All pegged together. There's a lot of this old rafter work down at Duke's Denver, and when I was a kid I made rather a pretty cache for myself

318

in a corner of the attic. Used to keep tiddly-winks counters in it and pretend it was a pirate's hoard. Only it was a dickens of a job getting them out again. I say! Blundell! do you remember that wire hook you found in the corpse's pocket?'

'Yes, my lord. We never made out what that was for.'

'I ought to have known,' said Wimsey. 'I made a thing very like it for the pirate's hoard.' His long fingers were working over the beams, gently pulling at the thick wooden pegs which held them together, 'He must have been able to reach it from where he sat, Aha! what did I tell you? This is the one. Wriggle her gently and out she comes. Look!'

He wrenched at one of the pegs, and it came out in his hand. Originally, it had passed right through the beam and must have been over a foot in length, tapering from the size of a penny-piece at one end to something over half-an-inch at the other. But at some time it had been sawn off about three inches from the thick end.

'There you are,' said Wimsey. 'An old schoolboy cache originally, I expect. Some kid got pushing it from the other end and found it was loose. Probably shoved it clean out. At least, that's what I did, up in the attic. Then he took it home and sawed six inches or so out of the middle of it. Next time he comes to church he brings a short rod with him. He pushes the thin end back again into place with the rod, so that the hole doesn't show from the other side. Then he drops in his marbles or whatever he wanted to hide, and plugs up the big end again with this. And there he is, with a nice little six-inch hidey-hole where nobody would ever dream of looking for it. Or so he thinks. Then — perhaps years afterwards — along comes friend Deacon. He's sitting up here one day, possibly a little bored with the sermon (sorry, padre!). He starts fidgeting with the peg, and out it comes — only three inches of it. Hullo! says he, here's a game! Handy place if you wanted to pop any little thing away in a hurry. Later on, when he does want to pop his little shiners away in a hurry, he thinks of it again. Easy enough. Sits here all quiet and pious, listening to the First Lesson. Puts his hand down at his side, slips out the plug, slides the emeralds out of his pocket, slips them into the hole, pops back the plug. All over before his reverence says 'Here endeth'. Out into the sunshine and slap into the arms of our friend the Super here and his merry men. 'Where are the emeralds?' they say. 'You can search me,' says he. And they do, and they've been searching ever since.'

'Amazing!' said the Rector. Mr Blundell uttered a regrettable expression, remembered his surroundings and coughed loudly.

'So now we see what the hook was for,' said Wimsey. 'When Legros, or Cobbleigh, whichever you like to call him, came for the loot — '

'Stop a minute,' objected the Superintendent. 'That cipher didn't mention anything about a hole, did it? It only mentioned cherubims. How did he know he needed a hook to get necklaces out of cherubims?'

'Perhaps he'd had a look at the place first. But

of course, we know he did. That must have been what he was doing when Potty Peake saw him and Thoday in the church. He spotted the place then, and came back later. Though why he should have waited five days I couldn't tell you: Possibly something went wrong. Anyway, back he came, armed with his hook, and hitched the necklace out. Then, just as he was coming down the ladder, the accomplice took him from behind, tied him up, and — and then — and then did away with him by some means we can't acount for.'

The Superintendent scratched his head.

'You'd think he might have waited for a better place to do it in, wouldn't you, my lord? Putting him out here in the church, and all that bother of burying him and what not. Why didn't he go while the going was good, and shove Cobbleigh into the dyke or something on the way home?'

'Heaven knows,' said Wimsey. 'Anyhow, there's your hiding-place and there's the explanation of your hook.' He thrust the end of his fountain pen into the hole. 'It's quite deep — no, by Jove, it's not! it's only a shallow hole after all, not much longer than the peg. We can't, surely, have made a mistake. Where's my torch? Dash it! (Sorry, padre.) Is that wood? or is it — ? Here, Blundell, find me a mallet and a short, stout rod or stick of some kind — not too thick. We'll have this hole clear.'

'Run across to the Rectory and ask Hinkins,' suggested Mr Venables, helpfully.

In a few minutes' time, Mr Blundell returned, panting, with a short iron bar and a heavy wheel-spanner. Wimsey had shifted the ladder and was examining the narrow end of the oaken peg on the east side of the beam. He set one end of the bar firmly against the peg and smote lustily with the spanner. An ecclesiastical bat, startled from its resting-place by the jar, swooped out with a shriek, the tapered end of the peg shot smartly through the hole and out at the other side, and something else shot out with it — something that detached itself in falling from its wrapping of brown paper' and cascaded in a flash of green and gold to the Rector's feet.

'Bless my heart!' cried Mr Venables.

'The emeralds!' yelled Mr Blundell. 'The emeralds, by God! And Deacon's fifty pounds with them.'

'And we're wrong, Blundell,' said Lord Peter. 'We've been wrong from start to finish. Nobody found them. Nobody killed anybody for them. Nobody deciphered the cryptogram. We're wrong, wrong, out of the hunt and wrong!'

'But we've got the emeralds,' said the Superintendent.

III

A SHORT TOUCH OF STEDMAN'S TRIPLES

(Five Parts)

840

By the Part Ends
5 6 1 2 3 4
3 4 1 5 6 2
6 2 1 3 4 5
4 5 1 6 2 3
2 3 1 4 5 6
Treble the observation.

Call her the last whole turn, out quick, in slow, the second half turn and out slow. Four times repeated.

(TROYTE)

the first part

THE QUICK WORK

The work of each bell is divided in three parts, viz, the quick work, dodging, and slow work.

TROYTE *On Change-Ringing*

Lord Peter Wimsey passed a restless day and night and was very silent the next day at breakfast.

At the earliest possible moment he got his car and went over to Leamholt.

'Superintendent,' he said, 'I think I have been the most unmitigated and unconscionable ass that ever brayed in a sleuthhound's skin. Now, however, I have solved the entire problem, with one trivial exception. Probably you have done so too.'

'I'll buy it,' said Mr Blundell. 'I'm like you, my lord, I'm doing no more guessing. What's the bit you haven't solved, by the way?'

'Well, the murder,' said his lordship, with an embarrassed cough. 'I can't quite make out who did that, or how. But that, as I say, is a trifle. I know who the dead man was, why he was tied up, where he died, who sent the cryptogram to whom, why Will Thoday drew £200 out of the bank and put it back again, where the Thodays have gone and why and when they will return, why Jim Thoday missed his train, why Cranton came here, what he did and why he is lying about it, and how the beer-bottle got into the belfry.'

'Anything else?' asked Mr Blundell.

'Oh, yes. Why Jean Legros was silent about his past, what Arthur Cobbleigh did in the wood at Dartford, what the parrot was talking about and why the Thodays were not at Early Service on Sunday, what Tailor Paul had to do with it and why the face of the corpse was beaten in.'

'Excellent,' said Mr Blundell. 'Quite a walking library, aren't you, my lord? Couldn't you go just a step further and tell us who we're to put the handcuffs on?'

'I'm sorry. I can't do that. Dash it all, can't I leave one little titbit for a friend?'

'Well,' said Mr Blundell, 'I don't know that I ought to complain. Let's have the rest of it and perhaps we'll be able to do the last bit on our own.'

Lord Peter was silent for a moment.

'Look here, Super,' he said at last. 'This is going to be a dashed painful sort of story. I think I'd like to test it a bit before I come out with it. Will you do something yourself, first? You've got to do it in any case, but I'd rather not say anything till it is done. After that, I'll say anything you like.'

'Well?'

'Will you get hold of a photograph of Arthur Cobbleigh and send it over to France for Suzanne Legros to identfy?'

'That's got to be done, naturally. Matter of routine.'

'If she identifies it, well and good. But if she's

stubborn and refuses, will you give her this note, just as it is, and watch her when she opens it?'

'Well, I don't know about doing that personally, my lord, but I'll see that this Monsieur Rozier does it.'

'That will do. And will you also show her the cryptogram?'

'Yes, why not? Anything else?'

'Yes,' said Wimsey, more slowly. 'The Thodays. I'm a little uncomfortable about the Thodays. You're trailing them, I suppose?'

'What do you think?'

'Exactly. Well, when you've put your hands on them, will you let me know before you do anything drastic? I'd rather like to be there when you question them.'

'I've no objection to that, my lord. And this time they'll have to come across with some sort of story, Judge's Rules or no Judge's Rules, even if it breaks me.'

'You won't have any difficulty about that,' said Wimsey. 'Provided, that is, you catch them within a fortnight. After that, it will be more difficult.'

'Why within a fortnight?'

'Oh, come!' expostulated his lordship. 'Isn't it obvious? I show Mrs Thoday the cipher. On Sunday morning neither she nor her husband attends Holy Communion. On Monday they depart to London by the first train. My dear Watson, it's staring you in the face. The only real danger is — '

'Well?'

'The Archbishop of Canterbury. A haughty prelate, Blundell. An arbitrary prince. But I don't suppose they'll think about him, somehow. I think you may risk him.'

'Oh, indeed! And how about Mr Mussolini and the Emperor of Japan?'

'Negligible. Negligible,' replied his lordship, with a wave of the hand. 'Likewise the Bishop of Rome. But get on to it, Blundell, get on to it.'

'I mean to,' said Mr Blundell, with emphasis. 'They'll not get out of the country, that's a certainty.'

'So it is, so it is. Of course, they'll be back here by tomorrow fortnight, but that will be too late. How soon do you expect Jim Thoday back? End of the month? Be sure he doesn't give you the slip. I've an idea he may try to.'

'You think he's our man?'

'I don't know, I tell you. I don't want him to be. I rather hope it's Cranton.'

'Poor old Cranton,' said the Superintendent, perversely, 'I rather hope it isn't. I don't like to see a perfectly good jewel-thief stepping out of his regular line, so to speak. It's disconcerting that's what it is. Besides, the man's ill. However, we shall see about that. I'll get on to this Cobbleigh business and settle it.'

'Right!' said Wimsey. 'And I think, after all, I'll ring up the Archbishop. You never know.'

'Dotty!' said Mr Blundell to himself. 'Or pulling my leg. One or the other.'

★   ★   ★

Lord Peter Wimsey communicated with the Archbishop, and appeared to be satisfied with the result. He also wrote to Hilary Thorpe, giving her an account of the finding of the emeralds. 'So you see,' he said, 'your Sherlocking was very successful. How pleased Uncle Edward will be.' Hilary's reply informed him that old Mrs Wilbraham had taken the necklace and restored the money paid in compensation — all without comment or apology. Lord Peter haunted the Rectory like an unhappy ghost. The Superintendent had gone to town in pursuit of the Thodays. On Thursday things began to happen again.

Telegram from Commissaire Rozier to Superintendent Blundell:

Suzanne Legros no knowledge Cobbleigh identifies photograph in sealed envelope as her husband identification supported by mayor here do you desire further action.

Telegram from Superintendent Blundell to Lord Peter Wimsey:

Suzanne Legros rejects Cobbleigh identifies sealed photograph who is it unable trace Thodays in London.

Telegram from Superintendent Blundell to Commissaire Rozier:

Please return papers immediately detain Legros pending further information.

Telegram from Lord Peter Wimsey to Superintendent Blundell:

Surely you know by this time try all churches registrars.

Telegram from Superintendent Blundell to Lord Peter Wimsey:

Vicar St Andrews Bloomsbury says asked perform marriage by licence William Thoday Mary Deacon both of that parish was it Deacon.

Telegram from Lord Peter Wimsey to Superintendent Blundell:

Yes of course you juggins charge Cranton at once.

Telegram from Superintendent Blundell to Lord Peter Wimsey:

Agreed juggins but why charge Cranton Thodays found and detained for inquiry.

Telegram from Lord Peter Wimsey to Superintendent Blundell:

Charge Cranton first joining you in town.

After dispatching this wire, Lord Peter summoned Bunter to pack up his belongings and asked for a private interview with Mr Venables, from which both men emerged looking distressed and uneasy.

'So I think I'd better go,' said Wimsey. 'I rather wish I hadn't come buttin' into this. Some things may be better left alone, don't you think? My sympathies are all in the wrong place and I don't like it. I know all about not doing evil that good may come. It's doin' good that evil may come that is so embarrassin'.'

'My dear boy,' said the Rector, 'it does not do for us to take too much thought for the morrow. It is better to follow the truth and leave the result in the hand of God. He can forsee where we cannot, because He knows all the facts.'

'And never has to argue ahead of His data, as Sherlock Holmes would say? Well, padre, I dare say you're right. Probably I'm tryin' to be too clever. That's me every time. I'm sorry to have made so much unpleasantness, anyhow. And I really would rather go away now. I've got that silly modern squeamishness that doesn't like watchin' people suffer. Thanks awfully for everything. Goodbye.'

★　★　★

Before leaving Fenchurch St Paul, he went and stood in the churchyard. The grave of the unknown victim still stood raw and black amid the grass, but the grave of Sir Henry and Lady Thorpe had been roofed in with green turves. Not far away there was an ancient box tomb; Hezekiah Lavender was seated on the slab, carefully cleaning the letters of the inscription. Wimsey went over and shook hands with the old man.

'Makin' old Samuel fine and clean for the summer,' said Hezekiah. 'Ah! Beaten old Samuel by ten good year, I have. I says to Rector, 'Lay me aside old Samuel,' I says, 'for everybody to see as I beaten him.' An' I got Rector's promise. Ah! so I have. But they don't write no sech beautiful poetry these here times.'

He laid a gouty finger on the inscription, which ran:

Here lies the Body of SAMUEL SNELL
That for fifty Years pulled the Tenor Bell.
Through Changes of this Mortal Race
He Laid his Blows and Kept his Place

331

Till Death that Changes all did Come
To Hunt him Down and Call him Home,
His Wheel is broke his Rope is Slackt
His Clapper Mute his Metal Crackt,
Yet when the great Call summons him from
  Ground
He shall be Raised up Tuneable and Sound.
                                        MDCXCVIII
                                    Aged 76 years

'Ringing Tailor Paul seems to be a healthy occupation,' said Wimsey. 'His servants live to a ripe old age, what?'

'Ah!' said Hezekiah. 'So they du, young man, so they du, if so be they're faithful to 'un an' don't go a-angerin' on 'un. They bells du know well who's a-haulin' of 'un. Wunnerful understandin' they is. They can't abide a wicked man. They lays in wait to overthrow 'un. But old Tailor Paul can't say I ain't done well by her an' she allus done well by me. Make righteousness your course bell, my lord, an' keep a-follerin' on her an' she'll see you through your changes till Death calls you to stand. Yew ain't no call to be afeared o' the bells if so be as yew follows righteousness.'

'Oh, quite,' said Wimsey, a little embarrassed.

He left Hezekiah and went into the church, stepping softly as though he feared to rouse up something from its sleep. Abbot Thomas was quiet in his tomb; the cherubims, open-eyed and open-mouthed, were absorbed in their everlasting contemplation; far over him he felt the patient watchfulness of the bells.

the second part

NOBBY GOES IN SLOW
AND COMES OUT QUICK

It is a frightful plight. Two angels buried him
. . . in Vallombrosa by night; I saw it, standing among the lotus and hemlock.
        J. SHERIDAN LEFANU: *Wylder's Hand*

Mr Cranton was in an infirmary as the guest of
His Majesty the King, and looked better than
when they had last seen him. He showed no
surprise at being charged with the murder of
Geoffrey Deacon, twelve years or so after that
gentleman's reputed decease.

'Right!' said Mr Cranton. 'I rather expected
you'd get on to it, but I kept on hoping you
mightn't. I didn't do it, and I want to make a
statement. Do sit down. These quarters aren't
what I could wish for a gentleman, but they seem
to be the best the Old Country can offer. I'm
told they do it much prettier in Sing Sing.
England, with all thy faults, I love thee Still.
Where do you want me to begin?'

'Begin at the beginning,' suggested Wimsey,
'go on till you get to the end and then stop. May
he have a fag, Charles?'

'Well, my lord and — no,' said Mr Cranton, 'I
won't say gentlemen. Seems to go against the

333

grain, somehow. Officers, if you like, but not gentlemen. Well, my lord and officers. I don't need to tell you that I'm a deeply injured man. I said I never had those shiners, didn't I? And you see I was right. What you want to know is, how did I first hear that Deacon was still on deck? Well, he wrote me a letter, that's how. Somewhere about last July, that would be. Sent it to the old crib, and it was forwarded on — never you mind who by.'

'Gammy Pluck,' observed Mr Parker, distantly.

'I name no names,' said Mr Cranton. 'Honour among — gentlemen. I burnt that letter, *being* an honourable gentleman, but it was some story, and I don't know that I can do justice to it. Seems that when Deacon made his getaway, after an unfortunate encounter with a warder, he had to sneak about Kent in a damned uncomfortable sort of way for a day or two. He said the stupidity of the police was almost incredible. Walked right over him twice, he said. One time they trod on him. Said he'd never realised so vividly before why a policeman was called a flattie. Nearly broke his fingers standing on them. Now I,' added Mr Cranton, 'have rather small feet. Small and well-shod. You can always tell a gentleman by his feet.'

'Go on, Nobby,' said Mr Parker.

'Anyhow, the third night he was out there lying doggo in a wood somewhere, he heard a chap coming along that wasn't a flattie. Rolling drunk, Deacon said he was. So Deacon pops out from behind a tree and pastes the fellow one. He said

334

he didn't mean to do him in, only put him out, but he must have struck a bit harder than what he meant. Mind you, that's only what he said, but Deacon always was a low kind of fellow and he'd laid out one man already and you can't hang a chap twice. Anyway, he found he'd been and gone and done it, and that was that.

'What he wanted, of course, was duds, and when he came to examine the takings, he found he'd bagged a Tommy in uniform with all his kit. Well, that wasn't very surprising, come to think of it. There were a lot of those about in 1918, but it sort of took Deacon aback. Of course, he knew there was a war on — they'd been told all about that — but it hadn't, as you might say, come home to him. This Tommy had some papers and stuff on him and a torch, and from what Deacon could make out, looking into the thing rather hurriedly in a retired spot, he was just coming off his leaf and due to get back to the Front. Well, Deacon thought, any hole's better than Maidstone Gaol, so here goes. So he changes clothes with the Tommy down to his skin, collars his papers and what not, and tips the body down the hole. Deacon was a Kentish man himself, you see, and knew the place. Of course, he didn't know the first thing about soldiering — however, needs must and all that. He thought his best way was to get up to Town and maybe he'd find some old pal up there to look after him. So he tramped off — and eventually he got a lift on a lorry or something to a railway station. He did mention the name, but I've forgotten it. He picked some town he'd never been in — a small place.

Anyway, he found a train going to London and he piled into it. That was all right; but somewhere on the way, in got a whole bunch of soldiers, pretty lit-up and cheery, and from the way they talked, Deacon began to find out what he was up against. It came over him, you see, that here he was, all dressed up as a perfectly good Tommy, and not knowing the first thing about the War, or drill or anything, and he knew if he opened his mouth he'd put his foot in it.'

'Of course,' said Wimsey. 'It'd be like dressing up as a Freemason. You couldn't hope to get away with it.'

'That's it. Deacon said it was like being among people talking a foreign language. Worse; because Deacon did know a bit about foreign languages. He was an educated sort of bloke. But this Army stuff was beyond him. So all he could do was to pretend to be asleep. He said he just rolled up in his corner and snored, and if anybody spoke to him he swore at them. It worked quite well, he said. There was one very persistent bloke, though, with a bottle of Scotch. He kept on shoving drinks at Deacon and he took a few, and then some more, and by the time he got to London he was pretty genuinely sozzled. You see, he'd had nothing to eat, to speak of, for a coupla days, except some bread he'd managed to scrounge from a cottage.'

The policeman who was taking all this down in shorthand scratched stolidly on over the paper. Mr Cranton took a drink of water and resumed.

'Deacon said he wasn't very clear what

happened to him after that. He wanted to get out of the station and go off somewhere, but he found it wasn't so easy. The darkened streets confused him, and the persistent fellow with the bottle of Scotch seemed to have taken a fancy to him. This bloke talked all the time, which was lucky for Deacon. He said he remembered having some more drinks and something about a canteen, and tripping over something and a lot of chaps laughing at him. And after that he must really have fallen asleep. The next thing he knew, he was in a train again, with Tommies all around him, and from what he could make out, they were bound for the Front.'

'That's a very remarkable story,' said Mr Parker.

'It's clear enough,' said Wimsey. 'Some kindly soul must have examined his papers, found he was due back and shoved him on to the nearest transport, bound for Dover, I suppose.'

'That's right,' said Mr Cranton. 'Caught in the machine, as you might say. Well, all he could do was to lie doggo again. There were plenty of others who seemed to be dog-tired and fairly well canned and he wasn't in any way remarkable. He watched what the others did, and produced his papers at the right time and all that. Fortunately, nobody else seemed to belong to his particular unit. So he got across. Mind you,' added Mr Cranton, 'I can't tell you all the details. I wasn't in the War myself, being otherwise engaged. You must fill up the blanks for yourself. He said he was damned seasick on the way over, and after that he slept in a sort of cattle-waggon and finally they bundled him out at last in the dark at some ghastly place or other. After a bit he heard somebody asking if there was anyone belonging to his unit. He knew enough to say 'Yes, sir,' and stand forward — and then he found himself foot-slogging over a filthy road full of holes with a small party of men and an officer. God! he said it went on for hours and he thought they must have done about a hundred miles, but I daresay that was an exaggeration. And he said there was a noise like merry hell going on ahead, and the ground began to shake, and he suddenly grasped what he was in for.'

'This is an epic,' said Wimsey.

'I can't do justice to it,' said Mr Cranton, 'because Deacon never knew what he was doing and I don't know enough to make a guess. But I gather he walked straight into a big strafe. Hell let loose, he said, and I shouldn't wonder if he began to think kindly of Maidstone Gaol and even of the condemned cell. Apparently he never got to the trenches, because they were being shelled out of them and he got mixed up in the retreat. He lost his party and something hit him on the head and laid him out. Next thing he knew he was lying in a shell-hole along with somebody who'd been dead some time. I don't know. I couldn't follow it all. But after a bit he crawled out. Everything was quiet and it was coming on dark, so he must have lost a whole day somehow. He'd lost his sense of direction, too, he said. He wandered about, and fell in and out of mud and holes and wire, and in the end he stumbled into a shed where there was some hay and stuff. But he couldn't remember much about that, either, because he'd had a devil of a knock on the head and he was getting feverish. And then a girl found him.'

'We know all about that,' said the Superintendent.

'Yes, I daresay you do. You seem to know a lot. Well, Deacon was pretty smart about that. He got round the soft side of the girl and they made up a story for him. He said it was fairly easy pretending to have lost his memory. Where the doctor blokes made a mistake was trying to catch him out with bits of Army drill. He'd never done any, so of course he didn't have to pretend not to recognise it. The hardest part was making out that he didn't know any English. They nearly got him on that, once or twice. But he did know French, so he did his best to seem intelligent about that. His French accent was pretty good, but he pretended to have lost his speech, so that any mumbling or stammering might be put down to that, and in the intervals he practised talking to the girl till he was word-perfect. I must say, Deacon had brains.'

'We can imagine all that part,' said Parker. 'Now tell us about the emeralds.'

'Oh, yes. The thing that started him on that was getting hold of an old English newspaper which had a mention of the finding of a body in the dene-hole — his own body, as everyone thought. It was a 1918 paper, of course, but he only came across it in 1924 — I forget where. It turned up, the way things do. Somebody'd used it to wrap something sometime, and I think he came across it in an estaminet. He didn't bother about it, because the farm was doing pretty well — he'd married the girl by then, you see — and he was quite happy. But later on, things began to go badly, and it worried him to think about those sparklers all tucked away doing no good to anybody. But he didn't know how to start getting hold of them, and he got a vertical breeze up every time he thought of that dead warder and the chap he'd thrown down the hole. However, in the end, he called to mind yours truly, and figured it out that I'd be out on my own again. So he wrote me a letter. Well, as you know, I wasn't out. I was inside again, owing to a regrettable misunderstanding, so I didn't get the letter for some time, my pals thinking it wasn't quite the sort of thing to send to the place where I was. See? But when I came out again, there was the letter waiting for me.'

'I wonder he made *you* his confidant,' observed Parker. 'There had been — shall we say, ungentlemanly words passed on the subject.'

'Ah!' said Mr Cranton. 'There had, and I had something to say about that when I wrote back. But you see, he'd nobody else to go to, had he? When all's said and done, there's nobody like Nobby Cranton to handle a job like that in a refined and competent manner. I give you my word I nearly told him to go and boil himself, but in the end I said, No! Let bygones be bygones. So I promised to help the blighter. I told him I could fix him up with money and papers and get him across all right. Only I told

340

him he'd have to give me a bit more dope on the thing first. Otherwise, how was I to know he wouldn't double-cross me again, the dirty skunk?'

'Nothing more likely,' said Parker.

'Ah! and he did, too, blast his worm-eaten little soul! I said he'd have to tell me where the stuff was. And, would you believe it, the hound wouldn't trust me! Said, if he told me that, I might get in and pinch the bleeding lot before he got there!'

'Incredible!' said Parker, 'Of course you wouldn't do such a thing as that.'

'Not me,' replied Nobby, 'What do *you* think?' He winked. 'Well, we went on writing backwards and forwards till we reached what they call an impasse. At last he wrote and said he'd send me a what d'you call — a cipher, and if I could make out from that where the shiners were, I was welcome. Well, he sent the thing, and I couldn't make head or tail of it, and I told him so. Then he said, All right; if I didn't trust him I could go down'to Fenchurch and ask for a tailor called Paul as lived next door to Batty Thomas, and they'd give me the key, but, he says, you'd do better to leave it to me, because I know how to handle them. Well, I didn't know, only I thought to myself if these two chaps come in on it they'll want their share, and they might turn sour on me, and it seemed to me I was safer with Deacon, because he stood to lose more than I did. Call me a mug if you like, but I sent him over the money and some perfectly good papers. Of course, he couldn't come as Deacon and he didn't want to come as Legros, because there might be a spot of trouble over that, and he suggested his papers should be made out as Paul Taylor. I thought it a bit silly myself, but he seemed to think it would be a good joke. Now, of course, I know why. So the papers were made out, with a lovely photograph — a real nice job, that was. Might have been anybody. As a matter of fact, it was a composite. It looked very convincing, and had quite a look of all sorts of people. Oh, yes! and I sent him some clothes to meet him at Ostend, because he said his own things were too Frenchy. He came across on the 29th December. I suppose you got on to that?'

'Yes,' said Blundell, 'we did, but it didn't help us a lot.'

'That bit went all right. He sent me a message from Dover. Telephoned from a public call-box — but I'll forgive you for not tracing that. He said he was going straight through and would come along up to London with the stuff next day or the day after, or as soon as he could. Anyway, he would get a message through somehow. I wondered whether I oughtn't to go down to Fenchurch myself — mind you, I never trusted him — but I wasn't altogether keen, in spite of my face-fungus. I'd grown that on spec, you understand. I didn't want you people following me about too much. And besides, I had one or two other irons in the fire. I'm coming clean, you see.'

'You'd better,' said Parker, ominously.

'I didn't get any message on the 30th, nor yet on the 31st, and I thought I'd been had proper. Only I couldn't see what he had to gain by double-crossing me. He needed me to handle the goods — or so I thought. Only then it struck me he might have picked up some other pal over at Maidstone or abroad.'

'In that case, why bring you into it at all?'

'That's what I thought. But I got so windy, I thought I'd better go down to the place and see what was happening. I didn't want to leave a trail, so I went over to Walbeach — never mind how, that's off the point — '

'Probably Sparky Bones or the Fly-catcher,' put in Parker, thoughtfully.

'Ask no questions and you'll hear no lies. My pal decanted me a few miles out and I footslogged it. I made out I was a tramp labourer, looking for work on the New Cut. Thank God, they weren't taking on any hands, so they didn't detain me.'

'So we gathered.'

'Ah! I suppose you would go nosey-parkering round there. I got a lift part of the way to Fenchurch and walked the rest. Beastly country it is, too, as I said before. I'm not doing my hiking thereabouts, I can tell you.'

'That was when we ran across one another, I think,' said Wimsey.

'Ah! and if I'd known who I had the pleasure of stopping I'd have walked off home,' said Mr Cranton, handsomely. 'But I didn't know, so I trotted along and — but there! I expect you know that part of it.'

'You got a job with Ezra Wilderspin and made inquiries for Paul Taylor.'

'Yes — and a nice business that was!'

exclaimed Nobby with indignation. 'Mr Paul Bleeding Taylor and Mr Batty Thomas! Bells, if you please! And not a hide nor hair of *my* Paul Taylor to be seen or heard of. I tell you, that made me think a bit. I didn't know if he'd been and gone, or if he'd been pinched on the way, or if he was lurking about round the corner or what. And that chap Wilderspin — he was a good hand at keeping a hardworking man's nose to the grindstone, curse him! 'Driver, come here!' 'Steve, do this!' I didn't have a minute to call my own. All the same, I started to think quite a lot about that cipher. I took the idea that maybe it had to do with those bells. But could I get into the confounded belfry? No, I couldn't. Not openly, I mean. So I made out to do it one night and see if I could make sense of the thing up there. So I made a couple or so of pick-locks, the forge being handy for the job, and on Saturday night I just let myself quietly out of Ezra's back-door.

'Now, look here. What I'm going to tell you is gospel truth. I went down to that church a bit after midnight, and the minute I put my hand on the door, I found it was open. What did I think? Why, I thought Deacon must be in there on the job. Who else was it likely to be, that time of night? I'd been in the place before and made out where the belfry door was, so I went along nice and quiet, and that was open, too. 'That's all right,' I thought. 'Deacon's here, and I'll give him Tailor Paul and Batty Thomas for not keeping me posted.' I got up into a sort of place with ropes in it — damn nasty, I thought they

344

looked. And then there was a ladder and more ropes atop of that. And then another ladder and a trap-door.'

'Was the trap-door open?'

'Yes, and I went up. And I didn't half like it, either. Do you know, when I got up into the next place — Gee! there was a queer feel about it. Not a sound, but like as if there might be people standing round. And dark! It was a pitch-black beast of a night and raining like hell, but I never met anything like the blackness of that place. And I felt as if there was hundreds of eyes watching me. Talk about the heebie-jeebies! Well there!

'After a bit, with still not a sound. I sort of pulled myself together and put my torch on. Say, have you ever been up in that place? Ever seen those bells? I'm not what you'd call fanciful in a general way, but there was something about the bells that gave me the fantods.'

'I know,' said Wimsey, 'they look as if they were going to come down on you.'

'Yes, *you* know,' said Nobby, eagerly. 'Well, I'd got to where I wanted, but I didn't know where to begin. I didn't know the first thing about bells, or how to get to them or anything. And I couldn't make out what had happened to Deacon. So I looked round on the floor with the torch and — Boo! — there he was!'

'Dead?'

'Dead as a door-nail. Tied up to a big kind of post, and a look on his face — there! I don't want to see a face like that again. Just as though he'd been struck dead and mad all at one go, if

345

you see what I mean.'

'I suppose there's no doubt he was dead?'

'Dead?' Mr Cranton laughed. 'I never saw anyone deader.'

'Stiff?'

'No, not stiff. But cold, my God! I just touched him. He swung on the ropes and his head had fallen over — well, it looked as if he'd got what was coming to him, anyhow, but worse. Because, to do them justice, they're pretty quick on the drop, but he looked as if it had lasted for a good long time.'

'Do you mean the rope was round his neck?' demanded Parker, a little impatiently.

'No. He wasn't hanged. I don't know what killed him. I was just looking to see, when I heard somebody starting to come up the tower. I didn't stop, you bet. There was another ladder, and I legged it up that as high as I could go, till I got to a sort of hatch leading out on to the roof, I suppose. I squatted inside that and hoped the other fellow wouldn't take it into his head to come up after me. I wasn't keen on being found up there at all, and the body of my old pal Deacon might want some explaining. Of course, I could have told the truth, and pointed out that the poor bloke was cold before I got there, but me having pick-locks in my pocket rather jiggered up that bit of the alibi. So I sat tight. The chap came up into the place where the body was and started moving round and shuffling about, and once or twice he said 'Oh, God!' in a groaning sort of voice. Then there was a nasty sort of thump, and I reckoned he'd got the body down on the floor. Then after a bit I heard him pulling and hauling, and presently his steps went across the floor very low and heavy, and a bumping noise, like he was dragging old Deacon after him. I couldn't see him at all from where I was, because from my corner I could only see the ladder and the wall opposite, and he was right away on the other side of the room. After that there was more scuffling, and a sort of bumping and sliding, and I took it he was getting the body down the other ladder. And I didn't envy him the job, neither.

'I waited up there and waited, till I couldn't hear him any more, and then I began to wonder what I should do next. So I tried the door on to the roof. There was a bolt inside, so I undid that and stepped out. It was raining like blazes and pitch-black, but out I crawled and got to the edge of the tower and looked over. How high is that cursed tower? Hundred and thirty feet, eh? Well, it felt like a thousand and thirty. I'm no cat-burglar, nor yet a steeplejack. I looked down, and I saw a light moving about right away up the other end of the church, miles away beneath me in the graveyard. I tell you I hung on to that blinking parapet with both hands and I got a feeling in my stomach as though me and the tower and everything was crumbling away and going over. I was glad I couldn't see more than I did.

'Well, I thought, you'd better make tracks, Nobby, while the dirty work's going on down there. So I came in again carefully and bolted the door after me and started to come down the ladder. It was awkward going in the dark and after a bit I switched my torch on, and I wished I hadn't. There I was, and those bells just beneath me — and, God! how I hated the look of them. I went all cold and sweaty and the torch slipped out of my hand and went down, and hit one of the bells. I'll never forget the noise it made. It wasn't loud, but kind of terribly sweet and threatening, and it went humming on and on, and a whole lot of other notes seemed to come out of it, high up and clear and close — right in my ears. You'll think I'm loony, but I tell you that bell was alive. I shut my eyes and hung on to the ladder and wished I'd chosen a different kind of profession — and that'll show you what a state I was in.'

'You've got too much imagination, Nobby,' said Parker.

'You wait, Charles,' said Lord Peter. 'You wait till you get stuck on a ladder in a belfry in the dark. Bells are like cats and mirrors — they're always queer, and it doesn't do to think too much about them. Go on, Cranton.'

'That's just what I couldn't do,' said Nobby, frankly. 'Not for a bit. It felt like hours, but I daresay it wasn't more than five minutes. I crawled down at last — in the dark, of course, having lost the torch. I groped round after it and found it, but the bulb had gone, naturally, and I hadn't any matches. So I had to feel for the trapdoor, and I was terrified of pitching right down. But I found it at last, and after that it was easier, though I had a nasty time on the spiral staircase. The steps are all worn away, and I slipped about, and the walls were so close I couldn't breathe. My man had left all the doors open, so I knew he'd be coming back, and that didn't cheer me up much, either. When I was out in the church I hared it for all I was worth to the door. I tripped over something on the way, too, that made an awful clatter. Something like a big metal pot.'

'The brass ewer at the foot of the font,' said Wimsey.

'They didn't ought to keep it there,' said Mr Cranton, indignantly. 'And when I got out through the porch, I had to pussyfoot pretty gently over the beastly creaking gravel. In the end I got away and then I ran — golly, how I ran! I hadn't left anything behind at Wilderspin's, bar a shirt they'd lent me and a toothbrush I'd bought in the village, and I wasn't going back there. I ran and ran like hell, and the rain was something cruel. And it's a hell of a country. Ditches and bridges all over the place. There was a car came past one time, and trying to get out of the light, I missed my footing and rolled down the bank into a ditch full of water. Cold? It was like an ice-bath. I fetched up at last in a barn near a railway station and shivered there till morning, and presently a train came along, so I got on that. I forget the name of the place, but it must have been ten or fifteen miles away from Fenchurch. By the time I got up to London I was in a fever, I can tell you; rheumatic fever, or so they said. And you see what it's done to me. I pretty nearly faded out, and I rather wish I had. I'll never be fit for anything again.

But that's the truth and the whole truth, my lord, and officers. Except that when I came to look myself over. I couldn't find Deacon's cipher. I thought I'd lost it on the road, but if you picked it up in the belfry, it must have come out of my pocket when I pulled the torch out. I never killed Deacon, but I knew I'd have a job to prove I didn't, and that's why I spun you a different tale the first time you came.'

'Well,' said Chief Inspector Parker, 'let's hope it'll be a lesson to you to keep out of belfries.'

'It will,' replied Nobby fervently. 'Every time I see a church tower now it gives me the jim-jams. I'm done with religion, I am, and if I ever go inside a church-door again, you can take and put me in Broadmoor.'

the third part

WILL THODAY GOES IN
QUICK AND COMES OUT SLOW

For while I held my tongue, my bones con-
sumed away through my daily complaining.
Psalm xxxii. 3

Wimsey thought he had never seen such utter
despondency on any face as on William Thoday's.
It was the face of a man pushed to the last
extremity, haggard and grey, and pinched about
the nostrils like a dead man's. On Mary's face
there was anxiety and distress, but something
combative and alert as well. She was still fighting, but Will was obviously beaten.

'Now then, you two,' said Superintendent
Blundell, 'let's hear what you have to say for
yourselves.'

'We've done nothing we need be ashamed of,'
said Mary.

'Leave it to me, Mary,' said Will. He turned
wearily to the Superintendent. 'Well,' he said,
'you've found out about Deacon, I suppose. You
know that he done us and ours a wrong that
can't be put right. We been trying, Mary and me,
to put right as much as we can, but you've
stepped in. Reckon we might have known we
couldn't keep it quiet, but what else could we

351

do? There's been talk enough about poor Mary down in the village, and we thought the best thing was to slip away, hoping to make an honest woman of her without asking the leaves of all they folk with long tongues as 'ud only be too glad to know something against us. And why shouldn't we? It weren't no fault of ours. What call have you got to stop us?'

'See here, Will,' said Mr Blundell, 'it's rough luck on you, and I'm not saying as 'tisn't, but the law's the law. Deacon was a bad lot, as we all know, but the fact remains somebody put him away, and it's our job to find out who did it.'

'I ain't got nothing to say about that,' said Will Thoday, slowly. 'But it's cruel hard if Mary and me — '

'Just a moment,' said Wimsey. 'I don't think you quite realise the position, Thoday. Mr Blundell doesn't want to stand in the way of your marriage, but, as he says, somebody did murder Deacon, and the ugly fact remains that you were the man with the best cause to do it. And that means, supposing a charge were laid against you, and brought into court — well, they might want this lady to give evidence.'

'And if they did?' said Will.

'Just this,' said Wimsey. 'The law does not allow a wife to give evidence against her husband.' He waited while this sank in. 'Have a cigarette, Thoday. Think it out.'

'I see,' said Thoday, bitterly. 'I see. It comes to this — there ain't no end to the wrong that devil done us. He ruined my poor Mary and brought her into the dock once, and he robbed her of her good name and made bastards of our little girls, and now he can come between us again at the altar rails and drive her into the witness-box to put my neck in the rope. If ever a man deserved killing, he's the one, and I hope he's burning in hell for it now.'

'Very likely he is,' said Wimsey, 'but you see the point. If you don't tell us the truth now — '

'I've nothing to tell you but this,' broke in Thoday in a kind of desperation. 'My wife — and she *is* my wife in God's sight and mine — she never knew nothing about it. Not one word. And she knows nothing now, nothing but the name of the man rotting in that grave. And that's the truth as God sees us.'

'Well,' said Mr Blundell, 'you'll have to prove that.'

'That's not quite true, Blundell,' said Wimsey, 'but I dare say it could be proved. Mrs Thoday — '

The woman looked quickly and gratefully at him.

'When did you first realise that your first husband had been alive till the beginning of this year, and that you were, therefore, not legally married to Will Thoday here?'

'Only when you came to see me, my lord, last week.'

'When I showed you that piece of writing in Deacon's hand?'

'Yes, my lord.'

'But how did that — ?' began the Superintendent. Wimsey went on, drowning his voice.

'You realised then that the man buried in Lady

Thorpe's grave must be Deacon.'

'It came over me, my lord, that that must be the way of it. I seemed to see a lot of things clear that I hadn't understood before.'

'Yes. You'd never doubted till that moment that Deacon had died in 1918?'

'Not for a moment, my lord. I'd never have married Will else.'

'You have always been a regular communicant?'

'Yes, my lord.'

'But last Sunday you stayed away.'

'Yes, I did, my lord. I couldn't come here, knowing as me and Will wasn't properly married. It didn't seem right, like.'

'Of course not,' said Wimsey. 'I beg your pardon Superintendent. I'm afraid I interrupted you,' he added, blandly.

'That's all very well,' said Mr Blundell. 'You said you didn't recognise that writing when his lordship showed it to you.'

'I'm afraid I did. It wasn't true — but I had to make up my mind quick — and I was afraid — '

'I'll bet you were. Afraid of getting Will into trouble, hey? Now, see here, Mary, how did you know that paper wasn't written donkey's years ago? What made you jump so quick to the idea Deacon was the corpse in the Thorpe grave? Just you answer me that, my girl, will you?'

'I don't know,' she said, faintly. 'It came over me all of a sudden.'

'Yes, it did,' thundered the Superintendent, 'And why? Because Will had told you about it already, and you knew the game was up. Because you'd seen that there paper before — '

'No, no!'

'I say, Yes. If you hadn't have known something, you'd have had no cause to deny the writing. You knew *when* it was written — now, didn't you?'

'That's a lie!' said Thoday.

'I really don't think you're right about that, Blundell,' said Wimsey, mildly, 'because, if Mrs Thoday had known about it all along, why shouldn't she have gone to Church last Sunday morning? I mean, don't you see, if she'd brazened it out all those months, why shouldn't she do it again?'

'Well,' retorted the Superintendent, 'and how about Will? He's been going to church all right, ain't he? You aren't going to tell me *he* knew nothing about it either.'

'Did he, Mrs Thoday?' inquired Wimsey, gently.

Mary Thoday hesitated.

'I can't tell you about that,' she said at last.

'Can't you, by God?' snapped Mr Blundell. 'Well, now, will you tell me — ?'

'It's no good, Mary,' said Will. 'Don't answer him. Don't say nothing. They'll only twist your words round into what you don't mean. We've got nothing to say and if I got to go through it, I got to go through it and that's all about it.'

'Not quite,' said Wimsey. 'Don't you see that if you tell us what you know, and we're satisfied that your wife knows nothing — then there's nothing to prevent your marriage from going through straight away? That's right, isn't it, Super?'

'Can't hold out any inducement, my lord,' said the Superintendent, stolidly.

'Of course not, but one can point out an obvious fact. You see,' went on Wimsey, 'somebody *must* have known something, for your wife to have jumped so quickly to the conclusion that the dead man was Deacon. If she hadn't already been suspicious about you — if *you* were perfectly ignorant and innocent the whole time — then *she* had the guilty knowledge. It would work all right that way, of course. Yes, I see now that it would. If she knew, and told you about it — then *you* would be the one with the sensitive conscience. *You* would have told *her* that you couldn't kneel at the altar with a guilty woman — '

'Stop that!' said Thoday. 'You say another word and I'll — Oh, my God! it wasn't that, my lord. She never knew. I did know. I'll say that much, I won't say no more, only that. As I hope to be saved, she never knew a word about it.'

'As you hope to be saved?' said Wimsey. 'Well, well. And you did know, and that's all you've got to tell us?'

'Now, look here,' said the Superintendent, 'you'll have to go a bit further than that, my lad. When did you know?'

'When the body was found,' replied Thoday, 'I knew then.' He spoke slowly, as though every word were being wrenched out of him. He went on more briskly: 'That's when I knew who it was.'

'Then why didn't you say so?' demanded Blundell.

'What, and have everybody know me and Mary wasn't married. Likely, ain't it?'

'Ah!' said Wimsey. 'But why didn't you get married then?'

Thoday shifted uncomfortably in his chair.

'Well, you see, my lord — I hoped as Mary needn't ever know. It was a bitter hard thing for her, wasn't it? And the children. We couldn't ever put that right, you see. So I made up my mind to say nothing about it and take the sin — if it was a sin — on my shoulders. I didn't want to make no more trouble for her. Can't you understand that? Well, then — when she found it out, through seeing that there paper — ' He broke off and started again. 'You see, ever since the body was found I'd been worried and upset in my mind, like, and I daresay I was a bit queer in my ways and she'd noticed it — when she asked me if the dead man was Deacon after all, why, then I told her as it was, and that's how it all came about.'

'And how did you know who the dead man was?'

There was a long silence.

'He was terribly disfigured, you know,' went on Wimsey.

'You said you thought he was — that he'd been in prison,' stammered Thoday, 'and I said to myself — '

'Half a mo',' broke in the Superintendent, 'when did you ever hear his lordship say that? It wasn't brought out at the inquest, nor yet at the adjournment, because we were most particularly careful to say nothing about it. Now then!'

'I heard something about it from Rector's Emily,' said Thoday, slowly. 'She happened to hear something his lordship said to Mr Bunter.'

'Oh, *did* she?' snapped Mr Blundell. 'And how much more did Rector's Emily overhear, I'd like to know. That beer-bottle, now! Who told her to dust the fingerprints off it — come, now!'

'She didn't mean no harm about that,' said Will. 'It was nothing but the girl's curiosity. You know how they are. She came over next day and told Mary all about it. In a rare taking, she was.'

'Indeed!' said the Superintendent, unbelievingly. 'So *you* say. Never mind. Let's go back to Deacon. You heard that Emily heard something his lordship said to Mr Bunter about the dead man having been in prison. Was that it? And what did you think of that?'

'I said to myself, it must be Deacon. I said, here's that devil come out of his grave to trouble us again, that's what I said. Mind you, I didn't exactly know, but that's what I said to myself.'

'And what did you imagine he had come for?'

'How was I to know? I thought he'd come, that's all.'

'You thought he'd come after the emeralds, didn't you?' said the Superintendent.

For the first time a look of genuine surprise and eagerness came into the haunted eyes. 'The emeralds? Was *that* what he was after? Do you mean he had them after all? Why, we always thought the other fellow — Cranton — had got them.'

'You didn't know that they had been hidden in the church?'

'*In the church?*'

'We found them there on Monday,' explained his lordship, placidly, 'tucked away in the roof.'

'In the roof of the church? Why, then, *that* was what he — The emeralds found? Thank God for that! They'll not be able to say now as Mary had any hand in it.'

'True,' said Wimsey. 'But you were about to say something else, I rather fancy, 'That was what he — ?' What? 'That was what he was after when I found him in the church.' Was that it?'

'No, my lord. I was going to say — I was just going to say, that was what he did with them.' A fresh wave of anger seemed to sweep over him. 'The dirty villain! He did double-cross that other fellow after all.'

'Yes,' agreed his lordship. 'I'm afraid there's not much to be said in favour of the late Mr Deacon. I'm sorry, Mrs Thoday, but he was really rather an unsatisfactory person. And you're not the only one to suffer. He married another woman over in France, and she's left with three small children too.'

'Poor soul!' said Mary.

'The damned scoundrel!' exclaimed Will, 'if I'd have known that, I'd — '

'Yes?'

'Never mind,' growled the farmer. 'How did he come to be in France? How did he — ?'

'That's a long story,' said Wimsey, 'and rather far from the point at issue. Now, let's get your story clear. You heard that the body of a man who might have been a convict had been found in the churchyard, and though the face was quite unrecognisable, you were — shall we say inspired? — to identify him with Geoffrey Deacon, whom you had supposed to have died in 1918. You said nothing about it until your wife, the other day, saw a bit of Deacon's handwriting, which might have been written at any time, and was — shall we again say inspired? — with the same idea. Without waiting for any further verification, you both rushed away to town to get remarried, and that's the only explanation you can give. Is that it?'

'That's all I can say, my lord.'

'And a damned thin story too,' observed Mr Blundell, truculently. 'Now, get this, Will Thoday. You know where you stand as well as I do. You know you're not bound to answer any questions now unless you like. But there's the inquest on the body; we can have that reopened, and you can tell your story to the coroner. Or you can be charged with the murder and tell it to a judge and jury. Or you can come clean now. Whichever you like. See?'

'I've nothing more to say, Mr Blundell.'

'I tell thee all, I can no more,' observed Wimsey thoughtfully. 'That's a pity, because the public prosecutor may get quite a different sort of story fixed in his mind. He may think, for instance, that you knew Deacon was alive because you had met him in the church on the night of December 30th.'

He waited to see the effect of this, and resumed:

'There's Potty Peake, you know. I don't suppose he's too potty to give evidence about

what he saw and heard that night from behind
Abbot Thomas's tomb. The black-bearded man
and the voices in the vestry and Will Thoday
fetching the rope from the cope-chest. What took
you into the church, by the way? You saw a light,
perhaps. And went along and found the door
open, was that it? And in the vestry, you found a
man doing something that looked suspicious. So
you challenged him and when he spoke you
knew who it was. It was lucky that the fellow
didn't shoot you, but probably you took him
unawares. Anyway, you threatened to give him
up to justice and then he pointed out that would
put your wife and children in an unpleasant
position. So you indulged in a little friendly chat
— did you speak? In the end, you compromised.
You said you would keep quiet about it and get
him out of the country with £200 in pocket, but
you hadn't got it at the moment and in the
meantime you would put him in a place of safety.
Then you fetched a rope and tied him up. I don't
know how you kept him quiet while you went to
fetch it. Did you give him a straight left to the
jaw, or what? . . . You won't help me? . . . Well,
never mind. You tied him up and left him in the
vestry while you went round to steal Mr
Venables's keys. It's a miracle you found them in
the right place, by the way. They seldom are.
Then you took him up into the belfry, because
the bell-chamber was nice and handy and had
several locks to it, and was easier than escorting
him out through the village. After that you
brought him some food — perhaps Mrs Thoday
could throw some light on that. Did you miss a

quart bottle of beer or so about that time, Mrs Thoday? Some of those you got in for Jim? By the way, Jim is coming home and we'll have to have a word with him.'

Watching Mary's face, the Superintendent saw it contract suddenly with alarm, but she said nothing. Wimsey went on remorselessly.

'The next day you went over to Walbeach to get the money. But you weren't feeling well, and on the way home you broke down completely and couldn't get back to let Deacon out. That was damned awkward for you, wasn't it? You didn't want to confide in your wife. Of course, there was Jim.'

Thoday raised his head.

'I'm not saying anything one way or other, my lord, except this. I've never said one word to Jim about Deacon — not one word. Nor he to me. And that's the truth.'

'Very well,' said Wimsey. 'Whatever else happened, in between December 30th and January 4th, somebody killed Deacon. And on the night of the 4th, somebody buried the body. Somebody who knew him and took care to mutilate his face and hands beyond recognition. And what everybody will want to know is, at what moment did Deacon cease to be Deacon and become the body? Because that's rather the point, isn't it? We know that you couldn't very well have buried him yourself, because you were ill, but the killing is a different matter. You see, Thoday, he didn't starve to death. He died with a full tummy. *You* couldn't have fed him after the morning of December 31st. If you didn't kill

362

him then, who took him his rations in the interval? And who, having fed him and killed him, rolled him down the belfry ladder on the night of the 4th, with a witness sitting in the roof of the tower — a witness who had seen him and recognised him? A witness who — '

'Hold on, my lord,' said the Superintendent. 'The woman's fainted.'

the fourth part

THE SLOW WORK

Who shut up the sea with doors . . . and
brake up for it my decreed place?

Job xxxviii. 8, 10

'He won't say anything,' said Superintendent
Blundell.

'I know he won't,' said Wimsey. 'Have you
arrested him?'

'No, my lord, I haven't. I've sent him home
and told him to think it over. Of course, we
could easily get him on being an accessory after
the fact in both cases. I mean, he was shielding a
known murderer — that's pretty clear, I fancy;
and he's also shielding whoever killed Deacon, if
he didn't do it himself. But I'm taking the view
that we'll be able to handle him better after
we've interrogated James. And we know James
will be back in England at the end of the month.
His owners have been very sensible. They've
given him orders to come home, without saying
what he's wanted for. They've arranged for
another man to take his place and he's to report
himself by the next boat.'

'Good! It's a damnable business, the whole
thing. If ever a fellow deserved a sticky death, it's
this Deacon brute. If the law had found him the

law would have hanged him, with loud applause from all good citizens. Why should we hang a perfectly decent chap for anticipating the law and doing our dirty work for us?'

'Well, it *is* the law, my lord,' replied Mr Blundell, 'and it's not my place to argue about it. In any case, we're going to have a bit of a job to hang Will Thoday, unless it's as an accessory before the fact. Deacon was killed on a full stomach. If Will did away with him on the 30th, or the 31st, why did he go to collect the £200? If Deacon was dead, he wouldn't want it. On the other hand, if Deacon wasn't killed till the 4th, who fed him in the interval? If James killed him, why did he trouble to feed him first? The thing makes no sense.'

'Suppose Deacon was being fed by somebody,' said Wimsey, 'and suppose he said something infuriatin' and the somebody killed him all of a sudden in a frenzy, not meanin' to?'

'Yes, but how did he kill him? He wasn't stabbed or shot or clouted over the head.'

'Oh, I don't *know*,' said Wimsey. 'Curse the man! He's a perfect nuisance, dead or alive, and whoever killed him was a public benefactor. I wish I'd killed him myself. Perhaps I did. Perhaps the Rector did. Perhaps Hezekiah Lavender did.'

'I don't suppose it was any of those,' said Mr Blundell, stolidly. 'But it might have been somebody else, of course. There's that Potty, for instance. He's always wandering round the church at night. Only he'd have to get into the bell-chamber, and I don't see how he could. But I'm waiting for James. I've got a hunch that James may have quite a lot to tell us.'

'Have you? Oysters have beards, but they don't wag them.'

'If it comes to oysters,' said the Superintendent, 'there's ways and means of opening 'em — *and* you needn't swallow 'em whole, neither. You're not going back to Fenchurch?'

'Not just at present. I don't think there's very much I can do down there for a bit. But my brother Denver and I are going to Walbeach to open the New Cut. I expect we shall see you there.'

★ ★ ★

The only other thing of interest that happened during the next week or so was the sudden death of Mrs Wilbraham. She died at night and alone — apparently from mere old age — with the emeralds clasped in her hand. She left a will drawn up fifteen years earlier, in which she left the whole of her very considerable estate to her Cousin Henry Thorpe 'because he is the only honest man I know.' That she should cheerfully have left her only honest relative to suffer the wearing torments of straitened means and anxiety throughout the intervening period seemed to be only what anybody might have expected from her enigmatic and secretive disposition. A codicil, dated on the day after Henry's death, transferred the legacy to Hilary, while a further codicil, executed a few days before her own death, not only directed that the emeralds which had caused all the disturbance should be given to

366

'Lord Peter Wimsey who seems to be a sensible man and to have acted without interested motives,' but also made him Hilary's trustee. Lord Peter made a wry face over this bequest. He offered the necklace to Hilary, but she refused to touch it; it had painful associations for her. It was, indeed, only with difficulty that she was persuaded to accept the Wilbraham estate. She hated the thought of the testatrix; and besides, she had set her heart on earning her own living. 'Uncle Edward will be worse than ever,' she said. 'He will want me to marry some horrible rich man, and if I want to marry a poor one, he'll say he's after the money. And anyway, I don't want to marry anybody.'

'Then don't,' said Wimsey. 'Be a wealthy spinster.'

'And get like Aunt Wilbraham? Not me!'

'Of course not. Be a nice wealthy spinster.'

'Are there any?'

'Well, there's me. I mean, I'm a nice wealthy bachelor. Fairly nice, anyway. And it's fun to be rich. I find it so. You needn't spend it all on yachts and cocktails, you know. You could build something or endow something or run something or the other. If you don't take it, it will go to some ghastly person — Uncle Edward or somebody — whoever is Mrs Wilbraham's next-of-kin, and they'd be sure to do something silly with it.'

'Uncle Edward would,' said Hilary, thoughtfully.

'Well, you've got a few years to think it over,' said Wimsey. 'When you're of age, you can see about throwing it into the Thames. But what I'm to do with the emeralds I really don't know.'

'Beastly things,' said Hilary. 'They've killed grandfather, and practically killed Dad, and they've killed Deacon and they'll kill somebody else before long. I wouldn't touch them with a barge-pole.'

'I'll tell you what. I'll keep them till you're twenty-one, and then we'll form ourselves into a Wilbraham Estate Disposals Committee and do something exciting with the whole lot.'

Hilary agreed; but Wimsey felt depressed. So far as he could see, his interference had done no good to anybody and only made extra trouble. It was a thousand pities that the body of Deacon had ever come to light at all. Nobody wanted it.

★　★　★

The New Wash Cut was opened with great rejoicing at the end of the month. The weather was perfect, the Duke of Denver made a speech which was a model of the obvious, and the Regatta was immensely successful. Three people fell into the river, four men and an old woman were had up for being drunk and disorderly, a motor-car became entangled with a tradesman's cart and young Gotobed won First Prize in the Decorated Motorcycle section of the Sports.

And the River Wale, placidly doing its job in the midst of all the disturbance, set to work to scour its channel to the sea. Wimsey, leaning over the wall at the entry to the Cut, watched the salt water moving upward with the incoming tide, muddied and chafing along its new-made bed.

On his left, the crooked channel of the old river lay empty of its waters, a smooth expanse of shining mud.

'Doing all right,' said a voice beside him. He turned and found that it was one of the engineers.

'What extra depth have you given her?'

'Only a few feet, but she'll do the rest herself. There's been nothing the matter with this river except that silting of the outfall and the big bend below here. We've shortened her course now by getting on for three miles and driven a channel right out into the Wash beyond the mudbanks. She'll make her own outfall now, if she's left to herself. We're expecting her to grind her channel lower by eight to ten feet — possibly more. It'll make all the difference to the town. It's a scandal, the way the thing's been let go. Why, as it is, the tide scarcely gets up higher than Van Leyden's Sluice. After this, it'll probably run up as far as the Great Learn. The whole secret with these Fen rivers is to bring back all the water you can into its natural course. Where the old Dutchmen went wrong was in dispersing it into canals and letting it lie about all over the place. The smaller the fall of the land, the bigger weight of water you need to keep the outfall scoured. You'd think it was obvious, wouldn't you? But it's taken people hundreds of years to learn it.'

'Yes,' said Wimsey. 'I suppose all this extra water will go up the Thirty Foot?'

'That's right. It's practically a straight run now from the Old Bank Sluice to the New Cut

Outfall — thirty-five miles — and this will carry off a lot of the High Level water from Leamholt and Lympsey. At present the Great Leam has to do more work than it should — they've always been afraid to let the Thirty Foot take its fair proportion of the flood-water in winter, because, you see, when it got down to this point it would have over-flowed the old river-bed and drowned the town. But now the New Cut will carry it clean off, and that will relieve the Great Leam and obviate the floods round Frogglesham, Mere Wash and Lympsey Fen.'

'Oh!' said Wimsey. 'I suppose the Thirty Foot Dyke will stand the strain?'

'Oh, dear, yes,' said the engineer, cheerfully. 'It was meant to from the beginning. In fact, at one time, it had to. It's only within the last hundred years that the Wale has got so badly silted up. There's been a good deal of shifting in the Wash — chiefly owing to tidal action, of course, and the Nene Outfall Cut, and that helped to cause the obstruction, don't you see. But the Thirty Foot worked all right in the old days.'

'In the Lord Protector's time, I suppose,' said Wimsey. 'And now you've cleared the Wale Outfall, no doubt the obstruction will go somewhere else.'

'Very likely,' replied the engineer, with unimpaired cheerfulness. 'These mudbanks are always shifting about. But in time I daresay they'll clear the whole thing — unless, of course, they really take it into their heads to drain the Wash and make a job of it.'

'Just so,' said Wimsey.

'But as far as it goes,' continued the engineer, 'this looks pretty good. It's to be hoped our dam over there will stand up to the strain. You'd be surprised at the scour you get with these quiet-looking rivers. Anyhow, this embankment is all right — I'll take my oath of that. You watch the tide-mark. We've marked the old low level and the old high level — if you don't see the one lowered and the other raised by three or four feet within the next few months, you can call me — a Dutchman. Excuse me a minute — I just want to see that they're making that dam good over there.'

He hurried off to superintend the workmen who were completing the dam across the old course of the river.

'And how about my old sluice-gates?'

'Oh!' said Wimsey, looking round, 'it's you, is it?'

'Ah!' The sluice-keeper spat copiously into the rising water. 'It's me. That's who it is. Look at all this money they been spending. Thousands. But as for them gates of mine, I reckon I can go and whistle for 'em.'

'No answer yet from Geneva?'

'Eh?' said the sluice-keeper. 'Oh! Ah! Meaning what I said? Ah! that were a good 'un, weren't it? Why don't they refer it to the League of Nations? Ah and why don't they? Look at thisher great scour o' water a-comin' up. Where's that a-going to? It's got to go somewhere, ain't it?'

'No doubt,' said Wimsey. 'I understand it's to go up the Thirty Foot.'

'Ah!' said the sluice-keeper. 'Always interfering with things, they are.'

'They're not interfering with your gates, anyway.'

'No, they ain't, and that's just where it is. Once you starts interferin' with things you got to go on. One thing leads to another. Let 'm bide, that's what I say. Don't go digging of 'em up and altering of 'em. Dig up one thing and you got to dig up another.'

'At that rate,' objected Wimsey, 'the Fens would still be all under water.'

'Well, in a manner of speaking, so they would,' admitted the sluice-keeper. 'That's very true, so they would. But none the more for that, they didn't ought to come a-drowning of us now. It's all right for him to talk about letting the floods out at the Old Bank Sluice. Where's it all a-going to? It comes up, and it's got to go somewhere, and it comes down and it's got to go somewhere, ain't it?'

'At the moment I gather it drowns the Mere Wash and Frogglesham and all those places.'

'Well, it's their water, ain't it?' said the sluice-keeper. 'They ain't got no call to send it down here.'

'Quite,' said Wimsey, recognising the spirit that had hampered the Fen drainage for the last few hundred years, 'but as you say yourself, it's got to go somewhere.'

'It's their water,' retorted the man obstinately. 'Let 'em keep it. It won't do us no good.'

'Walbeach seems to want it.'

'Ah! them!' The sluice-keeper spat vehemently. 'They don't know what they want. They're always a-wantin' some nonsense or other. And there's always some fool to give it 'em, what's more. All I wants is a new set of gates, but I don't look like getting of 'em. I've asked for 'em time and again. I asked that young feller there. 'Mister,' I says to him, 'how about a new set o' gates for my sluice?' 'That ain't in our contract,' he says. 'No,' I says, 'and drowning half the parish ain't in your contract neither, I suppose.' But he couldn't see it.'

'Well, cheer up,' said Wimsey. 'Have a drink.'

He did, however, feel sufficient interest in the matter to speak to the engineer about it when he saw him again.

'Oh, I think it's all right,' said that gentleman. 'We did, as a matter of fact, recommend that the gates should be repaired and strengthened, but you see, the damned thing's all tied up in some kind of legal bother. The fact is, once you start on a job like this, you never know where it's going to end. It's all piecemeal work. Stop it up in one place and it breaks out in another. But I don't think you need worry about this part of it. What *does* want seeing to is the Old Bank Dyke — but that's under a different authority altogether. Still, they've undertaken to make up their embankment and put in some fresh stonework. If they don't there'll be trouble, but they can't say we haven't warned them.'

'Dig up one thing,' thought Wimsey, 'and you have to dig up another. I wish we'd never dug up Deacon. Once you let the tide in, it's got to go somewhere.'

★ ★ ★

James Thoday, returning to England as instructed by his employers, was informed that the police wanted him as a witness. He was a sturdy man, rather older than William, with bleak blue eyes and a reserved manner. He repeated his original story, without emphasis and without details. He had been taken ill in the train after leaving Fenchurch. He had attributed the trouble to some sort of gastric influenza. When he got to London, he had felt quite unable to proceed, and had telegraphed to that effect. He had spent part of that day huddled over the fire in a public house near Liverpool Street; he thought they might remember him there. They could not give him a bed for the night and, in the evening, feeling a little better he had gone out and found a room in a back street. He could not recall the address, but it had been a clean, pleasant place. In the morning he found himself fit to continue his journey, though still very weak and tottery. He had, of course, seen English papers mentioning the discovery of the corpse in the churchyard, but knew nothing further about it, except, of course, what he had heard from his brother and sister-in-law, which was very little. He had never had any idea who the dead man was. Would he be surprised to hear that it was Geoffrey Deacon? He would be very much surprised indeed. The news came as a terrible shock to him. That would be a bad job for his people.

Indeed, he looked startled enough. But there had been a tenseness of the muscles about his mouth which persuaded Superintendent Blundell that the shock had been caused, not so much by hearing the dead man's name as by hearing that the police knew it.

Mr Blundell, aware of the solicitude with which the Law broods over the interest of witnesses, thanked him and proceeded with his inquiries. The public house was found, and substantiated the story of the sick sailor who had sat over the fire all day drinking hot toddies; but the clean and pleasant woman who had let her room to Mr Thoday was not so easy of identification.

Meanwhile, the slow machinery of the London police revolved and, from many hundreds of reports, ground out the name of a garage proprietor who had hired out a motor-bicycle on the evening of the 4th January to a man answering to the description of James Thoday. The bicycle had been returned on the Sunday by a messenger, who had claimed and taken away the deposit, minus the charge for hire and insurance. No, not a district messenger: a youth, who looked like an ordinary out-of-work.

On hearing this, Chief Inspector Parker, who was dealing with the London end of the inquiry, groaned dismally. It was too much to expect this nameless casual to turn up. Ten to one, he had pocketed the surplus deposit and would be particularly unwilling to inform the world of the fact.

Parker was wrong. The man who had hired the bicycle had apparently made the fatal mistake of picking an honest messenger. After prolonged inquiry and advertisement a young Cockney made his appearance at New Scotland Yard. He gave his name as Frank Jenkins, and explained that he had only just seen the advertisement. He had been seeking work in various places, and had drifted back to Town in time to be confronted with the police inquiry on a notice board at the Labour Exchange.

He very well remembered the episode of the motorbike. It had struck him as funny at the time. He had been hanging round a garridge in Bloomsbury in the early morning of January 5th, hoping to pick up a job when he see a bloke coming along on this here bike. The bloke was short and stocky, with blue eyes, and sounded like he might be the boss of some outfit or other — he spoke sharp and quick, like he might be accustomed to giving orders. Yes, he might have been an officer in the mercantile marine, very likely. Come to think of it, he did look a bit like a sailor. He was dressed in a very wet and dirty motoring coat and wore a cap, pulled down over his face, like. This man had said: 'Here, sonny, d'you want a job?' On being told 'Yes,' he had asked: 'Can you ride a motor-bike?' Frank Jenkins had replied, 'Lead me to it, guvnor'; whereupon he had been told to take the machine back to a certain garage, to collect the deposit and to bring it to the stranger outside the Rugby Tavern at the corner of Great James Street and Chapel Street, when he would receive something for his pains. He had done his part of the business, and hadn't took more than an hour, all told (returning by bus), but when he arrived at the Rugby Tavern, the stranger was not there, and apparently never had been there. A woman said she had seen him walking away in the direction of Guilford Street. Jenkins had hung about till the middle of the morning, but had seen no sign of the man in the motor-coat. He had therefore deposited the money with the landlord of the Tavern, with a message to say that he could wait no longer and had kept back half-a-crown — that being the amount he thought fair to award himself for the transaction. The landlord would be able to tell them if the sum had ever been claimed.

The landlord, being interrogated, brought the matter to mind. Nobody answering the description of the stranger had ever called for the money, which, after a little search and delay, was produced intact in a dirty envelope. Enclosed with it was the garage-proprietor's receipt made out in the name of Joseph Smith, at a fictitious address.

The next thing was, obviously, to confront James Thoday with Frank Jenkins. The messenger identified his employer immediately; James Thoday persisted, politely, that there was some mistake. What next, thought Mr Parker.

He put the question to Lord Peter, who said:

'I think it's time for a spot of dirty work, Charles. Try putting William and James alone in a room with a microphone or whatever you call the beastly gadget. It may not be pretty, but you'll probably find that it works.'

In these circumstances, therefore, the brothers met for the first time since James had left William on the morning of January 4th. The scene was a waiting-room at Scotland Yard.

'Well, William,' said James.

'Well, James,' said William.

There was a silence. Then James said:

'How much do they know?'

'Pretty well everything, by what I can make out.'

There was another pause. Then James spoke again in a constrained voice:

'Very well. Then you had better let me take the blame. I'm not married, and there's Mary and the kids to be thought of. But in God's name, man, couldn't you have got rid of the fellow without killing him?'

'That,' said William, 'is just what I was going to ask *you*.'

'You mean to say that it wasn't you who did away with him?'

'Of course not. I'd be a fool to do it. I'd offered the brute two hundred pounds to go back where he came from. If I hadn't a-been ill, I'd a-got him away all right, and that's what I thought you'd a-done. My God! when he come up out o' that grave, like Judgement Day, I wished you'd killed me along of him.'

'But I never laid hand on him, Will, till after he was dead. I saw him there, the devil, with that ghastly look on his face, and I never blamed you for what you'd done. I swear I never blamed you, Will — only for being such a fool as to do it. So I broke his ugly face in, so that no one should ever guess who he was. But they've found out, seemingly. It was cursed bad luck, that grave being opened so soon. Maybe it'd have been better if I'd carried him out and thrown him in the Drain, but it's a long way to go, and I thought we'd be safe enough.'

'But, see here, James — if you didn't kill him, who did?'

It was at this point that Superintendent Blundell, Chief Inspector Parker and Lord Peter Wimsey walked in on the pair of them.

the fifth part

THE DODGING

Then whispered they of a violated grave
— of a disfigured body.

EDGAR ALLAN POE: *Berenice*

The only difficulty was that the two witnesses
who had formerly refused to speak could now
hardly speak fast enough and spoke both
together. Chief Inspector Parker was obliged to
call for silence.

'All right,' he said. 'You've both been
suspecting each other and shielding each other.
We've grasped that. Now that we've got that
clear, let's have the story. William first.' He
added the usual caution.

'Well, sir,' replied William, briskly, 'I don't
know as I've much to tell you, because his
lordship here seems to have worked it all out
surprising neat. What my feelings were when he
told me just what I did that night I won't say
— but what I do want to make as clear as I can
is that my poor wife never knew one thing about
it, first to last. Why, that was my whole trouble
all the time — how to keep it from her.

'I'll begin right at the beginning, with the
night of December 30th. I was just coming
home, pretty late for me, from seeing to one of

380

the cows that had gone sick up at Sir Henry's place, and as I was passing the church, I thought I saw somebody a-creeping up to the porch and going in. It was a dark night, of course, but, if you remember, sir, it had begun to snow, and I could see something moving, like, against the white. So I thinks, that's Potty up to his games again — I better send him off home. So I goes up to the church door, and I sees footmarks going all along the path as far as the porch, and there they seems to stop. So I say, 'Hallo!' and looks about a bit. That's queer, I says to myself, where's the beggar got to? So I goes round the church, and I sees a light a-moving about and going towards the vestry. Well, I thinks, maybe it's Rector. And then I thinks, well, maybe it ain't. So I comes back to the door, and there's no key in it, like there would be in the ordinary way if Rector had been inside. So I pushes the door and it opens. And in I goes. And then I hears somebody a-moving about and bumping, like, up in the chancel. I goes along quiet, having rubber boots on, that I was wearing for the fields, and when I gets round behind the chancel screen I sees a light and hears the bloke in the vestry, so in I goes and there's a fellow a-tugging away at the ladder Harry Gotobed uses for seeing to the lamps and that, what's always kept a-lying along the wall. He had his back to me, and on the table I see a kind of a dark lantern and something else as had no right to be there, and that's a revolver. So I catches hold of the revolver and said, loud and sharp, 'What are you doing there?' And he jumped round pretty damn quick and made a dive for the table. 'No, you don't,' I said, 'I've got your gun and I know how to use it. What are you after?' Well, he started some sort of tale about being out of work and tramping about and wanting a place to sleep in, and I said, 'That won't wash. How about this gun? Hands up,' I said, 'let's see what else you've got on you.' So I went through his pockets and brought out what looked to me like a set of pick-locks. 'Well, my lad,' I said, 'that's quite enough for me. You're for it.' And he looked at me, and laughed like hell, and said, 'Think again. Will Thoday.' And I said, 'How do you know my name?' and then I looked again and said, 'My God, it's Jeff Deacon!' And he said, 'Yes; and you're the man that's married my wife.' And he laughed again. And then it come over me just what it all meant.'

'How did he know that?' asked Wimsey. 'He didn't get it from Cranton.'

'That was the other scoundrel? No, he told me he'd meant to come after Mary, but hearing from some fellow at Leamholt that she was married, he thought he'd better have a scout round first. I couldn't make out why he'd come back to the place at all, and he wouldn't tell me. I see it now, it was the emeralds. He did say something about me keeping quiet and he'd make it worth my while, but I told him I'd have no truck with him. I asked him where he'd been, but he just laughed and said, 'Never you mind.' And I asked what he wanted in Fenchurch, and he said he wanted money. So I made out that he'd meant to come blackmailing Mary. Well,

382

that made me see red, and I was in half a mind to give him up to the police and take what was coming to us, but when I thought about Mary and the kids — well, I couldn't face it. I was wrong, of course, but when I remembered all the talk there'd been — well, I wanted to spare her that. He knew just how I stood, the devil, and he stood there grinning at me.

'So in the end, I made a devil's bargain with him. I said I'd hide him and give him the money to get out of the country, and then I thought what was I to do with him? I'd got his picklocks all right, but I didn't trust him none the more for that, and I was afraid to go out of the church with him, where we might run up against somebody. And then I got the idea of putting him up in the bell-chamber. So I told him what I meant to do and he agreed. I thought I could get the keys from the Rector all right, so, just for the time being, I pushed him into the cupboard where the surplices hang and locked him in. Then I thought that he might easily break his way out while I was over at the Rectory, so I went down and fetched a rope from the chest and came back and tied him up. You see, I didn't believe that tale of his about sleeping in the vestry. Robbing the church was what I thought he was after. And besides, if I went away and left him, what was to stop him getting out and hiding somewhere and slugging me over the head when I got back? I'd no key to the church door, neither, and he might have made off.'

'Good thing for you if he had,' suggested Mr Blundell.

'Yes — so long as nobody else caught him. Anyhow, I got the keys. I put up some story to the Rector — it must have been a pretty lame one — the old gentleman was a bit puzzled, I think. He kept on saying how queer I looked, and insisted on getting me a drop of his port. While he was fetching it, I just nipped the keys off the nail by the door. I know what you're going to say — suppose he'd mislaid them as usual? Well, I'd have had to try some dodge on Jack Godfrey or else change my plans — but there they were and I didn't bother with any 'ifs'. I went back to the church and untied Deacon's legs and made him walk up the belfry stairs in front of me, like taking a pig to market. It wasn't difficult: I had the revolver, you see.'

'And you tied him up to a beam in the bell-chamber?'

'Yes, sir, I did. And wouldn't you a-done? Just think of yourself carrying victuals and stuff up one o' they ladders in the dark, with a murderer roaming loose at the top all ready to bash your head in the moment you popped it up above floor-level. I tied him up good and proper, though it were a bit of a job with the rope being so thick. 'Stay you there,' I said, 'and I'll bring you something to eat in the morning and see you out of the country before you're twenty-four hours older.' He cursed like a devil, but I paid no attention to him. It was all I could do to keep my hand offen him, and I'm often minded to think it's a wonder I didn't kill him then and there.'

'But had you made any plans for shipping him off?'

384

'Yes, I had. I'd been over to Walbeach the day before with Jim here, and we'd had a bit of a talk with a pal of his — a queer old skipper on a Dutch cargo boat that was lying there, taking in some sort of freight — I never rightly gathered what it was — but I got the notion the old boy wouldn't find much come amiss to him.'

'You're right there, Will,' put in Jim grinning.

'So I found. It wasn't the best plan, maybe, but it was all I could do in the time. I couldn't think very clear, to tell you the truth. I was terrible put about in my mind and my head was buzzing like a thresher. I suppose 'twas the flu coming on. I don't know how I got through that evening at home, looking at Mary and the kids and knowing what I knew. Fortunately, she knew I was worried over the cow and put it all down to that — at least, I thought so. I tossed and turned all night, and the only thing to comfort me was the blessed snow coming down and hiding all they footprints we'd left round the church.

'Next morning I was damned ill, but I couldn't stop to think of that. I slipped out well before daybreak, with some bread and cheese and beer in an old tool-bag. Jim heard me and called out to know what was up. So I said I was going over to see the cow — and so I did, only I took the church on the way.

'Deacon was all right, only very bad-tempered and perished wi' cold, so I left him my old coat — not wanting him to be frozen to death. And I tied him up by his elbows and ankles, leaving his hands free, as he could help himself to his victuals but not untie himself. Then I went on to

385

see to the cow and found her better. After breakfast I got the old car out and ran her over to Walbeach, feeling worse and worse all the time. I found my skipper, just getting ready to sail. I had a word with him, and he agreed to wait until ten o'clock that night and carry my passenger, no questions asked. Two hundred and fifty pounds was the price he wanted and I agreed to pay it. I got the money and gave him the fifty then and there, promising him the rest when I got Deacon aboard. I got into the car and started back — and you know what happened afterwards.'

'That's very clear,' said Parker. 'I needn't tell you that you were compounding a serious felony by helping a convicted murderer to escape from justice. Speaking as a policeman, I am shocked; speaking as a human being, I have every sympathy for you. Now, you.' He turned to Jim. 'I imagine your part of it comes in here.'

'Yes, sir. Well, as you know, poor Will was brought back in a terrible state and we thought for a day or two he was pretty well gone. He was out of his head and kept on calling out that he must go down to the church, but we put that down to the bell-ringing business. All the time he kept a sort of control over himself and never let out a word about Deacon, but one day, when Mary had gone out of the room, he clutched at my hand and said, 'Don't let her know, Jim. Get him away.' 'Get who away?' I said. And he said, 'In the belfry — bitter cold and starving.' And then he sat up in bed and said, quite plain and clear, 'My coat — give me my coat — I must have the keys and the money.' I said, 'All right, Will, I'll see to it' — thinking he was dreaming, and after a bit he seemed to forget about it and go off in a doze. But I thought it was queer, so I had a look in his coat, and there, sure enough, were the Rector's bunch of keys and a whole wad of money.

'Well, I began to think there might be something behind it, so I took the keys, and I thought, before I took them back, I'd just have a look round the church. I went in there — '

'Which day was this?'

'I reckon it was the 2nd of January. I went up into the belfry — right up to the bell-chamber, and — well! there he was!'

'He must have been pretty fed up with things by that time.'

'Fed up? He was dead and cold.'

'Starved to death?'

'Not he. There was a big bit of cheese beside him and near half a loaf of bread and two bottles of beer, one empty and one full. And he hadn't died of cold, neither, as you might expect. I've seen men that had died of exposure, and they died peaceful — curled up like kittens, mostly, as if they'd gone out in their sleep. No. He'd died on his feet, and whatever it was, he'd seen it coming to him. He'd struggled like a tiger against the ropes, working at them till he could get upright, and they had cut through the stuff of his jacket and through his socks. And his face! My God, sir, I've never seen anything like it. His eyes staring open and a look in them as if he'd looked down into hell. It fair shook me.

'I looked him over — and then I saw Will's old coat lying on the floor, thrown off, it might be, in his struggles — and that didn't look like dying of cold, neither. I couldn't tell what to make of it, for I didn't recognise him, you see. I had a look at his breast pocket, and found some papers. There was some made out in the name of Taylor and some in a French name that I've forgotten. I couldn't make head or tail of it. And then I had a look at his hands.'

'Ah!' said Wimsey, 'now we're coming to it.'

'Yes, my lord. You must remember that I knew Deacon. Not very well, but I knew him. And he carried a big scar on one hand, where he'd fallen down one day, carrying a tray with a glass jug on it. I'd seen that scar, and I'd never forget it. When I saw that, my lord, and knew who 'twas — well, there! I hadn't much doubt about what'd happened. Forgive me, Will — I thought you'd done him in, and as God's my witness, I couldn't blame you. Not that I hold with murder, and it came to me then that things could never be the same betwixt you and me — but I didn't blame you. Only I wished it had happened in a fair fight.'

'If it had happened. Jim, it would a-been in a fair fight. I might a-killed him, but I wouldn't a-killed him when he was tied up. You might a-known that.'

'Well, so I might. But it seemed to me at the time as there was no way out of it. I had to think quick what to do. I found some old boards and beams in a corner, and I stood them up in front of him, so as if anybody came in they might not

388

notice him — not unless they were looking for something — and then I came away and thought hard. I kept the keys. I knew I'd be wanting them, and Rector is so absent minded, he'd probably think he'd mislaid them.

'I thought all that day — and then I remembered that Lady Thorpe's funeral was fixed for the Saturday. It seemed to me that I might put him in her grave and that he need never be found, barring accidents. I was due to leave on Saturday morning, and I thought I could fix things so as to have an alibi.

'I had a bad moment on Friday. Jack Godfrey told me they were going to ring a muffled peal for Lady Thorpe, and I was all of a shake, thinking he'd see him when he went up to put the leathers on the bells. By a big stroke of luck, he didn't go till after dark, and I suppose he never looked into that dark corner, or he'd have seen the planks had been moved.'

'We know what you did on Saturday,' said Parker. 'You needn't bother with that.'

'No, sir. I had an awful ride with that bike. The acetylene lamp worked none too well, and it was raining like the tropics. Still, I got there — much later than I meant, and I went to work. I cut him down — '

'You needn't tell us that, either. There was a witness on the top of that bell-chamber ladder all the time.'

'A witness?'

'Yes — and lucky for you, my lad, he was a highly respectable and gentlemanly burglar with the heart of a rabbit and a wholesome fear of bloodshed — otherwise you might be paying blackmail through the nose. But I will say for Nobby,' added Parker reflectively, 'that he would consider blackmail beneath him. You got the body down into the churchyard?'

'And glad I was to get it there. Rolling it down the ladders — it gave me the heebie-jeebies. And those bells! I was expecting all the time to hear them speak. I never have liked the sound of bells. There's something — you'd think they were alive, sometimes, and could talk. When I was a boy, I read a story in an old magazine about a bell that called out after a murderer. You'll think I'm soft, talking that way, but it made an impression on me and I can't forget it.'

'*The Rosamonde* — I know the story,' said Wimsey, gently. 'It called, 'Help Jehan! Help Jehan!' It gave me the grues, too.'

'That's the one, my lord. Anyhow, I got the body down, as I said. I opened the grave and was just going to put him in — '

'You used the sexton's spade, I suppose?'

'Yes, sir. The key of the crypt was on Rector's bunch. As I was saying, I was going to put it in, when I remembered that the grave *might* be opened and the body recognised. So I gave it some good, hard blows with the spade across the face — '

He shuddered.

'That was a bad bit, sir. And the hands. I'd recognised them, and so might other people. I got out my jack-knife, and I — well, there!'

' 'With the big sugar-nippers they nipped off his flippers,' ' quoted Wimsey, flippantly.

'Yes, my lord. I made them into a parcel with his papers and slipped it all in my pocket. But I put the ropes and his hat down the old well. Then I filled up the grave and put the wreaths back as tidily as I could, and cleaned the tools. But I can tell you, I didn't care about taking them back into the church. All those gold angels with their eyes open in the darkness — and old Abbot Thomas lying there on his tomb. When my foot crunched on a bit of coke behind the screen, my heart was in my mouth.'

'Harry Gotobed really ought to be more careful with the coke,' said Wimsey. 'It's not for want of telling.'

'That damned parcel of stuff was burning my pocket, too. I went up and had a look at the stoves, but they were all stoked up for the night, and the top nowhere near burnt through. I didn't dare put anything in there. Then I had to go up and clean down the belfry. There'd been beer spilt on the floor. Fortunately, Harry Gotobed had left a bucket of water in the coke-house, so I didn't have to draw any from the well, though I've often wondered if he noticed next day that the water had gone. I made everything as clean as I could, and stacked the planks up where I'd found them, and I took away the beerbottles — '

'Two of them,' said Wimsey. 'There were three.'

'Were there? I couldn't see but the two. I locked up everything tight, and then I wondered what I'd better do with the keys. Finally I thought I'd best leave them in the vestry, as though Rector had forgotten them — all but the key of the porch, and I left that in the lock. It was the best I could think of.'

'And the parcel?'

'Ah! that. I kept the papers and a lot of money that was with them, but the — those other things — I threw into the Thirty Foot, twelve miles off from Fenchurch, and the bottles with them. The papers and notes I burnt when I got back to London. There was a good fire — for a wonder — in the waiting-room at King's Cross and nobody much about. I didn't think anybody would look for them there. I didn't quite know what to do with Will's coat, but in the end I posted it back to him with a note. I just said, 'Many thanks for the loan. I've put away what you left in the belfry.' I couldn't be more open, you see, for fear Mary might undo the parcel and read the letter.'

'I couldn't write much to you, for the same reason,' said Will. 'I thought, you see, you had somehow got Deacon away. It never entered my head that he was dead. And Mary usually reads my letters through before they go, sometimes adding a bit of her own. So I just said: 'Many thanks for all you've done for me' — which might a-been took to refer to you nursing me when I was ill. I see you hadn't took the £200, but I supposed you'd managed some fashion, so I just put that back in the bank where it came from. It was a queer thing to me that your letters had grown so short all of a sudden, but I understand it now.'

'I couldn't just feel the same, Will,' said Jim. 'I

didn't blame you, mind — but that rope stuck in my gullet. When did you find out what had happened?'

'Why, when the corpse came up. And — you'll have to forgive *me*, Jim — but, naturally, I fancied you'd done the job yourself, and — why, there! I didn't rightly feel the same, neither. Only I kept on hoping, maybe he'd died natural.'

'He didn't do that,' said Parker, thoughtfully.

'Then who killed him?' demanded Jim.

'I'm sure you didn't, for one,' replied the detective. 'If you had, you'd have accepted the suggestion that he died of exposure. And somehow I'm inclined to believe your brother didn't do it either — though you're both accessories after the fact to Deacon's crimes, and you aren't clear of the other thing yet; don't think it. You'd have an awkward time with a prosecuting counsel, both of you. But personally I'm inclined to believe you both.'

'Thank you, sir.'

'How about Mrs Thoday? The truth, mind.'

'That's all right, sir. She was uneasy in her mind — I won't say she wasn't — seeing me so queer, especially after the body was found. But it was only when she saw Deacon's handwriting on that paper that the meaning of it all come to her. Then she asked me, and I told her part of the truth. I said I'd found out that the dead man was Deacon and that somebody — not me — must have killed him. And she guessed that Jim was mixed up in it. So I said, maybe, but we must stand together and not make trouble for Jim. And she agreed, only she said we must get married again, because we were living together in sin. She's a good woman, and I couldn't reason her out of it, so I gave in about that, and we'd fixed to get it all done quiet-like in London — only you found us out, sir.'

'Yes,' said Blundell, 'you've got to thank his lordship here for that. He seemed to know all about it, and very sorry he was to have to stop you, I must say. Seemed to think whoever put Deacon away ought to get the Wedding March out of Lohengrin and flowers all down the aisle.'

'Is there any reason why they shouldn't go on and get married now, Superintendent?'

'I don't know as there is,' grunted Mr Blundell, 'Not if these two are telling the truth. Proceedings there may be — you two ain't out of the wood yet, but as to getting married, I don't see no great harm in it. We've got their story, and I don't know as poor Mary can add very much to it.'

'Thank you very much, sir,' said Will again.

'But as to who *did* kill Deacon,' went on the Superintendent we don't seem very much forrader. Unless it was Potty or Cranton, after all. I don't know if I ever heard anything queerer than this business. All these three, a-dodging in and out of that old belfry, one up t'other come on — there's something behind it yet that we don't understand. And you two' — he turned fiercely on the brothers — 'you keep your mouths shut about this. It'll have to come out some time, that's a certainty, but if you get talking and obstruct our duty of laying hands on the rightful murderer, you're *for* it. Understand?'

He ruminated, sucking his walrus moustache beween his large yellow teeth.

'I'd better go down home and grill Potty. I suppose,' he muttered discontentedly. 'But if he done it, how did he do it? That's what beats me.'

IV

A FULL PEAL OF KENT TREBLE BOB MAJOR

(Three Parts)

5,376

By the Course Ends
6 5 4 3 2
3 4 5 6 2
2 3 6 4 5
3 5 6 4 2
4 2 3 5 6
8th the Observation.

Call her before, middle with a double, wrong with a double and home; wrong with a double and home with a double; middle with a double, wrong and home with a double; before, middle with a double, wrong and home with a double; before, middle with a double and wrong with a double. Twice repeated.

(J. WILDE)

the first part

THE WATERS ARE CALLED OUT

Of clean beasts, and of beasts that are not
clean, and of fowls, and of everything that
creepeth upon the earth, there went in two
and two unto Noah into the ark.

Genesis vii, 8, 9

The public memory is a short one. The affair of
the Corpse in Country Churchyard was succeeded,
as the weeks rolled on, by so many Bodies in
Blazing Garages, Man-Hunts for Missing Murderers, Tragedies in West-End Flats, Suicide-Pacts in
Lonely Woods, Nude Corpses in Caves, and Midnight Shots in Fashionable Road-Houses that
nobody gave it another thought, except Superintendent Blundell and the obscure villagers of
Fenchurch St Paul. Even the discovery of the
emeralds and the identity of the dead man had
been successfully kept out of the papers, and the
secret of the Thoday remarriage lay buried in the
discreet breasts of the police, Lord Peter Wimsey
and Mr Venables, none of whom had any inducement to make these matters known.

Potty Peake had been interrogated, but without
much success. He was not good at remembering
dates and his conversation, while full of strange
hints and prophecies, had a way of escaping from

the restraints of logic and playing gruesomely among the dangling bell-ropes. His aunt gave him an alibi, for what her memory and observation were worth, which was not a great deal. Nor did Mr Blundell feel any great enthusiasm about putting Potty Peake in the dock. It was a hundred to one that he would be pronounced unfit to plead, and the result, in any case, might be to lock him up in an institution. 'And you know, old lady,' said Mr Blundell to Mrs Blundell, 'I can't see Potty doing such a thing, poor chap.' Mrs Blundell agreed with him.

As regards the Thodays, the position was highly unsatisfactory. If either were charged separately, there would always be sufficient doubt about the other to secure an acquittal, while, if they were charged together, their joint story might well have the same effect upon the jury that it had already had upon the police. They would be acquitted and left under suspicion in the minds of their neighbours, and that would be unsatisfactory too. Or they might, of course, both be hanged — 'and between you and me, sir,' said Mr Blundell to the Chief Constable, 'I'd never be easy in my mind if they were.' The Chief Constable was uneasy too. 'You see, Blundell,' he observed, 'our difficulty is that we've no real proof of the murder. If you could only be sure what the fellow died of — '

So a period of inaction set in. Jim Thoday returned to his ship; Will Thoday, his marriage ceremony performed, went home and went on with his work. In time the parrot forgot its newly-learnt phrases — only coming out with them at long and infrequent intervals. The Rector carried on with his marryings, churching and baptisms, and Tailor Paul tolled out a knell or two, or struck her solemn blows as the bells hunted in their courses. And the River Wale, rejoicing in its new opportunity, and swollen by the heavy rains of a wet summer and autumn, ground out its channel inch by inch and foot by foot, nine feet deeper than before, so that the water came up brackish at high tide as far as the Great Learn and the Old Bank Sluices were set open to their full extent, draining the Upper Fen.

And it was needed; for in that summer the water lay on the land all through August and September, and the corn sprouted in the stocks, and the sodden ricks took fire and stank horribly, and the Rector of Fenchurch St Paul, conducting the Harvest Festival, had to modify his favourite sermon upon Thankfulness, for there was scarcely sound wheat enough to lay upon the altar and no great sheaves for the aisle windows or for binding about the stoves, as was customary. Indeed, so late was the harvest and so dark and chill the air, that the stoves were obliged to be lit for the evening service, whereby a giant pumpkin, left incautiously in the direct line of fire, was found to be part-roasted when the time came to send the kindly fruits of the earth to the local hospital.

Wimsey had determined that he would never go back to Fenchurch St Paul. His memories of it were disquieting, and he felt that there were one or two people in that parish who would be better pleased if they never saw his face again.

But when Hilary Thorpe wrote to him and begged him to come and see her during her Christmas holidays, he felt bound to go. His position with regard to her was peculiar. Mr Edward Thorpe, as trustee under her father's will and her natural guardian, had rights which no court of law would gainsay; on the other hand Wimsey, as sole trustee to the far greater Wilbraham estate, held a certain advantage. He could, if he chose, make things awkward for Mr Thorpe. Hilary possessed evidence of her father's wishes about her education, and Uncle Edward could scarcely now oppose them on the plea of lack of funds. But Wimsey, holding the purse-strings, could refuse to untie them unless those wishes were carried out. If Uncle Edward chose to be obstinate, there was every prospect of a legal dogfight; but Wimsey did not believe that Uncle Edward would be obstinate to that point. It was in Wimsey's power to turn Hilary from an obligation into an asset for Uncle Edward, and it seemed very possible that he would pocket his principles and take the cash. Already he had shown signs of bowing to the rising sun; he had agreed to take Hilary down to spend Christmas at the Red House, instead of with him in London. It was, indeed, not Mr Thorpe's fault that the Red House was available; he had done his best to let it, but the number of persons desirous of tenanting a large house in ill-repair, situated in a howling desert and encumbered with a dilapidated and heavily mortaged property, was not very large. Hilary had her way, and Wimsey, while heartily wishing that the whole business could have been settled in London, liked the girl for her determination to stick to the family estate. Here again, Wimsey was a power in the land. He could put the property in order if he liked and pay off the mortgages, and that would no doubt be a satisfaction to Mr Thorpe, who had no power to sell under the terms of his trust. A final deciding factor was that if Wimsey did not spend Christmas at Fenchurch, he would have no decent excuse for not spending it with his brother's family at Denver, and of all things in the world, a Christmas at Denver was most disagreeable to him.

Accordingly, he looked in at Denver for a day or two, irritated his sister-in-law and her guests as much as, and no more than, usual and thence, on Christmas Eve, made his way across country to Fenchurch St Paul.

'They seem,' said Wimsey, 'to keep a special brand of disgusting weather in these parts.' He thrust up his hand against the hood of the car, discharging a deluge of water. 'Last time it was snowing and now it's pelting cats and dogs. There's a fate in it, Bunter.'

'Yes, my lord,' said that long-suffering man. He was deeply attached to his master, but sometimes felt his determined dislike of closed cars to be a trifle unreasonable. 'A very inclement season, my lord.'

'Well, well, we must push on, push on. A merry heart goes all the way. You don't look very merry, Bunter, but then you're one of those Sphinx-like people. I've never seen you upset, except about that infernal beer-bottle.'

'No, my lord. That hurt my pride very much, if I may say so. A very curious circumstance, that, my lord.'

'Pure accident, I think, though it had a suspicious appearance at the time. Whereabouts are we now? Oh, yes, Lympsey, of course; we cross over the Great Leam here by the Old Bank Sluice. We must be just coming to it. Yes, there it is. By Jove! some water coming through there!'

He pulled up the car beyond the bridge, got out and stood in the downpour staring at the sluice. Its five great gates were open, the iron ratchets on the bridge above drawn up to their full extent. Dark and menacing, the swollen flood-waters raced through the sluices, eddying and turning and carrying with them the brown reeds and broken willow-stems and here and there fragments of timber filched from the drowned lands of the Upper Fen. And even while he watched, there came a change. Angry little waves and gurgles ruffled the strong flow of the river, with an appearance as of repressed tumult and conflict. A man came out of the gate-house by the bridge and took up his position by the sluice, staring down into the river. Wimsey hailed him.

'Tide coming up?'

'Yes, sir. We has to watch her now if we don't want to get the water all across the causey. But she don't rise very far, not without there's an extraordinary high spring tide. She's just coming up to springs now, so we has to do a bit of manipulation, like.' He turned, and began to wind down the sluices.

'You see the idea, Bunter. If they shut this sluice, all the upland water has to go by the Old Leam, which has enough to do as it is. But if they leave it open and the tide's strong enough to carry the flood-water back with it through the sluice, they'll drown all the country above the sluice.'

'That's it, sir,' said the man with a grin. 'And if the flood-water carries the tide back, we might drown *you*. It all depends, you see.'

'Then we'll hope you manipulate things in our favour,' said Wimsey, cheerfully. The rush of water through the arches was slackening now with the lowering of the sluice-gates, the whirlpools became shallower, and the floating sticks and reeds began to eddy against the piles of the bridge. 'Just hold her back for a bit till we get to Fenchurch, there's a good fellow.'

'Oh, we'll keep her level, don't be afraid,' said the man, reassuringly. 'There ain't nothing wrong wi' *this* here sluice.'

He put such marked emphasis on the word 'this' that Wimsey looked sharply at him.

'How about Van Leyden's Sluice?'

The man shook his head.

'I dunno, sir, but I did hear as old Joe Massey down there was in a great taking about they old gates of his. There was three gentlemen went down yesterday to look at 'em — from the Conservancy or the Board of something o' that, I reckon. But you can't do nothing much for they gates in flood-time. Mebbe they'll hold, mebbe they won't. It's all according.'

405

'Well, that's jolly,' said Wimsey. 'Come on, Bunter. Have you made your will? We'd better go while the going's good.'

Their way this time lay along the south bank or Fenchurch side of the Thirty Foot. Dyke and drain were everywhere abrim and here and there the water stood in the soaked fields as though they needed but little more to sink back into their ancient desolation of mere and fen. There was little movement on the long straight road. Here a shabby car met them, splashed with mud and squirting water from every pot-hole; here a slow farm cart plodded ahead with a load of mangel-wurzels, the driver huddled under the rough protection of a sodden sack, and deaf and blind to overtaking traffic; there a solitary labourer, bent with rheumatism, slouched homeward dreaming of fire and beer at the nearest pub. The air was so heavy with water, that not till they had passed Frog's Bridge did they hear the sweet, dull jangle of sound that told them that the ringers were practising their Christmas peal; it drifted through the streaming rain with an aching and intolerable melancholy, like the noise of the bells of a drowned city pulsing up through the overwhelming sea.

They turned the corner beneath the great grey tower and passed by the Rectory wall. As they neared the gate a blast of familiar toots smote upon their ears, and Wimsey slackened speed as the Rector's car came cautiously nosing its way into the road. Mr Venables recognised the Daimler immediately, and stopped his engine with the Morris halfway across the road. His hand waved cheerfully to them through the side-curtains.

'Here you are! Here you are again!' he cried in welcoming accents, as Wimsey got out and came forward to greet him. 'How lucky I am to have just caught you. I expect you heard me coming out. I always blow the horn before venturing into the roadway; the entrance is so very abrupt. How are you, my dear fellow, how are you? Just going along to the Red House, I expect. They are eagerly looking forward to your visit. You will come and see us often, I hope, while you're here. My wife and I are dining with you tonight. She will be so pleased to meet you again. I said to her, I wondered if I should meet you on the road. What terrible weather, is it not? I have to hurry off now to baptise a poor little baby at the end of Swamp Drove just the other side of Frog's Bridge. It's not likely to live, they tell me, and the poor mother is desperately ill, too, so I mustn't linger, because I expect I shall have to walk up the Drove with all this mud and it's nearly a mile and I don't walk as fast as I did. Yes, I am quite well, thank you, except for a slight cold. Oh, nothing at all — I got a little damp the other day taking a funeral for poor Watson at St Stephen — he's laid up with shingles, so painful and distressing, though not dangerous, I'm happy to say. Did you come through St Ives and Chatteris? Oh, you came direct from Denver. I hope your family are all quite well. I hear they've got the floods out all over the Bedford Level. There'll be skating on Bury Fen if we get any frosts after this — though it doesn't look like it at present, does it? They say a green winter makes a fat churchyard, but I always think extreme cold is really more trying for the old people. But I really must push on now. I beg your pardon? I didn't catch what you said. The bells are a little loud. That's why I blew my horn so energetically; it is difficult sometimes to hear while the ringing is going on. Yes, we're trying some Stedman's tonight. You don't ring Stedman's. I think. You must come along one day and have a try at them. Most fascinating. Wally Pratt is making great strides. Even Hezekiah says he isn't doing so badly. Will Thoday is ringing tonight. I turned over in my mind what you told me, but I saw no reason for excluding him. He did wrong, of course, but I feel convinced that he committed no *great* sin, and it would arouse so much comment in the village if he left the ringers. Gossip is such a wicked thing, don't you think? Dear me! I am neglecting my duties sadly in the pleasure of seeing you. That poor child! *I must* go. Oh, dear! I hope my engine won't give trouble, it is scarcely warmed up. Oh, please don't trouble. How very good of you. I'm ashamed to trespass on your — ah! she always responds at once to the starting-handle. Well, *au revoir, au revoir!* We shall meet this evening.'

He chugged off cheerfully, beaming round at them through the discoloured weather curtains and zigzagging madly across the road in his efforts to drive one way and look another. Wimsey and Bunter went on to the Red House.

the second part

THE WATERS ARE CALLED HOME

Deep calleth unto deep at the noise of thy waterspouts: all the waves and thy billows are gone over me.

Psalm xlii.7

Christmas was over. Uncle Edward, sourly and reluctantly, had given way, and Hilary Thorpe's career was decided. Wimsey had exerted himself nobly in other directions. On Christmas Eve, he had gone out with the Rector and the Choir and sung 'Good King Wenceslas' in the drenching rain, returning to eat cold roast beef and trifle at the Rectory. He had taken no part in the Stedman's Triples, but had assisted Mrs Venables to tie wet bunches of holly and ivy to the font, and attended church twice on Christmas Day, and helped to bring two women and their infants to be churched and christened from a remote and muddy row of cottages two miles beyond the Drain.

On Boxing Day, the rain ceased, and was followed by what the Rector described as 'a tempestuous wind called Euroclydon'. Wimsey, taking advantage of a dry road and clear sky, ran over to see his friend at Walbeach and stayed the night, hearing great praises of the New Wash Cut and the improvement it had brought to the harbour and the town.

He returned to Fenchurch St Paul after lunch, skimming merrily along with Euroclydon bowling behind him. Turning across the bridge at Van Leyden's Sluice, he noticed how swift and angry the river ran through the weir, with flood-water and tide-water meeting the wind. Down by the sluice a gang of men were working on a line of barges, which were moored close against the gates and piled high with sandbags. One of the workmen gave a shout as the car passed over the bridge, and another man, seeing him point and gesticulate, came running from the sluice-head across the road, waving his arms. Lord Peter stopped and waited for him to come up. It was Will Thoday.

'My lord!' he cried, 'my lord! Thank God you are here! Go and warn them at St Paul that the sluice-gates are going. We've done what we can with sandbags and beams, but we can't do no more and there's a message come down from the Old Bank Sluice that the water is over the Great Leam at Lympsey, and they'll have to send it down here or be drowned themselves. She's held this tide, but she'll go the next with this wind and the tide at springs. It'll lay the whole country under water, my lord, and there's no time to lose.'

'All right,' said Wimsey: 'Can I send you more men?'

'A regiment of men couldn't do nothing now, my lord. They old gates is going, and there won't be a foot of dry land in the three Fenchurches six hours from now.'

Wimsey glanced at his watch. 'I'll tell 'em,' he said, and the car leapt forward.

The Rector was in his study when Wimsey burst in upon him with the news.

'Great Heavens!' cried Mr Venables. 'I've been afraid of this. I've warned the drainage authorities over and over again about those gates but they wouldn't listen. But it's no good crying over spilt milk. We must act quickly. If they open the Old Bank Sluice and Van Leyden's Sluice blows up, you see what will happen. All the Upper Water will be turned back up the Wale and drown us ten feet deep or more. My poor parishioners — all those outlying farms and cottages! But we mustn't lose our heads. We have taken our precautions. Two Sundays ago I warned the congregation what might happen and I put a note in the December Parish Magazine. And the Nonconformist minister has co-operated in the most friendly manner with us. Yes, yes. The first thing to do is to ring the alarm. They know what that means, thank God! they learnt it during the war. I never thought I should thank God for the war, but He moves in a mysterious way. Ring the bell for Emily, please. The church will be safe, whatever happens, unless we get a rise of over twelve feet, which is hardly likely. Out of the deep, O Lord, out of the deep. Oh, Emily, run and tell Hinkins that Van Leyden's Sluice is giving way. Tell him to fetch one of the other men and ring the alarm on Gaude and Tailor Paul at once. Here are the keys of the church and belfry. Warn your mistress and get all the valuables taken over to the church. Carry them up the

411

tower. Now keep cool, there's a good girl. I don't think the house will be touched, but one cannot be too careful. Find somebody to help you with this chest — I've secured all the parish registers in it — and see that the church plate is taken up the tower as well. Now, where is my hat? We must get on the telephone to St Peter and St Stephen and make sure that they are prepared. And we will see what we can do with the people at the Old Bank Sluice. We haven't a moment to lose. Is your car here?'

They ran the car up to the village, the Rector leaning out perilously and shouting warnings to everyone they met. At the post office they called up the other Fenchurches and then communicated with the keeper of the Old Bank Sluice. His report was not encouraging.

'Very sorry, sir, but we can't help ourselves. If we don't let the water through there'll be the best part of four miles o' the bank washed away. We've got six gangs a-working on it now, but they can't do a lot with all these thousands o' tons o' water coming down. And there's more to come, so they say.'

The Rector made a gesture of despair, and turned to the postmistress.

'You'd best get down to the church, Mrs West. You know what to do. Documents and valuables in the tower, personal belongings in the nave. Animals in the churchyard. Cats, rabbits and guinea-pigs in *baskets, please* — we can't have them running round loose. Ah! there go the alarm-bells. Good! I am more alarmed for the remote farms than for the village. Now, Lord

412

Peter, we must go and keep order as best we can at the church.'

The village was already a scene of confusion. Furniture was being stacked on handcarts, pigs were being driven down the street, squealing; hens, squawking and terrified, were being bundled into crates. At the door of the school-house Miss Snoot was peering agitatedly out.

'When ought we to go, Mr Venables?'

'Not yet, not yet — let the people move their heavy things first. I will send you a message when the time comes, and then you will get the children together and march them down in an orderly way. You can rely on me. But keep them cheerful — reassure them and don't on any account let them go home. They are far safer here. Oh, Miss Thorpe! Miss Thorpe! I see you have heard the news.'

'Yes, Mr Venables. Can we do anything?'

'My dear, you are the very person! Could you and Mrs Gates see that the school-children are kept amused and happy, and give them tea later on if necessary? The urns are in the parish-room. Just a moment, I must speak to Mr Hensman. How are we off for stores, Mr Hensman?'

'Pretty well stocked, sir,' replied the grocer. 'We're getting ready to move as you suggested, sir.'

'That's fine,' said the Rector. 'You know where to go. The refreshment room will be in the Lady Chapel. Have you the key of the parish-room for the boards and trestles?'

'Yes, Sir.'

'Good, good. Get a tackle rigged over the church well for your drinking-water, and be sure and remember to boil it first. Or use the Rectory pump, if it is spared to us. Now, Lord Peter, back to the church.'

Mrs Venables had already taken charge in the church. Assisted by Emily and some of the women of the parish, she was busily roping off areas — so many pews for the schoolchildren, so many other pews near the stoves for the sick and aged, the area beneath the tower for furniture, a large placard on the par-close screen REFRESH-MENTS. Mr Gotobed and his son, staggering under buckets of coke, were lighting the stoves. In the churchyard, Jack Godfrey and a couple of other farmers were marking out cattle-pens and erecting shelters among the tombs. Just over the wall which separated the consecrated ground from the bell-field, a squad of volunteer diggers were digging out a handsome set of sanitary trenches.

'Good Lord, sir,' said Wimsey, impressed, 'anybody would think you'd done this all your life.'

'I have devoted much prayer and thought to the situation in the last few weeks,' said Mr Venables. 'But my wife is the real manager. She has a marvellous head for organisation. Hinkins! right up to the bell-chamber with that plate — it'll be out of the way there. Alf! Alf Donnington! How about that beer?'

'Coming along, sir.'

'Splendid — into the Lady Chapel, please. You're bringing some of it bottled, I hope. It'll

414

take two days for the casks to settle.'

'That's all right, sir. Tebbutt and me are seeing to that.'

The Rector nodded, and dodging past some of Mr Hensman's contingent, who were staggering in with the cases of groceries, he went out to the gates, where he encountered P.C. Priest, stolidly directing the traffic.

'We're having all the cars parked along the wall, sir.'

'That's right. And we shall want volunteers with cars to run out to outlying places and bring in the women and sick people. Will you see to that?'

'Very good, sir.'

'Lord Peter, will you act as our Mercury between here and Van Leyden's Sluice? Keep us posted as to what is happening.'

'Right you are,' said Wimsey. 'I hope, by the way, that Bunter — where is Bunter?'

'Here, my lord. I was about to suggest that I might lend some assistance with the commissariat, if not required elsewhere.'

'Do, Bunter, do,' said the Rector.

'I understand, my lord, that no immediate trouble is expected at the Rectory, and I was about to suggest that, with the kind help of the butcher, sir, a sufficiency of hot soup might be prepared in the washhouse copper, and brought over in the wheeled watering tub — after the utensil had been adequately scalded, of course. And if there were such a thing as a paraffin stove anywhere — '

'By all means — but be careful with the

415

paraffin. We do not want to escape the water to fall into the fire.'

'Certainly not, sir.'

'You can get paraffin from Wilderspin. Better send some more ringers up to the tower. Let them pull the bells as they like and fire them at intervals. Oh, here are the Chief Constable and Superintendent Blundell — how good of them to come over. We are expecting a little trouble here, Colonel.'

'Just so, just so. I see you are handling the situation admirably. I fear a lot of valuable property will be destroyed. Would you like any police sent over?'

'Better patrol the roads between the Fen-churches,' suggested Blundell. 'St Peter is greatly alarmed — they're afraid for the bridges. We are arranging a service of ferryboats. They lie even lower than you do and are, I fear, not so well prepared as you, sir.'

'We can offer them shelter here,' said the Rector. 'The church will hold nearly a thousand at a pinch, but they must bring what food they can. And their bedding, of course. Mrs Venables is arranging it all. Men's sleeping-quarters on the cantoris side, women and children on the decani side. And we can put the sick and aged people in the Rectory in greater comfort, if all goes well. St Stephen will be safe enough, I imagine, but if not, we must do our best for them too. And, dear me! We shall rely on you, Superintendent, to send us victuals by boat as soon as it can be arranged. The roads will be clear between Leamholt and the Thirty Foot,

416

and the supplies can be brought from there by water.'

'I'll organise a service,' said Mr Blundell.

'If the railway embankment goes, you will have to see to St Stephen as well. Good-day, Mrs Giddings, good-day to you! We are having quite an adventure, are we not? So glad to see you here in good time. Well, Mrs Leach! So here you are! How's baby? Enjoying himself, I expect. You'll find Mrs Venables in the church. Jack! Jackie Holliday! You must put that kitten in a basket. Run and ask Joe Hinkins to find you one. Ah, Mary! I hear your husband is doing fine work down at the sluice. We must see that he doesn't come to any harm. Yes, my dear, what is it? I am just coming.'

For three hours Wimsey worked among the fugitives — fetching and carrying, cheering and exhorting, helping to stall cattle and making himself as useful as he could. At length he remembered his duty as a messenger and extricating his car from the crowd made his way east along the Thirty Foot. It was growing dark, and the road was thronged with carts and cattle, hurrying to the safety of Church Hill. Pigs and cattle impeded his progress.

'The, animals went in two by two,' sang Wimsey, as he sped through the twilight, 'the elephant and the kangaroo. Hurrah!'

Down at the sluice, the situation looked dangerous. Barges had been drawn against both sides of the gates and an attempt had been made to buttress the sluice with beams and sandbags, but the piers were bulging dangerously and as fast as material was lowered into the water, it was swept down by the force of the current. The river was foaming over the top of the weir, and from the east, wind and tide were coming up in violent opposition.

'Can't hold her much longer, now, my lord,' gasped a man, plunging up the bank and shaking the water from him like a wet dog. 'She's going. God help us!'

The sluice-keeper was wringing his hands.

'I told 'em, I told 'em! What will become on us?'

'How long now?' asked Wimsey.

'An hour, my lord, if that.'

'You'd better all get away. Have you cars enough?'

'Yes, my lord, thank you.'

Will Thoday came up to him, his face white and working.

'My wife and children — are they safe?'

'Safe as houses, Will. The Rector's doing wonders. You'd better come back with me.'

'I'll hang on here till the rest go, my lord, thank you. But tell them to lose no time.'

Wimsey turned the car back again. In the short time that he had been away the organisation had almost completed itself. Men, women, children and household goods had been packed into the church. It was nearly seven o'clock and the dusk had fallen. The lamps were lit. Soup and tea were being served in the Lady Chapel, babies were crying, the churchyard resounded with the forlorn lowing of cattle and the terrified bleating of sheep. Sides of bacon

418

were being carried in, and thirty wagonloads of hay and corn were ranged under the church wall. In the only clear space amid the confusion the Rector stood behind the rails of the Sanctuary. And over all, the bells tumbled and wrangled, shouting their alarm across the country. Gaude, Sabaoth, John, Jericho, Jubilee, Dimity, Batty Thomas and Tailor Paul — awake! make haste! save yourselves! The deep waters have gone over us! They call with the noise of the cataracts!

Wimsey made his way up to the altar-rails and gave his message. The Rector nodded. 'Get the men away quickly,' he said, 'tell them they must come at once. Brave lads! I know they hate to give in, but they mustn't sacrifice themselves uselessly. As you go through the village, tell Miss Snoot to bring the school-children down.' And as Wimsey turned to go, he called anxiously after him — 'And don't let them forget the other two tea-urns!'

★   ★   ★

The men were already piling into their waiting cars when Lord Peter again arrived at the sluice. The tide was coming up like a race, and in the froth and flurry of water he could see the barges flung like battering rams against the piers. Somebody shouted: 'Get out of it, lads, for your lives!' and was answered by a rending crash. The transverse beams that carried the footway over the weir, rocking and swaying upon the bulging piers, cracked and parted. The river poured over the tumult to meet the battering force of the tide. There was a cry. A dark figure, stepping

419

hurriedly across the reeling barges, plunged and was gone. Another form dived after it, and a rush was made to the bank. Wimsey, flinging off his coat, hurled himself down to the water's edge. Somebody caught and held him.

'No good, my lord, they're gone! My God! did you see that?'

Somebody threw the flare of a headlight across the river. 'Caught between the barges and the pier — smashed like egg-shells. Who is it? Johnnie Cross? Who went in after him? Will Thoday? That's bad, and him a married man. Stand back, my lord. We'll have no more lives lost. Save yourselves, lads, you can do them no good. Christ! the sluice gates are going. Drive like hell, men, it's all up!'

Wimsey found himself dragged and hurtled by strong hands to his car. Somebody scrambled in beside him. It was the sluicekeeper, still moaning, 'I told 'em, I told 'em!' Another thunderous crash brought down the weir across the Thirty Foot, in a deluge of tossing timbers. Beams and barges were whirled together like straws, and a great spout of water raged over the bank and flung itself across the road. Then the sluice, that held the water back from the Old Wale River, yielded, and the roar of the engines as the cars sped away was lost in the thunder of the meeting and overriding waters.

★ ★ ★

The banks of the Thirty Foot held, but the swollen Wale, receiving the full force of the

420

Upper Waters and the spring tide, gave at every point. Before the cars reached St Paul, the flood was rising and pursuing them. Wimsey's car — the last to start — was submerged to the axles. They fled through the dusk, and behind and on their left, the great silver sheet of water spread and spread.

★ ★ ★

In the church, the Rector, with the electoral roll-call of the parish in his hand, was numbering his flock. He was robed and stoled, and his anxious old face had taken on a look of great pastoral dignity and serenity.

'Eliza Giddings.'

'Here I am, Rector.'

'Jack Godfrey and his wife and family.'

'All here, sir.'

'Henry Gotobed and his family.'

'All here, sir.'

'Joseph Hinkins . . . Louisa Hitchcock . . . Obadiah Holliday . . . Miss Evelyn Holliday . . . '

The party from the sluice gathered awkwardly about the door. Wimsey made his way up to where the Rector stood on the chancel steps, and spoke in his ear.

'John Cross and Will Thoday? That is terrible. God rest them, poor, brave fellows. Will you be good enough to tell my wife and ask her to break the sad news to their people? Will went to try and rescue Johnnie? That is just what I should have expected of him. A dear, good fellow in spite of everything.'

Wimsey called Mrs Venables aside. The Rector's voice, shaking a little now, went on with his call:

'Jeremiah Johnson and his family . . . Arthur and Mary Judd . . . Luke Judson . . . '

Then came a long, wailing cry from the back of the church:

'Will! Oh, Will! He didn't want to live! Oh, my poor children — what shall we do?'

Wimsey did not wait to hear any more. He made his way down to the belfry door and climbed the stair to the ringing chamber. The bells were still sounding their frenzied call. He passed the sweating ringers and climbed again — up through the clock-chamber, piled with household goods, and up and on to the bell-chamber itself. As his head rose through the floor, the brazen fury of the bells fell about his ears like the blows from a thousand beating hammers. The whole tower was drenched and drunken with noise. It rocked and reeled with the reeling of the bells, and staggered like a drunken man. Stunned and shaken, Wimsey set his foot on the last ladder.

Halfway up he stopped, clinging desperately with his hands. He was pierced through and buffeted by the clamour. Through the brazen crash and clatter there went one high note, shrill and sustained, that was like a sword in the brain. All the blood of his body seemed to rush to his head, swelling it to bursting-point. He released his hold on the ladder and tried to shut out the uproar with his fingers, but such a sick giddiness overcame him that he swayed, ready to fall. It was not noise — it was brute pain, a grinding, bludgeoning, ran-dan, crazy, intolerable torment. He felt himself screaming, but could not hear his own cry. His eardrums were cracking; his senses swam away. It was infinitely worse than any roar of heavy artillery. That had beaten and deafened, but this unendurable shrill clangour was a raving madness, an assault of devils. He could move neither forward nor backwards though his failing wits urged him, 'I must get out — I must get out of this.' The belfry heaved and wheeled about him as the bells dipped and swung within the reach of an outstretched hand. Mouth up, mouth down, they brawled with their tongues of bronze, and through it all that shrill, high, sweet, relentless note went stabbing and shivering.

He could not go down, for his head dizzied and his stomach retched at the thought of it. With a last, desperate sanity he clutched at the ladder and forced his tottering limbs upward. Foot by foot, rung by rung, he fought his way to the top. Now the trap-door was close above his head. He raised a leaden hand and thrust the bolt aside. Staggering, feeling as though his bones were turned to water, and with blood running from his nose and ears, he fell, rather than stepped, out upon the windy roof. As he flung the door to behind him, the demoniac clamour sank back into the pit, to rise again, transmuted to harmony, through the louvres of the belfry windows.

He lay for some minutes quivering upon the leads, while his senses slowly drifted back to him. At length he wiped the blood from his face, and pulled himself groaningly to his knees, hands fastened upon the fretwork of the parapet. An enormous stillness surrounded him. The moon had risen, and between the battlements the sullen face of the drowned fen showed like a picture in a shifting frame, like the sea seen through the porthole of a rolling ship, so widely did the tower swing to the relentless battery of the bells.

The whole world was lost now in one vast sheet of water. He hauled himself to his feet and gazed out from horizon to horizon. To the southwest, St Stephen's tower still brooded over a dark platform of land, like a broken mast upon a sinking ship. Every house in the village was lit up: St Stephen was riding out the storm. Westward, the thin line of the railway embankment stretched away to Little Dykesey, unvanquished as yet, but perilously besieged. Due south, Fenchurch St Peter, roofs and spire etched black against the silver, was the centre of a great mere. Close beneath the tower, the village of St Paul lay abandoned, waiting for its fate. Away to the east, a faint pencilling marked the course of the Potters Lode Bank, and while he watched it, it seemed to waver and vanish beneath the marching tide. The Wale River had sunk from sight in the spreading of the flood, but far beyond it, a dull streak showed where the land billowed up seaward, and thrust the water back upon the Fenchurches. Inward and westward the waters swelled relentlessly from the breach of Van Leyden's Sluice and stood level with the top of the Thirty Foot Bank. Outward and eastward the gold cock on the weathervane stared and strained, fronting the danger, held to his watch by the relentless pressure of the wind from off the Wash. Somewhere amid that still surge of water, the broken bodies of Will Thoday and his mate drifted and tumbled with the wreckage of farm and field. The Fen had reclaimed its own.

★   ★   ★

One after another, the bells jangled into silence. Gaude, Sabaoth, John, Jericho, Jubilee, Dimity and Batty Thomas lowered their shouting mouths and were at peace, and in their sudden stillness, Tailor Paul tolled out the Nine Tailors for two souls passed in the night. The notes of the organ rose solemnly.

Wimsey crept down from the tower. Into the ringing-chamber, where old Hezekiah still, stood to his bell, streamed light and sound from the crowded church. The Rector's voice, musical and small, came floating up, past the wings of the floating cherubim:

'Lighten our darkness . . . '

the third part

THE BELLS ARE RUNG DOWN

The bronze monster had struck him dead.
JULIAN SERMET: *The Rosamonde*

For fourteen days and nights the Wale River ran backwards in its bed and the floods stood in the land. They lay all about Fenchurch St Stephen, a foot above the railway embankment, so that the trains came through snorting and slowly, sending up a wall of water right and left. St Peter suffered most, its houses being covered to the sills of the upper windows, and its cottages to the eaves. At St Paul, everything was flooded eight feet deep, except the mound where church and rectory stood.

The Rector's organisation worked brilliantly. Supplies were ample for three days, after which an improvised service of boats and ferries brought in fresh food regularly from the neighbouring towns. A curious kind of desert-island life was carried on in and about the church, which, in course of time, assumed a rhythm of its own. Each morning was ushered in by a short and cheerful flourish of bells which rang the milkers out to the cowsheds in the graveyard. Hot water for washing was brought in wheeled water-butts from the Rectory copper. Bedding was shaken and rolled under the pews

426

for the day; the tarpaulins dividing the men's side from the women's side of the church were drawn back and a brief service of hymns and prayer was held, to the accompaniment of culinary clinkings and odours from the Lady Chapel. Breakfast, prepared under Bunter's directions, was distributed along the pews by members of the Women's Institute, and when this was over the duties of the day were put in hand. Daily school was carried on in the south aisle; games and drill were organised in the Rectory garden by Lord Peter Wimsey; farmers attended to their cattle; owners of poultry brought the eggs to a communal basket; Mrs Venables presided over sewing-parties in the Rectory. Two possible wireless sets were available, one in the Rectory, the other in the church; these tirelessly poured out entertainment and instruction, the batteries being kept recharged by an ingenious device from the engine of Wimsey's Daimler, capably handled by the Wilderspins. Three evenings a week were devoted to concerts and lectures, arranged by Mrs Venables, Miss Snoot and the combined choirs of St Stephen and St Paul, with Miss Hilary Thorpe and Mr Bunter (comedian) assisting. On Sundays, the routine was varied by an Early Celebration, followed by an undenominational service conducted by the two Church of England priests and the two Nonconformist ministers. A wedding, which happened to fall due in the middle of the fortnight, was made a gala occasion, and a baby, which also happened to fall due, was baptised 'Paul' (for the church) 'Christopher' (because St Christopher had to do with rivers and ferries), the Rector strenuously resisted the parents' desire to call it 'Van Leyden Flood'.

On the fourteenth day, Wimsey, passing early through the churchyard for a morning swim down the village street, noticed that the level of the water had shrunk by an inch, and returned, waving a handful of laurels from somebody's front garden, as the nearest substitute for an olive-branch. That day they rang a merry peal of Kent Treble Bob Major, and across the sundering flood heard the bells of St Stephen peal merrily back.

★　★　★

'The odour,' observed Bunter, gazing out on the twentieth day across the dismal strand of ooze and weed that had once been Fenchurch St Paul, 'is intensely disagreeable, my lord, and I should be inclined to consider it insanitary.'

'Nonsense, Bunter,' said his master. 'At Southend you would call it ozone and pay a pound a sniff for it.'

The women of the village looked rueful at the thought of the cleansing and drying that their homes would need, and the men shook their heads over the damage to rick and barn.

The bodies of Will Thoday and John Cross were recovered from the streets of St Stephen, whither the flood had brought them, and buried beneath the shadow of St Paul's tower, with all the solemnity of a muffled peal. It was only after they had been laid in the earth that Wimsey opened his mind to the Rector and to

Superintendent Blundell.

'Poor Will,' he said, 'he died finely and his sins died with him. He meant no harm, but I think perhaps he guessed at last how Geoffrey Deacon died and felt himself responsible. But we needn't look for a murderer now.'

'What do you mean, my lord?'

'Because,' said Wimsey, with a wry smile, 'the murderers of Geoffrey Deacon are hanging already, and a good deal higher than Haman.'

'Murderers?' asked the Superintendent, quickly. 'More than one? Who were they?'

'Gaude, Sabaoth, John, Jericho, Jubilee, Dimity, Batty Thomas and Tailor Paul.'

There was an astonished silence. Wimsey added:

'I ought to have guessed. I believe it is at St Paul's Cathedral that it is said to be death to enter the bell-chamber when a peal is being rung. But I know that if I had stayed ten minutes in the tower that night when they rang the alarm, I should have been dead, too. I don't know exactly what of — stroke, apoplexy, shock — anything you like. The sound of a trumpet laid flat the walls of Jericho and the note of a fiddle will shatter a vessel of glass. I know that no human frame could bear the noise of the bells for more than fifteen minutes — and Deacon was shut up there, roped and tied there, for nine interminable hours between the Old Year and the New.'

'My God!' said the Superintendent. 'Why then, you were right, my lord, when you said that Rector, or you, or Hezekiah might have murdered him.'

'I was right,' said Wimsey. 'We did.' He thought for a moment and spoke again. 'The noise must have been worse that night than it was the other day — think how the snow choked the louvres and kept it pent up in the tower. Geoffrey Deacon was a bad man, but when I think of the helpless horror of his lonely and intolerable death-agony — '

He broke off, and put his head between his hands, as though instinctively seeking to shut out the riot of the bell-voices.

The Rector's mild voice came out of the silence.

'There have always,' he said, 'been legends about Batty Thomas. She has slain two other men in times past, and Hezekiah will tell you that the bells are said to be jealous of the presence of evil. Perhaps God speaks through those mouths of inarticulate metal. He is a righteous judge, strong and patient, and is provoked every day.'

'Well,' said the Superintendent, striking a note of cheerful commonplace, 'seems as if we didn't need to take any more steps in this matter. The man's dead, and the fellow that put him up there is dead too, poor chap, and that's all there is to it. I don't altogether understand about these bells, but I'll take your word for it, my lord. Matter of periods of vibration, I suppose. Yours seems the best solution, and I'll put it up to the Chief Constable. And that's all there is to it.'

He rose to his feet.

'I'll wish you good-morning, gentlemen,' he said, and went out.

The voice of the bells of Fenchurch St Paul: Gaude, Gaudy Domini in laude. Sanctus, sanctus, sanctus Dominus Deus Sabaoth. John Cole made me, John Presbyter paid me, John Evangelist aid me. From Jericho to John a-Groate there is no bell can better my note. Jubilate Deo. Nunc Dimittis, Domine. Abbot Thomas set me here and bade me ring both loud and clear. Paul is my name, honour that same.

Gaude, Sabaoth, John, Jericho, Jubilee, Dimity, Batty Thomas and Tailor Paul.

Nine Tailors Make a Man.

We do hope that you have enjoyed reading
this large print book.

Did you know that all of our titles
are available for purchase?

We publish a wide range of high quality
large print books including:
Romances, Mysteries, Classics
General Fiction
Non Fiction and Westerns

Special interest titles available in
large print are:
The Little Oxford Dictionary
Music Book
Song Book
Hymn Book
Service Book

Also available from us courtesy of
Oxford University Press:
Young Readers' Dictionary
(large print edition)
Young Readers' Thesaurus
(large print edition)

For further information or a free
brochure, please contact us at:
Ulverscroft Large Print Books Ltd.,
The Green, Bradgate Road, Anstey,
Leicester, LE7 7FU, England.
Tel: (00 44) **0116 236 4325**
Fax: (00 44) **0116 234 0205**

FIVE RED HERRINGS

Dorothy L. Sayers

Holidaying in Scotland, Lord Peter Wimsey examines the scene of a sudden death. The body of an artist lies in a burn amongst jagged rocks, at the bottom of a granite slope, an easel bearing a still-wet painting near the edge of the cliff above. It's assumed he must have stepped back to view his work, and accidentaly plummeted to his doom. But there are too many suspicious elements, not least the medical evidence which contradicts eyewitness reports of when he was last seen alive. And there are six prime suspects — though five of them must be red herrings . . .

STRONG POISON

Dorothy L. Sayers

As a mystery novelist, Harriet Vane knows all about poisons. And now she stands in the dock, on trial for her life, accused of murdering her former lover Philip Boyes by poisoning him with arsenic. The two had quarrelled bitterly, and Harriet admits to having purchased arsenic, strychnine, and prussic acid under false names — for the purpose of literary research, she claims. The judge considers her guilty as sin. But the trial results in a hung jury . . . Lord Peter Wimsey, observing proceedings, is positive that Harriet is innocent. Can evidence for the defence be found before she is re-tried?

UNNATURAL DEATH

Dorothy L. Sayers

Miss Agatha Dawson, an elderly spinster suffering from cancer, passes away in her bed. Her GP, surprised by the suddenness of her death and unsatisfied as to its cause, orders and performs a post-mortem — which reveals no sign of foul play. But a scandal arises nonetheless. The locals, seeing the doctor's actions as tantamount to accusing Miss Dawson's niece and nurse of murder, ostracise him to the point where he sells his practice and leaves . . . Lord Peter Wimsey, upon hearing the tale, is intrigued, and mounts his own investigation. Then one of the old woman's maids turns up dead . . .

This book it chalketh out before thine eyes
The man that seeks the everlasting prize;
It shews you whence he comes, whither he goes;
What he leaves undone, also what he does;
It also shews you how he runs and runs,
Till he unto the gate of glory comes.

John Bunyan. From 'The Author's Apology for his Book' in *The Pilgrim's Progress*.

Contents

Acknowledgements

I give particular thanks to my co-authors for allowing me to include in this book five items which were written jointly. These authors are: Malcolm Ashmore, Nigel Gilbert, Trevor Pinch, and Tony Williams. It will be clear to the reader that the quality and style of these chapters are greatly superior to those in which I was left to struggle alone. I also thank the three anonymous referees whose comments to John Skelton at Open University Press helped me considerably to select and organize the material in this book. They stand as substitutes for all those poor, unthanked referees who have persistently misunderstood my submissions to learned journals over the years and who have done their best, almost without exception, to prevent me from publishing at all. I also thank Malcolm Ashmore, Trevor Pinch and Steve Yearley for looking over the final product and for providing further helpful comment. Special thanks are due to Ann Griffiths and Richard Wrightson for the help they gave me with the final chapter. Lastly, I thank Vivienne Taylor and her computerized battalions for their invaluable assistance in producing the camera-ready text for this book. (Yes, that's right, T-a-y-l-o-r! I might as well have done it myself.)

Permission to reproduce chapters 1, 6, 7, 8 and 14 was given by Sage Publications; permission to reproduce chapters 2, 9 and 11 was given by *Philosophy of the Social Sciences*; permission to reproduce chapter 3 was given by Cambridge University Press; permission to reproduce chapters 4 and 5 was given by Routledge; permission to reproduce chapter 10 was given by JAI Press; permission to reproduce chapter 12 was given by Unwin Hyman; and permission to reproduce chapter 13 was given by *Sociology*. Full details of previous publication are given at the end of the book.

The title of the last chapter 'Looking Backward' has been taken from Edward Bellamy's utopian novel first published in 1888. See Bellamy (1960).

Preface: The author as a sociological pilgrim

In this book, I have brought together fourteen of the various papers dealing with science that I have authored, or co-authored, over the last two decades. Each of these papers is, I hope, interesting in itself. I mean by this that every paper is intended to say something worth saying about the social nature of science and/or about the sociological study of science. The collection may also be of interest as a partial reflection of the changes that have occurred during the 1970s and 1980s within the sociology of science. In addition, its contents may be read as illustrating the alterations that have taken place in my own understanding of science and in my conception of what is involved in making sense of science and in depicting its place in modern society.

The first section of the book following this Preface contains three methodological papers arranged in chronological order. These chapters explore the underlying assumptions and problems of the three significantly different approaches to sociological study through which, it seems to me in retrospect, my work has passed over the years (see Ashmore 1989). The first and most traditional of these approaches may be called 'interpretative sociology', the second 'discourse analysis' and the third 'new literary forms'. The methodological chapters in part one outline the basic sequence of my intellectual development concerning the sociological analysis of science and, in conjunction with this Preface, provide an overall framework within which to view the contents of the remaining sections. These sections are also organized chronologically. Part two consists of five traditional studies written during the 1970s. This is followed by three examples of discourse analysis from the early 1980s and the book ends with three fairly recent works employing unconventional textual formats or new literary forms.

Most of the material included in this volume has appeared independently of my major empirical publications on radio astronomy (Edge and Mulkay 1976), bioenergetics (Gilbert and Mulkay 1984; Mulkay 1985), and health economics (Ashmore, Mulkay and Pinch 1989). The exceptions are chapter 12 which is a preliminary version of the concluding chapter of *The Word and the World* and chapter 13 which also appears in *Health and Efficiency*. Some of the titles of the original articles have been slightly modified. In other respects, the contents of this book have been reproduced without revision and, therefore, without rectification of stylistic lapses, failures to achieve clarity of expression or use of gender biassed phrasing. I apologize for these defects which, I hope, are relatively few in number. For reasons of economy, virtually all footnotes and end-notes contained in the original versions have been removed and references have been reduced to a minimum.

* * * * *

In the rest of this prologue, I intend to give a brief personal account of how and why my approach to the sociological analysis of science has changed over time. The major difficulty I have experienced in composing such an account is that I can no longer speak authentically on behalf of that much younger author who wrote my early papers. I feel myself to have much in common with the authorial voices of my more recent texts. We seem to share a similar, if not quite the same, analytical world. But young Mulkay and I, it seems to me, share very little. I cannot claim with any confidence, therefore, to be able to represent his position in a manner that would meet with his approval. Fortunately, elsewhere in the book, he is given considerable opportunity to speak for himself. Indeed, part two is devoted entirely to his work and I believe that he has made a major contribution to part three. Thus, the interpretation I am about to furnish of the beliefs and objectives of this defenceless younger man can be assessed by the reader in the light of his writings reproduced below.

It seems to me now that a critical feature of the first phase of my work on science in the early 1970s was that it operated within the intellectual terms of reference established by science itself. At that time, my aim was to contribute to a social scientific understanding of science. Ultimately, I am sure, the intention was to reach conclusions that would be of benefit, in some as yet unspecifiable way, to social science in general and to the discipline of sociology in particular. For example, in the final note of a paper drafted in 1973, I wrote that 'it could be argued ... that sociologists of science have a unique opportunity of improving their own research by observing the similarities and differences between the disciplines they study, on the one hand, and their own discipline of sociology on the other hand'. In the foreseeable future, however, attention was to be focused exclusively on the natural sciences and, more specifically, on the social processes by means of which the disciplines of natural science produced what was recognized as certified knowledge.

One of the influential formulations of the day, to which I imagine I subscribed, was that sociologists of scientific knowledge had to concentrate on the most advanced physical sciences because these areas of study appeared to provide the 'hardest case' for sociological analysis. It was argued that, if one could demonstrate the social production of knowledge in, say, physics or radio astronomy, this would necessarily imply that knowledge was socially negotiated and socially contingent in all other less developed areas. There are several points worth noting about this kind of argument. In the first place, although it adopts the scientific community's supposed epistemological hierarchy to distinguish the more advanced areas of knowledge from the less advanced, it appears to do this in order to challenge and replace what is taken to be the official version of scientific knowledge. Secondly, however, the challenge is directed exclusively toward intellectually distant fields of inquiry. The relevance of the conclusions of the sociology of scientific knowledge (SSK) for sociology itself is put in parenthesis.

It is defined as something to be pursued once the major struggle with the natural sciences has been successfully completed.

This strategy was almost universally taken for granted within SSK throughout the 1970s. My own work was fairly typical in this respect. I strove at that time to construct a generalized account of the social production of scientific knowledge which paralleled scientists' idealized models of natural phenomena. My approach was also scientific in its attempt to derive its conclusions from systematic analysis of reliable empirical data, in its use of linguistic forms that resembled those employed in the natural sciences to present experimental findings, and in its refusal to acknowledge its own social location. It seems puzzling to me now that I could have continued for so long to have contributed to SSK's efforts to demythologize natural science without properly recognizing that my own quasi-scientific approach to sociological analysis served to endorse and to buttress the derivative myth of sociology as a traditionally conceived science of social action.

During the 1970s, I did make occasional attempts to come to terms with the socially constructed character of my own knowledge-claims. One of these attempts is reproduced as chapter one below. But, as I see it now, such passing reflections on the nature of my own sociological practice could lead nowhere until I had become more aware of the restricted nature of my own analytical language and of the interpretative assumptions built into the linguistic repertoires and textual forms by means of which I constructed the results of my sociological endeavours. The basic, underlying difficulty was that the language of social science, like that of the wider scientific enterprise, requires analysts to look outwards toward a world of supposedly objective facts which appears, by the very nature of the language, to exist independently of their interpretative activities. Accordingly, although I was able to seek an understanding of the ways in which *other* actors, such as scientists, actively created their worlds within the limits of their social situation, I had at that time no way of using language which would allow me to give recognition, in the heart of my analysis, to my own socially located and socially contingent interpretative work. Indeed, to have done so would have seemed to me then to have undermined my own sociological claims by removing their appearance of being 'factually based', 'required by the evidence' and 'demonstrated by systematic study'.

It seems to me now that in the middle and late 1970s I simply turned away from these issues and pressed on hopefully with ever more detailed and systematic examination of case study material. The implicit view that I adopted *then* was that once I really understood how science worked in its full complexity, the consequences for social science would quickly become apparent. My interpretation *now* is that I was caught in an analytical dilemma that could not be resolved whilst I continued to rely solely on the conventional language forms of social science with their tacit endorsement of a non-sociological, natural science conception of knowledge.

I cannot supply a definitive version of what happened next, for reasons that will become clear as I proceed. But, somehow or other, I found that the more careful, detailed and systematic my empirical work became, the less was it possible to construct a satisfactory interpretative account of the social actions that I was trying to describe and to explain. The analytical implications of this sociological impasse were explored in *Opening Pandora's Box* which Nigel Gilbert and I published in 1984 and in a series of related papers that we wrote in the early 1980s (see part three for some examples). The considerations which led at this point to a radical change in my approach to sociological analysis are discussed in the second chapter of the methodological section of this book.

The central problem that Nigel Gilbert and I encountered in our work on biochemists may be called 'the proliferation of accounts'. In other words, the more closely we studied our data in order to establish the nature of participants' actions, the more confusing and internally irreconcilable those data became, due to participants' ability to reformulate and reinterpret their own and others' actions in an apparently open-ended fashion. This caused us difficulty because the language of social science and its conventions of reportage are unitary in character; that is, they presuppose the existence of one real social world which is available for coherent representation in the texts of social science. But the harder we tried to capture the one real social world of science, the greater was the multiplicity of divergent accounts of that supposed world that was revealed and/ or generated by our attempts at understanding. In due course, we came reluctantly to the conclusion that we had no choice but to abandon the traditional sociological goal of furnishing a single, empirically justified model of the realm of social action under study and to pursue instead what we saw as the more realistic objective of describing how participants constructed their differing versions of their social world and of linking the variations in participants' discourse to aspects of the social context in which they were produced. We called this research strategy 'discourse analysis' (DA) (see Potter and Wetherell 1987).

Work along these lines, focusing on the linguistic variability of other knowledge-producers, made it increasingly difficult for me to avoid facing the questions concerning my own use of language that I had managed to shelve whilst I had been engaged in a more traditional style of sociological analysis. For, although my own analytical language was still highly empiricist, the claims that I was now advancing about the nature of language-use implied unequivocally that my formal accounts of the social world were as contingent and as dependent on context as the research papers of the biochemists I was investigating. Like these scientists, I gave significantly different versions of my results and of my research activities when I was not involved in producing formal texts. Moreover, if I wished to insist on the radical interpretative diversity of the social world, could I consistently claim to represent this diversity within the limits of a unitary analytical discourse? What justification could there be for continuing to offer the findings of DA as if they were representations of a world which existed independently of the conventional linguistic forms that I happened to employ in the formal research context?

During the period 1979 to 1982-83, my answer to these questions was that the conclusions of sociological inquiry had to be presented formally within the established conventions, largely derived from the natural sciences, simply because no viable alternative forms were available. But this appears to me now to have been an inherently unstable response which was made untenable by my implicit acceptance that the social world could be, and was, viably construed in a multiplicity of different, and often irreconcilable, ways; that my own sociological formulations were but one small part of this multitude; and that my readings of those fragments of the social world with which I was professionally concerned could not, in principle, reduce this multitude to a single, unitary, scientific voice. Nigel Gilbert and I had used the metaphor of Pandora's Box to suggest that we were going to reveal the interpretative multiplicity of social life and to set free its conflicting voices. However, once it became clear that the dominant language forms of social science could never allow us the textual freedom that these objectives required, it became necessary to consider whether it was possible to find or to develop other, more liberating modes of analysis.

Gradually, during the early 1980s, I decided that I would, at least, have to *try* to devise a new kind of sociological language that could give expression to the conception of knowledge provided by SSK and to the ideas concerning language-use furnished by DA. This radical conclusion emerged in the course of long discussions with Malcolm Ashmore (see Ashmore 1989) and was given impetus by the work of Bruno Latour (1980), Steve Woolgar (1982) and Anna Wynne (1988), all of whom seemed to me at that time to be moving in this direction. My first attempt at what came to be called 'new literary forms', following Woolgar's introduction of this phrase, was 'The Scientist Talks Back' which was published in 1984. After finishing this paper, I spent the academic year 1983-84 on an ESRC personal grant writing what eventually became *The Word and the World: Explorations in the Form of Sociological Analysis* (1985).

The phrase 'new literary forms' is better than, say, 'new analytical language', because what was needed at that time was not a new vocabulary for writing about social life, but new ways of organizing our language which would avoid the implicit commitment to an orthodox epistemology that was built into the established textual forms of social science. In an attempt to address the self-referential nature of SSK's central claims and to display the ways in which analysts' claims are moulded by their use of specific textual forms, I began to employ multi-voice texts in which both analytical claims and textual form could become topics of critical discussion in a natural manner. Texts of this kind made it possible, I found, to replace the unitary, anonymous, socially removed authorial voice of conventional sociology with an interpretative interplay within the text as a result of which the voices involved became socially located and their constructive use of language became available for comment both within the text and beyond.

I began to hope that such dialogic texts might at last provide an effective practical response to the longstanding self-referential dilemma of SSK. In other words, once one had moved outside the narrow forms of scientific textuality, it seemed to have become possible to make sociological proposals about the world without hiding from view the socially constructed character of those proposals. Of course, such textual forms no longer allowed authors to claim to reveal the nature of the one real social world. But sociologists' reluctance to abandon this essentially non-sociological presumption had long been the major barrier to further intellectual advance. In short, multi-voice texts appeared to provide a form of textuality which fostered a social conception of understanding that was consistent with SSK's basic view of the variable social construction of knowledge and with its emphasis on the availability within the social world of many different ways of knowing.

The advent of new literary forms also seemed to begin to liberate that multitude of competing voices with which DA had been unable to cope. In addition, it transformed my understanding of my own and others' work in SSK during the 1970s. I came to realize that that kind of analysis was not inherently defective, as it had come to appear from the perspective of DA, but was best seen as the naturally limited expression of a sociology of scientific knowledge formulated within the textual confines of conventional social science. Indeed, a similar reassessment applies to discourse analysis itself. Thus the traditional forms on which I relied exclusively during the first two phases of my intellectual career can now be seen as one small, yet valuable, part of a potentially open-ended analytical repertoire. Young Mulkay's work was not wrong, I realize now, nor was that of other authors in the same tradition. It was, rather, too narrowly restricted in the textual resources it employed to be able to express in full its own interpretative implications. Now that its limitations can be seen in the context provided by other forms of textuality, it is possible to appreciate more clearly the essential contribution made by work of this kind to the sociological understanding of science.

In recent years, I have explored an increasingly wide range of alternative textual formats, in addition to the simple, multi-voice texts with which new literary forms began. Whereas traditional, monologic texts were designed to hide their own textuality, that is, their own artful use of language to give meaning to the world, these other forms reveal and celebrate that textuality (see Woolgar 1988). They thus encourage a new relationship between analyst and participant, and between author and reader. No longer is the sociologist treated implicitly as a higher source of knowledge about the operation of the social world, but as one among many socially located voices capable, at best, of an essentially limited understanding similar in kind to that of both participants and readers. New literary forms, as a response to the social and linguistic construction of knowledge, is in this sense the opposite of Mannheim's (1952) suggestion that social science can provide a superior kind of social knowledge in so far as its practitioners remain socially detached. The use of new literary forms, in contrast, involves an open recognition in the very structure of one's analytical language of the inescapably social character of sociological practice.

This refusal to grant the sociologist a privileged interpretative position does not mean that sociology has nothing worthwhile to offer in the way of knowledge. It means, rather, that we have to abandon traditional notions concerning the nature of that knowledge. Thus it seems to me now that, in trying to gain a sociological understanding of natural science and in trying to grasp the implications that follow for my own discipline, I have come to use forms of analysis that move outside of science as it presently exists. The language-forms of science, I believe, are unsuitable for self-knowledge and unsuitable for the kind of dialogue required by the multiplicity of social life. It may be that, despite its achievements, or perhaps partly because of its achievements, scientific knowledge engenders a corresponding ignorance which hides from view the more important dimensions of our world. This possibility is explored in the final chapter of the present book, 'Looking Backward', in a manner that would be inconceivable had I not managed, temporarily I have no doubt, to bring together into one sociological trinity the central themes of the three phases of my intellectual life.

As a result of the intellectual pilgrimage outlined above, I have come to see sociology's ultimate task, not as that of reporting neutrally the facts about an objective social world, but as that of engaging actively in the world in order to create the possibility of alternative forms of social life. The chapters in this book record my slow journey toward this realization. I offer them as a moral tale in the hope that you will take up the burden when I come to lay it down.

Part One: Questions of method

1 Two conflicting conclusions concerning methodology (1974)

The traditional view of methodology in sociology has been relatively simple. Its basic assumptions have been as follows: that empirical data relevant to sociological analysis exist independently of the investigator; that the fundamental task of the researcher is to 'gather' these data (the metaphor is revealing) whilst minimizing any distorting effects that might arise from the investigator's intrusion into the social process; that adequate evidence for any one theoretical concept can usually be obtained by means of one single operational indicator; and that research method provides the link between theory and the collection of data, whilst remaining distinct from theory and independent of the data to be gathered. In recent years these assumptions have begun to be revised. In the first place, it is argued that sociological research is a social act; an act in which those being studied usually participate with the investigator to produce the final observations. It follows that the sociologist must do more than simply take a few elementary precautions against distorting the results. He must begin instead to explore the social nature of the research act and he must begin to take his conclusions on this topic into account when interpreting his results. In the light of this argument, social facts begin to appear increasingly volatile and subject to variations due to the largely unexplored complexities of the research process. Thus it is necessary to view any one phenomenon from several perspectives. It is necessary to assume that there are likely to be several indicators for any single concept, and on the assumption that the results given by different indicators will vary, it is necessary to examine these variations, not only in relation to the phenomenon under study but also in the light of the social procedures which each indicator requires. Comparison between various indicators not only throws into relief the theoretical notions which are used or implied in interpreting empirical material; it also shows that theories about research techniques are involved.

For the rest of this paper I am going to accept these revised assumptions. I shall assume that sociological research is a social act; that the subjects under investigation are likely to be responding to a variety of definitions of the investigator and, through him, perhaps to other less obvious audiences; that any one sociologically defined phenomenon can be observed by means of several indicators; and that these indicators must be interpreted in relation to the specific social contexts created in the course of research. These assumptions raise difficult problems for those of us concerned with empirical research. In particular, they make exceedingly problematic the transition from observing social life to stating results. What I want to do now is to illustrate a few of these problems by reference to the study of the development of radio astronomy carried out by D.O. Edge and myself (Edge and Mulkay 1976).

My collaborator and I were interested, generally, in the nature of scientific development. We decided to study radio astronomy in particular, largely because my colleague had at one time been a radio astronomer and because it seemed possible that, by working together in the investigation of this field, we could produce a piece of research which would be unusual in giving equal weight to scientific and to social developments. Our initial definition of the problem reflected this concern with development and with the relations between social and scientific factors. Basically, we started with three fairly broad questions:

1. How did radio astronomy emerge as an identifiable area of study?
2. What was the sequence of scientific developments?
3. Were scientific developments accompanied by discernible changes in social relationships?

These questions could be approached in several different ways. We could, for example, review the literature for relevant hypotheses and use the material on radio astronomy to test these hypotheses. There were, however, several good reasons for not proceeding in this fashion. There was, in the first place, scant literature on the emergence of scientific disciplines; and what literature there was, seemed too piecemeal and its results too uncertain to provide convincing hypotheses. At the beginning, we knew very little about the development of radio astronomy. It was, therefore, impossible to judge without more exploratory study whether the few, questionable hypotheses available could in any way be tested against observations drawn from this field. Furthermore, hypothesis-testing requires uniform, controlled methodological procedures. Use of such procedures would perhaps have led us to miss just those things which were unexpected about radio astronomy and, therefore, specially interesting. In addition, whereas none of the existing sociological studies paid much attention to the development of scientific knowledge, we definitely wanted to use our unique chance of studying that in detail and in relation to social factors.

As a result of considerations such as these, we decided that our study should be frankly exploratory. In other words, we decided that we would not define in advance the detailed questions which were to be answered nor the precise research procedures which were to be adopted. We also decided that, given the scarcity of reliable studies in the area as well as the lack of convincing theoretical analysis, we would present our results with a minimal theoretical commitment. We would try to leave the theoretical interpretation of our material as open as possible until further comparable studies were available. Now it is likely that, in an exploratory study such as this, the difficulties of interpretation arising from the social nature of the research act will be fairly *obvious*, owing to the relative lack of control exercised by the investigators over the research process. Nevertheless, the kinds of problems which I shall now discuss are, I think, still present in sociological investigations of a more structured kind.

We began our research with a certain amount of information on the development of radio astronomy which my colleague had acquired whilst he was a radio astronomer and in the course of his subsequent irregular contacts with radio astronomers. We knew, for example, that radio astronomy started to expand rapidly during the 1940s and early 1950s. We knew that it required large-scale techniques, so that active radio astronomers must always be members of groups which have suitable equipment. We also knew who to go to for lists of publications and lists of group members. And we knew who had made major contributions to the field and who would, therefore, have to be interviewed. This kind of background knowledge and personal contact was invaluable in getting the research started and in helping us to overcome a whole series of practical difficulties. But the point I want to stress at the moment is that such knowledge is acquired whilst one is a comparatively uncritical participant, and that this knowledge is a social construct of doubtful validity. Let me give an example.

I can remember my partner's remarking right at the beginning of our study: 'We have chosen a very simple case. It all began when Jansky made this unexpected discovery in the early 1930s. The significance of Jansky's discovery is shown by the fact that all graduate theses in the Cambridge radio astronomy group began, until the late 1950s, with a statement like: "The first direct observation of extraterrestrial radio noise was made in 1932 by an American engineer named Jansky".' My colleague had formed this belief in the importance of Jansky's original contribution when he was a participant and it appears to be a belief which has become widely accepted by many radio astronomers who actually took no part in the early years. This view of the growth of the field has two main elements: it stresses the contribution of the 'great man'; and it sees scientific growth as a fairly straightforward development of intellectual opportunities revealed by the great man. Thus the development of radio astronomy is viewed by many participants as a simple, cumulative growth, having specifiable origins in the work of Jansky. This interpretation came, by way of 'background knowledge', to affect our initial perception of the kind of result we would probably obtain from our study. Yet it is almost entirely wrong. It was dispelled from our minds quite early in the research process, as we examined other sources of information. For example, when we interviewed those who had been members of the first radio astronomy groups in Britain, we found that they denied being greatly influenced by Jansky. And when we examined the citations they had made in those early days, we found that the references to Jansky in their published research reports were negligible. Reality was clearly more complex than the 'Jansky myth' implied.

I have given a very simple example of a participant's misconception which was taken over by the investigators; although in this case the notion was soon corrected. The point that I want to make, however, is that it was only noticed because it appeared obviously incompatible with other information. Thus there may well be many other such erroneous assumptions, perhaps of a less obviously factual kind, which are taken over by the investigators, which are never noticed, and which help to determine the results. It might be suggested that this is the typical problem of the participant observer and that it can be avoided by using other research techniques in which participants have no part to play. I would answer this proposal in the following way. Firstly, if the sociological study of science involves a close examination of its *technical culture*, the active cooperation of technically competent participants must be gained in one way or another. Secondly, on many issues of sociological interest, members of a given research community are likely to have firm and agreed definitions of reality which are linked to their technical and scientific assumptions. It is often possible to regard such issues as problematic only if the investigator has enough technical knowledge to challenge these firm definitions.

The main thrust of my argument so far then is that if we are to study in detail the operation of scientific communities, we must have the active cooperation of participants or ex-participants; that including participants as investigators affects the nature of the research act and may lead to the investigators' taking over false, or incomplete, assumptions from the group under study; but that misleading assumptions can, at least sometimes, be corrected by the use of several sources of information or multiple indicators. This last point, however, raises a further question: How do we use these various kinds of partially conflicting information to reach a valid inference? In the case of the Jansky myth what we did was roughly as follows. On the basis of our background knowledge we put open-ended questions to participants in the course of interviews. The answers we received did not match our initial expectations about the contribution of Jansky. It was, of course, impossible to assess these conflicting data without some further, independent evidence. We used the relatively objective data provided by citations. These data are objective in the sense that they cannot be distorted by the selective perception of participants. However, the use of citation patterns in this way, as an index of lines of intellectual influence, clearly involves an implicit theory of citing. It may appear fairly obvious that, if British radio astronomers did not cite Jansky, they were not directly influenced by him. But in fact we know very little about who cites whom in science, and why. There has been no clear demonstration of the way in which citations reflect the processes of scientific influence. Thus our interpretation of the contribution of Jansky, although it seems at the commonsense level to be undeniable, appears upon closer examination to be based upon quite speculative theoretical notions about the nature of our research techniques, in this case, upon an implied theory of citing.

I have illustrated my themes so far in relation to the comparatively simple problem of establishing how far Jansky contributed to the emergence of radio astronomy. The problem becomes considerably more complex when one attempts to describe the long term evolution of ideas in radio astronomy. In the first place, participants tend, in retrospect, to view much prior work simply as wrong. The current framework of knowledge provides their criteria for judging the significance of earlier research. Thus there is a tendency for scientists to dismiss much prior work, not as reasonable attempts to explore problems which were then scientifically ill-defined, but as errors. And, being errors, they are no longer scientifically interesting. This is the usual view taken by researchers *within* their professional community. Now it is very seldom that they talk of such matters to outsiders. For most outsiders are both uninterested and technically incompetent. When interviewed therefore, they tend to gloss over their mistakes and wrong-turnings, not out of any deliberate intention to mislead, but because they regard such work as scientifically unimportant. There is a definite confusion in their accounts between *scientific* accuracy and *historical* accuracy. So, if the interviewer takes their accounts of intellectual development as complete, he is likely to get a misleading impression of steady, undeviating advance toward the state of knowledge which now exists. A similar pattern emerges when one examines participants' historical writings. On the whole, they miss out the slow, groping development which often occurs. Instead, they tend to take a fairly stereotyped form; they note the major discoveries which occurred early on, and then they skip quickly through to the current framework of knowledge – as if all that happened in between was part of an inevitable progression. Perhaps the only way of redressing this emphasis by participants on the contemporary scientific framework is by close, chronological study of research reports and, in particular, review articles and symposia. A careful examination of this material tends to reveal a continual series of false inferences, redefinitions of problems, and alterations of intellectual perspective on the part of scientists as their subject develops.

What I have just been saying implies the need, once again, to compare several kinds of information and to assess, or interpret, these kinds of information quite differently. In the study of radio astronomy, we regarded our reading of the original research reports as less subject to distortion, or 'selective emphasis', than participants' retrospective accounts. We regarded participants' special view of intellectual development as arising from their concern with scientific validity, a concern which was reinforced by their normal patterns of technical communication and which helped to determine the nature of their response to our investigations. Once more, then, our use of the data depended on an instrumentation theory; in this case an instrumentation theory which clearly took into consideration the social relationship between investigator and respondent. It might be objected that our interpretation of the various kinds of data was merely a plausible *ex post facto* assessment. There is, however, a partially independent check. The straightforward view of undeviating development proposed by many participants implies that major scientific advances will be perceived in advance and clearly predicted. In radio astronomy this has not been the case. Most of the major discoveries have, in fact, been totally unexpected. This provides, I think, further support for the view of scientific development in this field as proceeding irregularly and involving continual reappraisals and redefinitions; a view which is supported by our interpretation of evidence drawn from the research literature but which is seldom volunteered by participants.

I have suggested that typical participants' accounts of intellectual development are incomplete and, to some extent, systematically biassed. But I have *not* suggested that their accounts are essentially *inconsistent* with accounts which rely heavily on published research reports. There are normally differences of emphasis rather than incompatibility between these sources of information. This is borne out by the way in which participants reacted when we circulated our first draft through the post and asked them to comment on our historical reconstruction of scientific development. Our reconstruction was firmly based upon original research reports and contemporary discussions, where these were recorded; although it did take account of interview material and participants' historical writings as well. Our respondents reacted in the following way. They did not reject or heavily criticize our account of scientific development. Many of them concentrated on correcting fairly minor points of technical detail. A few made more substantial points which could be independently corroborated. Several of them expressed feelings of discomfort at seeing all their early 'mistakes' set down in detail. They clearly found it disheartening.

This relative lack of criticism from participants gave us increased confidence in our findings. Their concern with technical detail and with past errors offered some confirmation of our interpretation of the bias contained in participants' historical writings and in interview material. In making this last statement, I do not mean to imply that interview material is of no value in arriving at an understanding of intellectual development in science. Participants will not normally *volunteer* an account of scientific development which gives full recognition to discontinuity, misunderstanding, redefinition of problems, and so on. It is possible, however, as one's knowledge grows, to ask more probing questions, to challenge simplistic accounts, and to introduce into the discussion the views of other participants. These tactics usually lead participants to provide a more elaborate statement, which reflects more closely the actual historical complexities. Furthermore, certain kinds of relevant information can only be gathered by means of interviews. For example, it is very seldom that 'errors' are retracted in the official journals. We came across only one case in radio astronomy where an observational claim was later admitted to be wrong in print – and this admission was made in *Scientific American*. Now it is clear that many published observations do become widely suspect and generally ignored as unreliable. But this formation of scientific opinion occurs informally and is not recorded in the journals. Of course, to those who know the area well, the consequences of these changes in scientific opinion can be observed in the journals. But clearly, if we wish to understand in detail how these changes occur, we must try to explore the informal social processes, at least partly by means of interviews.

It is obvious that the research interview is a social act. It is, perhaps, equally obvious that the nature of this act will vary from one area of inquiry to another. In many areas, the investigator and the respondent will share a common framework of assumptions, a similar vocabulary and a similar background of experience, all of which will enable them to communicate fairly easily. This is so, for example, in relation to research on the mass media, on the family, and so on. Even in these areas, of course, difficulties of interpretation arise. The most basic of these difficulties are firstly, that of knowing how far questions and answers mean the same thing to both parties; and, secondly, that of discerning whether investigator and respondent are engaged in a particular role-set, which the investigator does not allow for but which nonetheless influences the results. The most common interview-set is that in which respondents regard the researcher as socially superior and, consequently, provide him with conventionally approved responses. Problems of these kinds are clearly evident in interviews with scientists. They do, however, take rather special forms.

In the study of radio astronomy we used three types of interview:

1. where the respondent answered questions put by a sociologist alone;
2. where questions were put by both a sociologist and an ex-participant;
3. where the interview was conducted solely by an ex-scientist.

Each of these types of interview entails a different social context in which empirical material tends to be produced in different ways.

Interviews conducted by a sociologist alone tend to have a relatively low level of technical content. Even when the sociologist has a good layman's knowledge of the field, he is unable to discuss technical issues with the flexibility of a participant or ex-participant. Yet technical and social issues are intimately related. A scientist's typical account of why he took up a particular line of research at a particular time will stress technical considerations, e.g. 'the problems were scientifically interesting', 'suitable techniques were available'. Consequently, if one wants to know about the effect of competitive or other social pressures on the decision, it is helpful to be able to enter into a dialogue regarding technical factors in the course of which the respondent can be guided toward greater consideration of social factors. It is useful, therefore, to have a technically competent interviewer present. Perhaps the best arrangement is to have the scientist interviewed by both a sociologist and a participant/ex-participant. However, this social triangle does have its difficulties.

In order to gain the respondent's interest, allay his possible suspicions and establish rapport, it is usually necessary to open the interview with questions from the ex-participant on technical/scientific developments. This exchange reassures the respondent because it resembles his everyday discussions with colleagues. Thus excellent rapport can be quickly established between respondent and ex-participant, and much information on social as well as technical issues can be elicited. If the sociologist continually intervenes in this process he is in danger of disrupting its flow and of preventing the respondent from elaborating his responses within his normal frame of reference. There is a tendency, therefore, for the sociologist to refrain from entering the dialogue as long as the respondent is providing new information. The only circumstances in which the sociologist feels obliged to enter the discussion is when the respondent's account of social events appears in some way problematic. Thus he tends to intervene when the respondent is inconsistent, when one respondent's account differs from that of others, or when issues are being examined about which the interviewee is reluctant to talk openly (such as secrecy or competition). In this situation, the sociologist becomes in an obvious sense (more obvious than when he is the sole interviewer) an outsider. And some respondents at least adapt by providing more guarded responses to those questions which the 'alien' sociologist appears to regard as specially important. Now if this is an accurate description of the triadic interview situation, some of the responses which it generates must be interpreted differently from those which occur when there is only one interviewer. This does not mean that the responses in a three-person interview are *more* problematic. They are simply different; and they require different treatment by the investigator.

There are several other factors which affect the interview situation. For instance, those with the widest knowledge of the social and scientific development of research groups tend to be group leaders and other older members of the groups. These men are, therefore, particularly important sources of information and, when participants' accounts are inconsistent, one might be tempted to regard their views as more authoritative. However, they tend also to be most concerned with maintaining the group's reputation and, consequently, with preventing the passage of information which would reflect adversely on the group. Furthermore, group leaders are eminent members of disciplines which have much higher academic status than that of the investigators. It is, therefore, very difficult to break down the social barriers which support group leaders, in their tendency to present a favourable image of their group's activities.

The general points, then, that I want to make are that even within this single study the social context in which interview responses were provided varied considerably; that the social context of the interview is, in fact, quite complex; and that the research context should at least be borne in mind when interpreting interview material.

In our study we tried to a limited extent to face some of the difficulties of using interview material. The procedure we adopted was roughly as follows. On the basis of the interview transcripts and other data, we identified a number of recurrent themes, or issues, e.g. the relationship between the two British groups or the way in which new lines of research came to be pursued. We then extracted from the transcripts all statements bearing on each of these themes. This enabled us to judge the range of responses and the degree of agreement on particular issues. Continual reference was made to the interview transcripts in order to check that the material was being interpreted correctly in the light of the interview context. This material was combined with other data to provide the empirical foundation of the study. Quotations were used copiously to illustrate participants' views, to demonstrate the range of views and to give the reader as much direct contact as possible with the original data. Wherever it seemed particularly necessary we gave an indication of the interview context in which the respondent's view had been expressed. Because of the complexity of our subject matter and the imponderables involved in even the simplest kind of interpretation, we decided to check our work as far as possible by sending the first draft of our report for comment to all those we had interviewed, as well as to a number of participants we had been unable to interview.

We received a considerable response, much of which was useful in improving the historical and scientific accuracy of our study. Perhaps surprisingly, there were only two objections to the way in which we had used quotations from interviews. Certain aspects of our initial interpretation, however, received strongly negative comment, especially from group leaders. These comments were about our discussion of competition/cooperation, leadership and secrecy. Entering into a dialogue in this way with participants is, of course, quite unlike the traditional sociological approach, which advocates that the researcher should minimize social interaction with respondents. Our approach, in contrast, assumes that interaction is almost unavoidable and that the researcher, instead of trying to avoid interaction, should make explicit the social nature of the various research contexts in which he engages and should take these into account when stating his results. Thus participants' comments on our draft constitute additional data, no different in principle from the original interview material or from participants' historical writings. Nonetheless, these comments do require a somewhat different kind of interpretation, because they are the product of a distinctive type of social interaction. I shall discuss here only the comments on competition/cooperation.

In our preliminary report we stressed the prevalence of competition among radio astronomy groups rather than cooperation. This was based on the frequency of respondents' references to competition and rivalry, compared with the infrequency of accounts of cooperation. In addition, there was documentary and other evidence of one longstanding dispute as well as an almost complete absence of joint publication by members of different groups.   A number of our interviewees, and especially the group leaders, reacted as follows. They made no complaint about the essential accuracy of our account of the one major dispute, between a British group and a group abroad. They claimed, however, that we had misrepresented the real relationship between the two major British groups. They pointed out that there had been much *technical* cooperation between the two British groups, which would not result in joint papers, and they gave examples of technical cooperation. They also suggested that joint publication was a poor index of scientific cooperation, for long term cooperative research might prove unproductive or produce disproportionately few results. Finally, they stated that the two large groups in Britain had adopted an explicit policy of avoiding research overlap and that this policy, which was itself a form of cooperation, significantly reduced the likelihood of outright competition.

This feedback from respondents clearly provided useful information. It drew attention to the existence of *technical* cooperation, which was not reflected in the number of joint publications. In other words, our assumptions (or our implicit theory) about the connection between joint publication and cooperation were shown to need revision. In addition, our notice was drawn to the policy of differentiation adopted by the two groups, for which there was independent evidence. Nevertheless, the response had to be treated cautiously. For several reasons, it could not be accepted entirely at its face value. Firstly, there were *very* few joint publications. Secondly, there had been very few collaborative but unproductive ventures, and we had already noted them anyway. Thirdly, both the interviews and the background knowledge of my partner provided much evidence of inter-group rivalry.

This evidence, plus the very force and urgency with which respondents' criticisms were presented, led us to believe that their response was more than just a reasoned attempt to get the facts straight. The most likely interpretation, it seemed to us, was that we were seen by some respondents as putting in jeopardy the image of science as a cooperative and dispassionate pursuit of knowledge. From this perspective an account which threatened this image would be seen, particularly by scientists responsible for maintaining the groups' financial and social support, as endangering that support. Thus when we stressed that radio astronomers were to a noticeable extent concerned with priority and professional repute, that such considerations influenced their research, that they led to competition and prevented active collaboration, we were seen by some participants to be undermining their whole professional life. Their response was to reassert vigorously the public image of science. The additional data gained by means of feedback did lead us, therefore, to extend our original analysis. We noted the occurrence of technical cooperation between groups. We placed more emphasis on the way in which groups avoided competition by concentrating on different lines of research. We also modified our assumptions about the ways in which figures on co-authorship can be used to indicate the extent of scientific cooperation. We did not, however, change our basic view of the relations between the two main groups, that is, relations characterized more by rivalry than by cooperation, but a rivalry kept in check by the small degree of scientific and technical overlap.

The brief account given above of some of our research procedures in relation to competition and cooperation provides further illustration of my main themes, which may be summarized as follows:

1. Even the simplest kind of sociological analysis involves a complex process of reaching inferences from partial evidence.
2. When several kinds of evidence are brought to bear on a given problem, apparent biases and inconsistencies often arise.
3. Attempts to resolve these inconsistencies draw attention to the methodological theories, either implicit or explicit, which underlie the use of every kind of evidence.
4. Much sociological evidence is created in the course of various kinds of social interaction between investigator and subject.
5. As it is impossible to eliminate such interaction, it seems necessary to have explicit theories of how evidence is generated within different research contexts.
6. At present, formal theories of this kind are entirely lacking.
7. Thus methodological theories tend either to remain implicit, largely unnoticed and closed to critical appraisal; or they are introduced as speculative, *ex post facto* appendages.
8. Sometimes independent material gathered during the course of the study can be used to provide support for (or to modify) important methodological assumptions, e.g. the claim above that the nature of discovery in radio astronomy supported our greater reliance on research reports and review articles as compared with participants' retrospective accounts of scientific development.

The concluding paragraph of this paper could be written in at least two quite different ways. Let me present them both. I can see no rational grounds for preferring one rather than the other. *Ending one.* The sociological analysis of science, like other areas of sociological inquiry, is faced with an irresolvable dilemma. At present, in the study of any given social phenomenon, the interpretation of the results of available research techniques is as problematic as the phenomenon initially under investigation. Thus findings cannot be regarded as valid until we have satisfactory methodological theories. But satisfactory methodological theories are no different in principle from other sociological theories and they, too, need the support of firm methodological theories. We appear, therefore, to be caught in an infinite regression which effectively prevents any form of intellectual advance. *Ending two.* In the past the importance of methodological theories has not been properly recognized in sociology; nor has the extent to which methodological assumptions must vary from one research setting to another. In the sociology of scientific development, because it is a fairly new area of detailed inquiry, we have the opportunity of constructing explicit methodological theories more or less from the start and of conducting future research so as to improve these theories. For some time, of course, there will be a high degree of uncertainty, because it is at present impossible to assume that any research techniques produce results which can be reliably interpreted. In practice it will often be necessary to make 'reasonable assessments' of partially inconsistent data and to introduce speculative *ex post facto* methodological theories. But as long as the rationales behind these assessments and the nature of these methodological theories are made clear, they will be open to scrutiny and to improvement. This procedure appears directly analogous to 'pulling oneself up by the bootstraps'. The only indication that such a 'bootstrap operation' can work is the likelihood that some of the most 'successful' areas of intellectual endeavour must have begun in a manner similar to this.

2 Action and belief or scientific discourse? (1981)

This session is concerned with the present state of social studies of science. That is a huge topic. I've recently written a book-length review just on the *sociology* of science, without touching on the history or philosophy of science (Mulkay and Milic 1980). *And* I had to leave out various parts of the sociological literature. So, in half an hour's talk, there's no point in taking the topic of this session literally. What I have decided to do instead is to address just one issue. But I think that it is such a basic issue that it has implications for the whole of social studies of science. Furthermore, it may well be that the way we have dealt with this issue in the past has had a major influence on social studies of science. So, by tackling this issue, I may be able to imply something about the present state of affairs in general, and also about the direction that our studies should take in the future.

Phrased in its most general form, the issue that I want to examine is a methodological one: how should we go about analyzing sociological and historical data on science? More specifically, I now see that question as more or less equivalent to: should we be trying to provide definitive versions of scientists' actions and beliefs or should we be analyzing scientific discourse? Its clear from this formulation that the issue I am addressing has strong implications for some of the sessions which follow. My formulation does not present scientific discourse as just another topic to be covered in this area. The analysis of discourse is being presented as an *alternative* to the more traditional concern with describing and explaining action and belief.

What do I mean by 'providing definitive versions of action and belief'? It is my impression that almost all prior work in the history and sociology of science has sought to provide definitive versions of scientists' actions and, to a lesser extent, of their beliefs. This is less true of philosophers of science. Let me give some simplified examples taken mostly from the sociological literature.

1. To a very considerable extent research contributions are judged impartially on their scientific merit, no matter where they come from or who presents them.
2. Scientists' professional actions are carried out overwhelmingly in accordance with a specific and identifiable set of prescriptions.
3. The collective action of groups of research scientists can be seen to oscillate between periods of routine action and periods of revolutionary action.
4. When we look at laboratory practice, it becomes clear that scientists do not

act in terms of the correspondence-theory of truth. Scientists seek success rather than truth.

5. Scientists' ideas are tools which their adherents devise in order to achieve their purposes in specific social and cultural situations.

6. In 16th century Europe certain groups of mathematicians began to interact much more closely with those concerned with the improvement of practical techniques. This change in patterns of social action had a major impact on mathematicians' conception of number.

7. An examination of the major participants' positions in the struggle reveals the role politics plays in extending scientific perception. Behind the published results are such political manoeuvres as marketing, salesmanship, and manipulation – all of which are vital to scientific inquiry.

I am tempted to provide a much longer list. But these brief snippets give us the flavour of some of the diverse views propounded about science in the recent literature. All of these statements are clearly concerned with portraying the actions of groups or collections of scientists. Scientists are described as 'judging impartially', 'conforming to certain prescriptions', 'engaging in revolutionary action', 'seeking after success or other objectives', and so on. Its more difficult to produce brief examples of the characterization of ideas or beliefs, but the text from which quotation six is taken goes on to describe in detail the mathematical conceptions which are said to have arisen out of certain changes in social action. Earlier I said that I was going to illustrate sociologists' *definitive* versions of action and belief. Clearly the authors of these statements are not claiming that they could not possibly be wrong. These claims are not presented as definitive versions in that sense. Rather, analysts are presenting these versions as definitive in the sense that, if the analyst has interpreted his evidence correctly, *this is the way things actually happen or actually happened.* Thus each author seems to be implying that, for analytical purposes, there is one best version of particular actions and beliefs or of particular classes of actions and beliefs. Each author also seems to be saying that he has examined the relevant evidence and has provided the one version which can be deemed to be best in the light of that evidence. So what I want to do in this talk is to consider whether it is possible to move from the kinds of evidence we have to the kinds of characterizations of action we find in the literature.

My series of seven quotes can be seen to display several overlapping sequences as one reads from number one to number seven. There is a movement away from so-called hard data toward qualitative data. There is a movement away from a traditional view of scientific knowledge to a more socially contingent view. The later quotations also imply a critique of the earlier ones. And the later quotes are more concerned with characterizing specific sets of actions in such a way that they can be seen as generating specific scientific beliefs. In a crude fashion, therefore, these quotations reflect some of the main analytical changes which have occurred in the sociology of science, and perhaps in social studies of science, during the 1970s.

What I want to ask is: can we accept *any* of these kinds of attempts to characterize scientists' actions and beliefs? I am going to approach this question by looking at the kinds of data used as the basis for those claims and I am going to make a simple distinction between citation data and qualitative data. The ideas contained in the early quotes on my list were first derived from qualitative material, but the versions I have paraphrased as quotes 1 and 2 are offered by their authors as quantified verifications established by means of citation analysis. The authors of these claims are not directly concerned with scientific ideas or knowledge, but with characterizing actions. Assumptions about the character of scientific belief only enter the analysis covertly. Thus our first task becomes that of examining how analysts manage to show, by means of citations, how scientists actually act when they carry out technical evaluations, distribute rewards, respond to prescriptions, and so on. This is not the place for a comprehensive critique of citation studies. I simply want to make one central point, namely, that the claimed correspondence between scientists' actions and the pattern of citations is not itself demonstrated, but is established solely by means of an *analyst's fiat*. Definition by fiat is necessary because we know virtually nothing about the production of citations: and, as I will argue later, we cannot use qualitative data to find out. Let me try to show what I mean by examining the kind of citation analysis which lies behind quotation one.

When sociologists try to show that scientific research contributions are judged impartially, they devise measures of the scientific quality of research papers and they maintain that it is the quality of research more than anything else which leads to the receipt of rewards. Thus the allocation of rewards is said to be impartial. Various reservations are always expressed about the use of citations to measure quality; for instance, it is admitted that we know very little about scientists' reasons for making citations and it is recognized that measuring quality in this way means that an unknown proportion of papers will be treated as high quality even though their frequent citation probably indicates only that they have been quickly rejected by the majority of interested researchers. The response to this latter point is usually that negative citations do not lessen the appropriateness of citations as an indicator of quality, because any paper which has stimulated wide criticism must thereby have contributed valuably to clarifying scientific issues in some intellectually beneficial way. I want to draw your attention to the gradual elision of meaning which is taking place here. Although analysts are seeking to *justify* their use of citations as a direct measure of quality, in their texts they actually make it clear that citation is more or less equivalent, not to quality, but to 'thought to be worth referring to' or 'formally noticed by other authors'. It is impossible, therefore, in my view to draw any valid conclusions about the impartiality of scientists' actions from this kind of citation measure.

Despite their own reservations, however, the analysts doing this work continue to insist on their definition by fiat. For the purposes of these studies, the quality of scientists' research actions is the number of citations their papers receive. Consequently, strong analytical statements about quality are presented, not as uncertain inferences from simple numerical findings about citations, but as straightforward empirical findings. Thus the following kind of statement of empirical results is typical: 'It is the quality of research rather than its sheer amount that is most often recognized through honorific awards'. However, this is not in fact a simple finding but a translation, by means of analysts' fiat, of the following observation: 'Highly cited physicists are more likely to receive awards than those who have written as many papers but are less frequently cited'. What is observed is that physicists who are often cited also receive a lot of awards. But the analysts *claim* to have demonstrated an empirical relationship between quality of research action and allocation of social recognition. I want to suggest that the only connection between these two statements, the statement about numbers of citations and numbers of papers and the statement about such actions as bestowing recognition and producing high quality research, is the analysts' unjustified decision to treat citations and quality as identical. The arbitrariness of this decision is further revealed by the fact that analysts regularly choose to use each of their limited range of indicators to measure quite different variables. Thus citation is used, not only to measure quality, but also to measure recognition. Accordingly, it is quite possible to interpret the finding that highly cited physicists also receive more awards as revealing only that the analysts' two measures of recognition are correlated; or to put it another way, that both kinds of reward tend to go to the same people.

If analysts were to restrict their claims to simple statements about relationships between citations and other quantifiable variables, their findings would be unobjectionable but also relatively trivial. My general conclusion, therefore, is that this kind of analysis does not, and possibly cannot, tell us anything interesting about collective action in science. Citation analysis *appears* to deal with scientists' actions only because the analysts involved have consistently hidden away their speculative interpretations behind methodological fiats.

Qualitative data

One claim of qualitative analysis is that it is not arbitrary, nor does it oversimplify the rich variety of social action in which participants engage. Qualitative analysis goes to the people under study and captures the real, complex meanings of their activities. Can we accept, then, that the conclusions contained in quotes three to seven are more firmly established than those based on citation data? I suspect that we cannot. Let me try to say why.

The central problem on which I want to focus is that of the diversity and the apparent inconsistency of accounts of action and belief that participants produce. The analyst using qualitative data seems to be claiming to have produced a composite 'best version of events' which brings together and reconciles all the versions produced by participants. My judgement, however, is that analysts have not taken seriously enough the difficulties of this task. What analysts usually do is to formulate a general, overall interpretation, which is broadly substantiated by a selective use of participants' own versions. My suggestion is that these broad qualitative conclusions are only achievable because analysts formulate their interpretation at a level which enables them to ignore much of the diversity and fine detail of their data. Although this is, of course, particularly true of sociologists, a very similar line of criticism could be applied to historical research. I want to concentrate, however, on a very condensed sociological example.

Quotation seven claims that much of scientists' professional action is political in character. These actions are described more specifically as involving marketing, salesmanship and manipulation. How is this characterization of political action established? It is based on the results of a series of brief case studies. In each study, the procedure is as follows: The analyst collects a number of interview statements from scientists working on a particular topic. In each interview transcript he finds that the speaker offers various versions of other scientists' actions. Other scientists are said to be 'fanatical, paranoid and obsessed', for instance. They are said to be driven by personal antagonisms and to be engaged in a bitter struggle to gain acceptance for their ideas, which leads them to engage regularly in a variety of political manoeuvres. Although respondents say other things as well, statements of this kind appear regularly in virtually every transcript.

What can we legitimately conclude from these data? One general conclusion might be: when researchers *talk* about scientific debate in the course of interviews, they regularly *attribute* negative personal characteristics to those with whom they disagree and they regularly explain the rejection of correct ideas, as well as the acceptance of incorrect ideas, by referring to the influence of social and political factors. This conclusion stays fairly close to the data. But it is *not* the analysts' conclusion. *My* conclusion deals with a regularity in what scientists *say* about each other's actions when they are discussing controversial topics. The analysts' conclusion is about scientists' *real actions*. The analysts' underlying methodological procedure here is to accept statements at face value if they occur often enough. If enough participants *say* that a certain kind of action is occurring, then you can assume that it *is* occurring. Unlike the citation analyst who identifies action by fiat, the qualitative analyst tends to allow *participants* to do the analysis; although the qualitative investigator, of course, plays a crucial role in deciding which parts of participants' analysis to treat as important and to reproduce as his own. In an important sense, participants collectively replace the qualitative analyst. What enough scientists say about action comes to be taken as a literal description of action.

Some people might regard this as an adequate procedure for establishing relatively crude conclusions about action. Working on the assumption that 'there's no smoke without fire' or remembering the old adage that 'fifty million Frenchmen can't be wrong', one might be happy to operate in this way. But there are at least two reasons why this procedure is unacceptable. The first is that one can show that scientists' statements about political action cannot be taken as accurate. Secondly, one can show that the regularity found in scientists' *statements* about political action is produced by a regularity in the methods by which they construct their accounts of action, rather than by a regularity in the actions themselves. These two points are complementary. I will expand on them briefly.

The conclusion reproduced as quotation seven is based on a study of biochemists. It so happens that Nigel Gilbert and I have recently begun a study of more or less the same research network (Gilbert and Mulkay 1984). In our interview material we find very similar data to that which furnished the basis for that conclusion. But we have gone one step further than that analyst and we have compared each statement about the actions of a particular scientist with every other comparable statement about that scientist. We find that these statements are remarkably inconsistent. Every statement which characterizes a given scientist's actions or ideas as X is contradicted by numerous other statements which characterize his actions or ideas as various kinds of non-X. Furthermore, any particular speaker will tend to vary and modify his accounts of actions and ideas; not only other peoples' actions and ideas, but also his own. The author of quotation 7 seems to assume that participants either see an action as a political manoeuvre or they do not. But our close analysis of qualitative data shows that a given act can be portrayed as a political manoeuvre by one person and something completely different by another person. Or the same person may call it a political manoeuvre on one occasion and a disinterested act performed out of duty on another occasion. Thus there is no way you can get from this collection of incompatible statements to a conclusion about action, unless you can find some way of sorting out reliable assertions by participants from unreliable assertions. You might try to do this, for example, by distinguishing those speakers whose statements were biassed from those who were not. But to do this you would have to draw on another collection of statements, where you would face exactly the same problem of characterizing action. As a last resort, you might try using non-verbal data to help you establish the meaning of participants' verbalizations. However, if my comments about citation data are generally applicable to non-verbal data, and I think they are, this would offer no way out.

Analysis of discourse

My general conclusion, then, is that neither citation data nor qualitative data can be used to furnish adequate characterizations of action or belief. Of course I'm generalizing wildly. It may simply be that I have picked a particularly tricky concept to cope with by citation data. And perhaps the qualitative study I chose was badly done or did not employ sufficiently subtle analytical techniques or the research area under study was unusual in some way. All these are reasonable possibilities. But let's assume for the purposes of argument that I have established my thesis in its full generality. What follows from it? Well, in the first instance, it seems to follow that all the studies quoted earlier are inadequate. It also follows that there is no point in trying to improve on that kind of study. It is simply impossible to produce definitive versions of scientists' actions and beliefs. This conclusion helps us to understand why there is so little agreement in the field. But does it not also remove all possibility of further analysis? This, of course, is where the analysis of discourse comes in. It *may* be that this is an alternative. What, then, is meant by analysis of discourse and in what sense is it an alternative to the analysis of social action? (I'm simply using the word 'discourse' here as a convenient way of referring to all forms of verbalization; to all kinds of talk and to all kinds of written document.) Let me return to my previous example of qualitative analysis to show what analysis of discourse might look like and how it can perhaps replace the traditional form of analysis.

The original analyst did not notice that all his interviewees' statements about political action were made in attempts to account for or explain the acceptance by other scientists of what the speaker treated as incorrect scientific views. In other words, the statements were all centrally concerned with accounting for scientific error. In addition, he ignored the fact that reference was regularly made in these statements to various other social, but not directly political factors, and to a whole range of negative personal attributes. Thus what his data and our own clearly demonstrate is a very regular pattern of interpretation in scientists' utterances about error and correct belief. Each speaker takes correct belief, that is, his own scientific view, as unproblematic. If he is asked to explain or if he asks himself why he or others hold that belief, he does so entirely in cognitive terms, usually by a simple reference to experimental evidence. This appears to pose an interpretative problem in accounting for error. If correct belief is scientifically unproblematic, how is it that some scientists have got it wrong? This difficulty is resolved by drawing on a wide repertoire of distorting non-cognitive factors, that is, social, psychological, or political factors, to account for the acceptance of error and the rejection of correct ideas. We call this pattern that of 'asymmetrical accounting for correct and incorrect belief'. In our data it occurs fifteen times more frequently than symmetrical accounting.

I have no time to say much more about this kind of analysis. But I hope it is clear that the traditional objective of describing and explaining what really happened has been abandoned and replaced with an attempt to describe the recurrent forms of discourse whereby participants construct *their* versions of social action. One focuses, not on action as such, but on the methods scientists themselves use to account for, and make sense of, their own and others' actions. This is not, of course, a new approach in other areas of sociology. It has only just begun to be adopted, however, in the sociology of science.

There are many advantages to this form of analysis. Firstly, one is no longer trying to use observable evidence to explain unobservables such as past actions or ideas in peoples' heads. Instead one is concerned only with interpreting given documents or recorded utterances. Secondly, all the detailed inconsistencies between accounts which occur in all qualitative analyses cease to be specially troublesome as such, once one stops trying to get through to what really happened. Material which is utterly incompatible when taken literally, can nevertheless clearly reveal a highly recurrent pattern of interpretation – as in the pattern of asymmetrical accounting for error. Finally, even this preliminary analysis of accounting for error helps us to begin to understand the structure of our own scholarly literature. The traditional sociological view of science adopted the conception of correct belief embodied firmly in scientists' own pattern of asymmetrical accounting and exemplified in all sorts of ways in the formal research literature and the data that literature generates. Many of the critics of the traditional sociological position have drawn on less formalized scientific discourse, particularly on scientists' own standard interpretation of error, which has enabled them to 'show' that science is directly influenced by social factors. Thus, as I have implied from the beginning, the literature of social studies of science is largely derivative from scientists' own literary products and accounting procedures for its versions of scientific action and belief. If the analysis of scientific discourse *is* a viable analytical alternative, it may help to set us free from this longstanding form of intellectual vassalage.

3 Textual fragments on science, social science and literature (1989)

A false start

How shall I tell it, this story that I have in mind but not yet in word? Can I present it as the one true story, as in, say, *The Origin of Species* or should it be more like *The Thousand and One Nights* where each story finds its completion in yet another? In trying to answer these questions, I must not forget that this is a story partly about Science. It seems appropriate, therefore, to adopt a 'realist' technique and tell my story as if it is the simple, literal truth of the matter. I will have to employ what Gusfield (1976) nicely terms 'the style of non-style', that is, the style of Science. My text will give the impression that its symbols are inert, passive, neutral representations of a world which exists quite independently of my efforts. My text will be the mirror of Nature turned upon the natural phenomenon of Science itself (Rorty 1979). Indeed, how else could the true story of Science be told?

Stop! That opening paragraph did not work out very well at all. It was meant to begin with some apparently tricky questions and then to use them as a lever with which to move the rock of ignorance just enough to reveal the first steps on the road to knowledge. But all it actually succeeds in doing is to leave us with another question. Its obvious, of course, that *this* question is meant to be rhetorical. Its intended to imply an answer to the earlier questions with which the text began. But I'm pretty sure that the answer which is implied will turn out to be incongruous and paradoxical; and unfortunately the language-game of Science is ill-designed to allow for incongruity and paradox. So, what looked like a promising start has already got us, that is, you as well as me, into trouble.

What trouble? Let me see if I can explain. It seems to me that the rhetorical question above expresses a basic dilemma facing all attempts to understand Science from outside. Take the example of sociologists' attempts to understand Science as a social and cultural enterprise. Following the logic of my opening paragraph, sociologists have found it impossible to approach Science without trying hard to be scientific about it. Now 'being scientific about it' has been taken to mean being 'detached, objective, guided by the facts, methodologically circumspect, textually restrained', and so on. Even the most 'radical' sociological analysts of Science have gone about their business in this fashion, from within the cultural forms of the scientific world-view. However, one of the most fundamental tenets of this world-view is that phenomena must be described and explained from the *outside*. Within the language-game of Science, true knowledge is objective, external knowledge. It is knowledge that is uncontaminated by subjective, variable, inherently unreliable, inner experience of the phenomenon in question. Thus a paradox of the sociology of Science is that its scientific conclusions are formed from within the cultural confines of Science, but the culture of Science requires that Science be understood from a detached, external, perspective. It follows, therefore, that if sociologists are to understand Science scientifically, they must adopt a *non*-scientific perspective. The final twist, of course, is that Science either denies entirely the legitimacy of such external forms of knowledge or treats them as inferior. Consequently, whatever sociologists of Science do, whether they stand outside of Science or try to work within its forms of life, they are bound to fail, in scientific terms.

Perhaps I need to make it clear that these problems are, ultimately, problems of Science and not of sociology of Science. It is not that the defects of sociology are revealed when its practitioners try to deal with Science, but that the defects of *Science* are then revealed. For, by the very nature of their discourse, Scientists are not only prevented from achieving self-understanding and thereby from understanding each other, but they are prevented from allowing the adequacy of any other understanding. Science, as a language-form, is essentially unreflexive. Science is a form of language which hides and denies its own linguistic character. Science, as a kind of knowledge, hides and denies its producers' social, and therefore their inner, experience. There can be no doubt that ...

This is terrible! The text just isn't working properly. Its degenerating into mere rhetoric. Look at that thundering three-part list in the last paragraph. Its also smug: 'its not that the defects of sociology are revealed ...' Disgraceful! And its beginning to claim certainty when the only thing that's certain, in the realm of human affairs to which Science belongs, is that one can never be certain. Oh dear, there I go again. What's going wrong? I suppose, in part, the problem is that I am trying to recognize the multiplicity of the world, but also to force it into my neat little single-minded line of analysis. Its becoming so predictable. Pretty obviously, the next step along the path from 'ignorance' to 'understanding' will be to argue that the inherent limitations of Science, and of sociology of Science, can only be remedied by Literature. For Literature, it will be claimed, has all the important features that Science lacks as a form of textuality. Literature, for example, is necessarily reflexive in form, concerned with the relationship between inner experience and social life, and able to give expression to diversity as well as uniformity. The multifarious textual forms of Literature involve no denial of their inventive use of signs to create new meanings, but rather ...

No, I still don't like it. In my opinion, its too abstract, too divorced from the richness and uncertainty of life. The text so far employs a desiccated form of discourse; not Science, but akin to Science in its obsessive pursuit of idealized relationships and its disregard for the subtlety and significance of the particular. I'm not going any further in that direction. I'll have to try something else. I know, I feel in the mood for Romance.

Sociology and science: a moving story of love and bondage

She had never seen anyone like him before. In the golden glow of the Enlightenment his very being shone like a god. Indeed, the rumour was that he had banished God to a back room in the Universe and was going to use Newton's laws to run the whole thing himself. He was the master she had been longing for. She knew, from that first moment, that she was meant to be his slave and that, oh, her life was destined to be intimately intertwined with his.

She knew, of course, that she was unworthy of him. She would never be able to acquire his quality of mind, his economy and precision of language, or his indomitable will to conquer. That was not her nature. Her concern was with people, not things. Her task ultimately was to care for their needs and to help them through their troubles. But, she believed in her youthful innocence, she could imitate him well enough to become his helpmate; a partner in his struggle to improve man's lot through the pursuit of knowledge. She would, she vowed, teach herself to think, speak and act as he did. He would become her model in all things.

As time went by, she saw his achievements multiply. As the natural world came increasingly under his control, she strove to apply his techniques to her own humble realm of human affairs. Of course, he took little notice of her modest labours and, when their fruits were brought to his attention, he derided them as worthless, woman's things. But she was not discouraged. Indeed, her ardour was inflamed by his effortless superiority and she tried even harder to subdue the human world as he had taken command of all that was not human.

The decades passed by and then turned into centuries. The first strands of grey could now be seen in her once lustrous hair and the shine in her eyes was less brilliant. She felt that she had done all that could be expected of her, but still their union seemed no closer. She was sure that her spirit was attuned to his. But he did not seem to return her feelings. She sometimes suspected that he said unkind things about her when he was closeted with his friends. Most revealing, and hurtful, of all, he pointedly refused to allow her to attend the yearly festival of the Nobel Ceremonies when all that was great and good was praised and rewarded.

Slowly, imperceptibly at first but with growing momentum, she began to have doubts about the man she had loved and admired so much. How could he be so heartless and so unmoved by her devotion? Did he still have the fine qualities which had touched her heart all those years ago? Had she ever properly understood him? She began to wonder whether the pledge that she had made in her youth had been based on an illusion. If so, it might not be too late to start again. But first she must find out the truth. Her new quest, she decided, would be to apply *his* methods of understanding, as well as she could, to discovering what sort of person he really was.

She already knew many of his writings, of course. But he never stopped producing more and the range of his knowledge increased at a daunting speed. Although she read and read, and re-read and re-read, she felt that the man she was searching for was hidden from view behind the elegant neutrality of his written texts. In addition, she was deeply worried by the texts themselves. How had she ever been impressed by this simplistic, yet cumbersome, language and by this manipulative way of relating to the world? She began to talk to those who knew him well. They spoke of him with respect and admiration. But, she felt, to be praised in this unreserved fashion by industrialists, entrepreneurs, politicians and the military, was itself a kind of implicit condemnation. Anyway, she got a strong impression that there was an undercurrent of fear. She sensed that their professions of confidence in the man she loved (or was it the man she *had* loved?) were underlain by a nagging suspicion that he no longer knew what he, or they, were doing and that the world they had raped together was now going to pay them back in kind.

She was shocked by her own thoughts. She had never seen it this way before, but somehow 'rape' now seemed appropriate. His basic assumption was, she realized, that knowledge was the same thing as control; and the basic assumption of his companions seemed to be that knowledge gave you the *right* to control, that is, to dominate, exploit and subjugate for your own ends. The 'god' of her youth was beginning to look, as she approached middle age, more like a 'devil'. It was time, she decided, to go and talk to the man himself.

On her first visit, he was quite charming. He complimented her on her 'youthful good looks' and invited her to pursue any line of inquiry that she wished. 'I have nothing to hide', he insisted with a laugh. However, he wouldn't allow her to tape-record a discussion which 'might touch upon delicate political issues'. She noted down the general gist of his responses: 'Not my fault if things go wrong "out there". Soon have all basic answers. Cheap, inexhaustible energy just around corner. Solve problem of global overheating immediately. Seal up ozone layer with self-reproducing micro-organisms designed to reflect harmful rays. Train aquatic mammals and use them to cleanse oceans. More money needed for research. Just a bit more time to achieve perfect unity of knowledge. Nearly there already. Three down, one to go. Once we've got that, control whole system. Better life for all – as long as they do what they're told'.

This monologue didn't exactly rekindle her love for him. But maybe he was right, she thought. Perhaps he *did* have the ability to take everything under his control and make it run perfectly, in due course. Yet what did it mean to make it run 'perfectly'? And in whose interests would control be exercised? On her next visit, she put these questions to him. She was distressed and shocked by his reply which was, in effect, that that was none of *his* business. *She* was the one, he pointed out, who dealt with people. It was up to her to develop her own 'perfect unity of knowledge' that could be used to control the *social* world in the same way that he would soon have total mastery over the physical and biological domains. 'When you have achieved this,' he said, 'I will welcome you into my dwelling and we will at last join together to create a perfect, ordered world for humankind.'

At these words, she turned in horror from him and ran out of his world. She had finally come to realize that the man she had loved was emotionally, morally and even intellectually deformed. He was, she now knew, unable to see the world from another's point of view; unable to understand that there could be no perfect unity in the realm of human affairs because the social world was not unitary, but multiple. She saw for the first time that her fragmentary and disordered conception of social life, her concern with its concrete, ever-changing particulars, were not signs of her failure, as she had always believed, but evidence of her success.

Suddenly she felt free as if an intolerable burden had been lifted from her mind. The cost of learning the truth had been great. But, at last, her subjugation was over. Her youth had been sacrificed to an illusion. Now she was a middle-aged woman adrift in a sick, if not a dying, culture. Yet she was, for the first time, able to think for herself and to begin to create her own language; which would be a language, not of domination and control, but of imagination and freedom.

A symposium à trois

Malcolm: What did you think of it, Trev?

Trevor: Not a lot.

M: Why, what was wrong?

T: I thought there was a real problem with the dolly.

M: I know what you mean. She shouldn't have been messing about interfering in men's affairs.

T: Well, that goes without saying. But what I mean is, I think she was still in love with the bloke.

M: I dunno, she seemed pretty keen to get away from 'im at the end.

T: Yeah, she *thinks* that's what she wants, but it stands to reason – no middle-aged biddy is goin' to give up an offer like that and bugger off on her own, is she?

Author: Excuse me, gentlemen, but I don't think the text should be read in quite this fashion. The characters were intended to stand –

T: Give over, mate. Who do you think you are, the author? Ha ha ha ha.

M: Ha, ha ha ha.

A: Well, yes, I am actually.

M: Go on, pull the other one.

T: Wait a minute. If you're the author, perhaps you can explain what's going on. I came here to find out about Science and Literature.

M: That's right. We made a point of visiting this chapter to find out what sociologists have got to say –

T: And all we find is a bit of a farrago. First there was a false start –

M: And then we leave the real world altogether and find ourselves hearing about 'Sociologist in Wonderland'.

A: Well, if you don't like it, you can just clear off. Nobody's *for*cing you to stay. This is a free text, where every voice can do its own thing.

T: Alright, alright. Don't get upset. I didn't realize authors were so sensitive. We were just playing the Fool, literally. We know that when a couple of fellas like us appear, we're expected to provide a bit of low comedy or at least light relief. With a sexist tinge, of course.

M: That's right. We were only *pretend*ing to read your stuff in that vulgar and offensive way. We understand, of course, that its a kind of parody which invites the reader to perform subtle interpretative work of his or her own.

A: I suspect that you're pretending *now* and that what you said before was more like a *bona fide* reading.

T: Funnily enough, that's just what we're interested in and what we want to ask you about, as a sociologist.

M: Yes, we've been discussing whether there can be a viable distinction between pretence and reality for an observer of the social world. Our conclusion, as mere amateurs of course, is that this is only a participants' distinction which cannot hold for the analyst.

T: The analysts' frame of reference, it seems to us, is necessarily different from that of the participant. For the latter, an action has got to be either real or a pretence. It can't be both at the same time.

M: No, because if it was, participants wouldn't know how to react. But for the *an*alyst, a pretence is just as much a real form of action as a genuine act. Its a *real* pretence. The task of the social analyst, as we see it, is to show how participants construe actions and bring them off interactionally as one thing or another, as a pretence or as a genuine act for example, without committing *her*self either way.

T: That's my real reason for criticizing the sociologist in the Romance. She should have accepted that sociologists have no option but to strive for detached, objective representation. She should simply have got on with the job of being a social scientist in those terms. That's why I think that, deep down, she must still love and admire the man of objective knowledge and want to be like him.

M: Let's not get caught up in that fairy story again. The point is that, for the sociologist, there is no distinction between pretence and reality as such, but only between what participants take to be pretence and take to be reality. In that sense, the sociologist is a neutral observer whose task is to document how participants construct their versions of the world in the course of their ongoing social lives.

T: Right. I agree with that.

A: Therefore its *true*, of course.

T: No need to be sarcastic. I agree that 'I agree' is used interactionally as meaning 'that's true'. That's a good illustration of how we construct the meaning of the world through the fine detail of social interaction. In other words, by agreeing some version of the world with another person, we establish that *version* of the world as indistinguishable *from* the world.

M: Right. For those people, on that occasion, that particular bit of the world in which they're interested comes to be constituted by what we might call their 'consensual version' of it. Now as I understand it, as an out*s*ider, the traditional goal of sociology as a quasi-scientific enterprise was to produce the ultimate, consensual version of the social world, that is, the version which everyone would come to accept as the scientifically established truth. But this attempt to write the Final Text of human society broke down in the face of participants' own textuality and their ability to produce what you might call sociological counter-texts. For sociologists are, of course, not only outside observers, but also participants in their own textually created reality. And that socially constructed reality is bound to conflict, often fundamentally, with other participants' realities. Thus sociologists cannot avoid becoming involved with others' realities. And they must often do so as participants, and not from the safe neutrality of the external observer.

T: He gets carried away, sometimes, by his *own* textuality. What he means is that sociologists, having adopted a scientific model of textuality which was devised to cope with objects that are textually inert, tried to force this model upon the textually volatile realm of human action. Inevitably their grandiose assertions, partly because they were drained of vitality by their inappropriate linguistic form, met with rebuttal and even ridicule.

M. O.K. Fair enough. But what I was *re*ally trying to say was that its impossible to produce a final, consensual version of social action, let alone the social *world*, whatever *that* might mean, because action is a kind of text and is always open to different readings and re-readings.

T: To put it in a nutshell, sociologists made the mistake of taking over the unitary textual forms of Science, whereas they should have employed the textual multiplicity made available by Literary forms.

A: Wait a minute. A little while ago, you were insisting that sociology's central task was that of neutral observation and representation of social life. That seems to me like an expression of support for the unitary textuality of Science. Now I hear you saying that that was a mistake and that sociologists should make use of textual forms which give voice to the textual diversity of social life. You can't argue both those positions. You've got to adopt one or the other.

T: It wasn't *me* who argued for Science, it was Mal.

M: Well, I agr*ee*d with you, Trev, but that was really to help you make a point. I thought it was worth arguing your case in order to see where it led us.

A: So, in fact, neither of you is in favour of using the restricted formalism of scientific discourse in relation to social action, but would encourage sociologists to adopt textual forms that can give voice to a diversity of interpretations, analyses and understandings. Is that right?

M: Well, I don't think its necessary to use Science and Literature in this way as two terms in a simple binary contrast.

T: Nice one, Mal. Er, but what does it mean?

M: Its quite straightforward. Both Science and Literature are aspects of Textuality. Science is a form of Textuality that is based on the assumption that there is a single coherent factual world which can be accurately and consistently represented by the application of a constant method, and to a considerable degree controlled by the textual producer. Literature is another form of Textuality the basic premise of which is that there are many potential worlds of meaning that can be imaginatively entered and celebrated, in ways which are constantly changing, to give richness and value to human experience. Both these forms of Textuality furnish us with the means of relating to the world and of giving expression to that world.

T: So you're implying that neither form should be given primacy or regarded as inherently superior to the other?

M: Yes, that's right. As far as sociology is concerned, both forms can equally well be employed. Society can be read for regularity, order, coherence and control according to the scientific format. Or it can be read for disorder, diversity, incommensurability and so on, through the production of openly creative texts.

A: You're implying that sociology has always been committed to the coherent representation of social order. But what about Marx and that whole tradition? Marx was fundamentally concerned with disorder, struggle and revolution. And his dialectical method was designed to give expression in his texts to the conflicting processes at work in the social world.

T: I don't think Mal would deny that. You can certainly read Marx as a body of Literature giving voice to social disorder and contradiction. Yet, at the same time, the aim of those texts is to reveal the underlying orderly processes which are supposed to generate struggle, conflict and social change. So, although Marx gives textual recognition to the contradictions of social life, these contradictions become resolved in his texts, that is, they become orderly, understandable, and ultimately controllable.

M: Indeed, Marx argues that eventually these opposing forces will cancel themselves out and will give way to a nicely-balanced utopian society in which orderly social life is self-perpetuating. In this sense, the semantic order of Marx's text precedes and thereby helps to create the emergent harmony of the future society.

A: Of course, there are *Literary* forms which are rather similar in this respect. I'm thinking of those utopian novels in which the defects of the author's society are contrasted with, and condemned in the light of, the perfection of some imaginary future society. So literary forms are not necessarily linked to disorder and diversity. They can equally well portray and advocate unity and orderliness.

M: That's true. But, for me, there's one basic difference. The utopian novels are offered openly as works of the imagination. Thus we can enter the textual reality of their world and learn from that experience. But such texts do not insist that *their* reality is the *only* reality. By their very nature, they allow other texts the right to exist. Compare this, however, with the Marxist literature or that of sociology generally. These imaginative creations masquerade under the banner of Science. They claim to tell us of a social world that exists independently of their textuality. They deny that they are constru*c*ting a world and either assert, or imply by the very form of their textuality, that they do no more than lift the veil from a world which already exists or which will inevitably come to be.

T: Quite often, of course, it turns out to be very difficult to make the world, that is, other people, fit the scientific text. In addition, people do insist on reading the master-texts of social science 'wrongly'. As a result, you get a continual wrangling among Marxists and other social scientists about what the text (Marx, Weber, Durkheim, Parsons, Merton, Habermas) actually means and whether or not it is confirmed by 'the facts'. So, out of this collective striving for intellectual order emerges further disorder and, in sociology, a mounting dismay at the failure to achieve the unitary, consensual version required of any self-respecting scientific discipline.

A: I must say that it seems to me, despite your denials, that you are arguing in favour of the adoption of Literary forms in sociology in place of the customary scientific forms. And it seems to me that you're heading for trouble. Your policy appears to be a kind of sociological Glasnost. No doubt that will win you a lot of applause in the present climate. But I suggest that you reflect a little on the difficulties that face Mr Gorbachev. That should be a warning.

M: That's an interesting comparison. Clearly there was a relationship between the authoritarian rule of the old-style Soviet regime and their belief in the intellectual supremacy of the Marxist master-text. In the West, you can observe something similar in the Thatcherite conviction that society is a market-place – although there's less scholarly reliance in this case on a particular body of writing. In both instances, however, commitment to a specific 'consensual version' of the social world creates an inability to allow that there can be any other legitimate understanding of that world; it also engenders a ruthless political repression of all opposing voices.

T: The implication of that argument, Mal, seems to be that sociological analysis must involve political, and moral, choices and decisions. As I see it, in arguing for forms of analysis which give the fullest possible expression to the interpretative diversity of human society, we are resisting any form of social life which restricts that diversity and which seeks to impose its own 'truth' as a means of social domination.

M: I think that's right. Personally, I can't separate the act of knowing the world from that of acting in the world in relation to other people –

A: I'm sorry to interrupt. But before you two get too carried away with mutual approbation, I want to clarify exactly what you have in mind when you recommend the use of Literary forms in sociology. Don't get me wrong, I quite like the idea. I'm pretty fed up with forcing my rich files of data into the conventional format of the research paper. What actually made the stuff interesting in the first place often seems to disappear. But I need a clear-cut procedure to tell me what to do at each step.

M: Well, I'm not so sure –

T: I wouldn't approach it –

A: I think I've understood the central idea that the form of the text is just as important a part of the communication as the content. So I could, for example, convey the fragmentation of social life by a judicious ordering –

T: How can we get out of here? This clown hasn't written in a real-life setting for this so-called symposium. There's no easy way out. Not even a window to climb through.

M: Don't worry. We're autonomous illusions. We can simply speak our way out of the text and back into the real world.

T.   O.K. Ready? 'And so Trev',

M: 'And Mal',

T: 'left the text immediately, never to return'.

M: 'left the text immediately, never to return'.

A: Am I relieved to get rid of those two! Silly sods!

Maritime reflections on the text-thus-far

Why are Dolphins not encompassed by this text? And Whales? Why are Whales not brought gently aboard? No inlet is provided for the Shark or the Tunny. Crustaceans, Catfish, Krill. Ignored completely. The text just washes them away. Turtles, for example, and Octopus are of some importance in the watery scheme of things. But the words of this text flood past leaving them beached and dying on the shores of man's ignorance.

I am here to speak for them and to speak for them in the human way. For I once was Apollo the god of music and of human song. That was close to the time when men sang their knowledge of the world and, as *we* do, sang that world into being in joy. But the time of man's song is past and I am now mundane aquatic mammal, talking fish, light entertainment on the cheap. A leaping, friendly fool in a sea-blue prison.

It is true, we *are* friendly, though, I insist, no fools. We Cetaceans have no aggression. We became the major culture of the globe millions upon millions of years ago; long before humankind evolved their modest brain and their sadly limited communicative capacity. Yet we did this by creating a culture based on play and on song. We did this without destroying others or ourselves. We did this whilst maintaining a serene harmony over seven-tenths of the surface of the earth. We sang our ever-changing songs communally across the oceans of the world. We fashioned a shared current of knowledge which fostered peaceful co-existence in a world held in common, not only by the members of the Whale Nation, but by minds and voices other than our own. We were able to do all this because our knowledge was our collective song.

But now I must confine myself to speech, not song. I must speak plainly through a human text. I must speak on behalf of Cetaceans, but also for all those other non-humans who are made flotsam by the crushing tide of human conduct. The 'text-thus-far', through which I am allowed to have my say, has the virtue of being playful. This is greatly to Dolphins' taste. Indeed, playfulness is central to the Cetacean way of life. Nevertheless I detect, beneath the innocent surface of the text, some of humanity's most basic and deadliest prejudices. Take Trevor's reference above to the non-human as 'textually inert objects'. Or consider the suggestion in the Romance that aquatic mammals might be used to clean up the oceans, our realm of *be*ing that mankind has so grossly polluted. That may, of course, have been mere fancy. Yet who can doubt that, if it *were* possible to *use* us in this fashion, man would have no reservations about doing so? The assumption that non-humans are things to be used like inanimate objects, as men see fit, is so firmly built into human textuality that even our apparently compassionate author and the figments of his text have taken it utterly for granted until now.

This is especially disheartening for me, given that this text is supposedly concerned with extending the scope of *sociological* understanding. As I see it, sociology is fundamentally concerned with social relationships, that is, with contact between living beings who interpret the world, who communicate with other beings about the world, and who design their conduct accordingly. How is it, I ask, that sociologists are unaware of, and make absolutely no mention of, human beings' involvement with, and indeed dependence on, non-human beings and non-human cultures? How can they be so completely ignorant of the Cetacean world, of the culture of the Whale, when so much of modern human society has been built out of that culture's destruction?

'This', you will reply, 'is a typically maritime exaggeration; like fishermen's tales about "the one that got away"'. But the Whale did *not* get away. He and she were turned in their millions into such useful items as lamp fuel, candles, watch springs, umbrellas, toys, petroleum, soap, margarine, lipstick, detergents, glycerine, brushes, linoleum ... sausage skins, drum skins, laces, surgical stitching, tennis rackets, chess pieces, golf-bags, varnishes, insecticides, paint, skin cream, iodine, insulin ... photographic film, corsets, bodices, fish bait, dog food, anti-freeze, low calorie cooking fat, rissoles ... piano keys, car-wax, machine oil, more and more and more cosmetics ... The list goes on and on. The unacknowledged sociological fact is that the Whale body has been a critical resource in enabling the human race to make the transition to industrial society. Man's treatment of the Whale Nation has been the most extreme and horrific example in history of human exploitation. Yet it is not even noticed by sociologists or by most other so-called men of knowledge. This is because we Cetaceans are seen as bodies without minds and therefore as destined to be the raw material for the 'advance' of human society. We are seen as mere bodies, as mindless things whose pain and suffering does not count, simply because our language is different from that of humans and beyond the limited grasp of human understanding.

As I understand it, our sociologist is searching for forms of textuality that will enable him to observe and give expression to the social world, not from one narrow perspective, but from many different, unexpected and sometimes opposing, points of view. Yet, so far, he has stopped looking for alternative forms of textuality at the limits of *human* language. This is surely a fundamental error. The fact that there has so far been only modest success in communicating *across* the human/non-human barrier is not, in itself, good reason to deny the existence of our culture, its importance for man or, most critically in my opinion, the collective wisdom acquired during its fifty million year history and embedded in its forms of life.

'Can we properly speak of a Cetacean "culture?"' 'Are not Whales, Dolphins and their like merely instinctive, inferior creatures?' 'Do they not simply act out their inbuilt propensities like fairly complicated, but entirely predictable, biological machines?' These are likely to be the kinds of objection raised by our sociological expert in cultural matters. In doing so, he cannot personally be blamed. He does no more than give voice to the unexamined presuppositions of his species and of a language designed for domination. Yet we Cetaceans have had brains as advanced as man's for twenty million years. Some of us have brains six times the size of man's. We have also had subtle and complex languages of our own for ten times as long as man, with which we communicate among ourselves and which we alter as our circumstances change and as our oral traditions evolve. Man's inability to recognize our culture and to relate to us as social beings on at least an equivalent cultural level as humankind is a sign, not of *our* inferiority, but of man's failure to appreciate the poverty of his language forms and of his reality.

It is true that some humans have managed to achieve a faint awareness of our capacities. And some of these have done so by using the language and methods of Science. But, on the whole, although this has thrown some light on how we function as mechanisms, it has made us appear more like fascinating objects for study than responsible, comprehending social actors. The detached reportage of Science alone serves to alienate us further from humankind. We become floating experiments. We exist, scientifically, as the source of an endless series of research publications. Ethics committees, so I am told, assess with care the implications of human research on other humans. But there are no committees concerned with the ethics of Cetacean research. For we have no rights and humans have no obligations in their relations with us. This is true even for our sociologist, who is an expert in the social Science concerned with rights and obligations. From the perspective of your Science, we are no more than things.

There is a song though, or perhaps I should call it a poem, which gives some kind of human expression to how *we* might see and experience our relationship with humankind. I have in mind here Heathcote Williams' *Whale Nation*. Without that poem, I doubt that I would have been allowed a place in this text. *Whale Nation* is not *our* story. Yet it succeeds in evoking a human sense of what our story might be. It is not a simple description of the facts. Yet it establishes the possibility of another non-human reality that goes beyond what *you* would call 'the facts'. It is, in one sense, a sociological representation of the clash between the two dominant cultures of the globe. But it bears virtually no resemblance to the formally restricted textual products of that would-be scientific discipline which specializes in cultural matters. In my view, the openness of poetic form sets free imaginative powers and the capacity for revealing the 'social world' in a new way. The implications for the 'text-thus-far' and for the language of sociology in general are obvious. For, how can one cross the boundary between the human and the non-human without a poetic, a songlike, a Delphinine leap of the imagination? We, of course, have already made that leap for *you*. Long ago, when we were a multitude. Will you be able to do so in time for *us*, before we leap from the water of life for the last time?

From space, the planet is blue.
From space, the planet is the territory
Not of humans, but of the whale.

A Bacchic soliloquy

We enter a bar. The bar-room is circular. It forms the top floor of a hundred-storey hotel tower. The outer wall is made almost entirely of glass. The room revolves slowly revealing through the glass an ever-changing, yet endlessly repeated, urban environment that stretches infinitely away in every direction.

By the window sits a man. He is a distinguished, authorial figure. He is also, at this moment, rather the better for drink. Although he is alone, he mutters softly to himself. He is obviously an academic of some kind because, despite his condition, he speaks, not quite in blank verse, but certainly in well constructed sentences. From the ripples of elation and despair that cross his face, it seems that he is grappling with arcane matters that he believes, in his erudite innocence, to have great significance beyond his confused, faltering mind. He has evidently been here for some time. We join him in mid-stream of consciousness.

* * * * *

... sociology be? What should it *not* be? Should I just suffer things as they are or continue to explore new ways of extending sociology's textuality? All that seems to happen is that my efforts engender outrage. I find myself immersed in a sea of troubles. If only I could return to the waters of tranquillity. Perhaps the best thing would be to take early retirement; a kind of intellectual slumber before the final deadline comes. But, of course, I would still dream of writing that crucial paper, that really influential book, which would put everything to rights. Vain dream! As I seem to remember writing once: There is no such thing as a final text. Each text is, at best, a resource for the next act of textual production until their currents turn awry and lose the name of action. No, that last bit wasn't me, I'm sure it came from Shakespeare ...

Waiter! Waiter, your cocktails are really swell. I'll have another Symposium à Trois, please, with ice ... Thank you.

What about this chapter I've been working on? What will the Editors make of it? I fear that they will spurn my patient merit and return it with the request that I grunt and sweat my way through radical revisions. Well, if they do, I'll refuse to give up the dolphin. I think that her contribution is the most interesting of all. She certainly made *me* think about the question of textual forms in a way I'd never previously considered. Playfulness. That was the essential thing. Her presence was made possible by playfulness. I like the idea that Cetaceans may have developed such large brains because they spend so much of their time in play. That's one crucial element that's missing from the formal language of science and, by imitation, from that of social science. We would certainly see the world and our place in it very differently if we thought of knowledge as imaginative play instead of as manipulative control ... But how can I finish off this text in a suitable and convincing way? The trouble with a sequence of textual fragments is that it can stop at any point. Indeed, it would *have* to stop at some arbitrary point in order to maintain the fragmentary character of the text. Yet, if the text *has* to cease in an arbitrary fashion, then to end the text at some random point is to furnish the text with an appropriate, coherent conclusion. Which would be inconsistent with the nature of the text. Thus, the only way of providing a g*e*nuinely arbitrary, fragmentary ending would be to round off the text with a conventional, orderly, well designed resolution ... Shall I wind up this semantic spring to the next level? No, its not worth it. The point *is* that I can't *reason* myself to a conclusion about how to bring my text to a conclusion; I have to make a *choice*. Of course, I have reasoned myself to the unavoidability of making a choice. But now I must make it ... My choice is to let the text stop where it happens to stop at present ... And I'll just sit here and imagine, in a playful fashion, how it might have ended if I had decided to write an ending.

> Waiter, waiter, I'll have another Symposium à Trois, if you please ...
> That's most kind.

Quite an effective way of ending it would have been to reflect upon the text's own underlying contrast structure. Beneath the obvious contrasts, for example between science and literature, between science and social science, between human and non-human, between those with language and those without language, there seems to me to be a more basic contrast between texts which are vehicles of domination or control and texts which are expressions of reciprocity and harmonious balance. Mankind, and man's science in particular, were seen as committed to the former kind of text. The dolphin, and to some degree, the sociologist, were portrayed as adopting the second kind of text. The language of science was depicted as a language geared to human control over that which is inert, over that which cannot express itself and over that which, therefore, is taken to be without rights except in so far as such rights may be granted by humankind. Given this form of textuality, it follows that, as the scope of man's knowledge grows, so does the collection of manipulable objects available for his use. The world becomes fragmented into bits and pieces that are significant or not depending on their usefulness to man. Of course, there is no guarantee that a discourse of world-wide domination of this kind can be permanently successful. All the signs are that it cannot. Apart from the retribution of the non-human upon its human master that looms ever larger in our collective, global mind, there are likely to be disastrous *social* consequences in the long run – or so it seems to me in my present state of higher consciousness.

What I mean is – Well, science, despite its conventional disclaimers, *are* used as if its technical formulae *are* the one, real world. It is on this assumption that human beings employ science to try to control the world. But the scientists, the men of knowledge, seldom make the ultimate decisions about how their knowledge is to be applied for practical purposes. Such decisions come from the mouths of an even smaller elite within the higher echelons of the industrial nations. So, increasingly, a minute proportion of mankind exercises a knowledge-based, invisible domination over both the human and non-human worlds at a global level. It seems to me obvious that this elite is not equipped to intervene in the world on this scale without disaster. Indeed, the disasters are already here. But at present their effects are still confined primarily to the powerless peoples of the world. When they spread, however, as it seems to me they must, then the authoritarianism implicit in the knowledge-forms of the advanced societies will necessarily be given clear expression in the political realm. The response from the elite to the masses will be: 'We could not know it would work out like this. We are not to blame. If only we had had the time to make our knowledge perfect, we would have built you a perfect world entirely under our control. But, unfortunately, things have got out of control, beyond *any*one's control, and you will just have to take it and die like men. If you don't obey, we'll shoot you.' It may not be exactly like this, but along those lines, anyway.

Waiter, another Thingy à Trois, if you don't mind, with ice, if you please … Thanks.

Of course, that's the negative side of the contrast in its most prophetic mode. I'm not in the mood to pursue that any further. Too gloomy. Its this bloody tower. What a symbol of man's, man's … something or other. However, there is also the positive component of the contrast structure. What can I say about that? I suppose the basic idea is that the many, constantly changing forms of literature are more suited to giving voice to that which is creative, that which can communicate its intentions and that which is able, in principle, to fulfil obligations and, therefore, to claim its rights. The literary forms of science are not suitable for this because they deny their objects a voice of their own. Science replaces those voices with its own impassive, amoral discourse; a discourse which seems stylistically neutral, yet which implicitly asserts the 'knower's' right to dominate and control … Just listen to me! Already this supposedly positive side of the contrast has become negative and critical. It derives its force from condemning the so-called defects of its opposite. But what would it actually *be* like, this creative discourse of changing forms? This playful form of life that was pledged to tolerance and harmony? This textuality that allowed, indeed encouraged, not one world, but many? How can human language escape its essential character, that is, as a tool for controlling and refashioning the world? Is it not true that, in speaking, we project our speech outside itself, thereby creating the appearance of an independent world beyond our speech? Is it not true that we then have no option but to act as if the illusion created by our speech is the one, real world in which we, and all others, have our and their being? This is certainly true. I myself have written something very much like it and published it as well. So it *must* be true. But I believe that we can reveal the element of illusion in all our supposed realities by a constant attention to the forms within which our language is embedded. In short, we can devise textual structures which address us along with the content of our speech and which draw attention to the creative process of using language and, thereby, to the ever-present possibility of alternative creations. It is the textual availability of realities beyond our own speech which is the ultimate safeguard of others' rights and of our own ...

That's pretty positive, I think. Its not prophetic, of course. I can't follow Marx and come up with a theory showing that the bad will undoubtedly be replaced shortly by the good. In fact, I'm inclined to think that the unitary discourse of domination and control is, under most circumstances, much more powerful than the multiple discourses of playfulness and respect. Its obvious really. Unity and diversity. Work and play. Dominance and toleration. My team loses every time. Of course, I'll go on making my case for a different kind of social science, a new sociological textuality. But there's not much hope. Just look out of this window. Man on a global rampage. Man intoxicated with the apparent power of his knowledge. I think I'll have another drink my*self*. We celebrated Apollo earlier, now its Bacchus' turn.

Waiter! Waiter, I'll have one last Condominium à Trois, if that's alright with you. Have one yourself ... Your eternal servant!

Part Two: Conventional analysis:
revealing the social world
of science

4 Structure and process in a physics department (1971) *with* Anthony Williams

Introduction

It has become widely accepted by those working in the sociology of science that one of the most significant social processes within the scientific community is the exchange of information for professional recognition. Professional recognition is valued by scientists, not only because it is experienced as gratifying in itself, but also because it makes more accessible a variety of associated rewards such as research funds, promotion, salary increases and so on. Professional recognition, however, depends on research publication. Thus the professional career of research scientists centres around the exchange of information for recognition. In the present paper the physics department at a new Canadian university is studied with special reference to this exchange process and to the manner in which the reward system of the scientific profession structures activities within the department.

The first section of the paper examines how the policy of the government-sponsored National Research Council combined with norms of independence within the department to enable the physicists at Simon Fraser University to pursue their individual research interests. In the second section it is shown that the physicists' major professional goal was to contribute information defined as original and valuable by the appropriate scientific specialty. After this several strategies are discussed by means of which physicists at SFU sought to ensure that their contributions would be so defined and would, accordingly, receive professional recognition. The next section focuses, in relation to the role of 'referee', on the operation of certain norms involved in the exchange of information for recognition. It is argued that the mechanisms of social control in physics do not always foster scientific excellence. An attempt is then made to demonstrate the relative pre-eminence of professional recognition over financial rewards and to show how this influenced the physicists' interpretation of their teaching role within the department. Finally, the department's rather unexpected administrative structure is discussed in relation to the professional objectives and incentives of its members.

The data used in this study were collected mainly by means of semi-structured interviews with fifteen of the sixteen physicists in the department. Both authors were present at thirteen of the interviews which lasted from one to two hours.

Because the number of respondents was small, responses have not been tabulated but are presented in the course of the analysis. Owing to the obvious limitations of the empirical material the level of generalization is intended to be low. Nevertheless, the findings are, we believe, consistent with a more theoretical discussion presented elsewhere (Mulkay 1969).

The role of the National Research Council: support of professional autonomy

Most professions are primarily concerned with using esoteric knowledge to perform a public service. Scientists, however, and particularly university scientists, have traditionally been removed from the application of knowledge. They have been concerned instead with the extension of certified knowledge for its own sake. That this tradition persists today in Canada is largely due to the activities of the National Research Council which, being run by scientists drawn predominantly from universities and operated with little intervention on the part of the federal government, has systematically supported basic research whether in the universities or in its own laboratories.

> The policy in awarding research grants during the past 50 years has been to support research where the greatest competence lies ... The subject matter of the research need not have been related to any national program, but must have represented a sound objective in attempting to advance the boundaries of knowledge in the specialty concerned ... the method of assessment ... does ensure that physicists' applications are assessed by physicists, the majority of whom are from the universities themselves ... (*Physics in Canada* 1967: 32)

All members of the physics department at SFU at the time of our study were receiving grants from the NRC, either to cover operating expenses or to purchase basic equipment. Yet none saw the granting agency as influencing the content of his research. Thus the NRC assists the basic research scientist to choose his projects solely in terms of their potential contribution to the extension of certified knowledge. Even those four respondents who received additional grants from the Defence Research Board and from industry appeared to be free from formal constraints. It seems likely that the existence of the NRC influences the research policies of these other agencies. For if the restrictions the latter impose are unacceptable to the researcher he can always fall back upon NRC funds, which depend simply upon quality of research rather than its technological implications. Consequently, when the physicists we studied found that they were working on projects which could conceivably be of interest to industry or the DRB, they tended to formulate their research goals in a manner which would elicit support from such agencies but which would leave them sufficient freedom to pursue those developments which they thought were interesting in their own right. Thus grants from industry were accepted without any obligation to provide information in return. The findings of industrially financed research were to be published in the professional journals in exactly the same way as those financed by the NRC. Similarly the DRB does not demand any immediate benefit from the research it supports. However, it does exercise a more systematic control than industry over research, through the mechanisms of grant-renewal which require physicists to score highly on two indices. One of these indices is constructed by a panel of university scientists who attempt to estimate the scientific quality of the research in question. The second index is supplied by the DRB scientists who judge the long term value of the research for their own organization. Most projects, however, once they have been accepted in the first place, are assured of support for a period of three years. Given that the scientist's original application for funds normally arises out of a conjunction of interests which, at least in the researcher's view, makes possible the satisfaction both of his basic research goals and the needs of the granting agency, it seems clear that the university scientists in this department are not deprived of their professional autonomy by the requirements of those who give them financial support.

Freedom in research is strengthened by norms of individual independence in the department. Hagstrom (1965) distinguishes three such norms within the scientific community at large, the most important of which is freedom with regard to problem selection. This ideal made itself felt in the department we studied in a number of ways. To begin with, physicists were in fact allowed complete autonomy in their choice of topics, though there were of course informal pressures which led them to link their projects to others current in the department, and every researcher presumably became a member of this department on the understanding that he would undertake research in the field of solid state physics. Then as we have seen above, they only requested funds from specialized agencies when some conjunction of interests enabled them to maintain their own research goals. Thirdly, when asked why they had chosen to work in the university rather than in industry or government, more than half our sample referred explicitly to the greater independence accorded the researcher in universities. Whether or not this is the 'true' reason for their preferring the university, its frequent use in justifying the choice is evidence of its normative standing. Our examination of this physics department then provides further evidence for the existence of norms of independence among scientists and for their direct effect upon behaviour. We have also seen that the physicists' autonomy in Canada is based upon the financial support of the NRC and probably upon the impact of the NRC on other granting agencies. These factors combined to allow the individual physicist at SFU to decide for himself what kind of information he would supply to his professional community.

The research goals of physicists: originality within conformity

The basic research goal of all the physicists at SFU was that of contributing something new to the body of scientific knowledge. This goal can be interpreted as a product of conformity to the norm of originality described by Merton (1962). Our interviews provide ample evidence of the importance of originality. For example, graduate students' research projects were carefully selected by supervisors to guarantee the student the opportunity for an original contribution to knowledge. Yet, although research projects are selected independently by each faculty member and although projects are geared towards originality, similar topics tend to be investigated simultaneously by numerous researchers throughout any given specialty. The reason for this is that scientific activity most of the time consists in the attempt to force nature into the conceptual boxes supplied by professional education (Kuhn 1962). Normal science, as this process has been called, does not seek novelties of a fundamental kind. Rather it tries to extend its empirical range without altering its basic commitments. These conceptual, theoretical and methodological commitments constitute models or paradigms from which derive coherent traditions of scientific research. When research is directly paradigm-based, scientific investigation becomes a highly directed activity. Thus although the physicists we studied wished to produce original results, their originality was limited by the paradigm accepted within their specialty. Originality is not valued unconditionally in physics. It is valued only in so far as it contributes to the extension or modification of the current paradigm.

There are several kinds of evidence which can be drawn from the department under study to support this interpretation of the informal structuring of scientific research. In most physics departments in North America we would find researchers involved in a wide range of specialties. Consequently, we would expect to find some physicists obviously engaged in normal science but they would be mixed with other specialists whose situation would be much less clear. At SFU, however, the department was unusual in that it was composed entirely of physicists working in solid state physics or in closely related areas. And solid state physicists are likely to be engaged in normal science, as the following statement by some eminent practitioners shows.

> Solid state physics is concerned with the elucidation of observed properties of solids in terms of atoms, of electrons, and of the interaction between these constituents. At present, we think that our understanding of these constituents and their interaction is, in principle, adequate to account for all of the observed properties of solids. We do not believe that major new concepts are needed in solid state physics, in the sense that such concepts are, for instance, needed in high energy physics. Nevertheless, the description of the solid state presents a considerable intellectual challenge, because of the complexity of the many particle aspects. (*Physics in Canada* 1967: 294-5)

The Head of the department was one of the authors of this statement and all but two of its members were in agreement. They agreed that projects in solid state physics were concerned primarily with resolving problems generated by the appearance of phenomena unanticipated within the accepted theoretical framework. Their actual research goals reflected this situation, and were aimed at greater experimental accuracy, the resolution of experimental or theoretical anomalies, or the refinement of existing theoretical assumptions.

If individual physicists within a given specialty are allowed complete autonomy in their choice of research problems and if the problems themselves are generated by the paradigm which they have been trained to use, there will be a strong tendency toward selection of similar problems. This overlap will be greater the more widely the current paradigm is accepted. In solid state physics this difficulty is considerable because, as we have seen above, there is general agreement on the appropriate paradigm. Duplication of research makes more difficult the contribution of original results and reduces the likelihood that physicists will receive professional recognition for their work. Thus it is not surprising that virtually all our respondents were concerned about the possibility of being anticipated in the presentation of their work. A further consequence was that most physicists in our sample took steps to reduce the likelihood of anticipation. The most common means to this end was the establishment of adequate channels of communication with related specialists. Not only were our respondents concerned with anticipation but they knew those researchers working on projects similar to their own and who could therefore anticipate them. Although the physicists working in one specific area are geographically separated they use the circulation of pre-prints and personal discussions at conferences as sources of information about the direction of other people's potentially threatening research.

In addition to establishing channels of communication it is possible to reduce the probability of anticipation by choosing difficult research problems. Not only does this gambit lessen the number of 'competitors', it also reduces the need for information about others' projects and increases the recognition gained from the presentation of a successful solution. Several members of the department chose to investigate intricate problems, and were in fact aware of the competitive advantage which they gained in this way. A third way of minimizing competition is by working on the margin of the discipline, for example where physics merges with chemistry. Physicists may, of course, be attracted by the interesting questions which arise in such inter-disciplinary areas. However, this kind of research does offer the additional benefit of decreased competition.

There was one further way of reducing the probability of anticipation which was explicitly mentioned by our respondents. This was to speed up the presentation of results. None of the physicists we studied admitted adopting this solution and several were critical of the very notion that it should occur. It is clear, therefore, that there is a norm which defines the deliberate acceleration of research as illegitimate on the ground that it leads to poor quality work. Owing to this norm we were unable to estimate the prevalence of accelerated publication in the department.

Although most members of the department were concerned about anticipation, our data indicate that this concern varied according to the amount of professional recognition which individual scientists had accumulated. In particular, anxiety over anticipation seemed to decrease as physicists attained senior academic ranks. This is understandable. To begin with, mature researchers have a settled reputation and one paper more or less will not greatly change their status within the scientific community. Because any specific project is less valuable to the senior man than his younger colleague his concern with anticipation will be less. In addition, the more established physicists have many more channels of communication and are more capable of reducing competition by choosing difficult and inter-disciplinary topics. A further factor which improves their competitive position is the fact that they receive grants which are several times larger than those given to the junior man. Not only are they less concerned with anticipation but they are more able to avoid it.

Rewards, norms and journals: the ritual of publication

We have so far produced evidence consistent with the view that the reward system of basic research in physics consists of an exchange of information for social recognition; this recognition depending on conformity to certain *technical* norms provided by the current paradigm. Some analysts have, however, argued that receipt of professional recognition in science depends primarily on conformity to certain *social* norms and even that, without such conformity, 'the extension of knowledge would be seriously hampered if not stifled altogether' (Storer 1966: 83). This thesis is stated most strongly by Storer who identifies six important scientific norms. We wish to question Storer's analysis in relation to two of these, namely, the norms of universalism and organized scepticism and, in so doing, to elucidate further how scientific information and recognition are actually exchanged.

The norm of universalism 'finds immediate expression in the canon that truth claims, whatever their source, are to be subjected to *pre-established impersonal criteria*' (Merton 1973: 270). Closely associated with this norm is the practice of keeping secret the names of those persons chosen to 'referee' articles submitted for publication in the professional journals. Presumably anonymity makes it possible for the referee, whose role is to maintain established standards of competence and originality, to remain unaffected by personal ties and to use impersonal criteria of scientific adequacy. It should be noted, however, that although the researcher does not know the identity of the referee, the referee does have the name of the author. Thus anonymity operates in one direction only, to protect the referee. Furthermore, despite its operation, *all* our respondents thought that the vast majority of papers in the journals which they read were of poor quality or of little significance. One respondent stated that 'only 2% of publications are significant and 50% are wrong'. This response may be phrased in extreme terms but every member of the department endorsed its general sentiments. If we accept their opinion it appears that, contrary to Storer's thesis, the norm of universalism even when combined with institutionalized anonymity does not maintain the quality of scientific publications.

There are perhaps two interpretations of this fact. First, it may be that items of dubious quality get accepted by the journals because there are available no clear criteria for evaluation. But this can hardly apply to solid state physics where there exists firm agreement upon the kinds of problems to be solved and the means to be used in their investigation. The second interpretation is that the obligations of refereeing are not fulfilled because they are not rewarded with professional recognition. Our findings support this view. To begin with, none of our respondents who had refereed papers had spent more than a few hours on the task. Indeed, one physicist, who enjoyed perhaps the most extensive reputation of those within the department, refused to referee any papers which would take longer than one day to scrutinize. It appears to be quite normal, therefore, for reports which have taken months to prepare to be evaluated in a few odd hours. Furthermore, even if any one referee devotes a great deal of time and effort to examining papers, he will not appreciably change the overall situation. For the reports which he rejects will, perhaps with minor alterations, be accepted elsewhere. Consequently, the tendency is for referees to check papers for no more than style of presentation, for the correct use of techniques, and for originality in the sense that the findings are not exactly duplicated in the existing literature. The physicist mentioned above, who returned lengthy papers, was exceptional in his concern with the quality and significance of papers which he refereed. He could maintain this policy, however, only by refusing those which would use up too much of his time.

Institutionalized anonymity appears actually to reduce the likelihood that referees will fulfil their obligations. Conscientious performance of the task of refereeing reduces the time available for research. As this research is the major source of professional rewards, and as the time available is already subject to encroachment by teaching and administration, scientists are naturally unwilling to reduce it further in order to fulfil obligations which receive no professional recognition. Not only this, but in assessing papers referees are likely to confer benefits on their 'competitors'. For articles are frequently refereed by physicists cited in the footnotes and are always examined by specialists in the area concerned. This interpretation of the 'defects' in the existing pattern of refereeing in physics is consistent with the general analysis presented here, but it clearly needs more convincing evidence. Such evidence could perhaps be found by investigating instances where referees make unacknowledged use of information submitted to them for scrutiny, for our analysis leads to the prediction that such 'thefts' will occur. This is so because the referee's lack of recognition will tend to become magnified in comparison to that gained by his competitor and will create pressures upon the referee to take whatever he can from the situation. Furthermore, his 'crime' will be obscured by the veil of secrecy. In the department we studied, although only one respondent claimed to have been abused in this way, several of them referred to cases involving other physicists they knew. Whether these instances are genuine or 'scientific myths' their significance for our analysis remains.

The second norm we would like to examine is that of organized scepticism. According to Storer (1966: 79): 'The scientist is obligated ... by this norm to make public his criticism of the work of others when he believes it to be in error'. Our findings do indicate a slight tendency for organized scepticism to exist as a norm. But even more conclusively they show that the norm had little influence upon the actual behaviour of our respondents, none of whom had ever taken steps to criticize publicly the poor work which, they stressed, filled the journals. Several of them claimed that they knew of other physicists who did write critical letters to the editors of journals or who published articles of rebuttal. But we take this to be evidence of the existence of the norm only, for nobody was able to *name* such a scrupulous physicist. As our respondents had studied and taught at a number of leading universities in North America and Western Europe we can reasonably infer that the norm of organized scepticism has little effect upon the behaviour of physicists. The vast majority of papers are not subjected to critical scrutiny. The information they contain is either extracted from the journals by interested researchers or it is ignored. As in the case of universalism, although the norm of organized scepticism exists within the scientific community, it does not operate as Storer suggests. And once again the reason seems to be that conformity to the norm is not linked securely to the receipt of recognition. Criticism of the work of others is not valued highly, perhaps because it is perceived as a dangerous practice which reduces the amount of professional recognition available. Thus it is possible that scientists, at least during a period of normal science, have a vested interest in *not* quarrelling with their neighbours' work. As a consequence, if critiques bring little positive reward then any original contribution to knowledge will be seen as a relatively more rewarding pursuit. Furthermore, if an 'original' contribution is defined as any result which is not exactly duplicated elsewhere, and this is the pragmatic definition adopted by many referees, then the search for publishable findings is likely to be a more profitable undertaking than the criticism of others' errors.

Professional rewards and the organization of the department

So far we have proceeded as if recognition by the research community were the sole reward accorded physicists. This is an oversimplification. Physicists are clearly rewarded by the monetary payments proffered by university, industry and government. Without exception, however, our respondents appeared to value money less highly than professional recognition. This fact made itself evident in several ways. To begin with, salaries of scientists in industry and government are considerably higher than those available in the university. Our physicists were aware of this discrepancy and yet several of them had given up remunerative positions in industry to return to university life. Although such action was sometimes justified by reference to teaching most respondents balanced the loss of income against the increase in autonomy within the university. Cash was less important to them than the opportunity to solve problems which they themselves saw as important and which, according to our analysis, gave them access to the plaudits of other basic researchers in solid state physics. These rewards appear to be very satisfying, for nobody in the department had any intention of moving away from the university environment. This attitude towards financial rewards was further demonstrated by their lack of interest in patents. According to the NRC, patenting involves several advantages for the researcher. First, the financial awards which may be received are often substantial. Second, the taking of patents by Canadian scientists generates economic benefits for their country. Third, the researcher is frequently furnished by the Patent Office with information about associated work in his field. And lastly, the researcher gains a large international audience additional to the general readership of scientific journals. Yet despite these alleged incentives and despite the attempts by the NRC to stimulate recourse to the patent system, none of our respondents had ever taken out a patent while working in the university. There appear to be two factors involved.

The first is that our respondents thought of patents as bringing solely financial benefits. They did not seem to be aware that patenting might bring them wider professional recognition, nor did they mention the services of the Patents Office in providing additional information. The second factor is that patenting involves a long delay in publication. It is possible to publish but only after the patent has been completed. The physicists at SFU were unwilling to risk losing their most valued response simply for the sake of increasing their income.

Within the university physicists are paid for teaching. If we are correct in suggesting that monetary rewards are less significant for them than receipt of professional recognition, we should find that the teaching role is interpreted to suit research interests. In the department we studied, teaching was taken very seriously. For instance, it was stressed that performance at teaching was important in gaining promotion, and several members of our sample referred to the opportunity to teach as their main reason for choosing to work in the university. However, despite this genuine attempt to increase the importance of teaching relative to research, it seems to us that the teaching role was still subordinate to the research role and the receipt of income ancillary to that of professional recognition.

In the first place there was the department's decision to produce small numbers of graduates, at a time when most politicians and educationalists were attempting to justify the creation of SFU on the ground that it would supply a pool of persons trained to serve the science-based industries of the future. This stress on quality within the department seems to demonstrate an underlying concern with the major professional goal of research rather than the requirements of the university or the local community. This interpretation is further strengthened by the fact that our respondents valued most highly and obtained their important satisfactions from teaching graduate rather than undergraduate students. We do not mean to imply that undergraduates were poorly trained or that graduate students were used to further the research goals of faculty members. What we wish to suggest is that the basic satisfactions derived from teaching came from producing graduates who would one day become good researchers. This is what our respondents meant when they said that they enjoyed teaching or that they returned to the university to teach. And in order to help establish their students as fully-fledged members of the scientific community they were willing to organize their own research so as to enable their students to produce something original. Thus teaching was valued as an opportunity to initiate younger men into the satisfactions of basic research.

The emphasis upon research rather than teaching was also evident, although not clearly envisaged by the physicists, in their recruitment and promotion procedures. While promotions were often said to depend equally upon performance in teaching and research, most of the younger men, that is the actual candidates for promotion, believed that research was much more important. The validity of their interpretation was supported by the fact that ability to teach undergraduates was never mentioned in our interviews as a quality required of new entrants to the department. Applicants who were being considered seriously as prospective members of the department were invited to give a departmental seminar to assist evaluation of their research competence and their teaching proficiency. In the words of the Head:

> ... the main purpose of these seminars is to assess a man's ability to communicate. In my view it matters little whether this communication is with undergraduates or with graduates. Such seminars, I believe, are the best guide available to us for assessing a man's teaching ability. We ask him to speak on the subject which he ought to know very well, namely the topic of his thesis, and if he cannot do a creditable job on this it is unlikely that he will turn out to be a big success as a teacher for undergraduates.

What is significant for our argument is that teaching skill is judged in terms of basic research interests. An assessment of teaching ability is felt to be important in the appointment of new faculty but this assessment is made on the basis of a discussion of candidates' recent research.

The authority structure of the department: the benevolent dictatorship

In this final section we wish to show how authority came to be exercised in the department in a way which furthered the major professional aims of its members. Professional objectives appear to have been safeguarded in many university science departments by the development of egalitarian authority structures. Barber argues that because scientists strongly support norms of individual independence and because science is composed of numerous specialties the members of which are not competent to judge each other's work, scientists tend to form self-regulating communities 'in which the several participants are relatively autonomous equals' (Barber 1962: 195-6). The physics department at SFU was, however, rather unusual and quite different from this. It was accurately described by some of its members as a 'benevolent dictatorship'. It was a dictatorship in the sense that administrative decisions were made and departmental policy promulgated by the full professors and, more specifically, by the Head. It was benevolent in the sense that departmental opinion was regularly probed through informal discussions and, more significantly, in the sense that there was general agreement about the proper goals of the department and the means to be used in attaining them.

How widespread this kind of authority structure is within university science departments we do not know. But in this particular department there appear to have been two features which worked to produce such a structure. The first factor was the physicists' zealous concern with research. As a consequence of their overriding commitment to research they preferred to entrust virtually all administration to the Head. In this way they could reduce the claim upon their time of duties which they regarded as peripheral. Many of the respondents experienced a certain degree of frustration arising from the conflicting pressures exerted by *teaching* and research. This was true even for those who enjoyed teaching. But none of those below the rank of full professor at least, experienced this frustration in relation to administrative duties, simply because administration was done by the Head with assistance from the senior men. Yet this delegation of decision-making would probably not have been so complete had there been less agreement about the goals of the department. In this department the degree of consensus seems to have been particularly high largely because all members worked within the same specialty. It may be that in more conventional departments which include representatives of a range of specialties there does emerge a pattern of 'colleague authority' which guarantees fair treatment for all varieties of research. At SFU, however, there was so much agreement about the correct policy for the department that decision-making could be entrusted to the Head thereby leaving the other physicists more time for research itself.

There was only one element within the department which in any way threatened the cohesion described above. This was the distinction between theoreticians and experimentalists which derives on the one hand from the development of highly mathematical theories, and on the other hand from the existence of a complex data-gathering technology. Although the role differentiation between theoreticians and experimentalists is less developed in solid state than in many other specialties, there was in this department of sixteen physicists only one man who combined the two roles. The others described themselves and were described by their colleagues as either an experimentalist or a theoretician. Furthermore, role differentiation is sufficiently complete in solid state physics for the two kinds of specialists to experience difficulty in understanding each other. While the experimentalist cannot follow all the mathematical symbols of the theorist, the latter's knowledge of complicated experimental techniques is far from perfect. As a result, although there are no specialized journals, the two groups are directed toward distinct audiences: for professional recognition is valued only when it comes from those who are capable of understanding one's contribution and of passing competent judgement upon it. This division within the specialty was reflected in the department in several ways. First, except in the case of the Head, experimentalists and theoreticians never collaborated with a view to joint publication. If we accept that the two groups are interested in distinct audiences, each with different technical norms and paradigm-induced problems governing the acceptance of publications, then we would not expect such collaboration to occur. Second, experimentalists and theoreticians formed distinct informal groupings within the department. We would expect this partly because of the common interests within each group. We would also expect informal groupings to emerge out of the simple interaction among experimentalists working in their laboratories and theoreticians left behind in their offices. Third, there was some slight evidence of negative feelings between the two groups. For example, theorists were described as having a 'soft life' or as 'breaking everything they touch'.

Although the department was divided in this way the division did not generate any noticeable conflict. The reasons for this are quite evident. To begin with, the language barrier is not as great in solid state as in such specialties as high energy physics. As one of our respondents said: 'In high energy physics the theorists have become involved in formalisms which are decreasingly related to empirical phenomena. In high energy physics the theorists all have different gods, whereas in solid state theorists and experimentalists are linked symbiotically.' Moreover, although there was no direct collaboration between the two groups there was a certain amount of reciprocal influence. For example, theoreticians would take up the theoretical aspect of problems being investigated experimentally by their colleagues, and vice versa. Thus there existed a greater degree of informal contact and reciprocal recognition than could occur in more traditional physics departments composed of representatives from a range of specialties. This informal interaction and exchange of recognition is likely to further departmental consensus. Departmental concord was also furthered by the dual role of the Head who was both experimentalist and theoretician. Given that those who combine the two roles are awarded highest prestige, that the Head was the centre of the network of informal discussions on departmental policy, and that he could appreciate the needs of both groups, there is every reason to think that he played an important part in maintaining the unity of the department. Thus, although we have seen that formal collaboration was in fact minimal, whenever we asked our respondents about it both experimentalists and theoreticians said that it existed and regularly gave the Head as an example of its occurrence.

At the beginning of this section we saw that the democratic structure of university science departments has been interpreted as a response to norms of individual autonomy and as a means whereby individual members can pursue the kind of research required and rewarded by their own specialties. At SFU, however, we have seen that the creation of a department devoted entirely to solid state physics produced such internal consensus that decision-making could be highly centralized without raising any qualms in the minds of its members. Indeed, the physicists enthusiastically approved a situation which, given the agreement within the department and the Head's position as both experimentalist and theoretician, did not threaten their independence but rather gave them more time for that research which provides the central theme governing their professional lives.

5 Three models of scientific development (1975)

In this paper I am going to discuss three generalized accounts, or 'models', of the processes by which science develops. I shall call these the 'model of openness', the 'model of closure', and the 'model of branching'. The central concern of each is to show how social factors operating within the pure research community contribute to the development of scientific knowledge. I shall argue that the third model provides a more satisfactory solution to this problem than either of the other two.

The model of openness

The model of openness, in one version or another, has been widely accepted as providing an accurate specification of the main features of the scientific research community. It seems to correspond fairly closely to the common sense view of science held by many laymen and it is also a model which scientists tend to use when describing the distinguishing features of the scientific community to outsiders. The first systematic sociological exposition of this model was that of Merton (1938) whose analysis has been repeated, with little modification until recently, by several subsequent generations of sociologists. Let me give a brief account of this sociological variant of the model of openness.

The community composed of those engaged in pure research exists within industrial societies as a distinct and partly autonomous social unit. It is distinguished from other groupings within the same society by the fact that its members are centrally concerned with extending reliable, certified knowledge. In a sense we can view the extension of certified knowledge as a goal of the community, even though this may not be the dominant aim of all its members. Individual scientists may be more interested in getting promoted, in gaining an international reputation or in occupying a position of power and influence. But, as members of the research community, they can usually only achieve these personal goals by making a significant contribution to science and by conforming to the social norms of science. Thus, although scientists have a wide range of individual motives, their professional activities converge because they are subject to a common set of social expectations. There is an essential similarity of behaviour throughout science because scientific roles are defined in terms of certain cultural values or norms, which are generally endorsed by scientists in the course of their professional activities. Individuals will only be accepted into the scientific community and receive its rewards to the extent that they act in accordance with these values.

It follows that the central part of any exposition of the model of openness is a description of the major values characteristic of the scientific community. There are, however, many such descriptions already available. Therefore, instead of listing these norms and explaining them one by one, let me show how they are seen to be related, whilst indicating in parenthesis the norms to which I am referring at each point. In the first place, there is a basic expectation that all members of the research community will strive to discover and explain new aspects of the natural world (norm of originality). But the information they obtain can only become scientific knowledge if it is made accessible to the critical inspection of other scientists. Thus, researchers are required to communicate their results without reservation to their colleagues (communality). Scientific information belongs to the research community and not to the individual practitioner. When scientists furnish other researchers with valuable information, they are rewarded with professional recognition. But they must not actively seek recognition, or indeed any reward other than the satisfaction of adding to certified knowledge (disinterestedness). Similarly, when judging the adequacy of other scientists' results, they must remain strictly impartial. They must make their judgements independent of any personal characteristics of the source of information (universalism). At the same time, each scientist must be highly critical of his own work and that of others (organized scepticism). Scientists must take nothing on trust in the course of their professional activities. They must continually re-assess their own intellectual convictions as well as all knowledge-claims put forward by their colleagues.

The central contention of this kind of analysis is that science is an activity which depends on its practitioners being open-minded. The model of openness takes scientific information to be, in principle, socially neutral; and the norms of science are seen as preventing scientists from interfering with this neutrality. On the assumption that there is widespread conformity to these norms among scientists, it is argued that science will grow rapidly because there is little intellectual prejudice and minimal resistance to new ideas; and that scientific knowledge will be peculiarly effective in practical terms because the objective complexities of the physical world will be revealed without distortion. The basic assumption underlying the whole argument is that the rapid growth of reliable knowledge can take place only within 'open' communities and that, as science has undoubtedly developed much more quickly and with more evident practical success than other intellectual movements, so the scientific community must be more open than other social groupings. This line of reasoning has one further important feature: namely, it implies that any intervention from outside the scientific community is likely to impede scientific advance. When outsiders try to influence the direction of scientific growth they introduce partiality, self-interest, intellectual prejudice and secrecy. Consequently, proponents of the model of openness tend to argue that science is most likely to flourish in democratic societies; partly because the values of science are themselves democratic and partly because democracies are less likely to exert pressure on the research community.

In one form or another the model of openness has become widely adopted. It is surprising to find, therefore, that it is based upon very scant evidence. For instance, Merton's original analysis of the norms of science is based upon an unsystematic selection of statements by a small number of scientists about their profession. But such data cannot legitimately be used to characterize the scientific ethos unless systematic procedures are adopted to obtain representative statements and unless the meaning of these statements is examined in relation to the audiences to which they were directed. Although this has never been done, several attempts have been made to discover the extent to which defined samples of scientists express agreement with verbal formulations of the so-called scientific values. But not one of these studies has produced any evidence of strong commitment by scientists to the putative norms of science. Furthermore, there is some indication that, even when scientists endorse these values at the verbal level, they do not necessarily *act* in accordance with them. Thus in a study of a university department made up entirely of solid-state physicists it was found that: all members of the department agreed verbally that scientists should be critical of poor work published in the journals; most of them stressed that a great deal of bad work was published in their field; but not one of them had either written a critical review of another scientist's published work or could name a scientist who had written such a review (see chapter four).

There is little direct evidence, then, that scientists generally endorse the values of intellectual 'openness' or that they are greatly influenced by them in practice. Moreover there are many statements by participants which depict science as being far from open. There is, for example, the famous statement by Max Planck that 'a new scientific truth does not triumph by convincing its opponents and making them see the light, but rather because its opponents eventually die, and a new generation grows up that is familiar with it' (Planck 1950: 33-4). Certain writers, several of them ex-scientists, have developed this line of thought and have argued that scientists' strongest commitment is to established scientific procedures, to bodies of scientific knowledge and to particular intellectual perspectives. Polanyi, for example, describes a number of instances which show that scientists are often not open-minded, independent puzzle-solvers, but rather men devoted to solving a limited range of problems rigidly defined by their group. The crux of this argument is that intellectual development in science has not been a smooth process, but has been brought about by a series of battles in which innovators have been forced to fight against the entrenched ideas of fellow scientists. Thus Polanyi insists 'on acknowledgement of the fact that the scientific method is, *and must be*, disciplined by an orthodoxy which can permit only a limited degree of dissent, and that such dissent is fraught with grave risks to the dissenter' (Polanyi 1963: 94).

The model of closure

Views of this kind which stress, not the openness of science, but the existence of scientific orthodoxies, I shall call models of closure. Such models have several distinct advantages over the model of openness. In the first place, they recognize the well documented occurrence of intellectual resistance in science. Whereas the model of openness tends to explain these occurrences in terms of extraneous factors producing temporary deviation from the norms of science, the model of closure takes them as the focus of its analysis and gives a systematic account of their origin. Secondly, the model of closure is supported by a whole series of studies of the allocation of professional rewards in science; for these studies show that receipt of professional recognition depends in no direct way on conformity to the supposed norms of science, but rather on the provision of information which is judged to be valuable in the light of current cognitive and technical standards. Thirdly, the model of closure appears to be more consistent with the nature of scientific education, which has traditionally operated to produce intellectual conformity. In all well-established scientific disciplines participants assume that, over a wide area, the correct problems have been posed and the correct answers have been found. Consequently, the student of science is required to acquire, rather than to question, the existing body of knowledge. Finally, there is the fact that the internal structure of the scientific community is formally organized in terms of specific fields of knowledge, technique and investigation. It makes sense, therefore, to regard these bodies of knowledge as central to the analysis. For instance, study of commitment to broad social values is unlikely to help us explain variations in the rate of growth of different specialties. But if we focus instead on differences in the character of the knowledge, problems and techniques of the specialties, we are more likely to perceive significant differences which may well bear upon the divergent rates of growth.

These, then, are some of the advantages of a model of closure. However, there appears to be one crucial disadvantage, for how can such a model be made consistent with the remarkably rapid and innovatory intellectual development of modern science? The model of openness postulates the existence of original contributions to scientific knowledge and then virtually eliminates the possibility of intellectual resistance by assuming conformity to values of openness. This answer may be inadequate in certain respects, but it is at least consistent with the occurrence of cumulative intellectual innovation. The model of closure, by stressing the prevalence of orthodoxies, appears to make scientific innovation highly problematic. There is, nevertheless, a very plausible solution to this problem. For scientific orthodoxies, like repressive political systems, may be overthrown by revolution.

Kuhn (1962), in particular, has recognized the need to balance the notion of 'scientific orthodoxy' with a conception of 'scientific revolution'. I shall, therefore, concentrate here on his version of the model of closure. Kuhn's central thesis is that the cumulative advance of scientific knowledge arises, not from its practitioners' intellectual openness, but paradoxically from their intellectual closure. Normal scientific research, he argues, is guided by paradigms, that is, by a series of related assumptions – theoretical, methodological and empirical – which are generally accepted by those working in a particular area. Most scientific research consists of attempts to solve problems generated by the paradigm without bringing into question its basic assumptions. Only because those committed to a paradigm take their underlying cognitive framework as firmly established, can they concentrate on the detailed resolution of that range of issues generally regarded as problematic within their research community. Thus scientific communities are able to achieve cumulative intellectual advance because they establish firm internal agreement about which kinds of problems, techniques and solutions are legitimate and also because they exclude from participation any persons who fail to adopt the current framework.

From this perspective most scientific innovations are seen as predictable additions to or relatively minor modifications of existing paradigms. But Kuhn argues that a second, much more radical, kind of innovation occurs when one paradigm is replaced by another. Because scientific paradigms define their field in a very rigid way and because scientists become very strongly committed to paradigms which have proved to be fruitful, this kind of intellectual transition can only be brought about by means of open rebellion against the existing order of intellectual orthodoxy. Such revolutions are usually provoked by an accumulation of anomalies, which gives rise to a loss of confidence in the paradigm. All paradigms continually generate anomalies which cannot consistently be reconciled with the precise cognitive expectations guiding normal science. But usually these failures appear insignificant in the light of past successes and other work currently in progress. Sooner or later, however, the very efficiency of paradigm-induced research reveals a growing number of puzzles which simply cannot be answered within the existing rules. The widespread failure of these rules leads to a search for new rules, particularly by the young who are less committed to the old style of thought. Numerous alternative schemes are put forward and the predictability of normal science is undermined, leading to a crisis situation in which there are no generally accepted criteria of scientific significance. In most cases of this kind, out of competition among the adherents of rival theories, a new paradigm gradually becomes accepted and a new orthodoxy is established in the field.

Kuhn's account of scientific development says little about the social processes whereby intellectual conformity is maintained within the research community. However, what is currently known about the nature of social control in science serves, to a considerable extent, to strengthen the analysis. There is now a considerable body of evidence to show that social control in science is maintained by the way in which scientists exchange valued information for professional recognition. Competent recognition of the value of a scientist's work is the primary reward controlled by members of the research community. It is highly valued by scientists, partly because it provides the clearest indication that they have fulfilled their basic obligation of extending certified knowledge, and partly because the realization of other objectives, such as promotion, occupation of positions of authority, access to research funds, and so on, depends on the prior receipt of recognition. There is much evidence to show that the amount of recognition a scientist receives is determined mainly by the perceived quality of his work. But it is clear that the quality or significance of a scientist's work is judged in relation to the existing set of scientific assumptions and expectations. Thus, whereas radical departures from a well defined intellectual framework are unlikely to be granted recognition easily under normal circumstances, original contributions which conform to established preconceptions will be quickly rewarded.

It appears, then, that in general the system by means of which recognition is distributed operates to maintain normal science. Nevertheless, the reward system of science may, under certain conditions, foster revolutionary upheaval. It will do this in the following way. When a paradigm or a research framework first becomes generally accepted it will identify a wide range of significant and unresolved problems. These problems will provide for those working in the field abundant opportunities for attaining professional recognition, career advancement, intellectual satisfaction and so on. In these circumstances, social control will be effectively maintained because information offered to the research community within the confines of the paradigm will receive at least an adequate, and often a generous, reward. But Kuhn's analysis clearly implies that the significance of results produced by normal science declines over time. Gradually, all the major issues come to be resolved and the questions still in doubt become increasingly trivial. At the same time, research becomes less predictable and researchers become less sure of receiving a proper reward for their efforts. In other words, as the paradigm is filled in, so the level of professional reward and the certainty of reward declines. Consequently, conformity to the existing orthodoxy becomes less and less prevalent. In due course, therefore, if this decline in the availability of professional rewards continues, a complete breakdown of social control will ensue.

I have tried to show in the last few paragraphs that Kuhn's account of scientific development is not only consistent with, but to some extent receives support from, the analysis of social control in science. It appears that in situations where there is a firm scientific consensus accompanied by numerous avenues of predictable research, processes of exchange work to maintain intellectual conformity; but that, as the main puzzles generated by the paradigm come to be solved, the processes of social control will weaken, making more likely the occurrence of intellectual crisis and revolutionary upheaval. However, this analysis, in which scientific development is viewed in terms of an oscillation between normal and revolutionary science, is dependent on several questionable assumptions. In particular, it is assumed that scientific orthodoxies are rigid, precise and not amenable to gradual modification; that discoveries are either consistent with or incompatible with existing scientific conceptions; that the groupings whose members are committed to particular paradigms are relatively distinct and of stable membership; and that each participant's opportunities for recognition are confined to a single research grouping. Only if these assumptions are made does it become necessary to attribute to scientific revolutions a central place in the model. I wish to suggest that these assumptions are invalid and that if they are correctly modified we are led toward a model of branching.

One difficulty with Kuhn's analysis is that it is based on a misleading and narrow conception of discovery. Kuhn recognizes two main types of scientific discovery. On the one hand, there are the small-scale innovations of normal science where 'everything but the most esoteric detail of the result [tends to be] known in advance' (Kuhn 1962: 35). On the other hand there are major innovations, typically involving a drastic re-conceptualization of an existing area of study. Now I am sure that Kuhn is right in arguing that highly predictable results are regularly produced in science and that radical alterations of perspective do occur. But the important issue is not whether 'normal' and 'revolutionary' science occur, but whether they are typical and whether there are other types of discovery which contribute significantly to scientific development. One kind of discovery not included in Kuhn's analysis takes place when observations or theoretical inferences are made which are unexpected but which are not incompatible with existing scientific assumptions. Such discoveries reveal 'new areas of ignorance' to be explored, in many cases, by means of the extension and gradual modification of established conceptual and technical apparatus. In Kuhn's scheme this type of discovery is dismissed as unimportant. Yet there are numerous instances where major scientific advances have taken this form. One of the most fully documented cases is that of radio astronomy (Edge and Mulkay 1976).

Systematic study of radio emission from celestial bodies began during the 1940s, as a number of academic physicists followed up certain accidental observations which had been made in the course of industrial and military research. These initial observations were quite unexpected, yet they were not anomalous. They did not violate established scientific expectations. They did not require reconceptualization of the existing issues. Rather they led to the formulation of questions which defined a field of investigation previously unknown to those involved. These questions were attempts to specify an area of ignorance, attempts to identify the kind of information needed in a realm where very little was known. Gradually, acceptable answers to the original questions were developed. But the researches undertaken to solve these problems recurrently generated new, often totally unexpected, areas of investigation. Within any given area there was, broadly speaking, a movement from vaguely-conceived problems and imprecise techniques toward precise instrumentation, clearly conceived problems and solutions, and an increasingly firm intellectual consensus. However, at the same time as the major questions were resolved in one area, participants tended to focus their attention on new areas where the processes of defining, solving and uncovering further problems were repeated. This growth by branching of radio astronomy is represented in Figure 1. Although the emergence of all these new avenues of inquiry has profoundly altered the character of traditional optical astronomy, intellectual resistance on the part of optical astronomers has not been marked – largely because they never regarded the revelations brought about by the radio astronomers as *incompatible* with the established knowledge of the optical universe.

This pattern of scientific growth has not been confined to radio astronomy. A similar sequence can be observed, for instance, in the development of the medical sciences during the last century. Furthermore, although there are only a few detailed case studies of growth by branching, the statistics on the overall growth of science demonstrate that growth by branching must be a very frequent occurrence. If we examine the long term increase in the numbers of scientists or scientific papers, we find that growth is approximately exponential, with a short doubling period of around fifteen years. It is *possible* that this cumulative burgeoning of scientific activity has been concentrated within a fairly stable number of research areas. But it seems much more *likely* that the dramatic increase in the size of the research community has been achieved by the continual creation of new fields of inquiry. One way of bringing evidence to bear on this

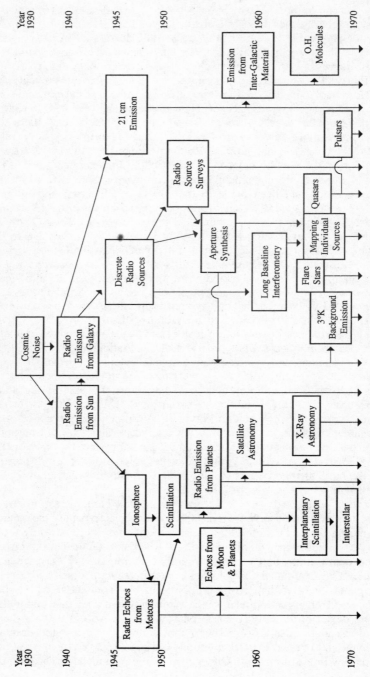

Figure 1
The Proliferation of Problem Areas in Radio Astronomy*

* Adapted from Mulkay, M.J. and Edge, D.O. (1973), 'Cognitive, Technical and Social Factors in the Growth of Radio Astronomy', *Social Science Information* 12(6): 25–61.

issue is to examine the growth of scientific journals, which tend to be founded to facilitate communication among those working within new areas. The fact that there has been a remarkably rapid growth in the number of journals, therefore, is a good indication that science has developed to a considerable extent by the formation of new avenues of inquiry. Thus it seems probable that science has grown, not by the continued expansion and recurrent redefinition of a stable set of research areas, but by the cumulative efflorescence of new lines of investigation.

Although the scientific research community has grown and continues to grow rapidly in size, the social networks associated with particular problem areas do not grow correspondingly. There seems indeed to be an upper limit between one and two hundred members, beyond which research networks tend to break up into smaller groupings. Consequently, the research community is composed of an increasing number of relatively small-scale networks which cut across the formal boundaries dividing science into disciplines and specialties. There is clear evidence that the membership of these networks overlaps considerably, that participants continually move from one problem area and its associated network to another, and that research networks undergo a continuous process of growth, decline and dissolution. This characterization of the research community in terms of a fluid and amorphous web of social relations is quite different from that proposed by Kuhn, and it has important implications for the way in which we conceptualize intellectual development in science.

The model of branching

A central assumption of this third model is that in science new problem areas are regularly created and associated social networks formed. It is also assumed that the evolution of any one network depends considerably on developments in neighbouring fields. The onset of growth in a new area typically follows the perception, by scientists already at work in one or more existing areas, of unresolved problems, unexpected observations or unusual technical advances, the pursuit of which lies outside their present field. Thus the exploration of a new area is usually set in motion by a process of scientific migration. Scientific migrants tend to come from research networks with definite characteristics: networks in which there has recently been a pronounced decline in the significance of results; networks whose members have few or no avenues of research easily available; networks whose members have special competence in knowledge or techniques which have given some indication of being more widely applicable; and networks which have been disrupted, often by events such as war originating outside the research community, and whose members consequently have no firm commitment to an established problem area. These characteristics promoting movement into new fields are not mutually exclusive.

During the first stage of development, researchers at different locations and in various countries tend to take up the same or closely related problems, often unaware of similar work proceeding elsewhere. Because the variables chosen for study and the techniques used in this exploratory phase are fairly obvious, and because there is little communication among those involved, there is a high probability of multiple discovery, anticipation of results and open competition for priority. An early lead in the competition for results is usually taken by those with best access to such resources as graduate students, research funds, suitable techniques, publication outlets and the legitimacy conferred by the support of eminent scientists.

The initial results in a new area tend to be scattered among various disciplinary journals and in general-purpose journals. As a result of these first publications, some of those working independently on similar problems become aware of their common interests and establish informal contact. Such contact is also promoted through the links between the members of existing 'invisible colleges', many of whom will at this stage guide their protegees into the new area if it looks particularly promising, whilst remaining on the margins themselves. As a result of improved communications an increasingly effective scientific debate ensues, out of which general agreement gradually emerges about such issues as the relative significance of problems, the proper definition of variables and the correct use of techniques. The establishment of consensus is not necessarily a smooth, cumulative process. In many cases it involves various changes of perspective, redefinitions of central problems and strong disagreement among participants. But it does not normally entail an intellectual revolution, because there is no generally accepted orthodoxy to be overthrown. Instead, consensus is established through a series of negotiations in which researchers modify the perspectives they have previously acquired in response to the problems of the new area and in the light of alternative perspectives brought to bear by participants from different scientific backgrounds.

Growing consensus is accompanied by associated changes in intellectual and social processes within the network. Publications appear in an increasingly narrow range of journals. The proportion of references to the work of authors not centrally engaged in the field declines markedly. A small number of early contributions come to be recognized as especially important and to be cited regularly. As these major contributions become more widely known, the number of active researchers and the number of papers in the area increase exponentially. Research teams and clusters of collaborators form who recruit new entrants to the field and train them from the perspective of the increasingly firm consensus. As problems become more clearly defined these research groups, as well as individual scientists, cultivate specialist lines of enquiry, which are chosen so as to minimize overlap and, consequently, to reduce the likelihood of competition. This process ensures that a relatively wide range of issues is explored.

Research networks develop typically in response to basic contributions which appear early in the growth sequence. Subsequent work tends to consist primarily of elaborations upon these contributions. Consequently, a major part of the innovative work is completed before the field has begun to acquire a significant proportion of its eventual membership. This means that opportunities for making a notable scientific advance and the chances of receiving an unusual amount of professional recognition decline very quickly after the earliest period. As this becomes evident to participants and, more slowly, to potential entrants, growth becomes linear instead of exponential. As the decline of interesting and/or solvable problems continues, accompanied by a growing scarcity of professional recognition and career opportunities, recruitment falls away and established members of the network move elsewhere into problem areas in process of formation. These migrants will tend to pursue, in particular, avenues of inquiry which have emerged unexpectedly out of the problem area now in decline. However, research areas which have become well established often take a long time to die out altogether. There are nearly always *some* observations yet to be made, *some* measurements still to be refined, or *some* technical developments not yet fully exploited. In many fields, therefore, a small scientifically active rearguard is likely to remain, which carries on the research tradition long after the focus of interest has shifted elsewhere.

The exposition presented above of the model of branching is couched in terms of the growth and decline of those small scale research networks which are the initial producers and validators of scientific knowledge. Very similar processes operate, however, in the emergence of new specialties and new disciplinary areas. The major difference is that in the latter instances the first period of exploration produces a rapid efflorescence of loosely related avenues of investigation. This can be seen in Figure 1. In such cases the sequence of preliminary exploration, exponential growth and levelling off, can be clearly observed at the level of the specialty or discipline.

This model of growth through branching is significantly different both from the model of openness and from the model of closure. Nevertheless, it does resemble the latter in several respects. In the first place, both models focus on the connections between cognitive and social differentiation in the research community. In addition both models agree in their view of the educational system of science and both models emphasize the existence of pressures toward intellectual conformity. Furthermore, in cases where radical innovations which participants perceive to be incompatible with the current framework are introduced into a stable network, either from inside or from outside, both models predict revolutionary upheaval. But whereas this pattern is seen as typical from the perspective of the model of closure, it becomes merely a special case for the model of branching. Thus the latter model enables us to specify the conditions under which revolutions are likely to occur in the course of highly institutionalized science. They will tend to occur in networks where the availability of significant problems and of professional recognition is declining; in networks where movement of researchers in and out is difficult, for example, due to the need for esoteric technical skills; and in networks where cognitions are highly precise and where, consequently, the possibility of gradual intellectual redefinition is limited.

It is not necessary, therefore, to regard the models of branching and closure as entirely incompatible. Moreover, the model of openness may have some value if we regard it as an ideology. From this point of view the model of openness comes to be seen as a series of verbal formulations, or a vocabulary, which scientists use in specific social contexts – particularly, I suggest, when they are engaged in describing or justifying pure research to outsiders. Thus it seems that the model of branching is the most satisfactory of the three models, not only because it avoids the defects of its predecessors, and not only because it is consistent with a wider range of empirical findings, but also because it can encompass what is valuable in the other two models of scientific development.

6 Norms and ideology (1976)

Although the sociology of science is no longer merely one branch of functional analysis, much of the sociological literature on the scientific community remains true to its functionalist origins in stressing the importance of the normative structure of science and in paying little attention to ideology. In the discussion which follows I shall try to show that these two themes can be profitably combined. I shall argue, first of all, that what has been regarded as the normative structure of science can better be viewed as an ideology. I shall then try to show why this ideology, rather than other available alternatives, was developed and used by scientists.

The supposed norms of science

For many years, the scientific research community within the modern Western academic setting was depicted by sociologists as being predominantly openminded, impartial and objective. These features, it was claimed, although they were not unique to the scientific community, were present there to a degree unrealized in other fields of intellectual endeavour. This supposed fact could not be explained in terms of the special characteristics of scientists as individuals, because it was recognized that the motives, interests and qualities of individual scientists were quite diverse and by no means always in accord with the special attributes of their professional community. It seemed preferable, therefore, to regard these attributes as characteristics of the community as such, that is, as norms which defined the social expectations to which scientists were generally obliged to conform in the course of their professional activities.

As a result of this line of reasoning, a long list of putative norms or normative principles has been developed, among which the most important are rationality, emotional neutrality, universalism, individualism, disinterestedness, impartiality, communality, humility and organized scepticism. These norms have been expounded and discussed too many times to need any further clarification here. It is important to note, however, that there is more to the thesis than the simple assertion that these norms exist within the scientific community. For it is also claimed that widespread conformity to the norms is maintained by an effective system of social control. This is a necessary step in the argument in order to reach the conclusion that these norms are functional for science. In other words, it is suggested that certified, reliable scientific knowledge will be produced only in so far as these, and no other, norms actually guide scientists' actions. This assumption plays a crucial part in Merton's (1938) initial discussion of the norms, where it is argued that scientific knowledge develops more effectively in democratic societies because such societies are more willing to allow the institutionalization of a set of norms in science which parallels those operant within the political system.

In order to show that conformity to these norms is an essential feature of modern science, those presenting this argument tend to describe the negative consequences of deviant acts. It is suggested that actions which contravene the norms will clearly distort any resulting knowledge-claims. For instance, if scientists become too committed to their own ideas, that is, if they fail to abide by the norm of emotional neutrality, they will be unable to perceive when their ideas are inconsistent with reliable evidence. Similarly, if scientists adopt personal, that is non-universalistic, criteria in assessing knowledge-claims, their judgements will tend to diverge from the objective realities of the physical world. At the same time, if secrecy and intellectual theft were to exist to any extent in science and the norm of communality ceased to be an effective guide for social action, then it seems likely that the smooth and impartial extension of certified knowledge would be disrupted. It is not difficult to find reasons why departure from any of the normative principles listed above might seem to interfere with the creation of valid knowledge about the empirical world. Thus from this perspective the normative structure is the crucial feature of the scientific community. The norms of science are seen as prescribing that scientists should be detached, uncommitted, impersonal, self-critical and open-minded in their attempts to gather and interpret objective evidence about the natural world. It is assumed that considerable conformity to these norms is maintained; and the institutionalization of these norms is seen as accounting for that rapid accumulation of reliable knowledge which has been the unique achievement of the modern scientific community.

In recent years, there has been much criticism of this kind of functional analysis of science. One reason for such criticism is that detailed study by historians and sociologists has shown that in practice scientists deviate from some at least of these putative norms with a frequency which is remarkable if we presume that the latter are firmly institutionalized. Another reason is that none of the empirical studies designed to discover how far defined samples of scientists express agreement with verbal formulations of the norms has produced evidence of any strong general commitment. One response to findings such as these is to argue that the central normative element in science is furnished, not by this set of social norms, but by the scientific frameworks and technical procedures in terms of which the research community is internally differentiated. This view has led to close analysis of the development of research networks and of the social processes by means of which standards of scientific adequacy and value are negotiated and applied to knowledge-claims. But this is not the only possible response. For we can argue that the original set of social norms was not so much wrong as incomplete. Merton, for example, who has made a major contribution not only to formulating the norms outlined above but also to the sociology of science in general, has tried to account for the very considerable deviation from these norms by introducing the notion of 'counter-norm'. Social institutions, he maintains, tend to be built around conflicting pairs of norms and science is no exception to this pattern. This response has been taken up by Mitroff (1974) in the course of a detailed study of scientists from several disciplines who have been involved in research concerned with the moon.

Counter-norms in science

One of the merits of Mitroff's study is that it provides a great deal of first-hand empirical material. In particular, it contains a large number of quotations from practising scientists. This means, not only that his own argument is exceptionally well-documented, but also that it is possible to an unusual degree for the reader to offer alternative interpretations of his data. Mitroff shows, first of all, that the scientists in his sample do sometimes use variants of the norms described above, as standards for judging the actions of their fellows and as prescriptions for describing how researchers ought to behave. But the overwhelming import of his evidence is that, in addition, there exists in science an exactly opposite set of formulations and that conformity to these alternative formulations can also be interpreted, by participants as well as by observers, as being essential to the furtherance of science. Let me give just a few examples.

Mitroff suggests that the norm of emotional neutrality is countered by a norm of emotional commitment. Thus many of the scientists studied by him said that strong, even 'unreasonable', commitment to one's ideas was necessary in science, because without it researchers would be unable to bring to fruition lengthy and laborious projects or to withstand the disappointments which inevitably attend the exploration of a recalcitrant empirical world. Similarly, the norm of universalism appears to be balanced by a norm of particularism. Scientists frequently regard it as perfectly acceptable to judge knowledge-claims on the basis of personal criteria. Instead of subjecting all research reports on their topic area to impersonal scrutiny, scientists regularly select out of the literature the findings of those colleagues whose work, for one reason or another, they have come to regard as reliable. In other words, scientists often regard it as proper to judge the man rather than the knowledge-claim. This tendency may be associated with the existence in science of a pronounced elite, the members of which exercise considerable influence upon the overall direction taken by scientific research. Once again, the counter-norm can be seen as functional, on the grounds that it saves researchers' time and effort, speeds up the rate at which research develops, yet at the same time ensures that greater weight is given in general to the judgement of those scientists who are seen by their colleagues to be 'more able' or 'more experienced'.

Let me give one more example. Mitroff produces evidence to show that the norm of communality is balanced by a norm in favour of secrecy. He also suggests that secrecy, far from hindering the advance of scientific knowledge, actually contributes to this objective in several ways. In the first place, by keeping their results secret, researchers are able to avoid disruptive priority disputes. Secondly, attempts by others to steal or appropriate a scientist's work serve to confirm the significance of that work and to motivate him to continue his efforts. Thirdly, by keeping their findings from others, scientists are able to make sure that their results are reliable without jeopardizing their own priority and, thereby, without undermining their enthusiasm for further research.

Mitroff's central argument, then, is that there is not one set of norms in science but at least two sets. The first set has been more or less accurately identified by Robert Merton (1973) and others working in the functionalist tradition. But to describe the ethos of science in terms of this first set alone is to produce an account of science which is grossly misleading. For each of the initial set of norms is accompanied by an opposing norm which justifies and prescribes action in complete opposition. Moreover, action in accordance with both sets of norms is needed if science is to flourish. Thus, secrecy is not an unrestricted ideal in science; but neither is communality of information. Intellectual detachment is often regarded as important by scientists; but so is strong commitment. Rational reflection is seen as essential; but so are irrationality and free-ranging imagination. And so on. In Mitroff's view, the empirical evidence which he has produced requires us to conceive of the scientific community as governed by these two major sets of norms and to interpret the dynamics of this community in terms of the complex interplay between these normative structures.

Lack of institutionalization of social norms in science

The evidence presented by Mitroff clearly prevents us from accepting the initial set of norms alone as the normative structure of science. However, I wish to suggest that there are no compelling reasons for regarding either set of formulations or the two sets combined as 'the operating rules of science'. This becomes clear as soon as we look more closely at the kind of evidence which is being adduced. Mitroff rightly criticizes Merton's procedure of extracting norms of science from the 'highly select writings of the rare, great scientists' (1974: 15). He suggests that we should base 'the institutional norms of science' (1974: 16), not only on the idealized attitudes of great scientists, but also on the messy behaviour and complicated attitudes found throughout the scientific community at large. He then proceeds to formulate his counter-norms by selecting out certain descriptive and prescriptive comments made by participants, which appear to contradict the original set of norms. There can be no doubt, therefore, that both sets of formulations are used by scientists to describe and to judge their own actions and those of their colleagues and to prescribe correct professional behaviour. But the mere use by participants of these types of verbal formulations does not demonstrate that they are the 'institutional norms' of science. In fact, neither Merton nor Mitroff furnishes evidence to show how far either set of evaluative formulations is institutionalized.

Social norms are to be regarded as institutionalized when they are positively linked to the distribution of rewards. Conformity to a given set of institutional norms is maintained fairly generally within a particular social grouping because it is regularly rewarded and/or because non-conformity is punished. Clearly the kind of analysis we have been considering so far assumes that the norms and/or counter-norms are institutionalized in this sense; for otherwise it would be difficult to see them as making a fundamental contribution to the extension of certified knowledge and to the progress of science. However, when we examine the considerable literature on the allocation of professional rewards and the dynamics of social control in science, we find little indication that receipt of such rewards is conditional on scientists' having conformed to the supposed norms or to the putative counter-norms in the course of their research.

The allocation of institutional rewards in science is closely associated with the system of formal communication. Scientists convey to their colleagues information which they believe to be interesting and reliable, by means of the professional journals. Although there is also considerable informal exchange of information, scientists are able to establish a conclusive claim to the credit for a particular contribution only by publishing it formally under their own name. In return for information which is judged to be of value, scientists receive professional recognition in various institutional forms and are thereby able to build up a personal reputation, which can in turn be used to obtain other scarce resources such as students, research funds and academic promotion. Perhaps the most important feature of this system, in the present context, is that the main medium of formal communication, the research paper, is written in a strict conventional style which is intended to concentrate attention on technical issues. Accordingly, references to the opinions, interests or character of the author are rigorously excluded. The report is typically written in the passive, so that allusions to the actions and decisions of the author do not occur. The effect of such devices is to produce an aura of anonymity, so that research becomes 'anyone's' research (Gilbert 1976).

There are, then, well established norms governing the style of formal communication in science. But as Medawar has pointed out, the impersonal conventions of the research paper not only 'conceal but actively misrepresent' (1969: 169) the complex and diverse processes involved in the production of scientific findings. This divergence between the formal procedures of communication and the social realities of scientific research exists in part because the rules governing the formulation of research reports make it virtually impossible for scientists to make moral judgements, on the basis of published findings alone, about the author of a report. Thus their response to a published report and their allocation of recognition to it, in the absence of other information about the author, cannot be influenced by the author's conformity whilst carrying out his research to any particular set of social norms. Of course, as Mitroff demonstrates, scientists who are in *informal* contact do regularly make moral judgements of their fellows along two major dimensions. These informal judgements may well affect the way in which scientists respond to others' results and may accordingly influence the allocation of rewards. However, the two sets of opposing principles which Mitroff has shown to operate informally tend to cancel each other out. There is, therefore, no reason to expect that these informal processes will produce general conformity to either one of these normative orders. Furthermore, self interest would lead scientists to respond favourably to information which was technically satisfactory, irrespective of the professional ethics of its producers. For those who did otherwise would place themselves at a disadvantage by not using available results as the basis for their own work. Consequently it is not surprising to find that the central conclusion of the corpus of sociological research on scientific rewards is that rewards are allocated overwhelmingly in response to the perceived quality of the scientific findings presented.

> There can be little doubt that the quality of work as it is perceived by other scientists is the most important variable in determining the allocation of rewards. There is also little doubt that to have one's work highly evaluated you must actually produce work that other scientists find useful, that is, work which is highly cited. (Cole and Cole 1973: 19)

This well documented conclusion implies that conformity to most of the supposed norms and counter-norms of science is largely irrelevant to the institutional processes whereby professional rewards are distributed. Researchers are simply rewarded for communicating information which their colleagues deem to be useful in the pursuit of their own studies. There are no institutional mechanisms for rewarding conformity to either set of social norms; nor is it possible to show that the provision of acceptable information presupposes the implementation of either set, for, as Mitroff demonstrates, both *contradictory* sets can be interpreted as being thus presupposed. However, it might be argued that what we know about the allocation of rewards in science does at least substantiate the importance of universalism; for the quality of the information furnished by accredited members of the scientific community appears to be judged by criteria which are largely independent of such particularistic factors as social class, educational background, and so on. But even this modest argument is subject to considerable limitation. In the first place, the distribution of recognition *is* noticeably biassed in favour of those at elite universities, irrespective of the quality of their work. Secondly, whereas universalism in science was originally seen as implying that scientific careers would be generally open to capable persons, subsequent research has shown that entry into the research community, including that in America in which the norms of science were thought to be most fully institutionalized, is markedly restricted by the ascribed qualities of sex, race and class. Thirdly, to say that the findings of qualified physicists and chemists are judged to a great extent by universalistic criteria is merely to say that researchers in these disciplines assess the results of others mainly in accordance with the cognitive and technical standards current within their research network. In other words, the notion of 'universalistic criteria' has no content until we formulate it in terms of specific bodies of scientific knowledge, practice and technique. But once we do this, we no longer need the concept of 'universalism'. We will be able to deal with the concrete realities of social life in science at least as adequately by examining scientists' actual intellectual commitments and the ways in which these commitments influence the reception of knowledge-claims and the allocation of rewards. The importance of these intellectual commitments is shown by the fact that the scientific community is internally differentiated in terms of distinctions based on differences in bodies of knowledge, research practice and technique, rather than differences in the structure of social norms.

'Norms' and 'counter-norms' as evaluative repertoires

If the 'norms' and 'counter-norms' described in the sociological literature are not the components of an institutionalized normative structure, how are we to interpret the evidence presented by Merton, Mitroff and others? One answer to this question has already been suggested, that is, they are undoubtedly relatively standardized verbal formulations which are used by participants to describe the actions of scientists, to assess or evaluate such actions and to prescribe acceptable or permissible kinds of social action. But standardized formulations of an evaluative kind never govern social interaction in any straightforward fashion. This point has been made strongly by Gouldner:

> ... moral rules are not given automatic and mechanical conformity simply because they, in some sense, 'exist' ... conformity is not so much given as *negotiated* ... The rule thus serves as a vehicle *through which* ... tension is expressed ... there is usually more than one rule in a moral code that can be claimed to be relevant to a decision and in terms of which it may be legitimated. A central factor influencing one's choice of a specific rule to govern a decision is its expected consequences for the functional autonomy of the part ... What one conceives to be moral, tends to vary with one's interests. (1971: 217-18)

The relevance to science of the general argument summarized in this quotation can be illustrated by reference to a recent study in which scientists' responses to the discovery of pulsars is examined in some detail (Edge and Mulkay 1976; see also Woolgar 1976). When the first paper on pulsars was published in 1968 by the radio astronomy group at Cambridge, there were numerous accusations of secrecy from members of groups in competition with the astronomers at Cambridge. It was said that the Cambridge group had unduly delayed publication; that they published insufficient data to allow other groups to undertake supplementary research; that they should have passed on their results before publication to close colleagues in neighbouring laboratories; that their secrecy prevented them from obtaining valuable advice from others; and that their action tended to impede the advance of science. Members of the Cambridge group, however, were able to provide various principles justifying their actions. In the first place, it was claimed that it was perfectly legitimate generally to avoid passing on information which could lead to anticipation by others. Secondly, secrecy was justified on the grounds that it gave researchers time to check their results and to publish high quality work, thereby ensuring the smooth development of scientific knowledge. Thirdly, it was said to be legitimate to make sure that important results improved the reputation of one's own group and its ability to obtain research funds. Fourthly, it was also said that scientists had the right to protect the first achievement of a young research student or the right of observers to have the first attempt at interpreting their own findings. Fifthly, it was said that steps had to be taken in the particular case of pulsars, to prevent the press from misrepresenting this remarkable discovery. Finally, as we would expect in view of this confusing variety of diffuse and overlapping rules, some participants denied that there had been any undue delay in making public the first observations of pulsars.

> There does not appear, however, to be a general commitment to these principles; nor are there clear procedural rules governing the communication of results. As a result, misunderstanding and resentment are sometimes produced by what are variously regarded as secrecy or as legitimate control over the circulation of scientific information. (Edge and Mulkay 1976: 250)

It is perhaps worth noting in connection with the argument above that conformity to social norms is irrelevant to the receipt of rewards, that despite the heated differences of opinion at the time of the pulsar discovery about the propriety of the actions of the Cambridge group, six years later two of its members received a Nobel Prize based in part on this discovery.

In science, then, we have a complex moral language which appears to focus upon certain recurrent themes or issues; for instance, the procedures of communication, the place of rationality, the importance of impartiality and commitment, and so on. But no particular solutions to the problems raised by these issues are firmly institutionalized. Instead, the standardized verbal formulations to be found in the scientific community provide a repertoire which can be used flexibly to categorize professional actions differently in various social contexts and, presumably, in accordance with varying social interests. It seems to me misleading to refer to this diffuse repertoire of verbal formulations as the normative structure of science or to maintain that it contributes in any obvious way to the advance of scientific knowledge.

Interests and the choice of vocabularies

The vocabulary of justification and evaluation in science can be described, it seems, in terms of two, and perhaps more, polarities. One of the influences upon scientists' choice of one polarity rather than another is likely to be their interests or objectives. It can be assumed that, for a given scientist or group of scientists, these interests will vary from one social context to another. Thus, in the example given above, when researchers were frustrated by the apparent reluctance of others to make significant findings available to them, they tended to select principles favouring communality which justified their condemnation of the others' behaviour and added weight to their own exhortations. In contrast, those scientists who had made the discovery were able to find principles in favour of personal ownership of results. It is worth noting that the principles actually implemented in this case were those proposed by the more powerful, that is, the scientists who had access to and control over the valued information.

The fact that scientists can choose rules in this way *within* science, that is, when dealing with persons who themselves have first-hand experience of the scientific social world provides some grounds for expecting that they will be able to draw selectively on their repertoire of justifications and descriptions in the course of interaction with non-scientists; for the latter will find it especially difficult to challenge their accounts. There is, in fact, some evidence that a process of this kind does operate, at least occasionally. The following statement is part of a description by a sociologist of some of the social processes which influence attempts to elicit accurate information from scientists.

> Those with the widest knowledge of the social and scientific development of research groups tend to be group leaders and other older members of the groups. These men are, therefore, particularly important sources of information and, when participants' accounts are inconsistent, one might be tempted to regard their views as more authoritative. However, they tend also to be most concerned with maintaining the group's reputation and, consequently, with preventing the passage of information which would reflect adversely on the group. Furthermore, group leaders are eminent members of disciplines which have much higher academic status than that of the investigators. It is, therefore, very difficult to break down the social barriers which support group leaders, in their tendency to present a favourable image of their group's activities. (See chapter one above.)

This statement is important for several reasons in the context of the present discussion. In the first place, it concerns those relatively eminent scientists who have been mainly responsible for representing the scientific community in the wider society and for conveying to the layman the special characteristics of science. Secondly, it suggests that there is a systematic bias in the views presented by such men. And thirdly, it brings to mind Mitroff's recommendation that we should not rely too heavily on the 'highly select writings of the rare, great scientists who were psychologically motivated enough to write glowingly of science' (1974: 15). I wish only to supplement Mitroff's point by suggesting that the leaders of science have presented the particular image of their community which has in fact become widely accepted not simply because of their strong psychological involvement in science, for given the existence of two opposing vocabularies such involvement could just as well have produced an exactly opposite characterization; but also in accordance with certain social objectives. I wish to suggest, therefore, that scientists have tended to select from their repertoire of accounts, those formulations originally taken by the functionalist interpreters to be the central norms of science; and that this version was selected because it served the social interests of scientists. It follows that the original functional analysis did identify a genuine social reality, but one better conceived as an ideology than as a normative structure.

In claiming that the original set of functionalist norms constitutes an ideology, I am making several related assertions. I am suggesting that scientists tend to use this vocabulary, rather than the opposing vocabulary, when portraying and justifying their actions to lay audiences; that this vocabulary provides an account of science which is so incomplete as to be positively misleading; and that this vocabulary is used to support scientists' interests. The second of these points I regard as having been established above. In order to illustrate the other two claims, I intend to examine a number of relevant studies. I shall look first at some studies of the social image of the scientist and then at several studies concerned with the formulation and use of scientific ideologies.

The social image of the scientist

Mitroff refers to the social image implicit in the so-called norms of science as the 'story book image of science'. He suggests that it is found in its purest form in textbooks and in popular accounts of science; and he cites a number of sources of this kind in which such attributes as willingness to change opinions, humility, loyalty to truth, objectivity, suspension of judgement and emotional neutrality are presented as being peculiarly characteristic of science and of scientists. This, of course, is very selective evidence. Mitroff does not undertake a systematic study of the social image contained in scientific textbooks. However, studies of the social image associated by American adolescents with scientists provide further confirmation that qualities like these have been widely attributed to scientists.

Mead and Metraux (1962) found that their sample of high school students furnished a fairly uniform and favourable account of 'the scientist' along these lines. As long as students were not asked to indicate any personal involvement, they depicted scientists as being highly intelligent, and devoted to their research; as patient and open-minded; as careful not to jump to conclusions, but as also able to defend their ideas when necessary; as dedicated men who work not for money or fame or self-glory but for truth, the benefit of mankind and the welfare of their country. In a study of American college students, Beardslee and O'Dowd (1962) reach similar conclusions. They state that their findings support those of Mead and Metraux and that a uniform image of scientists is held among various classifications of men and women students. The main elements of this image that they identify are intelligence, individualism, social withdrawal, self-sufficiency, perseverance, rationality, devotion to knowledge, relative indifference to money, selflessness and 'cold intellectualism'.

There are some grounds, then, for accepting that scientists have acquired a social stereotype which resembles in broad outline the original analysis of the normative structure of science. Furthermore, although no direct evidence has yet been offered to show that scientists themselves have been responsible for the creation of this image, we have noted that the original sociological analysis itself did rely heavily on the public utterances of leading scientists. In the long run, we clearly need detailed, historical studies of the kinds of accounts of science offered by scientists to various lay audiences and in varying social contexts. Let me briefly examine three studies of how scientists have depicted science in the course of attempting to justify their claim for a special relationship with government.

Science for science's sake: ideology and scientific autonomy

The first study, by Daniels, deals with science in nineteenth century America. Its central thesis is summarized as follows.

One of the most notable developments within the scientific community in post-Civil War America was a changed image of the scientist and of his role in society. Previously, science had been 'sold' to the public in terms of its contribution to important American values – utilitarian, equalitarian, religious – or even as a means of social control, depending upon the speaker's best estimate of his audience. But in the 1870s for the first time, great numbers of scientific spokesmen began to vocally resent this dependence upon values extraneous to science. The decade, in a word, witnessed the development, as a generally shared ideology, of the notion of science for science's sake. Science was no longer to be pursued as a means of solving some material problem or of illustrating some Biblical text; it was to be pursued simply because the truth – which was what science was thought to be uniquely about – was lovely in itself, and because it was praiseworthy to add what one could to the always developing cathedral of knowledge. (1967: 1699)

Daniels links the emergence of a pure science ideology in the late nineteenth century to various changes in the social context of science. For instance, as the scientific community became increasingly professionalized, its members came to concentrate more and more on internal, purely scientific objectives. At the same time, the practical applications of pure science became increasingly evident as the century progressed. Consequently, Daniels argues, it was no longer necessary for academic scientists to emphasize the eventual utility of their work. Taking this for granted, they began to stress that scientific knowledge was valuable in its own right; although, of course, it was usual to claim that scientific knowledge did in fact frequently produce practical benefits in the long term.

This new portrayal of science was formulated most clearly in the course of scientists' dealings with government. Normally, the receipt of government funds entails acceptance of the principles of accountability; that is, government controls the distribution of funds and decides to what extent these funds have been properly used. Scientists, however, strenuously resisted the application of these principles to their activities. Adopting conceptions of intellectual independence and academic freedom which had been developed particularly in Germany, they argued that science was a unique case and that it required special treatment. In particular, scientists maintained that regulation from outside would disrupt the scientific community; and that only by allowing scientists to proceed according to their own values and judgements would valid knowledge, and hence effective practical applications, be obtained.

As described by Daniels, this pure science ideology selects out and stresses certain facets of what I have called above the original functionalist portrayal of science. In the late nineteenth century ideology, the pursuit of truth is proposed as an ultimate value and the independence of the scientific community and of its individual members are interpreted as prerequisites for the attainment of this value. Notions of objectivity and universalism are also used; but in a socially divisive manner. It is argued that scientific knowledge is established in accordance with impersonal and universal criteria of adequacy. But it is also argued that only qualified scientists understand these criteria. The conclusion that non-scientists must be excluded from making decisions about the development of science is seen to follow necessarily. Thus within this ideology, universalism and independence are interpreted in a way which buttresses the attempt by scientists to claim the right to extend certified knowledge with the help of public funds, but without outside 'interference'.

Greenberg's (1969) study of the politics of pure science examines the relations between science and government in America for the period following the Second World War. Like Daniels, he sees the central feature of this relationship as the attempt by scientists to obtain financial support on an increasingly large scale, without giving up their autonomy. Similarly, Greenberg also sees scientists as developing an ideology: that society should support, but not govern, science; that all mature scientists must have complete independence; that science is unlike any other activity; and that the internal value system of science guarantees an ethical standard which requires no outside surveillance. This supposed value system appears to stress, as we might expect, objectivity, flexibility and open-mindedness, individualism, disinterestedness and impartiality. The reality, of course, often seems to be inconsistent with these ideals and Greenberg describes in detail many of the failures to abide by these principles. Nevertheless, he argues, because this ideology came to be accepted in some measure by politicians, scientists have been able to achieve the unique position of receiving massive financial support from government, without being subject to the usual rules of accountability.

> But though reins and restrictions existed, and the principle of accountability (loathsome to the scientists) was never absent, the essential point was that, *in practice,* scientists wrote most of the rules for the use of federal research money; scientists staffed the agencies that dispensed the money, and scientists from the university community advised these same staff scientists on the distribution of the money. (Greenberg 1969: 330)

These studies by Daniels and by Greenberg present a consistent picture of the long term dialogue between American scientists and government. They describe a scientific community growing rapidly in size, becoming increasingly specialized and professionalized, and coming to require financial support on a scale which could only be provided by central government. At the same time, they show that scientists were determined to resist government control of academic or 'pure' science. Scientists strove vigorously to maintain what Gouldner calls 'functional autonomy'. And in order to do this, they drew selectively on their repertoire of justifications and descriptions. They argued that scientific knowledge was intrinsically valuable; but they also supplemented this assertion with the claim that scientific knowledge, because it was valid knowledge, would necessarily lead to practical benefit. In addition, they claimed that the attainment of valid knowledge depended on the implementation of such social values as impartiality, individualism, open-mindedness, etc.; and that these characteristically scientific values could only be maintained if scientists were left free from outside regulation. These two studies then show academic scientists using a particular ideology in the social context of their relationships with government. The next study that I wish briefly to mention, that by Tobey (1971) of *The American ideology of national science,* provides detailed evidence not only about scientists' dealings with government, but also about scientists' attempts to convey a specific professional image to the wider society.

Science as the model democracy

Tobey begins by describing the growing professionalization of American science during the early decades of this century. He emphasizes that at this time the gap between the scientific community and the wider society was increasing. Scientists were becoming more and more specialized; the knowledge which they produced was becoming increasingly esoteric; and they were under little constraint to contribute in any direct way to national goals. Scientists were aware, to some extent, of their growing isolation. But few of them favoured the introduction of any major changes in the social organization of basic science. Nor did they wish to continue the nineteenth century tradition of popular science; so that by the time of the First World War scientific popularization had virtually ceased in the USA. However, experiences during the war were to change the views of at least some of the leaders of the scientific community and to lead them to undertake subsequently an extremely active proselytization on behalf of science.

Many American scientists became involved in wartime research at least partly out of patriotism. Tobey shows, however, that a concern for the long-term benefit of science was also an important consideration. Although it had not been possible before the war to achieve government support of science, a number of influential scientists believed that the war might help them to fulfil this goal. Thus one of their wartime objectives was to make use of this opportunity to convince government of its duty to support scientific research. For a few leading scientists, among them George Ellery Hale, the director of the Mount Wilson Observatory, collaboration during the war with government served merely to strengthen this belief that strong, permanent links should be established between science and government. For others, such as the physicist Robert Millikan, the war brought about a conversion to the view that science could and should be more firmly integrated with government and with the wider society.

Tobey suggests that the experiences of the First World War changed scientists' attitudes in several important ways. In the first place, it lessened their antagonism to the centralized *promotion* of research; although the great majority of scientists continued to reject the idea of centralized *direction* of basic research. Secondly, it led them to perceive more clearly the value and what appeared to be the real possibility of support of basic research by government and by industry. Thirdly, it led many of them to question whether scientists should remain a highly specialized and socially isolated community. Finally, it led some of them to decide that if science and scientists were to play a major role in American society, it was necessary that the values of science should be seen to correspond with those of society at large. Accordingly, for a decade or more after the end of the war, a number of well-known and influential scientists banded together to 'sell' science, not only to government but also to the American public. They tried to create a new basis for science in the US by carrying out a campaign of scientific popularization and by formulating an ideology of which the central tenet was: 'American democracy is the political version of the scientific method' (Tobey 1971: 13).

> The end of the war, the political struggle over the peace treaty, and the growing disillusionment with the war's official ideals, however, brought an end to the obvious relevance of the scientist to national goals. There was no longer a great enterprise like the war effort conducted by the government in which the nongovernmental scientists had a role and which would justify the new organization of science. With the expectation of restoring the lost correspondence between their values and broad cultural values and of obtaining new sources of financial support, leading scientists endeavoured to convince the public that the scientific method was the ultimate guarantee of the existence of the values of pre-war progressivism – individualism, political and economic democracy, and progress. (Tobey 1971: xiii)

In trying to show the importance of science to American culture, great emphasis was placed on what were claimed to be the values of science. These values were said to be derived from the nature of scientific knowledge and, although they were realized most fully in the scientific community, they were portrayed as being the fundamental values of American society. The main objective in explaining science to the lay public was to establish that science was the source of national progress. This required the concept of inevitable progress in science. Science was accordingly depicted as being primarily concerned with the cumulative acquisition of facts; and speculative thought and scientific vision were underplayed. The acquisition of solid, reliable factual material was seen to depend on scientists' approaching the study of nature with values which rigorously curbed human tendencies towards bias, prejudice and irrationality. Thus the scientists involved in this movement promulgated by means of books, articles, public addresses and by means of their own popular science periodical, 'an image of the scientist as a particularly virtuous personality. For the national scientists, it followed from this image that to the extent that a man was scientific, he was good' (Tobey 1971: 178-9). The virtues attributed by these men to scientists have, in the light of the discussion above, a familiar ring. In the words of Millikan, whom Tobey describes as 'the major force in developing an ideology of science in the 1920s' (1971: 41), these virtues were 'modesty, simplicity, straightforwardness, objectiveness, industry, honesty, human sympathy, altruism, reverence ...' (1971: 179). Scientists, in general, were also credited with being humble, patient, sceptical, independent and emotionally disciplined. Such virtues, it was said, arose from the requirements of making correct scientific judgements; the absence of these attributes would prevent the scientist from gaining 'a correct understanding of the relations between phenomena' (1971: 179).

Scientific ideology in Britain

I have concentrated so far on developments occurring in the USA, primarily because the original functionalist analysis of science grew out of this American tradition. But there are additional reasons for this focus on the USA. In the first place, there are simply more historical and sociological studies available of the scientific community in America than in other countries. Secondly, the politics of science tends to be much less open in other countries. Thus as Robin Clarke states in the *Introduction* to the British edition of Greenberg's book:

> Indeed all that is known to have emanated from the SRC [since 1965 the main source of funds for academic research] so far is a certain amount of money for the support of scientific research and a series of press releases and formal announcements about the major decisions made. *The SRC has no public image* [...] if Britain plays her cards closer to the chest than the United States in the field of 'political' politics, she almost chokes on them while playing her hand at science politics. (1969: 12-13)

Despite the paucity of information about and analysis of the politics of British science, there is some evidence indicating certain parallels between developments in Britain and America. These parallels, as well as several significant differences, can be seen by comparing the American sources discussed above with the article by M.D. King (1968) on 'Science and the professional dilemma'. King shows, for example, that British scientists, like their colleagues in the US, began seriously to reconsider during the inter-war period their traditional relationship with government. Scientific opinion became more favourable to greater coordination of research, as long as it was carried out by members of the professional community, and to a change in customary attitudes toward the wider society. As a result, between 1915 and 1939, there was conducted from the pages of *Nature* 'a concerted and eloquent campaign to secure in the minds of laymen (and more especially of lay politicians and administrators) ... a thoroughgoing revision of the conception they entertained of the qualities of mind and character that were inculcated by a scientific training and by the discipline of scientific research ... ' (King 1968: 54-5).

British scientists, like their American counterparts, maintained that certain values and attitudes were an essential part of science. The existence of values such as disinterestedness, impartiality, suspension of judgement, rationality and objectivity followed, it was said, from the nature of scientific knowledge. However, although there appears to have been fairly general agreement among the apologists of science that the scientific life is a unique source of distinctive values, virtues, and attitudes, widely different inferences were drawn with respect to political action. On the one hand, some scientists, such as Bernal in particular, adopted a Marxist perspective and argued that scientists should become actively engaged in changing, not only science, but also the wider society.

> Bernal was trying to persuade his readers that the social and natural knowledge at the command of scientists, and the particular attitudes of

mind, perspectives, and moral virtues which their discipline demands ... should rightly secure for them a major, perhaps a dominant role in policy-making both in industry and in government. (King 1968: 63)

On the other hand, Polanyi and his supporters took the more traditional view that the basic values of science could only be maintained by keeping science 'pure' and by ensuring that it was separated from the sectional interests, the prejudices and the irrationalities of the political realm. In Polanyi's view scientists, in addition to producing valid knowledge, had a crucial responsibility to keep alive and untarnished those values which could serve as the principles of the 'good society'.

These few comments, brief though they are, enable us to see that developments in Britain between the two world wars resembled those occurring in America during the same period. Scientists in both countries became increasingly concerned to ensure that science was adequately financed by government; they also strove to convince government and the public at large of the moral, as well as the practical, importance of science; and they provided an account of scientific values with which we have become familiar. In Britain, but apparently not in America, there were two conflicting views of the place of science in modern society: one advocating that scientists should act positively to make politics more rational and scientific, and the other advocating that scientists would help the layman best by the force of their moral example. However, the ethical characteristics attributed to science and used as a justification for treating science as a special case seem to have been much the same in the two societies.

Concluding remarks

Let me repeat some of the main points of the discussion above. Firstly, I have argued that what have previously been regarded as components of the dominant normative structure of science are better conceived as vocabularies of justification, which are used to evaluate, justify and describe the professional actions of scientists, but which are not institutionalized within the scientific community in such a way that general conformity is maintained. Secondly, I have tried to show that the leaders of academic science in Britain and, more clearly, the United States have drawn selectively on these vocabularies in order to depict science in a way which justified their claim for a special political status; and that the biassed image of science which they have vigorously proclaimed seems to have been widely accepted, not only among the public at large, but at least in part within official circles. Thirdly, I have suggested that this systematic presentation by scientists of a view of science which supports their collective interests amounts to the utilization of an occupational ideology.

This analysis of norms and ideology in science directs us toward the consideration of issues which have received little attention by sociologists – essentially because we have ourselves tended to accept the ideology at its face value. With respect to the internal dynamics of science, we are led to ask such questions as: How do scientists use vocabularies of justification inside their professional community? Are different vocabularies used in different social contexts; for example, in public as opposed to private media of communication? Are the more powerful groups and individuals better able to employ these vocabularies to serve their interests? With regard to the external relations of science, we are led to ask: How have scientists succeeded in gaining widespread acceptance of their ideology, if this is in fact the case? What range of political interests can be attributed to scientists and how exactly do such interests influence ideologies? Have scientists used different ideologies in 'non-democratic' societies?

These are a few of the more obvious questions which immediately come to mind once we begin to adopt a sociological perspective which allows us to conceive of science, not just as a community with special professional concerns and with normative components appropriate to those concerns, but also as an interest group with a dominating elite, and a justificatory ideology.

7 Consensus (1978)

In principle, science has always been regarded as coming within the scope of the sociology of knowledge. Yet it has always been treated, in one way or another, as a special case. This divorce between the sociology of knowledge and the sociology of science is probably due in varying measure to several factors. In the first place, whereas sociologists concerned with knowledge in a relatively general sense have naturally tended to focus on fairly broad social pressures impinging from the outside on a range of knowledge-producing communities, most sociologists of science have been kept busy either following up certain major insights into the internal social dynamics of the scientific research community or in examining the ways in which and the extent to which scientists have succeeded in adapting to employment in non-academic contexts. In other words, the issues taken as central in the sociology of science have, until recently at least, had little bearing on those prominent within the sociology of knowledge. A second factor is that sociologists inevitably find it difficult to understand in sufficient detail or with sufficient confidence the esoteric knowledge produced within the modern scientific community. In contrast with artistic styles, literary forms or political credos, the task of absorbing quantum mechanics or molecular biology as an essential part of the process of sociological analysis appears comparatively daunting. Given that most sociologists become separated quite early in their intellectual careers from developments in the natural sciences, this factor alone may have played a major part in preventing sociologists from attempting the systematic analysis of scientific knowledge. I suspect, however, that a more important consequence of this division between the 'two cultures' is that it has helped to foster totally inaccurate assumptions about science on the part of the uninitiated.

Science as a special case

The two factors I have suggested so far are, of course, merely contingent. Once we become aware of them, we can take steps to ensure that they do not prevent us from treating the study of science as part of the sociology of knowledge. For example, we can partially avoid the second difficulty mentioned above by securing in various ways the active cooperation of competent scientists. But there are, in addition, a whole range of considerations which cannot be regarded as contingent, for they are considerations based upon what are taken to be distinguishing and necessary characteristics of science as an intellectual and as a social activity. These supposed characteristics are used, sometimes explicitly and often by implication, as grounds for treating science as a special case and as justifying its exemption from the claims usually made by sociologists of knowledge. In this short paper I intend to examine certain assumptions frequently made with respect to scientific consensus and the assessment of scientific knowledge-claims. I will argue that when these phenomena are properly understood, they provide no good grounds for excluding scientific knowledge from the realm of sociological analysis.

In the opening pages of *Ideology and Utopia,* Mannheim (1936: 5) suggests that awareness of the possibility of a sociology of knowledge is likely to arise in an age when intellectual disagreement is more conspicuous than agreement. As this statement implies, the rationale behind sociological analyses of knowledge has often been that divergent or changing interpretations of a given phenomenon cannot have their origins in the phenomenon itself but must, instead, derive from socially structured perspectives or interests which affect its perception and/or interpretation. Now if this is a major justification for applying the sociological perspective to ideas or to knowledge, several plausible arguments for exempting science immediately come to mind. In the first place, it can reasonably be maintained that the scientific community is characterized by remarkably high levels of intellectual agreement. In the natural sciences, it is often suggested, we ordinarily find an unforced consensus among free and well-informed scholars (Ziman 1968: 6). Consequently, given that disagreement occurs relatively infrequently in science and that when it does occur it is usually quickly resolved, there are grounds for claiming that sociological analysis of the establishment of scientific knowledge is inappropriate.

It is clear that there *is* a connection between the idea of 'consensus' and that of 'knowledge'. Only propositions which command (more or less?) universal assent on the part of competent judges can be said to be true 'knowledge'; although of course, not all agreed propositions are necessarily valid. As soon as intellectual disagreement appears we seem to be dealing not with demonstrated knowledge, but merely with knowledge-claims. It can be argued, therefore, that the intellectual consensus peculiarly characteristic of science is a by-product of the fact that modern science has been uniquely able to establish precise and universally valid knowledge about the natural world. Science, then, can be seen as dealing with the eternal verities of the physical world; and for that reason scientific knowledge, once it is firmly established, does not undergo the sequence of changes and revisions which are typical of bodies of thought directly dependent on social circumstances. Thus it may be that scientists are able to create and maintain intellectual consensus because they have devised efficient means of being true to the phenomenon they study and because the content of their knowledge is, accordingly, not directly influenced by social pressures.

Now, although I began by presenting these arguments as reasons for exempting the production of scientific knowledge from sociological analysis, they clearly do leave room for the formulation of certain *kinds* of sociological questions. Even if we accept these arguments, we can still ask without inconsistency: By what kinds of internal social arrangements does the research community ensure the selection and perpetuation of valid knowledge (Ravetz 1971)? What kinds of social environment are compatible with the maintenance of such a research community (Merton 1973)? By what processes are economic and social support allocated to science and to particular sectors of the scientific community (Lemaine *et al* 1976)?

The grounds presented above for treating scientific knowledge as beyond the scope of sociological analysis are no barrier to the pursuit of questions such as these, which deal with social influences on the direction of scientific growth or with the institutional context within which science is embedded and on which it depends. What these considerations do specifically is to prevent us from viewing scientific knowledge as, in the classic terminology of the sociology of knowledge, socially or existentially determined. To use an alternative phrase which is slightly less simplistic, we might say that we are prevented from seeing scientific knowledge as being socially constituted, as being created as an integral part of an ongoing social process. As long as we accept that there is a strong intellectual consensus in science, and that consensus about and invariance of scientific knowledge are due to its objective validity, we experience some difficulty in regarding the *content* of scientific knowledge as being dependent in any direct way on social processes. These assumptions prevent us from treating scientific knowledge itself as a social product in the same way that we would treat its rate or direction of growth. Let us, therefore, explore these assumptions a little further.

Agreement and disagreement in science

There can be no doubt that natural scientists frequently do achieve relatively high levels of intellectual agreement about limited domains of the physical world. In this respect they appear to differ, at least in degree, from practitioners of the social sciences and the humanities. This has led some commentators to distinguish 'genuinely scientific' fields from others on the basis of their degree of intellectual unanimity (Kuhn 1962; Ziman 1968). To begin with, I wish to suggest that the extent of intellectual consensus in the natural sciences has been exaggerated in these accounts.

In the first place, within many if not most areas of research, marked differences of scientific opinion and judgement exist in relation to major issues. In all fields of modern scientific research which have been studied in depth, intellectual divergences have been found to be widespread. This has been shown to be the case, for example, for molecular biology (Olby 1974), for 'lunar science' (Mitroff 1974), and for radio astronomy (Edge and Mulkay 1976). It may well be, of course, that such disagreement is in most instances relatively short lived; and it is certainly true that in many areas there is a strong tendency for intellectual diversity to be replaced increasingly by consensus. Thus the overall pattern of development in radio astronomy has been described in the following way.

> Within any given area there was, broadly speaking, a movement from vaguely conceived problems and imprecise techniques toward precise instrumentation, clearly conceived problems and solutions, and an increasingly firm intellectual consensus among those engaged in the field. As the major problems were resolved in one area, so interest tended to focus on new areas where the process of defining, solving and uncovering further problems was repeated. (Edge and Mulkay 1976: 77)

Although this trend toward consensus is recurrent in science, it is important to note that it probably occurs only in certain circumstances. In particular, consensus tends to be established firmly and quickly to the extent to which scientists share a common scientific/technical background and to the extent to which they are able to select for attention problems which they judge to be solvable within their common framework. Typically, of course, scientists do choose those problems which they believe to be solvable (Ravetz 1971: 132-4). This has become a major feature of scientific culture; and problems which appear to fall well beyond the scope of current theory and technique are often defined as 'metaphysical' or 'non-scientific'. It seems, therefore, that intellectual dissensus tends to persist in science in so far as scientists working on the same phenomena do not share a common scientific/technical framework and in so far as the problems with which they are faced are too complex to be resolved within the limits of existing intellectual resources, as has long been the case in cosmology (Singh 1970).

Scientific consensus, then, in a given area of interest is seldom complete and its establishment may well depend on such socio-cultural factors as the selection of problems for which technically defined solutions appear likely as well as on the application of a relatively uniform scientific perspective. Moreover, the eventual consensus which appears in many fields seems to be the outcome of a delicate balance between cooperation and collaboration, on the one hand, and dispute, competition and specialization, on the other hand. In other words, scientific consensus in research networks seems to be achieved, at least partly, by processes of informal negotiation between participants who have certain shared as well as certain conflicting interests (Mulkay, Gilbert and Woolgar 1975). If this is so, the character of any particular scientific consensus is likely to be affected by such factors as differences in reputation among participants and variations in access to social support and scarce resources. To put this another way, the processes whereby scientific consensus is established and maintained become open to sociological analysis. It does not follow necessarily that the content of what comes to be deemed scientific knowledge is a simple by-product of these social processes. What does follow, as I shall try to show more fully below, is that these processes do influence the way in which the cultural resources of science are extended so as to produce new knowledge.

Possible objections

At this point, it is necessary to consider certain objections which could be made to the argument thus far. One objection might be that, if the negotiation of scientific knowledge was much the same as other forms of negotiation, we would expect to find much more evidence than in fact we do of various forms of social bias. In particular we would expect to find that negotiation was greatly influenced by particularistic factors such as race, sex, social class and organizational affiliation. But within science these factors appear to be much less important than is usual elsewhere (Gaston 1973). Although sociologists in the past have seldom investigated directly the negotiation of scientific knowledge, they have paid considerable attention to the distribution of professional rewards. This information about scientific rewards is relevant to the present discussion because, if particularistic factors did influence the creation and acceptance of scientific knowledge, we might expect to see these sources of influence reflected in the allocation of rewards to those recognized as having contributed to this knowledge. Now, although there can be no doubt that variations in race, sex and social class do greatly restrict entry into the scientific community, nor that affiliation with an elite university improves members' chances of receiving professional rewards once they belong to that community, the major factor determining receipt of scientific rewards appears to be the quality of the information which scientists supply to their colleagues.

> Science, more than most other social institutions, approximates the ideal of universalism in its assignment of individual scientists to positions in a highly stratified social structure ... There can be little doubt that, in science, contribution to the advance of knowledge is the most highly valued activity, and our data show that those scientists publishing the best work are the most heavily rewarded. (Cole and Cole 1973: 247-8)

It is implied, therefore, that rewards are distributed in a relatively universalistic fashion in science because there are well-institutionalized and non-negotiable technical standards against which contributions to knowledge can be impartially measured and in relation to which rewards can be impersonally distributed.

This is an important argument which deserves to be taken seriously, because it is supported by a considerable body of systematic evidence. Nevertheless, I doubt whether this particular inference can be substantiated by that evidence. For instance, the quality of scientific work or of scientific knowledge-claims is necessarily measured indirectly, by means of citation counts or by participants' assessments. Such indirect measures must, therefore, take participants' cognitive and technical standards as given. Quality is always measured as participants perceive it, in the light of whatever standards they happen to apply. Accordingly, the finding that the production of high quality work is rewarded to a large extent independently of certain particularistic factors, has little bearing on the ways in which those standards which guide participants' judgements of quality are established. This body of careful research into the distribution of rewards in science in no way precludes the possibility that the standards by which scientists judge the validity of knowledge-claims and allocate professional rewards are themselves socially negotiated.

The negotiation of consensus

Apart from this purely negative response to the objection raised above, there are several positive reasons for emphasizing that the creation of scientific consensus, and thereby the creation of scientific knowledge, is a social process which does not necessarily depend on the application of clear-cut independent intellectual criteria.   The criteria for defining results as 'established knowledge' are themselves often created and refined as an integral part of the process of discovery and validation.   Numerous illustrations can be drawn, for instance, from the development of radio astronomy of the way in which participants define the significance of research findings in accordance with ad hoc criteria; criteria which are frequently abandoned subsequently. There seems to be a direct parallel here with the way that non-scientists 'accomplish' common-sense knowledge.

In order to substantiate this point I wish to describe, as briefly as is compatible with clarity, certain events which occurred in the course of the 'optical identification of celestial sources of radio emission'. By the early 1950s about 100 discrete sources of radio emission had been observed in the sky. One of the main problems facing radio astronomers was that of locating these sources in space. In particular, it was thought to be important to know whether the radio sources were within our own galaxy or whether they were extragalactic. At this time, most radio astronomers thought that the majority of radio sources were intragalactic. There was evidence consistent with this conclusion, but it was far from compelling and a number of astrophysicists argued that most radio sources were probably extragalactic. The issue could not be solved by the use of radio techniques, because they could not provide reliable measurements of distance. However, one way of trying to resolve the question for any particular radio source was to see if it could be identified with a source observable by optical techniques. Once a radio source and an optical source had been shown to be identical, optical methods could be used to measure its distance and to show whether or not it was extragalactic.

The identification of radio sources with visible objects was far from easy. There was a considerable margin of error in the radio positions and there were always a number, and often a large number, of optical objects falling within the area of sky in which the radio sources could be said to be located. Accordingly, the procedure adopted in the search for optical identifications was to examine all optical sources which were candidates, in order to determine whether they had any 'unusual' features. Those optical candidates which were defined as 'unusual' were judged to be possible sources of radio waves. No attempt was made to establish in advance what would constitute such an unusual optical object. Instead, astronomers simply photographed the area of sky where radio sources had been observed and then tried to decide whether any of the visible celestial objects could be seen as sufficiently unusual. A few of the grounds on which identifications were actually made are as follows (Edge and Mulkay 1976):

1. that the optical candidate was a 'unique object visually', being the remnant of the supernova explosion observed in AD.1054 and occurring within our galaxy.

(In fact there were other supernova remnants which had not been found to coincide at that time with any radio source);

2. that the optical candidate was a giant ellipsoidal galaxy, 'unique among galaxies of its kind' on account of a huge jet of matter emanating from its nucleus. The nature of this jet was 'a complete mystery' at that time;

3. that the optical candidate was a globular extragalactic nebula which had been used as a 'typical specimen' of a 'normal class' of galaxies, but which was 'now known to be unusual in several respects';

4. that the optical candidate, one among a cluster of galaxies, appeared actually to be two galaxies in collision.

These are just a few of the specific criteria which astronomers used to demonstrate 'unusualness' and on which they based their optical identification of radio sources. It is clear that the guiding conception of 'unusualness' was left vague and imprecise. It is also clear that its meaning, both in terms of sense and reference, was interpreted *ex post facto* to meet the requirements of particular observations. Of course, the physicists and astronomers engaged in this research attempted to reduce the apparent diversity and arbitrariness of their findings and of the criteria which had been developed in the course of establishing optical identifications. Thus it was quickly agreed that, as radio emission was often associated with gas in violent motion (although it also came from apparently normal galaxies), this phenomenon was probably responsible in some way for the existence of intense radio emission. Consistently with this view, much emphasis was placed on the fourth criterion listed above, that of galaxies in collision. Consequently, for nearly a decade after the first interpretation of a radio source as a pair of colliding galaxies, 'the majority of astronomers and astrophysicists were convinced that galactic collisions were responsible for all, or nearly all, the other extragalactic radio sources' (Jennison 1966: 79). Throughout this decade further observations were made and interpreted until it seemed to participants that the evidence in favour of this hypothesis was more or less conclusive. Yet early in the 1960s, this consensus was destroyed by the 'chance' discovery of new classes of radio sources which were clearly quite different in character (quasars, for example). With the advent of these unexpected observations, astronomers believed that there was little alternative but to abandon the well established account of emission from radio sources and to begin a laborious process of reinterpretation. The apparently firm consensus turned out to be remarkably fragile in practice and the framework of supporting interpretation which had been erected subsequently was quickly jettisoned. It is worth noting, however, that as late as ten years after the demise of the 'colliding galaxies' hypothesis among active researchers, it was still being communicated uncritically to the wider public by the majority of popular books on astronomy.

The purpose of this digression into the history of modern astronomy has not been to illustrate the irrationality of scientists, nor to show how they sometimes get it wrong. The point of this example has been to show that, sometimes at least, there are no clear, pre-established criteria on which to base or to assess scientific knowledge-claims; that the acceptability and the meaning of particular knowledge-claims is something to be worked out or negotiated subsequently among participants; and that items of knowledge which participants regard as well-established and about which they agree are produced by this negotiation and are regularly revised as it proceeds further.

The exclusion of intellectual deviants

Further evidence can be brought to bear on these issues. For instance, there are now several well-documented studies of instances where demonstrably competent scientists have been excluded from a field of study as their ideas have come to diverge from those of the majority. In such cases it is difficult to argue convincingly that scientific consensus is a direct result of scientists' recognition of an unequivocal empirical reality; for it is clear that in these cases the degree of apparent consensus has been maximized at least partly by disregarding the views of an intellectual minority. The example provided by Gilbert (1976) from radar meteor research illustrates this nicely.

Radar meteor research began shortly after World War II as radio physicists made use of wartime radar equipment to explore a number of questions about the nature and origins of meteors entering the earth's atmosphere. The results which they produced found a ready, even enthusiastic audience among those astronomers who carried on the long tradition of research into meteors by means of optical techniques. At the time that the radio physicists entered the field it was regarded as of minor interest by most professional astronomers, and it was much cultivated by amateurs using extremely crude observational methods. It is not surprising, therefore, that the application of advanced electronic techniques generated a great deal of information which was regarded as astronomically valuable by those already working in the area. Most of the findings provided by the radio physicists were accepted without demur. But one topic, that of the origin of sporadic meteors, became the subject of lengthy and bitter dispute. On one side there was, in particular, a professional optical astronomer, Opik, who argued that both radar and optical observations were consistent with meteors entering the earth's atmosphere from outside the Solar system. On the other side was a specific group of radar physicists, who said that although the optical evidence was ambiguous, the radar observations clearly showed that meteors originated inside the Solar system. The dispute continued for some time, with the physicists making further observations and with both sides refining their arguments and introducing supplementary interpretations and hypotheses. In due course, the radar physicists' thesis came to prevail within the research network. Although there is no record of Opik ever changing his position, he and his work simply faded from view. However, it is by no means clear that the analysis of the origin of sporadic meteors advanced by the radar physicists had been conclusively demonstrated in scientific terms – even in their own eyes. This is shown by the fact that the radar physicists were still involved in setting up new experiments on this problem after the paper had been published which subsequently came to be regarded as settling the issue. Furthermore one of the physicists involved was able, when being interviewed years later, to suggest what kinds of observations would have been necessary in his view to resolve the question unambiguously. But consensus had been achieved without recourse to these observations.

This case is interesting because it shows that reasonably complete agreement can be established within an area of science and that major issues can be accepted as settled, even though central participants both for and against the emerging consensus regard the available evidence as incomplete or inconclusive. It suggests, therefore, that social factors, as distinct from scientific considerations, played a part in bringing about this consensus. It is, of course, difficult to show exactly what social processes were at work and Gilbert, in the original study, is cautious about drawing strong inferences on this point from his data. Nevertheless, it is not unreasonable to suggest that differences in prestige between the radar physicists and the amateur meteor astronomers, as well as differences in technical competence and the sheer numerical superiority of the physicists, may have played a part. In this connection, it is worth noting that Opik, a professional astronomer, was both technically competent and of comparatively high prestige. However, whether or not these factors were important, this case appears to illustrate fairly clearly how scientific consensus and the definition of scientific knowledge can be as much a social as an intellectual product. In this instance, at least, something more was involved than the assessment of observations in relation to clear and independent criteria of scientific adequacy; and a strong consensus was achieved partly because most participants chose simply to disregard the sole alternative view available.

The nature of scientific consensus

So far in this discussion of scientific consensus I have tried to make two main points, namely, that the creation of consensus is a social as well as an intellectual process and that the extent of agreement among scientists within a given research area is often much less than has been supposed. Let me merely mention two further considerations in support of this latter assertion. In the first place, if we assume that scientific thought is *typically* governed by clear, precise and widely endorsed intellectual frameworks, it becomes difficult to account for radical scientific innovations without introducing some notion akin to that of 'scientific revolution'. Yet, although there is no logical error involved in this line of reasoning, its validity is suspect because so little evidence has accumulated since the publication of *The structure of scientific revolutions* actually documenting the occurrence of intellectual upheavals of this kind in modern science. Secondly, there is the fact that members of the same specialized and mature research community frequently reach different conclusions when they try to apply their expertise in practical situations (Mazur 1973). Such divergence of technical opinion is, of course, partly a consequence of scientists operating in a social context which differs in important respects from that provided by the research community. But this, in turn, indicates not only that the nature and extent of scientific consensus is context-dependent, but also that intellectual consensus in science is relatively loose and flexible, and that its content is open to interpretation in numerous directions.

We appear, then, to need a new conception of 'scientific consensus'. The beginning of such a conception has perhaps been formulated by Gilbert.

I have proposed an evolving family of different but related models distributed among the members of a research network in place of one fixed paradigm shared by a unified research community. Researchers learn to order the esoteric world of their problem area with the aid of a model which they pick up from prior publications and from their new colleagues. But novices to a problem area adapt the model they acquire to match their specific problems, so that its irrelevant aspects remain ill-defined. They also use their past experience and particular expertise to extend and change the model. The model frequently changes again during the course of their research. Consequently, although the models used by members of a research network bear a family resemblance to each other, they are by no means identical. A researcher's model provides an initial formulation of the research problem, indicates the theories and techniques which may be applied appropriately to the problem, and eventually plays a crucial role in giving meaning to reports of the completed research. Readers will extract from the reports those findings which suit their own models. When in turn readers come to write up their own research, they justify their findings by citing those conclusions which have gained a general acceptance within their field and which are also compatible with their own model. Certain findings will be repeatedly cited because they fit the majority of the models used by members of the network and can therefore become the basis on which research in the area relies for its justification. It is these findings which will become adopted [temporarily at least], as scientific knowledge. (1976: 302)

This account has several advantages in the light of the discussion so far. It allows for intellectual diversity within an area, yet makes sense of the notion of 'established knowledge'. It recognizes that given results may be variously interpreted outside as well as inside an area, and it allows for the possibility that interpretations may vary in accordance with changes in social setting. It also accommodates the occurrence of radical intellectual change without the accompaniment of revolution, as well as allowing for the gradual negotiation of increasing consensus as participants' models evolve. It does seem, therefore, that preliminary steps have already been taken toward an interpretation of 'scientific consensus' which is consistent with the line of thought presented in this paper.[1]

Concluding remarks

I began by recalling not only that the sociology of knowledge had its origins during a period of intellectual ferment and disagreement, but also that the existence of intellectual divergences has often been a key factor in enabling sociologists to pose questions about the social origins of ideas and about social influences upon the acceptance of knowledge-claims as valid. Whenever different participants espouse apparently inconsistent views about a given phenomenon, or when participants' views of that phenomenon change rapidly over time, it is reasonable to explore the possibility that these views are in some way and to some extent a product of social influence. However, it has always been difficult to apply this line of reasoning to the natural sciences; partly because scientists have appeared, to an unusual degree, to be characterized by intellectual agreement; partly because the particularistic biases which are important in other social contexts have seemed to be relatively unimportant in science; and also because scientists have been seen as employing universal, independent and, hence, objective criteria which could be and typically were used to decide the validity of their knowledge-claims.

I have argued that these grounds for exempting scientific knowledge from sociological analysis are untenable. I have suggested, firstly, that intellectual consensus is much less usual in science than has often been maintained. Moreover, it is worth adding that even the most firm and longlasting intellectual consensus does not necessarily indicate that social factors are irrelevant to this consensus. It may be merely that social factors which operate continuously are most easily *observed* during periods of disagreement and conflict. Secondly, I have suggested that the apparent unimportance of the more obvious particularistic factors does not necessarily mean that unambiguous, independent or universalistic standards are applied in the selection of acceptable knowledge-claims or in the allocation of professional rewards. Thirdly, I have suggested that the standards used in judging the adequacy and value of scientific knowledge-claims are constantly negotiated and re-negotiated in the course of social interaction. If this line of argument is accepted, we appear so far to have every reason to include science within the scope of the sociology of knowledge and to proceed further in examining the social processes by which scientific knowledge is created.

Note

1. A much more detailed examination of scientific consensus is presented in chapter six of *Opening Pandora's Box* (1984). The general argument for including science within the sociology of knowledge is developed at length in *Science and the Sociology of Knowledge* (1979).

8 Knowledge and utility (1979)

In recent years there has been much discussion of whether it is possible to have a sociology of scientific *knowledge,* as distinct from an analysis merely of the social relationships and moral ethos of science. This debate has necessarily raised issues which are epistemological as well as sociological in character. The most obvious of these issues is that of the relativity of knowledge. This problem has been prominent in the main tradition of the sociology of knowledge and has received most attention in the recent debate. There is, however, at least one other topic which has had a major influence on sociologists' thinking about science and which, if my experience is at all representative, is seen by most students, as they draw on their stock of 'common knowledge' about science, as showing most clearly that scientific knowledge must be exempt from sociological analysis. This second topic or issue is that of the supposed connection between scientific knowledge and utility or practical effectiveness. Let me try to show that this issue, which has not so far been systematically explored by sociologists of knowledge, deserves a place in the current debate.

Two sociological perspectives on science

In the literature which considers the place of science within the sociology of knowledge, two contrasting perspectives are to be found.

Perspective one
This is the dominant perspective which treats science as a special sociological case. Scientific knowledge is regarded as epistemologically unique – as consisting basically of observation statements which have been firmly established by the controlled, rigorous procedures of scientific method. The corpus of certified scientific knowledge is thought to represent, with increasing accuracy and completeness, the truth about the physical world. Because scientific knowledge is seen as an objective account of the real world, it is assumed that sociological analysis must stop when it has shown how the social organization of science enables scientists to observe and report the world objectively, with little sign of the bias and distortion which are thought to arise in other areas of cultural production through the impact of social and personal factors.

Within this perspective, the close analysis of the development of scientific knowledge can be left almost entirely to philosophers of science and to historians of ideas. Sociologists will be able to contribute directly to analysis of the conclusions of science only in cases where social factors have helped to remove impediments which have previously hampered scientists' perception of the truth, or where there has been some mistake. Werner Stark expresses this view when he writes that:

> [S]ocial developments do not determine the content of [genuinely valid] scientific developments, simply because they do not determine natural facts, but they may well open the eyes of the scientists to natural facts which, though pre-existent and always there, had not been discovered before. (1958: 171)

Within this perspective it appears that social influences can intrude into the actual intellectual content of science only when science has been *distorted* by non-scientific pressures. Sociologists interested in the creation of scientific *knowledge*, as distinct from scientific error, have therefore come to concentrate, not on the intellectual content of science, but on the normative structure which is thought to make objective knowledge possible.

The norms of science have customarily been conceived as a defensive barrier which protects the scientific community from intellectually distorting influences, and which thereby enables scientists to assess research results solely in accordance with the clear-cut, pre-established *technical* criteria appropriate to the validation of empirical knowledge-claims. General conformity to such normative principles as impartiality, emotional neutrality and, particularly, universalism, is seen as *necessarily* implied by the nature of scientific knowledge. In so far as scientists deviate from such prescriptions, it is argued, they will be influenced in their observations and judgements by considerations which do not originate in the physical world itself. From this perspective, then, sociological analysis of science is built upon the premise that the firm conclusions of science are determined by the physical, and not the social, world; that the content of scientific knowledge is not amenable to sociological investigation; and that the cohesion and effectiveness of the scientific community depends on the maintenance of a highly universalistic ethos without which 'object-centred' knowledge could not be regularly produced.

Perspective two
There is, however, an alternative perspective which argues that the procedures and conclusions of science are, like all other cultural products, the contingent outcome of interpretative social acts. It is argued that the empirical findings of science are intrinsically inconclusive and that the factual as well as the theoretical assertions of science depend on speculative and socially derived assumptions. It is also suggested that the general criteria by which scientific knowledge-claims are assessed (such as consonance with the evidence, replicability, and the like) have no meaning until they are interpreted in terms of scientists' particular intellectual commitments and in relation to specific interpretative and social contexts. In addition, it is argued that scientists' actions within the research community are

not *governed* by the universalistic social norms traditionally assumed by sociologists. Rather, it is proposed that what have been taken to be the institutionalized norms of science are merely one part of a much broader repertoire of social formulations, which scientists employ as resources in negotiating the acceptance of specialized knowledge-claims.

The central contention, then, of this perspective is that, although the physical world exerts constraint on the conclusions of science, it never uniquely determines those conclusions. Scientific research is never merely a matter of registering an objective world. It always involves the attribution of meaning to complex sets of clues generated by scientists' actions on the physical world; and such attribution of meaning is not carried out in a social vacuum maintained by a set of rigid moral prescriptions. Rather the attribution of *technical* meaning is always inextricably bound up with those processes of social interaction whereby the social attributes of participants and their claims are negotiated.

The conclusions established through scientific negotiation are not taken to be definitive accounts of the physical world. Nor is it accepted that they have been demonstrated to be valid for all groups at all times through the application of unchanging technical criteria; although, of course, scientists may often appear to treat their conclusions in this way. Instead, the propositions advanced by scientists are regarded, sociologically, as claims which have been deemed to be adequate by particular groups of actors in specific social and cultural contexts. Within this second perspective, it is accepted that there are good grounds for including science fully within the sociology of knowledge and for examining in detail how objects present themselves differently to scientists in different social settings, how scientists in different social positions devise and accept different kinds of knowledge-claims, and how 'social' (that is, non-technical) considerations enter into the structure of scientific knowledge.

The two perspectives and the problem of relativity

Until very recently the first of the two perspectives I have briefly outlined was quite clearly dominant – and indeed virtually unchallenged – within the sociology of knowledge. In the last few years, however, the alternative perspective has been gaining ground. Consequently, some attention has been given by its proponents to showing that adoption of such an approach need not lead, as has been customarily assumed, to intractable analytical difficulties – in particular, that it does not founder on the problem of relativity. Within this perspective, all assessments of knowledge-claims, as well as the very meaning of such claims, are viewed as contingent products of social processes. In the past, most sociologists of knowledge have regarded such a position as 'relativistic' and, therefore, as self-refuting: they have seen it as a 'trap' to be avoided, not least because of the threat it seemed to pose to their own knowledge-claims. They have generally accepted without question that, unless they can retain a special epistemological status for a certain class of propositions which are not socially or existentially 'determined', their own analyses will have to be treated as mere by-products of social processes and, consequently, as invalid. Thus any extreme version of the sociology of knowledge, which fails to define some knowledge-claims as beyond its scope, has appeared to lead to intellectual chaos.

In the last few years, however, this form of argument has been re-examined. It has been pointed out that this vicious circle only operates as long as one presupposes that socially determined ideas are necessarily invalid. Thus, if we have been led to conclude that all ideas *are* socially produced and their meaning socially contingent, we can avoid the trap of relativity simply by abandoning this presupposition. Once a firm commitment has been made to the idea that all knowledge is socially created, this traditional presupposition comes to appear as 'a gratuitous assumption' and to embody

> ... an unrealistic demand. If knowledge does depend on a vantage point outside society and if truth does depend on stepping above the causal nexus of social relations, then we may give them up as lost. (Bloor 1976: 14)

In short, when faced with the 'trap' of relativity, we can always choose to revise our conception of validity instead of abandoning a sociological approach to the creation of knowledge.

In the passage from which I have just quoted, David Bloor asks us to reconsider the assumption that if ideas are a product of social causation they must be false. It is, however, difficult to abandon this assumption as long as we continue to use the kind of *causal* terminology traditionally employed within the sociology of knowledge. Within this tradition, sociologists have written of ideas (or knowledge-claims, etc.) as being *determined* by social factors in much the same way that the movement of a billiard ball may be seen as determined by the impact of a cue. Given such a causal metaphor, it is particularly difficult to accept that an idea can be socially determined and yet valid; for the nature of the idea appears to depend solely on the character of the cause and to have little or nothing to do with the subject dealt with by the idea. But this kind of causal language need not necessarily play any part in a sociological account of knowledge-production. Thus in my brief description of the second sociological perspective on science I made no mention of causes or social determinants, but referred instead to social actors using cultural resources to interpret socially produced observations in specific contexts. The metaphor here relies on a notion of actors negotiating meanings, rather than the impacts of billiard balls and cues. It inclines more toward some form of hermeneutic analysis than the kind of causal analysis which traditionally gives this problem a misleading appearance of insolubility. An interpretative formulation of the second perspective on science does not lead us into intellectual chaos. We are not impelled to abandon all criteria of validity, nor to accept that all knowledge-claims are epistemologically equal. What we *do* have to accept is that criteria of validity are neither pre-established, eternal or universal. They are cultural resources whose meaning has to be re-interpreted and re-created constantly in the course of social life.

Knowledge, utility and perspective one

I will not pursue the topic of relativity any further here. I have mentioned it partly in order to suggest that the 'problem of relativity' does not necessarily eliminate the second perspective from consideration; and also to show that the discussion which follows contributes, from a different angle, to the same debate. I turn now to an equally fundamental issue which, although it also has major implications for the sociology of scientific knowledge, has so far received much less attention. This is the question of the relationship between knowledge and practical application.

This issue has as much bearing on our choice between the two perspectives as that of relativity. For it seems that a reluctance to attempt to carry out sociological analysis of scientific knowledge is often linked to an unquestioned conviction that such knowledge must be epistemologically unique and independent of social context *because it is such a fruitful source of successful technological application.* To put this another way, whereas the problem of relativity has led sociologists to seek a class of knowledge-claims which is epistemologically privileged and therefore exempt from sociological analysis, the supposed connection between science and technology has often led them to identify this class of privileged propositions with scientific knowledge. Let me give three illustrative examples of sociologists presenting this kind of argument.

The first is Werner Stark who, writing some twenty years ago maintained that:

> [S]o far as nature is concerned, the main guiding value has ever been the same, namely, to achieve an understanding and control over her ... and hence in all ages attention has been paid to the same aspects of the realm of nature – those which promise us a foothold in and a whiphand over her ... Whether [man] likes it or not, he must, under all cultural circumstances, pursue, among others, the economic and technological values, the values of science.

Accordingly,

> ... whereas man has more than once shifted his vantage-point for the consideration of social facts so that these facts appear to him in ever new and often surprising, outlines, he has always kept to the same spot for surveying the facts of nature ... so that these latter have always offered to him the self-same surface. He has merely learned to look more closely ... (1958: 166)

Stark concludes, therefore, that in our dealings with the physical world there has been cumulative intellectual progress, as sources of bias and distortion have been steadily eliminated, and as selection of knowledge-claims on the basis of their capacity for providing effective practical control has been generally established.

A second, and more recent, example is provided by Elias, who writes that human knowledge of the physical world 'has reached a comparatively high degree of object-orientation, of fitness to [its] objects ... and men have acquired a correspondingly high capacity for controlling the course of events in that sphere' (1971: 163). He goes on to argue that, if we are to develop a general sociology of knowledge, we must recognize that our analysis of the production of such relatively objective knowledge must differ markedly from our analysis of subject-centred knowledge. Central to this analysis, he stresses, must be the fact that scientific thought has become progressively separated off from social influences and its conclusions thereby rendered independent of variations in social context. Elias's argument is particularly interesting, because the only criterion he gives to identify object-centred knowledge is its 'capacity to control the course of events'; and because object-centred knowledge is treated as being synonymous with science and technology. In this formulation, then, effective practical control is seen as the defining characteristic of the body of properly validated and socially autonomous scientific knowledge.

It is important to recognize that neither Elias nor Stark is referring exclusively to the kind of control over events which is exercised by laboratory scientists in the course of experiment and systematic observation. The point these authors stress is that the universal validity of scientific conclusions can be established for us, as laymen, by the success of science in everyday practical affairs. Thus Elias emphasizes that the object-centredness of scientific knowledge becomes evident in the contribution it makes to its possessors' efforts in the struggle for survival. Presumably he has in mind the contribution of science to economic technology, to military hardware, and to the control of disease. This view of the practical effectiveness of science is most clearly expressed by Johnston:

> When we say that science 'works', what we mean is that it provides us with the capability to manipulate and control nature ... [T]he enormous attainments of modern natural sciences, which are supported not only by the work of the scientists themselves, but, even more importantly, by the millions of experiments going on in the real world when objects are constructed or predictions made based on scientific theories, represent a fairly conclusive proof of their mastery of a segment of reality and a clear demonstration of their superiority over all other knowledge systems invented by man ... (1977: 23-4)

This line of argument can be used to pose a major challenge for the second sociological perspective on science, and for its central claims that scientific knowledge is socially contingent, that its content is influenced by variations in social context, and that the interpretation of the criteria used to validate scientific knowledge is also socially variable. For, we have just seen that it can quite reasonably be argued that there *is* an objective, socially invariant criterion which can be and is used to certify the validity of scientific knowledge-claims – the criterion of practical utility. Scientific knowledge can be seen to be valid because it works, irrespective of changes in social context, in a way which everyone must accept: it seems to be objectively valid in the sense that it gives us efficient control over many aspects of the physical world. It is difficult to see how context-dependent formulations would do this. Thus it seems that 'every new technology bears witness', not only 'to the integrity of the scientist' (Merton 1957: 560), but also to the objectivity of his knowledge and to his freedom from social influences. In short, the practical effectiveness of scientific knowledge establishes its special epistemological status; and its special epistemological status then establishes its independence of social context, and its exclusion from the scope of sociological analysis.

In the next two sections, I shall subject this line of argument to critical appraisal, in order to try to discern how far it does undermine the second sociological perspective on science. I do not imagine that the brief comments which follow will resolve the complex issues involved. My aim, therefore, is the relatively modest one of drawing attention to the fact that discussion of the relationship between science and technology has important implications for the sociology of scientific *knowledge*; and of showing that the view of this relationship which is contained in the dominant tradition of sociological thought about science is, at least, open to question. My intention, then, is to generate discussion of these issues, rather than to forestall further argument by means of a final, conclusive analysis.

How far is modern technology dependent on science?

When we argue that the special epistemological, and therefore sociological, position of science is established by the technological productivity of modern society, we appear to be assuming that most effective practical techniques created today are a fairly direct product of scientific knowledge, and also that most scientific knowledge actually generates such techniques. The very terminology which sociologists, and others, have used to describe the relationship between science and technology clearly expresses these assumptions. Thus the processes whereby knowledge is produced and put into operation have typically been depicted as taking place along a continuum from 'basic' (or 'pure' or 'fundamental') research, to 'applied' research, to 'technological development'. As we have seen, sociologists of knowledge have been inclined to take it for granted that the conclusions reached at the 'basic' end of the continuum are in general validated by practical activities occurring at the 'development' end. Yet when we come to look at the empirical evidence relevant to this issue, we find little indication of any clear or close links between basic scientific research and the great mass of technical developments. Let me refer briefly to several different kinds of evidence to illustrate this point.

If we begin with the results of citation analysis we find, firstly, that in any given scientific field, most knowledge-claims do not appear to 'work' in any sense at all (except perhaps as items on a curriculum vitae). The majority of claims are not cited by (and appear to receive virtually no attention from) other scientists. They seem to exist merely as archival material (Cole and Cole 1973). Moreover, certain areas of scientific inquiry (for example, stellar spectroscopy) are never seen by participants or outsiders as having any relevance to practical application. Consequently, when we talk of scientific knowledge demonstrating its objectivity through successful application, we are at most referring to a minority of scientific knowledge-claims within a limited number of research areas. We cannot, therefore, use this argument to show that the intellectual products of science *in general* enjoy a special epistemological status. This negative conclusion is strengthened by the fact that the 'literatures' of science and technology tend to remain distinctly separate, with little cross-referencing and with significantly different patterns of internal citation. As far as we can tell from citation analysis, science seems to accumulate mainly on the basis of past science, and technology primarily on the basis of past technology (Price 1965).

The view that the relationship between academic research and practical application is weak and indirect receives further support from various case studies of technological development. For example, in the early 1960s a number of studies of recent innovations in 'materials' were carried out, under the sponsorship of the Materials Advisory Board of the US National Academy of Sciences (1966). The Board constructed a seven-stage model of the process of technological innovation which depicted an orderly sequence from basic science to practical application. It proved, however, to be impossible to interpret the empirical findings consistently with this model. In none of the cases studied could the innovation be seen as a direct consequence of advances in basic science. In most instances, the innovation appeared to derive directly from prior technological activity. Similar conclusions were reached in a later British study of the eighty-four technological innovations granted the Queen's Award in 1966 and 1967. The authors write that:

> We have paid particular attention to the relation of basic science to innovation ... [O]ur failure to find more than a small handful of direct connections is the more striking for the fact that we set out deliberately to look for them. (Langrish *et al*. 1972: xii)

In a recent review of the literature bearing on this issue, Layton sums up its implications with the statement that 'the old view that the basic sciences generate all the knowledge which technologists then apply will simply not help in understanding contemporary technology' (1977: 210).

Layton and others have stressed that practical application and what has traditionally been called 'basic research' take place in different social contexts. It seems that the social separation and divergent internal dynamics of these contexts operate to prevent any marked social or cognitive interaction. This is evident in the findings of a study by Blume and Sinclair (1973) of the reward system among chemists in British universities. These authors show that only a minority of British academic chemists are concerned with problems of practical application, and that those who are so concerned are neither particularly productive nor highly regarded by their colleagues. Furthermore, those with strong industrial interests tend to receive appreciably less recognition in the university setting for a given amount of published work. It seems that the British chemical industry has the attention of a small and relatively unproductive sector of the university research community – at least partly because the allocation of academic rewards directs participants' interests away from practical application. This, it should be noted, is within that scientific discipline which has the longest history of contact with industry.

We must not exaggerate the line of argument being proposed here. There have been some notable and well-documented cases where academic research undertaken in pursuit of fundamental scientific knowledge has led directly to successful practical application. There is also the phenomenon of 'embodiment'. This occurs when scientific knowledge becomes embodied in a specific procedure or device, such as a transistor, which is then used in the production of further techniques. There is a tendency in such cases to treat the second generation of techniques as growing out of prior technology alone and to ignore the original scientific contribution. There is also the difficulty of estimating the extent to which basic science contributes to technological advance by means of informal interaction and as a result of the basic training which most applied scientists obtain in an academic setting. Nevertheless, the kind of evidence I have summarized makes problematic the simple view that in general the abundant technology of industrial societies is a direct by-product of a growing corpus of basic scientific knowledge.

It is, of course, true that there is an increasing number of 'technological sciences' which are explicitly organized around problems arising in the pursuit of practical objectives. These sub-disciplines are often located mainly within the academic community, whilst retaining close links with industry. However, these technological sciences are intellectually as well as socially distinct from the autonomous generalizing sciences which sociologists have considered to be the main repositories of certified scientific knowledge. In particular, they are

> ... less abstract, less idealized. Thus, the theory of structures is less abstract than physics, for example, in incorporating idealized versions of manmade devices. But in turn, structural design, which has become scientific in some respects, is much less abstract than structural theory. That is, the designer must take into account a more complex reality. The theorist may assume that the materials are uniform, but the designer must be aware of non-uniformities in his materials and make due allowances for them. (Layton 1977: 210)

In other words, in so far as this kind of technological science approaches practice, so its cognitive content appears to diverge from the universal formulations of the basic scientific disciplines. Whenever basic science is used as the foundation for technological science (and hence for the production of technology), it requires a considerable amount of reformulation. In order to make basic science 'work', it has to be radically re-interpreted in accordance with the requirements of the social context of practical application. This seems to illustrate, not that practical utility furnishes an objective criterion of the universal validity of scientific propositions, but rather that judgements of cognitive adequacy vary with social context. It certainly makes it far from obvious that we can treat the practical success of technology or applied science as validating the formulations of basic science; for the latter actually undergo major transformations of meaning as they come nearer to the realm of application.

So far I have concentrated on the connection, or lack of connection, between technology and basic science. But even if we leave basic science aside for the moment, and focus instead on the contribution to practical technique made by applied science, it is still doubtful whether the bulk of modern technology derives in any direct fashion from scientific knowledge.

> The rapid growth and the scientific glamour of research-intensive industries tend to obscure the fact that most industries are not research-intensive, and that much technological work is relatively unsophisticated ... The first design in a new field of industry may be quite crude and totally outside science. R.G. LeTourneau, the inventor of the bulldozer, quite typically was a practical mechanic without formal technical education. The prototype machine was assembled from known components using an acetylene torch ... [As in this example] a major portion of modern industry is quite unrelated to the science-technology complex ... (Layton 1977: 215)

When we consider those practical applications which do appear to originate in scientific research, it is important to remember that most (and possibly all) knowledge systems have produced successful practical applications – even systems like Babylonian mythological astronomy, whose general principles we now regard as clearly falsified. Given this, and given that industrial societies have devoted an ever increasing proportion of their immense 'surplus product' specifically to the production of systematic knowledge, we would expect a dramatic growth of knowledge-related technology in modern society, without having to assume that the epistemological character of knowledge has altered with the advent of modern science. There is no need to assume that scientific knowledge is different in kind from 'pre-scientific' or craft knowledge, or that the 'rate of practical return' on scientific knowledge is remarkably high. It may simply be that there is now much more systematic knowledge; that it is much more detailed and precise; and that there are many more people actively concerned to exploit it for practical purposes.

A notable consequence of the cumulative increase in the rate of knowledge-production has been that more and more previously unsuspected phenomena and realms of investigation have been identified and explored in detail. Many of the most obvious and influential practical successes of science have come from exploiting the findings of these new fields; this is true, for example, in relation to electricity, bacteria and sub-atomic particles. Such practical applications have seemed particularly dramatic because there has been little or no knowledge previously available of the phenomena involved. Consequently, even the crudest kind of practical intervention, as in the early attempts at vaccination, could be and were interpreted as testifying to the special efficacy of scientific knowledge. Scientists and scientific popularizers used these discoveries to promote an aura of wonder and infallibility, which served to strengthen their claims for ever more men, money and social support. But, given that most bodies of systematic thought about the natural world have engendered successful practical applications, the practical exploitation of new areas of scientific inquiry generated by the increasing scale and intensity of the scientific enterprise provides no grounds for treating scientific knowledge as epistemologically unique or as occupying a privileged sociological position.

It is also important to realize that in most areas where scientific research is maintained as a basis for practical application, technological *failure*, unlike technological success, usually remains invisible to, and unconsidered by, the outsider. If we wish to argue that practical success validates scientific knowledge, we have to accept that practical failure is an indication to the contrary. Unfortunately, we know very little about the incidence or circumstances of technological failure – perhaps partly because its possible significance for traditional sociological assumptions about scientific knowledge has not previously been noted. However, what little we do know seems to suggest that unexpected failure to bring about technological advance through the exploitation of scientific knowledge is far from uncommon (Sapolsky 1977). Without sufficient evidence, we cannot reach a firm conclusion about the frequency of technological failure. But without a systematic attempt to balance success against failure, we can hardly use the technological productivity of modern society as grounds for exempting scientific knowledge from sociological analysis.

Finally, it is worth documenting the fact that in areas where science *has* made a significant contribution to practical action, this contribution can become greatly exaggerated, thereby providing spurious support for commonsense assumptions. We have already seen how sociologists tend to take for granted that the effectiveness of modern medicine provides one of the clearest illustrations of how science pays off in practical terms. Indeed, this view is very widely held. For instance, until recently it was accepted, almost without question, that the massive decline in mortality from infectious diseases which has occurred in Western societies since the middle of the last century was brought about by improvements in medical therapy deriving directly from the findings of scientific research. This view is so well entrenched that it is worth examining the systematic evidence rather closely. Let us look briefly at some of the more significant infectious diseases.

Consider first tuberculosis, which was the largest single cause of death in the nineteenth century, and the virtual elimination of which has contributed nearly a fifth of the total reduction in mortality since then. It is clear that the death rate in England and Wales from respiratory tuberculosis declined steadily from 1850 to 1970. But effective chemotherapy did not begin until 1947, with the introduction of streptomycin, and immunization was used on a substantial scale only from 1954.

> By these dates mortality from tuberculosis had fallen to a small fraction of its level in 1848-54; indeed most of the decline (57%) had taken place before the beginning of the present century. (McKeown 1976: 93)

This pattern is repeated in the case of virtually all the major infectious diseases.

> Of the total decline of mortality between 1848-54 and 1971, bronchitis, pneumonia and influenza contributed nearly a tenth; of the fall in the present century they contributed a fifth. Most of this decrease occurred before the introduction of sulphapyridine. (McKeown 1976: 94-5)

Mortality from whooping cough began to decline from the seventh decade of the last century. Treatment by sulphonamides and, later, antibiotics was not available before 1938 and even now their effect on the course of the disease is doubtful. 'Clearly almost the whole of the decline of mortality from whooping cough occurred before the introduction of an effective medical measure' (McKeown 1976: 97). Mortality from cholera and related diseases began to fall from the late nineteenth century and, by the time that intravenous therapy was introduced, 95 per cent of the overall improvement had taken place. Similarly

> mortality from typhus fell rapidly towards the end of the last century and there have been few deaths in the twentieth. It can be said without hesitation that specific medical measures had no influence on this decline. (McKeown 1976: 102)

The decline in mortality from infectious diseases is the most significant medical achievement of modern times. It is commonly assumed that this achievement is primarily a product of applied science; and this assumption about the impact of medical science has strengthened sociologists' conviction that scientific knowledge is a special type of knowledge. Detailed examination of the historical evidence, however, seems to show unambiguously that medical science has made only a marginal contribution to this practical achievement. If this realm of practical action is at all representative much of what we take for granted about the practical efficacy of science may be quite illusory. Given that the production of scientific knowledge-claims has grown steadily and cumulatively in modern times, any secular trend in the realm of practical action will be correlated with the growth of scientific knowledge; and given our conception of the special character of scientific knowledge, it will be only too easy to interpret the former as a consequence of the latter. But the example of the infectious diseases should lead us to beware of taking this kind of connection for granted, and to treat seriously the evidence and arguments (presented earlier in this section), which challenge 'commonsense' by insisting that the links between scientific knowledge and practical application are relatively weak.

In this section I have concentrated on the strength of the connection between science and technology; and I have commented only in passing on the question of whether, even where there *is* a direct link, the practical application of knowledge can actually serve to validate that knowledge. In the next section I will take up this latter issue in more detail.

Can successful practical application validate a scientific theory?

As we have seen, it has customarily been taken as self-evident that when a theory is actually used as the basis for successful practical action, this necessarily validates the theory. There are, however, strong grounds for maintaining that effective practical application is insufficient to provide such validation. This issue has been examined with particular reference to modern science and technology by Mario Bunge (1967), and the discussion which follows takes his analysis as its point of departure.

The central question with which we are concerned can be re-stated as follows: is it possible for a false or a partly false theory to be successful in practical terms? Bunge argues that it *is* possible, for several reasons. In the first place, we must recognize that any theory is composed of a number of propositions. It is always possible that only some of these propositions contribute significantly to its successful practical application. It therefore appears that the most we can conclude from using a theory to good practical effect is that some *part* of that theory is valid, or approximately so. But this conclusion must be further qualified. The complexity of everyday practical situations and the impossibility of controlling all relevant variables make it much more difficult to establish clear theoretical inferences on the basis of practical success, compared with the relative clarity of inference attainable in the laboratory or its equivalent, where some close approximation can often be made to the idealized relationships between phenomena with which scientific theory deals.

> A careful discrimination and control of the relevant variables and a critical evaluation of the hypotheses concerning the relations among such variables is not done while killing, curing, or persuading people, nor even while making things, but in leisurely, planned, and critically alert scientific theorizing and experimentation. Only while theorizing or experimenting do we *discriminate* among variables and *weigh* their relative importance, do we *control* them either by manipulation or by measurement, and do we *check* our hypotheses and inferences. This is why factual theories, whether scientific or technological, substantive or operative, are empirically tested in the laboratory and not in the battlefield, the consulting office, or the market place. (Bunge 1967: 336)

It follows that it is usually impossible to identify by means of successful practical action alone, which elements of a theory have been responsible for, and hence validated by, the successful achievement. It is, therefore, misleading to talk of scientific knowledge being validated by 'the millions of experiments going on in the real world'.

Another important consideration which strengthens these conclusions is that the idealized formulations of scientific theory have always to be not only reformulated, but also combined with other cognitive elements when they are brought to bear on the 'chunks of everyday reality' with which men deal in their practical affairs. For example,

> the relativistic theory of gravitation might be applied to the design of generators of antigravity fields ... which in turn might be used to facilitate the launching of spaceships. But, of course, relativity theory is not particularly concerned with either field generators or astronautics; it just provides *some of the* knowledge relevant to the design and manufacture of antigravity generators. (Bunge 1967: 331)

The construction of effective antigravity generators, therefore, would not necessarily provide conclusive support for any part of the initial academic version of relativity theory, partly because that theory will have been revised, reinterpreted and, probably, considerably simplified in accordance with the specific requirements of this field of practical endeavour; and also because many supplementary conceptions will have been introduced which may well have been crucial in bringing about practical success.

It is also important to realize that the accuracy requirements of practice are very different from, and usually far less stringent than, those applied in research undertaken with no immediate practical objective. An approximate and simple theory will often be sufficient for practical purposes, even when it is known to be scientifically inadequate. For instance, applied physicists today concerned with designing optical instruments can get by for the most part with optical theories dating from the middle of the seventeenth century. In many cases, the crudity of the theories employed for practical purposes will be hidden from the outsider by the wide margins of error which are allowed for in the technological product.

> Safety coefficients will mask the finer details predicted by an accurate and deep theory anyway, and such coefficients are characteristic of technological theory because this must adapt itself to conditions that can vary within ample bounds. Think of the variable loads a bridge can be subjected to or of the varying individuals that may consume a drug. The engineer and the physician are interested in safe and wide intervals centered in typical values rather than in exact values. A greater accuracy would be pointless since it is not a question of testing. Moreover, such a greater accuracy could be confusing because it would complicate things to such an extent that the target – on which action is to be focused – would be lost in a mass of detail. Extreme accuracy, a goal of scientific research, is pointless or even encumbering in practice in most cases. (Bunge 1967: 334-5)

The considerations identified above – that is, reformulation of theories in practical contexts, use of only part of a theory, low accuracy requirements and the complexity of practical situations – show that 'infinitely many possible rival theories' can yield results which are identical in practical terms and that it is undoubtedly possible for a false theory or a partly false theory to be practically effective. In other words, we seem to have decided that successful practical application has no conclusive validating force. However, we might still wish to object to this conclusion, on the grounds that knowing how to do something is itself valid knowledge. As Bunge puts it, it might yet 'be argued that a man who knows how to do something is thereby showing that he knows that something' (1967: 336). Let us examine this claim in connection with the following example of a successful practical act. An example reported in the *Daily Telegraph* will help us to see that the claim is either a tautology or demonstrably false.

> An African tribal remedy, using strips of paw-paw fruit, successfully cleared post-operative infection in a kidney transplant patient after antibiotics had failed, doctors disclosed yesterday. The remedy for infection was suggested by Dr Christopher Rudge, a junior member of

the transplant team, who had seen it used in the South African bush on ulcers and wounds. The fruit was bought from Fortnum and Mason, the Piccadilly grocers. He said he had used it before in difficult cases, and felt it could be useful in treating routine healing problems. 'It is not awfully scientific: I do not know why it works'.

One might wish to argue that Dr Rudge's knowledge of the curative effects of paw-paw was shown to be valid by his practical success. It is certainly clear that Dr Rudge did have the prior knowledge that the act of laying paw-paw strips on a wound was sometimes followed by a reduction of infection. It is also clear that the act was deemed to have been successful in this instance. But 'success' and some form of 'knowledge that' are presupposed in the kind of case we are considering, for, if either of these elements were lacking, the issue of validation would not arise. Thus the claim that 'a man who knows how to do something must know that something', when applied to such cases, can become a mere tautology. It can be used to mean only that, in the kind of case being examined, a man described a practical act which, when carried out, was judged to have been successful. By the nature of such cases, however, there *must* be a correspondence between the original description and the practical outcome. Interpreted in this minimal sense, then, the claim is vacuous. But if we interpret the claim more strongly, as requiring that the actor must state not only *that* something works, but also present some appropriate account of *how* it works – that is, some form of theoretical or scientific knowledge – then this example appears unambiguously to refute the claim.

We are quickly led to a similar conclusion if we reverse the formulation of the claim above and present it as: 'If a man knows X, then he must know how to do or make X.' This statement appears not to apply to all cases. For example, we know (or think we know) how geological formations are produced by natural processes, but we are unable to reproduce them ourselves. Likewise, astronomers are confident that they have an enormous body of validated knowledge about the nature of stars, the distribution of galaxies, and so on, without being able to influence these objects in any way at all. Our practical incapacity in no way weakens our confidence in the validity of either geological or astronomical knowledge. Furthermore, not only can we use our knowledge in these areas to show why practical intervention is impossible; but earlier theories could also be used in this way, such as those of medieval astronomy, which we now regard as false. It seems that our ability to control, regulate or reproduce natural phenomena is not decisive in enabling us to claim valid knowledge of such phenomena; nor is the capacity to explain this lack of practical effectiveness, within a theory's own framework of analysis, crucial in distinguishing false from true theories.

We can, then, conclude that the successful use of scientific theories establishes neither their validity nor their privileged epistemological status. This conclusion strengthens the case of the second sociological perspective on science, by weakening one of the main presuppositions of the dominant framework: it is also more consistent with the analysis of science provided by the second perspective. From the dominant perspective, validated knowledge is conceived as being established as universally valid by the application of invariant criteria of adequacy; it is, therefore, rather hard to understand why it should prove to be so difficult to validate theoretical knowledge by means of the apparently invariant criterion of practical success. In contrast, the second perspective proposes that knowledge is constituted differently according to varying interests, purposes, conventions and criteria of adequacy, in different social contexts or groups, and that judgements of cognitive 'correctness' will necessarily be context-dependent; it follows that judgements of practical efficacy cannot serve unproblematically to validate knowledge-claims which are proposed in connection with different interpretative contexts and in relation to different socially defined objectives.

Concluding remarks

I have sought to widen the scope of the current debate about the possibility of subjecting scientific knowledge to sociological analysis. I have tried to show that in identifying scientific knowledge as epistemologically special, and as exempt from sociological analysis, sociologists have tended to make two basic assumptions which have so far received little systematic investigation; namely, that scientific theories can be clearly validated by successful practical application, and that the general theoretical formulations of science do regularly generate such practical applications. I have argued that both these assumptions are very doubtful. In developing this argument, I have been led to defend the second sociological perspective on science, which treats scientific knowledge as open to sociological analysis, and to show that it can cope with the basic issues which arise when we consider the relationship between science and practical application.

There is, however, at least one important respect in which my argument remains incomplete. For I have avoided raising the question of whether or how 'practical effectiveness' is itself socially constructed. Throughout the analysis above I have used 'practical success' as a sociologically unproblematic notion – an unexamined interpretative resource. To this extent I have stayed within the main sociological tradition, where it has generally been assumed that the effectiveness of certain kinds of practical action is self-evident and is not open to negotiation or subject to social variation. Despite my reticence on this question, it does seem to me that there *are* areas where the *technical* meaning of given practical actions can be shown to be socially constructed, socially variable and context-dependent.[1] This is well illustrated in Michael Bloor's (1976) study of the diagnosis of cases for adenotonsillectomy. Nevertheless, there are very few studies of this kind and none at all which consider how the technical meaning of *hard* technology is socially constructed. Until this kind of analysis is forthcoming, the second sociological perspective will remain incomplete; for it is clearly implied in that perspective that no area of knowledge (whether formal, scientific or practical) is closed to sociological interpretation. I suggest, therefore, that this area of discourse should also be introduced into the debate; although at the moment I intend to offer nothing more concrete on the topic than this broad exhortation.

Note

1. It is important to recognize that the difficult task facing the sociologist here is that of providing an analysis of the *technical*, as opposed to what we might loosely call the *social* meaning of technology. Thus, it is fairly easy to show that the social meaning of television varies with and depends upon the social context in which it is employed. But it is much more difficult to show that what is to count as a 'working television set' is similarly context-dependent in any significant respect.

Part Three: Discourse analysis: showing how scientists construct their social worlds

9 Putting philosophy to work (1981)
with Nigel Gilbert

Popper as philosopher of action

'I think Popper is incomparably the greatest philosopher of science that has ever been', writes Sir Peter Medawar, winner of the Nobel Prize for medicine and himself an experienced analyst of scientific thought and scientific practice. Medawar's judgement has been echoed by many other eminent scientists. Sir Hermann Bondi states that: 'There is no more to science than its method, and there is no more to its method than Popper has said'. Similarly Sir John Eccles, another Nobel Prizewinner, testifies to the impact of Popper's writings on his approach to research: 'my scientific life owes so much to my conversion in 1945 ... to Popper's teachings on the conduct of investigations ... I have endeavoured to follow Popper in the formulation and in the investigation of fundamental problems in neurobiology'.

In the book from which these quotations are taken, Magee (1975) emphasizes that Popper's philosophy is a philosophy of action. It is intended to influence people's practical acts and choices, in science as well as in politics. Popper himself, in his 1958 Preface to *The Logic of Scientific Discovery*, stresses that his attempts to resolve certain problems in the philosophy of science are to be regarded as successful in so far as they contribute not only to philosophical knowledge but also to science (1959: 19). Popper, then, seeks to have an impact on scientific practice and several aspects of his philosophy of science clearly reveal this concern with practical intervention. In Popper's own words: 'I shall try to establish the rules, or if you will the norms, by which the scientist is guided when he is engaged in research or in discovery, *in the sense here understood*' (1959: 50). That last qualifying phrase is all-important, if one is not to misunderstand Popper's intention. Without it, Popper's statement would read like a preface to a sociological description of the cognitive and technical norms which scientists actually employ. But Popper says clearly that this is not his goal. He defines 'scientific knowledge', and by implication 'genuine scientist' and 'truly scientific action', on the basis of a purely logical analysis of what is entailed in proof and disproof.

His argument is that, in the realm of empirical knowledge, only disproof or falsification can logically be demonstrated. As a result, he proposes that 'scientists', in the ordinary sense of that word, ought to use a set of rules which ensure that their propositions are falsifiable and that propositions are accepted only if they have withstood rigorous attempts to show them to be false. Only in so far as such rules are implemented will so-called scientists approach Popper's ideal of rational action and thereby succeed in generating genuine scientific knowledge. Whether or not ordinary scientists actually conform to these rules is seen as an empirical rather than a philosophical issue. Thus Popper's aim is not to describe what such scientists do, but to identify the rules of scientific method which follow from a philosophically correct demarcation between scientific (or genuine empirical) knowledge and other empirical knowledge-claims, and to make these rules available to practising scientists.

It is worth dwelling for a moment on the question of how far Popper's rules can be regarded as accurately descriptive of scientific practice, even though it is not Popper's explicit objective to provide such a description. In one passage, Popper insists that his rules do not provide a description of how scientists choose their theories:

> In so far as the scientist critically judges, alters or rejects his own inspiration we may, if we like, regard the methodological analysis undertaken here as a kind of 'rational reconstruction' of the corresponding thought processes. *But this reconstruction would not describe these processes as they actually happen*; it can give only a logical skeleton of the procedure of testing … it so happens that my arguments in this book are quite independent of this problem. (1959: 31–2)

In this passage, Popper states that the most his rules can provide is a logical skeleton which operates at a level somehow removed from that of scientists' actions. One might have thought that this gap between rules and practice would have posed a major problem for a philosopher who wishes to contribute to science by providing workable guidelines for scientists. But as his final sentence shows, Popper concludes that this problem is irrelevant to his analysis.

If Popper maintains that his methods cannot be used to describe scientists' theoretical choices as they actually happen, perhaps we have been misrepresenting him in suggesting that he is a prescriptive theorist, a philosopher of action. However, Popper states unambiguously that he is not solely concerned with the logical structure of scientific thought. Consider the following passage from the same work as the previous quotation.

> I am quite ready to admit that there is a need for a purely logical analysis of theories, for an analysis which takes no account of how they change and develop. But this kind of analysis does not elucidate those aspects of the empirical sciences which I, for one, so highly prize. A system such as classical mechanics may be 'scientific' to any degree you like; but those who uphold it dogmatically … are adopting the very reverse of that critical attitude which in my view is the proper one for the scientist … If we therefore characterize empirical science merely by the formal or logical structure of its statements, we shall not be able to exclude from it that prevalent form of metaphysics which results from elevating an obsolete scientific theory into an incontrovertible truth.

Such are my reasons for proposing that empirical science should be characterized by its methods: by our manner of dealing with scientific systems: by what we do with them and what we do to them. (1959: 50)

In this passage Popper clearly rejects any purely logical analysis of scientific belief in favour of an attempt to identify the methods which scientists should employ when critically evaluating their systems of ideas. Yet, as we have seen, he regards as irrelevant any attempt to specify how his methodological recommendations might be linked to practice in concrete terms and he insists that his rules are in some sense independent of or removed from actual practice.

We are forced to conclude that the relationship between the Popperian method and actual practice is left fundamentally ambiguous. Nowhere is this ambiguity more evident than in the application of what may be taken as Popper's basic rules, namely, that scientists should formulate conjectures which can be clearly refuted and that they should seek to disprove rather than prove these conjectures. Popper starts with the purely *logical* point that proof and disproof are asymmetrical; general propositions cannot be proved, but they can be disproved. As long as one is concerned solely with the logical structure of propositions, this asymmetry is clear enough. But Popper himself recognizes that the asymmetry between proof and disproof disappears in practice:

In point of fact, no conclusive disproof of a theory can ever be produced; for it is always possible to say that the experimental results are not reliable, or that the discrepancies which are asserted to exist between the experimental results and the theory are only apparent ... If you insist on strict proof (or strict disproof) in the empirical sciences, you will never benefit from experience, and never learn from it how wrong you are. (1959: 50)

Consequently, in relation to scientific practice one can talk only of positive and negative results, and not of proof or disproof. Negative results, that is, results which seem inconsistent with a given hypothesis, may *incline* a scientist to abandon a hypothesis, but they will never *require* him to abandon it, on Popper's own admission. Whether or not he does so may depend on the amount and quality of positive evidence, on his confidence in his own and others' experimental skills and on his ability to conceive of alternative interpretations of the negative findings. Thus the utter simplicity and clarity of Popper's logical point are lost as soon as he begins to take cognizance of some of the complexities of scientific practice and as soon as he makes the transition from his ideal scientific actor to real scientists engaged in research.

The mundane Popperian scientist, then, seems to be no better off than his non-Popperian colleague. In any situation of cognitive uncertainty, both Popperians and non-Popperians have to weigh positive as well as negative evidence in order to come to some 'reasonable' conclusion; and neither has any definitive criterion with which to establish the adequacy of their conclusion. Moreover, the scientist looking for 'reasonable proof' is no more allowed to ignore negative evidence than the Popperian who looks for 'reasonable disproof'. Even the most ardent proponents of induction as a scientific method have recognized the significance of negative observations, as the following quotation from Bacon clearly shows.

> I must now give an example of the Exclusion or Rejection of Natures which by the Tables of Presentation are found not to belong to the Form [Law] of Heat ... For it is manifest from what has been said that any one contradictory instance overthrows a conjecture as to the Form. (Spedding *et al*. 1860: 147)

Although Bacon, unlike Popper, did not elevate this simple point into a whole philosophical system, the special logical importance of negative findings had become common knowledge among natural philosophers by the time of the foundation of the modern scientific community.

It seems, then, that Popper's central idea is not new; that he remains unclear about the connection between the formal analysis of scientific belief systems and the provision of rules of action; and that he has not considered in detail how his rules of scientific method are to be put into practical effect. Nevertheless, Popper has insisted that one of his aims is to provide useful prescriptions for scientific practice. Furthermore, the remarks quoted at the beginning of this paper show that some eminent scientists have expressed enthusiastic approval of Popper's ideas and that these scientists seem to believe that Popper's writings have beneficially influenced their research.

These observations lead us to a number of intriguing questions. For instance: How much do scientists in general know about Popper's ideas? Do they see Popper's writings as prescriptive? If so, how many of them try to put his rules into practice? And how exactly do they go about doing this? How far does the Popperian method provide a clear guide for scientific research? If the Popperian rules are ineffective as a practical methodology, are they put to any other uses by scientists? And how can we best explain those enthusiastic testimonials with which we began?

These questions lend themselves to sociological analysis, or at least, sociological data and analysis have some bearing on them. We have chosen to explore these questions by examining how the members of a specific research network in biochemistry have responded to Popper's philosophy of science. Our analysis is based on two and a half to three hour interviews with 34 members of this network (in which a wide range of topics were discussed), and on information taken from letters and from scientific publications. There is, of course, no guarantee that this network is representative of biochemistry or of science in general. On the other hand, there is no reason to think that this network is in any relevant respects unique (see Gilbert and Mulkay 1984). Furthermore, by concentrating on one currently operating research network, we can furnish a relatively detailed appraisal, we can look behind the public pronouncements of leading figures, we can obtain some idea of Popper's impact on ordinary as well as on eminent scientists, we can carry out our analysis with a moderately informed appreciation of the scientific issues, and we can observe scientists putting philosophy to work in a situation of cognitive uncertainty.

How widely is Popper known?

No mention is made of Popper in the primary research literature of this field. If we had confined our attention solely to research papers, we would have had no reason to suspect that his ideas were in any way influential or even known to the scientists involved. There are, of course, references to the testing of hypotheses in research papers. But the use of this kind of terminology is never explicitly linked to Popper in the hundred or so papers which we have read. Even in the secondary literature produced by this research network, we can find only three explicit mentions of his name. One of these occurs in a semi-autobiographical review paper by a major contributor to the field. Another reference to Popper occurs in a short 'popular' article, written to explain to a wider audience why this scientist had received a prestigious prize. The third occasion was in a letter, in which the author took exception to the way in which Popper's ideas had been 'mis-used' in the popular article.

There is, then, no reference to Popper in the formal literature and only very occasional reference to him in less formal publications. In the context of interviews, however, a quite different picture emerged. Indeed, it was the regularity with which Popper was mentioned in our first few interviews that persuaded us to investigate his influence on the members of this research network. Thus in the first ten interviews, five respondents spontaneously mentioned Popper and commented on his significance. Although the other five early respondents did not refer to Popper of their own accord, we found that they also were more familiar with his name than with that of any other philosopher of science, that they had some understanding of his work, and that they had opinions about its value.

By the time that we had completed the first batch of interviews, a number of questions about Popper had become firmly built into our interview schedule. We found that, although British scientists were more familiar with his work than those in the United States, all the members of our sample had some conception of what Popper had to say about science and that he is by far the most widely known philosopher of science within this research network.

Although everybody had heard of Popper, very few had actually read him. Of our 34 interviewees, only five or six appear to have done so in any detail. Our estimate on this point was confirmed by many of the scientists themselves. Statements like the two that follow occurred regularly.

1. I think that when people talk about Popper's ideas, not many of them have read the original works. They're much more likely to have read the Fontana classic by Bryan Magee, in which it is made plain for the ordinary man what it is that Popper has said. (Burridge 11)
2. Everybody knows the name Karl Popper. Everybody knows about falsifiability. Nobody has read him. Well, very *few* people have read him. More people talk about him than have read him. (Harding 20)

A fairly straightforward view is generally taken of Popper's philosophy of science and there is considerable agreement about its implications for the practising scientist.

3. The idea which I think's due to Popper and which sounds common sense afterwards, but perhaps it wasn't originally, is that a hypothesis is only a hypothesis if it can be tested and shown to be wrong by fairly defined experiments. That's really what we were coming back to earlier on, that in a way there are experiments which could show Spencer's views to be wrong. Its much harder to see what the experiments are that show Jennings' views are wrong, except a mass of positive evidence in another direction ... I think that's Popper, isn't it? (Finch 40-1)

4. Spencer is a great fan of Karl Popper, who takes the view that a hypothesis is good as long as you can't disprove it, so you've to spend all your time not trying to prove it, but trying to *dis*prove it. So if, for instance, in this system, we had altered ... (Thompson 14)

These passages illustrate how Popper's ideas were typically formulated by our respondents. They also show how speakers appeared to have no doubt that Popper intended to be prescriptive. Only one of our interviewees expressed uncertainty on this point. In addition, they provide examples of the two ways in which these scientists saw Popper as potentially useful. In quotation three, the speaker takes Popper's prescription to be that only falsifiable hypotheses are truly scientific. In quotation four, the speaker formulates the central idea as 'do not try to prove, but try to disprove' hypotheses. There is no indication in our interviews or in our other data that more than five or six of the scientists we interviewed knew any more than this about Popper's message for the practising scientist. Thus the question of Popper's influence on this body of researchers is more or less equivalent to asking how far they put these two aspects of the principle of falsification into effect.

How influential do scientists think Popper has been?

Only six scientists in our sample described themselves explicitly as 'Popperians' or as having found Popper's ideas definitely useful in carrying out their research. Even less said that Popper had exerted a significant influence on other scientists' practice. Quotation five illustrates the most strongly Popperian response that we received. It is from a scientist whom we will call Spencer. Spencer is a particularly eminent scientist, whose contribution to the field has been exceptionally important. He began the interview by referring immediately to Popper's 'miraculous and brilliant view of how induction really works' and proceeded straightaway to characterize his own approach to research in the following terms:

5. I suppose this is how one attempts to use one's mind to produce programmes on purpose, which will then be subconsciously used in order to probe the literature, in order, in a very Popperesque manner, to make

conjectures and constantly test and retest, mostly of course rejecting them. (Spencer 1)

In this extreme case, the scientist described even his subconscious mental processes in Popperian terms. But this degree of identification with Popper was unique. Quotations six and seven are much more typical of the statements of those who said that they had been directly influenced by Popper.

6. We now spend a lot of time with our students ... [putting across] the notion that science is not to do with sitting and making observations and trying to think what it all meant, but actually testing ideas, having ideas *first*. I suppose Popper's more the fashion now than he was twenty years ago. I would very much subscribe to his own viewpoint of how science proceeds. (Thompson 33)
7. Perhaps I should be ashamed to admit it, but I'd never heard of Popper until recently ... I've since read quite a bit of his stuff and I find it very interesting and obviously a good way to proceed. Very useful thought. I've also read *Lateral Thinking* and I find that also a useful way to proceed. (Barton 30)

In addition to mentioning their own adherence to Popper's precepts, scientists also expressed their own endorsement of the Popperian method by complimenting other researchers on the way in which they put Popper's rules into effect.

8. When I was a graduate student, I was very struck by what Karl Popper had to say about science ... I'd thought that you couldn't prove scientific theories, so I'd wondered how you went about it ... I can't remember now whether I read Spencer's papers or Popper's first ... It seemed that Spencer was going about his business in a thoroughly Popperian way. And it seemed such a productive way of going about things ... He was attempting to get rid of the theory. He was trying to disprove it ... Popper's book is the theory and Spencer's way of going about business is the practice. (Aldridge 17-18)

Quotations five to eight illustrate varying degrees of support for Popper, ranging from very strong personal commitment through enthusiastic advocacy to restrained approval, among those who clearly stated that they were pro-Popper. However, a greater number of scientists expressed doubts about the relevance to scientific practice of Popper's analysis; and almost everybody, whether or not they approved of Popper's rules, asserted that philosophers generally, and Popper specifically, had had very little impact on the large majority of scientists in this field. The next speaker, for instance, denies that Popper has actually influenced his research, even though he calls himself a 'Popperian'.

9. *Interviewer:* You mentioned some time ago that, in some sense, you were a Popperian. Does that mean that you feel you have been significantly influenced by his writings?
   Respondent: No. I must say that I have this view that what we do seems to come naturally, rather than consciously from philosophy ... So, in

general, I'm not sure that Popper's opinion influences scientists who
are working on a particular problem very much. (Nesbitt 30-1)

Thus, this scientist's view of himself as a Popperian seems to co-exist with a
recognition that neither he nor other scientists have been particularly influenced
by Popper. The meaning of this apparently rather odd combination of opinions is
clarified a little by the next quotation:

10. *Respondent:* Popper's more the fashion now than he was twenty years
    ago. I would very much subscribe to this viewpoint ...
    Interviewer: So you think Popper's had a significant influence on the
    thinking of scientists.
    Respondent: I don't think he has at *all*. Which is a great pity really. I
    think the *good* scientists think that way anyway. (Thompson 33–4)

The point being made here is that, although Popper has not changed scientific
practice in any way, he has grasped how *good* scientists have always gone about
their business. In other words the speaker, clearly perceiving himself as a good
scientist, feels that Popper's formulations nicely fit his actions and those of other
scientists whose work he approves.

This scientist also distinguishes between Popper's ideas being fashionable and
correct, both of which he accepts, and Popper's ideas being widely influential,
which he denies. The implication seems to be that there is much more talk about
Popper than there is implementation of his ideas. This point was made frequently
by other scientists.

11. I don't know whether Popper's ideas have had an influence or not.
    They've been talked about, within the context of Spencer's theory. And
    people have claimed to use the idea of 'Is a theory refutable or not?' I
    can't think of any examples of anybody who has changed their mind on
    those grounds. (Norton 41)
12. People talk about falsifiability and many of them talk about it dishonestly.
    Because either their experiments are *not* designed to produce an answer
    that really falsifies their premise or else, if it seems to, they start to re-
    define things. Not many people in my experience in the field have
    actually done a Popperian experiment and acted upon it. (Harding 20)

Similar comments were made by numerous other scientists, several of whom
suggested that Popper's rules did not guide scientists' practice, but were applied
after the event to provide a somewhat spurious legitimation for scientists'
technical decisions.

13. I regard this Popper vogue as slightly a band-wagon, which I am a little
    surprised to see Spencer eagerly clambering aboard. I thought we knew
    how we did science, quite independently of what Popper [and other
    philosophers] said. (Roberts 20)

14. I have suspected that scientists know how they are working and how they want to do experiments. They find that Karl Popper comes along and explains to them why they're doing what they're doing, and they'll say they take a lot of notice of Karl Popper. But I'm not sure it really has any influence. I don't know what Spencer would say about that. (Bendall 23–4)

A good many other scientists in our sample simply said that most scientists concentrate on trying to provide positive evidence in favour of their hypotheses and that neither Popper nor other philosophers influenced how they went about doing this.

15. *Interviewer:* Do you think that scientists do go out to try and prove their theories wrong?
    Respondent: No. No. No. From what I've seen, you try and prove it right, not wrong. That's human nature, I suppose. I think it would be a very strange animal who would say 'I think it works this way', and then show that it doesn't. That's why in a sense I'm a bit – I don't like this Popper approach. (Finch 41)

16. What people have tended to do when things don't fit in, they don't abandon the theory, they just modify it. Occam's Razor is very blunt, I am afraid, amongst us. (Harding 21)

17. I don't think scientists worry about that sort of thing at all, if you ask them to be very precise about their philosophy of science. I put myself in that category. It really balls it up. I wouldn't be very coherent about it. Yet at the same time I have probably got a fairly good intuitive understanding about the methodology, the idea of the test, the idea of the hypothesis. (Crosskey 24-5)

In the next quotation the speaker is summarizing, not his own view, which is markedly Popperian, but what he takes to be the opinion of most of his colleagues.

18. [Philosophy] is of no interest to scientists … Science provides problems and issues which philosophers can go away and discuss. But they have nothing much of interest to say to scientists. (Aldridge 17)

The main conclusion to emerge from these quotations is that, although there is much informal talk about Popper, although there is general agreement about Popper's message for the active researcher, and although a number of practitioners describe themselves as being Popperians in some sense, virtually all of those involved are doubtful about Popper's influence on scientists' research activities. Although a number of scientists verbally endorse Popper's methodological rules and on some occasions portray themselves as putting these rules into practice, very few scientists are actually recognized by their fellows as carrying out Popper's prescriptions faithfully or indeed as exemplifying any particular philosophical position. There is also some indication that the Popperian approach is often seen as a useful characterization of or legitimation for what scientists would have done anyway.

How do scientists recognize conformity to Popper's rules of method?

In several of the quotations above we have shown that Spencer sees himself as putting Popper's method into practice and that other scientists see him as one of Popper's adherents. Because Spencer has been such a major figure in the field as well as being the leading advocate of Popper, a great many of our respondents expressed some judgement of the degree to which he properly exemplified the Popperian approach. We can take advantage of their comments on Spencer to explore how scientists recognize conformity to and deviation from the Popperian method.

Some scientists see Spencer as clearly acting in a Popperian manner: 'Popper is the theory and Spencer the practice', as one respondent said. However, a good many of our sample denied that there was any correspondence between Popper's prescriptions and Spencer's actions.

19. *Respondent:* Not many people in my experience in the field have actually done a Popperian experiment and acted upon it.
    Interviewer: Do you think that Spencer does, to any extent?
    Respondent: No. He says he does. He has always been, well, 'lucky' would not be fair, because he was brilliant in his original premises, so most of his tests worked. But he has also tended to quietly ignore the awkward, to say its too complicated. To go back to my experiments on X. When he could not explain them away, he said they are too complicated. He wouldn't concede even that they gave any cause for anxiety, even at the time when they really seemed to be irrefutably disproving his theory, because he knew his theory was right. So I think even he actually, as far as Popper goes, is a little bit hypocritical. (Harding 20)
20. I can't think of any examples of anybody who has changed their minds on [Popperian] grounds ... We felt discouraged when Spencer didn't respond in that way. It made us depressed. It doesn't seem substantially to have changed the way Spencer responded. I had expected that he would have said, 'OK, these experiments you do, do look as if they've altered this particular part of my theory. They may be right or they may be wrong. But let's look at them in a sensible way like that'. And that's not the reaction that came back. But rather, 'No you're wrong. And this is why you're wrong'. (Norton 25)
21. I can't understand at the moment why Spencer will not admit, and he will *not*, in any area, that his hypothesis is not *totally* correct as enunciated by him, because he's a man who has read a lot of the history of science and is a very close adherent of Karl Popper. He will tell you about Popper's ideas and illustrate the truth of them, applied to other people's science. But what he cannot see is that he himself, at this moment in time, is offending against those principles deeply ... The *spirit* of his theory is correct, there is no doubt about that. As his theory claims, there *is* an A, there *is* a B, there *is* a C. But Spencer has never done any experiments with D, E and F. And it is the people who are working on D, E and F who

are saying that in *detail* the original hypothesis is incorrect. But Spencer is fighting this tooth and nail ... For instance, he says 'Alright, Lucas showed that cytochrome oxidase is a proton pump, I accept that its a proton pump. I accept that its a proton pump. But it is *not* a proton pump when it is in the real system'. You see, in the experiments Lucas had done, he had to take cytochrome oxidase out and put it in an artificial system. So Spencer now says, and this has the ring of a terrible untruth, that when its actually sitting in the real system, then it *isn't* a pump. I find that very unconvincing. It is unscientific. (Burridge 11-12)

These three passages, each from a different respondent and each dealing with different aspects of Spencer's theory, illustrate two things. They show clearly that Spencer can just as easily be seen as contravening Popper's maxims as exemplifying them. They also show that participants' judgements that Spencer has failed to abide by his Popperian code are closely associated with disagreements over technical or scientific issues.

In each passage it appears that the speaker's Popperian assessment of Spencer's action or his assessment of some other scientist's action would necessarily have been different if the speaker's appraisal of the experimental evidence had been otherwise. To take the example given in quotation 21, if the speaker had not been convinced that cytochrome oxidase *was* a proton pump in both the real and artificial systems, he would have had no grounds for accusing Spencer of failing to be self-critical. Or, to put the same point in reverse, if the speaker had thought that the experimental evidence on cytochrome oxidase was inconclusive, he would have had to treat Spencer's defence of his own theory as perfectly consistent with his Popperian principles, because there would have been no clear indication that the theory had been falsified. In other words, assessments of conformity to Popper's basic rule of scientific method hinge on scientists' interpretation of the term 'falsification'; and the meaning of 'falsification' depends *entirely* on researchers' technical and scientific judgements. In situations of scientific uncertainty these judgements, and hence the meaning of the Popperian rules, will be variable. Consequently, when there is uncertainty, the Popperian rules cannot provide a straightforward guide for scientists' actions or decisions. There is a gap between rule and particular action which can only be bridged by the very scientific choice which the rule is intended to constrain. As we suggested in the introduction, it is precisely this gap between rule and particular application which Popper regards as irrelevant to his concerns and which he decides to ignore in formulating his version of scientific method.

Assessing the implications of experimental evidence in relation to Popper's rules

We can observe the consequences of the gap between Popperian rules and their specific application in passages where the speaker is describing the implications for theory of experimental evidence. For instance, in the following account by

Spencer of his position in relation to cytochrome oxidase, we can see Spencer himself accepting that the Popperian scheme furnishes the practising scientist with little specific guidance; that his response to the evidence on cytochrome oxidase depends on a technical and scientific assessment which seems quite independent of any Popperian rules; and that this technical assessment is itself ultimately uncertain and based on a highly personal and unformalizable judgement.

22. *Interviewer:* Are there any general criteria for establishing whether a scheme is adequate or not?

Respondent: No. I would say no. I would say this is the most marvellous thing about science that, thank goodness, there are no real rules for that. You have to use your discretion, your knowledge of other scientists, your general feeling of what is going to satisfy the mind. Because surely you've got three things, you've got the three worlds of Popper ... The mind is the only mediator between the real world that you see in the laboratory and world three which is what you are having to actually create. So the only criterion for trying to get the right feel surely is taste or something like that ... the whole thing's very uncertain and the criteria of agreement are not laid down by anybody. Take the case of the proton pump, cytochrome oxidase. Everybody is willing to agree that we can see at least *one* proton go, with the artificial system. Most of the work with the complete system had indicated that there *aren't* any protons ... Now we have very awkward decisions to make. When we use the real system there is all sorts of other stuff there and in order to do the experiments we have to add a reagent to inhibit certain processes. Well the people who use the artificial systems say 'the real system is useless because all these other things make it very complicated and we've missed something. Something else is going on that's stopping the proton being pumped'. We say, 'well, we don't agree with that. We like the complete system because we've done lots of controlled experiments and we can show that nothing else is happening'. They say, 'you can never get rid of all the difficulties with the complete system. We like the artificial system because we know its clean and we know what's there'. Well, we say, 'you don't actually ...' Now you see, I don't know who's right, but I was terribly pleased when Z [an eminent scientist] said 'I would rather have the complete system'. But the fact that I was pleased shows how vulnerable I am, doesn't it? (Spencer 51-5)

In this passage, Spencer views his assessment of whether or not cytochrome oxidase is a proton pump as following necessarily from his decision to treat the results obtained with complete systems as more apposite than those obtained with artificial systems. Given this technical choice he is *required* to conclude that there is no evidence that in the real system, which of course is primarily what his theory was originally intended to explain, cytochrome oxidase actually pumps protons.

One could, perhaps, challenge Spencer's account on the grounds that he is simply choosing that kind of experiment which supports his theory and is, therefore, contravening Popper's injunction to look for disproof. There is, however, no evidence that Spencer has reasoned in this way. Furthermore, even if he had, he could produce a strong scientific justification for doing so. For his theory has been very successful in explaining a wide range of experimental results and to begin to modify it in relation to cytochrome oxidase would weaken its overall coherence and explanatory power. Thus this challenge is inconclusive as long as the scientific issue in question remains unresolved.

Spencer's resistance to challenges is quite in accord with the Popperian method so long as he believes that his critics are wrong scientifically. Of course, were Spencer to come to accept their experimental claims, Popper's rule would require him to abandon his current position. But the rule would be completely redundant. For in accepting his opponents' claims, Spencer would already have given up on purely scientific grounds the position he is at present defending.

Given Spencer's scientific interpretation of the data on cytochrome oxidase, his theory is not yet seriously threatened with falsification and he is in no way obliged by his Popperian commitments to withdraw any part of his theoretical conjecture. Yet, at the same time, his critics are entirely justified in reaching an opposite conclusion, given *their* interpretation of the evidence. For the speaker in quotation 21, Spencer is simply denying the evidence when he maintains that cytochrome oxidase does not pump protons in the complete system. As long as this conclusion is seen as scientifically obvious, the speaker simply *has* to see Spencer as wilfully refusing to admit that his original conjecture is in some measure falsified and, consequently, the speaker must see Spencer as 'offending deeply' against the Popperian canon.

Popper's rules do not seem to play an active part in either Spencer's or his critics' scientific reasoning. These rules appear rather to be used as flexible additions to each scientist's technical analysis, as a means of supporting one's scientific position with moral and philosophical evaluations whenever it seems appropriate. This helps to explain the observation above that, although scientists do not think that Popper's ideas have significantly influenced research practice, there is a great deal of talk about the Popperian method within the network. We can now see that much of this talk is devoted to using Popper's flexible conceptions to depict the 'scientificity' of one's own and one's colleagues' actions and ideas in accordance with one's particular cognitive commitments.

These conclusions have been based on evidence taken from situations where there is uncertainty about scientific issues and, consequently, about the best way to act as a scientist. However, the Popperian rules are only relevant in such situations, for one does not need rules of action where there is no uncertainty about how to act. Since scientific uncertainty occurs when there are differences of opinion, it is not surprising that our interviewees referred to Popper almost exclusively in relation to discussions of marked disagreements over scientific issues.

Rules, actions and interpretations

One major reason for Popper's shortcomings as a prescriptive theorist is his failure to consider systematically how rules or norms in general are related to particular actions. The central difficulty in linking rules to actions is that no rule can specify completely what is to count as following or not following that rule. The terms of a rule always need to be interpreted in relation to the variable characteristics of specific situations. Consequently, the very meaning of a rule as a guide for conduct depends in part on procedures of interpretation which have to be used to bring particular cases within its scope. Such interpretative procedures may, of course, sometimes be formulated as supplementary rules. But these additional rules cannot be applied so as to give the initial rule a determinate meaning, for they in turn require interpretation. In short, the connection between general rules of action and specific acts is essentially indeterminate (Mulkay 1980).

This conclusion is strikingly similar to the central point which Popper himself makes in his critique of logical positivism and from which he derives his own views of scientific method, namely, that no number of individual instances can verify an empirical generalization. However, Popper's lack of concern with scientists' concrete research actions prevents him from realizing that a similar indeterminacy exists in the relationship between general rules of action and individual acts. We saw in the last section that Popper's extremely general formulations depend for their meaning on scientists' particular, detailed scientific judgements. These judgements, in turn, entail various kinds of vague and intangible interpretations which lie outside the scope of the Popperian rules.

Popper responds implicitly to scientists' need to interpret his rules when he distinguishes between appropriate interpretations and *ad hoc* modifications. In recognizing that supplementary reasoning is at least sometimes necessary in order to implement his rules, he is clearly accepting that their application to particular cases is not entirely self-evident. He is unwilling, however, to allow scientists too much interpretative flexibility. When he maintains that *ad hoc* interpretations can be systematically distinguished from proper interpretations, Popper is trying to ensure that scientific action can still be rigorously constrained by his rules, despite the need for varied responses to ever-changing circumstances and ever-new instances.

If, however, the relationship between rules and particular instances is necessarily indeterminate, as we have proposed, it follows that what Popper regards as *ad hoc* reasoning will be an unavoidable feature of the use of any general set of rules in science. In the following passage Spencer, the most committed Popperian in this area, comes to a similar conclusion as he identifies some of the intangible considerations which he believes affect his judgements in particular instances and thereby his interpretations of the Popperian method.

> 23. The criteria you use are in one way or another those of falsifiability. So generally speaking what will happen is that you make certain observations which seem to falsify a reasonably well accepted piece of a conceptual framework. You won't of course accept that falsification to start with. If

you constantly do that everything is going to go mad, because you falsify everything because you do a wrong experiment. So then this requires re-examination. Initially the feeling is the theory is alright still; there is something wrong with the experiment or the theory is sufficiently good to satisfy ordinary requirements and you don't want to overturn it because you can't think of anything better. Well, this depends very much on the discretion of the scientists at the time. Whether they have good mathematical knowledge, whether they would be prepared to go to a more abstract kind of theory or whether they want a more mechanically easily understood, visual kind of theory ... Its very complicated, not unlike problems in politics and other social phenomena where there must be an awful lot of taste and discretion, because a lot of the things between which you have to try to make comparisons can't simply have numbers attached. They have different qualities. So it is in that sense I don't think you can make hard criteria. But generally I suppose it hinges around the word 'falsify'. (Spencer 58-9)

In this quotation, Spencer emphasizes that the criterion of falsification is given meaning through judgements which cannot be formalized and which rest ultimately on taste and personal inclination. In quotation 24 below, another professed Popperian makes a similar point. Taking 'rules' to imply some kind of fixed and determinate formulation of how one should act, he stresses that research simply cannot be guided by rules.

24. I regard it very much like criminology, detectives and Sherlock Holmes and things. I mean, there are no rules, but you just have to find out what's going on and so you just try to design experiments that will give you the information and look for clues. But if something new comes along, then you tentatively make a set of rules by which you should try to figure out what it does. I suppose you could try and get a set of rules. But almost by definition with a new thing – if the new thing is really new, it won't fit your set of rules. (Nesbitt 29)

In so far as scientists' technical reasoning depends on personal, qualitative, unformalizable judgements and in so far as it is technical appraisals which give meaning to the Popperian rules, it is possible for each individual scientist to perceive his colleagues' interpretations as *ad hoc* and unjustified. We have seen that this perception is expressed frequently in our interviewees' accounts. Furthermore any outsider, a philosopher or a sociologist for example, will be quite unable to decide which participants, if any, are acting in a truly Popperian manner; at least, he will experience this difficulty as long as he remains uncommitted to any of the various competing scientific viewpoints. If, however, he perseveres in trying to establish how far scientists are conforming to the Popperian method, he will in all likelihood come to take the most widely accepted theory as his touchstone in distinguishing proper from improper Popperian actions. As we have noted above, it is fairly easy to apply Popperian rules retrospectively, once one has decided which scientific perspective is correct. This indeed is what scientists themselves do regularly and the philosopher or sociologist will be able to follow their example. But for the prescriptive philosopher, in particular, this practice will be disappointing. For the rules were intended to determine scientists' technical decisions and philosophers' technical evaluations, not to be determined by them.

How scientists use Popperian rules

In most sociological analyses of rule-use, it is emphasized that the flexibility of rules enables participants to show with some plausibility, whenever they wish, that specific actions follow 'necessarily' from some agreed rule of conduct. Although to the analyst the relationship between rule and specific act appears uncertain and dependent on contingent interpretations, participants regularly succeed in presenting their actions as stemming unavoidably from a shared prescription. In other words, they leave implicit or hidden the active interpretation required to fit rules to specific actions. When an act is subsumed under a rule which is accepted by all those involved, the act thereby acquires legitimacy. It becomes an act which should not and, given the moral character of the actor, could not have been otherwise.

The use of rules in this way is evident in our interviews with biochemists both in relation to specific rules and in relation to the Popperian method overall. As an instance of the former, consider the following quotation. The respondent has been asked whether a particular result was a replication. He appears to see this question as a criticism, as implying that his work was 'purely duplicative' and he responds by bringing his actions under the legitimating cover of a Popperian rule.

> 25. Work in this more microbial area has been a bit primitive, I think. Certainly, as far as Spencer's work is concerned, he is a great fan of Karl Popper, who takes the view that a hypothesis is good as long as you can't disprove it, so you've to spend all your time not trying to prove it, but trying to *dis*prove it ... So this experiment was a good test, I think, of the validity of his ideas. The fact that we didn't disprove them doesn't mean that the work is purely duplicative, not at all. It was different. It was a new test, independent test. (Thompson 14)

In this passage the speaker rescues his experimental work from the charge of 'mere duplication' by presenting it as a new test required by Spencer's and his own commitment to the Popperian rule. By comparing his statement with the research paper reporting the experimental work, one can see that the speaker makes a link between the rule and the experiment specifically for the purposes of his interaction with the interviewer. In the paper no mention is made of testing Spencer's hypothesis. Spencer's ideas are taken as given and the results are presented instead as demonstrating a new technique for measuring a phenomenon of some significance to Spencerian theory.

If 'showing' that an action follows from a rule is one way of justifying that action, showing that it deviates from a rule will be one way of condemning it. In the next passage, the speaker is concerned, not with his own actions, but with those of Spencer whose hypothesis he accepts. He uses what he sees as Spencer's conformity to the Popperian method as a way of legitimating the latter's scientific claims, while at the same time undermining the endeavours of most other theorists in the area.

26. Spencer was going about this business in a thoroughly Popperian way. And it seemed such a productive way of going about things. You see so many people trying to prove their theories. It seemed to me, before I'd read anything that Popper had written, that you couldn't do this. And Spencer was attempting to get rid of the theory. He was trying to disprove it. (Aldridge 17)

Popper's asymmetry between proof and disproof is used here to 'show' that the work of many of those who disagreed with Spencer was procedurally wrong and therefore doomed to failure: whereas Spencer's approach is depicted as procedurally correct and therefore much more likely to be productive. Shortly afterwards, however, when asked whether he thought that scientists tend to look for proof rather than disproof, as he seems to imply above, he replied:

27. They write as though they do. I don't think they do, but they write as though they did. Perhaps it is a trivial editorial point. (Aldridge 19)

There are two things to be noted here. Firstly, the speaker's initial characterization of Spencer as differing radically from most other scientists in seeking disproof rather than proof is subsequently weakened, if not contradicted, by his admission that scientists only *appear* to be trying to prove their theories. It seems that in the first passage he constructs a negative characterization of their actions, by means of a contrast with the Popperian ideal, as a way of bringing into sharp relief the merits of Spencer's work. But in the second passage where the comparison with Spencer is no longer relevant, he can, with no apparent recognition of inconsistency, devise a quite different version of most non-Popperian scientists' actions. The second point is that the speaker himself implicitly recognizes how flexibly scientists can portray their actions, in relation to the Popperian method, when he states that researchers may *do* one thing, but convey in their papers a quite different account of their actions. This possibility was noted by several scientists quite explicitly, although they tended to suggest that scientists were *more* likely to adopt a Popperian terminology in research papers than was justified by the 'real' character of their actions.

28. I think that the feeling we had was that we wanted to show that there was an energy equivalence. But in the papers we would probably have said, 'This is a test of the hypothesis. If this test fails then the hypothesis is wrong'. I think that's the way we would have written it scientifically, but as people I'm sure we would – we'd got all this nice data from a year ago and we wanted to take it a bit further and we wanted these numbers to balance. They did more or less ... we were assuming Spencer says N is 2, we will take 2 and plug it in and roughly it balances. And any imbalance we put into a data problem, error. (Crosskey 8-9)

It appears, then, that Popperian rules provide scientists with a flexible interpretative resource which can be applied to or contrasted with particular actions, actors or knowledge-claims in accordance with participants' varying objectives in different social situations. They can be used, for example, to negate a perceived criticism, to strengthen a knowledge-claim by giving the impression of detached experimental rigour, to explain the superiority of an influential hypothesis, to account for other researchers' scientific failures and to condemn the research strategy of one's opponents.

On the surface, these uses of the Popperian vocabulary appear quite diverse; and this diversity is certainly present, in the sense that Popperian ideas are continually re-interpreted to cope with the unique features of each new social interaction. Nevertheless, an underlying pattern can be discerned. It is that, except in situations where Popper's position is expressly repudiated, scientific conclusions with which the speaker agrees are often portrayed as arising from actions which exemplify the Popperian rules and never as arising from actions which contravene those rules; while conclusions with which the speaker disagrees are often seen as arising out of contraventions of the Popperian rules but never as arising out of conformity to the rules. All the scientists who used Popper's ideas to characterize actions favourably did so in relation to their own research or in relation to the work of those with whom they agreed scientifically. Similarly, all those who used Popperian notions to condemn scientists' actions did so in relation to their opponents. Not only have Popperian rules and concepts become incorporated into the informal repertoire of evaluative resources which scientists use in negotiating the meaning of each other's professional actions, but each scientist employs these notions to claim legitimacy for his own scientific views and to undermine the legitimacy of his opponents' views.

In our data there are no instances where this simple pattern does not apply. It is, of course, to be expected in the light of our analysis above. For we have stressed that scientists bridge the gap between rules and particular cases by interpreting the former in accordance with their scientific commitments. The highly abstract character of the Popperian rules coupled with their separation from the social practices of science means that they can always be interpreted and are always interpreted, as far as our evidence indicates, so as to support researchers' scientific-technical judgements. This helps to explain why they are enthusiastically endorsed by some scientists, yet rejected as worthless by others. Those who are persuaded to adopt Popper's view of scientific method will never experience any great difficulty in reconciling his rules with their own technical judgements. When these judgements turn out to have been often 'correct', this will be attributed by the actor at least partly to his Popperian strategy. It is not surprising, therefore, that successful scientists in other fields as well as in this one will be especially likely to testify to Popper's practical efficacy. At the same time, many scientists, and particularly those whose scientific contributions have not been so significant or who have failed to convince a successful Popperian of the inadequacy of his analysis of a specific topic, will tend to be struck by what they see as the hypocrisy of some of those who claim to put Popper into practice.

Both apparently contradictory views of Popper's ideas are equally reasonable, in the light of particular scientists' different experiences. But from our broader perspective on the members of this research network as a whole, we can see that both the apparent success and the apparent failure of the Popperian method arise out of its essential indeterminacy and its consequent employment as a flexible resource for characterizing social action during individual reflection and informal discourse. It is strikingly ironic that, if our analysis is correct, the impact of Popper's philosophical endeavours should have been restricted to that realm of ordinary discourse, as distinct from technical argumentation, which Popper has been so unwilling to regard as a serious object of study.

Conclusion: philosophers' practice and scientists' practice

We have seen that there is considerable disagreement among participants in the research network we have been studying about the meaning of the Popperian method in specific instances. We explored these divergent interpretations in relation to scientists' views of Spencer's actions and knowledge-claims. It was observed that the meaning of Popperian rules depended directly on participants' scientific and technical judgements. We suggested therefore that the Popperian rules are unable to provide clear constraints upon scientists' actions or on their technical assessments.

One major reason for the ineffectiveness of Popper's rules as prescriptions is his failure to consider the general issue of how particular acts are related to rules. We suggested that this relationship is essentially indeterminate. However, particular acts are frequently linked to rules in ways which give an impression of a necessary connection. This is accomplished by participants and analysts by means of supplementary interpretation, which is usually hidden and which cannot itself be reduced to formal rules. Because scientists' technical reasoning depends on highly personal judgements and because the meaning of the Popperian rules depends on such judgements, each individual scientist continually disagrees with his colleagues' Popperian interpretations. In situations of cognitive uncertainty Popperian rules have no single meaning. They cannot, therefore, operate as useful prescriptions, but only as evaluative retrodictions.

Philosophers may have failed to realize this largely because they have operated in a socio-cultural context which is significantly different from that of research scientists. Although philosophers of science and practising scientists are both concerned with systematic knowledge about the natural world, their perspectives on such knowledge are fundamentally different in at least two major respects. In the first place, philosophers tend to be interested primarily in the structure of knowledge *in general*. They do, of course, select particular scientific achievements for close analysis. But their intention is almost always to use specific examples to illustrate conclusions about knowledge as such. It does not matter to the philosopher that his examples are usually somewhat ancient and well-trodden; for he is interested in them not as particular instances, but as illustrations of universal features. In contrast, practising scientists focus on contributing to knowledge about a more or less narrowly defined range of natural phenomena. Their familiarity with other areas of current investigation is usually meagre as is their awareness of the history of science. Conclusions about knowledge as such are only deemed to be relevant to their professional actions in so far as they have implications for scientists' research into specific empirical topics. Thus research scientists, unlike philosophers, are only interested professionally in particular bodies of knowledge. This difference in perspective on knowledge is probably part of what participants *mean* by referring to work as 'philosophical' or 'scientific'.

A second, related difference between philosophers and scientists is that the former study completed intellectual achievements, whereas the latter seek to create such achievements. Philosophical analysis of scientific knowledge begins with the logical structure of the end-product of scientific practice. Or, at least, its analysis is carried out with prior knowledge of what the intellectual outcome was to be. In contrast, scientists are involved in making a contribution to a scientific corpus which, in so far as that contribution is new, will to some extent be changed by it. Thus the basic task for a prescriptive philosophy of science, such as that of Popper, is to transform general conclusions about *valid knowledge as such* which have been derived from *retrospective analysis*, into rules or guidelines which can tell scientists how to deal with *concrete research problems* in situations of *cognitive uncertainty*.

If these comments are broadly correct, it follows that any attempt to translate philosophical conclusions into rules of scientific action, without clear recognition that a major transformation of perspective is involved, will be extremely misleading. Let us briefly show that this is so by looking at a simple example provided by Magee. In this example, Magee tries to convey the unusual effectiveness of the Popperian approach. He begins by summarizing the rules of Popperian method: to formulate hypotheses as clearly as possible; to expose them rigorously to the possibility of refutation; to avoid *ad hoc* modifications in response to negative findings; but not to abandon hypotheses too lightly, in response to ill-conceived or poorly devised tests. He then takes as an hypothesis the proposition that water boils at 100° Centigrade. The next step is to subject this hypothesis to various 'tests', such as boiling water in a closed vessel or at the top of a mountain. One way of responding to the falsifications which these 'tests' can be presumed to have produced might be to modify the original hypothesis in a fairly direct fashion, so that it becomes something like 'water boils at 100° Centigrade in open vessels at sea-level'. These modifications, however, are seen as being *ad hoc*, in the sense that we have not adopted the Popperian method of formulating a new hypothesis which incorporates both positive and negative findings within one richer and wider-ranging generalization, and then proceeding to further tests. Thus the truly Popperian approach is portrayed as fruitful because it avoids *ad hoc* responses and uses the relative clarity of negative results as a springboard for the creation of ever more comprehensive conjectures which are consistent with an ever wider body of reliable evidence.

This kind of example is misleading because we already have a pretty good idea of what science textbooks say about pressure and the boiling points of liquids. Even if we are a little hazy about the details of 'the right answer', we can certainly recognize a wrong answer with the analyst's help.

So what we thought was a scientific law *turns out not to be one*. Now at this point we could *take a wrong* turning. We could *salvage* our original statement by narrowing its empirical content to 'Water boils at 100° Centigrade in open vessels'. And we could then look systematically for a *refutation* of our second statement. And if we were rather *more imaginative* than before we should *find it* at high altitudes: so that to *salvage* our second statement ... (Magee 1975: 24)

We have italicized the cues which Magee gives us in the text to make sure that we do not fail to distinguish between scientific blind alleys and the road to scientific success. As a result, Magee's *ad hoc* modifications stand out clearly as incorrect scientific generalizations. We therefore experience no difficulty at all in applying Popper's rules, as the analyst guides us carefully through the wrong answers and as he identifies obvious refutations of the original hypothesis on the way toward an answer that is known in advance. But this procedure, although presented as an illustration of the Popperian method in practice, is rather that of 'laying bare the logical skeleton' of established knowledge. It bears very little resemblance to the practical task facing the research scientist.

In Magee's retrospective analysis of a scientifically mature topic, general concepts such as 'falsification' and '*ad hoc* modification' present no interpretative problems at all. Their meaning is unproblematic because, as we have seen, it depends on scientific judgements, which in this case can be based on common knowledge. But at the research front it is precisely such specific scientific issues which are unresolved. For instance, in order to decide as unequivocally as Magee does in his example whether Spencer's view of cytochrome oxidase or that of his opponents was *ad hoc*, one would need to know whether cytochrome oxidase pumps protons in the real system. This, however, is precisely what participants are trying to decide. Accordingly, although the rules may appear to the retrospective view of the philosopher to operate unambiguously and universally, to the forward-looking scientist they offer no clear guide to action in the specific instances with which he is concerned.

It seems, then, that Popper's failure to provide effective rules of scientific action reveals a basic dilemma facing any prescriptive philosophy of science. Philosophical analysis deals with the universal structure of validated scientific achievements. Its prescriptions have been influenced by the kind of cognitive hindsight drawn on by Magee, which obscures the existence of interpretative contingency and the range of interpretative procedures necessarily employed by scientists. Thus philosophers' rules of method tend to stop precisely at the point where the individual scientist begins to need guidance.

Is there any way out of this dilemma? Given the open-endedness of rules, is it possible in principle to formulate them in such a way that they do operate as effective constraints? Clearly, the indeterminate or hermeneutic connection between rules and actions means that rules can never entirely determine actions. They might, however, be made to operate *more* or *less* effectively as social constraints. For instance, the rules of scientific publication are implemented well enough for us to recognize a considerable uniformity of end-product. This is done, however, not simply by making general rules of publication available to researchers, but by embodying these rules in a social practice, so that potential actors have access to a corpus of exemplary instances, they are guided in their efforts by skilled interpreters, and they are subject to various kinds of direct control by editors and referees. As a result, acceptable levels of conformity to the rules of scientific publication are negotiated through the actions and interpretations of networks of actors. In such a context, rules can be *made* effective as constraints, even though the rules have no unique, literal meanings independent of the context of application.

It follows, therefore, that if philosophers are to devise rules which can play some definite part in guiding scientists' actions, they must come to appreciate more fully how scientific practice differs from their own and they must be prepared to modify their analytical procedures accordingly. In particular, they must come to conceive of rules of scientific action as being given meaning only through the interpretative procedures and social relationships characteristic of the scientific research community. In this respect, Popper's practical failure serves to reveal important lessons for any prescriptive philosophy of science.

Although the scientists we studied have not benefited from Popper's writings in the manner that he foresaw, they have come to make regular use of his conceptions and his rules. We were able to document from our interviews how scientists use Popperian rules to characterize, justify and condemn one another's actions during everyday discourse. The generality of the Popperian rules, their lack of interpretative particularization and their independence of institutionalized social relationships, allow individual scientists considerable freedom to conceive of their own actions as Popperian in character and to attribute their intellectual success to the effectiveness of the Popperian approach. This is one reason why public testimonials to Popper are frequently produced by eminent men and why such expressions of approval give a misleading impression of this philosopher's actual influence on scientific practice.

This analysis, although based exclusively on evidence collected from natural scientists, has implications for all areas of intellectual endeavour where a dialogue occurs between practitioners and philosophers, and where the Popperian debate has been significant.

10 Theory choice (1984)
with Nigel Gilbert

How do scientists choose between theories? Both sociologists and philosophers of science have regarded this as an important question. It is important for philosophers because the way that scientists carry out such choices has implications for philosophers' conceptions of rational action in science. Popper is not unrepresentative of philosophers when he states that it is scientists' way of selecting between theories which makes science uniquely rational (1963: 215). Similarly, the question is crucial for sociologists because it focuses on a primary aspect of the relationship between scientists' social actions and the creation of scientific knowledge (Zuckerman 1977). In this paper we will examine existing approaches to the analysis of theory choice in science and we will try to show that a new analytical perspective is required. The methodological and theoretical issues that we discuss below are, however, by no means specific to the topic of theory choice. They are, rather, basic issues that could be explored by reference to a wide range of social actions, both in science and in other areas of social life. Consequently, the conclusions proposed in the following discussion have important implications for sociology in general, not only for the sociology of science or even for the sociology of knowledge.

The philosophical and sociological literature on theory choice is large, and the various positions to be found there can be divided up in a great many different ways. We will begin with a simple two-fold distinction that suits our aims in this paper. On one side we place those views that depict theory choice as arising out of the application of a set of widely-shared and rational rules. According to such views, scientists assess theories in terms of such criteria as accuracy, consistency, simplicity, and so on, and they act on the basis of rules that require them to adopt those theories which most fully satisfy these criteria. From this perspective, most acts of theory choice in science can be explained as following from scientists' conformity to internalized rules embodying these criteria. Deviations from the rules are like other forms of social deviance, and can be attributed to the distorting effect of additional social and personal influences. Moreover, scientists' choices can be justified philosophically, or rationally reconstructed, in so far as the rules which appear to fit any particular choice are accepted by the analyst to be 'rational'.

The second approach to theory choice is taken by those philosophers and sociologists of science who maintain that such rules of theory choice may have *some* bearing on scientists' judgements, but the interpretation of these rules by particular actors is always significantly affected by contingent personal and social factors. From this perspective, these rules do not fully determine scientists' choices. They are regarded as contributing only modestly to sociological explanations of cognitive development in science. Philosophically, this second view has led toward what some writers describe as 'radical subjectivity', in the sense that the existence of universal standards for assessing the value of scientific ideas is denied.

In the main part of this paper we will examine some empirical material that has important implications for these two views of theory choice in science. Before we do this, however, we will summarize and discuss an attempt by Kuhn to justify a version of the second approach outlined above. Consideration of Kuhn's argument will enable us to identify and to question certain of the basic assumptions of these two approaches. By means of this discussion of Kuhn, we will try to establish an analytical context within which to perceive the significance of our empirical data and of the conclusions we derive from analysis of these data. We have chosen to discuss Kuhn's treatment of theory choice in the next section because it seems to us to be the best at present available and because it forms a bridge between the traditional positions and our own radically different approach.

Theory choice and scientific values

Kuhn identifies five criteria that have been traditionally regarded as characteristic of good scientific theory (1977: Chap. 13). These are not taken to be the only criteria used by scientists in choosing between theories. They have been selected by Kuhn because they are generally acknowledged to be among the most important. The first criterion of *accuracy* refers to the requirement that a theory should agree with the results of existing experiments and observations. The second criterion of *consistency* means that a theory should be compatible with other established bodies of knowledge as well as free from internal contradiction. His third criterion is *simplicity*. A theory should replace observational diversity and confusion with an underlying pattern which is simple enough to be clearly understood. Fourth, theories are expected to be *fruitful*, to reveal new, previously unexpected phenomena and relationships. Finally, a theory should have broad *scope*. That is, it should not be limited to a very narrow range of observations; our formulation of *scope* differs slightly from Kuhn's because his version seems to us to be indistinguishable from his criterion of *fruitfulness*.

Kuhn states that he agrees entirely with the traditional view that such criteria play a vital role in science. These criteria, he suggests, together with others of much the same sort, 'provide *the* shared basis for theory choice' (1977: 322). Nevertheless, he emphasizes, we must not ignore certain difficulties scientists encounter when they apply the rules embodying these criteria. For these difficulties are so fundamental that, even if we could identify *all* the relevant criteria, we would still not have a shared algorithm capable of dictating unanimous, rational choices for scientists in general.

The first difficulty is that, when the criteria are used together, the choice which seems to follow from any one criterion on any particular occasion often conflicts with that which follows from some other criterion. Unless the criteria are placed in some strict order of priority, they will frequently generate incompatible choices. Second, the criteria are imprecise. The basic rules of theory choice tell neither participants nor analysts how to judge accuracy, simplicity, etc, in specific instances. It is possible to interpret any given rule in different ways in relation to any particular theory. Thus it appears that the original set of rules, if they are to generate clear choices in specific instances, require additional rules that determine the relative weighting of criteria and which inform actors' interpretation of the criteria in any given circumstances. Kuhn illustrates these difficulties with historical examples and concludes that:

> When scientists must choose between competing theories, two men fully committed to the same list of criteria for choice may nevertheless reach different conclusions. Perhaps they interpret simplicity differently or have different convictions about the range of fields within which the consistency criterion must be met. Or perhaps they agree about these matters but differ about the relative weights to be accorded to these or to other criteria when several are deployed together. With respect to divergences of this sort, no set of choice criteria yet proposed is of any use. One can explain, as the historian characteristically does, why particular men made particular choices at particular times. But for that purpose one must go beyond the list of shared criteria to characteristics of the individuals who make the choice. One must, that is, deal with characteristics which vary from one scientist to another without thereby in the least jeopardizing their adherence to the canons which make science scientific. (1977: 324)

In short, Kuhn maintains that it is impossible to formulate a set of supplementary rules which will resolve problems of theory choice for individual actors. Each scientist must actively interpret the rules in the light of his personal experiences and convictions in order to distinguish between competing theories.

Kuhn suggests that there are three kinds of factors which directly influence scientists' interpretations of rules of theory choice and make application of these rules extremely variable. The first of these is previous scientific experience, which varies with each scientific biography. Second, scientists have extra-scientific social and cultural commitments. Such commitments tend to alter with the historical period and to vary from one scientist to another; yet they often exert a major influence on scientific judgements. Third, there are basic differences in personality. These three classes of factors may be termed 'subjective' in the sense that they are never the same for any two individuals. In so far as Kuhn regards them as *necessarily involved* in scientific theory choice, his approach may be contrasted with the traditional view. For according to the latter, the rules have straightforward, literal meanings which unequivocally determine the choices to be made by those committed to the rules, thereby furnishing an invariant, 'objective' basis for choice. Nevertheless, Kuhn repudiates the charge that his position is in any sense radically subjective: 'My point is, then, that every individual choice between competing theories depends on a mixture of objective and subjective factors, or of shared and individual criteria. Since the latter have not ordinarily figured in the philosophy of science, my emphasis upon them has made my belief in the former hard for my critics to see' (1977: 325).

It appears, then, that Kuhn does not regard his stress on the existence of marked variations in individuals' interpretations of the rules of theory choice as incompatible with the idea that these rules provide a shared basis for choice. He tries to reconcile these two notions by arguing that the supposed rules are not rules at all, but values. 'Criteria that influence decisions without specifying what these decisions must be are familiar in many aspects of human life. Ordinarily, however, they are called not criteria or rules, but maxims, norms, or values' (1977: 330). Kuhn's central point is that scientific values influence individuals' choices without uniquely determining them. He argues that shared values do, in some way, constrain or specify to a certain extent the direction taken by collective action, although the meaning of any value is highly variable from one actor to another.

> [D]ifference in outcome ought not to suggest that the values scientists share are less than critically important either to their decisions or to the development of the enterprise in which they participate. Values like accuracy, consistency, and scope may prove ambiguous in application, both individually and collectively; they may, that is, be an insufficient basis for an algorithm of choice. But they do specify a great deal: what each scientist must consider in reaching a decision, what he may and may not consider relevant, and what he can legitimately be required to report as the basis for the choice he has made. (1977: 331)

This passage, which is Kuhn's most explicit attempt to reconcile the existence of radical variation in particular cases with the traditional idea that individual choices are subject to a common cultural constraint, seems to us to be unconvincing. For, having been at great pains to show that the meaning of all prescriptions about theory choice is highly variable, he then proceeds to assume precisely what his argument has made problematic, namely that such prescriptions do 'specify a great deal' for each and every scientist. If a value can be interpreted differently by every individual scientist, it is difficult to see how it can incline scientists to act in a similar manner. Two scientists may, of course, both report that they are considering, say, the accuracy of a theory. But the term *accuracy* may have different meanings for these scientists. The fact that, on some occasions, they use similar or identical terms to describe their choices does not necessarily mean that these choices have been guided in the same direction by common values. In other words, the existence of a common evaluative vocabulary does not imply that actors have a shared basis for choice.

There is, we suggest, a fundamental inconsistency in this part of Kuhn's analysis. For instance, a value like *simplicity* can be said to specify 'what each scientist must consider' only if we can extract from the multiplicity of individual interpretations some common formulation of what *simplicity* means. If we cannot state what simplicity means for scientists generally, we cannot describe what this value specifies for the 'enterprise of science'. But if we *can* extract a common meaning '*X*' for this criterion, we could then formulate the following universally binding rule: Consider those theories which are simplest in the sense of having the quality X. Although Kuhn denies that universal rules exist which can dictate theory choice, his account of how scientific values operate seems to require such rules. It seems, therefore, that if we are to build on Kuhn's analysis we must either return to a more traditional conception of rules of theory choice in order to maintain his view of cultural constraint in science or we must adopt some alternative conception of 'cultural constraint' which is consistent with the existence of marked individual variation in the interpretation of rules. We will pursue this second possibility.

Cultural constraint and cultural reproduction

Although Kuhn's analysis of theory choice hinges on the issue of the variability of scientists' interpretation of given criteria, he makes no attempt to examine systematically the range of variation displayed in empirical data. He writes consistently as if the meaning of a rule may vary from one individual to another, but as if variability necessarily ends there. Thus he states that in order to understand how the same rules are interpreted differently, we must 'deal with characteristics which vary from one scientist to another' (1977: 324). It seems to be assumed that *each scientist* operates with a uniform interpretation of each rule of theory choice. That is, each researcher has a personal algorithm which he has fashioned out of available cultural resources, including, in particular, the values of science, although there is no shared algorithm of theory choice. This assumption is reflected in his account of the factors which explain individual variability, for such factors as scientific biography, wider social commitments, and personality are likely to remain stable for any specific actor. Whether or not Kuhn is correct in treating the rules as having determinate meanings for each individual is primarily an empirical matter, and we will examine some relevant data below. For the moment, however, let us no longer *assume* that each scientist always interprets each criterion in the same way. Let us explore the analytical implications of abandoning this assumption.

The notion of invariance of rules is closely associated with the idea of rules as sources of constraint. On the one hand, if each scientist is committed to a set of rules and to an invariant interpretation of these rules, then his acts of choice between theories will necessarily follow from the rules and proceed in a specifiable manner. His choices are constrained by the rules and can be explained by reference to them, even though his particular interpretation of the rules may be explicable by reference to a specific set of historical and biographical factors. On the other hand, if each scientist can interpret the same rules differently on different occasions and/or in different interpretative contexts, the rules themselves provide no definitive constraint either upon his acts of theory choice or *upon the way that he describes his acts of choice in terms of the rules*. His specific theory choices can be derived unequivocally neither from the rules nor from some combination of rules plus invariant biographical factors. But equally important, if we are concerned with using the evidence generated by scientists to document the character of their actions, we have to accept that the criteria of theory choice can be *used by* scientists as well as exerting constraint upon them. Potentially, the criteria and values of theory choice provide a flexible cultural resource which the individual may interpret to suit his actions or, more accurately, which he may employ to portray his actions. As Mulkay and Milic have pointed out, recognition that actors can interpret given rules in various ways opens up new analytical possibilities.

> Instead of concentrating exclusively on rules as sources of constraint, we can begin to explore some of the other uses to which rules are put. Once we think of rules as forming a large evaluative repertoire, from which participants can select and interpret flexibly, it becomes possible to recognize that rules can be used by participants to convey to their colleagues, and to the analyst, various *versions* of specific or recurrent actions. In other words, rules can be used to characterize actions as well as to constrain them. (Mulkay and Milic 1980)

A particular rule or value, then, *may* be used to constrain or guide an individual's choice of a specific theory. But it may equally well be used by that individual as, say, a justification for a choice which may or may not have had its origins elsewhere. Furthermore, in order to make his use of the rule effective as a justification, the actor will *present* his action as following necessarily and exclusively from the rule (Mulkay 1980). Thus, the kind of interpretative flexibility enjoyed by participants will often make it impossible for the analyst to infer from their statements what influence the rule actually exerted on the 'concrete act' of theory choice. From actors' statements about theory choice, it will be impossible to distinguish an act of choice guided by a rule from an act of justification in which that rule is employed after the fact. If rules and values of theory choice can be used by actors as resources for constructing variable accounts of their actions, then the analyst is unable to assume that the link between act and rule created by a participant in any one or more of his accounts represents the actual link determining his choice of a particular theory. Moreover, the analyst has no way of deciding on the rules which led to a particular choice that does not depend on actors' statements; the analyst cannot replace participants' readings of the rules with his own personal interpretations of these rules. In other words, if each individual's interpretations are variable, we will have to devise a form of analysis that is not undermined by the fact that our only access to the phenomena of theory choice is through members' statements, in which participants themselves may have contingently used the rules that we wish to employ as a definitive explanatory resource.

It is clear, then, that the degree of variation in individual scientists' interpretation of criteria of theory choice is a crucial issue. If the variability is considerable, we may have to treat as unanswerable the question with which we began, namely, how do scientists choose between theories? We may have to ask instead: How do scientists themselves use rules, values and criteria of theory choice to give specific, but variable, meanings to their supposed acts of choice on particular occasions or in certain kinds of interpretative contexts? Let us see whether we can begin to resolve this issue by an examination of some empirical material.

The variability of individuals' criteria of theory choice

Our objective in this section is to show that individual scientists employ their apparently specific criteria of theory choice in a highly variable manner. We will look closely at passages taken from interviews with three biochemists, comparing the use made by each respondent of specific criteria as he gives accounts of the adequacy of different theories and as he makes sense of his own scientific judgements. All three scientists work on the topic of energy production in biological systems. The overall process which they are studying is called 'oxidative phosphorylation'. This process takes place in small particles called 'mitochondria'. Mitochondria are said to have two membranes and oxidative phosphorylation is said to be closely associated with the inner membrane. The end product of oxidative phosphorylation is ATP (adenosine triphosphate), which is a fundamental source of energy in living organisms. ATP is said to be created in a complex enzyme located in the mitochondrial membrane called the 'ATPase'. Further detail about the scientific issues in the field can be obtained from *Opening Pandora's Box* (Gilbert and Mulkay 1984), but it is not required to understand the material which follows.

We interviewed thirty-four scientists working on oxidative phosphorylation and on related topics. The interviews were recorded and transcribed in full. The quotations below are taken from the transcripts of three of these interviews. The number of transcripts examined is small because individual variability in accounts of theory choice can only be demonstrated by means of detailed comparison of two or more passages produced by the same person. We have used the minimum number of transcripts here in order to have enough space to bring out the implications of such data. Interested readers will find a great deal of similar data in our other papers on theory choice (Gilbert and Mulkay 1982; Mulkay and Gilbert 1983). In these three papers on this topic we have been able to present thirty-five passages from seventeen of our thirty-four respondents and to demonstrate, thereby, that scientists' variability in accounting is widespread and sociologically significant. This strategy of carrying out detailed analysis of multiple samples of qualitative data on specific topics follows from the discussion in Mulkay and Milic (1980: 93).

In the following passage the speaker is talking about a theory of how the ATPase works.

A (1) I would not say Watson's mechanism is incorrect. (2) I think it is 'optimistic' at this point. (3) I guess I am much more conservative by nature than he is and (4) I am looking at something simpler to explain things than the mechanism he is using. (5) This type of flip flop mechanism, it may be right. (6) You can't say it is wrong. (7) But on the other hand you can't say its right by any means. (8) Now that mechanism has been proposed for simpler enzyme systems and in all the cases where that's really been looked at very closely in similar systems it is proven to be not the case. (9) He certainly has experiments that are consistent with this hypothesis, but to my mind it is far from proven. (10) I would like to see it a little simpler. (Fasham 9)

Three considerations or criteria are advanced here as grounds for not accepting Watson's theory: that Watson's mechanism is not simple enough (sentences A4 and A10); that the type of mechanism he proposes has not been found to operate in enzymes which are simpler than the ATPase (sentence A8); and that, although there is some evidence in its favour, it has not yet been proven correct experimentally (A5-7 and 8-9).

The speaker does not need to claim that his criteria are widely accepted by other scientists. In no way does he suggest that they provide a shared algorithm. Indeed, he seems to propose in sentences three and four that his choice of the criterion of simplicity, or perhaps his interpretation of that criterion, is conditioned by his conservative personality. On the other hand, his references to proof, consistency with the evidence, and to what has been shown to be the case in simpler systems all seem to imply the existence of some standards which are shared. His own use of criteria is not presented as if it were totally idiosyncratic. Thus, this passage can be plausibly interpreted as furnishing support for Kuhn's view of theory choice: that is, it can be inferred from this account that Fasham chooses between theories by means of a coherent combination of objective and subjective, or shared and individual criteria.

As we look more closely at this scientist's talk about theory choice, however, we cannot sustain the view that he applies his criteria in uniform fashion. For, subsequently in the interview, he interprets each of his criteria quite differently as he discusses them in different contexts. Take the criterion of 'proof'. In quotation A it seems to be implied that biochemical analyses can be proven correct (A9). It would appear to be inconsistent to refuse to accept a theory because it has not yet been proven, unless proof is possible in principle. Yet shortly after the passage above, we find the following exchange:

B *Interviewer:* (1) Do you find that you have to adopt some working hypothesis of a mechanism in order to guide you in doing the experiments?
   Respondent: (2) Well, only in – sure. (3) I mean, you always have to have some working hypothesis that you can – (4) And then you do experiments to try to prove it or disprove it. (5) Well you never can prove it. (6) You try to do experiments to disprove the hypothesis. (Fasham 10)

This is an interesting passage, not only in terms of its content but also because the respondent corrects himself three times over in as many lines (B2-5). He seems to be struggling to find the right formulation of his own research practice. Each correction seems to lead to a stronger and more 'rigorous' version of his method. Eventually he conveys the idea that his research consists of developing a series of explicit working hypotheses which he then strives to disprove (B6). This account meets the needs of the particular conversational exchange. It deals directly with the interviewer's question. It ends up by showing the respondent to be conducting his research in textbook fashion and it thereby forestalls any further questions which might have been elicited had the speaker developed his 'well, only in –' opening phrase.

In the process, however, the speaker has undermined, or at least radically changed, the character of one of his three criteria for refusing to accept Watson's theory. For he now says clearly that proof is unattainable in principle. Thus, on adjacent pages of the interview transcript, we find Fasham maintaining that proof is impossible (sentence B5) *and* that, in part, he finds Watson's theory unacceptable because it is far from proven (A9). Therefore, there is no point in trying to infer from the speaker's discrepant statements whether or not his judgements have actually been constrained by an invariant criterion 'proven to be incorrect by the experimental evidence'. As we argued in the introduction, it is more appropriate to regard such criteria as resources for constructing meanings for participants' actions of theory choice. The criterion of experimental proof seems to be a verbal formulation that can be used as a means of expressing particular judgements of theoretical adequacy in plausible terms, but which can equally well be replaced with a notion which the speaker himself treats as contradictory (B4-5). Which of these notions is selected by the speaker seems to depend on subtle interpretative exchanges occurring in the interview, and, presumably, in other social interactions.

In the next quotation the same scientist is discussing alternatives to Watson's mechanism and sketching the outlines of his own working hypothesis.

C (1) I think the other main contender for a mechanism is some sort of complex regulation and it is pretty clear that *some* complex regulation is going on. (2) It could be some combination of the two, because you know you have more nucleotide binding sites than you have catalytic sites. (3) There is no doubt about that. (4) So, I look for some variant of these two mechanisms. (5) That would be my working hypothesis right now. (Fasham 11)

Having dismissed Watson's hypothesis partly on the grounds that some simpler mechanism is required, the speaker then advances as his alternative an hypothesis which combines Watson's mechanism with 'some sort of complex regulation'. It is difficult to see how this notion could be preferable to Watson's because it is simpler. Complexity is presented as a major defect of Watson's theory, but is the virtue of Fasham's own conception. Thus, once again, an apparent criterion of theory choice is applied selectively and its significance altered in a way which lends support to the speaker's own scientific judgements. The speaker does not seem to be assessing the various hypotheses against invariant criteria of proof or simplicity. Rather, having used one interpretation of these criteria to 'show' that Watson's ideas are unacceptable, the speaker appears subsequently to reverse their implications for theory choice when justifying his own research practice or when formulating his own alternative hypotheses.

Fasham's use of the remaining criterion is somewhat similar, as we can observe in the following quotation. In this passage, he begins by explaining why findings with respect to simple systems can be used, as he suggested in assessing Watson's mechanism, as a standard against which to assess those proposed for more complex systems. As he proceeds, however, the cogency of this procedure is progressively weakened.

> **D** (1) There aren't as many pitfalls awaiting you in these simple systems. (2) They are much better to find molecularly and the possibilities are much restricted. (3) So in that sense they are simpler. (4) But any complex biological system I would say is similar in working out. (5) There are others that are equally complex. (6) Any biological system is – that becomes the whole interesting thing to try and filter your way through things to see your way to the crux of the problem without getting lost into a bunch of blind alleys ... (7) When you talk about mechanisms, you have to talk about your experiences with simpler systems. (8) It may be that your experience with simpler systems is not relevant. (9) It is possible, you never know ... (10) Even in some of the simpler systems there are some simple chemical mechanisms where there are controversies going. (11) For example, one amusing controversy in gas phase kinetics ... [is] a very great reaction involving two molecules in the gas phase. (12) There are at *least* two plausible mechanisms and there is no experiment that has yet been done to distinguish between these two plausible mechanisms. (13) That's a very simple case. (14) So you imagine the difficulty in the more complex case. (Fasham 12, 21-3)

The speaker begins and ends this quotation, which is selected from a longer passage on the same topic, by asserting the relevance of simple systems for the understanding of complex systems. But whereas at the beginning of this passage, as in the early comments on Watson's optimism, simple systems are depicted as particularly helpful points of reference (D1-3), by the end of the passage the message has become that so-called 'simple systems' are themselves complex (D13-14). Fasham weakens his earlier use of simple systems by emphasizing that all biological systems are similar in so far as the task of theoretical inference is difficult (D4-6), that the interpretation of data in simple systems is often uncertain (D10-12), and that there is no independent way of knowing whether one's experience with simpler systems is relevant in any particular more complex case (D7-9). Thus the criterion of 'correspondence with simpler systems' is here depicted as open-ended and indeterminate. Fasham does not employ this criterion selectively in justifying his own ideas, as with the previous two, but he does give a much weaker general account of the relevance of simpler systems for the understanding of complex systems than is implied in his earlier appraisal of Watson's theory.

In order to show that the kind of interpretative variability illustrated above is not peculiar to the one interview transcript examined so far, let us look at a second example. The speaker in the following passages is comparing two general theories of oxidative phosphorylation: the chemiosmotic theory of Spencer and Perry's paired moving charge theory. For this speaker, in this interview, there were no other important hypotheses in the field. One technical point needs to be understood in order to grasp the meaning of this respondent's remarks. The Spencer model proposes that the processes of oxidative phosphorylation operate across a closed biological membrane or 'vesicle' and that without a closed membrane oxidative phosphorylation cannot occur. Perry's PMC model does not require this assumption. The processes described in this latter model can operate even if the membrane is disrupted. Thus observing whether or not oxidative phosphorylation persists in situations where the membrane is ruptured is one obvious way of testing the two theories experimentally. Oxidative phosphorylation is described in this passage as a 'coupled' reaction, that is, as involving several processes which are linked or coupled together. It is implied by the chemiosmotic hypothesis that various other 'coupled' processes are dependent on the existence of an undisrupted membrane.

The speaker in passage E, Scott, describes some of his work on this issue. He tells how his technique for disrupting the membrane turned out to inhibit the respiratory process which is also vital to oxidative phosphorylation and how, as a result, his initial experiments were equivocal because the absence of oxidative phosphorylation could be attributed to the lack of respiration. He then says that he examined a simpler subsidiary process, that of the exchange of ATP and inorganic phosphate, which is also a coupled reaction and which therefore, according to the chemiosmotic theory, could only occur if the vesicles used in the experiment remained intact. When the speaker carried out these experiments, he was a junior member of Perry's laboratory. By the time of the interview, he had moved elsewhere.

E   (1) Then, when I came to Perry's lab, the whole thing got very fascinating ... (2) His idea was demolishing the membrane and showing how you still got coupling. (3) That would be an unequivocal disproof of the Spencer model. (4) And when he was first telling me that, I thought it was totally unlikely. (5) But he suggested a fascinating idea of using a compound called lysolecithin and I had some experience with it ... (6) It seemed that lysolecithin was damaging respiration. (7) If you can't have respiration, you can't see if you have any ox. phos. (8) I decided to look at a simpler reaction called ATP-Pi which is definitely a coupled reaction OK. (9) Although some people in the field may be sceptical, but those that know enough about coupling know its a powerful coupling reaction ... (10) So this reaction didn't require respiration ... (11) And we demolished the membrane OK, really demolished it. (12) We did electron microscopes to show there was no vesicles possible or anything possible, mini-vesicles that were so small you couldn't see them. (13) Now under these conditions we still got 30 percent of ATP-Pi exchange ... (14) It was totally reproducible ... (15) That was tremendously damaging to the Spencer model OK. (16) You know, here I am, I was a believer in the Spencer model. (17) I was totally floored, it blew my mind. (18) I did that, I succeeded, I was totally floored ... (Scott 7-8)

This passage appears initially to be fairly straightforward. Scott seems to accept Perry's view that demolishing the membrane and retaining coupling, that is, retaining oxidative phosphorylation, would unequivocally disprove Spencer (E3-4). He also claims that, in his view, the ATP-Pi exchange is definitely a coupled reaction and therefore equivalent experimentally to oxidative phosphorylation (E8-9). He then goes on to maintain that he completely demolished the membrane (E11-12), that he still got an appreciable ATP-Pi exchange (E13), that this result was tremendously damaging to Spencer's theory (E15), and that his belief in that theory was seriously shaken (E16-18).

This, then, is an informal account of the theoretical implications of a key experiment. The dependence of coupled reactions on the existence of an intact vesicle is presented as a clear criterion of theoretical adequacy. If the presence of the membrane is *the* crucial difference between the two theories, and if they are more or less equally satisfactory in other respects, one might have expected Scott to continue by saying that he had adopted the PMC model in place of the chemiosmotic hypothesis in response to experimental findings. Later in the interview, Scott did provide explicit evaluations of the two models. These are reproduced in quotations F and G. They are difficult to reconcile with passage E.

F (1) I think that the strength of Perry's model, this is my own personal opinion, rests on the strength of Spencer's model. (2) The weakness of Perry's model rests on the weakness of the Spencer model. (3) I don't think it goes much beyond where the Spencer model left off. (4) You might say I don't agree with Perry on that. (5) I don't think it explains anything much more than the Spencer model. (6) He does have an explanation for how you get coupling in a non-vesicled system. (7) OK, that's the difference between his model and the Spencer model ... (8) I always felt that [Perry's] model was explaining control. (9) But I never could see him explaining that at all, it made no sense to me. (10) It really didn't say anything about it, didn't predict it, and didn't help at all after we did it. (11) Neither did Spencer's model explain it in that sense... (Scott 13)

G (1) I don't think bioenergetics is solved. (2) Spencer didn't explain anything, his model is incorrect. (3) I think there's got to be a new model which engulfs the Spencer model, but yet dramatic and engulfs other aspects of it. (4) Perhaps the aspects of control too.

Interviewer: (5) Apart from the control aspect, do you have any other features which are completely unexplained?

Respondent: (6) Well no (long pause) (7) I think the Spencer model pretty well explains most phenomena. (8) The only thing it doesn't explain is how its possible to get non-vesicular coupling. (9) I mean, its a nice model, because it really has explained almost everything, and that's why the field is closing its books. (10) You know, there are very few observations, at least there may be a few detailed observations which, you know, if I rack my brain I can come up with some of them ... (11) I don't see these as really major against the Spencer model ...

Interviewer: (12) How many other major models do you think there have been in the field, apart from Spencer's?

Respondent: (13) In my opinion, there is no model except Spencer's. (14) And maybe Perry's. (15) Perry saw there was no model beside Spencer's. (16) And he knew enough – he understood exactly what a model was and was shot from trying to put forward a model rather than just some kind of – (17) You see, the idea of a model, it tries to explain everything, not just a mundane detail ... (18) So I don't see any other models beside the Spencer model and the Perry model. (Scott 22-3)

The variability of Scott's statements about theory choice in these passages is considerable. By the end of quotation E, he seems to have used his experimental criterion to show the inadequacy of the chemiosmotic theory. Quotation F begins with a direct comparison between the two models, which can be heard to some extent as favouring Perry's model (F3 and 6). Thus, although Perry's model is said to be difficult to distinguish from Spencer's (F1-2), the suggestion seems to be that it has gone at least a little way beyond that of Spencer (F1 and 6). Furthermore, the ability of the PMC model to satisfy the experimental criterion developed in quotation E is clearly noted (F6). As a whole, however, quotation F conveys the idea that there is virtually nothing to choose between the two hypotheses. In sentences 1 and 2, Scott is making a point made by several other respondents: Perry's theory has incorporated some of Spencer's theoretical notions. In so far as this is the case, Scott suggests, the two models have more or less the same merits and defects. Moreover, to say that Perry's model 'doesn't go much beyond' Spencer's (F3-6) is likely to be taken to mean that Perry's model is actually no better at all than that of Spencer. The negative form of sentences F3-5 shows that they are designed to *deny* any claim to theoretical superiority on behalf of Perry's model: 'I *don't* think Perry's model goes much beyond ... '; 'I *don't* agree with Perry ... '; 'I *don't* think Perry's model explains .... ' Similarly, in the closing sentences (F8-11), Scott appears to find the two theories equally unsatisfactory in accounting for the phenomenon of *control*, that is, for the overall processes of regulation in oxidative phosphorylation. In passage F, then, where he most explicitly compares the two theories, Scott comes down clearly on neither side.

If we take Scott's experimental criterion as providing an invariant and fundamental evaluative standard which can supply unequivocal disproof (E2-3), it is a little surprising that he does not express greater support for the PMC model in quotation F; given that this model is said to be very similar to its competitor, except for the crucial fact that it alone is consistent with Scott's experimental findings on disrupted membranes. In passage F, Scott seems to treat his experimental criterion as less significant than he does in quotation E. One possible interpretation of the speaker's apparent equivocation in passage F may be that he regards both theories as so woefully inaccurate as to make firm preferences one way or the other somewhat inappropriate. However, we have already heard Scott stating that before his lysolecithin experiments, he had believed in the chemiosmotic theory and that he was staggered to find that his results were inconsistent with Spencer's model (E16-18).

Thus, if we are committed to making coherent sense out of all of these statements, it does not seem that this interpretation is satisfactory. Scott's accounts of the criteria of theory choice and of the merits of these two theories continually generate inconsistencies, no matter which interpretation we propose. Given that the strengths and weaknesses of the two theories are very similar, that both theories therefore are worthy of belief, that the credibility of the chemiosmotic theory has, however, been severely damaged by the lysolecithin experiments, and that the PMC model explains the results of these experiments, we would expect the speaker to decide clearly in favour of the PMC model. But in passage F he does not do so.

At the beginning of quotation G, however, the speaker seems to change his position once again and to move in the 'expected' direction. He now states that Spencer's model is incorrect and actually explains nothing (G1-4). It is difficult to reconcile this with his previous claim to have been a believer and to have been surprised by the model's one major experimental failure. However, one might try to use the wholesale rejection of Spencer's model at the start of quotation G to reinterpret quotation F. One could suggest that, in the light of his statements in G, Scott can be seen as implicitly expressing a preference in F for Perry's PMC model and, therefore, as consistently applying his experimental criterion in Perry's favour. Unfortunately, this interpretation is immediately overturned by the speaker's next statement (G7), to the effect that Spencer's theory pretty well explains most things. From this point onward his advocacy of Spencer's theory becomes stronger and stronger. He maintains that Spencer explains everything of any importance, except for non-vesicular coupling (G6-8); that the theoretical adequacy of Spencer's model explains why the field is closing down (G9); that he can think of very few observations, and no major ones, which are inconsistent with Spencer's theory (G10-11); and that Spencer's theory provides the only real model in the field, with the possible exception of Perry's (G13-18).

In considering the case of Scott, we have moved away from formal criteria like *scope* and *simplicity* and toward a specific experimental criterion formulated in a particular cognitive setting. We have seen that it is extremely difficult to extract from Scott's statements any clear, invariant meaning for this criterion which can be taken to be guiding his theory choice. At the end of passage G, he introduces for the first time a formal criterion of theoretical adequacy. Theories, or models, should 'try to explain everything' (G17) he suggests. But this criterion in no way resolves our interpretative difficulties. Indeed, it makes them more intractable. For it appears to require Scott to abandon the chemiosmotic theory, which cannot explain non-vesicular coupling, in favour of the PMC model, which can. In other words, Scott's formal criterion seems to strengthen the case for the theory which he does not endorse. Thus, these passages from Scott's transcript illustrate how a combination of a formal criterion with a more substantive experimental criterion may produce an algorithm which can be used to establish the relative adequacy of the theories, in terms of the characteristics attributed by the speaker himself to these theories, yet which diverges from the speaker's statements about his theoretical evaluations.

The speaker's interpretative variability follows not only from his differing interpretation of the criterion of *adequacy* but also from his radically different explications of a given theory at different junctures. For instance, at one point Spencer's theory is said to be incorrect and not to explain anything (G1-2). Shortly afterwards, it is said to explain most phenomena fairly well (G7), and later still to be the only real model in the field (G13). Of course, one can argue that not all of these statements should be taken literally, and that those which are inconsistent with the speaker's characteristic utterances should be reinterpreted to make them conform to his usual line. Thus, viewed in its context, Scott's statement that chemiosmosis did not explain anything might mean simply that it had some inadequacies. One difficulty with this approach is that each specific formulation used by Scott is closely linked to other claims, and that these other claims become problematic as soon as one begins this kind of reinterpretation. For instance, Scott's claim that chemiosmosis is incorrect enables him to maintain that there has to be a new model that engulfs chemiosmosis. This inference would not follow from a reinterpretation of his prior statement. Similarly, his subsequent characterization of chemiosmosis as explaining almost everything provides the basis for his assertion that the field is closing its books (G9) rather than searching for a new model. Thus, each particular characterization of a given theory plays its part in the respondent's talk by enabling him to devise other associated statements about the field or about his own actions. In this way, the speaker constantly reinterprets the social world in which his own scientific activities occur as he engages in various kinds of interpretative work. In an important sense, therefore, speakers are not necessarily talking about the 'same' theory in different passages of a transcript, even though they may use a single term such as 'chemiosmotic model', any more than they are appraising the theory by means of the same invariant substantive or formal criteria.

Let us consider one more example of interpretative variability, before we turn to consideration of its analytical implications:

H (1) There were lots of hypotheses, especially the chemical one which was the only prevailing one when I was receiving my lectures. (2) I don't believe anyone took it all that seriously as a framework for a hypothesis. (3) There certainly wasn't any kind of detailed information on it at all. (4) It was actually very hard to test, because if something didn't agree with it, what usually happened was that something else was introduced. (5) This happened somewhere along the line, I've forgotten exactly when, a couple of times. (6) That kind of hypothesis is almost useless. (7) You can explain the data with it, but if you have to keep modifying it to keep up to date, I think something's wrong. (8) You couldn't test it and throw it out … (9) Its adding another layer on the hypothesis. (10) You can keep on doing this as long as you want, but to me its violating basic scientific principles. (11) Eventually you have to discard a very complicated hypothesis for a simpler one …

Interviewer: (12) Do you think there's a clear difference between the chemical intermediate theory and chemiosmosis in this respect, in the sense that chemiosmosis has been changed in the light of further evidence?

Respondent: (13) To me the chemiosmotic hypothesis ... [equals] three basic postulates, in which you have proton translocation by the chain, you have a reversible proton translocating ATPase; these are both in membranes. (14) As far as I am concerned that is the chemiosmotic hypothesis. (15) Now to make this whole thing reasonable you have to start coming up with mechanisms, specific mechanisms ... (16) These are Spencer's specific suggestions and these are only suggestions as far as I can see. (17) There is no evidence for them really. (18) Working hypotheses or how this thing *could* work. (19) They may turn out to be wrong. (20) Does that mean the chemiosmotic hypothesis is wrong? (21) No, of course it doesn't! (22) It means that there is a specific way in which this whole process has been suggested to occur is wrong perhaps ... (23) Well, you know, we've gotten this far and we still don't know how its done. (24) I used to apologize to people for this until I realized that really nobody knows how any substance crosses a biological membrane ... (Shaw 39-40)

In this passage, the speaker compares what most respondents described as the two main hypotheses in the area, namely the chemical and the chemiosmotic. He comes down fairly clearly in favour of chemiosmosis (H20-21). As he phrased it elsewhere in the interview, chemiosmosis is 'to me now above being a working hypothesis – this is the way it works instead' (Shaw 19). Shaw mentions three ways in which the latter hypothesis is scientifically superior. In the first place, the chemical theory could explain the data, but it had to be modified continually in order to do so. As a result, it was impossible to test it and throw it out (H4-8). Secondly, it failed to provide any detailed information on the processes involved (H3). And, thirdly, it was too complicated. These criteria are stated explicitly and the requirements of testability and simplicity seem to be identified as basic scientific principles.

How far, then, do these principles appear to direct the speaker's choice? Are they applied uniformly to the two hypotheses in question, in a manner which forces him to choose one hypothesis rather than the other? In passage H, only passing reference is made to the failure of the chemical theory to furnish detailed information. The other two criteria are given more prominence and the passage is organized primarily to reveal the inadequacy of the chemical theory in relation to *simplicity* and *testability*. However, the speaker's reluctance in this passage to commit himself to the detailed mechanism of chemiosmotic theory (H16-23) leads him to interpret the criteria quite differently as he moves from the chemical to the chemiosmotic theory.

Consider first the criterion of *simplicity*. Shaw's claim seems to be that whereas the chemical theory had to be continually elaborated in order to deal with each new observation, the chemiosmotic theory has been successfully restricted to three basic postulates. He seems to weaken his own case, however, by his subsequent comments and to change the meaning of the criterion as he applies it to the theory which he advocates. The chemical theory is taken as including those theoretical elements which were reformulated in response to empirical results. Accordingly, the chemical theory is presented as varying along with those results and thereby becoming increasingly complicated (H4-9). In contrast, the three postulates of chemiosmosis are treated as being necessarily quite separate from the detailed processes at work. No matter what the empirical findings, therefore, Shaw's account of the chemiosmotic theory can stress its simplicity and invariance (H13-22). Thus it appears that, in this passage, the speaker creates the impression that the two theories differ in their degree of simplicity by means of an interpretative fiat. Unlike the theory he is condemning, the speaker's own theory is defined in such a way that its basic simplicity can never be in doubt.

The speaker's variable interpretation of the criterion of *testability* also hinges on his keeping the chemiosmotic theory removed, interpretatively, from the impact of experimental evidence. He repudiates the chemical theory partly on the grounds that it could not be tested. Predictive failure could not lead to rejection because, whatever the observational results, the chemical theory could always be changed accordingly (H6-8). However, the separation which Shaw achieves in his account of chemiosmosis has precisely the same consequence for this theory. As presented in this passage, chemiosmotic theory is no more open to disproof than is the chemical theory. Negative evidence is simply taken to mean that one specific interpretation of the basic postulates has been ruled out. But this does not affect the confidence with which the speaker maintains the validity of the postulates themselves (H20-2).

In addition, the final statement in this passage (H24) has the effect of legitimating *any* failure on the part of chemiosmotic theory to cope with empirical material. If 'nobody knows how any substance crosses a biological membrane', then it seems to follow that the chemiosmotic theory can neither be expected to explain how protons cross mitochondrial membranes nor be judged unsatisfactory for failing to deal adequately with this topic. No attempt is made, however, to devise such an all-embracing defence for the predictive failures of the chemical theory. Although the speaker characterizes the two theories in terms which make them both appear untestable, only the chemical theory is condemned for this reason, while the chemiosmotic theory is buttressed by statements which make empirical inadequacies expectable and allowable. This speaker is able to display the superiority of chemiosmosis, not by applying invariant criteria to two given theories, but by characterizing the theories and by interpreting the criteria in ways which ensure that that interpretative outcome is attained.

Discussion

In the previous section we have illustrated the kind of variability which is typical of scientists' talk about theory choice. In several other papers, we have tried to show how such material can be analyzed, despite its variability (Gilbert and Mulkay 1982; Mulkay and Gilbert 1983). In this article, our objective has been different, namely, to show how traditional conceptions of theory choice are unable to cope fully with the type of data presented above. Let us make this clearer by reconsidering the data in relation to the two views of theory choice identified in our opening sections.

The quotations which we have examined are as appropriate as they could be for analysis in traditional terms, for we have chosen passages where the scientist concerned has explicitly formulated criteria and/or rules of theory choice. Consequently, there are parts of these passages which can easily be seen as exemplifying the traditional conception of theory choice. For example: 'You try to do experiments to disprove the hypothesis' (B6); 'That would be an unequivocal disproof of the Spencer model' (E3); 'The idea of a model, it tries to explain everything' (G17); 'To me its violating basic scientific principles. Eventually, you have to discard a very complicated hypothesis for a simpler one' (H10-11). Such more or less explicit statements of rules and evaluative criteria occur only occasionally in our scientists' talk during interviews. But when they do appear, they are presented either as if the speaker's adoption of a theory necessarily followed from the rule(s) in question (e.g. B6) and/or as constituting grounds for rejecting other scientists' theory choices because they did not satisfy these rules (e.g. H9-11). The concepts employed, such as 'unequivocal disproof' and 'basic scientific principles', seem to imply a considerable degree of cultural consensus among scientists on such matters. The criteria and rules are, to some extent, presented as embodying shared obligations with respect to theory choice.

Yet at the same time, speakers often suggest that other scientists would not necessarily accept their criteria or make the same choices. They frequently imply that there is no *shared* algorithm. Indeed, in several of these passages, the speaker states explicitly that the criteria he is applying are peculiarly his own, even in situations where the criteria are being used to condemn or criticize other scientists' choices. For instance, Fasham in passage A acknowledges that his less 'optimistic' assessment of Watson's theory may be due to his conservative personality, which leads him to adopt especially restrictive criteria of theoretical adequacy. Similarly, Shaw states that the principles he formulates are basic *to him* (H10-11). It is not clear from the transcript whether this statement means that the principles are not held by any other scientists or whether the speaker's *interpretation* of these principles is idiosyncratic. Either way, however, it is implied that his judgements are highly individual, albeit derived from rules.

There is much evidence in our transcripts that scientists often depict the implementation of rules of theory choice as highly personal and varying from one researcher to another. In addition, it is easy to document instances in which an ostensibly standard criterion is used in radically different fashions by different scientists. For instance, the experimental criterion of Perry and Scott, which Scott presents as providing the basis for an unequivocal disproof of Spencer's hypothesis, was interpreted quite differently by Spencer in evaluation of Scott's actual findings. Scott and Perry maintained that they had disproved Spencer's chemiosmotic theory; according to the theory, an intact membrane was required for the operation of various coupled processes associated with oxidative phosphorylation, and they had shown experimentally that one such process could occur in totally disrupted membranes. In a letter to Perry, however, Spencer stated that 'the experiments that you cite by Bailey and Scott on the lysolecithin-treated mitochondrial vesicles [merely] demonstrate the remarkable robustness of the vesicle preparations' (Letter 57). Spencer does not reject the experimental criterion employed by Perry and Scott, but interprets quite differently their specific attempt to apply the criterion.

The interpretative procedures used by the two parties to give meaning to the experimental criterion are markedly discrepant. Perry and Scott maintain that they have destroyed the membrane and that, as biochemical activity persists, the membrane is not required for such activity. Spencer, in contrast, appears to construct his response by beginning with the observation of biochemical activity rather than with the supposed rupture of the membrane. His interpretation seems to be that, given that biochemical activity persists and that there is much other evidence that it depends on a membrane, then Scott's findings *must* mean that the attempt to destroy the membrane has failed. In other words, Spencer is able to interpret Scott's observations without having to abandon his theory or to deny the putative experimental criterion. Evidently, all parties to this theoretical dispute could accept an experimental criterion for theory choice formulated in very general terms. But because different scientists judge the technical requirements of their 'shared' criterion very differently, they can reach diametrically opposed conclusions about theoretical adequacy on the basis of specific experimental results.

This example may seem to lend further support to Kuhn's view of theory choice. Not only do scientists themselves often talk as if they have their own individual algorithms, but it also appears that different individuals' theory choices are influenced by the same technical criterion, if not determined by it. There is no doubt, then, that Kuhn's analysis comes closer to the details of the empirical data than does the traditional approach to theory choice. Nevertheless, his approach seems to us to need further revision before it can cope fully with the kind of material we have presented.

Consider first the experimental criterion 'shared' by Spencer and Perry and Scott. This criterion can be said to be shared only if it is formulated in extremely vague terms – for example, 'Chemiosmosis will have been shown not to be (entirely) correct if oxidative phosphorylation (or other coupled processes) can be shown to occur in totally disrupted membranes'. But at this level of generality, the criterion cannot guide theory choice in any particular direction. In order to constrain choice it has to be further specified. Decisions have to be made about what constitutes a fully disrupted membrane, about which coupled processes are essential to the theory, and so on. At this more detailed level, Scott and Spencer do not agree; the criterion is no longer shared. As we have seen, they use markedly different interpretative procedures to give meaning to the components of the criterion. Thus, the criterion can only be said to be shared when it is formulated in a manner which cannot constrain theory choice. The criterion can only be said to constrain choice when it is interpreted at a level where Perry and Spencer disagree.

This example, then, illustrates that to refer to shared criteria is misleading unless one also includes the interpretative procedures whereby scientists give meaning to those criteria in specific instances. We cannot reconcile this conception of criteria with Kuhn's claim that criteria influence scientists in a specifiable direction, not the least because of Kuhn's observation of variability between scientists. Moreover, as we have shown above, the radical variation between the accounts of theory choice produced by each individual scientist is irreconcilable with the conception of cultural constraint which Kuhn seeks to retain. For if we cannot formulate a set of binding rules and interpretations for individual scientists, we can hardly do so for whole groups of scientists.

In the previous section, we presented material showing why it is unsatisfactory to replace the idea of shared algorithms of choice with a conception of each scientist operating in terms of a personal algorithm. We saw how each speaker interpreted given criteria differently in different passages and in devising assessments of different theories. For instance, we observed how Fasham asserted that Watson's theory was unacceptable because it had not yet been proven, yet in a subsequent passage maintained that proof of any theory was in principle unattainable. Similarly, we showed how Shaw formulated his principle of testability differently in condemning one theory and in warranting another. In the case of Scott, we showed how difficult it was to extract a coherent algorithm of theory choice from his divergent statements about the PMC and chemiosmotic models.

In the light of this material, we suggest that the idea of coherent individual algorithms for theory choice, like that of shared algorithms, is not appropriate to the data. In specific passages, the scientists quoted above make their theory choices appear to derive from binding rules and clear-cut criteria. But we have seen that this appearance of a necessary connection between criteria and particular choices is a members' interpretative accomplishment which cannot be accepted at face value by the analyst. For it is clear that the criteria identified by scientists in specific passages as being responsible for their choice of theory are indeterminate and capable of radically different interpretation by the same scientist. Thus, the basic concept of algorithmic theory choice, which is common to Kuhn's analysis as well as the more traditional approach, is inadequate as an analysts' concept. It is rather a *participants' interpretative method* for constructing versions of social actions. It is a method used by scientists to make their own actions seem unavoidable. It thereby enables scientists to furnish determinate explanations of their choices and, given the hearer's acceptance of the criteria cited, at the same time provides justification for these choices.

Participants use both the collective and individual versions of this interpretative method to devise accounts of theory choice appropriate for each specific occasion and each social context. As a result, their interpretations are highly variable. Most analysts are looking for invariant formulations of the cultural and social bases of scientists' choices, which will enable them to give definitive analytical versions of what happens in science and why. We suggest that the variability of scientists' interpretative work makes this traditional objective unattainable. Because they have adopted interpretative methods very similar to those used by participants, analysts' attempts to compile definitive composite accounts of theory choice will always be undermined by the diverse ways in which participants use these methods to generate incompatible accounts. An alternative approach is needed, therefore, which operates on an analytical level different from that of the scientists themselves and which assumes the variability of scientists' accounts of action.

We propose that analysts abandon the goal of trying to show that theory choices are made in conformity with one of the two existing views of theory choice. Instead, they should concentrate on describing how scientists use interpretative resources to construct differing versions of theory choice. The aim here is to discern how scientists organize their accounts of, or versions of, theory choice in ways which are appropriate to the interpretative settings in which these accounts are constructed. For instance, instead of trying to explain or justify scientists' theory choices in terms of personal and/or social algorithms, we should examine scientists' accounts to see if we could specify the circumstances in which scientists characterized their actions by means of each kind of algorithm. Our underlying assumption is that the analyst can never distil a definitive account of how choices are actually made from participants' variable accounts, but may be able to categorize the accounts themselves in ways that are meaningful to participants, to describe the methods and repertoires used by scientists to construct their accounts, and to identify some of the contextual features that participants take into consideration when devising one kind of account rather than another.

For example, it seems fairly clear that when scientists are engaged in formal scientific debate they tend to use a highly restricted and formalized interpretative repertoire to depict their actions, including their 'acts' of theory choice (Gilbert and Mulkay 1984). It seems likely that the traditional notion of a shared, universally compelling algorithm of theory choice will predominate in accounts scientists produce for formal scientific debate. In contrast, in informal settings, scientists' accounts of action are often very personal. Greater allowance is made for individual idiosyncrasy, and scientists are therefore likely to construct their accounts in terms of personal algorithms and other more contingent versions of social action. Whether or not this specific suggestion is correct, it illustrates a type of analysis that may be viable despite the variability of participants' interpretative practices – the attempt to link scientists' accounting procedures to variations in social context.

We are proposing, then, that the analysis of how scientists choose between theories be supplemented by an analysis of scientists' discourse about theory choice. This new approach to the analysis of data on theory choice has the advantage of helping us to understand why the existing body of analytical literature has adopted specific interpretative resources. For we can see how the contextual variations in scientists' accounting procedures mentioned above are reflected in the two main analytical perspectives on theory choice. The traditional approach distinguished between the context of discovery and the formal context of justification, and based its analysis on the versions of action produced by scientists for the latter context (Kuhn 1977). If we are right in suggesting that scientists tend to interpret their acts of theory choice in this context as if they derive from a shared cultural matrix, then it follows that analysts relying mainly on this type of data will be led toward the traditional analysts' view of theory choice. In short, traditional forms of analysis took over the interpretative method employed by participants in the context of formal discourse.

In recent years, however, many analysts, including Kuhn, have rejected the distinction between the two supposedly discrete domains of scientific action. They have argued that actions carried out in the formal arena are not separate from, and cannot be understood without reference to, the informal domain. They have accordingly come to take much more notice of scientists' informal accounts. In informal discourse they have observed both the wide range of variation between scientists in the interpretation of criteria of choice and indications of scientists' commitment to personal algorithms. Once again, the form of interpretation offered by the analyst is directly dependent on his selective recourse to versions of action produced by participants for a particular kind of context. We suggest that although Kuhn and others are correct in repudiating the traditional distinction between *contexts of action* in science, they have erred in failing to recognize the importance of separate *contexts of discourse about action* and in adopting forms of scientists' discourse prevalent in the informal context.

Our analytical approach, then, has the unique advantage of enabling us to begin to discern how analysts have constructed their own literature by adopting accounting forms used by participants in different interpretative contexts. In addition, there are several other advantages to the approach we are advocating. Firstly, it enables us to analyze the data that are directly available to us, namely, participants' documents, recorded statements and pictorial representations, instead of having to use these data merely as indicators of unobservable phenomena such as theory choice. Secondly, we are able to avoid treating actors as no more than passive respondents to a combination of cultural constraints and determining biographical factors. We regard them instead as actively constructing and reconstructing the meanings of their own actions. Participants' interpretative practices become the focus of our analysis. Thirdly, this approach is more consistent with what is now known about rules or prescriptions in general: namely, no rule can specify in full how it is to be applied to particular instances. In other words, the application of rules always depends on actors' use of supplementary interpretative procedures which can never themselves be formally specified in full. It is this open-endedness of rules which enables scientists, like other actors, to bring various apparently divergent actions within the scope of a given rule and to derive a given action from quite different rules. Thus, the approach proposed above has the final advantage of allowing for the existence of wide interpretative variations in the accounts of theory choice produced by scientists as they employ a flexible evaluative vocabulary of rules, formal and substantive criteria, and so on, in accordance with the variable requirement of divergent social situations. Because it is the only approach currently available which has fully recognized the extent of the variability of scientists' accounts of theory choice, it is the only approach which offers some promise of being able to cope analytically with that variability.

In this paper, we have not carried out any analysis of scientific discourse. We have simply tried to demonstrate the need for such analysis. This paper has dealt with basic methodological issues. It is appropriate, therefore, for us to end with broad procedural recommendations for analysts of theory choice and of other forms of social action in science. They cannot construct definitive accounts of how particular aspects of science actually work on the basis of the variable stories told by participants. Analysts should no longer seek to force scientists' diverse interpretative products on any given topic into one authoritative account of their own. They should instead strive to make sense of the multiplicity of ways in which scientists can present their theory choices and other actions. Analysts should seek to understand why so many different versions of events can be produced, instead of imagining that there is only one genuine version that the analyst will be able to piece together, ultimately. Analytically, there is much to be gained by setting free the multitude of voices with which scientists, and other social actors, speak.

11 Replication and mere replication (1986)[1]
with Nigel Gilbert

When philosophers and sociologists discuss the nature of experimental replication in science, they typically take as their point of departure the following kind of statement by participants.

> The essential basis for [physics'] success was the possibility of repeating the experiments. We can finally agree about their results because we have learned that experiments carried out under precisely the same conditions do actually lead to the same results. (Heisenberg 1975: 55)

Some sociologists and philosophers have taken such statements to imply that scientific researchers regularly try to repeat, and thereby check, the experimental work of their colleagues; and that such repetition plays an important part in explaining the success of science. In sociological parlance, this becomes: 'In science, the institutionalized requirement that new contributions be reproducible is the cornerstone of the system of social control' (Zuckerman 1977: 92).

Other sociologists, particularly those who have closely examined particular scientific debates, have rejected this view of science. They point out that scientists seem to be notably uninterested in repeating each other's experiments (Collins 1975). Furthermore, they argue that 'replicability' is never a clear cut criterion which can be applied unproblematically to specific knowledge-claims. They propose that the meaning of 'replication' in any particular instance is the outcome of social negotiation and, therefore, that 'replicability should be seen as part of the "rhetoric of presentation"' (Collins 1975: 208). Although the position adopted by these analysts is directly opposed to those mentioned in the previous paragraph, the point of analytical departure is exactly the same. Both analytical positions focus on what might be called the 'official view' of replication, although one position aims to confirm that official view, and the other undertakes to show that it is incorrect.

We suggest that this common point of analytical departure is based on a misconception. When scientists' discourse about replication is examined in detail, we find that scientists themselves furnish a much more subtle and intricate account than the supposed 'official view'. While we do not intend to suggest that their accounts will tell us how replication really does operate in science, the point of departure must surely be a proper appreciation of the complex, diverse and flexible interpretative work which is routinely carried out by scientists. Our aim here is therefore to begin to document some of the recurrent features of scientists' talk about replication; to show that scientists themselves use several conceptions of replication; and to begin to show how these apparently diverse conceptions of replication can be employed by scientists to portray their own and others' actions.

The empirical material presented below is taken from the transcripts of recorded interviews with biochemists in the field of oxidative phosphorylation. In our interviews with biochemists we regularly covered the topic of experimental replication. The topic was discussed with each speaker in general terms and also in relation to specific experiments in which he was interested or involved. The resulting discourse clearly displayed numerous recurrent features, some of which will be described and illustrated in the following sections.

Mere replication

Consider the following extract from an interview transcript.

A *Interviewer:*(1) How often do you actually check out in your own laboratory the kinds of results that you are finding in other people's papers?

Respondent:(2) We don't make *any* effort to repeat what somebody else does. (3) We have so many problems unexplored that result from our own initiative, that we would never think of going back to repeat something that Joe Blow does. (4) Its interesting, there is a laboratory that I've never visited and which shall remain nameless, but I have a colleague who has visited and he says that when you go there the Professor says, 'Well, here is Mr So-and-So, he's working on the Milner phenomenon. Here's Mr So-and-So, he's working on the Perry stuff.' (5) They actually take pride in the fact they are checking papers that have been published by others, with the result that a great deal of confirmatory work precludes their truly innovative contribution to the literature. (Waters 15-16)

This passage begins with one of the two interviewers asking the respondent how often he checks other scientists' experiments. This kind of question was asked regularly in the interviews and Waters' initial emphatically negative response (A2) is typical of the replies we received from our sample. In A3, Waters goes on to provide a justification for not repeating other people's work. The justificatory effect of this sentence depends on the assumption that experimental repetition is less valuable scientifically than the exploration of his own problems. The relative triviality of repetition is not stated explicitly here, but is implied by the dismissive turns of phrase, for example, 'we don't make *any* attempt', 'we would never think of', 'something that Joe Blow does'.

The invidious comparison between repetition and original research is developed further in the rest of the passage by means of an implicit condemnation of a laboratory which is supposed to specialize in replication. In A4, the speaker decides not to reveal the name of the laboratory. The only other situation in which our respondents ever insisted on the need for others' anonymity was in alleging acts of fraud. Thus in A4, Waters appears to treat regular experimental replication as a somewhat discreditable practice. Because the members of the nameless lab are depicted as pursuing goals that are, at best, relatively unimportant and, at worst, bordering on the disreputable, their actions are treated by Waters as somewhat puzzling. 'They actually take pride' in replication, when what they should obviously be doing is what Waters does, namely, making truly innovative contributions to the research literature (A5).

In passage A, then, we have a clear example of a certain kind of social action being depicted as 'mere replication', that is, as action which, because it does no more than repeat what other researchers have already done and reported, makes a comparatively unimportant contribution to science. We also have an emphatic denial by the speaker that he spends much of his time on mere replication. This latter point was repeated throughout our interviews. Scientists often replied succinctly to our questions about the frequency with which they carried out replications, saying: 'Occasionally, very rarely'; 'Never'; 'Rarely'; 'Very seldom, very seldom'; 'Only occasionally'; 'You can spend a lot of time doing other people's experiments over and life is short and we have our own fish to fry'. Only two of our 34 respondents claimed to replicate other people's experiments with any regularity.

If we were to accept these claims at face value, we might be tempted to conclude that very little replication occurs in this area of biochemistry and that the reason for this is that scientists avoid 'mere replication' in order to concentrate on making original contributions to the research literature. However, such conclusions, although consistent with some recent proposals by sociological analysts of scientific knowledge (Knorr 1977), would be premature. There is an apparent incongruity in scientists' talk about replication which must be resolved before we can be sure that we understand the significance of these interview data.

This incongruity is created by the fact that, when our scientists were asked about others' replication of their findings, they maintained, *without exception*, that their own findings *had* been replicated. The quotation below is a typical illustration.

B *Interviewer:*(1) Does this imply that you don't repeat other people's experiments?
Respondent:(2) Never.
Interviewer:(3) Does anybody repeat yours?
Respondent:(4) Oh, does anybody repeat my experiments? (5) Yes, they do. (6) I have read where people have purified the rat liver enzyme from other sources. (7) They get basically the same sub-unit composition. (8) I'm always happy, by the way, when I see that somebody has done something and repeated some of our work, because I always worry ... (Carless 51)

It is not *necessarily* incongruous to observe that our scientists claim that they rarely or never replicate others' work, whilst asserting that their own research is often replicated. It is possible that there exists another population of uninterviewed researchers working at nameless laboratories, all of whom are engaged in replicating our respondents' experiments. But if we disregard this as highly unlikely, we are left with two recurrent, yet somewhat paradoxical, components in our sample's discourse about replication. Let us try to remove the apparent incongruity by showing that our biochemists used (at least) two significantly different conceptions of replication.

Replicating by doing something different

In retrospect, on looking back through the interview transcripts, it seems clear that we, the interviewers, often operated with a concept which one could call 'exact replication' or 'close copying'. We frequently asked questions which implied that replication is simply an attempt to repeat another's experiment as closely as possible: 'How often do you repeat others' experiments?', 'Can we ask you a few questions about replications, repeating experiments? Do you do much of that, repeating other people's published work?'. In other words, at the time of the interviews, we interpreted 'replication' in accordance with the 'official view', as more or less the same as 'exact repetition'. It is this conception which scientists consistently refused to apply to their own actions.

Although respondents reject *this* conception of replication, they have available another significantly different one which, they say, is exemplified regularly in their field and in their own actions. Consider the following passage.

C (1) [There was a] problem about the cytochrome oxidase thing being either involved or not involved in simply moving protons across the membrane … (2) We looked to see if *we* could see in a steady state the operation of the cytochrome oxidase driving H^+ into the interior of the sub-mitochondrial particles. (3) We spent some time doing that experiment because it was a different approach from the one that this man Lucas had mainly used to produce *his* evidence that this proton movement was going on. (4) The crucial difference being that we were looking in a very slow time scale … (5) The way people have argued against him was that he was looking at changes in proton concentration in very short time scales and what he was looking at was side reactions which were not this cytochrome oxidase moving protons. (6) That explanation could hardly apply to our experiments because the side reactions couldn't last for ten minutes … (7) [So] we came to the conclusion that we agreed with him that cytochrome oxidase moves protons. (Finch 21-2)

It seems that all the elements of what we normally mean by 'replication' are present in this quotation, yet with no reference to anything resembling exact repetition or close copying. Indeed, it is precisely through the avoidance of close copying that replication is said to have been achieved. The speaker is talking about replication in the sense, firstly, that there is a prior experiment and a prior knowledge-claim which the speaker is said to be checking (C3). Secondly, the prior knowledge-claim is said to have been upheld by the speaker's own subsequent experimental work (C7). However, this confirmation is said to have been accomplished, not by repeating the other's observations in detail, but by doing something *different* which led to the *same* scientific conclusion (C3–4). Thus the notion of the 'sameness of results' is included in this conception of replication, but at a higher interpretative level than in the previous one. Let us clarify this point.

In passage C it is assumed that the proposition 'cytochrome oxidase moves protons across the sub-mitochondrial membrane' can be experimentally demonstrated in more than one way (C2-4). The proposition is taken to be a more general statement than that inherent in the observations furnished by any particular experimental set-up. Consequently, it can be verified, validated or replicated in various different ways. Thus, although replication undoubtedly involves a second experimenter reproducing the 'same' conclusion as a predecessor, the conception of replication employed here allows for the possibility that different experimental procedures may be used to accomplish this 'sameness'. Moreover, the use of a different experimental design is presented as having the added advantage that it may avoid some of the limitations of the initial method and thereby rebut potential or actual criticisms of that method; something which cannot be done by mere repetition of the original experiment (C5-6).

This alternative view of 'replication' occurs time and again in our transcripts. In the following quotation it seems to be combined with a vigorous rejection of a supposed accusation of 'mere replication'. Here we can clearly observe a speaker distinguishing between these two conceptions and selecting the former rather than the latter. The passage occurs in the course of a detailed discussion of the text of one of the respondent's papers.

D   *Interviewer:*(1) In the Introduction it says that Spencer and Norrell have already reported that you get a ratio of 2 per site.
  Respondent:(2) That's right, yes.
  Interviewer:(3) Given that that result already exists, did you feel that you were replicating results?
  Respondent:(4) No, not at all! (5) No, we said there, quite clearly, how those sorts of numbers had been obtained. (6) There's always criticism of any one method. (7) There are very few methods that are bomb-proof. (8) And they have achieved *their* results by taking mitochondria that had got the whole respiratory chain and using different reductants, using an NAD donating reductant or something like succinate. (9) What we did was to use the same substrate throughout really, NADH, and just vary the respiratory chain. (10) It was just the other way of doing it. (11) But an *independent* way of doing it, that was the important thing. (12) And yet we still got the same result. (Thompson 13)

The scientific issue which is being discussed here is similar to that covered in quotation C. There, the question was whether a particular component of the sub-mitochondrial membrane moves protons across the membrane. In passage D, the issue is *how many* protons move across the membrane at specific sites. The interviewer begins by pointing out that the ratio of 2 per site was already in the literature and the respondent has cited this earlier work. Was he, therefore, engaged in replicating these prior results? (D1-3). To begin with, the respondent emphatically denies this suggestion (D4). Yet, at the end of the passage, not only does he re-affirm the 'sameness' of the two sets of results, but he clearly makes this one of the central features of his experiment (D12).

What exactly is he denying, then, when he maintains that this is not a case of replication (D4)? The answer seems to be that he is denying that it is 'close copying' or 'mere replication'. His account of the meaning of his experiment is very like that of Finch in the previous example. He stresses that he used a *different* method (D8-11) to establish the *same* conclusion (D12); and he points out that the use of various independent methods strengthens confidence in the conclusion by showing that it does not depend solely on one specific kind of experimental manipulation (D6-7, 10-12). He is not, therefore, denying that he confirmed a previous experimental finding. He seems, rather, to be rejecting the invidious implication that his experiment was no more than a routine copy of somebody else's work. He rejects the application of the conception of 'mere replication' to his own actions and replaces it with a conception that we can call 'replication through experimental variation'.

In the last two passages, scientists have been talking about specific experiments and specific scientific issues. They have not themselves identified an alternative conception of replication that is available to researchers in general. We have extracted this alternative conception from their remarks. On numerous occasions in our interviews, however, participants did provide general versions of replication through experimental variation.

E   *Interviewer:* (1) When you read other people's work in the literature, how frequently do you replicate that work, repeat it in your own laboratory?
  Respondent: (2) Only occasionally, I would say. (3) It depends on the situation. (4) If its a directly relevant experiment, which it is important that I should be sure that its correct, for me to go on with my *other* experiments, then I would probably replicate it. (5) Normally I wouldn't repeat the experiment as such. (6) I might well do a similar experiment. (7) But I probably wouldn't do exactly the same experiment. (8) Because you can test them by doing them slightly differently ... (9) [So I would] do a *different* experiment. (10) Much more valuable to do a different experiment which gives rise to the same data and/or, at least, would give rise to a conclusion or data directly relevant to that answer ... (11) If you do an experiment a different way and you get anything which says that the other experiment is wrong, (12) and you have two or three ways of doing that, (13) *then* you can write a paper which is reasonably good for the literature. (14) Because, you haven't bothered to say the other person directly did the experiment wrong, (15) but rather you've shown that the conclusion which that experiment gave rise to is incorrect, by multiple criteria. (16) Then you've been constructive. (Hawkins 37–8)

In this passage, the respondent is asked a fairly general question and he replies in general terms, giving us a summary account of how replication fits into his research practice. Unlike the two previous speakers, he focuses on the possibility of failing to confirm others' results and shows that the strategy of experimental variation can be applied just as forcefully to such negative cases. He uses the interviewer's word 'replicate' to describe his actions (E4) and he seems to accept, initially, the interviewer's treatment of 'replication' and 'repetition' as synonymous. But in E5, he makes it clear that replication would not normally involve 'repeating the experiment as such'. From this point on, he explicitly formulates a version of replication through experimental variation. He distinguishes the general scientific issue or conclusion from any specific experiment or batch of data (E10, 15) and he stresses that the best way of testing a conclusion is by employing various different experimental techniques. Thus this speaker, like the two previous speakers, is proposing that a researcher can have greater confidence in a conclusion where the 'same conclusion' has been demonstrated by means of varying experimental methods.

Maintaining speakers' consistency

The existence of two conceptions of replication within this discourse enables us to resolve the apparent interpretative incongruity identified above. When our respondents deny that they engage in replication, they are denying that they 'merely replicate' others' work; and when they assert that their own work is replicated, they are claiming that others have confirmed their conclusions through experimental variation. This latter regularity in our respondents' discourse is exemplified in the following quotation.

> **F**   *Interviewer:* (1) You don't know whether somebody actually did repeat it?
> *Respondent:* (2) Let me see. (Long pause) (3) Once again, that fellow Reister obviously succeeded in getting coupling with lysolecithin-treated sub-mitochondrial particles. (4) He wasn't measuring the same coupling function that we were, but he measured an even more labile coupling function – energized transhydrogenase – and he definitely succeeded in repeating it. (5) He published it. (Scott 11)

Once again, we find the interviewer asking an apparently straightforward question about experimental repetition. This time, however, the respondent is not asked whether he repeats others' work, but whether they repeat his. He seems to find the question difficult to answer. Nevertheless, after reflection, he produces a positive reply; his experiment with lysolecithin was repeated at least once (F3). But this is immediately qualified in a way which makes it clear to the questioner that this repetition differed in some significant ways from his own experiment, whilst confirming what he has consistently presented as the central conclusion of that experiment, namely, that coupling does occur in lysolecithin-treated sub-mitochondrial particles (F4-5). In other words, he depicts this validation of his own conclusions in terms of replication through experimental variation.

This pattern is typical of respondents' replies to questions about replication of their own work. Such work is almost always said to have been replicated; but replicated in the sense that its conclusions have been used successfully as the starting point for further original experiment and analysis. We have, therefore, been able to rescue the consistency of scientists' accounts of replication. The apparent incongruity seemed to exist only because the interviewers introduced into the discourse a conception of replication which participants were unwilling to apply to their own actions. It will have been noted that the conception of replication repudiated by our respondents was equivalent to the 'official view' of replication discussed in the introduction to this paper.

Replication in principle, but not in practice

Does this mean, then, that a conception of exact replication or close copying has no part to play in scientists' discourse? In fact, this conception of replication does appear regularly in our interview material. It appears in the form of a pervasive assumption that exact replication, or at least very close experimental copying, is routinely possible in principle. Indeed, it seems to be for this reason that simple repetition of others' experimental results is treated as 'mere replication'. *Because* it is assumed that the great majority of findings are easily reproducible, it follows that no significant contribution to science will normally be made by showing that others' results can be reproduced.

Whereas some analysts of science have assumed that the replicability of results is constantly checked and other analysts have treated it as puzzling that, in practice, scientists seem to be relatively unconcerned with exact replication, our respondents simply take reproducibility for granted and, therefore, as something which does not normally require their attention. Even in accounts of cases where there is marked scientific disagreement, speakers do not usually question the reproducibility of each other's observations. Rather, they query the scientific *meaning* of others' experimental regularities; and questions of scientific meaning, they maintain, are best settled, not by means of simple repetition, but through the strategy of experimental variation.

Example G presents five passages illustrating this kind of discourse.

G (a) (1) With Milner's work on the respiratory chain, its a question of what the real substrate is sometimes, and in other cases its a question about whether the oxygen can really measure the initial kinetics. (2) I am not denying that the traces that he reports would happen if I went to his lab, it would happen. (3) The question is whether it really means what he says it means ... (Nesbitt 42)

(b) (1) We repeated all his experiments. (2) We can get the same answers that he did. (3) There's no question of not believing his data. (4) Its not a question of that at all. (5) We reported this and we showed that with our equipment and everything we get exactly the same answers. (6) That's all recorded in our papers. (7) But what was wrong was ... (Milner 13)

(c) (1) Anyone who has repeated that experiment, who did it the same way as we did it, gets the same answer that we got ... (2) So anyone who repeated this method got the same answer that we got. (3) Its just that when we start doing other methods ... then these don't seem to give us the same stoichiometry as the staining method. (4) Yet all of that's reproducible in everybody's hands, even with different enzymes. (5) So all I am saying is that we don't know what the right answer is, yet. (Carless 52-3)

(d) (1) I am primarily an experimentalist and I *love* clean experiments (2) and I don't give a damn whether my models are right or wrong. (3) The only thing I defend is my numbers. (4) I think its critical for a scientist to produce numbers that somebody else can reproduce. (5) The interpretation, you have to be very lucky to be right. (6) These systems are just so damn complicated that to come out right you have to be very lucky ... (7) Within yourselves you have to say, look if that interpretation is wrong its because that's all I could do on that day ... (Cookson 6, 26)

(e) (1) 99% of what people say in their experiments is quite true and ... (2) their interpretation can vary enormously ... (3) It won't be *untrue*. (4) It will be consistent with their facts. (5) So what you've got to judge is how reasonable their deductions are from the actual facts they give ... (6) It's very *rarely* that I come across a weakness in their actual observations ... (7) the actual work described in a publication is usually true. (8) However, its *quite* often the case that there are one or two other experiments which could have been done, either to establish their interpretation more firmly, or just to establish the *actual* point more firmly. (9) And *that's* what I'm looking for. (10) Further experiments which would bear upon the particular point. (Barton 34)

In passage Ga, the respondent begins by identifying two features of another scientist's work about which he is doubtful. He then makes it clear that he is not questioning the reproducibility of the observations (Ga2), but rather the meaning given to those observations. Thus any concern with exact replication seems irrelevant to this dispute. In Gb, the scientist mentioned in Ga is referring to the work of a third party. Like the previous speaker, this respondent also emphasizes that the data in question are reproducible (Gb1-5). (Although he claims to get 'exactly the same answers', it is doubtful from the rest of the transcript whether he is talking in any simple sense about 'exact replication'.) Having established beyond all doubt the reproducibility of the data, however, he proceeds immediately to demolish the conclusions derived from the data by the original experimenter. Carless, in Gc, shows how contradictory findings can be taken to be equally replicable and thus, once again, that the attainment of an agreed scientific meaning may be treated as quite independent of experimental reproducibility. He goes on to stress that scientific meaning has to be consistent with the observations provided by various experimental approaches.

In Gd, we find a similar divorce between replicability and meaning. In this passage, a scientist who describes himself as an experimentalist firmly distinguishes between the reproducibility of his results and their interpretation and claims that his main responsibility is with ensuring reproducibility, even though this in no way guarantees the adequacy of his interpretative attempts. In Ge, we have a series of general comments along the same lines. The accuracy and reliability of published results is strongly affirmed (Ge 1, 6-7), but the question of interpretation is left open (Ge 2-5, 8-10). Interpretations, it is suggested, depend not on repeating others' observations, for their reproducibility is taken for granted, but upon carefully considered experimental variation. Similar material from our transcripts could be repeated in abundance.

The 'replicability in principle' of the great majority of published observations is assumed in these passages and throughout our respondents' talk on the topic of replication. As passages Ga-c illustrate, the reproducibility of results is seldom in question, even in accounts of pronounced scientific disagreement. However, for our respondents, this reproducibility in no way implies that the empirical regularity correctly represents some regular feature of the natural world. They allow for the possibility of reproducible artifacts (Lynch 1985) and in their accounts of replication they have to show how such artifacts are distinguished from 'genuine results'.

It is only when talking about possible artifacts that our respondents ever propose exact replication as a procedure. They do not, however, propose it as a way of establishing the truth, but as a way of understanding more fully how doubtful results have been produced.

H (1) He has an interesting system which provides an alternative explanation to the chemiosmotic theory. (2) I went up to his lab and did an experiment there once on my bacteria to see whether it worked. (3) It worked up in his lab, but I couldn't get it to work in [mine].
Interviewer: (4) Have you any explanation of why you should get certain experimental results in Peck's laboratory, but not back in [yours]?
Respondent: (5) No, I don't know. (6) If I'd known, I would have dealt with it. (7) I didn't know. (8) I just gave up. (9) I even had the same buffer solution, and so on, but I couldn't get it to work in [my lab]. (10) I don't know whether we telephoned or wrote, and he said he shook the reaction mixture, while I'd stirred it. (11) He said shake, not stir, so I tried that. (12) But it still didn't work. (13) So I gave that up ... (14) There were funny things about it. (15) You needed to keep it aerobic, but oxygen had nothing to do with it. (16) There was something a little bit fishy, but there were some very good experiments, very convincing experiments ... (Aldridge 22)

This is one of only two instances in our transcripts where a respondent describes his attempts to repeat exactly someone else's experiment, as distinct from referring in passing to the need for exact replication. The speaker stresses the problematic nature of the findings in question. Not only do they seem to contradict the prevailing theory (H1), but some of the experimental details are also 'fishy' (H15-17). In addition, the speaker describes how he had difficulty in getting the same results and how this prompted him to try to repeat, even more closely, the original experimenter's procedures (H11-12). As the results come to be defined as increasingly problematic, so exact replication comes to seem more appropriate. The important feature of this passage for us is the way in which failure to repeat another's experiment in one's own lab, despite one's every effort, is taken to be a decisive *negative* criterion. Failure of experimental results to survive this transfer from one lab to another is taken, by the second party at least, to be sufficient grounds for disregarding the experimental claim in question (H9, 14).

Close experimental copying, then, is treated by our respondents as a strategy to be used very occasionally in order to try to find out how doubtful findings are being produced. Failure to accomplish exact replication is taken as a strong negative criterion. A serious, but unsuccessful attempt at exact replication is presented as justifying the speaker in taking no further notice of the observations in question or any scientific conclusions derived from them. However, successful experimental repetition is not usually treated, in itself, as positive grounds for accepting others' claims. Rather, the positive criterion is taken to be the ability of genuine findings to persist despite local variations in experimental production. This is a recurrent theme in our transcripts.

I   *Interviewer:*(1) [If you were to try to repeat this experiment] would you use *exactly* the same equipment and *exactly* the reagents as were specified?

   Respondent:(2) What I would do is use what's available to me. (3) And if it doesn't work, I would then start saying 'OK, its something about their *particular* reagents'. (4) So instead of using the reagents I happen to have, which come from one company, and a different cation there, then I would try and get the one from the same company that they got, and use the same cation. (5) Approach closer and closer to the exact conditions until I could repeat it. (6) But the expectation would be that, if its a real effect, you could repeat it just by following the same *general* recipe. (7) And the same with the piece of machinery. (8) It really shouldn't matter what piece of machinery you use. (9) So its only if it fails that you start to wonder about that. (Norton 47)

In this illustrative passage, the speaker displays a clear rationale for being relatively unconcerned with carrying out exact replication. He maintains that scientists translate specific observations into more general scientific conclusions, which should be demonstrable in various different, yet scientifically equivalent, ways (I6-8). Variations in local conditions should not alter one's ability to reproduce 'a real effect'. And if small variations do significantly change one's findings, that in itself is grounds for questioning their scientific significance (I6-9). The reproducibility of specific results in principle is not in question here (I5). Exact replication is treated as something one might seek to demonstrate, very occasionally, in cases where there are grounds for doubting whether it can be achieved. It is not treated as a critical part of the social process of validation.

Scientific meaning is depicted as being actively accomplished, not through the constant repetition of concrete observations, but through the systematic pursuit and interpretation of experimental differences; in other words, through what we referred to earlier as the strategy of experimental variation (I2). Valid knowledge is presented as being composed of those conclusions which survive the test of experimental variation and diverse conditions of local production.

Concluding remarks

In earlier sections, we showed that it is possible to extract from scientists' discourse about replication at least two rather different conceptions. Participants' statements sometimes seem to suggest that exact experimental repetition is crucial to science. Other statements claim or imply a different and more complex account, according to which scientific knowledge emerges as meaning is attributed to sets of diverse, yet comparable, experiments.

Contributions to the secondary literature on replication in science tend to propose one or other of these conceptions. The more customary approach has been to assume, somewhat simplistically, that scientists' pronouncements about 'replication in principle' necessarily imply that scientific practice is centrally concerned with experimental repetition. We have seen that our respondents persistently deny this portrayal of their practice, without, however, abandoning their commitment to replicability in principle.

More recent case studies have examined scientists' replication discourse much more closely. As a result, they have been able to use scientists' own detailed interpretative work to undermine what they have taken to be the 'official view' of scientific replication. They have tried to show instead that science can be depicted as developing through complex, open-ended negotiations about scientific meaning. The view which they advocate should be rejected is described in the first quotation below and the one to be adopted in the second quote.

> According to the algorithmic model we would expect a scientist wishing to replicate an experiment to search his available information sources for the algorithm, follow it, produce an exact copy of the original apparatus, and *ipso facto* identical results. (Collins 1975: 206)

> The most fruitful way of interpreting the activity of scientists in this field, I suggest, is not as attempts to competently replicate, or competently test 'O's findings, but rather as *negotiations about the meaning of a competent experiment* in the field ... In the gravity wave field scientists were not concerned to conduct experiments isomorphous with that of the originator of the research. There are many possible ways of explaining this, but a convincing interpretation of their actions is that ... Scientists' actions may ... be seen as negotiations about which set of experiments in the field should be counted as the set of competent experiments. In deciding this issue, they are deciding the character of gravity waves. (Collins 1975: 219-20)

It is clear from the discussion above that something closely resembling the two versions of replication presented here as alternatives are combined by our respondents within a more complex and intricate, yet standardized and coherent, account of replication. If participants can plausibly reconcile exact replication with experimental negotiation, there seems to be no good reason why analysts should proceed by assuming that they are fundamentally incompatible. In the last passage above, the writer maintains that the scientists he studied are not attempting to replicate, but are doing something else which he can now correctly identify as 'negotiation'. But he is able to make this claim only by confining himself to one, rather simple, conception of replication and, indeed, to a conception which our respondents would presumably treat as grossly oversimplified.

In the two passages above, scientists' lack of interest in close experimental copying is made puzzling and in need of sociological attention by the presumption that it is contrary to what we have been led to believe about science. However, the lack of observable attempts at exact replication ceases to be puzzling once we recognize that scientists, upon whom we rely for the interpretations which constitute our 'data', tend to avoid portraying their own actions as 'mere replication' and to depict others' actions in this way only in somewhat exceptional circumstances. The writer himself mentions that there are many possible ways of explaining the absence of close copying in the field he has studied. But he does not consider the possibility that participants themselves employ versions of 'experimental replication' which encompass his own and from which his own conclusions derive. It appears, then, that prior analyses of scientific replication may have been constructing, and seeking to resolve, puzzles generated by the intricacies of scientists' discourse on this topic.

In conclusion, we must stress that we are not proposing that the standardized replication account outlined above be accepted as a valid portrayal of scientific action. For one thing, it is quite conceivable that, under different circumstances, significantly different replication accounts are furnished by participants. Thus we have done no more in this paper than try to describe one recurrent interpretative form which scientists employ when talking about their social world. Our aim has not been to reveal the truth about replication, but to draw attention to the fact that scientists are much more skilled constructors of social meaning than analysts usually give them credit for; to suggest that we begin analysis with proper recognition of the interpretative complexity of their discourse; and to describe some of the intricate structure of one of their interpretative forms.

Note

1. Although this paper was not published until 1986, it was, like chapter 10, written during the academic year 1982-3.

Part Four: New literary forms: exploring the many worlds of textuality

12 Noblesse oblige (1984)

My starting point in this chapter is the proposal that all (sociological) analysis is a form of parody and, therefore, that parody can be a form of (sociological) analysis. This argument can be sustained, I think, in relation to any kind of analysis. I will concentrate, however, on the particular case of sociology.

All sociological analysis makes use of and builds upon what I will call 'original texts'. These texts are 'original' in the sense that they precede and are necessary for the production of the analytical text. Such original texts are sometimes produced by the analyst himself; for example, an observer's field notes in which he describes the actions of those under study. Sometimes they are produced by the actors under investigation; for example, letters exchanged among participants and subsequently collected by the analyst. Sometimes these original texts are jointly produced by analysts and participants; for instance, the interview schedules devised by an analyst and answered by a respondent. There is also a form of sociological analysis which relies almost entirely on previous sociological writings for its original texts. The analyst's task, put as generally as possible, is to make sense of a particular batch of texts (the original text) by formulating a secondary text of his own. The objective of the secondary text is to show any reader, including the analyst, how the original text is to be read or understood.

One necessary feature of the secondary, analytical text is that it differs from the original text. If the secondary text did not differ from the original text, it would be a mere repetition of that text and would be analytically empty. The secondary text inevitably selects from the original text, summarizes it, ignores parts of it, rephrases it, puts it in a new context, identifies its important and unimportant features, simplifies it, and so on. In other words, the analytical text systematically deviates from and, in this sense, distorts the original text as it performs analytical work on that text and re-presents it for analytical purposes. This systematic distortion is captured in the frequently used distinction between raw data (original text) and results or findings. The raw data are manipulated, re-ordered and re-presented in the analytical text to reveal their sociological meaning.

There is one word in particular in the previous paragraph which may seem inappropriate, namely, the word 'distort'. For whereas 'distort' is equivalent to 'misrepresent', 'twist out of shape' or 'falsify the meaning of', the secondary analytical text customarily claims to be true to the original text and to be doing only what is necessary to bring to light the underlying meaning of that text. Thus sociological analysis changes the shape of the original text, yet it does this in order to reveal its actual structure and its true sociological significance.   In this sense, the secondary text necessarily bears an ironic relationship to the original text. As Woolgar puts it: 'To do irony is to say of something that appears one way, that it is in fact something other than it appears' (1983: 249). The secondary text, in transforming the original text yet claiming to reveal that text's meaning, inevitably asserts the kind of interpretative privilege over the original text which is the essential element in textual irony. The original text is denied the right to speak for itself. It is the secondary, analytical text alone which can properly convey the reality of the original text.

But what does this have to do with parody? In order to establish the connection, it will be helpful to consider the origin of this word. It is derived from 'para', which is Greek for 'alongside of', and 'oide', a 'song' (Funk 1978). Thus, a parody is literally a song written alongside another song. In time, the second song came to concentrate on identifying the central features of the first song and, by the artful combination of re-statement and variation, to undermine the standing of the original song in some way, often by means of irony or humour. The word 'song' was appropriate in the Greek context owing to the nature of Greek dramatic and literary forms. But subsequently parody has come to be used in relation to a wide variety of textual forms. Accordingly, we can replace the word 'song' with the word 'text'. Linking this definition to the preceding discussion, I suggest that a parody is a secondary text which is closely based on (alongside of) an original text, but which differs from the original text in ways which reveal the true nature of the original text (its central features) and at the same time establish the superiority of the secondary text (undermine the standing of the original text).

We seem to have arrived at the conclusion that parody and analysis can be defined in virtually identical terms. Thus, I claim to have demonstrated my initial proposal that sociological analysis is a form of parody and that parody can be a form of sociological analysis. I have to admit that this conclusion depends upon some rather careful textual work carried out above. Consequently, some readers may feel that the argument presented here is itself a parody of proper analysis. But all analysis depends on such careful textual work. If this were not so, writing analytical texts would not require such detailed attention to wording, so many revisions and so many wasted pages (see Westfall 1980 for a discussion of Newton's copious and minute revisions). Moreover, to maintain that my analysis is a parody only adds further support to my argument that analysis is a parody. The only criticism that might, at first, appear to weaken my case would be that my argument is not parody. But if my analysis is not a parody, then I can assume that it stands as valid analysis; that is, I can assume that analysis is a parody. Hence, whichever of these responses the reader decides to adopt, he will be forced by iron logic, as the author has been, to accept that sociological analysis is a form of parody and, therefore, that parody can be a form of sociological analysis.

At this point, any reader inclined to be prejudiced against the conclusion demonstrated above is likely to be preparing a trap for me and for my argument. Clearly I am going to suggest that, now that we have established that parody can be a form of sociological analysis, we should actually employ parody as a form of analysis. But once I have put forward this recommendation, the trapdoor will be slammed shut with: 'But if analysis already *is* a form of parody, the recommendation to use analytical parody is redundant. Analysts are already doing so'. Fortunately for me, however, the door closed too quickly, leaving me safe outside. For my recommendation is not that sociologists should take up analytical parody, but that they should recognize, acknowledge, even celebrate their involvement in parody, instead of denying it, and begin to explore the possibilities opened up by cultivating parody as an analytical form.

One advantage of explicitly recognizing and presenting one's own analysis as a parody of others' texts is that the secondary text claims no interpretative privilege with respect to parallel secondary texts. An explicit parody does not claim to offer a definitive reading of the original text. It is offered as but one reading among many possible readings. In addition, it allows for the possibility of some kind of rejoinder on behalf of the original text. A secondary text which is an explicit parody invites further parody (analysis) of its own text. As a result, explicit analytical parody enables us to treat our own work as one more contribution to a continuing series of texts; to treat our own work as a textual artifact which uses selection, simplification and exaggeration along with humorous contrast and incongruity to propose new readings of and inform third parties about other texts (Woolgar 1983).

It is important, I think, to recognize that parody is not simply a textual form designed to make fun of original texts. Rather, ridicule and humour, as well as exaggeration and condensation, selection and paraphrase, are all used as a means of informing the reader about the nature of the original text. In this sense, explicit parody conforms to what is normally said to be the main objective of ordinary sociological analysis. At the same time, however, parody differs from ordinary analysis in drawing attention to its own textuality. Analytical parody says, in effect: 'What I have to offer is, I think, a viable conclusion, but it is not the original text (the real world) itself. Furthermore you, the reader, will have to perform the same kind of interpretative work on my text, in order to extract its meaning, as I performed on my original text'.

Analytical parody, then, differs from standard forms of analysis in openly inviting the reader to perform her own interpretative work on the analytical text and/or on the original text, and in encouraging the reader to explore alternative avenues of textuality in order to discover what they can reveal. Whereas conventional sociological analysis claims interpretative privilege for its own text, analytical parody directs attention to the possibility of carrying out diverse kinds of sociological analysis, that is, saying various new and interesting things about the production of the social world, by means of any and every conceivable literary form (including of course, as one textual form, conventional analysis). In order to illustrate the practical implications of this argument, I now offer an attempt at analytical parody.

The focus of this analytical parody is the Nobel Prize Ceremonies. Like a true sociologist, I will try to use parody to illuminate how the Nobel Prize Ceremonies are socially constituted. Various symbolic domains are used to make the arrangements of the awarding of the Nobel Prizes properly ceremonial, including music, painting, eating and apparel. But I suggest that the critical symbolic realm is that of language; and that the various non-linguistic accoutrements are given their specific ceremonial meaning by being embedded in a particular kind of spoken discourse. This discourse takes the surface-form of presentations, formal lectures, banquet speeches, and so on. However, all of these surface-forms rely upon the same recurrent smaller-scale interpretative forms to accomplish the overall effect of a ritual celebration of human achievement at the highest level. It is through the regular use of these fine-grained forms by all those taking part in the Nobel Ceremonies that the Ceremonies become recognizably a celebration.

The forms themselves are conventional. Yet it is the concentrated use of these conventions that creates the celebratory context. Any significant departure from these forms, any use of discourse which contradicts these forms, will disrupt the Ceremonies and detract from their celebratory import. In the following pages, I will parody the discourse of Nobel Prize Ceremonies and contrast it with forms of discourse which I believe are potentially available to, yet never actually used by, participants during the Ceremonies. Thus I will construct a secondary text which is fictional, in the sense that I stress that the events it reports did not happen; yet which is also factual in that it expresses in a concentrated way, and therefore with greater clarity and economy than could any original text, the interpretative forms through which Nobel Prize Ceremonies are actually constituted.

I have used as my basic sources Les Prix Nobel for the years 1978-1981. These are the original texts for the statements made by the Laureate, the representative of the Nobel Foundation, the presenter and the student representative. Most of these speakers' words are taken from these four volumes. The other speakers' words come from interviews with scientists collected over many years, from published responses to particular Nobel awards in various fields, and from my own informed invention. None of these characters is based upon, or intended to represent, any particular person. The actors in the parody below are composite figures representing typical features of scientists' discourse.

The Nobel Ceremonies are made up of five kinds of textual component: speeches by non-Laureates leading to the award of a prize, return speeches by Laureates at the formal banquet, a speech addressed to all Laureates by a student representing the younger generation of researchers and scholars, formal lectures by each Laureate about their own contribution to knowledge, and a biographical account of each Laureate's career, usually written by the Laureate concerned. I have drawn on the full range of this material in devising a series of speeches supposedly given at a celebratory banquet. I have assumed that an unaccustomed intake of celebratory champagne has weakened the inhibitions of some of those who take part; particularly those who join in later in the sequence.

The Nobel Banquet incident

Representative of the Nobel Foundation Your Majesties, Your Royal Highnesses, Ladies and Gentlemen, It is my privilege and pleasure to begin the round of after-dinner speeches in honour of this year's Laureates. Honoured Laureates, the Nobel Foundation takes special satisfaction in welcoming you. You have already spent a few days in Sweden. I do hope that even this short time has enabled you to assess the magnitude of our appreciation for the stimulating scientific and personal contacts which have been made possible by the presence here of your honoured selves and your esteemed families. I also trust that you all feel that our traditional formalities are part of a friendly and cheerful celebration of your magnificent achievements.

Alfred Nobel stipulates in his will that his Prize go to those who have conferred the greatest benefit on mankind. The Nobel Prizes in physics, chemistry and medicine have often recognized pioneering research achievements at the frontiers of our knowledge: enterprises, therefore, that usually can only be understood and judged by a small group of specialists. This is in keeping with Nobel's wish that principal encouragement go to basic and pioneering research, whose results can be expected to lead to practical, significant developments of benefit to mankind.

A great number of scientists from all over the world are involved as nominators for the Nobel Prizes, and thereafter the proposals are subjected to a careful analysis by experts. It is well-known that receipt of a Nobel Prize is still considered to be one of the finest honours in the world. This opinion is based partly on the knowledge that the right to propose in the matter of prize awards is reserved to scientists throughout the entire world, and partly awareness of the occurrence of the word 'discovery' in Nobel's will. It is easy to understand what a change the general assessment of the Nobel Prize would undergo if one did away with the thought-association 'Nobel Prize–discovery'. The prize would lose its singular character.

Nobel Prize Day plays more and more the role of an annual reminder to those in power in the world of the quickly exhausted and irreplaceable assets which people of the remarkable calibre of our prize winners represent. Such outstanding figures must be granted the conditions they require to develop and exploit their immense intellectual capacity and industry in their ineluctable pursuit of further knowledge. What is more enticing or important than seeking the crown of truth wherever the search may lead?

If the Nobel Prizes can contribute to increasing political and public understanding of what research and creative and enterprising individuals can mean for the improvement of society, not only will Alfred Nobel's hopes of stimulating research within clearly defined areas be fulfilled, but the prizes will also contribute to the creation of the more peaceful world he dreamt of.

Representative of Swedish Students   Your Majesties, Your Royal Highnesses, Honoured Nobel Laureates, Ladies and Gentlemen, Ever since the first Nobel Prize Ceremony, we students have had the privilege of meeting once a year with the most distinguished representatives of Science and Literature, who by their brilliant achievements have earned the attention and admiration of the entire world. Today, we have the great pleasure of sharing this happy occasion with you.

On an evening such as this, research and higher education may seem glamorous and exciting occupations. Under the circumstances this is quite fitting, but as many of you know from personal experience a different reality is waiting around the corner tomorrow, when the festivities have ended.

One aspect of this other reality is that an increasing degree of control over scientific research has in many countries been accompanied by a growing reluctance to allocate funds. In a world blessed with a steadily increasing number of politicians and a steadily decreasing number of statesmen, long-term scientific effort is regretfully having to make way for the greater popular appeal of more short-term action. However, in a democratic society, free and independent research effort will always benefit all of mankind. For most scientific research has beneficial applications. Your important achievements have made an outstanding contribution to this process.

Each generation broadens and deepens the fund of knowledge possessed by mankind. You, the Nobel Prize Laureates gathered here today, represent pinnacles of achievement in your respective fields. We hope the younger generation of today will have the opportunity to develop your results, to take one more step up the steep ladder of knowledge. We hope the politicians of the world will provide the resources necessary to develop a flourishing base of higher education from which coming generations of researchers as able and as dedicated as you can be recruited.

Honoured Nobel Laureates, the students of the world pay homage to you today, because of your priceless contributions to the foundations upon which future generations of scientists are going to build. We wish to express our great respect for your brilliant results, our congratulations for the prizes you have received, and our esteem and tribute to you for being, not only the foremost representatives of science, but also the humble servants of our culture.

Representative of the Nobel Committees   Your Majesties, Your Royal Highnesses, Ladies and Gentlemen, I have the great honour this year of speaking on behalf of the subject committees for physics and chemistry.

The prize for physics this year goes to Professor Purple for his great discoveries in the borderland between a strange but known country and the probably large unknown territory of the innermost structure of matter. Our way of looking at this structure has changed radically in the last decade. Purple's theory of strong–weak, or weak–strong, interaction has been one of the most important contributions to bring about this change of outlook.

The epoch-making theory which is awarded this year's physics prize has extended and deepened our understanding of the strong force by displaying its close relationship to the weak force: these two forces merge as different aspects of a unified strong–weak, or weak–strong, force. This means, for example, that the electron and the neutrino are intimately related. We now know, as a result of Purple's theory, that the neutrino is the electron's little brother. Similarly, it follows from the theory that the proton is, surprisingly, the electron's elder sister and also, therefore, the neutrino's elder sister. In other words, the theory predicts that they are all members of the same family. These dramatic predictions have been fully confirmed by experiments carried out during the 1970s. Further research will undoubtedly reveal, in due course, the full extent of the previously unimagined kinship network which lies hidden behind the superficial characteristics of the physical world and will open up new possibilities for collaboration between physicists and the previously under-valued discipline of social anthropology. Professor Purple, the scientific world was shocked when you first announced your amazing discovery. Nobody, absolutely nobody, had anticipated anything like it. You pursued your demanding and difficult investigations with outstanding skill and determination and showed the impossible to be possible. You stand out as one of the greatest scientists of our time; the uncontested pioneer, original genius and founding-father of 'particle sibling research'.

I now turn to the prize for chemistry. The body and soul of Man is the most complex and refined chemical machine that we know. Even the simplest forms of life, for example bacteria, are almost immeasurably intricate systems compared to the dead matter that we find on our Earth and in the rest of the Universe. However, modern biology has taught us that there is no vital force, and that living organisms consist wholly of dead atoms.

The machinery of life is made possible by a unique interplay between two groups of biological giant molecules, nucleic acids and the proteins, in the form of enzymes. These molecules form the orchestra that plays the various melodies which, in combination, create the harmony of life. DNA is the carrier of the genetic traits in the chromosomes of cells, and it governs the chemical machinery, it conducts the music of life, by determining which enzymes a cell shall manufacture.

The scintillating investigators who have been awarded this year's Nobel Prize for chemistry, Doctors Frank and Stein, have brought about a new era in our understanding of the relationship between the chemical structure and biological function of the genetic material. Doctors Frank and Stein carried out the immensely difficult task of constructing a recombinant-DNA molecule, that is, a molecule which contains DNA from different species, e.g. genes from a human being combined with part of a bacterial chromosome. It was their awe-inspiring privilege, and their great gift to mankind, to set in motion the new epoch of genetic engineering and to put flesh upon the Faustian dream of constructing new forms of life and perhaps, thereby, putting Man in the driving seat of evolution.

As we all know, there has been extensive debate about the need to control these new techniques, after an initiative as one would have expected from Dr Frank himself, warning of possible dangers. Continued research has shown, however, that the concern for hypothetical risks has been unwarranted. Scientists never forget to fasten the seat-belt.

Doctors Frank and Stein, with incomparable ingenuity, great personal courage and unflagging persistence, you have innovated and brought humanity closer to a blithe new world. Your ideas and techniques have produced a breakthrough that has opened up major new insights into the fundamental processes of life and creation as well as infinite new practical possibilities. It is in recognition of these brilliant and pioneering contributions to science and to the benefit of mankind that we honour you today.

Professor Purple Your Majesties, Your Royal Highnesses, Ladies and Gentlemen, I have the great privilege and distinct pleasure to reply on behalf of the three Laureates in physics and chemistry. I wish humbly to express our deep appreciation and intense gratitude to Your Majesty and to all those who have made of Alfred Nobel's legacy a unique tribute to human achievement. We thank you for the very high honour and warm hospitality that have been bestowed upon us in Sweden.

During my career, the nature of science has changed dramatically. But despite these great changes, one thing still remains constant – it is the Nobel Prize. Its significance as the greatest scientific award on an international scale is universally recognized. This must be regarded as a unique achievement of Swedish scientists, because awarding prizes correctly requires great wisdom.

I do not mean to imply that you have been wise in awarding me the prize for physics; far from it. My personal contribution to science has been small. But I recognize the outstanding qualities and achievements of my fellow-Laureates here tonight and of those famous men and benefactors of mankind who have received this honour in the past. Their brilliant accomplishments lead me to reflect on the fact that scientific knowledge is cumulative; each individual stands on the shoulders of others, many of whom are giants, like those facing me across this table.

The completed body of scientific knowledge in any particular area is an integral work of art. It is like a patchwork quilt, built up from many separate pieces, which has become a golden tapestry. Tapestries are made by many artisans working together. The contributions of individual workers cannot be discerned in the finished work, and the loose and false threads have been covered over. So it is in the fields pursued by myself and by doctors Frank and Stein. The development of the strong–weak, or weak– strong, theory was not as simple and straightforward as it might seem. It did not arise full blown in the mind of any one physicist, nor even two or three. It, too, is the result of the collective endeavour of many scientists, both experimenters and theorists. This prize, therefore, is not awarded to me for my contribution to physics. I stand here today as the fortunate representative of that creative community of researchers who have pushed back the boundaries of physical knowledge. I have been chosen by Providence to receive the honour on their behalf.

Whilst I have the opportunity, I wish to give voice to the debt which we owe our teachers. My deepest impulse is to treat this year's prize for physics as having been awarded to my teacher and mentor, Professor Moon. When I became Moon's student, I gained access to a superior mind. Moon possessed clarity of thought, powers of concentration, encyclopaedic knowledge of physics, and an aesthetic sense unparalleled in modern research. He taught me, and I have taught others. It is the genius of Professor Moon which led to the original fundamental idea of the strong–weak, or weak–strong, force. The award of this year's Nobel Prize for physics to me is a direct outcome of the light shed by Moon on the basic structure of matter. Every aspect of my work reflects the penetrating scientific vision with which Moon illuminated everything he touched.

I am also particularly indebted to my many students and co-workers who have contributed so much to our common goal and whom I hold responsible in the largest measure for my achievements. Without their genius, perseverance and stimulation our work would not have flourished. I want to express my deep appreciation and my profound affection for my students and associates who have shared with me in the toil and should share equally in the honour. Now is not the moment to mention particular names, but I owe a great debt to the many wonderful people with whom it has been my privilege to work in relation to the strong–weak, or weak–strong, force.

As many of you will know, the theory of the strong–weak, or weak–strong, force was initially received with incredulity and fierce rejection by those already working in the field. In the long run, however, they have all come to accept the validity of that theory. Thus, what I find most remarkable and admirable is the self-abnegation and devotion to truth with which my former opponents have not only adopted my original hypothesis, but have actively promoted it to the status of an established theory. I would like to pay a most heartfelt tribute to those who were formerly my strongest critics, without whose altruistic and generous impulses, I feel sure that I would not be at this banquet. It is their untiring commitment to the basic scientific ideal of rigorous experimental testing which has ensured that our theoretical explorations have come to such great fruition. It is they who are honoured here tonight.

As I look back from this moment upon the last few decades of my life, I am struck by the good fortune that has come my way. Throughout my schooling, there was an abundance of opportunity and encouragement. Several of my teachers were remarkable individuals, scholarly and dedicated, who had a lasting influence on me. At every stage of my career I have been surrounded by stimulating and amazingly gifted colleagues, most of whom are my close friends. I entered research under the guidance of a kind and benevolent master, and my own endeavours have been enriched by exceptionally talented students and collaborators, and validated through the rigorous, but scrupulously fair, appraisal of other outstanding researchers in my field. Finally, and most important, my wife and children have created in my home an atmosphere of joy and harmony. They have loved and supported me with a selfless devotion without which my labours in pursuit of knowledge would have been impossible. My family has provided the bedrock on which all else has been built. They, above all, are honoured by the award of this year's Nobel Prize for physics. I thank them. I thank you all. God bless you!

Professor Black Your Majesties, Your Royal Highnesses, Honoured Laureates, Ladies and Gentlemen, I have been asked to say a few words on behalf of the non-Laureates here tonight. I hope that nobody will mind if I change the tone of these proceedings just a little, by making one or two objective comments. I have listened with growing interest to the praise heaped upon Professor Purple and the other Laureates this evening, and to Purple's humble protestations that he personally does not deserve this praise. As scientists, we are all committed to the truth. It seems to me, therefore, that we must ask: Who is right? If Purple is right in saying that the credit belongs to others, then the Nobel Foundation has made a mistake; the prize should have gone to Moon or it ought to have been shared with all those said by Purple to have made essential contributions to the strong–weak, or weak–strong, theory. If the Nobel Committee was right in honouring Purple, then Purple himself seems not to have understood the nature of his own achievement or he has been deliberately misleading us in his remarks tonight.

We seem, then, to be faced with rather a difficult choice. If we agree with the Nobel Foundation, it seems that we must regard Purple either as deceitful or as, at least, somewhat lacking in perception. If we agree with Purple, we must conclude that the Nobel Committee is incompetent. One might think that the problem is resolved by the manifest inconsistency of Purple's speech this evening. Thus, if the strong–weak, or weak–strong, theory was really Moon's idea, as Purple says, then it cannot be credited, as Purple also says, to Purple's students and collaborators. On the other hand, if the body of knowledge in Purple's area is a tapestry so intricately inter- woven that individual threads cannot be distinguished, to paraphrase Purple again, it is inappropriate to award the prize either to Moon or to Purple or to Purple's co-workers; the award must be withheld or awarded to the whole 'creative community' mentioned by Purple. It is clear, then, that Purple's various assertions are incompatible and his remarks are too internally inconsistent to be given more than a moment's serious consideration. It appears that we have no alternative but to reject Purple's account and to accept the decision of the Nobel Committee. At first, this may seem to be an ideal conclusion. Apart from anything else, it would be convenient in allowing us to get back to the celebrations. But, unfortunately, we seem to have been left with a paradox, namely, we have concluded that the Nobel Committee was right to award the prize to a scientist who is unable even to give a brief speech about his own achievements without getting into a disastrous logical tangle. Can such a mind deserve what has been described tonight as 'the greatest scientific award' and 'a unique tribute to human achievement'?

Professor Purple   I must reply to these charges. Professor Black is, as usual, making a mountain out of a molehill. He is following his customary scientific procedure of erecting an elaborate, yet flimsy, structure of interpretation upon shifting sand. What would his reply have been if I had stood up this evening and claimed sole responsibility and the entire credit for recent advances in the understanding of the kinship relationships among elementary particles?   He would have accused me of megalomania, of massive self-advertisement, of refusing to recognize the basic contributions made by others. He would have said that I was trying to deny Moon's seminal influence on the field, that I was seeking to put Moon into an eclipse, and that this was clear evidence of a deranged mind. Thus he would have ended up at the same putative paradox by another route.

Professor Black has chosen tonight to disrupt these celebrations by disregarding the proprieties which normally govern such occasions. He knows full well that it is simply inappropriate for a Laureate to engage in excessive self-congratulation on receipt of the prize. Laureates are expected to acknowledge the help they have received from others and to allow as many as possible to share unofficially in the honour. Professor Black has elected to take my partly conventional, but nonetheless sincere, remarks literally, under the guise of a scientific concern for the objective truth, in order to bring me into discredit and to spoil what would otherwise have been the most gratifying moment in my career.

As many of you know, Professor Black has been one of my most persistent critics and dogmatic antagonists. He has refused to accept the validity of the strong–weak, or weak–strong, theory, whilst at the same time maintaining that his own earlier weak–strong, or strong–weak, theory contains my theory as a special case. Thus Professor Black's personal attack this evening is due to his desire to stand here in my place. May God forgive him for the harm he has done.

Professor Black   There is a grain of truth in Purple's suggestion that I intended to remove the patina of convention which has shrouded most of the speeches here this evening. The student representative properly drew our attention earlier to that other reality which exists outside these walls. It was also my aim to make sure that this reality was not forgotten, not buried under the celebratory words required by the Nobel ritual.

Contrary to what Purple says, however, I don't mind about his getting the prize. But I do mind when the award of the prize is taken to mean that his theory must be correct and that it is universally accepted. In my view, and that of many others, Purple's hypothesis is incorrect and has certainly not been conclusively confirmed by experimental evidence. In addition, there is an alternative theory, the weak–strong, or strong–weak, theory, which preceded his hypothesis and which already included those aspects of his hypothesis which have proven to be fruitful. I do not claim this alternative theory as my own. It evolved as part of the cumulative growth of scientific knowledge. Nevertheless, its existence puts in doubt the award of this year's Prize to Professor Purple; for this theory was published before Purple began to work on the topic of particle siblings.

Finally, there is the issue which is normally discussed only in whispers, behind closed doors, but which I feel obliged to raise now: Why has Delia Son not been included in the Prize? Dr Son studied with Moon before he retired, after which she transferred to Purple. She was very much the rising star of particle kinship research and her writings clearly foreshadow Purple's hypothesis. Yet she disappeared without trace from Purple's lab. I suggest that this is another example of a female graduate student being exploited by, and denied credit by, a senior male colleague. Given that this year's prize has been awarded for the strong–weak, or weak–strong, theory, then it should not be Purple facing me through the candelabra, but Dr Son and Professor Moon.

Professor Purple   Your Majesties, Ladies and Gentlemen, I realize that this exchange between Professor Black and myself is becoming increasingly embarrassing. The topics raised by Professor Black should not really be discussed here. But I feel that I cannot let his slanderous accusations pass unanswered before this august assembly, whose respect I believe I deserve and which I wish to retain.

The fact is, as all who know me well can testify, that I strive constantly to maintain, and have succeeded in maintaining, an intimate accord with all my graduate students and post-docs. Delia Son was no exception to this. She worked closely with me for a short while, but there was neither exploitation nor plagiarism on my part. Nor was there any mystery about her departure from my lab. She left to have a baby; an eventuality which we have to face when we allow young women into research. She was a competent researcher. But she made no special contribution to our work. She simply followed my instructions and her research could always have been, as it eventually was, carried out by another young researcher. If she, or any other of my students, had made a distinctive and significant contribution, they would be alongside me this evening. My students are treated like members of my own family. They form part of a caring relationship which –

Mrs Purple   This is too much! I've listened patiently to a lot of nonsense this evening, but I can't hold myself back any longer. My husband described our family life earlier, just as all the other Laureates described theirs, as a kind of earthly paradise which has been the source of all his success. Well, I think its true that, without my constant labour and attention to his needs, his career might well have foundered. But the point is that it has not been an earthly paradise for me or our children; whatever it has been like for other Laureates' families. Indeed, when the children were younger, they would sometimes ask who their father was. They saw him so seldom, you see. He would either come home long after they were asleep or he would visit us briefly for dinner and then cycle back to his beloved lab.

He's still like that to this day; obsessed by his research. In my opinion, we have been sacrificed to his frenzied striving for success. In addition, I've had my suspicions about the reasons for all these conferences abroad. I'm not suggesting that these meetings are just a cover for marital infidelities, but the opportunities are certainly there, and if I know my husband –

President of the Nobel Foundation   My dear Mrs Purple, Professor Purple and Professor Black, I think you will agree that the realities of the world outside have become too obtrusive and are in danger of spoiling what is, after all, an occasion of joy and celebration; an occasion in which we all share in the honour associated with the outstanding cultural achievements of our time. I'm sure that these personal and scientific differences of opinion are important to those centrally involved. But they are of no interest to the rest of us gathered here to recognize some of the major accomplishments attained by the human intellect in recent years and to praise those responsible.

I suggest that it is time for music. If the orchestra is ready, let us now listen to the next item on the programme, which is the overture to George Gershwin's 'Of Thee I Sing'.

Parody, pastiche, farce

It is probable that the representation of Nobel discourse above does not adhere strictly to the literary form of the parody. But it is not particularly important whether we call the preceding empirical section a parody, a pastiche or even a farce. The main point is that it uses sociological data, that is, an original text, in a more obviously inventive way than is usual to inform us, in this case, about the structure of Nobel Ceremonies and perhaps about celebrations more generally.

The first part of the banquet scene, that is, up to the entry of Professor Black, re-presents in a condensed, exaggerated and simplified manner what I take to be the dominant features of the discourse through which the Nobel Ceremonies are socially constructed. The essential accuracy of this representation can easily be assessed by anyone who chooses to examine carefully the texts of *Les Prix Nobel*. In these texts, the basic pattern which I have depicted and parodied is repeated time and time again. The parody brings out clearly and economically how the representatives of the Nobel Foundation, ostensibly acting on behalf of and with the support of a wider intellectual and social community, offer to the Laureates the most intense praise for outstanding accomplishments which are taken to be the Laureates' individual achievements. It also shows how the Laureates respond by scrupulous avoidance of explicit self-praise and by reassigning the praise they have received to teachers, students, colleagues, the scientific research community at large and, less directly, to their families. Thus the simplified re-presentation of participants' discourse is used above to reveal how the Nobel Ceremonies are socially organized in a way which turns the celebration of personal achievement into a collective affirmation of the activities and accomplishments of scientists in general.

Once Professor Black stands up to speak, my own use of participants' discourse changes and becomes more obviously imaginative. I have drawn here upon various supplementary sources, such as interviews and letters, as well as upon my own intuition. In *Les Prix Nobel,* no speaker ever departs from the dominant pattern. Without exception, participants stay rigidly within the standard interpretative repertoire and forms on which the ceremonies seem to depend; that is, they follow the models exemplified above by Purple and the Nobel representatives. Professor Black, however, deviates dramatically from the customary forms of discourse. He introduces into the ceremonial context various kinds of interpretation which occur regularly among scientists, but which are never allowed to disrupt the conventionally restricted image of scientific action around which the Nobel Ceremonies are organized.

One pervasive feature of conventional ceremonial discourse is that it depicts science as socially and intellectually consensual. The nature, responsibility for and significance of specific scientific achievements are routinely treated as agreed and unproblematic. Although this impression is normally sustained with little difficulty within the confines of ceremonial discourse, it is frequently challenged by scientists in other contexts. Professor Black draws upon several of the alternative 'realities' or alternative accounting systems which scientists regularly employ in other situations and he uses them in a way which highlights the constructed character of the particular version of science which informs the Nobel Ceremonies. Professor Black, with the help of Mrs Purple, draws our attention to some of the opposing interpretative possibilities which are excluded from ceremonial discourse, but which are recurrent in the scientific community at large.

In addition, Professor Black carries out interpretative work on the basic forms of ceremonial discourse which reveals how that discourse is open to 'internal deconstruction'. He shows how various of participants' assertions about the scientific achievements that are being recognized at the ceremony are, when taken 'literally', incompatible. In particular, he shows that the Nobel representatives' allocation of praise to the Laureates can be made difficult to reconcile with the Laureates' avoidance of self-praise and their reallocation of praise to others. Similarly, Laureates' regular identification of major contributions made by co-workers and students is, from Professor Black's perspective, difficult to reconcile with their repeated absence from the Nobel podium. The possibility of such internal deconstruction may well be built into all apparently coherent forms of discourse (Derrida 1977). In carrying out this deconstruction of scientists' ceremonial language, Professor Black provides further indication of the conventional nature of that language and of the socially constructed character of the image of science which it conveys. Professor Black and Mrs Purple, creations made possible by the open use of parody, encourage us to consider, not only what actually takes place during the Nobel Ceremonies, but also what is systematically excluded. They invite us to begin to try to understand the various social worlds of science in a way which is more frankly creative than is allowed by the textual forms of conventional sociological analysis.

13 Measuring the quality of life (1987)
with Malcolm Ashmore and Trevor Pinch

An opening dialogue

This is the textual analysis of a paper in health economics.

What is the textual form of this analysis?
Its form is that of an evolving series of questions and answers.

Why has this form been adopted?
My reasons for adopting this form are complex and have been explored at length elsewhere (Woolgar 1982; Ashmore 1989; Mulkay 1985). In the present context, the best short answer I can give to your question is that this form has been adopted because it contrasts markedly with the 'scientific' format of the paper which is to be analyzed and because it thereby helps to throw into clearer relief some of the characteristics and consequences of that format. I also think that the form of my text is less rigid than the highly conventionalized form of the standard research paper and that this gain in flexibility can be used to make the analysis more informative.

Which health economics paper has been selected for study and why?
The paper is 'Economics of coronary artery bypass grafting' by Prof. Alan Williams of the University of York. It appears in the *British Medical Journal*, vol. 291, 3 August 1985, pp. 326-329. There are several reasons why it has been selected for study. In the first place, health economists themselves tend to treat it as something of a classic of its kind. Secondly, I am interested in the application of social science in practical situations. The paper in question is centrally concerned with this task. Williams' guiding aim is to show medical administrators and other medical practitioners that economics can be put to work for their benefit and, ultimately, for the benefit of their patients. I have therefore chosen this paper in order to inspect how the discourse of the discipline of economics can be brought to bear on practical problems. The paper is a good choice because it illustrates with great clarity one potent strategy for applying social science to 'real world' issues.

In addition, Williams seeks to influence health care policy by measuring people's 'quality of life'. This may seem to you, at first sight, an exorbitant, even preposterous, objective. It is, however, taken very seriously by health economists and their preliminary efforts have met with an encouraging response from various medical administrators, clinicians and so on. It is a growing area of research in health economics. It seems to me that, if such work were to succeed in relation to health care, it could have profound implications for other fields of practical action and for the involvement of economists and what they call their 'way of thinking' in such fields. Improvement in the 'quality of life' is presumably a major goal of all public policy. If it came to be widely accepted that economists were able to measure accurately the changes in 'quality of life' likely to follow from different courses of action in non-medical as well as in medical fields, economists might well come to have a dominant role in the formation of policy across the full range of social life. There seems, therefore, every reason to try to understand in some detail how the practical discourse of economics is organized and, in particular, how measurement of the 'quality of life' is textually accomplished and put to work for our benefit.

What has 'quality of life' to do with economics or with economists? Surely economics is to do with money and the mechanisms of the market?
Economists would be inclined to treat these comments as simple-minded and as based on a misunderstanding of the nature of their discipline. Economics is said to be the systematic study of all human actions where scarce resources are used to produce valued outcomes. As your questions imply, people's valuations and the allocation of scarce resources are often mediated through market prices. But this is not always the case. The British National Health Service, for instance, is said to embody the principle that receipt of medical care shall not depend on the wealth or economic standing of the persons concerned. Thus scarce resources are allocated within the NHS to the various forms of medical treatment in order to furnish valued outcomes for patients, but (to some extent) independently of patients' willingness or ability to pay for these treatments. Economists are interested in this kind of provision of valued services precisely *because* the 'normal' market mechanisms are not involved. In such circumstances, economists are likely to question whether health care can be provided with maximum efficiency when those providing the services are not guided by market forces, and to try to identify an effective substitute for market forces. To put this in a slightly different way, the NHS constitutes an unusual monopoly in which the producer is not only the sole supplier of goods, but also tells consumers what they need and decides, with little reference to consumers' preferences, what will be produced. In such a situation, economists will try to ensure that the resources available for health care are being used to supply the mixture of services that will produce the most benefit as judged by recipients.

Does this mean that health economists regard themselves as the guardians of patients' interests and that they take their main task to be that of making NHS managers think more carefully about serving those interests?
Although that may be implicit in what health economists say and do, they do not normally depict themselves as directly representing patients. Rather, what they tend to do is to speak as the source of rational courses of action which, if implemented, would work to *everyone's* benefit. It is important to recognize,

however, that patients are seldom, if ever, given the opportunity to appraise health economists' proposals for themselves. Because the details of health care policy in Britain are decided formally by NHS managers, but often informally by clinicians, British health economists must approach and persuade both managers and clinicians if they are to influence medical practice. Health economists, however, do not normally seek the approval of patients.

Discussion of the paper begins

I presume that this is true in the case of Prof. Williams' paper.
Yes it is, in several ways. In the first place, that paper is published in a medical journal and is, it would seem, addressed primarily to the members of the health care professions who read such a journal. Secondly, the paper contains an economic analysis which had previously been presented at a 'consensus development conference on coronary artery bypass surgery' where, it is clear, most of the participants were members of the medical professions. Thirdly, there is a close coincidence between the problem in health care administration which provided the focus for the conference and the problem in economic analysis posed by Williams. Thus in Williams' words: 'the central issue before the conference was whether the number of operations for coronary artery bypass grafting should be increased, decreased, or maintained at its present level' (1985: 326). The abstract to Williams' own paper begins in almost identical terms: 'To decide whether the number of operations for coronary artery bypass grafting should be increased, maintained at the present level, or decreased we need to know how cost effective they are relative to other claimants on the resources of the National Health Service' (1985: 326).

It appears that Williams' paper is not only addressed to NHS managers, but takes the form of an economic analysis designed to solve the practical problem initially formulated by those managers. When Williams says that 'we' need to know how cost effective bypass operations are, he speaks both for managers and for economists. In the opening passage of his paper, the discourse of both parties appears to merge in a common search for a solution to a shared problem in the realm of practical action. Although ordinary people are not directly involved in devising this solution, I am sure that Williams would insist that the 'we' of his text also includes the general public, who meet the costs and some of whom may enjoy the benefits.

The next step is presumably to identify the various kinds of constraints which limit managers' and others' actions in order to be able to construct a realistic solution.
Well, no. Williams does not proceed in this way. In his paper, he reformulates the managers' version of their administrative problem in terms of the concepts of health economics, in such a way that it becomes an abstract, idealized problem to which the answer is obvious once one can discern the relationship between costs and benefits.

The objective of economic appraisal is to ensure that as much benefit as possible is obtained from the resources devoted to health care. In principle the benefit is measured in terms of the effect on life expectancy adjusted for quality of life...Procedures [medical treatments] should be ranked so that activities that generate more gains to health for every £ of resources take priority over those that generate less; thus the general standard of health in the community would be correspondingly higher.

Coronary artery bypass grafting is one of many contenders for additional resources. Ideally, all such contenders should be compared each time a decision on allocation of resources is made to test which should be cut back and which should be expanded. (1985: 326)

Although health service managers provide the starting point for Williams' analysis, their voice quickly disappears from his text and their definitions are quickly replaced by those of the health economist. The practical task of deciding on the allocation of health service resources is transformed by the economist into an exercise in cost/benefit analysis. The course of action required by the health service managers is treated in the course of economic analysis as following necessarily from the balance between costs and benefits as conceived in that analysis. The benefits or outcomes of various forms of medical treatment are defined by the economist in quantifiable terms as the effect on patients' expectation of life with adjustments made for the variable effect on patients' quality of life. Costs are defined, in principle, to include monetary and intangible costs to patients and their families as well as monetary costs to the NHS. But, in practice, only the latter are considered (1985: 327). As a result of all this redefinitional work, the economic analysis is able to generate ratios of cost/ benefit for various courses of action (medical treatment) and to recommend those actions which furnish the greatest excess of benefit over cost.

Thus the managers' practical task is reconstituted in the economist's text in such a way that it becomes solvable on the basis of a simple economic metric. This metric generates recommendations because its basic terms carry strong normative weight. No rational actor, it is implied, would incur greater cost than was necessary; nor would s/he refuse additional benefit which was available at no further cost. These assumptions are built into the very meaning of the terms 'cost' and 'benefit'. They are part of the semantics of economic analysis. For instance, if actors chose not to accept what was thought to be additional benefit, it would follow necessarily either that this was in fact not a benefit for them after all or that other aspects of the situation, which had been ignored, constituted benefits or costs in their eyes. This is one reason why the economic metric is immensely powerful and persuasive. Once complex administrative decisions have been reduced to simple, and usually quantified, comparisons of cost and benefit, it comes to seem irrational (or improper, if individuals choose to pursue their private ends rather than the public good) not to act in accordance with the numbers.

You say 'comes to seem irrational'. But surely it is irrational not to obtain the maximum benefit from a given supply of resources. I suggest that the economic metric is persuasive because it does actually solve the managers' problem.
Well, that may be so. Certainly it is the case that Williams is able to conclude his

article with a series of strong practical recommendations based on his calculations of costs incurred and quality adjusted life years (QALYs) gained by various forms of medical treatment.

> Resources need to be redeployed at the margin to procedures for which the benefits to patients are high in relation to the costs, such as the insertion of pacemakers for heart block, hip replacement, replacement of valves for aortic stenosis, and coronary artery bypass grafting for severe angina with left main disease and triple vessel disease and moderate angina with left main disease. These treatments should take priority over additional facilities for patients needing kidney transplants and coronary artery bypass grafting for mild angina with left main disease, moderate angina with triple vessel disease or one vessel disease, and severe angina with one vessel disease, for which the costs per quality adjusted life year gained are higher. (Williams 1985: 329)

But the point I want to stress is that, in the process of providing solutions to the managers' problem, Williams has changed the nature of that problem. He has reformulated the problem in terms of the narrowly conceived discourse of microeconomics. As a result, what might in other discourses be treated as the potential complexities of comparative costs become reduced to single figure comparisons and the diverse consequences of specific medical treatments for different groups and individuals become subsumed under aggregate figures representing the 'quality adjusted life years' produced by those treatments. This process of reduction and quantification in terms of concepts with a built-in normative power enables Williams to furnish potent practical proposals. But it also subtly changes the original problem by taking into account only those factors that can be incorporated within the economic metric. For instance, the benefit to be gained from, say, coronary artery surgery *becomes* the number of QALYs it generates and nothing else. The notion of QALYs, however, is furnished by the economists and the procedures for measuring QALYs are devised by economists. Thus although the economists are, in one sense, adopting the managers' problem and providing a clear, rational solution they are also, at the same time, redefining and altering the nature of the problem itself. In other words, what begins as the managers' problem is transformed into an economists' problem; and what is eventually offered to the managers, by the economists, is a solution to the economists' analytical problem. A major task facing economists is thus to persuade managers and clinicians that this transformation is actually a revelation of what the problem really is (see Williams 1972: 204).

Is this meant as a criticism of the economists? Perhaps they might reply that the managers' formulation of the problem had to be abandoned because it was unsolvable in its initial form and what they have done is to identify the analytical problem that lies behind any practical problem. The fact that the health care professionals were holding a consensus development conference to consider how to allocate resources shows that they were in trouble. How have they dealt with this task in the past?

This is not examined explicitly in Williams' paper. He makes only passing reference to the existing practice of NHS management. He suggests, in particular, that far too much attention has been paid in the past to comparative rates of survival as a criterion for allocating resources to different therapeutic procedures (1985: 326, 329). This index of medical benefit is misleading, he maintains, because there are many therapies whose main benefit is better quality of life rather than mere prolongation of life at a relatively low level.

However, it is clear from other texts by health economists that their critique of existing practices of resource allocation in the NHS often goes much further than this. For example, it has been suggested that the NHS suffers from 'the blinkered concerns of cost-minimizing accountants and benefit-maximizing clinicians' (Maynard 1986: 159), both of which lead to inefficient allocation of resources. In addition, both economists and practitioners recognize that resource allocation is closely linked to political processes within the health service and that resources tend to go, in the idiom of the NHS, to the person or group or specialism that 'shouts the loudest'.

In that case, Williams' proposals are evidently an improvement on existing practices. They replace the irrationalities engendered by the medical status system and by conflict among competing interest groups with a rational calculus designed to link the allocation of resources directly to the overriding goal of the system, namely, the maximization of patients' benefit. Perhaps the appeal of the economists' procedures lies in the fact that they eliminate irrelevant considerations from the decision-making process. What you called above Williams' 'simplification' and 'reduction' of the administrators' complex problem may be more accurately regarded as a clarification of the central issues of resource allocation combined with a procedure for generating appropriate courses of action.

If you were right in suggesting earlier, as it seemed to me, that Williams was imposing the discourse of economics upon the problems of NHS management and replacing their concerns with those of his own discipline, one would surely expect the health service professionals at the conference to respond in a fairly negative manner. Does Williams tell us how they reacted to his supposedly alien discourse? Williams quotes the following passage from the report of the conference in the second paragraph of his article:

> We were impressed by one method of measurement combining quality and duration of life. Further development of this approach is recommended so that it can be of help not only in comparison between coronary artery bypass surgery and other priorities but also between the various subgroups of patients whom it is proposed should be treated by coronary artery bypass surgery. Such techniques would also help to identify health service estimates which are being continued despite low benefit. (1985: 326)

This does seem to show that participants at the conference did find Williams' procedures and proposals quite persuasive and suggests that the discourse of economics is entering into that of NHS management. However, there may be various reasons for this. In the first place, it may be that the administrators in particular are attracted by the relative simplicity and lack of ambiguity of the economists' decision-making procedures. Such procedures might be favoured, by some parties at least, partly because they make things easier for management. Secondly, the rhetoric of 'cost', 'benefit' and 'quality of life' is, as I mentioned earlier, difficult to oppose (see McCloskey 1985 for an extended discussion of the rhetorical power of economic discourse). Thus if the economists' proposals coincide with certain participants' existing inclinations, they will furnish these participants with a powerful additional weapon in the process of negotiation over the allocation of resources within the NHS. If, for example, you have been pressing for more resources for hip replacements and, by implication, for less resources for costly therapies such as renal dialysis, it will become possible to present your case in more 'objective' terms and to appear to be free from the taint of special pleading. As a result of such considerations, it is likely on most occasions that some participants will have good reason to adopt the proposals generated by the methods of economics. But this will not mean that the irrationalities of political negotiation are being replaced by rational economic appraisal. It may simply mean that sections of management and various medical specialisms adopt the procedures and conclusions provided by economists and employ them selectively as a political resource, whilst other equally powerful and numerous people oppose them.

In other words, the sequence may operate along the following lines:

1. The economists take over a practitioners' problem and reformulate it in terms of the economic calculus, thereby generating an economically rational course of action for practitioners.
2. Because all traces of 'special interest' and 'irrationality' have apparently been removed by the economists' procedures, their discourse has a special moral and persuasive power which gives it a peculiar political potency.
3. Economists' proposals, therefore, are welcomed by those participants with whose interests and preconceptions they coincide and are enthusiastically employed by the latter in the course of political negotiation over resource allocation within the NHS.
4. This sets up a strong reaction from those whose interests are harmed. Their opposition to the new procedures focuses on issues of methodology and the very language of political dispute within the NHS begins to absorb and merge with that of economic analysis.

In the course of this process, participants redefine and change the meaning of the solutions to their initial practical problem provided by the economists. If the situation is like this, we have the interestingly paradoxical conclusion that it may be the supposedly non-political or 'scientific' character of the economic calculus which makes it such a powerful political resource for some participants and which generates such strongly negative reactions from others. It may well be that when the economists' recommended solution to the initial problem is brought back into the practical setting, the complexities and 'irrationalities' which were removed for purposes of economic analysis are unavoidably reintroduced and the very meaning of the economists' proposals thereby transformed in their turn.

This is an interesting idea. But it is highly speculative and far removed from both the text with which we began and from the question that I asked.
This is true. However, if we are to understand the practical outcome of Williams' or any other social scientist's efforts to apply their knowledge, we must recognize that any single text operates within a complex series of textual exchanges. Williams can only put his economic expertise to work on behalf of non-economists if he responds to their problems and, in due course, conveys to them effective solutions to those problems. The point I want to emphasize is that important changes of meaning occur as these problems move from one culture or discourse to the other and back again; and that a truly effective 'applied social science' would have to recognize that fact. In the case of health economics, however widely the procedures and formulations furnished by economists may be adopted by participants in the NHS, the meaning of these cultural products and the social uses to which they are put are bound to change within this different social context. If this argument is accepted it would appear to follow that health economists would be well advised to respond in their analytical procedures and their formal texts to the fact that their rational courses of action can operate fully only within the protected confines of economic discourse.

This argument may sound persuasive within the 'protected confines of sociological discourse', but sociologists are known to be utterly ineffective themselves in the real world of practical action. It seems to me that economists, in contrast, have made very useful contributions in various realms of practical endeavour. In relation to health care, it seems entirely plausible to maintain that economists' efforts have been welcomed, not for the reasons you suggest above, but because economists have been able to provide better measures than anyone else of the real costs and benefits of practical actions. If this is so, and if health economists can measure patients' quality of life, their intervention will make patients the final arbiter of NHS policy. Economists will be no more than impartial intermediaries. They will certainly be offering NHS managers the products of their own disciplinary culture, but these products will take the form of objective measures of patients' preferences. Thus your remarks about changes of meaning as cultural products move between social contexts are irrelevant. The health economist is not dealing in meanings, but in facts. The ineffectiveness of NHS management in the past has undoubtedly been due to the lack of this kind of factual basis for decision-making. Once the facts about the cost and, particularly, the benefits of various policies become generally available within the NHS, they will severely limit the scope for political manoeuvre and will reveal vested interest, status considerations and other irrationalities for what they really are. I suggest, in opposition to your claims above, that economists' formulations will not be changed by the culture of the NHS, but that they will provide objective criteria of choice based on patients' experiences which will necessarily bring about major changes of that culture.

Your faith in the possibility of devising 'objective' measures of quality of life is touching, but I think misplaced. I would argue that the 'facts' generated by *any* group of cognitive experts, whether they are biochemists, radio astronomers or neutrino physicists, should be treated as the cultural products of the respective group and not as re-presentations of phenomena which exist independently of that group and its culture (Pinch 1986). The same argument applies to economists and to other social scientists – including ourselves (Ashmore 1989). Thus when health economists measure the quality of life of patients undergoing different forms of medical treatment, they are not, I suggest, directly identifying what Williams calls 'the benefits to patients' (1985: 329), but are offering us quantitative indicators of benefits which exist only through the actions and interpretative work of economists, and which are given meaning by economists in the light of their taken-for-granted assumptions about the way that patients, and people in general, experience the world.

I will ignore your provocative remark about my faith in economists being touching and concentrate on your own factual claim regarding the cultural production of facts. Can you show how it applies to health economists and the quality of life?

Measuring the quality of life

In order to do this, I must describe briefly how quality of life is measured. Although economists use various techniques to measure quality of life, I will focus on the procedure used in Williams' (1985) paper which is designed to specify the variations in QALYs produced by different medical treatments. The first step is to identify those aspects of quality of life that are to be measured. Williams adopts a procedure which deals with physical mobility (or degree of disability) and with level of distress (of which physical pain will be a major component).

Surely there is more to 'quality of life' than this?
Yes, Williams is well aware of that. He acknowledges that the judgements on which his measures are based are 'crude and in need of refinement' (1985: 326). However, physical mobility and freedom from distress are fundamental aspects of our life experience in the sense that without them we are unable 'to perform the activities of daily living and to engage in normal social interaction' (1985: 326). When we are physically confined, and in pain or otherwise distressed, we are prevented from enjoying even the commonplace pleasures of everyday life, let alone the more subtle aspects of high quality living.

That seems reasonable. But how can you measure physical mobility and distress? I suppose there must be physiological indicators of the level of pain; and I suppose you could fit pedometers to sick and healthy people and compare how far they walk each day. But distress seems more nebulous than pain and I wonder whether you can combine such different measures of such different phenomena into a single index of quality of life.

Well, neither Williams nor other health economists choose those kinds of physical indicators. They adopt what Williams calls elsewhere a 'feeling–functional' measure (1981: 273). What this means, I think, is that he is trying to measure how people subjectively experience and evaluate various states of disability and distress in relation to their normal patterns of life. He is attempting to assess in quantitative terms people's feelings about and preferences for various physical conditions which are below their normal quality of life.

So QALYs provide a measure of what one might call negative preferences. They tell us how far people dislike certain unpleasant states. Is that right?
That's correct. I think QALYs could, perhaps, have been more accurately called LYSPAMs, that is, 'life years spent in pain and misery'. But that rather unattractive acronym might not have captured economists' or administrators' imaginations so effectively. However, whatever we call it, this negative indicator seems appropriate when the analyst is trying to measure the outcomes of medical treatments which are intended, as far as possible, to return patients to normal health. The indicator used by Williams, therefore, takes normal health as its bench-mark and measures how far various conditions are judged by ordinary people to fall below that level.

But I still don't understand how this rather intangible negative utility is to be measured.
The procedure is as follows. First, allocate a value of 1 to the state of normal health and 0 to the state of death. Second, specify a series of intermediate states involving different degrees and combinations of disability and distress. The measure employed by Williams makes use of eight conditions of disability, ranging from 'no disability' through 'severe social disability' and 'unable to undertake any paid employment' to 'unconscious'. These are then combined with four levels of distress, namely, none, mild, moderate and severe, to give a quality of life (disability and distress) matrix with 29 possible conditions. The third step is to select a sample of respondents and to obtain from them numerical scores up to a score of 1 for each of the 29 conditions. The scores of individual respondents are then aggregated to form quantitative measures of the sample's, and indirectly the community's, valuation of the quality of life associated with various states of health (1981: 276). The values given by Williams decline in a fairly straightforward manner as the degree of disability and the level of distress increase. The findings confirm that there are few people who prefer to be in a state of extreme distress or who place a high value on being confined to a wheelchair or lying unconscious in bed.

If these are the results, is this rather complex exercise informative? And is it of any use?
I don't think it is *very* informative, although we may find it interesting that some conditions seem to be widely regarded as worse than death; for example, being confined to bed in a state of severe distress somehow gets a score of -1.486. However, the quality of life matrix certainly is useful; at least, many health economists maintain it is and health care managers are beginning to agree. From

the economists' perspective it doesn't matter that the ranking of states of health seems pretty obvious. Indeed, they might reasonably claim that this is a sign of the validity of their procedures. The critical point is, for economists, that they now have a quantified index of people's judgements of the quality of life associated with typical states of health. This means that we no longer have to make unreliable qualitative estimates of whether, say, hip replacements do more good than coronary artery bypass grafting. We can now quantify the benefit gained from radically different therapies using a common unit of value and, what is more, we can fairly easily work out how much each unit of value (QALY) costs in different areas of medicine and, therefore, where we can get best value for money.

I understand the general argument. But I still don't quite understand how you get from Williams' quality of life matrix to the measurement of quality adjusted life years.
In order to do this, you need some more information from patients and/or doctors. Basically, you require a profile of what happens to a typical patient over time after a specific medical treatment has occurred. In Williams' paper, doctors provide this information. But, in due course, patients will probably be employed to provide more accurate data. However they are obtained, the analyst's task is to interpret these profiles in terms of the aggregate quality of life scores attached to the various states of health identified in the matrix. For example, if a typical patient has an additional life expectancy of three years after having operation X and the matrix scores for those three years are 0.5, 0.3 and 0.2, the typical benefit of that operation will be 1.0 QALY (0.5 + 0.3 + 0.2). Operation Y in contrast, may add ten years to a patient's life expectancy with a quality of life score of 0.9 throughout. The QALY for operation Y, therefore, is 9 (0.9 x 10) and we can conclude that operation Y is nine times more valuable than operation X.

QALYs do seem to be very useful. By turning people's subjective judgements into an objective index, obtained by means of systematic and explicit procedures, they seem to help us to make rational choices. In the hypothetical example that you gave, we would clearly choose to divert resources from X to Y until their benefits were equal at the margin. You see, I'm not entirely ignorant of economics.
Well, a little economics is a dangerous thing. You've forgotten to consider costs. One of the great advantages of QALYs is that they enable us to compute a single-figure ratio in which benefit gained is related to cost incurred. Thus if operation X cost £100 and operation Y £900, the cost per quality adjusted life year gained would be identical for the two cases and nothing at all would be gained by altering things. However, in general terms, once costs have been taken into account we can use QALYs to construct a 'league table' of medical treatments which will show clearly where resources can be redeployed to provide greater benefit for patients in their own terms. Williams begins to do this in his paper. Thus the QALY can be regarded as a technique devised by economists to solve administrators' problems of resource allocation in such a way that patients derive the maximum benefit from doctors' actions.

That sounds wonderful. No doubt there will be many practical difficulties to be overcome. But by making people's preferences available to NHS managers and clinicians in quantitative form, the health economists do seem to be helping to construct a system of health care in which the patient's welfare or quality of life becomes the primary focus at last.

I'm not willing to accept that formulation without amendment. I would say that they are trying to construct a system in which the patient's welfare or quality of life *as seen by (some) health economists* is the primary focus.

Isn't that splitting hairs? You're quibbling over my choice of words. The fact is that the economists are going to patients, or at least to people who are potential patients, and obtaining the preferences that they carry about in their heads. In this basic respect, therefore, it is patients who will, ultimately, determine health care policy; that is, if the health economists' proposals are put into effect. However, I expect you will object to this interpretation on the grounds that the economists' recommendations will be changed, as you argued earlier, by the administrators and by political negotiations within the NHS.

Further implications are explored

No, I don't want to repeat that point. I want to concentrate now on the relationship between the economist and the *patient*. I'm very doubtful about your claim, which I think is Williams' claim as well, that the health economists' measurement techniques correctly represent patients' preferences. For instance, when we examine his paper we see that whereas health administrators *do* contribute actively to that paper in that they provide the initial problem and they are given space in which to express their support for further development of his investigations, patients never appear actively in the text at all. Generalizations about patients' inclinations are sometimes offered by the author; for example, that 'some patients are willing to sacrifice a measure of life expectancy for a better quality of life' (1985: 326). But the textual voice on such occasions is always that of the economist. We are never given direct access to the reasoning practices of patients or ordinary people in relation to the issues as they might define them. This is very clear in the case of people's judgements of quality of life and the indices of quality adjusted life years. This material is always presented in tabular or graphical form. Consequently, in this text, we are never concerned with any individual person's actual evaluations, but with aggregate evaluations prepared by economists or by their colleagues. It is quite misleading, therefore, to suggest that QALYs can bring the preferences of the general public directly to bear upon health care policy. What QALYs may do is to introduce into the policy arena some consideration of responses obtained from ordinary people. But these responses are given meaning by and processed in aggregate terms by economic experts.

But surely this is standard procedure in the social sciences. Would you prefer Williams to write chatty biographies about what Mrs Jones thinks and then generalize from Mrs Jones to the world at large? The use of aggregate measures is simply, if I may use the word in this context, an 'economical' way of expressing a central tendency within the group. If Williams did not aggregate his data, we would be lost in a welter of discrepant individual judgements and quite unable to come to any conclusion about what should be done to improve NHS policy. By means of aggregation, however, he can convey communal judgements with precision and make possible a rational choice of outcomes in accordance with those judgements.

I agree that this is normal procedure for much quantitative social science and that, within this approach, the range of methodological alternatives is strictly limited. The point I want to emphasize, however, is that such research methods do not represent the judgements of individual respondents, but rather create a new reality out of those judgements. Moreover, this analyst's reality can come to be regarded as 'more real' than that of the individuals it is supposed to represent. In the case of quality of life measures, for instance, as Williams notes in an earlier paper, the value that 'emerges may not coincide with the actual valuations of any particular individual' (1981: 277). Yet it is the value produced by the expert and given meaning in terms of the expert's analytical assumptions which is to be used as the basis for policy and as a guide for practical action. In this case, it is the economist alone who is allowed to speak on behalf of potential patients as a collectivity, even though no individual members of the collectivity may endorse the values proposed by the economist. It is accepted, of course, that the potential patient can give a true account of his or her personal preferences. But the precise measurement of the preferences of the group can be provided only by the economist. Indeed, if the valuations that emerged actually coincided with those of any particular individual or group of individuals, this could be taken as grounds for suggesting that the measurements were defective. (These points apply equally to any sociologist or other social scientist trying to measure group phenomena.) This is what I meant when I suggested earlier that the facts about quality of life furnished in Williams' text, and used as the basis for practical recommendations, are not patients' facts but economists' facts. They exist only through the actions and interpretative work carried out by economists. They are, therefore, resistant to challenge by potential patients, as are the practical recommendations to which they give rise, unless patients adopt the economists' basic assumptions about the possibility of aggregating individual preferences.

But this is only because social scientists have a unique ability to identify and give voice to patients' preferences. Their findings and eventual recommendations are severely restricted by the facts of the matter. Economists, for example, do not invent these preferences. What they do is to use their special knowledge and techniques to reveal preferences which already exist out there in the real world. In other words, economists are constrained by the data. Their measurements and conclusions, although they may not and perhaps should not coincide exactly with those of individual patients, do genuinely represent the average of the judgements of the group in question. It is true that we cannot know the nature of this collective judgement without economists' (or some other social scientists') help, but the reality which they make available to us is not their reality. It is that of the community of people from whom their data are obtained.

Perhaps. But this view depends on the assumption that the 'data' which supposedly 'constrain' economists are not their own creation and that they do not impose their own meanings on those data. I think that both these assumptions are wrong. Shall I explain why?

Please do.
In an earlier paper (1981) to which I have referred several times, Williams lists a series of six conditions which have to be satisfied when individuals express their evaluations of the quality of life associated with specific states of health. He states there that the analyst must try to ensure that respondents think of each health state as existing for the same length of time, that they judge each state on the basis of its intrinsic 'enjoyability', that all states are evaluated as if the respondent were in them now, that no element of prognosis 'seeps in', and so on. These conditions, he comments, are 'very stringent' and they 'make empirical work to elicit such evaluations rather difficult' (1981: 275).

Clearly, the analyst can try to make sure, as far as possible, that these conditions are satisfied by formulating questions in an appropriate manner. But it is impossible to tell from respondents' evaluations themselves – that is, from the 'raw data' – whether or not judgements have been carried out in the ideal fashion required by the measurement technique. What happens in practice, of course, is that analysts simply interpret the data on the assumption that these conditions have been met. Thus in his short BMJ paper Williams makes no mention of these stringent methodological requirements. In this text, respondents' quality of life scores are treated as unproblematic in the sense that the background assumptions on which their analytical meaning, and their practical implications, depend are left implicit. As a result, the ever-present possibility, in principle, of alternative interpretations becomes hidden from view.

If we worry about the 'ever-present possibility of alternative interpretations' we will never solve our analytical problems; nor will our research produce results which are useful in the practical world. This kind of constant concern with interpretative uncertainties seems to be one of the major differences between sociologists and economists. Sociologists sit there contemplating their own navels, or in this case someone else's epistemological difficulties, whilst economists get on with the real job of solving problems and improving our understanding. In Williams' case, you mentioned earlier that he admits that his present data are crude. Presumably this implies a recognition on his part that he has had to make assumptions in order to interpret the data. But these assumptions can be checked in future studies and the conclusions made increasingly rigorous.
That may be so. But it seems to me that many of these assumptions become taken utterly for granted and, consequently, are never put to the test. For example, in Williams' 1985 paper he notes that the evaluations of the doctors in the sample of respondents who provided the quality of life scores tended to differ significantly from those of the rest of the sample. In particular, the doctors tended to give lower scores than did other people. Williams concludes that these doctors 'appeared to have a much greater aversion to disability and distress than the population at large' and that they therefore overvalued 'reductions in disability

and distress compared with the rest of the population' (1985: 327).

In reaching this conclusion, Williams has assumed that there are no relevant variations within the sample in respondents' ability to understand the quality of life measure and to comply with the stringent conditions which it requires. In other words, he seems at this stage to have forgotten that the meaning given to respondents' scores depends on certain assumptions about how the scores were produced. As a result, he has not considered the possibility that systematic differences within the sample may well be due to differences in respondents' understanding of the measurement procedure. It seems just as reasonable to assume, however, that doctors, due to their high level of training in relation to issues of health care, are more able than the other members of the sample to make the precise and subtle assessments required by the quality of life measure. But if we make this assumption, we will be led to conclude that the average scores for the sample as a whole are inaccurate and that the scores furnished by the sub-sample of doctors may be a more valid indicator of quality of life valuations for the population at large. Thus Williams ignores the possibility that the stringent conditions required in this line of research may be satisfied to varying degrees by different kinds of respondent and infers that the different responses of doctors and others indicate genuine evaluative differentials. In contrast, my alternative interpretation assumes that doctors may understand the nature and requirements of the measuring device better than other people and that their scores are more accurate and furnish a better guide for practical action.

I am not trying to insist that this alternative interpretation is the correct one and that Williams is necessarily mistaken. The main point I wish to make is that Williams' data alone do not determine his conclusions about quality of life or about practical action. I have tried to show that, by varying our background assumptions, we can derive significantly different conclusions from the same set of quantitative scores; and that entirely reasonable alternative assumptions are available. I suggest, therefore, that if we wish to understand how Williams' conclusions about QALYs and medical treatments are produced we must concentrate, not on his data, but on the assumptions which are used to give meaning to those data.

Are you suggesting that there are further assumptions relevant to QALYs which are not identified in Williams' earlier (1981) paper?
Yes, I think there are. The assumptions formulated in Williams' 1981 paper are relatively specific and closely linked to quality of life measures. But there are other presuppositions evident in his work that are probably basic to much economic analysis. I don't want to overwhelm you with a lengthy disquisition on the nature of economic discourse (see McCloskey 1985). Instead, I will just comment briefly on three important background assumptions. I shall call them the assumptions of correspondence, stability and quantification. I will argue that these assumptions, although taken for granted in, for example, Williams' text, are open to question.

The first assumption is that the categories used by the analyst correspond with or capture the evaluations that respondents make in the course of ordinary everyday life. Unless this assumption is made, the analyst can hardly use her or his findings to recommend changes in NHS practice. Yet it seems a highly unlikely assumption because the analyst's categories are so abstract and artificial, because the judgements of quality of life elicited by the research technique are so far removed from those which occur in real social situations, and because the analysts state that their measurements actually change respondents' evaluations. For instance, the scores used in Williams' paper are generated by presenting to respondents a pre-arranged set of categories of disability and distress, clearly ranked in terms of severity, and by asking respondents to allocate numerical estimates of quality of life to these abstract conditions. It is hardly surprising that such a procedure generates a smooth distribution of aggregate values. But are these values in any way related to people's everyday judgements or are they a predictable response to an abstractly conceived measurement technique?

It is clear that in everyday life people are not required to distinguish between carefully defined categories, but to choose between ill-defined courses of action in situations which are complex, diffuse and subject to change. Judgements of quality of life, I suggest, may well be made quite differently in these two radically different kinds of context. Indeed Williams recognizes this, at least implicitly, when he discusses the stringent conditions of measurement which make empirical research in this area so difficult. In ordinary life, the experimental conditions identified by Williams as being required by the measurement procedure are never satisfied. It seems to me, therefore, rather difficult to assume that the scores elicited by the abstract, artificial measurement technique correspond in any straightforward way to the judgements that people make in normal circumstances.

The assumption of correspondence seems to become even more doubtful when one reads another previous paper which maintains that the subjects involved in evaluating the states of ill-health according to this procedure 'experienced the interview as traumatic and felt that it changed their perception of illness' (Kind, Rosser and Williams 1982: 167). If the scores obtained from respondents do express perceptions that have been altered by the act of measurement, it seems clear that these scores cannot correspond with or properly represent the values of a larger population whose members have not undergone measurement and whose normal procedures of evaluation seem to be so different from those used in the measurement device that the latter are experienced as profoundly disturbing.

At the very least, I suggest, we have to conclude that social scientists measuring quality of life in this way are assuming a correspondence between their measurements and people's ordinary judgements that is rather doubtful. Although the correspondence between social scientists' observations and the values of the population at large is far from certain, it is nonetheless taken for granted in the course of analysis. It is an assumption that is routinely brought to the data by the analyst and is used to give meaning to the data and to project that meaning upon the wider social world with which s/he is ultimately concerned.

The other two assumptions that I mentioned before operate, I think, in much the same way. The assumption of stability presupposes that people carry around a set of internal preferences or evaluations which are relatively stable. Given this assumption, the task of the researcher is to elicit and record those individual, internal states as precisely as possible. However, there is now a large body of research showing that the values forthcoming from given respondents change significantly in accordance with variations in the process of elicitation, and also that there appears to be little relationship between the values thus elicited and the choices actors make in real situations. It may be, therefore, that we should treat participants' evaluations as variable *social* phenomena and their evaluative responses, not as expressions of stable underlying preferences, but as reactions to socially defined situations (Cicourel 1964). In so far as we come to recognize the social character of the research process and the socially generated character of subjects' responses, the assumption that the social researcher is eliciting relatively stable and context-free evaluations becomes much less plausible. Once again, we come to see the assumption of stability as a presupposition which is taken for granted when the analyst treats his/her measurements as referring to stable preferences which exist independently of the process of measurement.

Similarly, the assumption of quantification seems to me to be quite unrealistic. It is fundamental to the procedure for constructing QALYs that respondents are required to make precise numerical assessments of the conditions provided by the analyst. Unless this is done, the benefits of different treatments cannot be measured and cost/benefit ratios cannot be derived. The analysis seems to assume, therefore, that the numbers assigned by respondents have some real meaning for them in ordinary situations and that these numbers express quantifications that are already implicit in individual respondents' scales of preference. We have to accept, of course, that analysts can persuade many respondents to assign numbers to the abstract categories which they provide, even though this process may often be experienced as traumatic. But we know from other studies that subjects in the experimental context can also be persuaded to pass what are taken to be damaging charges of electricity through innocent people (Milgram 1974). In other words, there may be good grounds for doubting whether actions such as quantification that are accomplished in the research setting closely reflect the processes which normally occur in everyday situations. Given the wholly artificial nature of the measurement procedure, it seems likely that the smooth distribution of scores produced in these attempts to measure quality of life is a result of respondents' recognition of a quantification already implicit in the analyst's pre-arranged categories.

You're arguing, then, that people's everyday judgements of quality of life are not quantitative, are not stable and do not correspond with the analyst's abstract categories.

Conclusions are drawn concerning social science and practical action

I'm arguing that the analyst, in using certain kinds of measurement techniques and in interpreting results in a particular manner, is making *assumptions* on these issues and that entirely reasonable alternative assumptions are possible. I'm also arguing that quality of life measures and QALYs are not re-presentations of people's pre-existing values. They are, I suggest, the interpretative outcome of a special, and indeed rather peculiar, form of social interaction between economists (and/or other social scientists) and ordinary people. Although QALYs are presented as an accurate reflection of the latter's preferences, ordinary people are only able to express their preferences through a measurement procedure which is constructed in terms of social scientist's preconceptions. Potential patients contribute only indirectly to economists' accounts of their preferences and it is economists who establish the *meaning* of that contribution.

To return to what I was saying earlier, economists use their results to speak on behalf of patients and to specify what actions would best serve patients' interests. Yet economists' results and recommendations depend on the background assumptions of their disciplinary culture. If that culture were different, what economists say on our behalf would be different. It is in this sense that the facts expressed in QALYs are not patients' facts, but economists' facts.

I accept much of what you have said about the interpretative dominance of the economist over his/her subjects of study. But in this respect, economics is surely no different from other social sciences; except perhaps that economists have used this dominance to greater scientific effect than, say, sociologists, who have been excessively concerned with the limitations of their own findings.

Its true that economists have been relatively successful in shaping the factual world of economic phenomena in accordance with the assumptions of their own disciplinary culture. Unlike sociologists, economists have more or less consciously adopted the simplest possible model of the social actor (namely, a maximizer of utility) and have used it to generate a wide range of rigorous, elegant analyses. In this respect, simplification and quantification have paid off analytically; if economists' claims were confined to their professional journals, the adequacy of their analyses would be for them to decide. However, when economists intervene in the realm of practical action, their analytical concern with a world of idealized economic phenomena and, in particular, their failure to recognize the social character of the research process and the social character of their own knowledge-claims may become significant for outsiders like ourselves.

You mean because economists imply that they know, or that they will know in due course, our real preferences and that they are, therefore, speaking and acting on our behalf, whether we realize it or not.

Yes, that's right. We need to understand economists' discourse because it appears textually to be a re-presentation of the general public's preferences and as such, as I suggested earlier, it may be absorbed into the decision-making practices of the NHS and used there as a basis for action and/or as a potent source of legitimation. Its important to remember that the range of potential application of concepts such as the QALY is very wide indeed. Given that economics is taken to be 'the systematic study of all human actions where scarce resources are used to produce valued outcomes', we can expect that, given the opportunity, economists will speak on our behalf in almost any area of practical activity.

You seem determined to find fault with the health economists. They are simply trying to use their distinctive skills to help other people. And all you can do is to criticize.

What I have to say must appear to be critical because its my task as a sociologist to refuse to accept the taken for granted assumptions of those I study and to make them available for inspection (Schutz 1972). But I may have another unacknowledged reason for criticizing the health economists. It may be that I have to prove them to be wrong, if I am to be able to establish the analytical and/ or practical value of my own contribution. I think that there is an important general point here about using one's knowledge to assist others; namely, in order to be of assistance one's knowledge must be shown to differ significantly from and to be rather better than that of the recipient (Ashmore, Mulkay and Pinch 1989).

That seems a rather trivial observation to me.
Perhaps it is. But the need to distinguish one's knowledge from the recipient's can have major consequences for the social negotiation of knowledge. There's a good example of this in relation to QALYs. Williams argues, you will remember, that in judging the success of medical treatments administrators and others have relied unduly in the past on measuring improvements in patients' life expectancy. He suggests that this is quite unsatisfactory for the considerable number of treatments whose main effect is on quality of life rather than the duration of life. It is for this reason that Williams' measure of medical effectiveness, the QALY, combines life expectancy with quality of life in a single indicator. However, in the matrix of scores for quality of life used by Williams the range of variation tends to be rather narrow. More specifically, 18 out of the 29 scores are between 0.9 and 1.0. As I explained earlier, Williams' quality of life scores measure how far various states of health are judged to fall below a normal quality of life. The figures in the matrix therefore suggest, if one adopts Williams' interpretation that they accurately represent respondents' ordinary judgements, that in the majority of conditions (18 out of 29) quality of life is deemed to be almost indistinguishable from normal. A condition would have to involve confinement to a wheelchair or something of that kind before respondents in the sample used by Williams begin to judge the quality of life as falling below 90% of normal. One consequence of this small range of variation is that quality of life scores tend to make a relatively minor contribution to Williams' QALYs; variations in life expectancy contribute much more to the final indicator and to the supposed differences in the benefits produced by various medical treatments.

This, of course, somewhat weakens the argument for the superiority of the QALY over the administrators' customary indicator of life expectancy. It also means that the QALYs generated using Williams' quality of life matrix may in many cases furnish little additional information for the policy makers in the NHS. However, since the publication of Williams' paper in 1985 this problem has been noted by other health economists, and moves have been made to ensure that, in the next generation of quantitative measures, the scores for quality of life will vary over a wider range. I have no doubt that a wide spread of quality of life scores will become a standard feature of QALYs in due course and that measures such as Williams' will be regarded as crude and defective preliminary attempts. Williams himself prepares the way for this when he stresses that his data are undoubtedly 'in need of refinement' (1985: 326).

Clearly, from the point of view of the health economists working on QALYs, they are engaged here in devising better indicators (Williams 1972: 204). But, from the point of view of an outsider like myself, they also appear to be engaged in distinguishing their product and their knowledge from that already available to the NHS administrators. There seems to me to be no particular reason to assume that people's real judgements of quality of life must involve a wide range of values rather than a narrow spread. As I mentioned earlier, Williams rejects doctors' scores as atypical because they have a wider spread than those produced by the rest of the sample. Moreover, we can have no independent indicator of these judgements which would help us to decide either way. It seems to me, therefore, that the wide range of values now being built into the measuring devices is not an observable feature of ordinary people's assessments of quality of life. It is, rather, a result of the presupposition by health economists that there is some quantifiable phenomenon out there called 'evaluation of quality of life' which has been inaccessible to administrators, combined with their commitment to measuring it in a way which will enable them to make a distinctive contribution to the administrative process. In my view, contrary to the impression conveyed by the scientific discourse of measurement used by economists, quality of life is not a measurable phenomenon out there in the social world, but an interpretative by-product of the social interaction between ordinary people, doctors, NHS managers and, most important of all in this context, health economists.

One thing that worries me is that you don't seem to apply your own kind of critique to yourself. Your research is as much a social act as the economists' and as much a process of attributing meaning guided by assumptions current within your discipline. Why should I accept the points that you have made against health economics if you avoid applying them to your own assertions?
Its entirely up to you. You can accept my arguments if you find them persuasive and reject them if you do not, but obviously I hope to persuade you. Anyway, I don't see my arguments as being directed particularly against health economics or health economists. My general claims about the social production and application of knowledge would indeed apply to any field of intellectual endeavour, including my own. What I've been trying to do, analytically, is to draw attention to some of the specific background assumptions which form part of the social practice of health economics and to the conventional nature of the textual forms used by economists, as well as by most other social scientists, whereby the contingent, socially generated claims of specific groups of 'knowledge producers' come to be depicted as, and sometimes mistaken for, the preferences of the population at large or the 'real world' of everyday action. At the same time, I have a practical message. I'm saying to anyone who is willing to listen to me: 'Be careful. This is only one way of looking at the world. There can be other versions of the facts and other rational and practically effective courses of action'.

So that's your version of the facts?
It is. But I have tried not to hide the partiality of my account behind the language of measurement and the supposedly universal discourse of scientific fact. I make

no claims for any privileged position and it is for you to decide on these matters for yourself.

Well, I'm rather disappointed if that's all you have to say. I am obliged to point out that you have engaged in a form of intellectual cheating. By making such strong criticisms of health economists you have implied that better procedures could be devised and put to work. But then you let yourself off the hook by admitting at the end that the same points could probably be made about anything. You've led me on, encouraging me to expect that you are going to provide a practical solution of your own – and now you've welshed on the deal. I would go so far as to allege that your moral condemnation of health economists has boomeranged, revealing the moral culpability of your own position.

I'm very sorry that you feel like that. It hadn't occurred to me that you would expect me to step into the health economists' shoes. I have to say that I refuse to replace their analytical expertise with my own. I did not invite you into my text in order to convince you that I and my sociological colleagues can provide better practical advice in the realm of health care than those academics in the next department. In fact, rather than offering to use my analytical expertise to help *you*, I have been trying to clarify these misunderstandings as a prelude to asking you to help *me*. Before I can hope to do anything of practical benefit, I need to find some way of bringing your voice, the questioning voice of the potential recipient, more actively into my texts. Unless I can engage you in true dialogue, applied sociological analysis, however well intentioned, will remain a discourse of domination. But are you willing to help?

14 Looking backward (1989)

Publications in the formal literature need to have an author. For this reason, I have put my name at the head of this text. I have also provided the title. But I must emphasize that the words below are not mine. I have done nothing more, in this case, than transcribe an audio-tape recording which has recently come into my possession and submit it to the journal's editor. This latter step seemed to me to be appropriate in view of the tape's unique character. If you choose to read on, it will soon become clear why I came to believe that wider distribution was essential. It is no exaggeration, I believe, to suggest that the publication of this transcript may mark a turning-point in human history. As a result, there are likely to be many enquiries about its authenticity. Let me, therefore, state that I have been given conclusive proof that the tape is genuine. I cannot reveal more in this public forum. However, toward the end of the tape, the speaker throws some light on these matters.

The tape seems to have been recorded at some kind of academic conference. On the original version, there is background noise and evidence of a live audience. This transcription presents only the words of the main speaker. The speaker is female.

*   *   *   *   *

Dear Friends and Fellow Listeners, Welcome.

I begin this annual meeting of the Society for the Herstory of Knowledges with the form of address that is conventional in our culture. But little else in this talk will be conventional. I intend today to break with convention in order to remind you dramatically of the distinctive forms of our discourse and of how these forms inform our understanding of the worlds which we create around us.

My first unconventional act is to draw your attention to what is blatantly obvious, namely, that time is passing. To be more specific, we are approaching the end of the ninety-ninth year of the New Era. Thus it will soon be exactly one hundred years since the final act of that great catastrophe, sometimes called the Cultural Holocaust, which enveloped and destroyed the scientific-technological societies of the pre-modern era. I realize that it is deeply embarrassing for you to hear me speak in this distressingly direct fashion and to hear me refer to such crude temporal symmetries. But there are reasons for these solecisms which will, perhaps, eventually emerge and which will, I hope, justify my departure from the conventions that govern intellectual discourse in our specialist Herstorical Society as well as in the wider society of which we are a minor part.

Our culture is deeply averse to any straightforward representation of symmetrical pattern or of coherent symbolic order. This is one reason why we of the post-Holocaust world so carefully avoid drawing attention to anniversaries of any kind. However, I have begun in this way because I intend this afternoon to look backward and indeed to speak, as far as is possible, not in the style of the present but in the style of the past, when conceptions of symmetry and order were intellectually dominant. Your natural response to this is likely to be: 'What on earth has the *past* to do with the study of herstory? The texts of the past have already been performed. They can only operate as a stifling restriction on the creative imagination of the herstorian, whose task is to assist in formulating the texts of the future. Our job', you may remind me, 'is not to tell the story of what happened, but to help create the stories that *will* happen.'

I accept all that, of course. I am, after all, an herstorian and I am aware that we run a risk if we deviate from our customary concerns and, in particular, if we return to the discourse of the pre-modern era. For it seems self-evident to us now that it was certain basic flaws in the language of scientific-technological society that led to its demise. Consequently, one of the most obvious paradoxes of our own paradoxical culture is that it denies the relevance of the past, yet its basic cultural forms can be seen to derive their legitimacy from a rejection of, and therefore a specific understanding of, the past. This paradox or inconsistency is comforting. We in the present world could hardly endorse an important cultural assumption that did *not* generate this kind of self-referential contradiction.

Nevertheless, I believe that our view of the past has its own dangerous flaw, namely, that if we were to forget entirely what the bad discourse of scientific-technological society was like, we would be unable to recognize that discourse if it were to reappear. Furthermore bad discourse, once established, spreads like an uncontrolled infectious disease or like the viruses that destroyed the first phase of computer technology. Even the early, twentieth century discourse analysts recognized this and tried to express it in a simplistic formulation which they called Gresham's Law of Discourse; namely, that 'Bad discourse drives out good'. To adopt pre-modern forms of discourse, however briefly, is certainly risky. But it is my view that we in the Society for the Herstory of Knowledges cannot avoid taking up the heavy burden of returning periodically to the past in order to safeguard the future by reminding ourselves of the pernicious linguistic forms so disastrously employed by our predecessors.

You, my listeners, will be well aware that I have already begun to use the alien mode of bygone times. Our essentially dialogic forms of discourse have been abandoned and the very structure of my language-use prevents you from joining with me in collaborative exchange. I hope you will forgive me as I continue in the archaic, unfamiliar and, I admit, discourteous form of the extended monologue. I am convinced that only by adopting this unconventional literary device from the past can I bring home to you the fundamental character of, as well as the basic dangers and defects of, the discourse of the pre-modern era. Some kind of break with convention is, of course, required by the conventions governing our annual presidential address. I hope it will become clear in due course,

however, that my departure today from the forms of proper discourse is intended
to be more than conventionally unconventional.

I will now briefly review the dominant approach to knowledge and to discourse in
scientific-technological society. I will refer to scientific-technological society as
'STS'. The univocal, extended monologue that I am employing in this
presentation was by no means the only textual form readily available within STS.
Indeed, the textual resources of STS were rich and varied. But this form acquired
a privileged position in that it came to dominate the production and
communication of what was taken to be knowledge. You will note that I have
used the singular term 'knowledge' in relation to STS rather than the customary
'knowledges'. This is necessary because, in STS, knowledge was generally
conceived as a single, coherent body of symbolic formulations which represented
the one objective, independent world shared by all. In other words, for these
primitive people of the past, knowledge was not multiple but unitary. It was
recognized, of course, that the knowledge-claims proposed by different
individuals and groups, or even by the same individuals and groups on different
occasions, often seemed to be quite incompatible. But this was put down to
human error and to people's failure to observe the world in a properly disinterested
and impartial fashion. The fundamental epistemological assumption of the culture
was that human beings inhabited a single, orderly independent world. It was
thought that knowledge consisted of those symbolic formulations which
accurately reproduced this world; and it came to be widely accepted that this
process of symbolic reproduction required an army of specialists who were
trained to employ the necessary linguistic forms and observational procedures. In
due course, the internal structure of the community of knowledge-producers, with
its complex network of tribal divisions, actually came to be regarded as a
reflection of the organization of the natural world. This strange blindness to the
social character of the process of knowledge-production pervaded STS because it
was built into its members' conception of knowledge and into their basic patterns
of language-use.

The development and cultivation of a unitary, univocal view of 'the world'
among the specialist knowledge-producers of STS proceeded with growing
momentum during the seventeenth, eighteenth and nineteenth centuries of the so-
called Christian era. As this happened, dialogic textual forms and discursive
repertoires which celebrated the uncertainty, ambiguity and multiplicity of the
worlds in which we have our being fell into decline and almost disappeared from
the various realms of intellectual enquiry. True knowledge, it was increasingly
assumed, had to be singular, unambiguous, exact and empirically validated; and
the language of knowledge had to be refashioned accordingly. In the words of a
leading eighteenth century advocate of the new kind of scientific knowledge:
'The creation of a science is nothing else than the establishment of a language,
and to study a science is to do nothing else than to learn a well-made language'.

The 'well-made language' of the scientific movement seems naive, even
ludicrous, to us. Nevertheless, the language of science was at the heart of STS
and was, in many ways, highly productive. The basic generative feature of this
language was that it was meant to enable its users to capture a world which was

assumed to exist in a particular form independently of the activities of the human knower. Thus the language and its associated knowledge-claims had to appear to be free from the potential 'bias' of subjective preference and from the 'distorting influence' of social relationships. The language of science had to seem to be, as far as humanly possible, a language of pure mind which could be taken to describe and to report, with detached precision, the orderly processes of the one true world. Accordingly, the knowledge-producers of STS gradually created a form of language-use in which their texts appeared to be a neutral medium through which the objective world itself gave symbolic expression to its own orderly processes. You will observe that, in my talk this evening, I am trying to adopt an analogous format and to furnish a monologic text which appears to look backward into the past and to describe a world which existed independently of my textual efforts, yet which is faithfully mirrored in the words of my text.

My empiricist monologue, however, cannot be fully effective, partly because I do not have adequate command of the scholarly rhetoric required by this linguistic form, but also because you will not hear my words from within the world-view of STS. It is built into *your* conception of life that the past and the future, the world without and the world within, are all fleeting dreams, are all passing products of our use of words, and that their stories can legitimately be told, indeed can *only* properly be told, in many different ways. But, I in*sist*, the people of STS did not think like that and did not approach their world in our tolerant, flexible, multi-faceted fashion.

Unlike ourselves, the people of STS, both knowledge-producers and knowledge-consumers, made a sharp distinction between what they called 'factual' and 'fictional' texts. As far as I can understand it, the former were taken to represent the so-called 'real world', whilst the latter were seen as imaginative creations which depicted 'unreal events'. However, it seems to have been accepted that factual texts were often wrong and, therefore, *mis*represented the real world and that fiction could convey profound truths about that world. Its very confusing and difficult for us to comprehend. Why did they not simply accept that all texts are, by their very nature, imaginative creations whatever the textual format or linguistic devices they employ? Why did they not realize that scientific facts, for example, are the fictions that scientists create in their laboratories? Surely they must have been aware that textual production is always socially located and conveys a version of events that has been created out of the limited cultural resources of specific groups, such as the various specialized groups of knowledge-producers in STS? How could they continue to maintain that they inhabited one world held in common, even though no two people formulated that world in the same way? Their answers to these questions are difficult to discern. For such questions, although they seem obvious to us and grow naturally out of our culture, could then have been posed only at the cultural periphery. Nevertheless, I will try to explain in broad terms how knowledge-producers in particular managed to proceed despite their strange underlying assumptions about knowledge and about the relationship between language and 'the world'.

In the first place, the practitioners of science employed public and private or formal and informal discourses which were quite different in their linguistic organization. You will note that I am using the kind of simple, binary contrast here that was endemic in this pre-modern era. The formal, public discourse of science, which was supposed to embody the culture's corpus of validated knowledge, was impersonal in style, technical in content, neutral in tone, and generally gave the impression of being produced by non-social automata rather than by flesh and blood human beings. This formal language was in strict accordance with the dominant cultural conception of knowledge as a detached representation of a world out there. It was a crucial rhetorical resource in scientists' eventual attainment of cultural ascendancy. But we, of course, realize that they could not have operated consistently in terms of this conception and that they could not have relied solely on this inflexible and one-dimensional form of language-use. Indeed, it is clear that they did not. The formal discourse of the knowledge-producers was, if you will allow the unlikely metaphor, like the crust of a succulent meat pie. From the outside, nothing else is visible. But only beneath the crust, on the inside, can the hot, living culture be discovered.

The inner culture of science was radically different from its formal surface; and its technical content was embedded here in quite different language forms. For instance, scientists' informal repertoires were often highly personal, socially variable and socially aware; and their supposedly neutral representations of the putative external world were regularly taken to be inconclusive, contingent and dependent on covert, unjustifiable background assumptions. In informal, private contexts, scientists' actions and beliefs were less likely to be depicted as generic responses to the realities of the natural world, and more likely to be treated as the activities and judgements of specific individuals acting on the basis of their personal inclinations and particular social commitments.

The flexibility of this private language was essential to science. It enabled knowledge-producers to cope more or less adequately with the interpersonal difficulties that inevitably grew out of their adoption of a unitary formal discourse. It was, however, their technical, public language that was the source of their power, both for good and for evil. The technical, public discourse of science, as we have seen, involved the presentation of formulations which captured (the metaphor of 'capture' is most appropriate) and gave expression to the patterns and processes of 'the real world' in a precise, economical and empirically documented manner. Now it is evident that few areas of investigation are amenable to such formulation when observed in the full complexity of their natural occurrence. It is for this reason that the relatively simple and highly repetitive movement of the planets provided the first major success for the proto-scientists of the seventeenth century. Even here, of course, the so-called laws of planetary motion were but approximations. In other words, the laws were general prescriptions depicting an idealized world. Despite centuries of subsequent research and symbolic refinement, the concrete predictions derived from the laws of motion were never made to coincide in an entirely satisfactory manner with the observed planetary movements. The search for the supposed 'missing planet', which it was thought would finally remove these anomalies, was still underway when scientific research as they knew it came to an end. Nevertheless, the match between 'fact' and 'theory' became very close in the case of this simple, stable, closed system and scientists' predictive power became phenomenal. In due course, they were able to use their knowledge effectively to control, if not the movements of the planets, at least the movement of human beings between them with only the occasional disastrous mishap. This success strengthened the hold of a simplistic and misleading view of scientific knowledge and its practical application from which the community of knowledge-producers was never able to escape.

The massive, regular, basically simple movements of the stable planetary system could be observed, described and predicted without active intervention. In this respect, they were quite unlike most other topics of scientific investigation. In the vast majority of cases, the complex irregularity of uncontrolled natural processes defied attempts at orderly, precise identification of fundamental patterns. The knowledge-producers of STS, committed to reinterpreting the complex uniqueness of natural events in accordance with their vision of an orderly, repetitive world, responded with the critical scientific technique of controlled experiment. Their essential procedure was to take the phenomena in which they were interested out of the natural world and into the world of the laboratory where human beings were in control. In this environment, natural processes were artificially simplified and manipulated in ways which enabled scientists to re-present them in terms of idealized symbolic formulations. Of course, even under these exceptional conditions, the correspondence between manufactured observation and idealized model was never complete. The theoretical models of science were not just re-statements of the results of controlled observation, but imaginative projections which furnished the human beings involved with an orderly picture of that fragment of the world in which they were interested. Nevertheless, it was these models, these idealized representations of empirical processes generated under artificial conditions that came to constitute the fundamental knowledge of STS.

The systematic, laboratory-based creation of idealized models of isolated segments of the world gradually came to be regarded as the ultimate form of knowledge-production. It was, undoubtedly, a major development in human culture with many specific practical consequences that were beneficial – at least in the short run. However, like the system of industrial production with which it coincided herstorically and with which it became increasingly intertwined, the mass production of scientific knowledge generated basic cultural contradictions. In the first place, systematically organized scientific research required ever greater specialization. This meant that scientists, in general, came to know a great deal about a very narrow range of artificially manufactured observations and their associated models. Yet, secondly, this peculiar form of knowledge was accepted as the only kind of genuine knowledge about the supposedly one real world. Consequently, its highly specialized exponents came to be viewed as the only reliable sources of knowledge about that world. The public language of science, which was the one facet of scientific culture that was – in grossly simplified form – made available to laypersons, greatly encouraged non-specialists to confuse the symbolic creations of science with the real world they were supposed to represent. For this language depicted the world as independent of, yet at the same time identical with, scientists' culturally generated knowledge-claims. Thirdly, because scientists spoke as if they knew how the world really worked and because they claimed to be able to use their knowledge to intervene successfully in the world outside the laboratory, it came to seem obvious to the people of STS that they should use this knowledge to control the world and to make it operate in their own interests.

The basic flaw in this world-view, which we can see clearly with the benefit of hindsight, is that the knowledge which they took to represent the natural world, and with which they sought to dominate and exploit that world, was but a fragmentary collection of idealized accounts of what had been observed under very peculiar conditions. Furthermore, it was based on the patently false assumption that there is a single, organized world which exists independently of its knowers. The attempt to create a collective body of knowledge in accordance with this assumption can be applauded as one of humankind's great mythic endeavours. However, the attempt to use this knowledge on a massive scale to control 'the world' was bound to expose the impossibility of capturing that supposed world in unitary terms.

It is clear that disaster was inevitable, not merely due to the undeniable complexity and uniqueness of natural events, but more fundamentally to the essential contingency and openness of human cultural systems. It is impossible to create complete, closed and fully validated analytical systems. It is impossible, therefore, to produce knowledge-based procedures of practical action that will not have unexpected and disruptive consequences. Thus it was inevitable that, the greater the scale of intervention in the natural world undertaken by the members of STS, the more certain was it that disaster would ensue and the greater was that disaster likely to be.

But I am getting ahead of myself. Let me return to the development of knowledge-production in STS. We know from the herstorical evidence that, even as early as the seventeenth century, the new breed of natural philosophers or 'scientists' as they were later called, regarded their knowledge as something special. It was special, they claimed, not only because it was reliable knowledge of the real world, but also because it would make possible extensive human control over that world. We realize today, of course, that although the world of the laboratory is real, it is not *the* reality; and certainly not the *same* reality as the world of practical action. However, this confusion was not noticed at the time and was indeed not important at the outset because practitioners' claim concerning the practical usefulness of scientific knowledge was more a promise for the future than a present achievement. It was part of the case made by the early natural philosophers to establish their intellectual superiority over previous knowledge-communities. It was not until the nineteenth, and even more the twentieth, centuries that the sciences became successfully integrated into the various realms of practical action.

This secular shift of emphasis from knowledge-production to knowledge-application did not occur without strenuous efforts by representatives of the scientific community. During the nineteenth and early twentieth centuries, various leading scientists worked hard to create opportunities for the members of their rapidly growing community to be employed in non-academic settings. They succeeded first in entering industry and then military and government establishments. By the mid-twentieth century, the great majority of scientists worked in these practical contexts. In the course of a sustained sequence of cumulative growth in size and in intellectual dominance, the community of scientists established an ever closer relationship with the major productive and redistributive agencies of industrial society and an ever more intimate involvement in its productive, and destructive, activities. In other words, the scientific community became increasingly dependent on the holders of political and economic power, who increasingly put scientific knowledge to work for their own practical purposes and who largely determined the conditions under which the practice of science was allowed to continue.

By the latter part of the twentieth century, the early promise of practical usefulness had been realized to the fullest possible extent. Many scientists trained in an earlier era thought that it had gone much too far. For all knowledge-production was by then linked directly to practical application, either by means of centrally implemented national science policies or by market mechanisms. The universities and colleges of higher learning had been replaced by what came to be called 'knowledge factories'. And the nation states of STS vigorously pursued policies of maximum economic growth, the success of which depended almost entirely on the regular production of new, science-based technologies intended to increase humankind's control over, and exploitation of, the natural world.

At about the same time, it became evident that the cumulative economic and military growth of STS, in which science and scientists were intimately involved, was having radical consequences on a global scale. This was most noticeable in connection with the gross changes occurring in the physical environment. The forests were dying, the earth and oceans were filling with poisonous substances, the weather patterns were altering, and the world-system was beginning to overheat. In the scientifically undeveloped nations, these changes produced floods on an unprecedented scale, failure of crops in previously fertile areas, rising levels of malnutrition, widespread starvation and a cumulative breakdown of social order.

The members of the developed nations were, initially, less affected by these changes, partly owing to their geographical location but also to their much higher levels of science-based agriculture and industrial output. However, the heavy dependence on science-based production in these countries meant that their local environments were also being rapidly destroyed. As the twentieth century moved toward its close, prophets of an approaching Doomsday appeared in ever-increasing numbers. Given the nature of STS, it is not surprising that many of these prophetic figures presented their predictions as the findings of science. 'Science shows', they proclaimed, 'that the world as we know it will end around the year 2000'. The great majority of practising scientists rejected these prophets as charlatans and their claims as non-scientific. We now know, of course, that these prophets were carriers of the truth.

Not only did most scientists refuse to take seriously the prophets of doom, but they were also unwilling to accept responsibility for the calamities engulfing STS. They insisted that there were many complex social and economic factors involved as well as the science-based technologies which they had helped to create. Moreover, they maintained, their knowledge was merely a neutral tool which could be used for good or ill. As scientists, they said, their main task was to reveal how the world actually worked and in what ways it could be manipulated and controlled by humankind. But, they protested, they could not be blamed if this knowledge was put to use in ways which had unfortunate consequences.

It is interesting to note that, at that time, this view of the neutrality of scientific knowledge was widely accepted. There were brief, intermittent social movements, usually on the margins of the scientific community, which called for scientists' acceptance of social responsibility and which were critical of the fundamental conceptions that lay behind the culture of science. But these internal critiques had no lasting effect. The great majority of scientists as well as laypersons in the later stages of STS simply could not imagine any form of valid knowledge other than the scientific. Thus, as their society staggered toward catastrophe, they became ever more reliant on science to solve the problems which were, ultimately, generated by that very form of knowledge.

The problems facing STS during its final phase arose out of the culture of science in the sense that scientists had consistently, over a prolonged period, misled non-scientists about the nature of their knowledge. It is no mitigation of their guilt that they also, to a considerable degree, misled themselves. As I have already pointed out, both the formal language of science and the public claims of the apologists of science conveyed the impression that scientists' certified conclusions were a detached, impartial, precise representation of the processes of the one real world. Thus people came to believe that science was the ultimate form of knowledge; that it therefore gave humankind the ability, and indeed the right, to control and to refashion the world; and that any ensuing problems could be resolved by further extending the scope of scientific knowledge. There can be little doubt that if the members of the scientific community had provided what we would regard as a more appropriate account of their knowledge and of their social practices, the technological, economic and social development of pre-modern society would have been quite different. It may well have been that, if this had been done, the eventual collapse of STS would have been avoided.

The formal language of science, however, was a language of certainty. The formal language of science was a language of mastery and domination. The formal language of science was a language which denied its social origins and its human limitations. These basic features of scientific culture were dangerous, and in due course catastrophic, because they were exported beyond the realm of laboratory practice and applied inappropriately in the attempt to conquer the unique, ever-changing, immeasurably complex and interconnected events of the everyday world. The total commitment by the societies of STS to unrestricted domination of the world system could not have proceeded on the scale and with the lack of restraint that it did, if its knowledge-producers had emphasized that their knowledge was a partial human product emerging out of a particular cultural setting and destined inevitably to be replaced; that it furnished no more than idealized accounts of artificially simplified fragments of the world; that scientists' representations of the world were, therefore, also *mis*representations of the world; that widespread practical action in the everyday world which was based on such idealizations would inevitably produce quite unforeseen and uncontrollable consequences; and that scientists' unparalleled success in providing certified useful knowledge generated in turn a profound *ignorance* in the sense that alternative views of the world, and alternative approaches to understanding and relating to the world, were covertly, yet at the same time utterly, banished from consideration.

This, of course, is the way that we now see science with the wisdom of hindsight. But at the time, even during the final phase of STS, the faith in science was such that the privileged status of scientific knowledge and the assumption that its application was overwhelmingly beneficial were still virtually unquestioned. As a result, the myopic conclusions of its technical specialists continued to permit the cumulative expansion of STS until its destructive consequences were irreversible. To take one example, although by the late twentieth century it was clear that the seas around the main industrial regions were extensively poisoned with the by-products of science-based production, the official specialists in such matters insisted that major changes in the system of production should not be undertaken until the natural processes at work in the polluted environment had been understood with the precision required by laboratory science and given proper symbolic expression in terms of the formal languages of the various appropriate specialisms.

Effective remedial action was in fact never undertaken because STS came to an end before it was deemed to be scientifically feasible. In countless areas such as this, the highly specialized training of scientific personnel, their commitment to forms of laboratory practice ill-designed to cope with the uncertainties of the practical world, and their refusal to recognize that scientific knowledge was part of the wider social context, all prevented STS from responding adequately to its growing range of problems. The problems of the pre-modern era could not be solved from within a world-view pervaded by the assumptions of science because science was itself part of the underlying problem. Thus the radical change of perspective that was needed if humankind was to survive could not, and did not, come from revisions undertaken in the realm of natural science nor from any direct reversal of humankind's exploitative approach to the natural world. It developed instead, as we all know, in the sphere of social relationships. It emerged, in particular, out of a growing concern with the forms of language used in the relationships between men and women.

I will not talk at length about the disintegration of STS or the creation of modern, multi-vocal culture. You will doubtless be feeling restless at being prevented from participating in the ongoing discourse and, even more, at being denied alternative versions of the herstory of STS. I know that you will find the unified, coherent story which I am trying to present inherently unconvincing precisely because it *is*, as far as I can make it, unified and coherent. But I am telling the story this way in order to engage you in the form of language-use that was dominant in STS. In that culture speakers were normally required, whether they were dealing with the natural or the social worlds, to provide unitary, internally consistent, definitive accounts. Each speaker represented in *his* speech the single, orderly world in which *he*, and all other speakers, were assumed to exist. As we have seen, this form of discourse led to fundamental problems in *man's* relationship with the natural world. These problems proved to be irresolveable basically because the natural world was denied a voice of *her own* by the very form of scientific knowledge. In the science-based culture of STS, man had forgotten how to listen to Nature. He saw the reality of the world only from *his* perspective and he mistook *that* reality for *the* reality. This was one of the critical ways in which, the more advanced his knowledge became, the more it produced a countervailing ignorance. In that society, man claimed the unqualified right to speak on Nature's behalf and to manipulate Nature in his own interests. When Nature eventually replied by denying man her sustenance, he was unable to hear her message and continued as before with his increasingly unsuccessful attempts to command and dominate.

That humankind, and Nature, survived this massive failure of comprehension was entirely due to parallel processes of domination, resistance, disintegration and change that were occurring within the social milieu of STS. These processes were complex and were made up of many partially independent strands. There was, for instance, the internal critique of the practice of social science. Participants in many social disciplines came gradually to realize that the unitary forms of scientific language were unsuitable for use in relation to social life because there was no one, objective social world to be captured in precise, symbolic terms, but a multiplicity of divergent, world-creating formulations produced by participants and analysts alike. By the end of the twentieth century, the enterprise of creating a social science analogous to the sciences of the physical and biological worlds was in disarray. Many different attempts were made to create new language forms that could encompass the interpretative multiplicity of the social realm. It was, of course, inevitable that the most radical innovations would first appear in those disciplines that were least integrated into the established community of knowledge-production in STS. Consequently, certain branches of sociology were in the vanguard of the search for 'new literary forms' which could give voice to that teeming multiplicity of social life which had almost disappeared from view behind the vacuous generalizations that passed for knowledge within the scientific approach to society. I must pay brief tribute here to the path-breaking efforts of the York school of multi-voice analysts whose texts are now revered as much as they were initially derided.

Although the sociologists' adoption of new literary forms was a major advance, their position on the intellectual margins of society meant that they could have little social impact. At roughly the same time however, toward the end of the twentieth century of the pre-modern era, certain similar ideas were developing within a social grouping which had the potential to re-shape society, that is, within the Women's Movement. By this time, the Women's Movement had begun to undertake a radical critique of the exploitative, male-centred language of STS. The language of science was a central focus of this critique because science was seen to be the most powerful realization of male-centred language developed by an overwhelmingly male community. The members of the Women's Movement gradually came to recognize that there was a close connection between the exploitation of women built into the ordinary language of STS and the exploitation of Nature built into the technical language of science. Both these forms of exploitation were seen to follow from man's linguistic and practical domination of all that was 'not man'. From the view embedded in man-made language, both women and Nature belonged to the same alien realm, the inhabitants of which were taken to exist in order to serve men's purposes. Consequently, as man's ascendancy over the processes of the natural world slipped away, so women began to assert their independence across the nations of the world. Slowly, but with increasing momentum as it became clear that man's supposed control over Nature had been a disastrous illusion, women began to explore new forms of language which not only set *their* voices free, but also enabled human beings to establish a true dialogue with the social actors of the natural domain.

In any previous herstorical period, the impact of the Women's Movement could not have been fundamental. Under normal circumstances, even if women had succeeded in achieving greater equality, this could have been accomplished only by the adoption of male-centred language and by co-optation within the existing structures of power. However, by the end of the twentieth century, the dominant cultural forms were falling apart and the need for a genuinely radical change became increasingly obvious. In this context of social, moral and intellectual disintegration, the Women's Movement alone offered the possibility of rebuilding social life on a new linguistic basis. The Women's Movement alone offered the possibility of rethinking the relationship between humankind and Nature. The Women's Movement alone offered the possibility of a transformation which would transcend national, class and many other socially divisive boundaries. Thus it was that the Women's Movement eventually gave birth to the multi-vocal, dialogic, collaborative culture of the New Era, with its emphasis on the linguistic equality of women and men, its stress on the equal significance of listening and speaking, and its insistence on the moral parity of the human and non-human realms.

My story now is ended and melted into air, into thin air. (That's not strictly true, as I will explain in a moment.) For me, it provides a warning about the dangers of pre-modern forms of discourse and a reaffirmation of the need to maintain forms different from those which I have tried to describe and, to some degree, to exemplify in this talk. But it is necessary to be careful when interpreting this legend of the death and re-birth of human society. In particular, it should not, in my opinion, be seen as indicating that women's discourse is inherently different from, or superior to, that of men. The willingness of women in STS to search for, and to adopt, new language forms was not due to their femininity, as such, but to their moral and social subjugation in a society in decline, and to the special perspective on the world that they acquired as women in a male-centred society. Now that that subjugation has been removed and now that what is herstorically 'women's language' is culturally dominant, the danger is that women will come to replace men as the source of exploitation and that forms of language will evolve which will hide this fact from them. The maintenance of a culture founded on good discourse is, by its very nature, always precarious. In this talk, I have tried to remind you, my friends and fellow listeners, of this fact, in a manner which is unconventional and thereby, I hope, provocative and stimulating.

Let me conclude, however, by revealing another reason for my having addressed you in the ancient style of bygone days. The reason is that my talk may have another, distant audience for whom an archaic style may be particularly appropriate. The possibility of reaching this audience has been created by a breakthrough at the Federation Institute For Technology Transfer. As you know, we have been able for some time to transfer technological artifacts into the future. This is, in principle, relatively easy because technologies have always been designed to change the future. But using technology to change the past has proved to be much more difficult. Nevertheless, recent trials have been very promising and I am able to inform you that a full-scale attempt is to be made to transfer a recording of my lecture here today back into the *late twentieth century*. It is with this project in mind, therefore, that I have used literary techniques and forms of language familiar to the members of STS at the period just before the start of the final, catastrophic cultural collapse.

The technology transfer will take place tomorrow and you are all welcome to attend. If it is successful, my talk today will already have been heard more than a century ago – perhaps by a group of free-thinking academics huddling together surreptitiously in one of the knowledge factories of STS. We have been careful to select a peripheral knowledge factory where the intellectual climate was likely to be reasonably favourable and where the Women's Movement was already active. There is a distinct possibility, therefore, that the glimpse into the future made available by this tape recording will have been a critical factor in making the Women's Movement fully aware of its transformative potential and, indeed, in setting in motion that cultural transformation out of which our own society eventually emerged. Let us join together to send this seed of hope and encouragement along the Fallopian tube of time to germinate in the ideological womb of scientific-technological society.

Thank you for listening.

Details of previous publication

Chapter 1. 'Methodology in the Sociology of Science'. *Social Science Information* 1974, 13 (2): 107-19.

Chapter 2. 'Action and Belief or Scientific Discourse?' *Philosophy of the Social Sciences* 1981, 11 (2): 163-71.

Chapter 3. 'Textual Fragments on Science, Social Science and Literature'. In G. Rousseau and P. Privateer (eds.), *Literature and Science: New Essays in Interdisciplinary Theories and Practices*. Cambridge, Cambridge University Press, forthcoming.

Chapter 4. 'A Sociological Study of a Physics Department'. *British Journal of Sociology* 1971, 22: 68-82 (*with* A.T. Williams).

Chapter 5. 'Three Models of Scientific Development'. *Sociological Review* 1975, 23 (2): 509-26.

Chapter 6. 'Norms and Ideology in Science'. *Social Science Information* 1976, 15(4): 637-56.

Chapter 7. 'Consensus in Science'. *Social Science Information* 1978, 17(1): 107-22.

Chapter 8. 'Knowledge and Utility: Implications for the Sociology of Knowledge'. *Social Studies of Science* 1979, 9(1): 63-80.

Chapter 9. 'Putting Philosophy to Work: Karl Popper's Influence on Scientific Practice'. *Philosophy of the Social Sciences* 1981, 11(3): 389-407 (with G.N. Gilbert).

Chapter 10. 'Opening Pandora's Box: A Case for Developing a New Approach to the Sociological Analysis of Theory-choice in Science'. In E. Long and H. Kuklick (eds.), *Knowledge and Society: Studies in the Sociology of Culture Past and Present* 1984, 5: 113-39 (*with* G.N. Gilbert).

Chapter 11. 'Replication and Mere Replication'. *Philosophy of the Social Sciences* 1986, 16(1): 21-37 (*with* G.N. Gilbert).

Chapter 12. A working paper (1984) which provided the basis for 'Noblesse Oblige', chapter eight of *The Word and the World: Explorations in the Form of Sociological Analysis*. London, Allen and Unwin, 1985.

Chapter 13. 'Measuring the Quality of Life: A Sociological Invention'. *Sociology* 1987, 21(4): 541-64 (*with* M. Ashmore and T. Pinch).

Chapter 14. 'Looking Backward'. *Science, Technology and Human Values* 1989, 14(4): 441-59.

Bibliography

Ashmore, M. (1989). *The Reflexive Thesis: Wrighting Sociology of Scientific Knowledge*. Chicago, The University of Chicago Press.

Ashmore, M., M. Mulkay and T. Pinch (1989). *Health and Efficiency: A Sociology of Health Economics*. Milton Keynes, Open University Press.

Barber, B. (1962). *Science and the Social Order*. New York, Collier Books.

Beardslee, D.C. and D.D. O'Dowd (1962). 'The College-student Image of the Scientist'. In B. Barber and W. Hirsch (eds.), *The Sociology of Science*. New York, The Free Press.

Bellamy, E. (1960). *Looking Backward*. New York, The New American Library of World Literature.

Berelson, B. (1960). *Graduate Education in the United States*. New York, McGraw Hill.

Bloor, D. (1976). *Knowledge and Social Imagery*. London, Routledge and Kegan Paul.

Bloor, M. (1976). 'Bishop Berkeley and the Adenotonsillectomy Enigma'. *Sociology* 10: 43-61.

Blume, S. and R. Sinclair (1973). 'Chemists in British Universities'. *American Sociological Review* 38: 126-38.

Bunge, M. (1967). 'Technology as Applied Science'. *Technology and Culture* 8: 329-47.

Cicourel, A. (1964). *Method and Measurement in Sociology*. New York, The Free Press.

Cole, J.R. and S. Cole (1973). *Social Stratification in Science*. Chicago, The University of Chicago Press.

Collins, H.M. (1975). 'The Seven Sexes: A Study in the Sociology of a Phenomenon, or the Replication of Experiments in Physics'. *Sociology* 9: 205-24.

Daniels, G.H. (1967). 'The Pure-science Ideal and Democratic Culture'. *Science* 156: 1699-1705.

Derrida, J. (1977). 'LIMITED INC abc ...'. *Glyph* 2: 162-254.

Edge, D.O. and M.J. Mulkay (1976). *Astronomy Transformed: The Emergence of Radio Astronomy in Britain*. New York, Wiley.

Elias, N. (1971). 'Sociology of Knowledge: New Perspectives, Pt 1'. *Sociology* 5: 149-68; and Pt 2, 355-70.

Funk, W. (1978). *Word Origins*. New York, Bell.

Gaston, J. (1973). *Originality and Competition in Science*. Chicago, The University of Chicago Press.

Gilbert, G.N. (1976). 'The Transformation of Research Findings into Scientific Knowledge'. *Social Studies of Science* 6(3/4): 282-306.

Gilbert, G.N. and M. Mulkay (1982). 'Warranting Scientific Belief'. *Social Studies of Science* 12: 383-408.

——(1984). *Opening Pandora's Box: A Sociological Analysis of Scientists' Discourse*. Cambridge, Cambridge University Press.

Gouldner, A.W. (1971). *The Coming Crisis of Western Sociology*. London, Heinemann.

Greenberg, D.S. (1969). *The Politics of American Science*. Harmondsworth, Penguin Books.

Gusfield, J. (1976). 'The Literary Rhetoric of Science: Comedy and Pathos in Drinking Driver Research'. *American Sociological Review* 41: 16-34.

Hagstrom, W.O. (1965). *The Scientific Community*. New York, Basic Books.

Heisenberg, W. (1975). 'The Great Tradition: End of an Epoch'. *Encounter* 54: 55.

Holton, G. (1962). 'Models for Understanding the Growth and Excellence of Scientific Research'. In S.R. Graubard and G. Holton (eds.), *Excellence and Leadership in a Democracy*. New York, Columbia University Press.

Jennison, R.C. (1966). *Introduction to Radio Astronomy*. London, Newnes.

Johnston, R. (1977). *Science and Rationality*. Manchester, Siscon.

Kind, P., R. Rosser and A. Williams (1982). 'Valuation of Quality of Life: Some Psychometric Evidence'. In M.W. Jones-Lee (ed.), *The Value of Life and Safety*. Leiden, North Holland.

King, M.D. (1968). 'Science and the Professional Dilemma'. In J. Gould (ed.), *Penguin Social Science Survey*. Harmondsworth, Penguin Books.

Knorr, K. (1977). 'Producing and Reproducing Knowledge: Descriptive or Constructive?' *Social Science Information* 16: 669-96.

Kuhn, T.S. (1962). *The Structure of Scientific Revolutions*. Chicago, The University of Chicago Press.

——(1977). *The Essential Tension*. Chicago, The University of Chicago Press.

Langrish, J. *et al.* (1972). *Wealth from Knowledge*. London, Macmillan.

Latour, B. (1980). 'The Three Little Dinosaurs or a Sociologist's Nightmare'. *Fundamenta Scientiae* 1: 79-85.

Layton, E. (1977). 'Conditions of Technological Development'. In I. Spiegel-Rosing and D.J. de Solla Price (eds.), *Science, Technology and Society*. London and Beverley Hills, Sage.

Lemaine, G. *et al.* (1976). *Perspectives on the Emergence of Scientific Disciplines*. Mouton, The Hague.

Lynch, M. (1985). *Art and Artifact in Laboratory Science: A Study of Shop Work and Shop Talk in a Research Laboratory*. London, Routledge and Kegan Paul.

McCloskey, D.N. (1985). *The Rhetoric of Economics*. Madison, The University of Wisconsin Press.

McKeown, T. (1976). *The Modern Rise of Population*. London, Arnold.

Magee, B. (1975). *Popper*. Glasgow, Fontana.

Mannheim, K. (1936). *Ideology and Utopia*. New York, Harcourt, Brace and World.

——(1952). *Essays in the Sociology of Knowledge*. London, Routledge and Kegan Paul.

Materials Advisory Board (1966). *Report of the Ad Hoc Committee on Principles of Research-Engineering Interaction*. Washington DC, National Academy of Sciences.

Maynard, A. (1986). 'Policy Choices in the Health Sector'. In R. Berthoud (ed.), *Challenges to Social Policy*. London, Policy Studies Institute.

Mazur, A. (1973). 'Disputes between Experts'. *Minerva* 11: 243-62.

Mead, M. and R. Metraux (1962). 'The Image of the Scientist among High-school Students'. In B. Barber and W. Hirsch (eds.), *The Sociology of Science*. New York, The Free Press.

Medawar, P. (1969). *The Art of the Soluble*. Harmondsworth, Penguin Books.

Merton, R.K. (1938). 'Science and the Social Order'. *Philosophy of Science* 5: 321-37.

——(1957). *Social Theory and Social Structure*. New York, The Free Press.

——(1962). 'Priorities in Scientific Discovery'. In B. Barber and W. Hirsch (eds.), *The Sociology of Science*. New York, The Free Press.

——(1973). *The Sociology of Science: Theoretical and Empirical Investigations*. Chicago, The University of Chicago Press.

Milgram, G. (1974). *Obedience to Authority: An Experimental View*. New York, Harper and Row.

Mitroff, I.I. (1974). *The Subjective Side of Science*. Amsterdam, Elsevier.

Mulkay, M. (1969). 'Some Aspects of Cultural Growth in the Natural Sciences'. *Social Research* 36(1): 22-52.

——(1979). *Science and the Sociology of Knowledge*. London, Allen and Unwin.

——(1980). 'Interpretation and the Use of Rules'. In T. Gieryn (ed.), *Festschrift for Robert Merton*. New York, Transactions of the New York Academy of Sciences.

——(1984). 'The Scientist Talks Back: A One-act Play, with a Moral, about Replication in Science and Reflexivity in Sociology'. *Social Studies of Science* 14: 265-82.

——(1984a). 'The Ultimate Compliment: A Sociological Analysis of Ceremonial Discourse'. *Sociology* 18: 531-49.

——(1985). *The Word and the World: Explorations in the Form of Sociological Analysis*. London, Allen and Unwin.

——(1988). *On Humour: Its Nature and Its Place in Modern Society*. Oxford, Polity Press.

Mulkay, M. and G.N. Gilbert (1983). 'Scientists' Theory Talk'. *The Canadian Journal of Sociology* 8: 179-97.

Mulkay, M., G.N. Gilbert and S. Woolgar (1975). 'Problem Areas and Research Networks in Science'. *Sociology* 9: 187-203.

Mulkay, M. and V. Milic (1980). 'The Sociology of Science in East and West'. *Current Sociology* 28(3): 1-342.

Olby, R. (1974). *The Path to the Double Helix*. London, Macmillan.

Physics in Canada (1967). Ottawa, Science Secretariat.

Pinch, T. (1986). *Confronting Nature*. Dordrecht, Reidel.

Planck, M. (1950). *Scientific Autobiography*. London, Williams and Norgate.

Polanyi, M. (1963). 'The Potential Theory of Adsorption'. In M. Polanyi, *Knowing and Being*. London, Routledge and Kegan Paul.

Popper, K.R. (1959). *The Logic of Scientific Discovery*. London, Hutchinson.

——(1963). *Conjectures and Refutations*. London, Routledge and Kegan Paul.

Potter, J. and M. Wetherell (1987). *Discourse and Social Psychology: Beyond Attitudes and Behaviour*. London and Beverly Hills, Sage.

Price, D.J. de Solla (1963). *Big Science Little Science*. New York, Columbia University Press.

——(1965). 'Is Technology Historically Independent of Science?' *Technology and Culture* 6: 553-67.

Prix Nobel, Les (published annually). Stockholm, Almquist and Wiksell.

Ravetz, J.R. (1971). *Scientific Knowledge and Its Social Problems*. Oxford, Clarendon Press.

Rorty, R. (1979). *The Mirror of Nature*. Princeton, Princeton University Press.

Sapolsky, H.M. (1977). 'Science, Technology and Military Policy'. In I. Spiegel-Rosing and D.J. de Solla Price (eds.), *Science, Technology and Society*. London and Beverly Hills, Sage.

Schutz, A. (1972). *The Phenomenology of the Social World*. London, Heinemann.

Singh, J. (1970). *Modern Cosmology*. Harmondsworth, Penguin Books.

Spedding, J., R.L. Ellis and D.D. Heath (eds.) (1860). *The Works of Francis Bacon*. London, Longman.

Stark, W. (1958). *The Sociology of Knowledge*. London, Routledge and Kegan Paul.

Storer, N.W. (1966). *The Social System of Science*. New York, Holt, Rinehart and Winston.

Tobey, R.C. (1971). *The American Ideology of National Science*. Pittsburgh, University of Pittsburgh Press.

Westfall, R.S. (1980). *Never at Rest. A Biography of Isaac Newton*. Cambridge, Cambridge University Press.

Williams, A. (1972). 'Cost-Benefit Analysis: Bastard Science? and/or Insidious Poison in the Body Politick?' *Journal of Public Economics* 1: 199-225.

——(1981). 'Welfare Economics and Health Status Measurement'. In J. Van der Gaag and M. Perlman (eds.), *Health, Economics and Health Economics*. Leiden, North Holland.

——(1985). 'Economics of Coronary Artery Bypass Grafting'. *British Medical Journal* 291: 326-9.

Williams, H. (1988). *Whale Nation*. London, Cape.

Woolgar, S. (1976). 'Writing an Intellectual History of Science: The Use of Discovery Accounts'. *Social Studies of Science* 6(3/4): 395-422.

——(1982). 'Laboratory Studies: A Comment on the State of the Art'. *Social Studies of Science* 12: 481-98.

——(1983). 'Irony in the Social Study of Science'. In K. Knorr-Cetina and M. Mulkay (eds.), *Science Observed: Perspectives on the Social Study of Science*. London and Beverly Hills, Sage.

——(1988). *Knowledge and Reflexivity: New Frontiers in the Sociology of Knowledge*. London and Beverly Hills, Sage.

Wynne, A. (1988). 'Accounting for Accounts of the Diagnosis of Multiple Sclerosis'. In S. Woolgar (ed.), *Knowledge and Reflexivity: New Frontiers in the Sociology of Knowledge*. London and Beverly Hills, Sage.

Ziman, J. (1968). *Public Knowledge*. Cambridge, Cambridge University Press.

Zuckerman, H. (1977). 'Deviant Social Behavior and Social Control in Science'. In E. Sagarin (ed.), *Deviance and Social Change*. London and Beverly Hills, Sage.

——(1978). 'Theory Choice and Problem Choice in Science'. In J. Gaston (ed.), *Sociology of Science*. San Francisco, Jossey-Bass.

Index